Property of the
STATE OF ILLINOIS
MARILLAC HIGH SCHOOL
NORTHFIELD, ILLINOIS 60093

Responsible health decisions, such as wearing life jackets, lower the risk of injury.

Making Healthy Choices

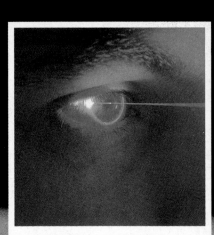

3. Your Sense Organs

HEATH

PERSPECTIVES ON

Health

Bud Getchell
Rusty Pippin
Jill Varnes

Stephen Podolsky, M.D., Medical Editor

Reviewed by
The American Academy
of Family Physicians

 D.C. Heath and Company
Lexington, Massachusetts / Toronto, Ontario

The American Academy of Family Physicians reviewed the text of the first edition of *Perspectives on Health* during the editing process and provided suggestions and recommendations to the publishers regarding the medical accuracy, internal consistency, and appropriateness of the text. The American Academy of Family Physicians is the national association of family doctors. It is one of American medicine's largest specialty groups, with more than 57,000 members in practice and training. Family physicians treat all ages and provide general medical care in the medical disciplines of internal medicine, pediatrics, obstetrics and gynecology, surgery, psychiatry and neurology, and community medicine. Membership in The AAFP requires completion of a minimum of 150 hours of approved continuing medical education every three years.

Stephen Podolsky, M.D., F.A.C.P., is Assistant Clinical Professor of Medicine at Harvard Medical School, Chief of Endocrinology and Metabolism at the Boston Veterans Administration Outpatient Clinic, and Consultant in Diabetes at the West Roxbury Veteran's Medical Center in Boston. Dr. Podolsky has published over 200 medical articles and his medical textbooks have been translated into several languages. He is also a Fellow of The American College of Physicians, The New York Academy of Sciences, and The Gerontological Society of America.

Copyright © 1992 by D.C. Heath and Company
All rights reserved. Certain portions of this publication © 1987, 1989, 1991.
No part of this publication may be reproduced or transmitted in any form by any means, electronic or mechanical, including photocopy, recording, or any information storage or retrieval system, without permission in writing from the publisher.

Published simultaneously in Canada.
Printed in the United States of America
International Standard Book Number: 0-669-26428-8

Teacher Reviewers

Gail F. Blackwell
Health Teacher
Pearce High School
Richardson, Texas

Marty Conklin
Health Teacher, Athletic Trainer
Edmond Mid-High School
Edmond, Oklahoma

John V. Davis
Coordinator, Science and Health Education
South Bend Community School Corporation
South Bend, Indiana

Jean R. Driggers
Chair, Physical Education and Health
North Clayton Senior High
College Park, Georgia

Robert H. Hager
Health Department Chair
Anaheim High School
Anaheim, California

Richard S. Jackman, Ed.D.
Health Teacher
Boston Latin School
Boston, Massachusetts

Linda B. Jones
Health Teacher
Seminole High School
Seminole, Florida

Elizabeth B. Lavender
Chair, Science Department
A.R. Johnson Health Science and Engineering
   High School
Augusta, Georgia

Jo Mancuso, Ph.D.
Chair, Physical Education and Health
Lyons Township High School
LaGrange, Illinois

Marcia C. Mason
Health Teacher
Albemarle High School
Charlottesville, Virginia

Billie McCann
Consultant, Health, Physical Education, and Recreation
El Paso Independent School District
El Paso, Texas

Dianne McCarthy
Health Teacher
Valley High School
Albuquerque, New Mexico

Glen McKendree
Health Teacher
Ocala-Forest High School
Ocala, Florida

Joe C. Miles
Health Education Instructor
Crockett High School
Austin, Texas

Marilyn Mitchell
Chair, Science Department
Worth County High School
Sylvester, Georgia

George R. Mulvaney
Health Teacher
Glens Falls High School
Glens Falls, New York

Bonnie Fontenot Nielson
Health Teacher
Albemarle High School
Charlottesville, Virginia

Edgar L. Reeves
Health Teacher
Westover High School
Albany, Georgia

J.H. Vickers
Health Education and Services
Orange County Public Schools
Orlando, Florida

Ann Meador Wells
Health and Physical Education Teacher
Princeton Senior High School
Princeton, West Virginia

Acknowledgments

TEXT

8 Adapted from *The Wellness Workbook,* by Regina Sarah Ryan and John W. Travis, M.D. Copyright © 1981. Used with permission of Ten Speed Press, Box 7123, Berkeley, CA 94707.

98 Adapted from the *Journal of Psychosomatic Research,* vol. 16, 1972. Reprinted with permission of Pergamon Press.

246 Adapted from "To Sleep the Good Sleep," *The Sciences,* December 1975, vol. 15, no. 9, page 25.

334 Adapted from *Down Syndrome,* 1985, page 9. Reprinted with permission of the National Down Syndrome Congress.

542 Adapted from *Information Please Almanac,* 1986, Houghton Mifflin Company, pages 100-102.

ILLUSTRATIONS

Fred Bigio and Fred Holz of B.C. Graphics: xiv (top), 515-537

Sue Lee: 18, 24, 29, 30, 31, 39, 41, 43, 47 (top), 52, 53 (top, bottom), 173, 183 (top), 183 (bottom), 197, 199, 202, 208, 242, 250, 310, 320, 323, 324, 350, 418, 442, 445, 498

Gordon Nealy: 216, 217 (bottom), 224, 229, 303 (top, bottom), 304, 322, 417, 437

Penny Pounder: 38, 47 (bottom)

Terry Presnall: 5, 7, 32, 51, 101, 120, 136, 158, 159, 160, 164, 179, 204, 229, 230, 245, 265, 269, 275, 292, 314, 328, 331, 334, 346, 355, 380, 422, 429, 443, 464, 479, 480, 481, 490, 492

Sue Solomon Seif/The Graphics Project: 172, 196, 200, 218 (bottom), 227, 237, 238, 239, 240, 302, 309, 315, 367, 373

Walter Stuart: 180, 181, 194, 198, 201, 236

Marcia Williams: Plates One, Two, Three, Six, Eight

Charles H. Boyter, D. Patrick Russell, and Marcia Williams of The Boston University Educational Media Support Center under the direction of Jerome Glickman, Boston University School of Medicine: xiv (bottom), 175, 217 (top), 225, Plates Four, Five, Seven

PHOTOGRAPHS

x (top) © Tom Tracy/Medichrome   xi (top) Barry L. Runk/Grant Heilman Photo   xii (top) Photo by Lennart Nilsson from *Behold Man,* Little Brown & Co., Boston, MA   xii (bottom) © Robert Isear/Photo Researchers Inc.   xiii David York/Medichrome   xvi–1 © Stephen Dunn/Focus West   1(inset) Mel DeGiacomo/The Image Bank   xvi (left) © Mary E. Messenger   2 Chris Luneski/Photo Researchers   5 © John D. Cunningham/Visuals Unlimited   6 © Mary E. Messenger   16 © Claudio Ferrar/Click/Chicago   19 Mary Ellen Lepionka   20 Carolyn Hine/The Picture Cube   21 © D.P. Hershkowitz/Bruce Coleman, Inc.   22 Andrew McClenaghan/Science Photo Library   25 (top) Gil Fahey/The Picture Cube   25 (center) Ed Reschke   25 (bottom) © Perry D. Slocum/Earth Scenes   26 (top, middle bottom left) L.V. Bergman & Associates   26 (bottom right) Ed Reschke   27 © Nubar Alexanian/Stock Boston   28 (top) © James Stevenson/Photo Researchers   28 (bottom) © Russ Kinne/Photo Researchers Inc.   31 Photos by Drs. R. William McNeill and Roger A. West, Seattle   36 Richard Hutchings   40 Photo by Lennart Nilsson from *Behold Man,* Little Brown & Co., Boston, MA   42 © David York/Medichrome   43 © K. Werner   44 (top) Charles Gupton/Southern Light   44 (bottom left) James H. Karales/Magnum Photos   44 (bottom right) © Herbert Gould/Medichrome   45 © Tom Tracy/Medichrome   46 Mel DiGiacomo/The Image Bank   49 (top) Photo by Lennart Nilsson from *Behold Man,* Little Brown & Co., Boston, MA   49 (bottom) Eunice Harrice/Photo Researchers Inc.   50 © E. Borreson 1985/Visuals Unlimited   58-59 © David Brownell   58 (left) Ken Sherman/Bruce Coleman   58 (right) © Owen Franken/Stock Boston   59 (bottom) © Will McIntyre/Photo Researchers   60 © Stock Imagery   61 Focus on Sports   62 Russ Lappa   63 The Bettmann Archive   64 © Wm. Floyd Holdman/The Stock Solution   66 (left, center) The Bettmann Archive   66 (right) UPI/Bettmann Newsphotos   68 (top) Ken Sherman/Bruce Coleman Inc.   68 (bottom) dph/Bruce Coleman Inc.   69 Bohdan Hrynewych/Southern Light   70 (top) J. Ballard   70 (bottom) Michael S. Renner/Bruce Coleman Inc.   71 © Eric Kroll/Taurus Photos   72 Lynn McLaren/The Picture Cube   75 © Tony Freeman   78 Lou Jones   80 (from left to right) © Owen Franken/Stock Boston, David Burnett/Stock Boston, © Frank Siteman/Stock Boston, © Owen Franken/Stock Boston   81 (right) Mark Sherman/Bruce Coleman Inc.   82 © Joe McNally/Wheeler Pictures   83 © T. Chan/Taurus Photos   84 © D.E. Cox/Click/Chicago   88 © Deni McIntyre/Photo Researchers Inc.   89 Read D. Brugger/The Picture Cube   91 Hank Morgan/Rainbow   100 Jean-Loup Charmet, Paris   103 © Joe McNally/Wheeler Pictures   104 © George E. Jones III/Photo Researchers Inc.   105 (top) © Hank Morgan/Rainbow   105 (bottom) © Don Smetzer/Click/Chicago   113 (left) © Alec Duncan/Taurus Photos   113 (right) © Jeff Reed/The Stock Shop   114 © Michael Melford/Wheeler Pictures   115 © Nubar Alexanian/Stock Boston   116 © Bruce M. Wellman/Stock Boston   119 © Jon Riley/The Stock Shop   121 © Derek Bayes/Click/Chicago   122 Dave Woodward/Taurus Photos   123 © Joseph Nettis/Photo Researchers Inc.   124

COVER CREDITS

Background: The Telegraph Colour Library/FPG International. **Left top to bottom:** Jacques Cochin/Photo Researchers, Lenart Nilsson from BEHOLD MAN © Little Brown photo courtesy Bonnier Fakta, Jeffrey Meyer/Stock Boston, Gregg Eisman. **Right top to bottom:** Alec Duncan/Taurus, Dan McCoy/Rainbow, John Anderson/TSW/Click Chicago

© John Moss/Medichrome **125** © Will McIntyre/Photo Researchers Inc. **128** Martha Stewart/The Picture Cube **129** © Ellis Herwig/The Picture Cube **130-31** © Frank Siteman/The Picture Cube **130** (left) © Jeffrey Meyers/Stock Boston **131** Philip Jon Bailey/The Picture Cube **135** Jeffrey Meyers/Stock Boston **140** Art Resource **142** Gilda Schiff/Photo Researchers Inc. **144** (top, top center) Barry L. Runk/Grant Heilman Photo **144** (bottom center) © Dr. E.R. Degginger **145** © Michal Heron **149** © David York/Medichrome **150** Lee Foster/Bruce Coleman Inc. **156** (left) Joseph A. DiChello Jr. **156** (right) © Robert Frerck/Click/Chicago **163** Schiffman/Gamma-Liaison **165** © Ann Hagen Griffiths/Omni Photo Communications **167** Robert P. Carr/Bruce Coleman Inc. **170** © Michael Phillip Manheim/The Stock Market **177** TRAVENOL LABS INC. **178** © Philip Jon Bailey/The Picture Cube **179** USDA/Science Source/Photo Researchers Inc. **180** Barry L. Runk/Grant Heilman Photography **181** L.V. Bergman & Associates **185** © Dan McCoy/Rainbow **190-91** Frank J. Staub/The Picture Cube **190** (left) © Richard Hutchings/Photo Researchers **190** (top right) © Lou Lainey **190** (bottom right) © Dan McCoy/Rainbow **191** © Frank Siteman/Taurus Photos **192** © Mary E. Messenger **195** Manfred Kage/Peter Arnold Inc. **203** Cary Wolinsky/Stock Boston **205** © Richard Hutchings/Photo Researchers Inc. **207** © Ed Reschke **211** Joseph A. DiChello Jr. **214** © Jacques Cochin/Photo Researchers Inc. **216** © Lou Lainey **218** From *Tissues and Organs: A Text-Atlas of Scanning Electron Microscopy* by Richard G. Kessel & Randy H. Kardon, W.H. Freeman and Co. © 1979 **219** © Lou Lainey **223** (top, center) © Biophoto Associates/Photo Researchers Inc. **223** (bottom) © Alfred Owczarzak/Taurus Photos **231** © Ulrike Welsh **234** Christian Petit/Photo Researchers Inc. **238** Photo by Lennart Nilsson from *Behold Man*, Little Brown & Co., Boston, MA **241** From *Tissues and Organs: A Text-Atlas of Scanning Electron Microscopy* by Richard G. Kessel & Randy H. Kardon, W.H. Freeman and Co. © 1979 **243** (top) © Fred Hossler/Visuals Unlimited **243** (bottom) © D. Johnson/Focus West **244** A.J. Wright/Taurus Photos **246** © D.P. Herskowitz/Bruce Coleman Inc. **247** © Dan McCoy/Rainbow **248** Courtesy of Northfield Mount Herman School/Lionel Delevingne **249** Courtesy of Wright State University, Dayton, Ohio **251** © Kenneth Karp/Omni Photo Communications **254** © Index Stock **265** © Frank Siteman/Taurus Photos **267** Cary Wolinsky/Stock Boston **268** © Owen Franken/Stock Boston **274** © Scott Legear/The Stock Shop **277** © Paul Shambroom/Photo Researchers Inc. **280** David S. Strickler/The Picture Cube **281** (top) © Martin M. Rotker/Taurus Photos **281** (bottom) Bob

Krist/Leo deWys, Inc. **282-83** Christian Delbert/The Picture Cube **282** (left) John Anderson/Click/Chicago **282** (right) Tony Freeman **283** Eric A. Roth/The Picture Cube **284** © Index Stock **286** © Lenore Weber/Taurus Photos **287** (top) © John Anderson/Click/Chicago **287** (bottom) © Junebug Clark/Photo Researchers Inc. **288** © Joseph Schuyler/Stock Boston **289** John Running/Stock Boston **290** (top) © Peter Charlesworth/Gamma-Liaison **290** (bottom) © Michael Amberger/The Stock Market **291** © David Lissey/Click/Chicago **293** © Owen Franken/Stock Boston **294** © John Anderson/Click/Chicago **295** © Charles Gupton/Stock Boston **296** © Marino Colmano/Gamma-Liaison **297** Cary Wolinsky/Stock Boston **300** Andy Levin/Black Star **308** J.D. Sloan/The Picture Cube **311** Dick Luria/Medichrome **313** © Tony Freeman **315** Ed Reschke **318** © David York/Medichrome **320** © David Scharf/Peter Arnold Inc. **321** Photos by Lennart Nilsson from *Behold Man*, Little Brown & Co., Boston, MA **325** Dittman/Rainbow **326** © Robert McElroy/Woodfin Camp & Associates **330** © Erich A. Roth/The Picture Cube **332** © Bill Longcore/Photo Researchers Inc. **333** © (top) Historical Pictures Service **333** (bottom) © Dan McCoy/Rainbow **334** © Jerry Howard/Positive Images **335** © David York/Medichrome **338** (left) © Bruce M. Wellman/Stock Boston **338** (right) © Frank Siteman/The Picture Cube **339** (top) Jeff Dunn/The Picture Cube **339** (bottom) Nicholas deVore III/Bruce Coleman, Inc. **340-41** Meri Houtchens-Kitchens/The Picture Cube **340** (top) © Coco McCoy/Rainbow **340** (bottom) Beverley Dixon **341** © Geoffrey Clifford/Wheeler Pictures **344** Culver Pictures, Inc. **345** © Coco McCoy/Rainbow **346** David Hurn/Magnum **347** © Russ Lappa **348** © Jan Halaska/Photo Researchers Inc. **350** © Michael G. Gabridge/Visuals Unlimited **351** © Gary Benson/Black Star **352** (left) © M. Zagaris/Focus West **352** (right), **354** © L.V. Bergman & Associates **356** © Edward Lettau/Photo Researchers Inc. **359** (right) © Don Smetzer/Click/Chicago **362** © C. Cloyd/Taurus Photos **364** (left) © John McGrail **364** (center) © Mary E. Messenger **364** (right) © Anthony Blake/Click/Chicago **366** Larry Day **369** © Mike Lacey **371** © Robert Frerck/Click/Chicago **374** © A. Glauberman/Photo Researchers Inc. **375** J. Ballard **376** Frank J. Staub/The Picture Cube **377** © Jim McHugh/Time Magazine **378** J. Ballard **379** Beverley Dixon **386** © Robert Isear/Photo Researchers Inc. **387** © Geoffrey Clifford/Wheeler Pictures **388** Steve Kagan/Gamma-Liaison **391** © Lawrence Fried/Magnum **392** © Jeff Rotman **396** (left) © Leonard Lee Rue III/Photo Researchers Inc.

Continued on page 576.

Contents

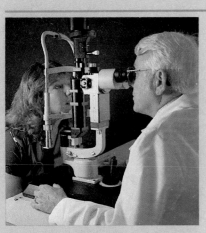

Authors

Leroy H. (Bud) Getchell, Ph.D., is Executive Director of The National Institute for Fitness and Sport in Indianapolis, Indiana, and Professor in the School of Health, Physical Education, and Recreation at Indiana University in Bloomington. Dr. Getchell is a nationally recognized lecturer and author on the subjects of exercise physiology, physical fitness, and wellness. He is the author of *Physical Fitness: A Way of Life, Being Fit: A Personal Guide,* and *The Fitness Book.* Dr. Getchell is a Fellow of the American College of Sports Medicine and a member of the Indiana Governor's Council for Physical Fitness and Sports Medicine.

Grover D. (Rusty) Pippin, Ph.D., a former high school health teacher and athletics coach, is now Professor and Director of Health Education at Baylor University in Waco, Texas. Dr. Pippin, a noted speaker and consultant in health and wellness, serves on the Board of Trustees of the Texas Association for Health, Physical Education, Recreation, and Dance. He has served on the Board of Governors of the Texas School Health Association. Dr. Pippin is currently a member of the Health Council of the Southern District of AAHPERD and is the Chairperson of the Texas Jump Rope For Heart task force.

Jill W. Varnes, Ed.D., a former high school health teacher and coach, is now Assistant Dean in the College of Health and Human Performance at the University of Florida in Gainesville. Previously she was employed as a Health Education Consultant with the Florida Department of Education. Dr. Varnes is the author of numerous journal articles on health and is currently Principal Investigator on a cancer prevention project with the National Cancer Institute. She has held numerous offices in professional organizations including President of Florida AAHPERD, and Vice President for Health of the Southern District AAHPERD. At the National level, she has served on the Board of Directors for the Association for the Advancement of Health Education and the AAHPERD Board of Governors.

Reviewers

Content Reviewers

W. Nicholson Browning, M.D.
Private Practice, Child Psychiatry
Lexington, Massachusetts

Henry E. Cooper, M.D.
Director, Adolescent Clinic
University of Colorado Health Sciences
Denver, Colorado

David E. Corbin, Ph.D.
Associate Professor, Health Education
University of Nebraska at Omaha
Omaha, Nebraska

Duane O. Eddy, Ph.D.
Dean, College of Applied Sciences
   and Technology
Ball State University
Muncie, Indiana

Helmi R. Fogels, D.M.D.
Assistant Dean and Chair, Department of
   General Dentistry
Tufts University School of Dental Medicine
Boston, Massachusetts

Neil E. Gallagher, Ph.D.
Chair, Health Science Department
Towson State University
Towson, Maryland

Mitchell Gilbert, M.D.
Clinical Fellow
Massachusetts Eye and Ear Infirmary
Boston, Massachusetts

Richard Gilbert, Ph.D.
Addiction Research Foundation
Toronto, Ontario, Canada

Paul R. Gilmore, M.D.
Assistant Professor of Medicine
Boston University School of Medicine
Boston, Massachusetts

Judith Hibbard, Dr.P.H.
Assistant Professor, Community Health
University of Oregon
Eugene, Oregon

Warren L. McNab, Ph.D.
Professor and Coordinator, Health Education
University of Nevada at Las Vegas
Las Vegas, Nevada

Louis J. Raffio, M.B.A.
Coalition of Digestive Disease Organizations
Westwood, Massachusetts

Warren E. Schaller, H.S.D.
Professor and Chair, Department of
   Physiology and Health Science
Ball State University
Muncie, Indiana

Richard G. Schlaadt, Ed.D.
Professor and Head, Department of School
   and Community Health
University of Oregon
Eugene, Oregon

David A. Sleet, Ph.D.
Professor, Health Science
San Diego State University
San Diego, California

Bill C. Wallace, Ed.D.
Professor and Chair, Division of Health
   and Safety
The University of Tennessee at Knoxville
Knoxville, Tennessee

Jack H. Wilmore, Ph.D.
Professor, Physical Education
The University of Texas at Austin
Austin, Texas

Wayne E. Wylie, Ed.D.
Assistant Professor, Health Education
Texas A & M University
College Station, Texas

Frances E. Young, M.H.E., Ph.D.
Health Education Consultant
Jacksonville, Florida

Tables and Charts

U N I T

1

1. Introduction to Health

2. Personal Care and Appearance

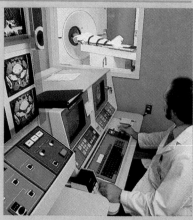

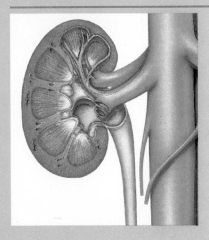

CHAPTER ONE

INTRODUCTION TO
HEALTH

Steve has gone over and over the rafting trip in his mind. He has anticipated the rush of the raft down the rapids, the breaking of the white water over rocks, the splash of cold water on his face. He has thought most about the laughter of his friends and how much fun the trip will be.

During the trip, Steve is likely to be so caught up in his adventure that he may not think about the possibility of an accident. He and his friends will wear life jackets and go with a guide who knows the river. By making these choices, they will reduce their risk of an accident.

Everyone makes choices about taking risks. The study of health, or your general physical and mental well-being, is all about making these choices wisely. The better you know your body and your mind, the better able you will be to make responsible decisions about your health.

Objectives

- Define *health* and *wellness.*

- List the four major factors that determine health.

- Define *life expectancy.*

- List five factors that relate to good health and tend to increase the average length of life.

- Explain how heredity can be a limiting health factor.

- Define *risk* and *statistics.*

- Explain the degrees of health and wellness on the Wellness Continuum.

- Explain how the decision-making model works.

Health Today

You probably know people you would label as *healthy*. They may be active in sports or they may walk to school, jog, or bicycle for exercise. They are likely to be trim and full of energy. They can handle the pressures of everyday activities without showing too much strain, and they project a positive outlook.

These people probably practice good health habits. By making good choices about diet, exercise, and their friendships with others, they are better able to enjoy their lives.

Health and Wellness

The word *health* can be used in a number of ways. In the past, health meant only the absence of disease or illness. Today, though, health has a broader meaning. **Health** is the state of your well-being that includes how you feel physically, mentally, and socially. **Wellness** is another term that describes this broader view of health. You can understand the need for a broader definition if you think about how health in your life is different from health in your grandparents' lives.

In 1900, the main causes of death were diseases that were spread by bacteria and viruses. If you had lived then, the danger of your dying from pneumonia would have been three times greater than the danger of your dying from cancer. Figure 1-1 compares the leading causes of death in 1900 and today.

The diseases that were most common in 1900 affected people of all ages. It is not surprising, then, that around 1900, the emphasis of health was on freedom from illness. Today many of the diseases that were common in 1900 can be prevented or cured by improved medicines and methods of sanitation. Most diseases now are likely to occur later in life. You as a teenager will probably not have to think about the same threats to your health as your grandparents did.

These improvements in health conditions mean that not only can you now enjoy a better life, but you also have a greater chance of having a longer life. Controlling diseases has increased

Health History

Childhood diseases were feared killers in the past. Between 1900 and 1904, measles, scarlet fever, whooping cough, and diphtheria together caused nearly as many deaths as cancer.

1900	Today	
All Ages	**All Ages**	**15-24 Year Olds**
Pneumonia and flu	Heart diseases	Accidents
Tuberculosis	Cancer	Homicide
Inflammations of the digestive tract	Stroke	Suicide
Heart diseases	Accidents	Cancer
Stroke	Lung diseases	Heart diseases
Kidney diseases	Pneumonia and flu	Birth defects
Accidents	Diabetes mellitus	Stroke
Cancer	Suicide	Pneumonia and flu
Childhood diseases	Liver diseases	Lung diseases
Diphtheria	Atherosclerosis	Diabetes mellitus

Figure 1–1 The leading causes of death in the U.S. Tuberculosis, which was the second greatest killer in 1900, was not even in the top ten by the 1980s.

the life expectancy in the United States. **Life expectancy** is the measure of the average number of years that a group of people may expect to live. Generally, people born more recently have higher life expectancies. Since 1900, the life expectancy in the United States has increased by more than 26 years. It has increased from 47 years for those born in 1900 to 74 years in 1981.

It is important to look also at some numbers that apply only to you. Figure 1-1 lists the main causes of death for people between the ages of 15 and 24. You will see that the first several causes are problems that you might prevent by taking more responsibility for your actions. This includes improving your emotional health and developing good habits such as wearing a safety belt and driving safely.

What Determines Health?

The United States Centers for Disease Control has identified four major factors that determine health. They are personal health behavior, biological influences such as heredity, the condition of the physical environment, and the quality of health care services.

Health Behavior Figure 1-3 shows the estimated percentage that each of these factors contributes to the combined ten leading causes of death. Personal health behaviors are factors in 51 percent of all ten major causes of death. **Health behaviors** are actions you take that affect your health.

A research study of over 7000 individuals reported seven health behaviors that promote good health and tend to increase average length of life. The seven factors are listed below.

1 Sleeping seven to eight hours daily
2 Eating breakfast almost every day
3 Rarely eating between meals
4 Maintaining normal weight
5 Not smoking cigarettes
6 Drinking alcohol in moderation, or not at all
7 Getting regular physical exercise

Those who practiced most or all of these behaviors tended to be in better physical and mental health than those who followed a few or none. People who are in good physical shape are better able to handle the pressures in their lives. People who have good mental health have a good self-concept.

Heredity Sometimes your ability to prevent diseases is limited by heredity and by other personal factors. **Heredity** is the passing of traits biologically from parents to child. If many of your family members have died of heart disease, you may be less able to prevent heart disease than someone whose family members have been free of heart disease. Sometimes a disability can keep you from being able to exercise regularly. Whatever your heredity or physical condition, though, you can improve your chance of having a lifetime of good health by choosing responsible health behaviors.

Figure 1–2 Life expectancy has increased steadily through this century. This child has a good chance of living longer than his grandparents.

Figure 1–3 Estimated contribution of the four major health factors to U.S. deaths from the 10 leading causes

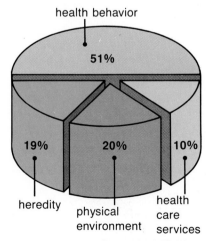

health behavior
51%

19%   20%   10%

heredity   physical   health
environment   care
services

Source: U.S. Centers
for Disease Control

Figure 1–4 Positive health behaviors such as regular physical exercise can lead to a longer, healthier life.

Physical Environment Your **physical environment** is your physical surroundings—any place in which you live, work, or play. Health threats in your physical environment may affect your personal health. Air pollution may increase your chance of developing lung disorders, or worsen a condition such as asthma. Scientists believe that air pollution might even cause some diseases such as cancer. Too much noise, very crowded living places, and infected food or water are examples of factors in the environment that can affect your health.

Health Care Services The quality of the health care you have available to you also helps determine the quality of your general health. If you can get regular medical and dental care, you may be able to prevent many health problems. Preventing an illness is almost always easier than curing one.

Lesson Review

Your health is a mix of factors in your life—physical, emotional, and social. Being aware of the four major factors that determine health will help you make decisions about positive health behaviors. Even though you cannot control all parts of your health, you can take responsibility for practicing as many positive health behaviors as possible.

1 Define *health*.

2 Explain *life expectancy*.

3 List the four major factors that determine health.

4 List five health behaviors that promote good health.

Making Healthy Choices

Some of the factors that determine health may seem to be beyond your influence. It is true that everyone has personal limits. Your heredity and sometimes your physical environment are not things you can change or control. However, you can still take responsibility for changing your behavior. This responsibility involves weighing the risks connected to the decisions you make.

What Is a Risk?

The possibility that something bad will happen is a **risk.** Risk also can be defined as the degree of danger that goes along with an opportunity. All risks have possible negative outcomes. However, some risks are worth taking. For example, suppose that you have the chance to join a school team. You risk a possible injury while playing to achieve the sense of accomplishment that comes with being on the team. You may decide that the pleasure of playing is worth the risk of injury. By being in good health, you can also reduce the risk of physical injury.

How can you determine the risks involved in an action? Many risks that relate to health choices have been studied. Scientists use statistics to measure these risks. **Statistics** is a branch of mathematics that helps determine the possibility, or odds, that something will occur. The information about the possibility is called **statistical risk** and can help you make healthy choices.

For example, statistics indicate that in this country the chance of dying from cancer is about 20 percent. In other words, two out of every ten deaths are due to some kind of cancer. Therefore, the risk of death from cancer is quite high. However, statistics also show that 80 percent of all cancers are related to things over which you have some control. In other words, you can make choices that will reduce your risk of developing cancer. These include such things as avoiding pollution, not smoking, and eating a diet high in fiber. If you do these things, you are less likely to develop cancer.

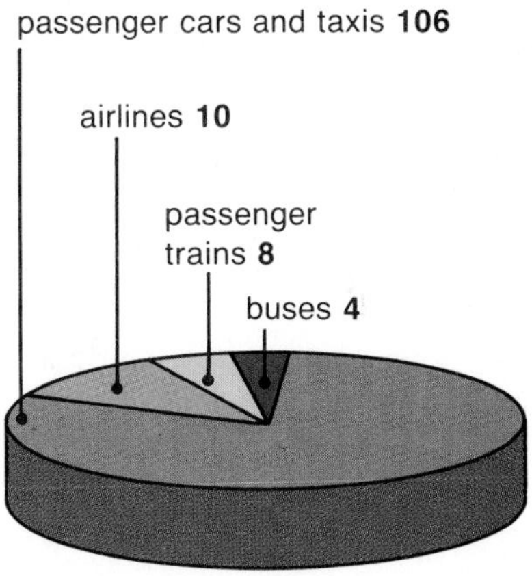

Fighting the Odds

A statistical risk is based on what has happened to a group of people in the recent past. But the risks can change. If enough people change their health behaviors, the statistics will also change. As you can see in Figure 1-1, as the behavior of the population changed between 1900 and today, so did the statistical risk of developing certain diseases.

Fighting the odds begins with each individual. For example, you may know that there is a history of diabetes in your family. Diabetes is a serious condition that may be brought on by being overweight. You may love sweets. But because you are aware of your danger of developing diabetes, you limit the amount of sugar you eat, and keep your weight down. You have evaluated the risk involved and have acted on it. To **evaluate** means to weigh or judge information. In understanding what can happen if you give in to your sweet tooth, you have evaluated the information you

passenger cars and taxis **106**

airlines **10**

passenger trains **8**

buses **4**

Deaths per ten billion passenger miles

Figure 1–5 A passenger mile is a mile traveled by one passenger. A train carrying 100 passengers for one mile travels 100 passenger miles.

Health Bulletin

While most people fear airplane accidents more than automobile accidents, the actual risks are quite different. Auto crashes kill so many people in a year that a full passenger jet would have to crash every day to equal the fatalities.

have. In deciding to give up sweets and maintain your weight, you have acted on your evaluation so that you have reduced your personal health risk.

Just as you act to reduce the health risk to yourself, you can also act to reduce health risks to others. For example, crossing the street involves some personal danger. You can reduce your risk by looking both ways, obeying traffic signals, and staying in the crosswalk. If you cross the street without looking, an accident may occur, causing injury to you. If the driver swerves to avoid you, other people may also be injured. Many other behaviors, such as driving habits, can put you and others at risk. It is important always to consider the injuries you might cause to other people as well as to yourself. Being responsible to others includes such things as staying away from people when you have an illness that can spread to others. This can be as simple as not going to school when you are ill.

In choosing your health behaviors, you will be taking both physical and emotional risks. It is important to remember that not all of these risks are life-threatening. Some health risks will not kill you, but they may prevent you from living to your full potential. Just as there are degrees of good health, so too, there are degrees of risk. Figure 1-6 shows some of the degrees of health and risk on a Wellness Continuum.

As you progress toward the right end of the continuum, you move in the direction of a higher level of physical, mental, social, and emotional health. At the same time, your health risks decrease. At the left of the scale are illness and early death. The health risks increase toward the left end of the continuum.

Now notice the middle area. This area is called the neutral zone. People at this point are not ill. But they are not especially well either. You probably know people at this stage. They may appear to be healthy. At least they do not appear ill. They attend their classes and get along well with their family. But they never seem to have any energy. They may eat too much. They are not very active in school or in sports. People in the neutral zone may

Figure 1–6 Traditional medicine cures illness, returning health to the neutral zone. Wellness includes overall physical, mental, social, and emotional growth and fulfillment.

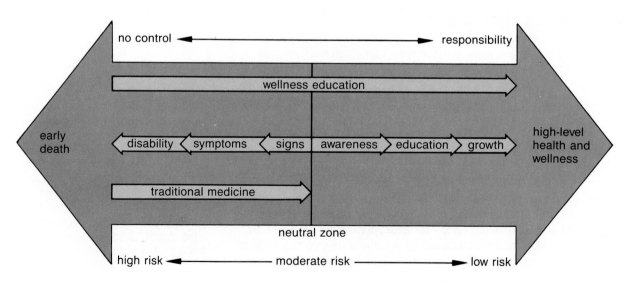

not have a very good self-concept. They seem to be just getting by. Even though the health risks at the middle of the Wellness Continuum are not fatal, they are chronic, or long-lasting. The effect of such health behaviors over a long time can be just as negative in later life as a disability or serious disease. People who live in the neutral zone of the continuum suffer daily by not living up to their potential.

Making Decisions

Evaluating the degree of risk may sometimes be comforting. It often helps to have a system for weighing things carefully. Figure 1-7 shows a model for decision-making that can help you make wise health choices. An example will show you how the model works.

State the Problem   Imagine that your friends, many of whom smoke cigarettes, are encouraging you to start smoking. Your best friend smokes and so do your parents. Your grandparents, who visit often, do not smoke and always ask your parents to quit. Every time you are with your friends, they want you to try a cigarette. You feel a great deal of pressure to start smoking. The problem, or decision you must make, is whether or not to smoke cigarettes.

Identify Your Options   You have many options. You can go along with your friends and begin to smoke on a regular basis. You can choose not to smoke. You could smoke only in the presence of your friends and not smoke at other times.

Choose One Option   Now think about your options. Select the one that you think you would like the best. You may not have a clear favorite. In this example, imagine that you do not want to smoke.

Evaluate the Outcomes   What would be the positive outcomes of that decision? You could feel the approval of your grandparents. You also might win approval from your parents, even though they smoke themselves. You would be free from the health risks that come from smoking. You would save money by not buying cigarettes. You would avoid the problem of stained fingers and teeth. And you would have greater endurance for sports and other activities.

Now consider the possible negative outcomes of your decision. Your friends may tease you. You might feel less grown up than your friends. Your friends may continue to pressure you to change your mind.

How might you reduce these possible negative outcomes? You could ignore your friends' comments. You could develop other talents to make you feel grown up. You could simply tell your friends that you are responsible for making your own decisions. You might even consider making new friends who do not pressure you to smoke.

Health Bulletin

Not all risks involve death. During their lifetime one out of three people is injured in a car accident badly enough to be disabled for at least a day.

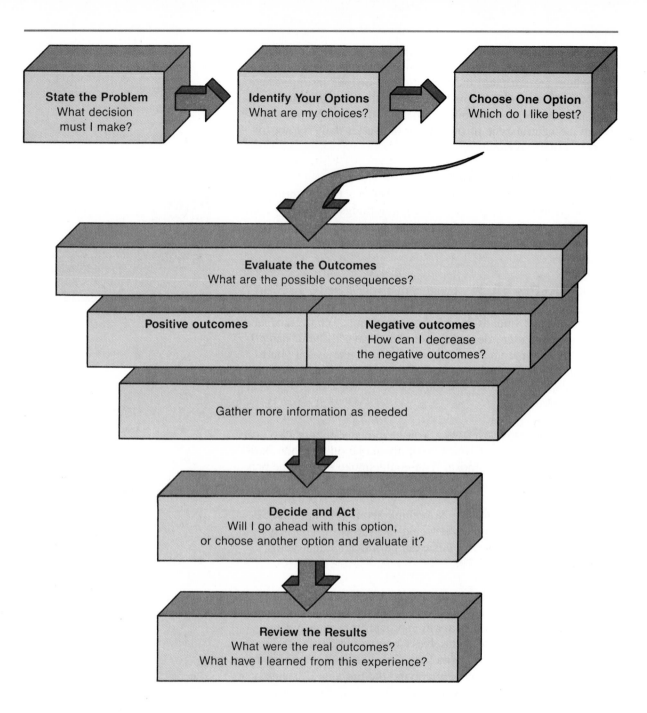

State the Problem
What decision must I make?

Identify Your Options
What are my choices?

Choose One Option
Which do I like best?

Evaluate the Outcomes
What are the possible consequences?

Positive outcomes

Negative outcomes
How can I decrease the negative outcomes?

Gather more information as needed

Decide and Act
Will I go ahead with this option, or choose another option and evaluate it?

Review the Results
What were the real outcomes?
What have I learned from this experience?

Figure 1–7 Making good decisions requires a method and practice. By using this model you will less often regret a hasty decision.

You may decide that you need more information before you can make a firm decision. You can go to the library to read books and articles about the effects of smoking on health. You can also ask people you respect, such as your family doctor. Once you have more information, you have to evaluate the positive against the negative outcomes.

Decide and Act If you feel the negative effects of smoking are stronger than the benefits, you will make the decision not to smoke. Your action will be to refuse cigarettes.

Review the Results Once you have acted, it is important to think about the results of your decision. Taking this last step in the model may either confirm your original decision or cause you to revise your thinking and make a new decision. You may even find that your friends respect your decision.

You can use this model to look closely at any health decision. Evaluating all of the possible outcomes will help you see all sides of even very difficult problems. By evaluating the outcomes before you act, you can change your mind and consider new options. You can avoid living through the outcomes of a poor choice.

Identifying Personal Health Risks

You have seen how you fit generally on the continuum of wellness and risks. Now is a good time to look at some specific personal health risks. On the next page you will find the Personal Health Inventory. It will help you identify more specifically what health behaviors you may need to change.

The inventory may call to your attention that you need to improve your diet. You may need to eat a wider variety of foods and avoid those that are high in salt, sugar, and fat. You may see that you need to exercise more often to maintain a normal weight and reduce stress. You may need to get more rest or try to express your emotions in positive ways. The inventory will encourage you to think about how you care for yourself and use health services. Finally, the inventory may make you think about some things related to health that might never have occurred to you. For example, you may never before have connected safety and the environment with health.

Take the Personal Health Inventory now. When you have finished the book, take the inventory again. It will show you whether what you have learned about health and wellness is helping you make healthy choices.

Health Bulletin

Do not rely on news reporting to learn about health risks. Although diseases such as heart disease, diabetes, and cancer kill many more people than do accidents and homicide, diseases receive far less coverage in the news.

Lesson Review

You are responsible for your own health. To act responsibly for your own health and that of others you should understand the risks involved in your decisions. Statistics can help inform you of risks. Using a model for decision-making can also help make sure that you consider many options. Making good health decisions and forming lifelong health habits now will help you maintain a high level of wellness throughout life.

1 Define *risk*.

2 What level of health risk is associated with symptoms of illness and disability?

3 Define *statistics*.

4 In the decision-making model, what is the next step after you identify the problem?

Personal Health Inventory

On a separate sheet of paper, write the numbers from 1 to 50. For the heredity section, write *yes* or *no* for each disorder.

Heredity	One of my close relatives has had:			
	1 heart disease	3 cancer	5 glaucoma	7 alcoholism
	2 high blood pressure	4 diabetes	6 asthma	8 mental illness

For the remainder of the inventory, write *usually* (or *always*), *sometimes*, or *rarely* for each statement. Respond to each statement with the word that best describes your typical behavior, not what you think you should do.

Mental Health		
	9	I allow myself to cry.
	10	I express feelings such as love, fear, and anger constructively.
	11	I have friends or relatives with whom I discuss problems.
	12	I keep anxiety from interfering with my activities at school or at home.
	13	I do not let stress build up and give me headaches or an upset stomach.
	14	I have hobbies that help me get away from daily tasks.

Nutrition		
	15	I eat a wide variety of foods, including meat, milk, fruits and vegetables, and breads and cereals.
	16	I avoid foods high in refined sugar.
	17	I avoid adding salt to my food.
	18	I avoid eating foods made with butter and other solid fats.
	19	I eat breakfast.
	20	I avoid eating between meals.

Physical Fitness		
	21	I do vigorous exercise such as running, swimming, or biking at least 3 times a week.
	22	I exercise to build muscle strength and endurance at least 3 times a week.
	23	I stretch to build flexibility.
	24	I warm up and cool down when I exercise.
	25	I enjoy some exercises or strenuous sports that I can continue with throughout my life.
	26	I maintain a healthy level of body fat, neither too much nor too little.
	27	I get 7 to 8 hours of sleep each night.

Substance Abuse		
	28	I avoid smoking cigarettes and using other forms of tobacco.
	29	I try to avoid the secondhand smoke of others.
	30	I avoid drinking alcohol.
	31	I avoid using illegal drugs such as marijuana, uppers, or downers.
	32	I avoid riding with a driver who is under the influence of alcohol or drugs.

Personal and Health Care	33	I brush and floss my teeth daily.
	34	I keep my skin and hair clean.
	35	I have my teeth checked twice a year.
	36	I see my family doctor every two years for a complete checkup.
	37	When under medical treatment, I follow my doctor's instructions about activities and using medications.
	38	I avoid using nonprescription medicines.
	39	I have my blood pressure checked once a year.
	40	I know the seven warning signs of cancer.
	41	I practice monthly self-examinations for cancer (breast exam for girls; testicle exam for boys).

Public Health	42	I walk, bike, or use public transportation whenever possible.
	43	I recycle such items as cans, paper, glass, clothes, and books.
	44	I avoid polluting the air with unnecessary smoke.

Safety	45	I use safety belts when driving or riding in a car.
	46	I obey traffic laws.
	47	I follow water safety procedures and can save myself or others from drowning.
	48	I use safety precautions when working with power tools, firearms, and other dangerous equipment.
	49	My home has safety features such as smoke detectors, outlet caps, and nonskid rugs.
	50	I know first aid methods to help others in an emergency.

Scoring

1 Questions 1–8: Give yourself 1 point for each question you answered *yes,* 5 points for each question you answered *no.*
   Questions 9–50: Give yourself 5 points for each question you answered *usually* (or *always*), 3 points for each *sometimes,* and 1 point for each *rarely.*
2 Add up all your points. The total is your inventory score.
3 Your score relates to the Wellness Continuum, Figure 1–6, as follows.

200 or higher   You are at low risk. You are practicing many good health behaviors.

100 to 199   You are in the neutral zone. You may not be ill, but you are at risk for long-term health problems. You are not getting everything you could out of life.

99 or lower   You are at high risk. In what sections did you answer *rarely* and *sometimes?* Pinpoint areas that need your attention, and find ways to lower your risk.

No matter what your score, you can make changes to increase your health. As you read this book, look for ways in which you can change your behavior to lower your health risks and improve your level of wellness. Now is the time to develop health habits for a good life.

Chapter Review

Vocabulary

evaluate	life expectancy	statistical risk
health	physical environment	statistics
health behavior	risk	wellness
heredity		

Using Vocabulary

Questions 1–10. On a separate sheet of paper, write the term from the column on the right that matches the phrase on the left.

1 action a person takes that affects his or her health
2 passing of traits biologically from parents to child
3 possibility that something bad will happen
4 information about the odds that something will occur
5 a broader view of health that includes prevention
6 to judge information
7 measure of the average number of years that people may expect to live
8 physical surroundings; place where you live, work, or play
9 branch of mathematics that helps determine the odds that something will occur
10 state of well-being

a wellness
b risk
c heredity
d life expectancy
e physical environment
f evaluate
g statistics
h health
i health behavior
j statistical risk

Interpreting Ideas

1 Compare today's broader definition of *health* with that of the past.

2 What is the neutral zone of the Wellness Continuum in Figure 1-6?

3 How has life expectancy in the United States changed since 1900? How can you account for this change?

4 According to the United States Centers for Disease Control, what are the four major factors that determine health?

5 How may air pollution affect a person's health? Name two other environmental factors that may affect your health.

6 How does the decision-making model help you make wise health choices? What are the steps in the decision-making model?

7 How can heredity be a limiting health factor?

8 What was the emphasis of health in 1900? Which diseases were most common then?

9 According to a recent research study, what seven factors promote good health and increase the average length of life?

10 If all risks have the possibility of a negative outcome, why do people take risks?

11 To what factors are most cancers related? What kinds of choices can reduce your risk of cancer?

12 How can you act to reduce health risks to others?

13 Where on the Wellness Continuum are health risks highest? lowest?

14 What effect does good physical health have on a person's ability to handle pressures?

15 How does the quality of health care help to determine the quality of a person's health?

16 How can you use statistical risk information to make healthy choices? What is the role of evaluation in making the choices?

17 When using the decision-making model, what do you consider in evaluating the possible negative outcomes of a decision? What do you do if you do not have enough information to make a firm decision?

18 What are the effects of improvements in health conditions in the United States?

19 Name two factors that determine health that may be beyond your influence. What responsibility can you take regarding these factors?

20 Describe the behaviors of people in the neutral zone of the Wellness Continuum. What is the cumulative effect of these behaviors?

Applying Concepts

1 What are the three leading causes of death for 15- to 24-year-olds? Hint: See Figure 1-1.

2 Of the seven health behaviors that promote good health and tend to increase average length of life, which two behaviors do you think are most important? Why?

3 Ann has an opportunity to join the soccer team. What risks are involved in playing? How can Ann reduce the risks?

4 Mike's father recently suffered a heart attack. Mike's grandfather died of a heart attack. How might Mike reduce the risk of heart disease?

5 Where on the Wellness Continuum is a 16-year-old girl who has begun to exercise regularly, lowered her fat consumption, and stopped smoking?

6 Dana gets regular checkups, avoids drugs, and eats an excellent diet of fruits, vegetables, whole-grain products, low-fat meats, and milk

products. He jogs five miles every other day and uses the rest of his waking hours to do homework and lift weights in his basement. How would you evaluate his health risk outlook, based on the Personal Health Inventory?

7 Using the Personal Health Inventory, determine how you can help to reduce health risks to others.

8 Do you think that allowing yourself to cry is a health risk or is a contribution to wellness? Explain.

9 Do you think that advertising in the United States helps to promote healthy behaviors? Why or why not?

10 What is the third leading cause of death among 15- to 24-year-olds, according to the table in Figure 1-1? Use the Personal Health Inventory to suggest three ways of reducing the number of deaths from this cause.

Projects

1 Sponsor a Wellness Day at your school. With the help of your teacher and classmates, design workshops to be conducted by health professionals throughout the day. For example, you might invite a doctor to conduct a workshop on sports injuries and their prevention, a psychologist to discuss depression and the prevention of suicide, and a gym instructor to demonstrate sports for cardiovascular fitness.

2 At your local library find out more about the current research on sleep. Are seven to eight hours of sleep necessary for health? Do some people need less sleep than others, and, if so, how do they otherwise differ from the rest of the population? Do sleep requirements change as a person gets older? What causes sleep disturbances and how may they be prevented?

3 After you take the Personal Health Inventory, create a Wellness Plan designed to improve your general well-being and reduce any health risks you may have discovered in taking the inventory. Once you start your plan, keep a daily written log in which you describe any or all of the following: how you feel, dietary changes, weight lost or gained, kinds of exercise begun or continued, sleep habits, and mood changes.

4 Find out the seven warning signs of cancer. Then construct a bulletin board on which you post the warning signs in bold letters; or create a pamphlet of information about cancer for distribution to students. You may wish to contact the American Cancer Society for additional information. Their phone number and address will be listed in your telephone directory.

The way you feel about yourself is reflected in the way you look. Careful grooming promotes a positive and appealing appearance.

CHAPTER TWO

Personal Care
& APPEARANCE

James whistled to himself as he got ready for the dance. The hot shower had made him feel clean and relaxed after tennis practice. As he dried his hair, he was glad that his hair fell neatly into place. Now that he had his braces off, he was pleased with the way he looked when he smiled.

As Gina looked in her mirror, she smiled too. Her hair was shiny. Her skin looked so much clearer since she had been swimming. Even though her skin was not perfect, she felt that she did not need much makeup. She liked the natural glow of her skin. Her smile seemed brighter than usual, maybe, she thought, because she felt good about how she looked. She was really looking forward to the dance.

Most people like to look their best. Exercising, eating a healthy diet, and resting properly all improve your appearance and outlook. Your appearance may influence how you feel about yourself, just as the appearance of others influences how you feel about them.

Objectives

- Identify the two main layers of the skin.
- List the four functions of the skin.
- Explain how nails and hair are related to skin.
- Identify common skin problems.
- Describe the three degrees of burns.
- Describe the ways to prevent skin cancer.
- Describe the four kinds of teeth and their functions.
- Explain why it is important to brush and floss teeth.

Your Skin, Nails, and Hair

Imagine that you are meeting of group of people for the first time. Your first impression of them is likely to be strongly influenced by their appearance. You will probably notice immediately if their skin looks healthy and if their hair and nails are clean and well-groomed. It is important to remember that others meeting you for the first time will also notice your skin, hair, and nails. A well-groomed appearance says a lot about what you think about yourself and determines what others think about you as well.

The Structure of Skin

Your skin is the largest organ of your body. An **organ** is a group of different kinds of cells that perform a certain function. Your skin has four main functions: protection, temperature regulation, waste removal, and sensation. As shown in Figure 2-1, your skin consists of an inner and an outer layer—the dermis and epidermis. The layer of tissue that binds the skin to the body is called the **subcutaneous layer** [*sub kyoo TAY nee us*]. The body often stores fat in the subcutaneous layer.

Figure 2-1 Structure of skin

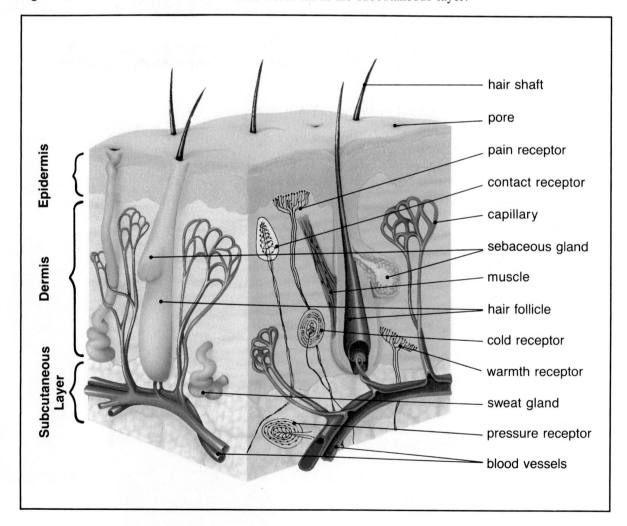

- hair shaft
- pore
- pain receptor
- contact receptor
- capillary
- sebaceous gland
- muscle
- hair follicle
- cold receptor
- warmth receptor
- sweat gland
- pressure receptor
- blood vessels

Epidermis

Dermis

Subcutaneous Layer

The Dermis   The inner layer of skin, called the **dermis** [*DUR mis*], contains most of the living structures of the skin— blood vessels, nerve endings, hair roots, and parts of sweat and oil glands. Near each shaft of hair are oil glands called **sebaceous glands** [*sih BAY shus*]. Sebaceous glands release an oil called **sebum** [*SEE bum*]. Sebum makes the skin moist and soft. Too little sebum can make the skin too dry.

The dermis is made up of loosely organized groups of cells that produce collagen. **Collagen** [*KAHL uh jun*] is an elastic fiber that gives skin strength and flexibility. The dermis also contains tiny nerve endings that respond to heat, cold, pressure, pain, and touch. These nerve endings allow you to feel the coldness of ice, the softness of a kitten, or the sensations of pain when you touch a hot stove.

The dermis also contains sweat glands. **Sweat glands** are glands that extend from the dermis to the outer layer of the skin. The sweat glands produce perspiration, which helps to cool the body. **Perspiration** [*PUR spuh RAY shun*] is a body fluid made up of water, salt, and wastes from your blood.

The sweat glands work together with tiny blood vessels in the dermis to help the body maintain a normal temperature. When the body is too hot, blood vessels near the skin expand. This allows more blood to come near the surface of the body to release heat. At the same time, the sweat glands increase their production of perspiration. The perspiration that is produced absorbs the extra body heat. As perspiration evaporates from the skin's surface, the body cools. This keeps the body from overheating. When the body is too cold, the blood vessels shrink. This helps keep warm blood away from cold skin. Keeping the blood warm helps maintain body heat.

The Epidermis   The thin outer layer of the skin is called the **epidermis** [*ep ih DUR mis*]. The epidermis is actually made up of many layers of living cells. Between the cells is a fatty material that acts as a seal between the cells to protect the skin against water loss. A substance called **keratin** [*KEHR uh tin*], which is a fiberlike material, fills the outer cells, making them strong and tough.

The cells in the outer portion of the epidermis are dead. You constantly shed that part of your skin. Dead skin cells can be rubbed off by your clothing, washing, or any movement that causes friction. Cells at the base of the epidermis are constantly dividing and making new cells. The new cells force the older cells to the skin's surface, replacing the ones that you shed. All of these cells are replaced every 28 days.

Have you ever looked closely at your epidermis with a hand lens or magnifying glass? On the surface of the epidermis are many tiny openings called **pores.** The sweat glands release perspiration through the pores. The pores also provide openings for the sebum, or oil, that is released from the dermis. Sebum coats the outer layer of the skin. This coating also contains an acid that keeps germs from entering the body.

Figure 2-2 Perspiration helps regulate body temperature.

Health Bulletin

If laid out flat, the skin would cover about 20 square feet. It weighs about seven pounds, more than twice the weight of the brain.

Figure 2-3 The greater the amount of melanin in the skin, the darker the skin.

Figure 2-4 Tips for healthy skin

1. Wash regularly.

2. Use skin care products in moderation.

3. Know the ingredients of any cosmetics or products you use.

4. Avoid soaking in a bath for long periods of time. Your skin will lose moisture.

5. Apply a moisturizer to skin after washing to help retain moisture.

6. Eat a balanced diet.

7. Avoid smoking.

8. Drink plenty of water.

9. Get plenty of sleep.

10. Protect your skin from cold weather and sunburn.

Skin Pigmentation   Substances in the lower part of the epidermis, called pigments, give color to the skin. **Melanin** [*MEL uh nin*], a brown pigment, is the most important. The more melanin in the epidermis, the darker your skin will be. Melanin helps block ultraviolet rays in sunlight, which can damage skin. As a result of exposure to sunlight, some skin makes more melanin. The skin becomes darker, or gets a tan. Melanin is not always evenly distributed in the body. In some people, melanin gathers in small areas, forming freckles.

Raised growths of brown pigment are called **moles.** Most moles are harmless. Sometimes, however, a mole can develop into a serious form of skin cancer. If a mole becomes irritated or changes in color, size, or shape, see your doctor immediately.

Birthmarks are marks on the skin that are caused either by enlarged blood vessels or extra pigment. They are usually present at birth. Many birthmarks eventually disappear. Covering birthmarks with makeup will make them less noticeable.

Skin Care

A glowing, smooth skin is one of the first things you notice about an attractive, well-groomed person. But looking neat and attractive is easier when you are healthy. You can keep your body healthy with responsible hygiene. **Hygiene** [*HY jeen*] is a set of healthful practices that help prevent disease. Hygiene includes good health habits, such as eating a variety of foods, exercising, getting enough rest, and keeping your body clean. Your hygiene program should also include careful choices of grooming products. Many of them have chemicals that can irritate the skin.

Regular washing will help keep your skin healthy and clean. Washing with a terry face cloth should help gently remove the top layer of dead cells. Most people have a combination of skin types, that is, some areas are oily and others are dry or normal. Washing oily areas more than once a day may be necessary. Figure 2-4 gives tips for healthy skin care.

Dry skin usually is not a problem among teenagers. But cold winter winds and dry hot air can rob the skin of its moisture. Creams or lotions that hold in moisture will protect dry skin. However, makeup may clog the skin's sebaceous glands and contribute to skin irritations.

Body odor occurs when bacteria come in contact with perspiration. Bacteria grow easily on the skin when it is warm and moist. Bathing or showering daily will cut down on body odor. Both deodorants and antiperspirants also help to fight body odor, but antiperspirants decrease or prevent heavy perspiration. Neither deodorants nor antiperspirants take the place of washing.

Hair and Nails

Your nails and hair are actually keratin-filled epidermis cells. Clear plates of these cells make up your fingernails and toenails. The nails themselves have no nerve endings or blood vessels. They serve as a buffer against blows and thus they protect the sensitive tips of your fingers and toes.

Figure 2-5 Baldness may be passed from father to son.

The hair shaft that emerges from the epidermis is made up entirely of hardened dead cells. Because the hair cells are dead, it does not hurt to have your hair cut. Hairs grow out of hair follicles deep in the dermis. **Hair follicles** are bulb-shaped roots that extend from the dermis up to the epidermis, as you saw in Figure 2-1. When hair cells form and push up from the deepest part of the follicle, they die and become filled with keratin.

Most of your body is covered with hair. Your hair protects you in several ways. The hair on your head helps to keep you warm. Hair helps keep dust and dirt out of your eyes, ears, and nose. Your eyebrows and eyelashes also help keep direct light out of your eyes.

Hair color is determined by the amount and kind of pigment in your hair, which, in turn, is determined by heredity. The shape of the hair shaft determines whether your hair is straight, wavy, or curly. The flatter the hair shaft, the curlier the hair. Straight hair has a round shaft. As you get older, the production of melanin slows down, causing gray or white hairs to develop. The age at which a person becomes gray is also hereditary.

As some men grow older their hair becomes thinner or they become bald. Baldness is the loss of the hair from the top of the head. Pattern baldness is caused by a combination of an inherited trait and the effects of a male hormone. It is the most common kind of baldness. Inherited hair loss occurs gradually as part of the normal aging process. Other forms of baldness can occur in both men and women and are related to illness. In these cases, the hair loss is usually temporary.

Hair Care

The key to keeping your hair looking healthy is to keep it clean, brushed, and free of tangles. Clean hair is easy to groom. One or two applications of your shampoo should be enough to cleanse the hair. Be sure to rinse your hair thoroughly after

Health Bulletin

Contrary to popular belief, baldness is not inherited only from the mother. It can be passed along from either the mother or the father.

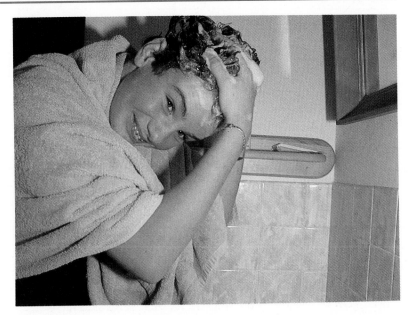

Figure 2-6 Washing and grooming help keep the scalp healthy.

shampooing and conditioning. Otherwise, your hair may look dull. Once you have washed and rinsed your hair, a wide-toothed comb should be used to comb it out. The best way to dry your hair is to let it dry naturally.

Regular brushing stimulates the circulation of blood to your scalp. It also removes dirt and spreads natural oils over the hair, helping it shine. Brushing 100 strokes every night, however, is not good advice. Excessive brushing or combing may damage the hair or scalp. Overexposure to a hair dryer, heated rollers, or curling irons can make your hair brittle and dry. Tight ponytails, cornrowing, permanent curling or straightening, dyeing, and bleaching can all damage the hair or scalp.

Many people choose to change their natural hair color. Products that dye, bleach, or strip hair color can leave the hair dry and brittle. Some hair dyes or bleaches also can be harmful to your scalp.

Hair Removal

Many people include hair removal in their grooming routine. Several methods may be used to remove unwanted hair from the body. Most of the usual methods are not permanent. Whatever method you use, be careful not to harm your skin.

When shaving, you may wish to soak the skin with a warm or hot towel. A lather of soap suds or shaving cream will help further soak the hairs and smooth the shaving process. This will keep you from removing too much of the epidermis along with the hair.

Some women prefer to use depilatories instead of shaving. A **depilatory** [*dih PIL uh tawr ee*] is a hair-removing cream, lotion, or spray. They may irritate the skin, so be sure to read carefully all directions on your product. It is safest to use depilatories only on the legs. Waxing has longer-lasting results than either shaving or using a depilatory. Waxing is a method of hair removal that in-

Health History
Czar Peter the Great of Russia did not like beards. He imposed a tax on beards, and then outlawed them in 1710.

volves the application of a warm waxy substance on the skin. After the substance cools and hardens, it is pulled off along with the unwanted hair.

Electrolysis [*ih lek TRAHL uh sis*] is a form of permanent hair removal that involves passing an electric current through each hair follicle. This should be done only by someone who is specially trained in electrolysis. Usually electrolysis is used on small areas, such as the upper lip. It is an expensive and sometimes painful procedure.

Caring for Hands and Feet

Washing with soap helps get rid of disease-causing germs that collect under the fingernails. Good nail care can also help prevent hangnails. A bit of loose cuticle is called a hangnail. A **cuticle** [*KYOO tih kul*] is the hard epidermis around the edge of a fingernail. To remove a hangnail, cut off the small bit of skin and rub lotion around the edge of the nail. Hangnails left ragged can become infected. When you trim your fingernails, you may want to shape them to be more attractive. To do this, use a nail file or an emery board when your nails are dry.

Infection can also result from ingrown toenails. An ingrown toenail is a painful condition in which a toenail cuts into the skin. Trimming the toenails in a straight cut can help prevent ingrown toenails. If an infection occurs, you should consult your doctor right away.

To prevent foot problems it is also important to wear shoes that fit properly. Shoes that do not fit can rub on the skin and cause hard, thick areas of keratin called **corns.** Corns are painful because they press on nerves and sensitive skin under them. Wearing better-fitting shoes and placing pads around the corns can help lessen the pressure.

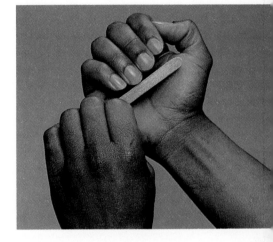

Figure 2-7 Trim nails are a sign of good personal grooming.

Lesson Review

Your skin is your largest organ and has several important functions. It helps keep germs from entering the body. It also helps regulate temperature and remove wastes. Knowing how to care properly for your skin, nails, and hair is an important part of developing and maintaining a healthy look. Care should be taken in choosing personal care products. Some with harsh chemicals can result in damage to the skin, nails, or hair.

1 What are four living structures found in the dermis?

2 What is the name of the outer layer of skin?

3 What is an advantage of melanin?

4 What is the substance in your fingernails that makes them tough?

5 List three healthful habits that contribute to good hygiene.

6 Name two ways you can help prevent body odor.

Treating Skin Problems

Skin problems are very common. Some stem from the natural processes that occur in your body as you develop into an adult. Others are caused by germs, injury, or environmental conditions. Some problems can be avoided and cared for through simple first aid. For more serious problems, you should see a dermatologist. A **dermatologist** [*DUR muh TAHL uh just*] is a doctor who treats skin disorders.

Acne

Acne is a skin problem very common in teenagers. It is related to the natural changes in the body during development, which cause an excess of sebum to be produced. The extra sebum causes blackheads, whiteheads, and pimples which are referred to as **acne.** A blackhead is a plug of hardened sebum in a pore. The blackhead is darkened not by dirt but by exposure to air. A whitehead is a plugged pore that is not exposed to air because the sebum has collected under the epidermis. Sometimes bacteria grow in the trapped sebum. This causes pimples to form. A **pimple** is a blocked pore that is inflamed and infected. It may be filled with pus.

For many years, scientists thought that greasy foods or chocolate caused pimples. Recent research, however, has shown that foods rarely cause acne. Acne may become worse through eating some foods though. The iodine in fish and many fast foods are examples. If you find that eating certain foods seems to increase your skin problems, avoid them.

Mild cases of acne can be treated by keeping the skin clean. Some dermatologists recommend washing the face with only a face cloth and warm water. Others suggest using only very mild soaps. You should also avoid picking or squeezing pimples and blackheads. Squeezing is likely to increase rather than relieve your problem, because it causes infection to spread.

If the acne is severe, you should consult your doctor. Serious cases of acne may result in scars. A doctor may prescribe various treatments, including the use of medicines. Overuse of some skin lotions can worsen the problem because they contribute to clogged pores. Use a cream or lotion only when suggested by your doctor. Fortunately, most people eventually outgrow their acne problems.

Figure 2-8 How a pimple develops

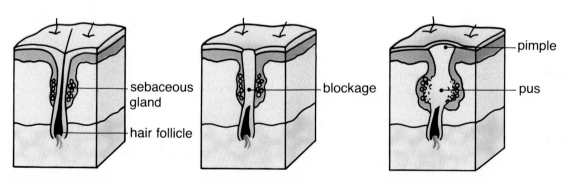

Dermatitis

The word used to describe redness and swelling of the skin is **dermatitis** [*dur muh TY tis*]. Dermatitis is not a disease but a skin condition that may result from many different causes.

An **allergy** is a reaction of the body to an irritating substance. Pollen, dust, plants, and animals are common causes of various allergies. You may eat, breath in, or brush against the allergy-causing substance. Some substances can affect your breathing or heart beat. At other times, your skin may be affected.

Eczema [*EK suh muh*] is a swelling and redness of the skin, including blisters and itching, usually caused by an allergic reaction. Sometimes it results from food, such as chocolate or tomatoes. **Hives** are bumps on the surface of the skin, usually caused by an allergic reaction to food or medicine. They may also be caused by emotional stress. The bumps may be small or cover large areas of the skin. Hives usually itch badly and burn. Your doctor may prescribe medicines to relieve the intense itching. If you think you have an allergic reaction, try to identify the cause so you can avoid it.

Dermatitis may be caused when a harsh or irritating substance touches the skin. Contact dermatitis, as it is called, can be caused by detergents, clothing, soaps, perfumes, hair dyes, and makeup.

One of the most common forms of contact dermatitis is a poison ivy rash. An oil in the sap of this plant causes the skin to turn red and blister, usually within 48 hours. Itching and burning usually occur. Some people even have headaches and fevers. With or without treatment, a poison ivy rash normally disappears within three weeks. The First Aid Manual of this book has some tips for immediate care of a poison ivy rash.

The oil in this sap is extremely potent. A single ounce of it can cause a rash on 28 million people. Even during the winter, the sap from a leafless broken vine can cause a reaction. The best way to avoid getting poison ivy is to avoid touching the plant. In Figure 2-9 you can see the three-leaf arrangement of the poison ivy and poison oak, and the fernlike leaves of poison sumac.

Skin Infections

Skin infections are problems caused by germs. They can generally be prevented by avoiding contact with an infected person or object. Different germs cause a variety of skin problems.

One of the skin infections caused by bacteria is an outbreak of boils. A **boil** is a hard, red lump that is tender to the touch and is caused by an infected hair follicle. Most boils will burst in about two weeks if left alone. Wet, hot compresses applied to the boil every few hours will relieve pain and encourage bursting. Do not pinch or mash a boil because this will spread the infection.

Another common bacterial infection is impetigo. **Impetigo** [*im pih TY goh*] is a skin infection caused by bacteria and characterized by small blisters that form yellow crusts. The infection spreads easily and enters the body through breaks in the skin,

Figure 2-9 Notice the leaf arrangements of poison ivy *(top)*, poison oak *(middle)*, and poison sumac *(bottom)*.

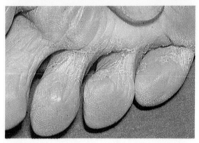

Figure 2-10 Ringworm *(above)* and athlete's foot *(below)* are fungal infections.

such as insect bites, cuts, and scrapes. The infected areas should be washed several times a day, enough to soak off any crusts. If it is more than a mild case, a doctor should be seen. Medicines are used to fight the bacteria both internally and at the site of the infection.

A wart is a skin growth caused by a virus. Warts are common in teenagers. Usually warts will disappear without treatment after several months. Warts that occur on the face, soles of the feet, or in the genital area should be examined and treated by a doctor.

Fungal infections are infections caused by a group of organisms, including yeasts and molds, that cause redness, itching, and flaking of the skin. The two most common types of fungal skin infections are ringworm and athlete's foot. Ringworm gets its name from the way it looks; it is not caused by a worm. **Ringworm** is a fungus that causes red, scaly, round patches. Ringworm can be transferred from person to person or from a pet to a person. It is not serious and is easily treated.

Athlete's foot is an irritating and sometimes painful fungal infection of the moist skin under and between the toes. The fungus causes the skin to become red, flaky, and itchy. Drying the feet well, using an antifungal cream or ointment, and wearing absorbent cotton socks will help to end the infection and prevent its return.

Scalp Problems

Small flakes of dead skin from the scalp are called **dandruff.** These flakes appear when the skin cells on the scalp grow very fast. Dandruff may be caused by mild forms of skin diseases, such as eczema or psoriasis, but it is usually not a serious problem. If regular shampooing and careful rinsing do not control the flaking, antidandruff shampoos may help. If the shampoo does not work after a few weeks of application, you may wish to see a dermatologist.

When tiny animals called lice infest the hair, the condition is called **pediculosis** [*puh dik yuh LOH sis*]. Lice feed on the scalp, causing it to itch. They may also cause a rash on the neck. Lice lay their eggs on hair shafts, as shown in Figure 2-11. The

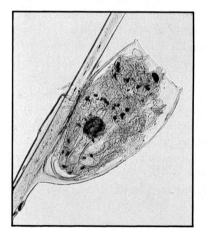
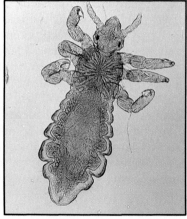

Figure 2-11 Nit on hair *(left)*; adult louse *(right)*.

eggs are called nits. Unlike dandruff, the nits cannot be shaken off. The spread of pediculosis can be reduced by not sharing clothing, combs, and brushes with others. If you discover lice in your hair, you can comb away the nits with a fine-toothed comb wet with vinegar. Then wash your hair with a special medicated shampoo.

Burns

Burns are caused by being in contact with hot objects, hot liquids or vapors, or with electricity or chemicals. Burns destroy the skin and affect the body's ability to fight infections. Burns also upset blood circulation. Burns are divided into first-degree, second-degree, and third-degree burns depending on the damage they cause. **First-degree burns** are burns that injure only the epidermis and heal without leaving scars. These might be caused by mild sunburn. **Second-degree burns** are burns that injure the epidermis and part of the dermis and may leave some scarring. Swelling and blistering are involved. Second-degree burns may be caused by such things as hot liquids, steam, or extreme sunburn. **Third-degree burns** are burns that go through all layers of the skin and affect the tissue underneath. The skin may look white, very red, or even black. Most third-degree burns do not heal themselves. The damaged skin usually has to be removed and new skin grafted on.

HEALTH + TECHNOLOGY

ARTIFICIAL SKIN—Every year about 10,000 people in this country die from severe burns. Severe burns allow the loss of water from the body. Once the protective covering of the skin is gone, the body is also in great danger of bacterial infection. When someone has been burned, the most important first step is to close the wound. The best way to close the wound is to transplant skin from another part of the victim's body. Unfortunately, some burns affect such a large area that transplanting the patient's own skin is not possible.

Fortunately, chemical engineers have recently developed a new product to help burn victims. This product is artificial skin. Artificial skin can quickly cover and protect large areas of burned skin. Artificial skin is a two-layer material made of tissue from cattle. It is only two-hundredths of an inch thick. This material guards against infection and the loss of fluids while the patient's skin grows back.

Over small wounds, artificial skin is eventually shed as the natural skin underneath heals. Over larger wounds, the artificial skins lasts up to 40 days before it breaks down and must be replaced. This new product may help save the lives of thousands of burn victims.

1 What two factors threaten burn victims?
2 What are some advantages of artificial skin?

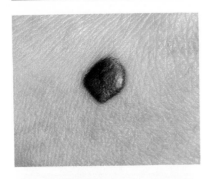

Figure 2-12 The risk of developing skin cancer increases with the length of exposure to ultraviolet light. Molelike growths of unusual color or shape can be one warning sign.

Skin Cancer

There are several different types of skin cancer. **Cancer** is an uncontrolled growth of cells that invade and destroy neighboring healthy tissue. Some skin cancers are small pink growths that increase in size, damaging surrounding tissues, but do not spread to other parts of the body. Other cancers begin as a lump that turns into an ulcer and may spread to other parts of the body. One common type of skin cancer is called **melanoma.** Melanomas are enlarged moles that bleed. They may be flat or raised and vary in size. This type of skin cancer usually spreads through the body.

Skin cancer can be cured if it is identified and treated early. It can also be avoided by not getting too much sun. Skin cancer is a long-term danger of exposure to ultraviolet rays. The risk of developing skin cancer increases with age, the number of years of exposure, and the number of sunburns.

Protection from Harmful Sun Rays

Brief exposure to sunlight stimulates your skin to produce vitamin D. Vitamin D is necessary for the healthy formation of bones and teeth. However, overexposure to the ultraviolet rays from the sun can damage your skin. Sunlamps at home and in tanning studios give off harmful ultraviolet rays just as the sun does. Good hygiene includes knowing how much sun you can get without harming your skin.

There are different preparations that protect your skin from sunlight, depending on your skin. These preparations are graded by numbers called sun protection factors (SPF). The higher the number, the greater the degree of protection. People with fair skin are wise to select a sunscreen with a value over 10. Darker-skinned individuals may be safe with a somewhat lower grade. When applying sunscreen, be careful to apply enough lotion to the nose, lips, shoulders, and knees, which burn more readily than other parts of the body.

Lesson Review

Most teenagers are affected by one or more of the common skin problems. However, many of the bad effects of these disorders can be lessened. Personal cleanliness, avoidance of the personal articles of an infected person, and prompt medical care of persistent problems can all help reduce the effects of skin problems.

1 Define *acne*.

2 What is eczema?

3 Poison ivy is an example of what type of skin problem?

4 Name two common fungal infections.

5 What kind of burn affects more than the layers of the skin?

6 What is the main cause of skin cancer?

Your Teeth

A bright smile begins with clean teeth. Strong, healthy teeth are important to your appearance as well as to your health. Chewing food properly aids digestion. Your teeth also affect how you speak and shape your face. People once thought that old age meant loss of teeth. But good dental care started early in life can help your teeth last a lifetime.

Structure and Function of Teeth

Each tooth in your mouth has three main parts: the crown, the neck, and the root. The **crown** is the part of the tooth that you see above the gum line. The **neck** is where the crown and root come together, which is just below the gum line. The **root** is the part of the tooth below the gum line that fits into the jawbone. You can identify these three main parts in Figure 2-13.

The tooth is made up of four kinds of tissue. **Enamel** [*ih NAM ul*] is a white, compact material containing calcium that covers the crown. Enamel is the hardest substance in your body. It is harder even than bone.

Beneath the hard enamel is dentin. **Dentin** makes up the body of the tooth, extending into the root, and is softer than enamel. The dentin holds the pulp. The **pulp** is soft tissue containing small blood vessels and nerve fibers. The pulp is housed in the center of the tooth and extends through canals in the roots into the jawbone. The soft tissue of the pulp cushions the nerves. The nerves are sensitive to heat, cold, pressure, and pain. The blood vessels nourish the tooth. The fourth kind of tissue in the tooth is cementum. **Cementum** [*sih MEN tum*] is a sensitive, bonelike material that covers the root of the tooth.

Your teeth have an important role in preparing food for use in your body. Each tooth performs a certain task. In Figure 2-13 you can see the **incisors** [*in SY zur*], the sharp front teeth used to cut

Figure 2-13 Structure and position of teeth

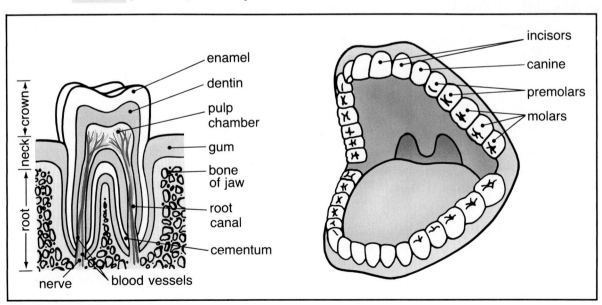

A tooth that is knocked out is not necessarily lost. If a knocked-out tooth can be reimplanted within 30 minutes, there is a 90 percent chance that it will survive.

Figure 2-14 Process of tooth decay

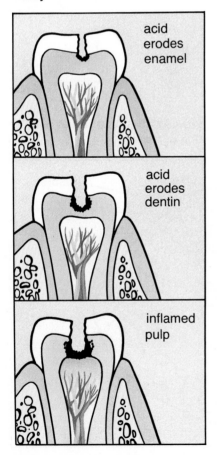

acid erodes enamel

acid erodes dentin

inflamed pulp

food. Notice their flat, sharp edges. The **canines** are pointed teeth that tear food into smaller pieces. They are also known as the cuspids. The **premolars** are teeth with double points that tear and crush food. **Molars** are large teeth with several rounded points that grind food into bits.

During each person's lifetime, two sets of teeth appear. The primary teeth, which make up the first set of teeth, form before birth. Usually all the primary teeth have grown in by age three. The permanent teeth, which make up the second set of teeth, begin to appear at about age six and continue to grow out over a period of years. As the permanent teeth grow in, the roots of the primary teeth dissolve. The permanent teeth gradually push out the remaining structures of primary teeth. Another 12 permanent teeth will grow in also.

Usually the first permanent teeth are the six-year molars. The six-year molars grow in behind primary teeth and do not replace any of them. These molars appear between the ages of six and seven years. The six-year molars help determine the positions of the other permanent teeth and give stability during the time primary teeth are lost and permanent teeth grow in.

The order of growth of the other permanent teeth is: the incisors, the canines, the premolars, and the second molars. The second molars grow in at about age 12. The third molars, or wisdom teeth, grow in behind the second molars if there is space. The wisdom teeth often appear between ages 17 and 21.

Dental Problems

The most common dental problems are decay and gum disease. Other dental problems involve the structure of the jaws and the spacing of the teeth.

Dental Caries   One of the most common diseases of humans is tooth decay, or **dental caries.** If left untreated, dental caries will eventually cause cavities. **Cavities** are the holes in enamel that result from decay.

Tooth decay begins with plaque. **Plaque** [*plak*] is a colorless layer of bacteria, saliva, and food particles. If left on the teeth, the bacteria break down starches and sugars, producing an acid that can destroy tooth enamel. The amount of sugar eaten is not the only important factor in decay. How long sugar remains in the mouth and how often sugar is eaten are important factors, too. This process of tooth decay is illustrated in Figure 2-14.

If the enamel of a tooth has been damaged, a dentist may recommend replacing the damaged area with a filling. A mixture of silver, tin, and mercury is often used. Before the filling is applied, the dentist removes all decay from the tooth. This prevents the bacteria from spreading decay deeper into the dentin and pulp of the tooth, which can be extremely painful.

In addition, infection may cause the pulp to die. A strong blow to a tooth also can result in such pulp damage. If the pulp dies, the tooth should be treated to save the tooth and to prevent bacteria from invading other healthy tissues.

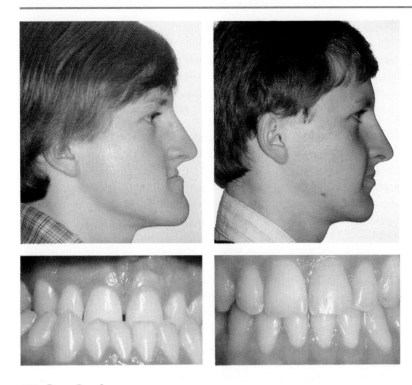

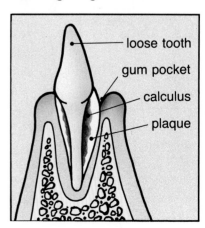

Figure 2-15 Malocclusion may be corrected with braces. Notice the profile of this person before and after treatment.

Malocclusion   Figure 2-15 illustrates the problems of overbite or underbite which are called malocclusions. A **malocclusion** [*mal uh KLOO zhun*] is a condition in which the upper and lower teeth do not line up properly when the mouth is closed. As a result, the teeth cannot bite, chew, or grind food correctly. This causes problems with digestion. Malocclusion may also impair speech. Because poorly aligned teeth are hard to clean, malocclusion can lead to dental decay or gum disease.

Most cases of malocclusion can be corrected by braces put on the teeth by a dentist or orthodontist. Severe cases of malocclusion may require surgery to improve the shape or size of the jawbones.

Periodontal Disease   Diseases of the gum are called **periodontal disease** [PEHR ee oh DAHN tuhl]. Periodontal disease is usually caused by calculus, or plaque, or both. **Calculus** is hardened plaque. The most common forms of periodontal disease are gingivitis and periodontitis. **Gingivitis** [*jin juh VY tis*] is an early stage of gum disease that may cause inflamed and swollen gums. The gums may also bleed easily during brushing. If untreated, gingivitis can lead to periodontitis.

Periodontitis [*pehr ee oh dahn TY tis*] is the later stage of gum disease that may cause chronic inflammation of the gum tissue and destruction of the bone tissue. See Figure 2-16. The margin of the gum begins to pull back from the tooth and a pocket forms. Pus may collect in the pocket, further irritating the gums and bone tissue. Bone loss may occur, causing the teeth to loosen. If the disease continues without treatment, the teeth will eventually fall out or need to be removed. If your gums bleed easily, consult your dentist.

Figure 2-16 Periodontitis is the later stage of gum disease.

Oral Cancers A cancer is abnormal, uncontrolled growth of cells that invades and kills other tissues. Oral cancer is characterized by the rapid growth of abnormal cells in the mouth. It may occur in several forms, including sores or lumps. Some abnormal growths of cells in the mouth are not cancer. **Leukoplakia** [*loo kuh PLAK ee uh*], for example, is a disease of the mouth marked by white patches on the cheek, gum, tongue, or lips. It is not a form of cancer, but may lead to cancer. If your doctor sees signs of leukoplakia, a sample of the tissue may be taken and examined for cancer cells. Early detection and treatment can help cure the problem. Use of any form of tobacco, including smokeless tobacco, and alcohol contribute to the development of oral cancer.

Dental Care

Good dental care begins with careful selection of the foods you eat. Eating balanced meals every day helps prevent dental decay. Daily care of your teeth is very important in both preventing decay and keeping your gums healthy.

Good oral hygiene involves brushing and flossing. Brushing your teeth thoroughly at least twice a day helps to remove plaque. Use a flat, soft toothbrush that can reach all of your teeth. Angle the toothbrush against the teeth and use short, gentle, back-and-forth strokes. Do this to the outside, inside, and tops of your teeth. To brush the insides of the front teeth, use the front end of your toothbrush in an up-and-down stroke.

Brushing cannot remove the plaque between your teeth. It also cannot clean under the gums. For this reason, you should floss

Figure 2-17 The graph shows the effectiveness of some methods of preventing tooth decay.

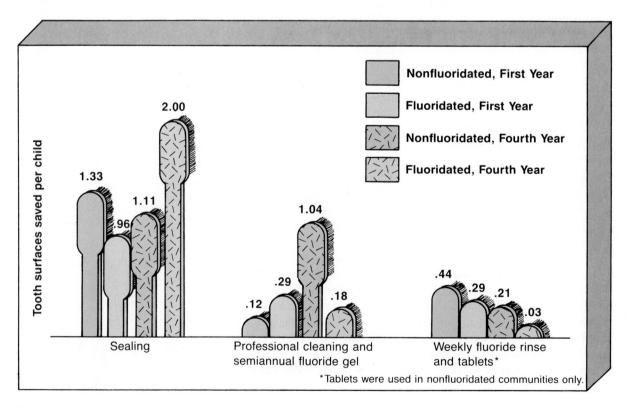

every day to remove plaque and food between the teeth and under the gums. To do this, wind about 18 inches of dental floss securely around your fingers as shown in Figure 2-18. Ease the floss between the gum and the tooth and gently scrape it along the inside of the tooth. This should be done carefully to avoid injury to the gums. Use a new section of dental floss as you clean each tooth. Rinse your mouth well with water.

Brushing and flossing also help keep the breath fresh. Bad breath can result when people do not take proper care of their teeth. If you regularly floss and brush your teeth and bad breath persists, you should see your doctor.

Fluoride has been found to be helpful in preventing dental problems. **Fluoride** [*FLAWR yd*] is a tasteless, odorless chemical that unites with tooth enamel to increase resistance to tooth decay. Many cities today add fluoride to their water supply. Where fluoridated water is not available, fluoride tablets, mouth rinses, or toothpaste can be used to help prevent tooth decay.

Dental Checkups   A regular dental checkup is vital for the prevention of tooth and gum disease. Checkups should be made on a regular basis, once or twice a year, or as often as your dentist suggests. Regular visits to the dentist make it possible to discover and treat problems early. Treatment will then be more effective and less costly.

A dentist will usually see that a number of tasks are performed. Professional teeth cleaning is one task. During the teeth cleaning, any calculus on the teeth is removed. A person who specializes in cleaning teeth is called a **dental hygienist.**

Your dentist will also x-ray your teeth, as needed. X-rays help to identify dental problems that cannot be seen with the eye. The dentist will also look closely at your teeth for signs of caries or gum problems.

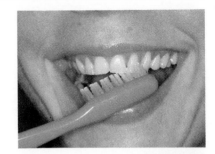

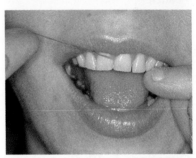

Figure 2-18 Healthy oral hygiene should include regular brushing and flossing.

Lesson Review

Your teeth are made of the hardest material in your body. They have different shapes which are related to their purposes in helping to break up food for digestion. Proper diet and oral hygiene can help prevent the most common dental problems. Braces are usually used to correct problems of bite. Proper care of the teeth includes regular brushing, flossing, and dental checkups.

1 What are the four kinds of tissue that make up teeth?

2 Name four main types of permanent teeth.

3 What is *plaque?*

4 What is another name for overbite or underbite?

5 What role does flossing play in oral hygiene?

6 Describe four steps that you can take to help keep your teeth and gums healthy.

Chapter Review

Vocabulary

acne	dermatologist	mole
allergy	dermis	neck
athlete's foot	eczema	organ
birthmark	electrolysis	pediculosis
boil	enamel	periodontal disease
calculus	epidermis	periodontitis
cancer	first-degree burn	perspiration
canine	fluoride	pimple
cavity	gingivitis	plaque
cementum	hair follicle	pore
collagen	hives	premolar
corn	hygiene	pulp
crown	impetigo	ringworm
cuticle	incisor	root
dandruff	keratin	sebaceous gland
dental caries	leukoplakia	sebum
dental hygienist	malocclusion	second-degree burn
dentin	melanin	subcutaneous layer
depilatory	melanoma	sweat gland
dermatitis	molar	third-degree burn

Using Vocabulary

Questions 1–12. On a separate sheet of paper, write the term from the column on the right that matches the phrase on the left.

1 brown pigment
2 condition in which lice infest the hair and feed on the scalp
3 form of permanent hair removal
4 hardened plaque
5 oil released by sebaceous glands
6 white, compact material that covers the crown of a tooth
7 bulb-shaped root that extends from the dermis to epidermis
8 redness and swelling of skin
9 condition in which upper and lower teeth do not line up properly
10 blocked pore that is inflamed and infected
11 body of a tooth
12 set of healthful practices that help prevent diseases

a hair follicle
b pimple
c enamel
d malocclusion
e sebum
f calculus
g melanin
h dermatitis
i dentin
j hygiene
k pediculosis
l electrolysis

Interpreting Ideas

1 Identify and describe the four kinds of tissue that make up teeth.

2 How does sugar promote tooth decay?

3 What are the four functions of the skin?

4 How do moles and birthmarks differ?

5 Why does dandruff appear? What measures can be taken to control dandruff?

6 Compare the three degrees of burns.

7 How does the dermis help to regulate body temperature?

8 How is each of the various kinds of teeth adapted for a particular function?

9 What steps can you take to maintain healthy teeth and gums? Why are brushing and flossing important?

10 How do tanning and freckling occur?

11 In what sense is acne an infection?

12 What kind of mole should be seen by a doctor?

13 How do eczema and hives differ?

14 Describe impetigo: its appearance, its cause, and its treatment.

15 Identify and describe the two most common types of fungal skin infections.

16 Identify and describe the two main layers of the skin. How are nails and hair related to skin?

17 How can you help prevent ingrown toenail?

18 Of what benefit to the scalp is regular brushing? List three grooming habits that can damage hair or scalp.

19 Describe melanoma. Generally, how can skin cancer be avoided?

20 In what ways do the primary and permanent teeth differ?

Applying Concepts

1 What functions of hair appear to be more closely related to the needs of people living in primitive times?

2 How can you explain a dramatic increase in perspiration and the onset of acne in a 14-year-old boy?

3 Why is it recommended that dental checkups begin at three years of age rather than at six years, when the permanent teeth begin to appear?

4 How can untreated malocclusion lead to periodontal disease?

5 What would you recommend as the best way to treat a mild case of acne? How would you care for a severe case of acne?

6 Why do you think that some people develop gray hair?

7 Don has bad breath. What steps can Don take to improve or eliminate this condition?

8 In each of the following situations identify the person's condition or disease and describe the steps that should be taken once a diagnosis is made: (a) Ellen has difficulty biting and chewing her food correctly. Lately she has had some digestive problems. (b) After showering, Cary noticed some redness and itching between her toes. (c) Rob, who has been using smokeless tobacco for two years, has noticed thickened white patches on his lips and tongue.

9 Describe skin changes under the following circumstances: (a) when you are cold; (b) when you are hot; (c) when you are worried; (d) when you have been exercising.

10 How would you outline a helpful strategy for improving a friend's acne?

Projects

1 In your school or local library find out more about warts. Are warts contagious? What are satellite warts? What are the methods of treatment? Can warts be contracted from the skin of toads?

2 Doctors can gather important data about the health of their patients by looking at their nails. Find out what kinds of information can be gathered in this way.

3 Create several humorous posters that illustrate tips for taking care of your skin, hair, nails, and teeth.

4 Set up a Personal Appearance Plan designed to improve one or two aspects of your appearance over an eight-week period. For each aspect that you decide to work on, write a goal for achieving it. If you have a problem with dandruff, for example, your goal may be to be rid of dandruff by a certain date. Then write down at least two steps that you intend to take in order to achieve your goal. For example: (1) Wash hair regularly with an antidandruff shampoo. (2) If condition has not improved after four weeks of regular washing with an antidandruff shampoo, see a dermatologist.

Your senses keep you in touch with your environment. They can help you understand and even shape the world around you.

CHAPTER THREE

YOUR
SENSE ORGANS

S arah loves the challenge of making pottery. Now, after much practice, she can place her hands in just the right place to make the shapes she wants. As she works, she likes the feel of the cool clay on her hands. She likes to listen to the soft whirr of the potting wheel. She likes the earthy smell of the clay. And when she has finished her work and her pots have been fired, she likes to see the soft colors of the glazes on her pots.

Sarah uses many of her senses in making pottery. She uses her sight, her hearing, her sense of touch, and her sense of smell. Have you ever imagined what life would be without your sense organs? Your eyes, ears, skin, tongue, and nose are precious gifts. These organs help you gain information about the world around you.

Objectives

- Describe the structure of the eye.
- Describe peripheral and stereoscopic vision.
- List four common vision problems and four common eye diseases.
- Explain the function of each of the ear's three parts.
- Explain how your ears help you maintain your balance.
- Identify the causes of hearing loss.
- Explain how eyes and ears may be protected.
- List the five sensations of touch.
- Name the four qualities of taste and locate the smell receptors.

The Eye

Your eyes are truly windows to the world. They can detect shape, color, brightness, and movement. Your eyes can read a novel or judge the curve of a baseball. They can watch a fiery sunset fade to dark or see a baby's beaming face.

The Structure of the Eye

The eye is a delicate organ. If people are to see well, all parts of the eye must function properly. The eye must be well protected. The bones of the head guard it from injury. The eyelids close out unwanted light and dirt. Tears from nearby ducts keep the eye's surface moist and clean.

A cross-section of the eye is shown in Figure 3–1. The eye is filled with a clear jelly in its center. This jelly is called the **vitreous humor** [*VIH tree uhs HYOO mur*]. Three layers of tissue surround the vitreous humor. The outer layer, which has tough tissues, protects the eye. The middle layer provides a network of blood vessels that nourish the eye. The inner layer contains cells sensitive to light that enable the eye to see.

Figure 3-1 Structure of the eye

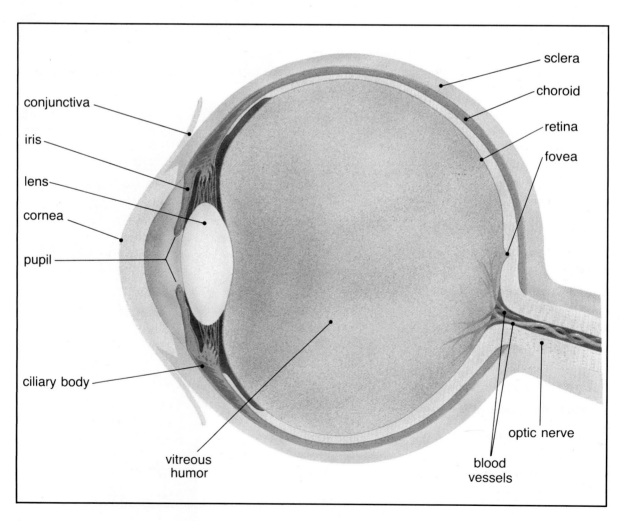

The Outer Layer When you look in a mirror, you can see the whites of your eyes. The **sclera** [*SKLER uh*], or the white of the eye, is a tough, fibrous tissue. The bulge in the front center of the eye is the cornea. The **cornea** is a clear, nearly circular structure that serves as a window to let light into the other layers of the eye. A thin layer of tears gives the cornea the necessary smoothness to be crystal clear.

The **conjunctiva** is a clear membrane that lines the insides of the eyelid. It also covers the front of the eye around the cornea.

The Middle Layer Light passes through the cornea to the pupil. The **pupil** is a round opening surrounded by muscles that regulate the amount of light that enters the eye. If the light is dim, the pupil enlarges. If the light is bright, the pupil becomes small to keep some of the light out of the eye. The size of the pupil is controlled by muscles in the iris. The **iris** is the colored circle surrounding the pupil which contains many tiny muscles. Depending on the amount and type of coloring it contains, the iris may appear brown, blue, green, or gray. The muscles in the iris receive their nourishment from blood vessels in the middle layer of eye tissue. The tissue that contains many blood vessels is called the **choroid.**

Behind the pupil, a lens is suspended by the middle layer of the eye. The **lens** is a flexible structure that aligns the light rays so that they come together in the inner layer of the eye. The point at which all of the light rays intersect is called the **focus.** The lens must constantly change shape to direct light rays to the proper focal point. The lens is naturally curved. However, tiny muscles allow it to flatten or curve more to focus on objects that are far away or nearby.

The Inner Layer After passing through the lens, light falls on the retina. The **retina** is the part of the eye that absorbs light rays and changes them into the electrical messages that then create images. The retina takes its name from the Latin word *rete*, which means a net. This refers to the network of blood vessels throughout the retina.

Receptors are nerve endings that send or receive signals. Receptors in the retina are sensitive to light and thus are called **photoreceptors.** Photoreceptors contain pigments that change when exposed to light. The process is similar to the way in which the chemicals on photographic paper change in the presence of light. But unlike photographic paper, the images made on the retina are not permanent.

There are two types of photoreceptors, as shown in Figure 3–2. These are rods and cones. The human eye contains about 120 million rods and 7 million cones. **Rods** are the cells that are very sensitive to light but which can only distinguish black from white. The rods allow you to see in dim light. Because the rods cannot distinguish color, you are unable to see colors at night.

Cones are photoreceptors that detect color, but are not very sensitive to light. Only during the day or in bright light is there

Health **History**
The iris of the eye is named for Iris, the mythological Greek goddess of the rainbow and messenger of the gods.

Figure 3-2   Photoreceptors of the eye

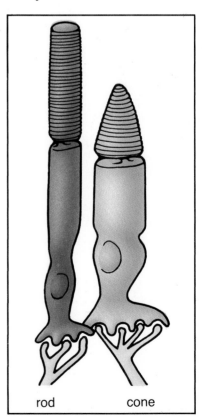

rod   cone

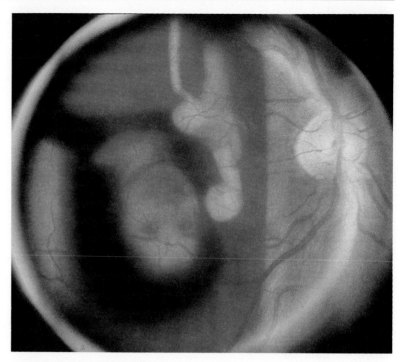

Figure 3-3 In this photograph of a retina, can you see the image of a young woman using a telephone?

enough light to stimulate the cones. Three different types of cones detect three different colors. Cones are receptive to reds, blues, and greens. Your eyes can mix these colors just as you do when you adjust the color on a television set. The mixture allows you to see a wide range of colors and shades of colors.

At the center back of the retina is a small yellow spot called the **fovea** [*FOH vee uh*]. The fovea contains a great concentration of cones, but it contains no rods. When you are in bright light, the fovea allows the eye to view things in great detail. Because it does not contain rods, however, the fovea does not provide clear images in dim light.

Another small area at the center of the retina contains neither rods nor cones. Thus, light landing on this spot, the blindspot, will not create an image. The **blindspot** is the point at which the optic nerve joins the eye.

How the Eye Sees

The cord of nerve fibers that carries messages to the brain is the **optic nerve.** When light strikes the rods and cones of the retina and causes chemical changes, the changes produce electrical messages, or nerve impulses. Nerve fibers at the base of the photoreceptors pass the impulses to the optic nerve, which relays the messages to the brain.

The brain must interpret these messages from the optic nerve. The process is similar to a computer arranging electrical signals into pictures on a video screen. As Figures 3–3 and 3–4 show, the image on the retina is upside down and reversed. Part of the brain's task is to process the information so that the vision matches the object being viewed.

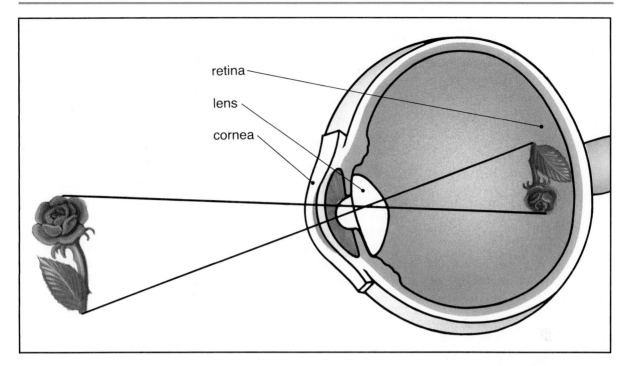

The brain must also coordinate the images received by each eye. Even though both eyes can focus on the same object at the same time, the views are slightly different. This is because the location of each eye is slightly different. With your eyes looking straight ahead, each eye is able to view objects within an oval-shaped pattern in front and to the side of the eye. The two patterns overlap, but they are not exactly the same. The process by which the brain puts these different images together is called **stereoscopic vision.** Stereoscopic vision allows you to see in three dimensions and to judge depth.

The slight difference in the location of each eye also creates peripheral vision. **Peripheral vision** [*puh RIF uh rul*] is the process of seeing objects at the sides of your eyes. Peripheral vision allows you to see out of the corners of your eyes.

Figure 3-4 The image on the retina is upside down and reversed.

Lesson Review

The eye is a delicate and complex organ. It can adjust and align light rays and process an image. It can turn the image to an electrical message and send that message to the brain for interpretation. Your eyes work together so that you can judge depth and see to the sides.

1 Describe the functions of the pupil and the iris.

2 What is the retina?

3 What are the two kinds of photoreceptors?

4 What does the optic nerve do?

5 Define *stereoscopic* and *peripheral vision*.

Correcting Eye Disorders

Your eyes are valuable organs. For this reason it is very important to have regular vision checkups and to recognize vision problems when they occur. Practicing good personal hygiene and choosing the correct treatment or lenses can help prevent many of these disorders.

Vision Checkups

During an eye examination, the doctor will look into each eye. By looking through the cornea, pupil, lens, and fluids directly at the retina, the doctor can check the clarity of the eye parts, the blood supply, and the structure of the retina. The doctor will also measure the pressure within the eye.

When your eyes are examined, you may be asked to read letters from an eye chart on a wall or in a machine. Figure 3-5 shows a Snellen chart. The Snellen chart has rows of letters. The letters in each row are smaller than those in the row above. During the exam, the vision of each eye will be checked. It is not uncommon for the vision of each eye to differ. If you can read the chart to the row marked 20/20, you have normal vision. The first 20 represents the number of feet from which you can read the letters. The second 20 represents the number of feet from which a person with normal vision could read the letters.

If you have 20/30 vision, your eyesight is slightly less than normal vision. You must stand at 20 feet to read what a person with normal vision could read from a distance of 30 feet. If your vision is 20/15, it is slightly sharper than normal vision. You can read at 20 feet what the person with normal vision can read only from a distance of 15 feet. A common vision checkup occurs before you are issued a driver's license. In most states, a driver must have corrected vision that is 20/40 or better.

Today many vision problems can be corrected. Most are corrected with eyeglasses or contact lenses. Some eye disorders respond better to one of these forms of correction than the other.

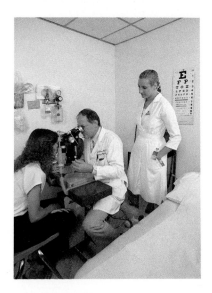

Figure 3-5   Regular vision checkups help preserve vision.

Vision Problems

Many people have vision problems because their eyes do not focus perfectly. **Nearsightedness** is a condition in which the retina is too far from the front of the eye, causing an image to come into focus in front of the retina rather than on it. For this reason, objects that are far away appear blurred, as shown in Figure 3-6. About one out of every five people is nearsighted. Nearsightedness usually can be corrected by placing a curved lens in front of the eye. The lens changes the direction of the light rays entering the eye. This enables the light rays to focus correctly on the retina. Figure 3-6 shows how a lens can correct nearsightedness.

Farsightedness is a condition in which the retina is too close to the front of the eye, causing an image to come into focus behind the retina rather than on it. Nearby objects appear blurred. A curved lens similar to the one shown in Figure 3-6 can help correct farsightedness.

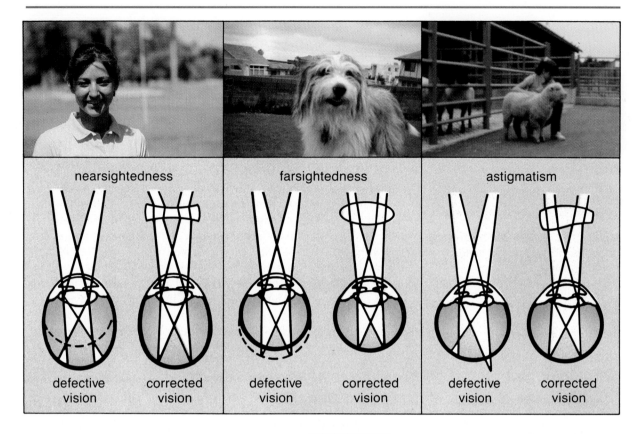

nearsightedness	farsightedness	astigmatism
defective vision — corrected vision	defective vision — corrected vision	defective vision — corrected vision

Astigmatism is another common eye problem. **Astigmatism** [*uh STIG muh tiz uhm*] is a disorder in which an irregularly shaped cornea or lens causes light rays to focus unevenly on the retina. Figure 3-6 shows how astigmatism distorts images.

Some vision problems can be caused when the muscles controlling the movement of the eyes do not work as they should. Sometimes these muscles do not keep the eyes pointed in the same direction. This may cause the eyes to be crossed. **Crosseye** is a condition in which the muscles pull one or both eyes toward the nose. A person with this muscle problem may experience double vision or have one eye dominate the other. Domination of one eye shuts down the vision in the other eye. Crosseye may be corrected with eye exercises, glasses, or surgery, but it must be detected early in life to preserve good vision.

Two vision problems that are caused by poor functioning of the photoreceptors are night blindness and colorblindness. **Night blindness** is a condition in which people do not have good vision in dim light. This problem is due to poor functioning of the rods. Night blindness may be caused by a diet that is too low in vitamin A or by damage to the retina.

People who have difficulty distinguishing colors are said to be **colorblind.** All or just some of their cones are not functioning properly. Most people with this disorder are unable to distinguish reds from greens. Colorblindness is a hereditary condition that occurs most often in men. About 8 of every 200 men, but only 1 of every 200 women, have some degree of color deficiency.

Figure 3-6 The shape of the eye or its parts can affect vision. Lenswear with a properly shaped lens will correct vision problems.

Figure 3-7   Braille is a system of raised printing that the blind read by touch.

Nearly one-half million people in this country have vision of 20/200 or worse. Those whose vision cannot be corrected by eyeglasses or contact lenses to 20/200 are said to be legally blind. Other people have partial blindness. This means that their vision is severely limited. The other senses can help perform some of the functions of the eyes. For example, fingers can feel raised letters to allow blind people to read.

Diseases of the Eye

As with any organ, the eye can be damaged by infections and diseases. A common infection that can harm the eye is a sty. A **sty** is an infection surrounding an eyelash. Bacteria collect at the base of the follicle, causing swelling and pain. Pain continues until the sty drains. This relieves pressure. Sties generally drain and heal in about a week. They can be treated with warm compresses. If a sty persists, it should be drained by a doctor.

Conjunctivitis, or pinkeye, is an inflammation of the inner lining of the eyelid. This lining touches the front outer layer of the eye. With conjunctivitis the white part of the eye may turn red and feel gritty. After the eye has been closed for a long time, a yellow fluid may collect and dry on the eye. Conjunctivitis is caused by bacteria, a virus, pollen, cosmetics, or other substances that come in contact with the eye. A doctor may prescribe medicines to help cure the infection. Since infections can be spread by fingertips or a cloth, good hygiene is especially important in preventing this eye problem. No one else should use the towel or washcloth of someone who is infected.

A **cataract** is a condition in which the eye's lens turns cloudy, causing total or partial blindness. The cloudy lens blocks light entering the eye. The most common cause of a cataract is aging, although some babies are born with cataracts. Injury, inflammation, or diabetes also may contribute to the development of a cataract. To improve vision, the clouded lens may be surgically removed. An artificial plastic lens may then be implanted in the eye.

A **detached retina** is the separation of the retina from the choroid, the nourishing middle layer of the eye. The early signs of a detached retina include flashes of light and loss of peripheral

Figure 3-8   During cataract surgery, a surgeon may remove the cloudy lens *(left)* and implant a plastic lens (right).

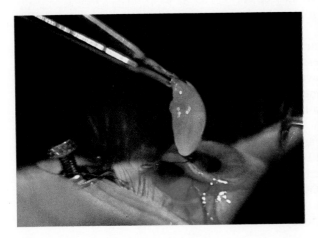

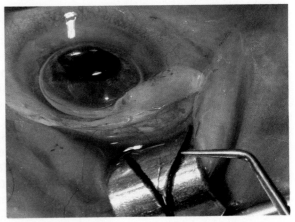

vision. Without proper treatment, eye damage and loss of vision will continue. Surgery also may be used to repair a detached retina, if the problem is identified early.

Some surgeons now perform corneal transplants to correct the sight of people with poor vision or even blindness. A **corneal transplant** is the removal of a damaged cornea and its replacement with healthy corneal tissue from a donor. The cornea is sewn in place with tiny stitches. There is a great need for corneas for corneal transplants. Many people will their eyes to eye banks for this purpose.

A very serious eye disorder is glaucoma. **Glaucoma** [*glaw KOH muh*] is a build-up of fluid pressure within the eyes, causing the eyes to become rigid. Glaucoma usually occurs when fluid fails to drain normally from the eye. The increased pressure inside the eye can damage the fibers of the optic nerve. Damage to this nerve may cause loss of peripheral vision and may eventually lead to blindness.

With glaucoma the loss of vision is gradual. Thus it may not be noticed until there is severe and permanent damage. The causes of glaucoma are not understood fully, but glaucoma may be hereditary. It is very important that people with a family history of this disorder have regular eye examinations. The disease occurs most often among people over the age of 40. A simple test that measures the pressure in the eye can detect glaucoma before permanent damage occurs. Often the disease can be controlled with medicines or surgery.

 ## Health *Careers*

Many different kinds of health care specialists work toward improving vision and keeping eyes healthy. Ophthalmologists [ahf thal MAHL uh jists] are medical doctors who specialize in eye care. After attending medical school, these doctors train for three or more years in the treatment of eye disorders. Ophthalmologists may test eyes and diagnose problems. Because they are doctors, they may also prescribe medicines. Ophthalmologists may perform surgery to correct eye problems.

An optometrist is another person qualified to prescribe corrective lenses. Optometrists are not medical doctors and therefore cannot perform surgery or prescribe medication. Optometrists must have a four-year degree from a certified college of optometry.

If you need corrective lenses, your prescription will probably be prepared by an optician. An optician is a skilled technician who cuts and shapes lenses. Opticians also fit eyeglasses and contact lenses. Opticians learn their skill by enrolling in a course in optical technology in a vocational school.

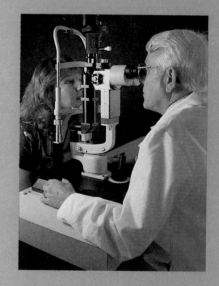

1 What is the difference between an ophthalmologist and an optometrist?
2 What kind of training is necessary to be an optician?

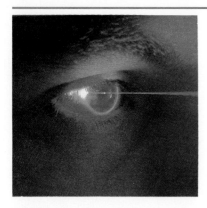

Figure 3-9   A laser may be used to perform eye surgery.

Health **History**

According to legend, the Chinese invented and used eyeglasses as early as 500 B.C. Marco Polo, who visited China in about 1275, reported seeing many Chinese wearing eyeglasses.

Eye Care

Although personal hygiene is very important in protecting eyes from infection and disease, wearing the proper safety glasses can also help. Each day, about 450 schoolchildren damage their eyes in accidents. While working at home or in school, people may wear safety glasses to protect their eyes from chemicals, light, or heat. During sports the use of proper equipment, such as helmets or goggles, can prevent injury.

Wearing the proper corrective lenses is also very important. The decision to choose eyeglasses or contact lenses depends on several factors. People will want to consider the kind of eye problem they have, their personal preferences, and the activities in which they participate. Those who prefer glasses have many styles to choose from. There are glasses in all colors and shapes as well as ones with darkened lenses for protection against glare.

Contact lenses may provide a wider field of vision than eyeglasses. This increases peripheral vision. For those who prefer contact lenses, many improvements have been made. For many years, contact lenses were made of hard, inflexible materials. They could be worn only for a short period of time. The hard lenses sometimes scratched the cornea. Some of these lenses irritated the eye by depriving it of oxygen.

New materials now make it possible for contact lenses to be worn longer periods of time because they allow oxygen to reach the eyes. These materials also make the lenses more adaptable in treating a variety of vision problems. A disadvantage of soft contact lenses is that they are more likely to cause infections than hard contact lenses.

People who wear contact lenses must take good care of them and clean them regularly. When changing lenses, users must be careful to have clean hands to prevent dirt or bacteria from getting in the eye. These can cause eye irritations and diseases. Any time contact lenses irritate the eyes, a doctor should be consulted to prevent further problems.

Lesson Review

Some vision problems require corrective lenses. Other problems need treatments with medicine or surgery. Many eye problems can be avoided through good personal hygiene. Protecting eyes from injury is also very important.

1 Define farsightedness and explain the causes of this condition. How is it corrected?

2 List three common vision problems.

3 What condition develops when the inner lining of the eyelid becomes inflamed?

4 What are some early signs of a detached retina?

5 What are two ways to prevent eye injury or infection?

The Ear

Whether you listen to rock, country, or classical music, your ears are the organs that allow you to enjoy the music. Your ears also are part of the body's warning system against danger and help you keep your balance. Proper care of the ears is very important. Even minor infections can cause hearing loss.

The Structure of the Ear

To understand the structure of the ear, study Figure 3-10. The outer ear is shaped perfectly to catch sound waves. The outer ear traps sound waves and passes them along a short tunnel to the middle ear. Sound then reaches the **eardrum,** which is a membrane stretched across the opening to the middle ear. The force of

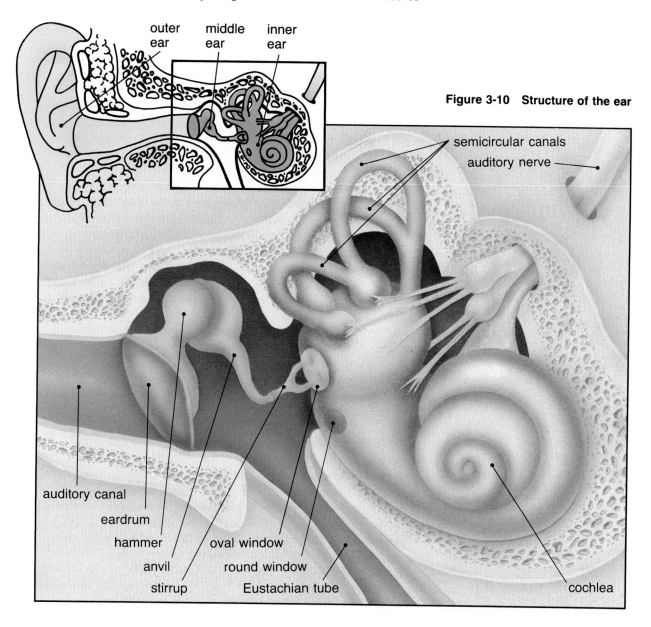

outer ear   middle ear   inner ear

Figure 3-10   Structure of the ear

semicircular canals
auditory nerve

auditory canal
eardrum
hammer
anvil
stirrup
oval window
round window
Eustachian tube
cochlea

the sound waves vibrates the eardrum. This begins a chain reaction as the sound waves pass along three tiny bones. They are the **hammer,** the **anvil,** and the **stirrup.** Their names reflect their shapes. The hammer is connected to the anvil, which, in turn, is connected to the stirrup.

In addition to their role in hearing, these bones protect the eardrum. If too much pressure is put on the eardrum, the pressure is passed from bone to bone. The pressure is then absorbed by the muscles attached to the bone.

Pressure also can be relieved by the Eustachian tube. The **Eustachian tube** [*yoo STAY shun*] stretches from the back of the nose to the middle ear. It lets air pass from the nose into the middle ear. This air helps keep pressure equal on both sides of the eardrum. You may have noticed a build-up of pressure while riding on an airplane or a carnival ride. Swallowing or yawning helps force air up the Eustachian tube. You may hear a popping sound in the ear as the air pressure changes.

The middle ear is separated from the inner ear by a membrane called the **oval window.** The stirrup moves in and out of the oval window. This movement also causes the fluid and the hair fibers lining the cochlea to move. The **cochlea** [*KAHK lee uh*] is a spiral tube shaped like a snail's shell that turns sound waves to nerve impulses and sends them to the brain. The cochlea is filled with fluid and lined with tiny hair fibers. At the base of these hairs are nerve endings.

You may also hear sounds that pass through the bones of the skull. The **round window** is an opening in the middle ear below the oval window that passes vibrations from the skull bones to the fluid of the cochlea. Like the eardrum, the round window is covered by a membrane that can vibrate.

The nerves in the cochlea that carry impulses to the brain form a network called the **auditory nerve.** Once impulses reach the brain, they are interpreted as sound. The brain can tell which direction sound waves come from by the part of the brain that is stimulated. Impulses from one ear travel to one part of the brain. Impulses from the other ear go to another part of the brain.

Balance

In addition to your sense of hearing, your ears also provide your sense of balance. Balance is a feeling of stability and body control. Your sense of balance comes from semicircular canals in the inner ear. The **semicircular canals** are fluid-filled tubes lined with tiny hairs. The hairs are connected to nerve cells. If you move or change the position of your head, the fluid and hairs move. This movement of the hairs stimulates the nerve cells, which send impulses to the brain. The brain coordinates this information with messages from other sense organs of the body. This process helps your body adjust so that you keep your balance, whether you are walking or riding a bicycle or an elevator.

Sometimes you feel dizzy when you move your head too quickly. This happens because of the rapid movement of fluid in the semicircular canals. Motion sickness is due to similar reactions in the inner ear. Motion sickness occurs most frequently while riding in a boat, plane, car, or carnival ride. It can cause nausea and headaches. Some people are more prone to motion sickness than others.

Common Ear Disorders

The most common problems of the ears are ear infections. Infections of the nose, throat, or Eustachian tube may spread to the middle ear. Swimming is a frequent cause of ear infections among teenagers.

Medicines may be prescribed to cure ear infections. In some middle ear infections, a doctor may make a small incision in the eardrum to reduce the pressure and pain in the ear. When this is done, the eardrum usually heals in 7 to 14 days with no scar. If the incision is not made, the eardrum may burst from too much pressure. A burst eardrum has ragged edges that form scars when they heal. Scarring prevents the eardrum from being able to flex easily. This may cause hearing loss.

Hearing loss also may be the result of excess wax in the canal of the outer ear. Glands along this canal release wax to help guard against infection. Usually the wax drains away. If wax hardens in the ear, a doctor may have to remove it. The doctor may also prescribe a wax softener to aid the natural cleansing process. Only a doctor should ever insert an object in the ear. Objects such as cotton swabs and hairpins could damage the eardrum and allow infection to enter the ear.

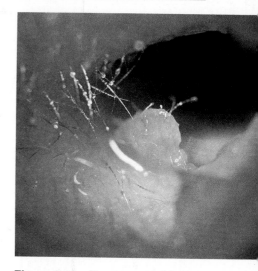

Figure 3-11 Ear wax can block the transmission of sound waves into the ear.

Hearing Impairment

Partial hearing loss is called **hearing impairment.** About 16 million people in the United States have some hearing loss. A total loss of hearing is called **deafness.** Deafness can be inherited or caused by injury or disease. Most hearing impairments are caused by infections, obstructions, or nerve damage.

Figure 3-12 Hearing aids such as the kind worn by these children can help the hearing impaired.

Obstructions may block sound waves traveling to the cochlea. If obstruction is the cause of the impairment, the hearing loss is usually not complete. It generally involves only one ear. Obstruction is a common cause of hearing loss in children. It may be due to a build-up of wax, bone blockage, or even something stuck in the ear.

Obstructed hearing also may be caused by an abnormal bone growth near the oval window. The bone may block the movement of the stirrup. The stirrup can no longer pass sound vibrations to the inner ear. This problem may be inherited. In eight out of ten cases, both ears are affected. Deafness may result, but surgery can cure many cases.

Another cause of hearing impairment is nerve damage. Nerve damage generally involves the hair cells in the cochlea or attached nerves. Nerve damage usually distorts hearing in both ears. Increasing volume generally distorts the sound waves even more. Exposure to loud noise can cause nerve damage. It may also occur with aging. This type of hearing loss is common among infants whose mothers had rubella (German measles) or another infection during pregnancy. The infection may enter the baby's blood before birth and settle in its ears, causing nerve damage.

Hearing impairments from obstruction or nerve damage may be gradual. Many people may not even realize they have a hearing impairment. You may want to ask yourself if your hearing has changed recently. Here are a few checks you can make.

Can you hear your teacher from the back of the room?
Do other people seem to mumble?
Are you often asking people to repeat themselves?
Do you seem to hear better out of one ear than the other?

Figure 3-13 The noise level of some sounds forces workers to wear protective earmuffs.

If you think you have a hearing problem, a doctor can check your hearing for an obstruction or nerve damage. People with partial hearing loss may be helped by an **audiologist** [*aw dee AHL uh jist*], a specialist in hearing problems and their treatment.

For many years, people with hearing loss have used lip reading and sign language to communicate. Sign language is communication involving the formation of letters and words with the hands and fingers. A hearing aid may enable some people to hear better. New surgical procedures and advances in electronics are making communication much easier for the hearing impaired.

Preventing Hearing Loss

To protect your hearing, you can limit your exposure to noise. Noise is intense and unnecessary sound. The level of sound is measured in units called **decibels** [*DES uh bulz*]. Your ears can become irritated and even damaged by too much noise. As shown in Figure 3-14, the risk of injury and hearing loss begins at 90 decibels. A typical rock concert measures about 110 decibels. Some jobs also present a risk of hearing impairment due to noise. As shown in Figure 3-13, ears can be covered to protect them from too much noise.

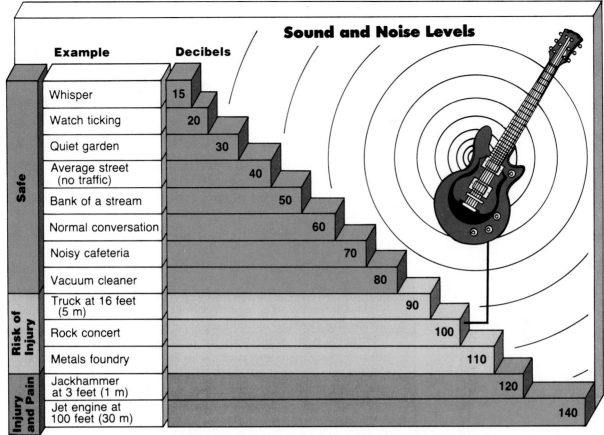

Sound and Noise Levels

	Example	Decibels
Safe	Whisper	15
	Watch ticking	20
	Quiet garden	30
	Average street (no traffic)	40
	Bank of a stream	50
	Normal conversation	60
	Noisy cafeteria	70
	Vacuum cleaner	80
Risk of Injury	Truck at 16 feet (5 m)	90
	Rock concert	100
	Metals foundry	110
Injury and Pain	Jackhammer at 3 feet (1 m)	120
	Jet engine at 100 feet (30 m)	140

CAUTION: The longer you listen to sounds louder than 80 decibels, the greater your risk of hearing damage.

Figure 3-14   Noise levels of some common sounds

Lesson Review

The ears can trap sound waves and change them into nerve impulses. These impulses are sent to the brain, where they are interpreted as sound. The ears also help you maintain your balance. But the ears must be protected. Infections should be cared for promptly. Nothing should be put in the ear since any foreign object may damage the eardrum. Ears also should be protected from excessive noise, since noise can damage the ear and even cause a loss of hearing.

1 Name the three bones of the middle ear.

2 Name the part of the inner ear that turns sound waves into nerve impulses.

3 What is the auditory nerve?

4 What are the two major causes of hearing impairment?

5 In what unit is sound measured?

6 Define *noise*.

Touch, Taste, and Smell

It is a cold snowy morning, but the blankets feel warm and soft. The smell of hot, crisp bacon begins to fill your bedroom. Should you stay in bed feeling warm and cozy? Perhaps you should head for your breakfast of sizzling bacon, buttered toast, and hot cocoa. Your decision will be influenced by your senses of touch, taste, and smell.

Touch

Your sense of touch includes five separate sensations—contact, pressure, cold, warmth, and pain. The receptors for touch are called tactile corpuscles. **Tactile corpuscles** are nerve endings that change shape in response to outside forces, sending impulses that travel to the brain or spinal cord. The different types of tactile corpuscles are shown in Figure 3-15.

In addition to the pain receptors located in the skin, you also have pain receptors in the outer layers of some internal organs. Pain near an internal organ signals that it is not working correctly. This information is important in helping doctors identify life-threatening diseases and injuries.

Different parts of the body are more responsive to the sensations of touch than other areas. This is because the tactile corpuscles are not scattered evenly in the body. They are arranged in clusters. The hairless parts of your body, such as fingertips, lips, and your tongue, are the most sensitive. The least sensitive area is the back of the shoulders. But in a spot no bigger than the size of a period on your fingertip, you have about 100 pressure receptors and 60 pain receptors.

The sustained loss of any of the sensations of touch may indicate a serious health problem. For example, the loss of feeling in the limbs could be a sign of poor blood circulation, which may be caused by a disease such as diabetes. Any loss of these sensations should be discussed with your doctor.

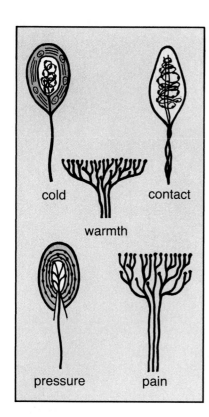

Figure 3-15   Sensory receptors of the body

Taste

Examine your tongue in a mirror. You will see that it is not smooth, but is made up of tiny bumps. Within these bumps are taste buds. **Taste buds** are tiny organs that contain taste receptors that respond to food. You have about 9000 taste buds on the tongue and in the back of your mouth.

In order to taste, receptors in the taste buds must be stimulated by particles of food carried in saliva. Food particles dissolved in saliva enter a tiny hole in the top of each taste bud. The food stimulates the nerve at the base of the taste bud. The nerve signals the brain, which identifies the taste.

Taste buds generally respond to four qualities in food. They identify bitter, sweet, salty, and sour tastes. Not all taste buds are sensitive to the same kinds of tastes in food. Figure 3-16 shows the location of the taste centers on the tongue. For example, taste buds that are sensitive to bitter foods are located at the back of the tongue. This is why some foods have a bitter aftertaste. You do not sense the bitterness until you swallow them. Many foods affect more than one taste center. Lemon drops, for instance, are both sweet and sour.

Smell

Like the senses of touch and taste, smell relies on the stimulation of receptors. **Olfactory nerve reactors** are receptors that are sensitive to smell. These are located in a small portion of the nasal cavity, as shown in Figure 3-17. You have receptors for as many as 50 different types of smells. Scientists believe that these receptors are activated by substances in the air. These substances stimulate the receptors as you breathe. The olfactory nerve receptors pass impulses to the olfactory bulb. The olfactory bulb relays signals to the brain, where the smell is identified.

Your sense of smell is linked closely with your sense of taste. One often affects the other. Food that smells good usually tastes good, too. At present, the connection between the two senses is not completely understood.

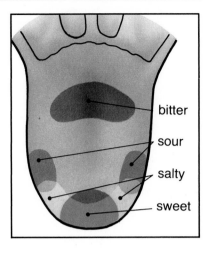

Figure 3-16 Centers of taste on the tongue

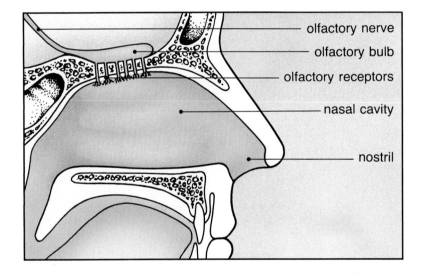

Figure 3-17 Structure of the olfactory organs

Lesson Review

The senses of touch, taste, and smell give you great pleasure and help protect you from danger. All of these senses depend on receptors sending messages to the brain. The brain interprets the messages and causes the body to respond. Even though the senses of smell and taste are related, they are, in fact, two separate senses.

1 What are the five sensations of touch?

2 Where are pain receptors located?

3 What are the four food qualities to which taste buds respond?

4 What other sense is linked with the sense of smell?

Chapter Review

Vocabulary

anvil	decibel	oval window
astigmatism	detached retina	peripheral vision
audiologist	eardrum	photoreceptor
auditory nerve	Eustachian tube	pupil
blindspot	farsightedness	receptor
cataract	focus	retina
choroid	fovea	rod
cochlea	glaucoma	round window
colorblind	hammer	sclera
cone	hearing impairment	semicircular canals
conjunctiva	iris	stereoscopic vision
conjunctivitis	lens	stirrup
cornea	nearsightedness	sty
corneal transplant	night blindness	tactile corpuscle
crosseye	olfactory nerve reactor	taste bud
deafness	optic nerve	vitreous humor

Using Vocabulary

Questions 1–15. On a separate sheet of paper, write the term from the right that matches the phrase on the left.

1 colored circle surrounding the pupil
2 structure that serves as a window for letting in light
3 layer of the eye that absorbs light rays and converts them to electrical impulses
4 nerve endings in the retina that send light signals
5 photoreceptor that detects color
6 membrane stretched across the opening to the middle ear
7 structure that lets air pass from the nose into the middle ear
8 photoreceptor that can only distinguish black from white
9 cord of nerve fibers in the eye; carries messages to the brain
10 structure that aligns light rays
11 opening that regulates how much light enters the eye
12 opening in the middle ear that passes vibrations to fluid of the cochlea
13 membrane that separates the middle ear from the inner ear
14 tube that turns sound waves into nerve impulses
15 network of nerves in the cochlea that carry impulses to the brain

a rod
b cochlea
c retina
d iris
e eardrum
f oval window
g lens
h optic nerve
i round window
j photoreceptors
k pupil
l cone
m Eustachian tube
n auditory nerve
o cornea

Interpreting Ideas

1 Identify and compare the two types of photoreceptors.

2 Identify each of the eye's layers and describe the main structures in each.

3 What are two causes of hearing impairment?

4 Identify and describe two vision problems that result from an inability to focus properly.

5 How does the ear help maintain balance?

6 How are middle ear infections caused? How can they lead to hearing loss?

7 Describe the cause of glaucoma. What is the test for glaucoma? the treatment?

8 What kinds of vision are created by the slight difference in the location of each of your eyes?

9 Describe the vision problems caused by poor functioning of the photoreceptors.

10 What is the function of ear wax? How may ear wax lead to hearing loss? How should ear wax be removed?

11 What happens when a person sustains the eye injury called detached retina?

12 What factors may contribute to the development of a cataract? How may it be treated?

13 Which parts of the body are the most sensitive to the sensations of touch? Why?

14 Identify and describe the function of each of the ear's three parts.

15 What are the five sensations that make up the sense of touch?

16 Identify the four qualities of food. Where on the tongue are the taste buds that are sensitive to each quality?

17 How might you discover that you have a hearing loss?

18 How can you see nearby objects as well as objects that are far away?

19 What are the causes, treatment, and prevention of conjunctivitis? of a sty?

20 List three ways to protect eyes from injury and disease.

Applying Concepts

1 Why is your sense of taste dulled when you have a bad cold?

2 When you eat food that is both sweet and sour, why would you notice its sweetness first? Hint: See Figure 3-16.

3 Why is it difficult to see anything in a dimly lighted room when you come into it from a brightly lighted place? Why do you tend to want to shut your eyes when you come into bright sunlight from a movie theater?

4 Why does your pupil look black?

5 Why is it dangerous to look directly at the sun?

6 As he does his homework, a friend listens to hard rock for several hours a day. Another friend continues to wear her contact lenses be-

yond the maximum number of hours prescribed by her ophthalmologist. What arguments would you use to convince your friends to discontinue these bad habits?

7 How could a head injury impair your sense of smell or taste?

8 Based on the following information, explain why albinos have very poor eyesight. In a normal eye, the pigment in the iris keeps most of the light entering the eye from passing through to the lens. Albinos lack this pigment.

9 Why would it be more accurate to say ''color deficient'' rather than ''colorblind''?

10 In your opinion, which of your senses is the most valuable? Why?

Projects

1 Demonstrate for yourself how the pupil regulates the amount of light that enters the eye. First, use a mirror to observe the size of your pupils. Then close your eyes for three minutes. What change do you observe in the size of your pupils when you open your eyes? Why did this change occur?

2 At your school or local library find out more about colorblindness. How is it detected? Why does it occur more often in males than in females? What kinds of problems may arise for colorblind people?

3 Sometimes your sensory receptors can trick you and lead you to make incorrect interpretations. For example, place your right hand in a pan of hot water, and your left hand in ice water. After a few minutes place both hands in lukewarm water. What happens?

4 At your school or local library find out how animals without outer ears, such as earthworms, snakes, and fish, are able to sense sound. How do bats use sound to find food in the dark? How do birds use sound to communicate?

Critical Thinking

ANALYZING ADVERTISING

"Mirror, mirror, on the wall, who's the fairest of them all?" asks the wicked queen in the popular children's story. This line is so memorable because most people would secretly like to be the "fairest of them all."

Advertisers know that personal appearance affects how you think about yourself and how others think about you. As a consumer, you need to know that advertisements for grooming products are designed to appeal to your desire to be popular and attractive.

The goal of an advertisement is to persuade you to purchase the product. Ads are cleverly designed to appeal to your need for an acceptable appearance.

When you see an advertisement, it is important to determine which material in the advertisement addresses your true grooming needs, and which information is given only to catch your attention. You need to distinguish the important facts from the unimportant information around them.

In other words, you need to learn how to identify the relevant information in an advertisement. Relevant information is information that is related to the matter under consideration, or that is pertinent to your decision. Materi-al that is not relevant is said to be irrelevant.

Here are some steps to help you separate relevant and irrelevant information:

Identify your needs Do you need a shampoo for oily hair, an antiperspirant that will not irritate sensitive skin, or a sunblock that will protect your skin?

Distinguish the stated purpose of the product What specific information does the advertisement present? For example, does an advertisement for a shampoo state that the product is useful for oily hair?

Compare the information in the advertisement with your needs Does the product fulfill your needs?

Ignore all the information that is not relevant to your needs Photographs of happy users, slogans, catchy phrases, and other forms of information are not useful if they are not related to your needs.

As an example, consider the advertisement for an imaginary toothpaste called Teensmile, shown at right. Which of the following statements about this product would be relevant to your decision about purchasing Teensmile?

a Teensmile is used by professional tennis players.
b Brushing with Teensmile keeps your confidence bright.
c Teensmile has a unique, patented, plaque-fighting formula that gives you a winner's edge.
d Teensmile is the exciting new toothpaste for the most exciting time of your life.

The correct answer to this exercise is (c). When selecting products for caring for teeth, it is important to fight plaque. By reducing plaque, you would be practicing good personal hygiene.

What about the other choices? Statement (a), that the toothpaste is used by tennis pros, provides you with no useful information about the effectiveness of the product. It does not tell you if these tennis players have good teeth, or if the product is effective in cleaning teeth. Since it is unlikely that toothpaste will affect your ability to play tennis, this statement is irrelevant.

Statement (b) contains very little information—it does not tell you how Teensmile will make you confident. Statement (d) is similar to statement (b)—it does not tell you how Teensmile will make your life exciting.

With practice, you will learn to identify the relevant information without needing to do a step-by-step analysis of every advertisement you encounter. By learning to distinguish the relevant information, you can avoid being unwittingly separated from your money while attempting to become the "fairest of them all."

To practice this skill, consider the following examples. On a separate sheet of paper, write the letter or letters of the statements that would be most relevant to your decision to purchase the product. In some cases, you may discover that the advertiser has given you no relevant information on which to base your decision.

1 Which of the following statements would be most relevant to your decision to purchase a skin medication called Datecare?

a Datecare is the skin cleanser for that best-date look.
b Datecare has a balanced formula of ingredients.
c Datecare removes dirt and oil.
d Datecare was developed by a leading authority at a famous resort.

2 Which of the following statements would be most relevant to your decision to purchase a cologne called Splash?

a Splash is formulated for men who care about their image.
b Splash gives an extra dash of elegance.
c It's a scent that lasts class after class.
d Splash will make you feel refreshed, together, and ready to face the world.

3 Which of the following statements would be most relevant to your decision to purchase Starface, a liquid makeup?

a Movie stars use Starface.
b It is a water-based makeup, effective for oily skin.
c It has a secret formula, developed by an Italian princess.
d Starface will make you a star on your own.

4 Which of the following statements would be relevant in your decision to purchase Calm, an antiperspirant?

a Calm will make you feel cool and collected all day long.
b Calm has been approved by a panel of experts.
c Calm is used by Olympic athletes.
d Calm was developed specifically for the stress that high school students must face every day.

2

4. Developing a Healthy Personality

5. Healthy Emotions

Mental **H**ealth

6. Managing Stress

7. Treating Mental Disorders

Learning to ski is a challenge for children.
Some take to it with enthusiasm, while others
are more cautious.

CHAPTER FOUR

DEVELOPING
A Healthy Personality

Just as you grow physically, so your inner self, or personality, also grows and develops. As it does, it affects how you act. Think of how different children act when they learn to ski. Some are bold and excited about their new adventure. Others are more careful. Some may even cry. The children behave differently because each has a personality that is different from all the others.

Many scientists have studied what forms the personality. Some parts of your personality exist at birth. But as you grow older other people, events, and your surroundings help shape your development as well. Good mental health will allow you to develop fully. It will help you become who you want to be. This involves knowing yourself, liking and trusting others, and being responsible for the choices you make.

Objectives

- Define *personality* and *mental health.*

- Explain how heredity and environment influence personality development.

- Name people whose research has influenced the understanding of personality.

- Identify the needs that must be met for the development of a healthy personality.

- Describe the main stages in the development of a mature personality.

- Identify the characteristics of a healthy personality.

- Distinguish between positive and negative attitudes toward life.

Influences on Personality

The word personality is used in a number of ways. Television and movie stars are called personalities. You may have heard that a lively classmate has "a lot of personality." In fact, everyone has a lot of personality. Your **personality** is the mix of how you feel, think, and behave that makes you different from others.

Personalities, like bodies, can be healthy or unhealthy. Positive mental health is an important part of wellness. **Mental health** is the state of well-being of the mind. In order to function at your highest level, you must feel good mentally and physically. Self-esteem is a vital part of mental health. People with positive self-esteem feel good about who they are and about their ability to face life's challenges.

At one time the study of personality centered on people who were not in good mental health. Today more is done to study the healthy personality. Scientists who study personality are called **psychologists** [*sy KAHL uh jists*]. In their studies psychologists have found two major influences that help shape the personality. Characteristics present at birth make up one area of influence. A person's surroundings make up the other area.

Heredity

Until the late 1800's, people thought that everyone's personality was already decided at birth. Whether you were shy, bold, clever, or lazy was believed to come from heredity. **Heredity** is the passing of characteristics biologically from parents to offspring. Heredity decides physical characteristics such as height and eye color. Heredity is the reason that children look like their parents.

Certain types of behavior are inherited by all people. These characteristics are called instincts. An **instinct** is an inherited pattern of behavior that does not need to be learned. For example, all babies are born knowing how to nurse. Nursing is an instinct. Although psychologists have studied many people, they have identified very few forms of behavior that are purely instinct.

Some scientists believe that people are born with certain feelings that guide the way they behave. The Swiss doctor Carl Jung was a leader in this belief. Jung wrote a book called *Psychological Types* in 1921. In it Jung identified two major personality types. One is the introvert. An **introvert** [*IHN truh vurt*] is a person concerned mostly with his or her own thoughts. A person who likes reading books more than attending parties might be called an introvert. An **extrovert** [*EHKS truh vurt*] is a person who is very interested in the world outside the self. A person who enjoys being with others more than being alone might be described as an extrovert. Many people are thought of as introverts or extroverts because they often behave in a certain way. But not all scientists believe that such behavior is inherited.

Studies have shown that some personality traits may be passed from parents to children. For example, children are likely to have levels of intelligence that are quite similar to those of their parents. **Intelligence** is the ability to learn and deal with change.

Figure 4-1 Newborns know by instinct how to nurse.

To determine the role of heredity in intelligence, scientists have studied identical twins. Identical twins have exactly the same heredity. Identical twins also tend to have very similar levels of intelligence. This is true even when the twins grow up in different surroundings. Scientists have also compared the intelligence of brothers and sisters. Brothers and sisters have similar but not identical heredity. Closer levels of intelligence were found between twins than between brothers and sisters. These findings suggest that heredity plays a very strong role in determining an individual's intelligence.

Other studies have shown that being good at art, at sports, or with languages may be passed from parent to child. Scientists agree that heredity plays a very important role in the development of personality. Most psychologists point out that a person's surroundings also greatly influence the way that inherited characteristics are expressed. For example, consider a child who inherits musical talent. If this child is given piano lessons, he or she may grow into a great musician. But if the child is never given music lessons, the inherited talent may never be developed.

Figure 4-2 Swiss psychiatrist Carl Jung believed people are born with feelings that guide behavior.

Environment

Even though you are born with many characteristics that shape your personality, others are learned from your environment. Your **environment** is the sum of all physical and social conditions in your surroundings. Your family, your school, and your community are part of your environment. How you behave in response to your environment is called **learned behavior**.

Your family has the major bearing on the way you behave. Parents begin a process of socialization from the time a child is born. **Socialization** [*soh shuh lih ZAY shun*] is the process of teaching behavior based on the beliefs and habits of the family and community. It takes in the teaching of religion, traditions, dress, and ways of behaving towards other people. For example, some families may be very affectionate. Other families may choose a more formal way of behaving toward each other.

Socialization takes place outside the home as well. Can you imagine life without all the influences you meet every day? Some of those are met in your community. Many different influences can be seen in the United States. This is because people from so many different lands have brought their own beliefs, traditions and customs. Some people who settled in Louisiana were used to playing joyous music and dancing at services in memory of a loved one. People today still do that. To people in other places this might not seem the right way to behave.

Other customs may be harder to pick out. You might not think about them unless you were with someone whose customs were different. For example, some groups of people think it is not polite to look straight into the eyes of those in authority. Other groups think that not meeting people's eyes is only a sign of shyness.

Another outside influence is your school environment. By sharing life from other places, classmates and teachers can broaden

Health Bulletin

Children are learning more outside the home today than in the past. By the time today's youngsters enter first grade, they usually have spent between one and three years in a classroom.

Figure 4-3 Children begin imitating adults very early in life.

what you have learned in your community. A good school environment can sometimes help children who inherit low intelligence improve in intelligence.

The process of socialization usually includes conditioning. **Conditioning** is the shaping of behavior with punishment or reward. For example, if parents turn away when a child shows off, the child may learn to boast less. When a child is praised for kindness, the child is likely to want to go on behaving that way.

Modeling is another way in which children learn. **Modeling** is the process of learning by imitating another person. The person whom someone watches and copies is called a **role model**. A child may learn to be helpful in the home, for example, by using an older brother as a role model. Socialization—community, home, and school—helps shape your ideas and ways of looking at life.

Lesson Review

Your personality is the unique mix of feelings, thoughts, and behavior that sets you apart from everyone else. The state of your mental health has a bearing on the way you feel, think, and behave. Good mental health is needed to have a healthy personality. Most scientists agree that both heredity and environment are important to personality development.

1 What is mental health?

2 Name two forms of socialization.

3 What is environment?

4 What is a role model?

Personality Development

Individuals develop at their own pace. Just as psychologists disagree about what most influences personality, they also have different ideas about the way personality develops. Most agree, however, that there are certain needs that must be met for people to grow up and to remain mentally healthy.

Theories of Development

There are many different theories, or ideas, about how the personality grows. One important theory was developed by the American psychologist Abraham Maslow. Maslow classified human needs into different groups, as shown in Figure 4-4. Maslow suggested that human needs form a kind of pyramid. This pyramid shows that lower, or more basic, needs must be met before higher needs can be satisfied. For example, according to Maslow, it is very hard to love other people before satisfying the need to feel safe. Although the changes between levels do not occur at specific ages, a person's needs become more complex as he or she matures.

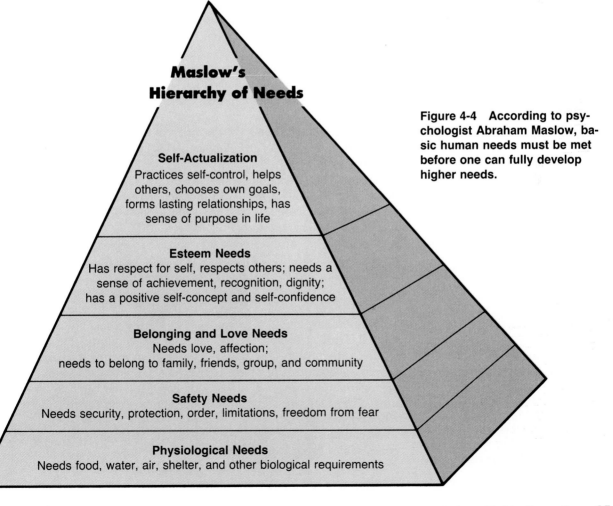

Maslow's Hierarchy of Needs

Self-Actualization
Practices self-control, helps others, chooses own goals, forms lasting relationships, has sense of purpose in life

Esteem Needs
Has respect for self, respects others; needs a sense of achievement, recognition, dignity; has a positive self-concept and self-confidence

Belonging and Love Needs
Needs love, affection; needs to belong to family, friends, group, and community

Safety Needs
Needs security, protection, order, limitations, freedom from fear

Physiological Needs
Needs food, water, air, shelter, and other biological requirements

Figure 4-4 According to psychologist Abraham Maslow, basic human needs must be met before one can fully develop higher needs.

Figure 4-5 Psychiatrist Sigmund Freud *(left),* **psychologist Jean Piaget** *(middle),* **and psychologist Erik Erikson** *(right)*

Three of the best-known theories of personality growth were developed by Sigmund Freud, Jean Piaget, and Erik Erikson. All three of these men believed that personality is formed in a series of stages. These stages typically occur at the ages shown in Figure 4-6.

An Austrian doctor, Sigmund Freud, studied human development at the beginning of the present century. He introduced a totally new way of looking at human nature. His theories were built on how childhood experiences, including sexual development, affect the child's personality. Freud believed that if a child has difficulty in one stage of development, the difficulties will also affect later stages of development. Freud identified five stages from birth to the middle of adolescence. **Adolescence**, from about age eleven to the late teens, is the time when children develop adult physical characteristics. According to Freud, at which stage does identification with role models begin?

Jean Piaget, a Swiss psychologist, was influenced by Freud's work as he worked on his own theories of development. He identified four stages of development. How are Piaget's stages different from Freud's?

Another researcher, the Danish-American psychologist Erik Erikson, named eight stages. Erikson described development from birth to late adulthood. According to Erikson, what happens during the adolescent years?

No one theory of development is accepted by everyone. But these theories and those of other scientists have led to a general understanding of how people grow and develop.

Infancy

From the beginning, a person needs love and affection. Studies have shown that babies who are not held and comforted are likely to have difficulty trusting others. They may have a hard time forming attachments to others later in life. On the other hand, babies who are touched, spoken to, and cared for can begin to build trust. They feel safe and start to learn that they can depend on other people.

Psychologist Rene Spitz studied two sets of children. He compared babies brought up by their mothers with those reared in orphanages since birth. Spitz found that children reared with a family's love are likely to be trusting and affectionate. Children

Health **History**

Last century many people believed that personality was determined by the shape of the head. The study of the bumps and hollows on the head was called phrenology. One of its followers was Queen Victoria, who requested phrenological examinations for her children.

Age	Freud Psychological Stages	Piaget Intellectual Stages	Erikson Social Stages
Birth to 1	*Oral Stage:* the child focuses on its mouth; is not aware of being separate from its mother	*Sensorimotor Stage:* child has not learned to speak; thoughts expressed through actions; learns that objects exist even when out of sight	*Basic Trust or Mistrust:* child's feelings of being loved will result in trust; mistrust leads to chaos
1 to 2			*Autonomy or Shame and Doubt:* praise for learning and control of bodily functions bring independence; criticism and neglect lead to shame and doubt
2 to 3	*Self-Control Stage:* child learns to control its body, including toilet training	*Preoperational Stage:* learns to speak by imitating others; later learns to read and write; has not yet learned to think logically; learns by trial and error	
3 to 4	*Self-Awareness Stage:* child becomes aware of self and its sexual identity; becomes aware of other people		*Initiative or Guilt:* praise for efforts leads to initiative, with development of memory and desire to begin learning adult roles; criticism results in guilt
4 to 5			
5 to 6			
6 to 7	*Socialization Stage:* child begins to identify with role models; boys identify with fathers, girls identify with mothers		*Industry or Inferiority:* feelings of worth and competence result in desire to learn and be productive; lack of industry or sense of self-worth leads to feelings of inferiority in comparison to others
7 to 8		*Concrete Operational Stage:* child views events from different perspectives; develops simple reasoning and problem solving abilities	
8 to 9			
9 to 10			
10 to 11			
11 to 12	*Full Awareness Stage:* adolescent becomes curious about opposite sex; is fully aware of self and prepares for adulthood	*Formal Operational Stage:* adolescent develops complex reasoning and problem solving abilities; beliefs and values take shape	
12 to 13			*Identity or Role Confusion:* sexual maturation and questions about identity lead to development of friendships; inability to separate from family results in adult role confusion
13 to 14			
Late teens			
Young adult			*Intimacy or Isolation:* shares self with others; inability to commit self leads to isolation
Middle adult			*Generativity or Stagnation:* has desire to contribute to community; is self-absorbed
Late adult & old age			*Integrity or Despair:* accepts fact of death and remembers life fondly; or fears death and feels sense of failure

Figure 4-6 Stages of mental development

Figure 4-7 Sharing comes easily to children who feel secure in their surroundings.

growing up in institutions, however, were usually less trusting and loving. This study and others like it have shown that loving experiences early in life help the development of self-confidence. Babies who feel loved are likely to develop into people who can give love to others in return. This is Erikson's Basic Trust or Mistrust Stage.

Babies soon begin to notice the world around them. They learn to recognize things and people by sight and sound. Most babies are interested in colorful or moving objects. They begin to want to explore their world and join in. They want to crawl, to walk, to speak. Encouragement, even at this early stage of life, is important for giving a child a sense of well-being. This adds to a child's eagerness to learn.

Childhood

The adults who care for the child provide the major influence during early childhood. At the same time, the child begins to want to be independent. Self-confidence, desire for achievement, and sense of self all develop during childhood. The child's environment affects the development of these characteristics.

Children gain a sense of achievement by successfully carrying out new activities. These activities may be doing puzzles, helping at home, and learning to read. Self-control becomes important, too. **Self-control** is being able to control your actions. Learning not to grab a favorite toy from a playmate, for example, needs self-control. If adults encourage self-control, children are likely to feel that they can get along with others.

During early childhood, children also begin the process of gender identification. **Gender identification** is having a sense of self that matches your sex. It is the awareness of being a girl or a boy. Parents usually serve as the chief models for gender identification. Girls are likely to copy their mothers, and boys are apt to copy their fathers. Later, girls and boys are likely to develop the manners and behavior of members of their own sex in their community. Note Freud's Socialization Stage in Figure 4-6.

It is important to good mental health for children to identify with their gender. It is also healthy for children to have choices that will keep them from being stereotyped because of their gender. **Stereotyping** is thinking that all members of a large group share the same characteristics in a fixed way.

There are many ways of stereotyping—by sex, by race, or by physical characteristics. The following three sentences are examples of stereotyping that may affect the way a child develops. *Boys do not like cooking. Japanese children are very clever. Nearsighted children are not good at sports.*

Stereotyping is not exact. It misses the fact that people are different. Children must accept their sex, race, and physical characteristics but they should not feel limited by them. A child who faces racial stereotyping may not develop a healthy sense of self-respect. But when the general atmosphere is encouraging, the child feels valuable and is more likely to become a responsible, considerate adult.

Adolescence

As an adolescent you may notice sudden mood swings. At one moment you may feel on top of the world. At the next you can be angry, lonely, or sad for no clear reason. This is partly because your body is changing as you grow into adulthood. But it is also because you are trying to become an independent person. You want to learn how to set your own standards and make your own decisions. During this stage of development, most teenagers ask themselves three key questions.

"Who Am I?" As a child, you probably did not question many of the thoughts and feelings you had. During adolescence you may no longer feel sure of who you are. If you were happy-go-lucky when you were in grade school but as a teenager find yourself feeling more serious, you may wonder which is the real you. This wondering is the natural way of searching for your own identity. Your **identity** is the particular parts of your personality by which you are recognized. Your identity is who you are.

Trying to understand yourself and express yourself fully can be both scary and exciting. You may sometimes feel like a stranger to yourself. You also may feel distant from people and activities you once enjoyed. Adolescents tend to look beyond their own families for new role models. Friends, teachers, or other people often offer new ideas and challenges. Belonging to a group of people your own age becomes more important. You may want to be with people who are like yourself. Groups of teenagers often like the same style of dress, use the same language, and listen to the same music. A group of people who are alike in one or more ways—usually in age and interests—is called a **peer group.**

Belonging to a peer group can have good results. Sharing experiences with friends, for example, may help you find out about your own identity. But it is also important to guard against too much pressure from your peers. **Peer pressure** is the urging from peers to follow the crowd. Some people may feel pressure

Figure 4-8 Peer influence becomes more important as teenagers seek social activities away from the family.

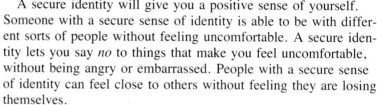

Figure 4-9 Obtaining a driver's license is one sign of independence that is important to many teenagers.

Figure 4-10 Graduation often marks the beginning of an independent life.

to smoke or drink alcohol like their friends. Sometimes no one encourages you to join in, you must feel you should. In both cases, peer pressure is at work. Giving in to peer pressure can influence how you feel about yourself.

A secure identity will give you a positive sense of yourself. Someone with a secure sense of identity is able to be with different sorts of people without feeling uncomfortable. A secure identity lets you say *no* to things that make you feel uncomfortable, without being angry or embarrassed. People with a secure sense of identity can feel close to others without feeling they are losing themselves.

"What Do I Believe?" This question involves the search for firm values. **Values** are beliefs and standards that you feel are important to live by. The question also looks at the role your conscience plays in the way you behave. Your **conscience** is the part of you that separates right from wrong. As a child, you probably accepted what your parents taught you. But as a teenager, you may want to know the reasons behind your parents' opinions and rules. You are becoming more aware of the different values held by other people, and you wonder what your own true beliefs are. This concern is addressed during Piaget's Formal Operational Stage, outlined in Figure 4-6.

You may question beliefs having to do with such large subjects as politics and social ills. But you are probably concerned also about what makes a good friend, the importance of being honest or hard-working, and how to please yourself without hurting others. Your adult personality will probably be a mix of some of the values you grew up with and ones you accept during adolescence.

"Where Am I Going?" Adolescence feels like an in-between period of life. In childhood you probably lived within a very organized environment. As a child in school, you may have lined up and marched to lunch as a class. You depended mostly on others to help you with problems. But as a teenager, you are beginning to break free of old limits. You want to experience the freedom of making your own choices. But you may find it a struggle.

As an adolescent, you will be trying to choose a way of life that agrees with your personality. You will begin to develop goals about the kind of career and the family life you wish to have. But all of this does not take place overnight. Adolescents often consider trying different paths before finding one that seems right. This exploration can prepare you for choosing your goals. Even in adulthood, though, you may want to change them if your interests change. While it is natural to seek one way of life, it is also wise to expect and prepare for change.

Young Adulthood

In your twenties and thirties, you will become legally independent. You will become responsible for yourself and your actions. You may finish college or trade school. You will get a job and support yourself. This usually means leaving home for a place of your own. Achievement in the working world and marriage usually are goals during this stage. Many people look forward to having children during this time.

Young adults have reached some emotional maturity. **Maturity** means the state of being fully grown. People who are mature know themselves fairly well and are able to make long-lasting ties with others. They can make responsible decisions and understand what may result from their actions.

For others, the twenties and thirties continue to be a confusing time. Some young adults may not feel ready for marriage. They may have trouble choosing a job that satisfies them. These people may need to look further before they reach a clear understanding of themselves and how they wish to live.

Some young adults have even more trouble. If experiences earlier in life left them with low self-esteem, their development may be slowed down. With low self-esteem, it is very hard to form close ties with others or to maintain lasting relationships. If people do not feel as worthy as they imagine others to be, it is difficult for them to gain a sense of achievement from their work. Without feelings of self-worth, the young adult may become self-centered and feel cut off from others. This is the Intimacy or Isolation Stage described in Figure 4-6. Being able to take responsibility for your actions needs a strong belief in yourself.

Middle Adulthood

Middle adulthood, usually from about age forty to sixty-five or seventy, often brings new satisfactions and new worries. Doing well in a job can give a great sense of achievement. Erikson's Generativity or Stagnation Stage describes the desire to give service to the community during this time of life. As greater responsibilities develop, this may be a time of financial worry. People may be trying to pay for their children's college educations, for example.

Figure 4-11 Many people marry during young adulthood.

Middle adulthood often is a time for reviewing life goals. You will have a better understanding of yourself and the world you live in. You will understand what is possible or impossible for you. This knowledge must be balanced against your earlier hopes and dreams. You may have to change your goals and ideas about the future based on what you have learned.

Even if you have obtained much satisfaction from family life or success at work, you may develop new needs, values, and beliefs. Entering a new adventure, even a difficult one, can be very rewarding. Changes often bring exciting new challenges and new drive.

Late Adulthood

In later years, usually after age sixty-five or seventy, the fact that life will not go on forever has become clear. For a few, those who may feel that some of their earlier dreams did not come true, this can be a difficult time. But many find that the later years are rewarding and can present many new challenges. People who have learned that life carries both happiness and sadness are likely to enjoy the present and remember the past fondly. You can see the chief concerns of late adulthood as viewed by Erikson in his Integrity or Despair Stage in Figure 4-6.

Late adulthood also can be a time of new choices, friendships, and interests. In fact, older people are often far busier than many young people think. Many are leaders in organizations and remain important to others. Some keep on working into their seventies or higher. Others serve as advisers or work on special projects. Some people take part in community affairs or volunteer organizations as they get older. The chance to follow more interests is also welcomed. These new and worthwhile activities can give great satisfaction. People can continue to learn, lead busy lives, and contribute to society well into their later years.

Figure 4-12 Healthy living increases the chances of enjoying an active and long life with the people you love.

Lesson Review

The work of psychologists and other scientists has added much to the understanding of personality. This work has shown how people grow and develop in stages. Each stage presents new questions and challenges. At each stage, certain needs must be met for individuals to develop and keep a healthy personality.

1 Name four people whose research has influenced the understanding of personality.

2 According to the research of Rene Spitz, what is necessary for a baby to develop a loving personality?

3 What are three important questions during adolescence?

4 What are three characteristics of a person who is emotionally mature?

5 What term describes a group of people of similar age and interests?

Taking Responsibility

Heredity and past experiences cannot be changed. People with healthy personalities know this. As they mature, they begin to take charge of their lives. In doing so, they often think about ways to make their lives better. Often this involves making changes in their own behavior and personalities. But first it helps to know what the characteristics of a healthy personality are.

Healthy Behavior

There are many healthy ways of managing your life. However, a few characteristics are usually present in a mentally healthy person. Such a person has a realistic self-concept, likes and trusts others, and takes responsibility for his or her own actions.

Your **self-concept** is your view of yourself and your role in life. When you have a realistic self-concept, you can see both your good points and your weaknesses. People who cannot see their faults are seeing only part of themselves. For example, a student may put off studying history fairly often. If she refuses to admit she has not studied when she fails a history test, she does not have a realistic self-concept. If your picture of yourself is not clear, your view of the world around you is likely to be unrealistic as well.

Having a positive self-concept, or feeling good about yourself, may be as important as having a realistic self-concept. Enjoying your good characteristics and being willing to work on or accept your faults means that you accept yourself. Accepting yourself is important to good mental health.

Being able to form close trusting relationships with other people is another sign of good mental health. People who cannot relate well to others are likely to feel lonely and unhappy. They may also find it difficult to be kind or fair to others. An inability to trust others often comes from a poor self-concept. If you think you are unlovable, it is hard to love others. You may feel that they will think you do not deserve love.

It is important to understand that certain ways of behaving cause certain results. Not blaming others for such results is taking responsibility for your own actions. This means you must be able to imagine the likely results of behaving in certain ways. Then you need to choose the action that will achieve the result you desire. When you decide for yourself how you will behave, you are likely to accept responsibility for what happens.

Making Changes

How do you know when changes will be helpful? Do you feel your life is in charge of you instead of your being in charge of it? If you can answer *yes,* you may wish to do some self-examination. **Self-examination** means stepping back and taking a look at yourself. Compare your good points, interests, and weaknesses with the characteristics of a healthy personality. You have the freedom to accept yourself as you are. Or you can work toward changing parts of yourself that you think need improvement.

In your self-examination, it helps to ask yourself some questions to narrow down the problem areas. Do you have problems that you ignore or count on someone else to solve for you? Do you feel embarrassed or ashamed of part of your personality? Do you have a hard time standing up to peer pressure when you really would like to do something different? Does your physical health seem to be affected by how you feel about yourself?

Once you have identified problem areas, you can begin to make changes. Sometimes just realizing you have a problem will allow you to change. Often, though, changing will progress slowly. This may be because you have developed habits or attitudes that keep you from achieving what you desire.

Breaking Habits A **habit** is an activity that you have repeated so often that you do not think before you do it. Once you have developed a habit, the action becomes automatic. Some habits are good ones. For example, brushing your teeth is a habit that promotes good health. Wearing a safety belt is another good habit. Any self-examination must include discovering your habits and deciding which ones you wish to change.

You may have physical habits such as grinding your teeth or biting your nails. These may harm your self-concept and be hard for others to live with. Other habits may have more to do with your personality. These might include interrupting or laughing at other people.

You were not born with any habits. They need not remain part of your behavior if you truly wish to change them. It will be hard at first. But just as habits are formed by repeating them, so they can be broken by repeatedly turning away from them.

If you decide that you want to change a habit, you will have to force yourself to stop and think each time before you do it. Set a goal to work on one habit at a time. Keep a daily record of your progress. You should reward yourself if you manage to avoid repeating your habit for a certain amount of time. Take one day at a time and do not give up if you find you slip back into the habit.

You may find it helpful to tell someone whom you trust that you wish to break a habit. For example, you might tell a friend you are trying to stop biting your nails. In this way you will have someone to remind you and encourage you.

Improving Your Attitudes Self-examination includes looking at your attitudes. An **attitude** is a state of mind toward something in particular or life in general. An attitude is an outlook. General attitudes can be grouped in two ways. A **positive attitude** toward life is the ability to see the best in a situation and to expect that good things are to come. A **negative attitude** toward life is always expecting the worst to happen.

If your self-examination shows you have a negative attitude about something, it may be helpful to think about how you came to have the attitude. Suppose you believe that you cannot make new friends. Perhaps when you examine this attitude you will see that it came from a few bad experiences when you were new in your school or neighborhood. It may have come from your family always describing you as the "shy" one. Having this kind of outlook about making friends may have become a habit that has resulted in a poor attitude.

One way you can try to change an attitude is to act as though you have the attitude that you wish to develop. Instead of thinking no one wants to talk to you, try starting conversations with others. Or invite them to do things with you. Instead of taking a teasing remark as though it were meant to hurt, try to tease back in a friendly way.

Very often you can improve an attitude by building on one good thing. This might be praise from someone you respect. Don't dwell on past mistakes. Instead, try to focus on positive achievements. Realizing that you have many benefits which other people lack may also help. Improvement in your self-concept may result from a new friendship. It may come simply from your deciding that you can be more in control of your life. However the improvement starts, the important thing is to recognize and enjoy the rewards that an improved attitude can bring. In this way your positive attitudes will be strengthened.

Figure 4-13 Some adults are trained to help you form a true picture of your personality.

Acceptance or Change In deciding whether to accept or try to change a part of yourself, remember that no one is perfect. All people have faults. Everyone makes mistakes sometimes. The effort to change should come out of a desire to be more comfortable with yourself and others. Your goals should not come from someone else's idea of success. Remember that even if you do decide that you would like to change something about yourself, it is not always possible. But taking a good look at a problem often leads to new ways of dealing with it.

Sometimes people close to you understand things about your personality that are hard for you to see. If you find it difficult to do a self-examination, you might ask your guidance counselor, coach, teacher, family doctor, or a member of the clergy for help. These people have the experience to help you understand yourself. It takes courage to try to change—and it also takes courage to accept what you cannot change. Both are forms of growth.

Lesson Review

People who are mentally healthy usually have a realistic self-concept, like and trust other people, and take responsibility for their own actions. Self-examination can help you discover some facts about your personality that you may wish to change. The growth of your personality, as well as the opportunities you create for yourself, will require many responsible choices.

1 What term describes your view of yourself and your role in life?

2 What is a positive attitude?

3 List four steps you can take to break a bad habit.

Chapter Review

Vocabulary

adolescence	instinct	personality
attitude	intelligence	positive attitude
conditioning	introvert	psychologist
conscience	learned behavior	role model
environment	maturity	self-concept
extrovert	mental health	self-control
gender identification	modeling	self-examination
habit	negative attitude	socialization
heredity	peer group	stereotyping
identity	peer pressure	values

Using Vocabulary

Questions 1–10. On a separate sheet of paper, complete each of these sentences with a term from the vocabulary list above.

1 The combination of characteristics that makes you different from anyone else is called your __?__.

2 Stepping back and taking a look at yourself is __?__.

3 A person who is more concerned with other people than with his or her thoughts and feelings would be classified by Jung as a __?__.

4 __?__ is a scientist who studies personality.

5 __?__ is the process by which certain characteristics are transmitted biologically from parent to child.

6 The shaping of behavior with punishment and reward is known as __?__.

7 Children who observe and then imitate their parents are learning through __?__. The person who is imitated is called the __?__.

8 __?__ is usually a time of sudden mood swings, when people first try to figure out their identity and their role in the world.

9 Your __?__ is your view of yourself and your role in life.

10 Your __?__ helps you to distinguish right from wrong.

Interpreting Ideas

1 How may belonging to a peer group be both positive and negative?

2 Describe three ways that children tend to learn certain behaviors.

3 What was the flaw in Jung's identifying individuals as personality types?

4 According to Maslow, what two kinds of needs must be met before a person can express love and affection?

5 In which of the following ways does self-control manifest itself in the young child: toilet training, learning to speak, sharing a toy, doing a puzzle?

6 According to Erik Erikson's theory of the eight life stages, in which age range do children develop a sense of competence?

7 Why does adolescence feel like an in-between period of life?

8 How can you account for the frequent mood swings during the teenage years?

9 Which is more likely to result in delayed development, lack of love early in life or a disappointing work experience in young adulthood?

10 In what sense are older people especially well-equipped to make a contribution to their community?

11 What are the two major factors that shape personality development?

12 Identify three characteristics of a healthy personality that are developed during childhood.

13 What characteristics describe a secure sense of identity?

14 According to the research of Rene Spitz, what is generally the early experience of children who are trusting and affectionate? of children who are less trusting and affectionate?

15 Which stage of life is characterized by a period of reviewing life goals?

16 In what ways may children develop a sense of achievement? Give specific examples.

17 During which stage of life is emotional maturity generally attained?

18 Why may stereotyping be harmful?

19 According to Piaget, when do simple reasoning and problem solving generally appear?

20 How does an introvert differ from an extrovert?

Applying Concepts

1 Describe some emotions and activities that are likely to concern a healthy eight-year-old, according to Freud, Piaget, and Erikson.

2 If a child's emotional need for love is not met, explain what could happen during adolescence, young adulthood, middle adulthood, and late adulthood as that person tries to form close relationships.

3 If a young adult finds it difficult to express love and affection, what, according to Maslow's theory, may we assume about the childhood experience of this person?

4 What are the advantages of taking responsibility for your own actions? If a young adult is not able to take responsibility for his or her own actions, what may be the basis for the problem?

5 Suppose a child is born with a tendency to act as a leader among playmates. Describe three environmental factors that might alter the child's tendency toward leadership.

6 After the Friday night dance at school, sixteen-year-old Nan gave in to peer pressure and drank two beers. After a self-examination of her behavior, Nan decided she wanted to be able to resist peer pressure. Which of the three characteristics of a healthy personality might Nan need to work on in order to make this change?

7 Why do scientists believe that heredity must be responsible for the striking similarities in intelligence between identical twins?

8 Which do you think is the more effective method of shaping behavior, conditioning or modeling? Why?

9 Some people believe that all girls are poor at math and science and all boys are inadequate in domestic roles, such as cooking or child-rearing. What factors may be responsible for these stereotypes?

10 Tom felt as if he would be miserable forever. He dreaded going to school, where he felt he had no friends. He hated the way he looked and behaved. List three ways that Tom could develop a better self-concept.

Projects

1 In this chapter you have studied just a few of the well-known systems of classifying behavior. Go to the library and look over some of the books on personality theory by other researchers. Select a theory of personality not covered in class. Prepare a ten-minute presentation on the theory to share with the class.

2 Produce a skit that shows how characters with healthy personalities approach problems and how those with a poor self-concept approach problems. Ask the audience to identify which of the characteristics of a healthy personality is present or is missing.

3 Set up a classroom debate, "Resolved: Environment Has a Greater Impact on the Personality than Does Heredity."

Appropriate expression of emotions helps maintain good physical and mental health.

CHAPTER FIVE

H E A L T H Y

Emotions

In a crowd at a football game, people experience many different emotions. Depending on how the game is going, some will feel happy, some angry, and some disappointed. The way people express their emotions is different. Some express themselves easily and harmlessly by cheering, booing, or yelling comments. Others may not be able to deal with their emotions in a healthy way. They may pick fights in the crowd or feel sad for hours if a game is lost.

Feelings about your own life are much more complex than those about a game. Your emotions can affect you physically. For example, they can make your heart beat faster or your palms feel sweaty. Often it is hard to handle your emotions, especially painful ones. Knowing appropriate ways to handle emotions is an important part of mental health.

Objectives

- List five emotions that most people experience.

- Identify several forms of love.

- Explain how anger can be helpful and identify two ways of dealing with anger that are harmful.

- Describe how fear may be helpful.

- Describe physical changes caused by emotions.

- Define *grief* and identify its five stages.

- Identify four defense mechanisms that are rarely constructive.

- Identify four defense mechanisms that are often constructive.

Emotions

Understanding your emotions, or feelings, is important to your mental health. **Emotions** are the strong, immediate reactions that you feel in response to an experience. They tell you whether what you experience is frightening or comforting, soothing or painful. If you are aware of your emotions, you can learn to express yourself constructively. For example, you may sometimes feel annoyed about a rule that seems pointless to you. If you understand why you are angry, you will be able to discuss your feelings more clearly.

Sometimes people think of emotions as mysterious. But emotions can be understood. The ability to understand and express your emotions builds your self-confidence and helps you to communicate well with others. It also helps you to understand others better. These abilities contribute to your mental health.

People in all societies and of all ages have emotions. Often they affect people in similar ways. The body responds to emotion. People who feel worried usually have a frown on their faces. Their muscles are tense. People who feel afraid, for example, may sit with their arms folded and legs crossed, as if they are protecting themselves. Certain emotions also cause physical changes. Your heart rate speeds up when you are angry. You perspire more when you are anxious. Emotions are powerful—they can make you sick, and they can help you to heal.

Some emotions, such as love, feel good. They enable you to feel attached to other people. They add to your sense of strength and give you a sense of hope. Other emotions, such as fear, can feel bad. They keep you from feeling pleasure and can even produce loneliness or emptiness. Emotions are not "good" or "bad" by themselves. All people—even the most mentally healthy individuals—experience many different emotions. How you deal with the feelings is what matters. In fact, difficult emotions can sometimes be handled in such a way that the result is good. You experience each feeling in your own way, and you may choose to express or to hide it.

Figure 5-1 Facial expressions of emotions are the same in all cultures. Can you identify the emotions shown here?

Love

A strong affection or deep concern for another person is **love.** Love can be communicated in many different ways. It is expressed through words, for example, or through touch or other

Figure 5-2 Love can be communicated in many different ways and can last for many years.

actions that show admiration and concern. Love often grows with time. The ability to love is one of the most pleasurable parts of living. All people have the ability to give love and the need to receive it.

Just as love is expressed in a variety of ways, there are also several types of love. Friendship is one form of love. You may think of friendship as just ''liking.'' But true friends feel loyalty toward each other and share interests and support. Such feelings and behavior are a form of love. The caring among parents, children, and brothers and sisters is another type of love. Family love is one of the strongest feelings human beings can experience. It grows out of many years of living together. And love in marriage, between a man and a woman, is one of the deepest kinds of love two people can share. This type of love involves promises to each other about all parts of life.

Some types of love are not felt toward individuals. You may love your country, for example. Respect for its values and the opportunities it offers may result in a patriotic feeling. Love of country can lead you to want to contribute to its well-being. Affection for humanity is another kind of love. It leads to a desire to be helpful, from assisting a stranger across the street to working in the community. Love is a bond that all humanity has in common.

Anger

All people feel anger at times. **Anger** is a strong feeling of displeasure. It ranges from annoyance to complete fury. It often causes a physical reaction. Besides an increase in heart rate, you might tremble when you are angry.

Anger may take different forms. Sometimes people feel angry out of frustration. **Frustration** is a feeling of disappointment. You feel frustrated when things are not the way you would like.

Hostility is another feeling of displeasure. It is a less strong form of anger. **Hostility** is feeling and behaving in an unfriendly

Health Bulletin

The facial expressions of emotions are the same in all cultures. Even children who are born blind smile and frown with these universal expressions.

Figure 5-3 Highly competitive environments can produce a great range of emotions from everyone involved.

way. Hostile people may make nasty comments. They may seem unkind. Hostility often is shown by going against the ideas of others. For example, if you feel hostile toward a friend you may refuse to speak to that friend.

Anger can sometimes be helpful. For example, if you see a friend being treated unfairly, you may feel angry. This anger may cause you to defend your friend and to defend what you believe to be right.

Your anger is your own response to a situation. Other people do not cause it. Anger can be handled in a constructive way. But two ways of dealing with anger are usually harmful: losing self-control and hiding your anger completely.

After working hard all summer mowing lawns, Mark was able to buy a bicycle. The next day he went to the garage to get the bicycle and go for a ride. He found the front wheel twisted out of shape so that the bicycle could not be ridden. Mark discovered that his younger brother, Tim, had taken the bicycle that morning without asking. Tim ran into a fire hydrant and twisted the wheel.

If Mark does not control his anger, he might take it out on Tim immediately. He might hit Tim or break something of his in return. Mark might even go out and kick the bicycle, out of frustration. On the other hand, Mark could refuse to express his anger at all. He might push it down inside him, leaving his relationship with Tim strained by unspoken anger.

Mark grabbed his tennis racquet and left the house. He hit tennis balls against the wall of the garage for a long time. Then he went to see his best friend and told him what had happened to his bicycle. Later that evening, Mark sat down with Tim for a talk. He told Tim how angry he was about what Tim had done. Tim agreed to use his allowance to get Mark's bicycle fixed.

Mark chose constructive ways to handle his anger. Physical activity and talking with an outside person both help to calm anger. They allow you to get the feeling under control. Waiting to talk with the person who made you angry is also a good idea. When you have calmed down, you can explain more clearly why you are angry. It is then easier to talk about the event and not just attack the other person. Calm talk usually leads to a better solution. It is easier to talk to someone who is calm than angry.

Fear

You feel fear when you believe you are in danger. **Fear** is a scared feeling. It can make you break into a sweat, your heart beat rapidly, or your hands and feet go cold. Your muscles also get tense. Your body gets ready to defend you against the threat.

Sometimes fear results from known dangers, such as fire or accident. Fear of real threats to your safety can be a helpful emotion. It warns you to jump out of the way of a moving car, for example. But fear can also be caused by something unknown. Some people are afraid of heights or being in a room without windows.

Anxiety is fear of the future or the unknown. Often it is fear of being hurt, or failing, or of losing something important to you.

Figure 5-4   People often express fear when danger threatens.

Anxiety makes you feel nervous and ill at ease. Your blood vessels may dilate, causing you to blush. Being anxious can make a "knot" in your stomach. This is because of changes in your digestive tract. You feel in danger, and you are not certain that you can handle it. Sometimes people have trouble figuring out what causes their anxiety. Some common causes of anxiety are tests in school, a first date, and giving a speech. What other situations make you anxious?

Everyone feels the various forms of fear from time to time. Because they cannot always be avoided, it is useful to know how to deal with them in healthy ways.

Rachel was given an assignment to make a brief speech to her English class. As the day for her speech approached, Rachel became more and more anxious. What if her speech were boring? What if her mind went blank in the middle of it? She got so nervous that studying for the speech became difficult. Rachel's heart beat faster just thinking about it, and her mind kept wandering.

Rachel could become so afraid of making the speech that she cannot sleep well; and she may lose her appetite. She may even feel sick and stay home on the day of the speech. On the other hand, Rachel might pretend that she feels fine about the speech. She may mention her anxiety to no one and not study very hard. She may walk to the front of the class and suddenly feel overwhelmed by the anxiety she has tried to ignore.

Rachel decided to discuss her fear about the speech with her parents. Her parents reminded her of other difficult events she had gotten through in her life. And they were sure the class would enjoy Rachel's speech. Together, the three of them agreed on a good study schedule for Rachel. They also had Rachel practice giving the speech in front of the family.

Rachel dealt with her fear in a healthy way. Admitting anxiety and talking it over increases understanding of the emotion. Once the reason behind the anxiety is clear, it is easier to create a plan for reducing it. In Rachel's case, sticking to a strict study schedule and practicing her speech helped reduce her anxiety.

When you feel fearful, it is best to admit the emotion and express it to someone who cares for you. Then you can develop a plan to deal with the threat you feel—whether real or imagined.

Jealousy and envy are emotions related to fear. **Jealousy** is the fear of losing something you already have. **Envy** is the fear that you cannot get what someone else has. People feel jealous, for example, when they are afraid of losing someone's love. Imagine that a good friend of yours pays attention to someone else. You may feel jealous, thinking it means your friend no longer cares for you. People feel envious when they wish they had something of someone else's. You may envy a classmate who has more expensive clothes than you, for instance. Occasional jealousy or envy is natural, but it is important to try to control them. They can lead to anger and may harm your relationships.

Grief

The death of someone you love or the divorce of parents are two events that can result in grief. **Grief** is a deep sorrow that is caused by the loss of someone or something that you cannot get back. The loss can be so painful that you feel empty and life seems meaningless.

Loss hurts. But it is a good reminder of your ability to love and form friendships. Without this ability, you would feel no grief, but you would feel no joy, either. Grief is a reminder of your ability to find meaning in your life.

Everyone experiences grief at some point. There are both healthy and unhealthy ways to get through it.

Miguel always had a special relationship with his grandfather. Whenever he visited, his grandfather took the time to ask Miguel how his school work was going. He often had good advice for Miguel and told him stories about his own boyhood. Sometimes they went to a ball game together. One day Miguel came home from school to find his mother upset. His grandfather had become ill. A few days later, Miguel's grandfather died.

Miguel might become so sad about his grandfather's death that he cannot think of anything else. He may refuse to do his school work or to join in activities with his friends. On the other hand, Miguel may refuse to think about his grandfather, since it makes him cry. While pretending to feel no pain, Miguel may decide that the risk in caring for someone is too great. He might hold himself back from people because of this experience.

At first, Miguel could not believe his grandfather was gone. Then he felt terrible pain during the first weeks after his loss. He cried often and could not sleep. He also began to feel angry at the world in general. He was especially angry with his grandfather for leaving him. At first he found it hard to do his school work or see his friends. But then he began to talk with his friends about the hurt he felt. He also expressed it to a teacher he especially liked. He did not feel like going out much, but he began to make himself do it. After a while, he grieved less. He still missed his grandfather, but he began to enjoy his memories of the good times they had shared.

Figure 5-5 Sharing feelings of grief is healthy behavior. The mourners will feel less alone.

Miguel managed grief in a healthy way. It hurts to lose some-one important, but it hurts worse to pretend it does not matter.

Grief is a process. Elisabeth Kübler-Ross, a Swiss-born psychiatrist, studied people's reactions to death. She identified five stages of grief, which are listed below.

1 *Denial*—The person denies that the death has occurred.

2 *Anger*—The person is angry over the loss and frustrated that the relationship with the loved one is over.

3 *Bargaining*—The person searches for ways to get back what has been lost.

4 *Depression*—The person feels hopeless and full of sorrow that there is no way to get back what has been lost.

5 *Acceptance*—The person accepts the loss and begins to look for meaning in other relationships and areas of life.

Other researchers have described the process of grief differently than Kübler-Ross. One scientist identified 10 stages of grief, as shown in Figure 5–6. It is important to let yourself go through the stages of grief. Only then can you accept what has happened. People sometimes feel despair along with grief. **Despair** is a feeling of complete hopelessness or loss of confidence. Despair can result if the grieving process is avoided or shortened. Sharing your feelings with others will make you feel less alone. It is also important to stay involved in your regular activities. This is hard to do at first. But slowly you will regain your pleasure in other interests.

Figure 5-6 Someone experiencing grief may not go through all of these stages, and may not go through them in the order shown.

Stages of Grief

Shock and Disbelief	Temporary retreat from hurtful event accompanied by feeling emotionally numb, which may last a few hours or days.
Emotional Release	May cry. Although crying is a healthy release, it may become hysterical.
Depression and Loneliness	Feels out of contact with daily events.
Physical Distress	May lose appetite, develop indigestion, high blood pressure, rapid heart beat, or changes in body temperature.
Panic	Actions may lack clear direction, sometimes accompanied by moments of disbelief.
Guilt	Feels guilty that nothing can be done to change the past relationship; regret and wishful thinking are common at this stage.
Hostility and Resentment	May express resentment toward doctors, friends, or even toward lost loved one.
Dejection	Unable to return to usual activities; all activities seem impossible and difficult.
Reconciliation	Begins positive steps to adjust to life without lost loved one.
Adaptation	Realizes that life can continue. Begins search for new relationships, but not as a substitute for lost loved one. New relations and activities will provide new reasons to continue living.

Guilt

People feel guilty when they behave or think in ways that do not match their values. **Guilt** is a feeling of having done something wrong. Stealing, for example, is an action that clearly conflicts with the standards of society. Thoughts that cause guilt are more difficult to recognize than actions. One example is angry thoughts about a loved person. Many people feel guilty when they are angry at someone they love, even though their anger may be reasonable on that occasion.

Guilt can be a helpful emotion. It can help you to live according to your conscience. And it can help you recognize when you have not lived up to your standards. You can then decide to do better. Everyone feels guilty sometimes. Learning to tell whether guilt is reasonable—and how to deal with it—will help your mental well-being.

Karen wanted a necklace to wear to a school dance. At last, she found the perfect necklace at a store. When no one was looking, Karen slipped it into her purse. At home that evening, she began to feel sorry about stealing the necklace.

Karen might feel so guilty that she decides she is a bad person. She could feel so awful that she decides she does not deserve to go to the dance. Instead, she stays home. On the other hand, Karen could decide that her behavior was not very bad. Guilty feelings are unpleasant, so she might ignore them. She may go ahead and wear the necklace to the dance.

Karen did not sleep well that night. In the morning she decided to tell her older sister what she had done. Her sister pointed out that even though stealing was wrong, Karen could correct her mistake. Karen decided to return the necklace to the store. After returning the necklace, she apologized to the owner of the store.

Karen handled her guilt in a constructive way. She dealt with her problem right away. Talking with her sister helped her understand why she felt guilty. Understanding why she acted as she did, and taking steps to right the wrong, were good ways of dealing with her guilt.

Lesson Review

All people experience emotions. Learning to understand and express your emotions in a constructive way is a sign of good mental health. Hiding or ignoring painful emotions only makes it harder to deal with them later.

1 Name five emotions that most people experience.

2 Identify three different forms of love.

3 What are two ways of dealing with anger that are usually harmful?

4 Describe some physical changes that might occur when you feel scared.

5 Identify Kübler-Ross's five stages of grief.

Defense Mechanisms

Some emotions, such as anxiety and grief, are not easy to live with. Even when you handle a difficult emotion in a healthy way, you may still feel pain. Most people develop defense mechanisms to defend themselves when they feel hurt. **Defense mechanisms** [*dih FENS MEK uh niz umz*] are methods of protecting yourself against further pain. They can help you get through difficulties and handle painful situations. Because defense mechanisms hide unwanted feelings, people are very often unaware that they are using defense mechanisms. This means that your behavior may seem confusing. You may become dependent on a defensive way of dealing with problems but not know it. If you examine the most common defense mechanisms, it may help you to recognize some of your own.

Defense mechanisms often serve a good purpose. Sometimes they are necessary for survival. But they can be used too often. When a defense mechanism continues to protect you from your true feelings, it stops being helpful.

Feelings must run their natural course. When a painful feeling is avoided for too long, the pain tends to become more difficult to work through. People must find their own balance between emotions and defense mechanisms. They need to find out whether their own defense mechanisms work for or against their long-term feeling of mental well-being.

Rationalization

People who rationalize are often unaware that they are hiding from the truth. Their actions seem right and reasonable to them. **Rationalization** *[ra shun uh lih ZAY shun]* is making an excuse for a mistake or failure. It is an attempt to preserve self-esteem and to avoid feelings of guilt. People are rationalizing when they make up a reason for something. They do this because the real reason is too painful to face.

Rachel was anxious about her speech because she was afraid she would fail. Suppose Rachel refuses to go to school that day and believes it is because she has the flu. She is rationalizing.

Rationalization can help maintain self-respect for a time. But facing reality and being honest about your feelings are better ways to build self-confidence.

Compensation

Covering up faults by trying to excel in other areas is known as **compensation.** Someone may become the class clown in order to hide a fear of being unpopular. This would be compensating. It usually occurs when people feel insecure and expect too much of themselves.

Karen stole the necklace because she is shy with boys and feels that nice clothes will make her more popular. Karen is compensating. It would be better if she were to try to make friends by being natural and cheerful. Clothes alone will not eliminate her shyness or attract friends.

Health History

The Austrian physician Sigmund Freud was the first to offer an explanation of defense mechanisms and the way they protect feelings.

Figure 5-7   Compensation has led many former athletes into broadcasting.

In some situations, compensation can be a helpful defense mechanism. It can lead you to develop your best abilities. For example, many disabled people compensate for their lack of ability in one direction by becoming very good at another activity.

Projection

Mark was angry at his brother Tim for wrecking his bicycle. Suppose Mark does not like his own anger, and imagines that Tim is angry at him instead. Because he is seeing his own feeling in someone else, Mark is projecting.

Projection is seeing your own faults or feelings in other people, even when they do not have them. People are projecting when they accuse others—whether silently or out loud—of having their own characteristics. This defense mechanism is used when people do not like what they see in themselves. They feel free of their faults if they see them in someone else instead.

Occasional projection is common and does not have to be a problem. But when used often, it can keep you from facing opinions you actually have about yourself. It also can keep you from understanding other people.

Identification

Feeling connected and similar to someone else is known as **identification.** Identifying with someone you admire is a defense mechanism that allows you to imagine you have the style or talents of someone else. This allows you to ignore your own faults. Miguel identified with his grandfather, who had played professional baseball. Through identification, Miguel felt very connected with his grandfather and his grandfather's interest in baseball.

Identification can sometimes be a healthy feeling. It is good to admire fine people and to try to develop qualities you respect in them. Identification can become a problem if you neglect your own personality growth.

Idealization

Sometimes people admire someone so much that they see the person as perfect. This is **idealization,** a defense mechanism that is an extreme form of identification. Idealization allows people to see others as they want them to be. But it keeps them from seeing others as they really are. This often happens in hero-worship of film or music stars whose real personalities and faults are hidden in a cloud of glamour.

Idealization is important in growing up. But it does mean you are exaggerating the good qualities of the other person. Not seeing people as they really are can lead you to expect too much from them. You then may be severely disappointed when you discover they have some faults.

Daydreaming

People often daydream in order to escape the frustration or hurt of difficult situations. **Daydreaming** is the creation of make-believe events that seem more pleasant or exciting than the real world. It is the living out in your mind of things you wish would happen. For example, you may wish to become better friends with someone you do not know well. If you are very shy—too shy to do anything about your wish—you might spend a lot of time imagining the friendship. Using your imagination in this way protects you from the anxiety of trying to develop real friendships. Your imagination serves as a defense mechanism.

Daydreams can be fun. They can also give you ideas for achieving your goals. They are obstacles when they serve as a substitute for reality. Then they keep you from taking action to make your dreams come true.

Reaction Formation

Have you ever pretended to be happy when you were really sad? **Reaction formation** is the expression of an emotion that is the opposite of what you truly feel inside. People use this defense mechanism to protect them against problems that might result if they expressed their real feelings.

Imagine that Karen is frightened by her guilt over stealing the necklace. She cannot face knowing that she did something wrong. Instead she brags to a friend about the necklace, pretending she is happy about it. Karen is using reaction formation.

Reaction formation can protect you from a painful feeling for a short time. But hiding your true feelings in this way is confusing to you and to people trying to understand you. Later on you will have to deal with your true feelings.

Regression

Suppose Mark is so upset about his broken bicycle that he kicks it. Instead of discussing his anger, he goes into his room and slams the door. He refuses to eat dinner with the family. By behaving in an immature manner, Mark is using regression.

Regression means to act in an immature way. People are regressing when they sulk or throw tantrums instead of expressing

Figure 5-8 Who are your heroes? Idealization involves thinking of people as perfect, without weaknesses or shortcomings.

Learning ways to manage a stress, including the stress of examinations, will help you achieve the goals you choose.

CHAPTER SIX

MANAGING STRESS

Most teenagers are familiar with stress. During tests or social situations, they may feel butterflies in their stomachs or feel their hearts pounding. Stress may make them feel anxious or even tired.

There are many ways to prepare for stress and deal with it positively. When stress builds up, though, some people may be unable to cope. They may begin to feel that their problems are too hard for them to solve. Some may even think about suicide. Suicide attempts among American teenagers now run as high as 1400 a day. Suicide is the second major cause of teenage deaths.

Learning how to manage stress is essential. Developing good friendships, exercising, and knowing how to say *no* to stressful activities will help. Stress can be managed.

Objectives

- Define *stress* and *stressors*.

- Identify positive and negative stressors.

- Identify the three stages of stress.

- Explain the connection between stress and psychosomatic illness.

- Define *depression*.

- Identify the kinds of stress that may lead to suicide.

- Identify the common warning signs of a potential suicide.

- Identify sources of help for a teenager who is considering suicide.

- Describe several strategies for managing or reducing stress.

Stress and Its Effects

Stress is as much a part of life as eating or sleeping. **Stress** is the body's response to a physical or mental demand or pressure. The physical and mental demands are called **stressors.** Physical stressors might be hunger, thirst, or cold. Feeling tired, maybe from overwork, can be a physical stressor. Certain drugs, such as tobacco or caffeine, cause physical stress, too. Mental or emotional stressors can trigger the same responses in the body that physical stressors do. Such stressors include worry about work or school and problems in relationships. Worry about money or poor health are other causes. Even happy events may be stressful.

Stages of Stress

When scientists first studied stress, they found a pattern to the body's physical reactions. They found that the body's response to stress is the same whether the stressor is physical or mental. Stress usually occurs in three stages: the alarm stage, the resistance stage, and the exhaustion stage.

Alarm Stage   As soon as you recognize a stressor, your body reacts. This quick physical warning is the **alarm stage.** When you feel fear, your body releases adrenaline. **Adrenaline** is a hormone that causes a rush of energy in times of danger. Your heart rate and breathing speed up. Blood rushes from your stomach and other internal organs to your arms, legs, and brain. The adrenaline has prepared you to fight with your greatest energy or to flee at your top speed. The body's immediate response to stress is called the **fight or flight response.**

Resistance   The second stage of stress starts when your body fights or flees. When your body works against the stress, it is at the **resistance stage.** Although you may not be able to fight or run, your body still works to resist a threatening stressor. In many cases, your body continues to respond as if it were in danger even after the stressor is gone.

In this stage, people cope with stress by using psychological defense mechanisms. These are sometimes called coping mechanisms. **Coping** means acting to correct a problem. Some mental coping behaviors are rationalization and denial.

Using a coping mechanism may help you control certain symptoms of stress. For example, you may be able to face a bad situation by joking instead of losing your temper. But you might not be able to stop your nervous perspiration. Few people can consciously stop the physical symptoms of stress.

Exhaustion   If stress lasts too long, you may move into the third stage of stress. In the **exhaustion stage,** the body's defenses against stress are used up. You are unable to fight, flee, or resist a threat in any way. Your body and mind are so tired you can no longer resist the stressor. During the exhaustion stage people often become ill.

Stress and Illness

As you know, stress causes many changes in the body. Stress can weaken the body and increase the risk of disease. Stress for long periods weakens the body's disease-fighting system. Some physical disorders that result from stress are psychosomatic. A **psychosomatic illness** [*SY kuh soh MAT ik*] is a physical disorder caused by stress rather than disease or damage to the body. Psychosomatic illnesses are real physical problems that may be triggered or complicated by stress. A psychosomatic illness is not, as many people believe, imaginary. It is simply a physical response to stress.

There are many kinds of psychosomatic illnesses with which you may be familiar. People may react in different ways. Sleep disorders are a common example. Worrying about something may make it hard to sleep. In some people, stress may result in sleeping much longer than usual.

The skin can be bothered by stress. Studies have shown that cold sores, acne, hives, and other skin disorders can be triggered by stressful situations.

Digestive problems also may be psychosomatic. The immediate response to stress includes slowing down the digestive process. This change may cause "butterflies" in the stomach. Nausea, vomiting, diarrhea, and constipation are also common results of stress.

Figure 6–1   The fight or flight response

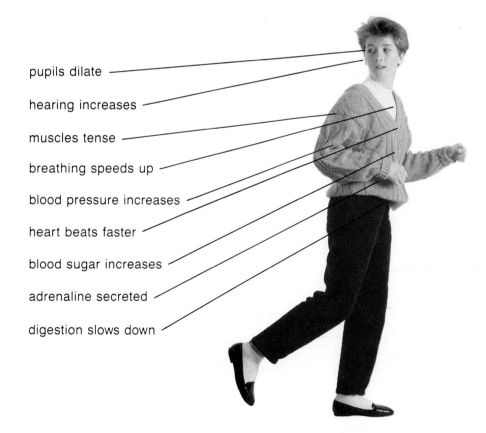

pupils dilate

hearing increases

muscles tense

breathing speeds up

blood pressure increases

heart beats faster

blood sugar increases

adrenaline secreted

digestion slows down

Ranking of Stressors by Senior High Students

Rank	Life Event	Frequency*	Life Change Units**
1	Getting married	10	101
2	Being pregnant and unwed	17	92
3	Experiencing the death of a parent	10	87
4	Acquiring a visible deformity	4	81
5	Going through parents' divorce	24	77
	Becoming an unwed father	23	77
6	Becoming involved with drugs or alcohol	226	76
7	Having a parent go to jail for one year or more	1	75
8	Going through parents' separation	29	69
9	Experiencing the death of a brother or sister	7	68
10	Experiencing a change in acceptance by peers	84	67
11	Having an unwed pregnant teenage sister	36	64
	Discovering that you are an adopted child	9	64
12	Having a parent remarry	19	63
13	Experiencing the death of a close friend	158	62
	Having a visible congenital deformity	14	62
14	Having a serious illness requiring hospitalization	26	58
15	Moving to a new school district	79	56
	Failing a grade in school	62	56
16	Not making an extracurricular activity	181	55
	Experiencing the serious illness of a parent	89	55
17	Breaking up with a boy friend or girl friend	411	53
	Having a parent go to jail for 30 days or less	5	53
18	Beginning to date	242	51
19	Being suspended from school	117	50
	Having a newborn brother or sister	30	50
20	Having more arguments with parents	351	47
21	Having an outstanding personal achievement	234	46
	Observing an increase in the number of arguments between parents	149	46
	Having a parent lose his/her job	51	46
22	Experiencing a change in parents' financial status	164	45
23	Being accepted at the college of your choice	49	43
24	Beginning senior high school	313	42
25	Experiencing the serious illness of a brother or sister	61	41
26	Experiencing father's increased absence from home due to a change in his occupation	70	38
27	Experiencing the departure from home of a brother or sister	199	37
28	Experiencing the death of a grandparent	144	36
29	Having a third adult added to the family	22	34
30	Becoming a full-fledged member of a church	100	31
31	Observing a decrease in the number of arguments between parents	179	27
32	Having fewer arguments with parents	180	26
	Having your mother begin to work outside the home	124	26

* Of the 913 people who took part in this study, this is the number of people who had this event happen to them.
** This is the average ranking people gave to these events.

Figure 6–2 The stress of an event is a result of how frequently an event occurs and how much adjustment the event demands.

An ulcer is another example of a digestive ailment often connected to stress. An **ulcer** is a hole or sore in the lining of the stomach or other parts of the digestive system. The acid in digestive juices causes ulcers. Stress may worsen this condition.

Various types of headaches, too, can be physical symptoms of stress. Tension headaches are caused by muscles that contract in the neck and scalp. A very severe headache sometimes caused by stress is a **migraine headache.** A migraine headache is preceded by temporary vision problems and is often accompanied by nausea. Just as muscles tighten during stress, so do arteries. When arteries to the brain tighten, the supply of blood may decrease. This causes the temporary vision problems. Then the arteries widen and pressure on the nerve endings in the artery walls causes the severe throbbing of a migraine headache.

The heart and blood vessels suffer most from high levels of stress. High blood pressure is often associated with stress. Stress can be deadly for a person who has high blood pressure.

Accumulation of Stress

Stress, especially mental stress, can accumulate. Overwhelming stress can destroy a person's physical health and mental well-being. Scientists have developed various scales to judge the level and effect of certain stressors.

The American doctor R. Dean Coddington made a list of 42 events that happen in the lives of many students. Coddington asked senior high students to tell him how often these events occur. The students also rated the events according to the amount of stress they felt each event caused. A **life change unit** is a unit of measurement for the amount of stress. Figure 6–2 lists some of the events and the average number of life change units rated by the students. What change did the students consider to be most stressful? Notice that some events are positive changes. Others are negative. Some are physical. Others are mental.

This scale of changes in life shows some useful things about stress. One is that many small stressful events in a short time may add up to more stress than a single, very stressful event. The higher a person's total on the scale, the greater the risk of serious health problems.

Lesson Review

Stress is the body's reaction to a physical or emotional strain. Too much stress may cause poor health. Scientists have done much to study the stages of stress. They also have helped people assess levels of stress for certain events or changes.

1 What is stress?

2 List four physical effects of stress.

3 What are the stages of stress?

4 List three examples of psychosomatic illness.

Suicide

Adolescence can be one of the happiest times of life. Yet it is also a time of accepting many physical changes and taking on new responsibilities. These changes can cause a great deal of stress. Teenagers may not know how to handle these new problems and feelings. These stresses may make them feel angry, frustrated, anxious, confused, or depressed.

Depression is a feeling of sadness, worthlessness, helplessness, or isolation. In its milder forms, it is often called the blues. Depression may be triggered by many different stressors. Loss of a loved one, illness, injury, aging, loneliness, and change of body chemistry are a few stressors that may cause depression.

Most people feel blue, depressed, or isolated from time to time. These feelings are usually temporary. For example, some people feel depressed on the weekend. But usually this feeling lasts only until they find something interesting to do.

Stress and Teenage Suicide

Sometimes the feeling of depression may last a long time. When depression does last a long time or when many things go wrong all at once, some teenagers may suddenly feel that nothing can ever go right again. They may even have thoughts of suicide.

I have made such a mess of my life. It seems as though the harder I try, the more things go wrong. I just do not seem to fit in anywhere. Kris just broke up with me. I guess I am just not as good-looking as the other guys. I will never be able to keep any girl friend. And my grades have slipped. Good grades are really important to Mom and Dad. I do not think I fit their idea of the perfect son. I feel lonely and, well—different. Nothing in my life right now seems worth the bother.

The boy who has just split up with his girl friend and whose grades are falling may be thinking about suicide. Suicide is not new among adolescents. What is new is the large increase in the numbers of teenage suicides. Teenage suicide has more than doubled in the last 30 years, and it is occurring at an earlier age. Why is this happening? The problem is very complex and there seems to be more than one cause.

Stress of Growing Up   For many teenagers, the stress of taking on more adult roles—growing up—brings up thoughts of suicide. Social pressures to feel attractive and accepted among friends are very strong. Having a steady boy friend or girl friend may take on great importance. Handling the growth or the break-up of such a friendship may be quite troublesome.

Pressures to succeed in school, in sports, or in a part-time job also increase. Teenagers may also be undergoing physical pressures that they may not understand. Changes in body chemistry may be responsible for their being cross, tired, or angry. They may tend to overreact. Physical changes may also cause marked differences in appearance. Trying to handle all these changes at once can be very stressful.

Health History

Teenage suicide is not a new phenomenon. Shakespeare wrote about it in his play *Romeo and Juliet.*

Figure 6–3   Romeo and Juliet

Stress of Loss Adolescence may be a time of learning to accept loss. The teenage boy in the story felt bad about losing a girl friend. He had also lost confidence that he could do well in school. Other kinds of loss might be the death of a close relative or the divorce of parents. Some teenagers feel great loss because they miss old friends after they have moved. When they feel sadness over a loss, it is important that teens talk over their feelings with a friend or a parent. This may help prevent deep depression or feelings of isolation that may lead them to think about suicide.

Stress to Succeed Most teenagers will be trying out many new roles in high school. They might, for example, try out for a school play. But they may find that other students are better actors than they are. The tendency to compare oneself to others is a natural thing, but it is important to remember that people excel in different ways. Failing in one area may mean only that they will excel in another.

Trying to get high grades or to score well on college entrance examinations can be very stressful. The stress of succeeding will certainly increase for teenagers who decide to attend college.

Helping Yourself and Others

When someone does commit suicide, the people closest to the victim are often taken by surprise. "Why didn't he say something?" they wonder. In most suicide cases, victims usually *do* give some clue within three months of their death. Eighty percent of teenagers who try suicide have mentioned it beforehand. But often the clues go unnoticed or are not taken seriously. Figure 6–5 lists some of the possible warning signs of suicide.

Many teenagers who consider suicide are loners who have problems gaining or keeping friends. Lacking friends, they also lack the social support they could use to help them manage their problems. Such teenagers may not have a positive self-image. They may tend to overgeneralize a problem. **Overgeneralization** is drawing a broad conclusion from one incident. For example, in the story the boy had lost one girl friend. He then drew the conclusion "I will never be able to keep any girl friends." He had overgeneralized.

People who consider suicide are often very critical of themselves. They often feel guilty or worthless. Failing in school, skipping classes, or having a hard time concentrating confirms their bad feelings about themselves. People who are very critical of themselves may personalize a problem. **Personalization** is the act of taking a remark or incident too seriously. For example, a teenager might feel guilty about his family's money problems. He might feel bad that he is not able to help more or feel that he is a burden because he needs clothing and food. He is personalizing and making himself feel responsible. When people begin to have negative feelings like these, they may feel very depressed. They may think about suicide.

Sometimes teenagers find that talking about their problem helps. If their depression is not too deep, a kind listener may help

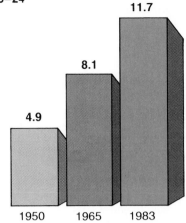

Suicides per 100,000 persons age 15–24

Source: U.S. Department of Health and Human Services

Figure 6–4 The tragic trend of suicide among young people.

Figure 6–5 Warning signs of suicide

Talking about suicide
Writing about suicide or feelings of hopelessness in journals, poems, or essays
Losing interest in friends, school, hobbies, favorite sports, personal appearance, or food
Giving away favorite possessions
Dropping all social inhibitions
Behaving emotionally by laughing, crying, or having explosive outbursts of temper without cause
Becoming suddenly accident-prone
Increasing use of drugs or alcohol
Possessing pills or weapons with which to commit suicide
Feeling depressed long after the loss of a loved one

Figure 6–6 Talking or listening to a friend in crisis can be the right help in preventing a tragedy. Below are other tips on how to handle a suicide crisis.

Take your friend's crisis seriously.
Get help immediately, but do not leave your friend alone.
If you are talking on the phone, keep talking until you get someone else to call for the police or fire department.
Do not deny that your friend has a problem.
Listen to your friend carefully.
Avoid statements such as "Don't worry," "There's nothing to worry about," or "Your problem's not really that bad."
Ask specific questions about the problem.
Afterwards, talk about the crisis with someone to relieve any anger, fear, loneliness, or guilt you may be feeling.
Ask your school guidance counselor to arrange a discussion group to help you and others deal with your feelings.

them rethink their concerns. Talking to the family doctor is a good approach. In some cases, a medical problem may cause feelings of depression.

If a medical problem does not exist, then counseling may be necessary. Many teenagers will want to talk to their parents first. Others may find it difficult to explain personal problems to their parents. Many schools have a staff psychologist to help. A school guidance counselor may be able to help or recommend someone, too.

Often, when there has not been enough help or when help comes too slowly, young people find themselves caught up in a friend's crisis and do not know how to stop it. Figure 6–6 offers some tips on helping a friend who is facing a suicide crisis.

Many towns have suicide hot lines or prevention and crisis centers to help potential suicide victims. These numbers are often listed at the front of the telephone book. Even though some small towns do not have suicide crisis centers, there is almost always someone who will listen and help. There will be a parent, teacher, clergy member, family doctor, or some other adult who cares.

Lesson Review

The stresses of adolescence can cause major changes in behavior and attitude. Feeling isolated and sad at times during these years is common. But long periods of depression or talking about death may be a warning of a suicide attempt. Two ways to help others are to learn to recognize the warning signs of suicide and to know where to get help for the person.

1 What is depression?

2 List three kinds of stress that are sometimes related to suicide.

3 List three warning signs of suicide.

4 What are four sources of help for teenagers who are thinking about suicide?

Dealing with Stress

While too much stress may cause illness, too little stress makes life dull. Nobody would want every day to be exactly the same with no challenges or risks. A life where nothing unexpected happens would be unchallenging.

Negative and Positive Stress

Stress can have both positive and negative results. When stress has a negative effect, it is called **distress.** People may feel distress when they are in new social situations. They may want to impress a special person at a party or to do especially well as they present a class project. Most people in stressful situations have similar physical reactions. Their hearts beat faster. They may feel a lump in the throat. Their hands may feel clammy, or their mouths may go dry.

Stress may also have positive effects. Stress that has a positive effect is called **eustress** [*YOO stres*]. An example of eustress might be learning a new sport. The activity is very positive. But most people will feel some stress because it is new. Figure 6–2 shows that even happy events can cause stress. It is important that people learn to increase their eustress and decrease their distress. Setting a comfortable level of stress and forming healthy habits for reducing stress can help.

HEALTH + TECHNOLOGY

BIOFEEDBACK THERAPY—When you are under stress, many parts of your body are affected. Such functions as heart rate, breathing, balance, and eye coordination are all influenced by stress. Most of these functions are controlled automatically by the central nervous system—you do not consciously cause the changes. But today biofeedback therapy is allowing people to bridge the gap between the body and conscious awareness.

During biofeedback therapy, special electronic equipment is attached by wires to different parts of the body. For example, an electromyograph is a machine that monitors the activity of muscles. The patient is able to know what is happening inside the body by observing changes in colored lights or listening to different sounds.

With biofeedback, the patient learns how to control the body's responses. For example, a patient may learn to relax the muscles that tighten and cause a headache. Biofeedback therapy has been used to lower high blood pressure and to control asthma. Thus biofeedback can help patients learn ways to counteract the effects of stress. With practice, the patient may learn to control the body systems without the need for the electronic equipment.

1 What is the purpose of biofeedback therapy?
2 What machine monitors the activity of muscles?

Your Level of Stress

Some people perform very well at high levels of stress. They seem to be forever on the go with meetings, sports, volunteer work, and hobbies. On vacations, they like to explore places where they have never been before, meet new friends, and seek excitement. Other people prefer to stay safely at home most of the time. They dislike risk and change. They enjoy following a regular routine, eating the same foods, and spending time with old friends. Most people fall in between these two extremes.

Think about the kind of schedule that makes you most comfortable. Do you feel tension when you increase your number of daily activities? **Tension** is an uneasy feeling caused by mental or emotional stress.

The best time to develop healthy habits for reducing stress is when you are not under much stress. Although you cannot know exactly what stressors you will face in the future, you can begin now to develop some ways to decrease your level of stress.

Reducing Stress

Have you ever been so involved in a project that you forgot the time of day or tried to ignore hunger? Did you wake up tired and exhausted the next day? People often push themselves hard to complete important tasks. But overloading schedules may lead to greater problems and stress. Taking on too much often results in unfinished tasks that demand attention.

One way to reduce stress is to identify the forms of stress that you have taken on voluntarily. Sometimes people take on too many tasks. They may want to be seen as helpful and active. But they may overwork themselves. Saying *no* can be a powerful way to reduce this kind of stress.

Three other ways to protect yourself against stress include maintaining good physical health, relaxing, and making friends.

Figure 6–7 Some people control themselves and others with confidence during stressful tasks.

Maintain Physical Health   The first step toward reducing the effects of stress on the body is to stay in good health. Good eating habits, plenty of rest, and adequate exercise help keep physical resources in shape. During times of high stress, eating well and sleeping well are very important.

Increasing exercise levels is also a good defense against stress. Exercise can increase your strength and endurance. Activities such as running, bicycling, or practicing tennis are also good ways to let off steam.

Relax   It is wise to save part of each day for relaxation. Even a few restful moments after lunch or dinner, for example, can have a refreshing effect. Listening to music, working on a hobby, or sharing time with a good friend are excellent ways to relax. Whatever the form of relaxation, the activity should make you feel calm. But if a hobby is too difficult, it may increase stress rather than lower it.

Reading can be very relaxing. A book can help you imagine you are in a different time or surroundings. Thoughts of a warm beach or the crisp cool air of a mountain can be like taking an instant vacation.

Playing sports for fun can also be relaxing. However, some competitive sports may actually increase feelings of stress. Of course, if you do not become too anxious about winning or losing, competitive sports can help you relax.

Some people enjoy taking a very hot bath to relax. Muscle relaxing techniques are also useful to relieve stress. You might try lying on your back with your arms at your sides. Relax your entire body into a comfortable position. Then imagine your arms growing heavy, having no energy of their own. Focus your attention on each part of the body. In turn, shift your attention from hands up to shoulders, from feet up to knees and hips, and so forth. When you feel one part lying totally relaxed, move on to the next. This exercise is good for a short break or for falling asleep at night.

Social Support   Friends are an important resource in coping with stress. It is easier to build friendships when things are going well than after stress has already built up. It is important to learn to share happy and sad feelings. Then, when stress does begin to mount, more friends are available to talk to. Friends may offer ideas that will help reduce stress. At the very least, they can often give encouraging support during a rough time. A strong support group of friends and adults is also one of the best defenses against stress.

Stress and Success

Moderate stress can help people achieve. It motivates them to learn, to change, or to take action. People feel good about themselves when they accomplish an important task. They may even feel ready to take on a new project or try a new challenge. But it is not good to have high levels of stress without relief from time

Figure 6–8   You may enjoy athletic activity as a method of releasing stress.

Figure 6–9   Relaxing with a hobby helps release stress.

to time. In order to maintain good mental and physical health, people must learn how to manage stress. Different strategies work for different people. Certain approaches to stress, however, are helpful to almost everyone. Preparation, taking one problem at a time, and coping with setbacks are ways to deal with stress.

Health Bulletin

Regular strenuous exercise increases the number of red blood cells that carry oxygen in the body. This means that more oxygen can be carried to the tissues, making a physically fit person less likely to tire easily from physical or emotional stress.

Preparation   When a difficult time is coming up, preparation is the best way to avoid high levels of stress. Of course, taking the needed action early is easy to talk about but hard for many people to do. Suppose, for example, that a teacher plans a test for Monday. Some students may torture themselves with worry all weekend about what will happen if they get a bad grade. This kind of worry is wasted energy—it accomplishes nothing. The best thing students can do is simply study for the test. This is something they can prepare for and control. Consider the different ways these students prepare for a class.

Jackson and Martha both had to give oral presentations in class. Martha worried about the presentation. But she did not do much library work on her topic. She also did not practice her talk before she gave her speech to the class. Jackson decided he would practice. First, he carefully researched his topic. Then he tape-recorded himself to pick out the rough spots.

Martha was not prepared for her presentation. She could not answer a question the teacher asked her during the talk. Martha became quite upset and had to cut short her talk. In class, Jackson was still a little nervous, but he knew his subject well. The longer he spoke, the more at ease he felt.

Because Jackson prepared for his stress, he handled it well. He felt confident. His anxiety was lessened. Since Martha's experience was upsetting, she may find the next speech assignment even more stressful.

One Task at a Time   A simple way to prevent stress is to tackle problems or tasks one by one. Making a list of jobs to be done in a logical order is a good start. Thinking a job through and then beginning may help to complete the next task on the list. Dividing a big job into smaller steps also helps. For example, a student who must do a term paper might research the topic, then outline the term paper, and then write. Finishing each step before starting the next one helps. It means there are fewer details to worry about at each step.

Coping with Setbacks   Everyone suffers setbacks from time to time. But some people seem to bounce back naturally and even turn setbacks into positive actions. Successful people do not avoid difficulty. Instead, they find ways to turn each difficulty into a new opportunity. Compare the following decisions of Maria and Richard.

Maria and Richard signed up for a required history course at their school. On their first test, both Maria and Richard failed. Richard was very upset about the possibility of failing the course.

Figure 6–10 Taking on more than you can handle will increase stress. Learn to deal with one problem at a time.

He immediately tried to transfer out of the class. He had an angry interview with both the history teacher and the school guidance counselor. Finally he switched to a study hall.

Maria was also upset at failing the test, but she took this to mean she had not worked hard enough. She asked her history teacher for help and studied as much as she could before the next test. Maria received an A on the second test and a B in the course.

Both Maria and Richard experienced the same stress of failure on their first history test. Richard gave up his chance to succeed in the class. He did not deal with his stress. Maria chose to keep working toward success. The stress of failing the first test did not defeat her. It motivated her to search for other ways to manage her stress and achieve her goal.

Lesson Review

Learning to manage stress helps prevent physical and mental problems. Each person, of course, must find a comfortable level of stress. Reading, exercising, and trying muscle-relaxing techniques are good ways to lower stress.

1 Define *distress*.

2 Define *tension*.

3 What are two ways to protect yourself against stress?

4 List three effective ways to relax.

5 List two ways to cope with high levels of stress.

Chapter Review

Vocabulary

adrenaline	exhaustion stage	psychosomatic illness
alarm stage	fight or flight response	resistance stage
coping	life change unit	stress
depression	migraine headache	stressor
distress	overgeneralization	tension
eustress	personalization	ulcer

Using Vocabulary

Questions 1–10. On a separate sheet of paper, write the term that most correctly completes the sentence.

1 The quick physical warning to which your body reacts is the __?__ stage of stress. (resistance, alarm, distress, exhaustion)

2 When a stress has a negative effect, it is called __?__. (distress, eustress, tension, alarm)

3 One digestive ailment connected to stress is a(n) __?__. (sleep disorder, migraine headache, outbreak of acne, ulcer)

4 A(n) __?__ may occur when arteries to the brain tighten, causing pressure on the nerve endings in the artery wall. (elevated blood pressure, migraine headache, bout with cold sores, ulcer)

5 In its milder forms, __?__ is called the blues. (tension, coping, distress, depression)

6 In the __?__ stage, the body's defenses against stress are used up. (distress, resistance, exhaustion, fight or flight)

7 A(n) __?__ is the unit of measurement for the amount of stress. (stress indicator, life change unit, adrenaline unit, alarm unit)

8 Overwork, extremely happy events, and worry about the need for love are all examples of __?__. (stressors, stress, eustress, coping)

9 When the body is under stress, the release of __?__ prepares the body for "fight or flight." (tension, hypothalamus, adrenaline, stressors)

10 A psychosomatic illness is __?__. (all in your head, a physical response to stress, caused by a pathogen, imaginary)

Interpreting Ideas

1 Compare the three stages of stress.

2 How does a coping mechanism help you control certain symptoms of stress?

3 Identify four stressors that may cause depression. When does depression become a serious problem?

4 Identify and describe three theories that may help explain what triggers teenage suicide.

5 What factors may produce physical stress? List several common physical reactions to stressful situations.

6 How may stress affect an ulcer?

7 How do moderate amounts of stress help people achieve?

8 Explain how stress may be related to high blood pressure and migraine headaches.

9 How do successful people cope with setbacks?

10 How does preparation help to reduce stress?

11 List four warning signs of suicide.

12 How can stress be measured? Are all the stressors in Figure 6–2 negative events?

13 Identify four strategies for managing and coping with stress.

14 Describe some sources of help for a teenager who is thinking of suicide.

15 How can you maintain physical health during times of high stress?

16 What skin disorders may be triggered by stressful situations?

17 How can friends help during times of stress?

18 Describe some common characteristics of the people who consider suicide.

19 What are three ways to protect yourself against stress that results from taking on too many tasks?

20 When is the best time for developing healthy habits to reduce stress?

Applying Concepts

1 An angry dog chases after you as you deliver newspapers. You begin to run and quickly outpace the dog. In this situation, what are (a) the stressor, (b) your immediate response to it, (c) the physiological changes that may accompany your response, and (d) the stages of stress that you are likely to go through?

2 Give reasons for agreeing or disagreeing with the following statement: Some stress is necessary to well-being, and a lack of stress can be harmful.

3 In a routine checkup, the patient complained of the following symptoms: headache, fatigue, and stomach distress. Recently, the patient had been fired from a job. The patient's doctor was able to rule out any organic disease through a series of tests. Are the patient's symptoms imaginary because there is no disease? How, then, might you explain the patient's symptoms? How might the doctor help this patient?

4 Describe an ideal world in which a person's habits and environment lead to physical and emotional well-being. Be specific about the amount of stress that should be present in the home, school, and sports. Describe the kind of diet, exercise, and relationships that would produce a sense of well-being.

5 Of the 42 events listed in the table in Figure 6–2, which is ranked with the greatest number of life change units? What life event do you think should be ranked highest? Why?

6 Generally, what is the message behind a suicide or a suicide attempt? Is it justifiable to betray the confidence of a friend who exhibits suicidal behavior? Why or why not?

7 Why, if the physical symptoms of eustress and distress are identical, is there a positive effect associated with eustress and a negative effect associated with distress?

Projects

1 Research the work of cardiologists Meyer Friedman and Ray Rosenman in which they describe the Type A personality. What are some characteristics of the Type A personality? What are the dangers of being a Type A? How are these dangers related to stress?

2 Create a program designed to relieve harmful stress in teenagers. Consider areas such as nutrition, exercise, and relaxation programs, and psychotherapy.

3 Design a funny bulletin board in which you create caricatures of personalities governed by stress: the chronic hurrier, the worrier with clenched fist and grinding teeth, the competitive challenger, the tense teenager. Tie each of these personalities to one or more physical symptoms

frequently produced by ongoing stress: heart attack, digestive complaints, headaches, high blood pressure.

4 Find out what is being done in your town or community to deal with suicidal crises. Are there hot-line numbers that can be used during a crisis? Are the Samaritans or similar groups active in your community? How would you counsel a friend contemplating suicide?

5 Design a pamphlet called *Suicide Myths and Facts*. One myth, for example, is that people who talk about suicide do not kill themselves. In your pamphlet this fact would follow the myth: Eight out of ten people who commit suicide tell someone that they are thinking about hurting themselves before they actually do it.

Group therapy with a qualified professional therapist is one way of treating mental disorders.

CHAPTER SEVEN

TREATING
Mental Disorders

Throughout history some people have suffered from mental illness. For many centuries, no one knew what caused mental disorders. A thousand years ago, for example, people with mild mental disorders were treated by many different methods. These included herbs, ceremonies, and lucky charms. Sometimes the people were kept in prison. In some cultures, people who had severe mental illnesses were thought to be possessed by the devil. These people were tortured or even burned at the stake as a way of destroying the devil in their bodies.

Today people who suffer from mental disorders are treated with the same care as those who suffer physical problems. Hospital care is prescribed when necessary. But the goal of any treatment is to help the mentally ill adjust to daily life so that they may live with other people.

Objectives

- Distinguish between organic disorders and functional disorders.

- Identify three kinds of mood disorders.

- Describe three personality disorders.

- Identify three anxiety disorders.

- Describe three different kinds of therapy for mental illness.

- Give examples of agencies that offer help for mental illness.

Causes of Mental Disorders

Any disease of the mind that affects the emotions, thoughts, or personality of an individual is a form of **mental illness.** The signs of mental illness may include changes in speech and difficulty in remembering things. A very different view or reaction to things can also be a sign of mental illness. For example, a person who laughs in response to a very sad event may be showing symptoms of mental problems. A **symptom** is evidence that may indicate a physical or mental illness.

At one time, people thought they could "catch" mental illness just as easily as a cold or flu. Most people stayed away from neighbors with mental problems. As scientists have studied the way people behave, they have learned that mental illness cannot be passed from person to person. Scientists have found two general classes of mental illness. These two classes are organic disorders and functional disorders.

Most research about mental disorders has been done by experts in psychology and psychiatry. **Psychiatry** [*sih KY uh tree*] is the medical study, treatment, and prevention of mental disorders. **Psychiatrists** [*sih KY uh trists*] are medical doctors who specialize in psychiatry. They differ from psychologists, who have practical training in psychology but are not medical doctors.

Health **History**

The Nobel Prize was awarded for research into mental disorders for the first time in 1949. Walter F. Hess, a Swiss researcher, received the prize for discovering how specific parts of the brain control specific organs of the body.

Causes of Organic Disorders

Mental illnesses that are chiefly the result of a physical cause are called **organic disorders.** Organic disorders are often due to physical abnormalities or chemical imbalances.

A chemical imbalance occurs when your body produces too much or too little of a chemical. A chemical imbalance in your body can affect normal thinking, feelings, attitudes, and behavior. A mental disorder can result. A tendency to develop a chemical imbalance is often inherited. In many cases, however, a person's environment plays a large part in causing mental illness.

Several mental disorders are related to chemicals that help the brain send its messages. These chemicals are produced by nerve cells. Nerve cells are constantly sending signals to other nerve cells. The chemistry of the brain is very complex. When something goes wrong with this process, a person's mood can be greatly changed. High fevers connected to other illnesses, or abuse of drugs or alcohol, may cause the trouble. Sometimes the mental change from the imbalance is permanent. At other times, it lasts until the chemical imbalance is corrected or controlled.

Sometimes changes in mood or reasoning may be signs not of mental illness but of physical illness. A physical checkup is very important when a person feels very depressed for no reason or notices a sudden change in personality. If a physical illness causes worrisome mental symptoms, the physical illness needs to be treated first. For example, a brain tumor may cause changes in personality, understanding, and speech. The mental disorder cannot be helped unless the tumor is treated.

Causes of Functional Disorders

Mental disorders that are not connected to physical causes are called **functional disorders.** They are emotional problems that stem from a person's environment. Painful childhood experiences and severe stress are two environmental factors that can lead to mental disorders.

Many scientists believe that your current mental state has been partly shaped by your childhood. Everything you heard, saw, and felt when you were a child influences your personality. Sometimes painful childhood events can lead to mental disorders.

The Austrian physician Sigmund Freud believed that childhood experiences were the most important influences on a person's mind. As you learned in Chapter 4, Freud believed that at each stage of development children have certain conflicts to resolve or problems to solve. If these conflicts are not resolved, a healthy personality cannot develop fully. In such cases, Freud believed, people are likely to develop mental disorders.

Most frequently, conflicts in childhood revolve around family, friendships, or school. If these conflicts are very painful or long-lasting, they can lead to mental disorders. Illness or death of a parent, brother, or sister may cause deep distress. Anyone who feels a lack of love from a parent suffers emotional pain. Other kinds of conflicts also may be caused by the divorce of parents or being left by a parent. Some children are mistreated. The emotional pain of being abused places the child at greater risk of developing a mental illness.

Extreme stress can also lead to mental disorders. As you read in Chapter 6, many events in life lead to stress, including prob-

Figure 7-1 A happy, secure childhood may help protect a person from developing mental illness later in life.

Figure 7-2 Some jobs involve more stress than others. Would you enjoy being a test pilot?

lems in the family, at work, or with friends. Mental stress makes people feel anxious, exhausted, and off-balance. Most people can cope with a certain amount of stress. But sometimes the stress is so great that a person cannot function normally. Mental disorders may result from severe, long-term stress.

Sometimes stress may be sudden and very powerful, as when someone experiences a trauma. A **mental trauma** [*TROW muh*] is a violent experience that damages a person's mental health. For example, witnessing a relative's death in a car accident or the horrors of wartime may cause a mental trauma. Such stress may increase a person's chances of becoming mentally ill.

Lesson Review

Much research has been done to discover the causes of mental illnesses. Many mental illnesses are organic disorders, which result chiefly from physical abnormalities or chemical imbalances. Functional disorders are emotional problems that stem from environmental factors such as stress or painful childhood events. A mental illness can result from a combination of inherited chemical imbalance and environmental factors.

1 What is psychiatry?

2 What is an organic disorder?

3 What is a mental trauma?

4 Name three causes of mental illnesses.

5 Give an example of a childhood conflict that may lead to mental illness.

Types of Mental Disorders

Everyone has occasional problems in dealing with emotions or relating to other people. But when these difficulties last for an unusually long time or interfere with normal daily activities, a person's mental health may be threatened. Millions of people experience some degree of mental disorders.

Chemical imbalance may be present in functional disorders, and a nonphysical cause, such as stress, may be present in organic disorders. Although constructive experiences and environment can help in fighting organic disorders, unpleasant and destructive experiences and environment can lead to functional disorders. Functional disorders include mood disorders, anxiety disorders, somatoform disorders, personality disorders, and dissociative disorders.

Organic Disorders

Organic mental disorders include some of the most common mental illnesses. Delirium and dementia most often affect adults. Other organic problems that can cause mental disorders may appear early in childhood.

Delirium [*dih LIR ee uhm*] is a mental disorder that involves confusion and a loss of awareness of the environment. Delirium may result from poisoning, high fever, or withdrawal from drugs

 ## Health *Careers*

Helping people with mental and emotional disorders can be a challenging and worthwhile occupation. A clinical psychologist may work with patients in a hospital, mental health clinic, or a private office. The psychologist uses tests to help determine the patients' problems and counsels patients with emotional or mental disorders. Strong communication skills and an ability to listen to others are necessary for a career in clinical psychology. Training for this career includes a college degree and a Ph.D. in clinical psychology.

Music therapists use songs and other forms of music to help patients change their behavior and understand themselves. Training includes a college degree and experience in an institution.

Occupational therapists help people with mental or physical disabilities develop job skills. For example, an occupational therapist may help a patient learn how to become a cook, and then help the patient find a job in a restaurant. Occupational therapists usually work with doctors, psychologists, or other members of a medical team. Occupational therapists must have a college degree in occupational therapy.

1. Name two types of therapists who work with people with emotional and mental disorders.
2. What type of training is necessary to become a clinical psychologist?

or alcohol. It may also be caused by fear or trauma. Delirious people are not sure what day it is, where they are, or who they are. Another sign of delirium is hallucination. **Hallucination** is seeing, hearing, or sensing something that does not exist. People who are hallucinating may see spiders on walls when none are there. They may also hear voices when no one is speaking.

Dementia [*dih MEN shuh*] is a severe and irreversible loss of mental ability. It is most common among elderly people. People with dementia have trouble remembering things. They forget names or conversations, and often lose their sense of judgment. They may also become quiet and withdrawn. One common type of dementia is Alzheimer's disease, discussed in Chapter 22.

Some forms of mental disturbance begin to show in early childhood. A very rare childhood mental disorder is infantile autism. **Infantile autism** [*AW tiz um*] is a condition in which children do not usually react to people or to their environment. If such children do respond, their behavior is strange. For example, when placed in an unfamiliar chair an autistic child may scream.

Hyperactivity is a condition in which a child is in constant movement and very easily distracted. Because hyperactive children have difficulty sitting still, completing tasks, and acting on instructions, they often have learning difficulties. Hyperactive children have trouble dealing with their environment. Thus they suffer a great deal of stress. Such stress may lead to functional disorders. Early treatment of this condition gets rid of the stressful symptoms and may quickly bring improvement.

Mood Disorders

Most people experience many moods. During one day, they may feel happy, sad, or angry. A **mood disorder** is a serious condition in which a single, often painful, mood rules the whole personality. Doctors today know a great deal about mood disorders and how to help people with them. Mood disorders often result from a chemical imbalance that can be treated with medicine. These disorders usually involve clinical depression or mania.

Clinical depression is a mental disorder in which there are ongoing deep feelings of worthlessness and hopelessness. People with clinical depression lose interest in almost all their usual activities. They feel very guilty about small matters and have a sense that they do not matter to anyone. Clinically depressed people often do not eat enough; or they eat too much. They often have trouble sleeping; or they sleep too much. They may have difficulty concentrating and therefore perform poorly at school or work.

A person who has a parent, brother, or sister with clinical depression is much more likely to develop clinical depression than a person whose relatives have not had this mental illness. But the individual's personality and environment may be able to overcome this. People suffering severe clinical depression often have thoughts of suicide. These people do not think that they will ever feel better. The risk of suicide increases when such people abuse alcohol or other depressant drugs.

Figure 7-3 Most people are depressed sometimes, but normally this mood soon changes to a happier one.

Mania can be thought of as the direct opposite of depression. **Mania** is an elated, impulsive mood. People with mania talk rapidly and feel very happy, or high. Sometimes they feel out of control. For example, they may buy things they cannot afford. Although manic people appear very happy, their extra energy can lead to violent behavior. Mania also ends in emotional and physical exhaustion.

Manic-depression disorder is a condition in which mania and clincial depression alternate. People experience mania followed by severe depression. These periods come and go, forming a cycle. For example, manic-depressive patients may feel normal. The next week they may start to feel "high," keep very busy, and go out all night. After a period of high energy, they may suddenly feel very depressed. Their energy disappears. They become so depressed that they do not want to go out. Next they may feel more like themselves, or they may become manic again. There is no general pattern to their mood shifts.

Anxiety Disorders

From time to time everyone feels anxious. Anxiety becomes a disorder when the fear lasts, is great, keeps someone from feeling any pleasure, or interferes with daily living. **Anxiety disorders** are a group of disorders in which anxiety is the main symptom. There are many kinds of anxiety disorders. They result from environmental causes.

Generalized anxiety is a constant state of anxiety with no single cause. Different people have different symptoms of generalized anxiety. Some shake or tremble. Others perspire and have pounding hearts, cold hands, and dry mouths.

Panic disorder is a sudden attack of terror that seems to have no cause but is usually connected with certain situations. Panic disorder feels like anxiety, only much worse. Sufferers have chest pains and their hearts beat faster. Trembling and feeling dizzy, they cannot breathe easily. Everything around them seems unreal. They fear going completely out of control or dying. In their efforts to control the terrible feeling of panic, people sometimes develop phobias.

A **phobia** is a constant, unreasonable fear of a situation or object. When such people are in the presence of whatever they fear, they are overcome with anxiety. Therefore, they try to stay away from what they fear. Claustrophobia is the fear of small enclosed spaces. Agoraphobia originally meant fear of big, open spaces. Now the term is used to mean the fear of leaving the home. These phobias often result from panic disorder. For example, a person who has a panic attack while driving a car may develop a phobia about driving. If people with panic disorder start avoiding many situations, they may develop agoraphobia in order to avoid any situation that could bring on an attack. Figure 7–4 lists some other phobias.

Obsessive-compulsive disorder involves the presence of unwanted thoughts, emotions, or behaviors. *Obsessions* are persistent thoughts that keep people from thinking about other things.

Health **History**

About 3000 years ago, Saul, the first king of Israel, suffered from symptoms that today might be diagnosed as clinical depression. During his periods of depression, Saul had young David play the harp to help change Saul's mood.

Figure 7-4 A phobia is an exaggerated, illogical fear.

Phobia	Fear of:
Acrophobia	heights
Aerophobia	flying
Agoraphobia	leaving home
Anthropophobia	people
Aquaphobia	water
Claustrophobia	closed spaces
Gephyrophobia	bridges
Mikrophobia	germs
Numerophobia	numbers
Nyctophobia	darkness
Ochlophobia	crowds
Ophidiophobia	snakes
Phonophobia	speaking aloud
Thanatophobia	death
Xenophobia	strangers
Zoophobia	animals

Compulsions are urgent, repeated behaviors. Compulsions are nearly always connected to obsessions. For example, people with an obsessive-compulsive disorder may worry about getting a terrible disease. They feel they must wash their hands—sometimes as often as 300 times a day. Immediately after washing, they begin to worry again. People with this disorder often worry so much about the thoughts or actions they cannot control that they are unable to carry out the activities of daily living.

Somatoform Disorders

The word *somatoform* is based on the Greek word *soma*, meaning body. A **somatoform disorder** [*soh MAT uh fawrm*] is a condition in which there are physical symptoms, but no physical illness. Although people with such disorders may believe they are suffering real disease, medical tests reveal no illness. Hypochondria is a somatoform disorder.

Hypochondria [*hy puh KAHN dree uh*] is a strong belief that one is ill when illness is neither present nor likely. People with hypochondria worry all the time about their imagined disease. Even doctors cannot make them believe that tests show they are healthy. For example, hypochondriacs often complain about multiple pains that come and go. They worry that they have serious diseases. They change doctors frequently, in order to find a treatment for their imagined disease. It is difficult to convince hypochondriacs of their mental illness.

Hypochondria is not the same as a psychosomatic disorder, which is a real physical pain or illness caused by stress or emotions. Migraine headaches caused by worry, or nausea caused by stage fright, for example, are psychosomatic disorders and not a form of hypochondria.

Personality Disorders

Personality traits that prevent people from interacting with others in a healthy way are called **personality disorders.** People with personality disorders do not have striking symptoms, such as illusion or hallucination. But their habits and behavior do keep them from feeling happy. They have trouble adapting to life and forming friendships. Once a personality disorder develops, it is difficult to change, even with professional help. There are several kinds of personality disorders.

Antisocial personality disorder is a condition in which a person has no respect for the rights of others. They usually have little or no feelings for other people. Often feeling bitter and cheated, people with this disorder believe that society's rules should not apply to them. Usually they conceal their bitterness by appearing confident and sincere. They may even be outwardly charming, while inside they feel cheated and believe they deserve whatever they can get. In other words, they say one thing and do another. As adults, they often become criminals.

Paranoid personality disorder [*PAR uh noyd*] is an unfounded suspicion and mistrust of others. Individuals with this disorder often keep their suspicions to themselves. In severe cases, their relationships may be damaged by their mistrust. Even after their suspicions are proved wrong, paranoid persons remain suspicious of others. For example, paranoid persons may believe they are being followed and change the locks on their doors.

Compulsive personality disorder is a state in which someone is constantly concerned with rules or standards. People with this disorder have difficulty changing the way they do things. Often they lack a sense of humor, and cannot express warm, loving emotions. Unable to really enjoy themselves, people with compulsive personality disorder can only express grim satisfaction when things seem right to them. Often they insist that others do things their way. When they are unable to control others, they become angry. Often these people overwork, valuing work above all else. Then they have little time for family and friends.

Schizoid personality disorder [*SKIT soyd*] involves a condition of deep withdrawal from other people. Persons with this disorder do not have warm feelings for others, yet criticism from others can easily hurt them. Thus they become withdrawn. Schizoid persons keep their feelings and thoughts to themselves. Such people have little desire to be involved with others and are often humorless and dull. Yet they feel lonely because they do not think other people have anything to offer them.

Passive-aggressive personality disorder causes people to resist cooperating with others. Such resistance is not out in the open. It is expressed indirectly. For example, a passive-aggressive person who does not want to help with party arrangements may promise to do so and then "forget." Passive-aggressive people do not openly refuse or express their anger. Instead, they show their resistance by failing to be reliable.

Figure 7-5 Overworking for long periods of time may be a symptom of a compulsive personality disorder.

Dissociative Disorders

Conditions in which the personality suffers sudden changes are called **dissociative disorders** [*dih SOH shee uh tiv*]. Usually people with these disorders forget who they are. Sometimes they believe they are someone else. In this way, they lose touch with themselves, becoming separated from their normal personalities.

Dissociative disorders are rare and usually result from terrible experiences, such as accidents or severe family circumstances. They may also result from extreme stress. By dissociating, these people are able to avoid facing extremely stressful events. They also help people avoid feelings with which they cannot cope.

Amnesia [*am NEE zhuh*] is the sudden inability to remember basic personal information. People with amnesia forget their names and where they live. They may not recognize family members or friends. For example, a fire that kills all but one person in a family may produce amnesia in the one who lives. Usually amnesia lasts for only a few days.

Multiple personality disorder is a condition in which a single person frequently changes between two or more separate personalities. This is a very rare illness. The central personality usually does not know about the other personalities. In fact, it may be hiding behind them. For example, one young woman was a kind and friendly person. Her second ''self'' was an unpleasant, noisy boy. Her third ''self'' was a quiet, frightened seven-year-old girl. This woman had been terribly abused in her childhood.

Multiple personality disorder can result from prolonged, severe childhood abuse or severe emotional trauma. In order to cope with the abuse or trauma the individual may develop different personalities. These new personalities cover up the pain felt by the central personality.

Figure 7-6   About one in every five Americans suffers from one or more mental disorders.

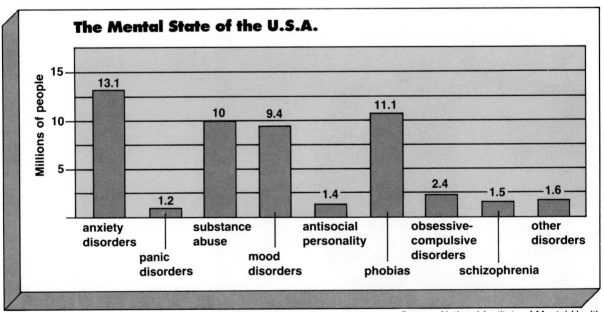

The Mental State of the U.S.A.

Millions of people

- anxiety disorders: 13.1
- panic disorders: 1.2
- substance abuse: 10
- mood disorders: 9.4
- antisocial personality: 1.4
- phobias: 11.1
- obsessive-compulsive disorders: 2.4
- schizophrenia: 1.5
- other disorders: 1.6

Source: National Institute of Mental Health

Schizophrenia

One severe mental disorder is **schizophrenia** [*skit suh FREE nee uh*]. People with schizophrenia severely distort reality and are deeply confused. They often have hallucinations, especially those of hearing voices. In some cases, people with schizophrenia feel they have magical powers or that others can read their thoughts. Some may withdraw from people. Others talk to themselves, wear bizarre clothing, or neglect their health. Schizophrenia usually begins between the ages of 15 and 25 and often affects more than one member of a family. It may come and go throughout life or, in severe cases, require lifetime hospital care. Although its cause is not fully understood, strong evidence points to a disturbance of important chemicals in the brain.

Figure 7-7 Louis Wain painted these pictures of cats while suffering from schizophrenia. The increasing distortion and violent colors reflect his disturbed mind.

Lesson Review

Delerium and dementia are organic disorders. Functional disorders include many forms of mental illness. Mood disorders affect how people look at life. Anxiety disorders cause people to feel very fearful. Somatoform disorders cause physically healthy persons to believe that they are ill. Personality disorders affect how people relate to those around them. Dissociative disorders cause people to forget who they are. A serious mental disorder, schizophrenia, causes patients to distort reality.

1 Name two kinds of organic mental disorders.

2 What is hallucination?

3 Name two symptoms of clinical depression.

4 What is a phobia?

5 Name three personality disorders.

6 What is amnesia?

Treating Mental Problems

For most people, hard times do not last. People with mental problems that last a long time need help. Today there are many kinds of help from which to choose. Only those people with grave mental disorders need to go into the hospital for extended care.

A common way to treat mental disorders is through psychotherapy. **Psychotherapy** [*sy koh THEH ruh pee*] is the treatment of mental, emotional, and nervous disorders without medication. It is based on communication between a person and a therapist. A **therapist** [*THEH ruh pist*] is a person who has been trained to treat an illness. A therapist may be trained as a psychologist or a psychiatrist.

Psychotherapy helps people understand their thoughts, feelings, and actions. This usually improves their mental health. There are many different kinds of psychotherapy. These include psychoanalysis and behavioral therapy.

Psychoanalysis

A process that tries to reveal the person's unresolved conflicts is **psychoanalysis** [*sy koh uh NAL ih sis*]. According to Freud, unresolved conflicts are the source of mental disorders. Many of these unresolved conflicts may lie in the person's **unconscious,** the part of the personality that is hidden from our own awareness. The psychoanalyst tries to discover the unresolved conflicts by having the client look at his or her childhood experiences, dreams, fantasies, and attitudes. Through psychoanalysis, doctors try to improve a client's self-awareness. They then use that self-awareness to decrease the client's conflicts.

Dan suffers from claustrophobia. This fear has begun to interfere with his job and other parts of his life. A marine biologist, Dan could study below the ocean's surface much more efficiently if he were not afraid to go underwater in small submarines. He decides to undergo psychoanalysis. During treatment, he discovers that early in life he was accidentally trapped inside a small cave while playing with friends.

Figure 7-8   A strong fear of small spaces would inhibit a marine biologist who must use a minisubmarine.

Although Dan had consciously forgotten the incident, a fear of small places resulted from his unconscious repressing the event. The psychoanalyst helped him to discover the cause of his fear. With this understanding, he may now be able to handle his problem more successfully.

Behavioral Therapy

Another form of psychotherapy helps individuals change their personal behavior. **Behavioral therapy** uses a system of rewards and punishments to encourage healthy changes in behavior. Behavioral therapists try to change problem behavior rather than focus on reasons for the problem. **Behavior modification** encourages good actions and discourages bad actions. This helps people develop positive behavior. Praise or treats may be given to the person as the problem behavior improves.

Instead of psychoanalysis, Dan may choose behavioral therapy. Rather than focusing on the cause of his problem, the therapist will try to change his habit of avoiding small, enclosed places. The therapist will use behavior modification to help Dan face his fears. The therapist may help Dan learn to relax through a conscious effort. Dan may then imagine himself to be in a small room, and try to relax at the same time. By repeating this many times, Dan learns to link small places with relaxation. Dan may also learn to feel proud each time he enters a small room without being afraid and may reward himself with small treats.

The goal of the therapist is to have Dan reward himself for entering small places by feeling relaxed or by other rewards. These rewards gradually change Dan's habits although he never discovers the cause of his claustrophobia.

Psychotherapy Techniques

All these types of psychotherapy may use various techniques to improve the person's condition. A therapist may use different types of psychotherapy and different techniques to fit the particular person's problem.

Play therapy studies and treats mental illness in children through observing them at play. Children show their thoughts, feelings, and conflicts while playing with different toys or puzzles. For example, a girl who unconsciously feels unloved by her father may break a male doll. To her, the doll may stand for her father. After seeing this happen, a therapist can help the child.

Many mental disorders can be helped by group therapy. In **group therapy,** a psychotherapist meets with several people who have similar problems. Usually six to twelve people meet in a group. They try to talk about their problems freely and honestly and advise each other. Therapy groups are formed to treat many kinds of mental disorders.

Family therapy is a form of group therapy in which all the members of a family are treated together. Psychodrama is another form of group therapy in which people act out certain roles to try to learn about their mental problems.

Chemotherapy

Today psychiatrists use many medicines in the treatment of mental disorders. **Chemotherapy** is the use of chemical medicines to treat disease. Tranquilizers, antidepressants, and even vitamins are used to treat clients with severe depression, manic-depression disorders, panic attack, and schizophrenia.

Medicines for mental disorders should be used only under the care of a psychiatrist. They need to be monitored closely. Medicines can correct chemical imbalances and reduce the symptoms of a mental disorder. They enable many people to feel better and lead normal lives. However, many personality problems still need to be solved through psychotherapy. Chemotherapy can greatly assist psychotherapy.

Chemotherapy may not always work. One reason is that it is difficult to find the right medicine and dosage for each person.

Health **History**

After World War II, doctors often used hypnotism to treat veterans suffering from amnesia. The hypnosis helped the veterans relive and relieve the emotional tensions experienced during the war.

Figure 7-9   In family therapy, family members try to learn how each one's behavior affects the others in the family.

Health Bulletin

The suicides of entertainment celebrities appear to trigger increases in the national suicide rate. Suicides increased 12 percent after the report of the suicide of Marilyn Monroe. Following the suicide of the comedian Freddie Prinze, suicide increased by 8 percent.

This can be a long, frustrating process. Another reason is that all strong medicines have side effects. People are sometimes bothered by the side effects of medicines used to treat their disorders. Chemotherapy has allowed thousands of patients to return to their homes and continue treatment without hospitalization.

Hospitalization

Today's psychiatric hospital is a place where most people receive help and then return home. Most patients stay only three to six weeks. Even so, the stay in the hospital can be emotionally painful. This is because patients must learn to accept their disorders and to cope with them. After going home from the hospital, many continue therapy to help them face life's challenges. In some cases of mental illness, the disease is often chronic and also must be controlled through medication.

Several kinds of people with mental disorders are helped by going into the hospital. These include people who are too depressed to take care of themselves; people so manic they cannot control themselves; and people likely to harm themselves or others. Those who need further tests also need to be in the hospital.

Hospitalization means protection for patients and their families. Patients receive specialized care in a safe environment. This includes diagnosis, psychotherapy, and, when needed, chemotherapy. Their environment is controlled; their time is structured. They are nearly always in the company of a member of the staff. If there is a high risk that they may harm others, they may live in locked wards until their condition improves.

Psychiatric hospitals have staff psychiatrists and psychologists who specialize in different mental disorders. Other staff members are also specially trained to help psychiatric patients. A major role of psychiatric nurses, for example, is to give patients emotional support. They also administer the medicines prescribed by psychiatrists. By observing patients' symptoms over time, these nurses can report the results of the treatment.

Psychiatric social workers provide family support and family therapy. Often they calm family members who are upset by the hospitalization and help them to accept the mental illness. They also report the patient's progress to the family. After patients are discharged, these social workers assist whenever problems arise.

Several kinds of therapy are a part of hospitalization. Many patients receive recreational therapy. **Recreational therapy** is pleasurable activity, such as sports and crafts, that helps patients express themselves creatively. **Occupational therapy** helps patients overcome their problems by teaching them practical skills. Therapy is individualized to meet each patient's needs.

Finding Help

There are early signs of many mental illnesses. Recognition of these signs in yourself or others may stop the development of worse mental problems. It is much easier to treat emotional problems early. It is therefore important to take notice of signs such as irrational fears, guilt, or irritability; poor concentration or

Figure 7-10 Occupational therapy helps psychiatric patients learn productive skills.

memory loss; withdrawal from friends and family; or deep feelings of hopelessness. Careful attention should be paid to signs of clinical depression, which may lead to suicide.

When you feel that you or someone you know shows signs of needing professional help, it is very important to tell your parents, school nurse, doctor, clergy member, or someone who can help you find good professional help. People with mental disorders can find help in many different places. Private therapy and hospitalization are not their only choices.

Community mental health centers offer various services. A new client can go there to seek advice on the treatment most suitable for a particular mental problem and to receive treatment. Recently discharged hospital patients can go for therapy. Troubled people who face a crisis and have nowhere to turn can also go to these centers. These centers will help arrange short-term or partial hospitalization. Partial hospitalization means that patients sleep in the hospital and work outside during the day. Patients may also sleep at home and spend the day at the hospital. Some community mental health centers also offer workshops about mental disorders.

Suicide prevention centers exist all over the country. They offer immediate help, usually by telephone. People feeling hopeless enough to consider suicide can call one of these centers. Staff members listen as long as distressed persons need to talk. In an emergency, they send someone to the caller's home. Then they try to arrange psychiatric treatment.

Many general hospitals have outpatient psychiatry centers. People with problems can make an appointment to be tested and treated. These centers offer psychotherapy and chemotherapy, as well as the services of psychiatric social workers and psychiatric nurses. Many hospital emergency rooms provide immediate care for persons undergoing mental crises.

Figure 7-11   Therapy can help people with problems such as depression.

Lesson Review

There are many effective treatments today for people with mental illnesses. Psychotherapy and chemotherapy are widely used. Hospitals, community mental health centers, suicide prevention centers, and outpatient psychiatry centers help those with mental problems. Awareness of the choices available for mental disorders helps you take responsibility for your own mental health. If you ever have a mental problem, knowing the treatments available will guide you in seeking help.

1 Name two different types of psychotherapy.

2 What is group therapy?

3 Name two kinds of people with mental disorders that are helped by hospitalization.

4 What kind of therapy teaches patients productive skills?

5 Name two places where people with mental disorders can find professional help.

Chapter Review

Vocabulary

amnesia
antisocial personality disorder
anxiety disorder
behavior modification
behavioral therapy
chemotherapy
clinical depression
compulsive personality disorder
delirium
dementia
dissociative disorder
functional disorder
group therapy
hallucination
hyperactivity

hypochondria
infantile autism
mania
manic-depression disorder
mental illness
mental trauma
mood disorder
multiple personality disorder
obsessive-compulsive disorder
occupational therapy
organic disorder
panic disorder
paranoid personality disorder
passive-aggressive personality
  disorder

personality disorder
phobia
play therapy
psychiatrist
psychiatry
psychoanalysis
psychotherapy
recreational therapy
schizoid personality disorder
schizophrenia
somatoform disorder
symptom
therapist
unconscious

Using Vocabulary

Questions 1-11. On a separate sheet of paper, write the term from the column on the right that matches the phrase on the left.

1 medical study, treatment, and prevention of mental disorders
2 unfounded suspicion and mistrust of others
3 emotional problem that stems from a person's environment
4 seeing, hearing, or sensing something that does not exist
5 violent shock that is damaging to a person's mental health
6 mental illness with a known physical cause
7 mood disorder characterized by an elated, impulsive mood
8 part of the personality that cannot be observed
9 person trained to treat an illness
10 severe and irreversible loss of mental ability
11 personality disorder that includes a withdrawal from reality, deep confusion, and sometimes hallucinations

a therapist
b organic disorder
c mania
d paranoid personality disorder
e schizophrenia
f hallucination
g psychiatry
h dementia
i mental trauma
j functional disorder
k unconscious

Interpreting Ideas

1 Compare the symptoms of mood disorders with those of personality disorders.

2 What is the difference between a functional disorder and an organic disorder?

3 Compare delirium and dementia.

4 Classify each of the following disorders as a mood disorder, a personality disorder, or an anxiety disorder: (a) clinical depression; (b) paranoid disorder; (c) obsessive-compulsive disorder; (d) panic disorder; (e) mania; (f) schizoid disorder.

5 Explain how Freud believed childhood experiences influence mental development.

6 What are the characteristics of schizoid personality disorder?

7 What is the role of psychodrama in therapy?

8 What is the goal of psychoanalysis?

9 Classify and compare amnesia and multiple personality disorder.

10 How does stress affect emotional health?

11 What is the difference between generalized anxiety and a panic disorder?

12 Describe the symptoms of hyperactivity in children. How may hyperactivity lead to a functional disorder?

13 What is the objective of behavioral therapy? How does it use behavior modification?

14 Identify and describe two main causes of mental disorders.

15 Name three kinds of therapy that are available to the patient in a psychiatric hospital.

16 Identify the symptoms of clinical depression. Given these symptoms, how is it possible for a person to be both manic and clinically depressed, as in manic-depression disorder?

17 What is thought to cause multiple personality disorder? Why does an individual develop different personalities?

18 Describe three kinds of treatment for people with mental illness.

19 Identify three kinds of agencies that offer help for mental illness.

Applying Concepts

1 The text states that environment plays a large part in determining whether people develop functional disorders. Do you agree with this observation? Why or why not?

2 At four years of age, Carlos would neither cuddle nor make eye contact with his parents or siblings. Most of the time he stared blankly into space and rarely responded to questions. Based on this description of his behavior, what disorder might you suspect that he has?

3 A 30-year-old woman washed her hands more than 100 times a day. It was not unusual for her to return home after having started for work in order to make sure she had left nothing cooking on the stove that could cause a fire. How would you classify her disorder? Give your reasons for your classifications.

4 A 14-year-old boy has recently been involved in starting small fires in old buildings, stealing food and inexpensive objects for "the thrill of it," and hurting household pets. What do you think this boy's behavior may mean? What may happen if he doesn't receive proper treatment?

5 A 15-year-old girl found it difficult to experience any satisfaction and pleasure, a condition known as anhedonia. Whenever she received a high mark on school work, for example, she discounted it as "just luck." When she was publicly recognized for saving a person from drowning, she dismissed it by saying, "Anyone else could have done the same thing." Into what main category of mental disorder would you classify her problem? What kind of treatment might be appropriate?

6 Name three undesirable habits or behaviors and describe how they might be changed through behavior modification.

7 Describe the kind of action you might take in the following situation: Your friend offers you his comic book collection, a cherished rock star poster, and several of his favorite record albums. During lunch period at school, you notice that he hardly touches his food, and he casually mentions how easy it would be to commit suicide with pills.

Projects

1 It is now generally accepted that the brains of people with schizophrenia are different, both structurally and functionally, from the brains of nonschizophrenics. Investigate several of the following theories about the cause of these brain differences: genetic causes, biochemical causes, nutritional causes, stress, infectious diseases, and family interaction. Which are the more generally accepted theories?

2 Make a survey of facilities and other resources available in your community to help people with mental disorders. You could interview a psychiatrist, a psychiatric nurse, a psychologist, or a psychiatric social worker. You might also visit a hospital or mental health clinic to find out what kinds of treatment are offered to patients and whether occupational and recreational therapy are available.

Critical Thinking

RESISTING PEER PRESSURE

Courtroom judges put on black robes before hearing evidence and making judgments. The rules of evidence in a courtroom are very strict. No one can give evidence that is based on rumor or hearsay.

Your peers sometimes act like judges by judging others on the basis of looks, ideas, and abilities. However, your peers seldom take the time to listen as carefully as a judge before reaching their decisions.

Peer judgments are a part of peer pressure. Most of the time you may not be aware of any pressure from friends and classmates. But there are times when you are uncomfortably aware of peer pressure. Peer judgments can influence your behavior and sense of self-esteem.

Observations, inferences, and judgments are three concepts that are often confused. Being able to distinguish among these three is one way of taking some of the pressure out of peer pressure.

Observation

Observation is the act of perceiving or seeing. Observations can be verified, or proven to be true. For example, if you say that it is hot outside, someone can verify this statement by checking a thermometer.

Observations include the information gathered by your own senses—seeing, hearing, touching, smelling, and tasting. But it is not necessary for you to make all observations by yourself. It is often possible to rely on the observations of others. Statistics in almanacs, the information presented in textbooks, and the news reports on television are all forms of information that can be verified.

Inference

An inference is a conclusion based upon an observation. Suppose, for example, that you look out the window and see that everyone is wearing a raincoat. From this observation, you could infer that it is raining outside. You would have made an inference based upon your observation.

Notice the difference between an inference and a direct observation. Inferences start with what has been observed—raincoats—and end with a conclusion. Because an inference is not a direct observation, it may be incorrect. For example, people could be wearing raincoats because it is chilly, not because it is raining.

Everyone makes hundreds of inferences every day. You probably make inferences when you observe other people. For example, suppose your teacher calls on a girl in your class. If the girl does not answer the question, you might infer that she does not know the answer. Have you observed that she does not know the answer? No. You have only observed her behavior. It is possible that she knows the answer, but is too shy to speak in class.

As you learned in Chapter 5, people express emotions in different ways. People also use different defense mechanisms to help them cope with emotions. Thus you cannot directly observe someone else's feelings. You can only infer their emotions from their behavior.

1 In the examples below, identify each statement as an observation or an inference.

a My brother likes to wear old clothes.

b Rick is the fastest sprinter ever to attend South High.

c I felt myself blush when the principal walked in.

d Juanita is so tall and thin that she could be a model.

Judgment

A judgment is an opinion. It is an expression of approval or disapproval of a person, action, or thing. Like inferences, judgments are not verified observations. But unlike inferences, judgments include an opinion that the subject being considered is either good or bad.

One form of judgment is the mark that your teacher gives you in a course. For example, if Tyrone receives A's on all his health tests, his teacher may give him an A for the term. The teacher has judged that Tyrone has a good understanding of the material in the course.

2 Identify each of the following statements as an observation, an inference, or a judgment.

a Phyllis is the top student in mathematics. She has the highest grades on all of the algebra tests.

b They must be going steady because they have been to three movies together.

c John was very angry—he raised his voice and slammed the door as he left the room.

d Matthew has a lovely singing voice.

e Angie can't be beaten. She has won the high jump in every track meet this year.

Unfounded Opinion

A teacher's judgment of a student's ability is based upon verifiable information, such as the student's performance in the classroom, on homework, and on tests. Thus a teacher's decision to give a student a certain grade is a form of reasoned judgment. Reasoned judgments are based on good observations and reasonable inferences.

Not all opinions are the result of reasoned judgments. Opinions without supporting observations are said to be unfounded. Unfounded opinions often play a part in peer pressure. For exam-

ple, consider this statement: "People who get good grades are no fun." This statement is unfounded because it is an overgeneralization. It is not based upon a thorough examination of all people who get good grades.

Unfounded opinions of other people are harmful for two reasons. Such judgments can make the person who is being judged feel bad. They may also be unfair because one person cannot know the reasons for another person's behavior.

3 In the following examples, identify which statements are reasoned judgments and which are unfounded opinions.

a Kit is a snob. He almost never talks to any of the other students in his class.

b People who go to that school don't dress the way we do. They don't care how they look.

c Carol speaks well and knows how to listen to other people. She would be a good candidate for student council.

d Sheri has failed two tests in English. She is a failure.

e Barry is on the football team, so he won't be interested in taking part in the school play.

4 For each of the statements in question 3 that you identified as being an unfounded opinion, state two reasons why the opinion may be incorrect.

U N I T

3

8. Understanding Nutrition

9. Planning a Diet

Nutrition

10. Digestion and Excretion

Cooking a balanced meal is fun when you
know how to apply the basics of nutrition.

CHAPTER EIGHT

UNDERSTANDING

NUTRITION

Your body needs food for life and good health. Foods come in many colors, textures, and flavors. Today in the United States a wide variety of foods can be found. Foods from around the world are available in supermarkets. Some people may eat Chinese-style food one day, Italian-style the next, and Mexican-style the day after.

Eating the right kinds of foods in the right amounts helps you to look, feel, and perform at your best. No one food provides all the nourishment you need to keep your body going. That is why variety is important. A lack of any of the six major nutrients can lead to poor growth and development, a lowered resistance to disease, and even death. Knowing the Four Food Groups helps you plan balanced meals. Understanding product labels helps in buying nutritious foods.

Objectives

- Identify the six groups of nutrients.

- Explain the importance of proteins, fats, and carbohydrates in the functioning of a healthy body.

- Explain the role of vitamins, minerals, and water in the functioning of a healthy body.

- Plan a nutritious diet using the Four Food Groups and the U.S.D.A. Dietary Guidelines.

- Interpret the information presented on a food label and be able to apply it when shopping for foods.

- Describe the functions of food additives.

Nutrients and Energy

The process by which the body takes in and uses food is called **nutrition.** Foods that promote good nutrition contain nutrients. **Nutrients** are substances found within foods that the body needs to work properly. There are six types of nutrients—carbohydrates, fats, proteins, vitamins, minerals, and water. Together they supply energy, regulate body functions, promote body growth, and repair body tissues. Each nutrient is important in one or more of these ways.

Carbohydrates, fats, and proteins, along with other important uses, are the nutrients that provide energy. You need energy for all activities, including riding a bike and taking a test. You also need energy for breathing, blood circulation, and other body functions, even while sleeping. When your body uses carbohydrates, fats, and proteins, energy is released. This energy is measured in Calories. A **Calorie** is a unit of heat energy. Using Calories as a way of measuring is useful in comparing the energy available from different foods. For example, an orange contains about 90 Calories while a hamburger contains about 250 Calories.

Carbohydrates

It is the night before a big marathon. The runners are being treated to a dinner by the race's organizers. The runners are happy to see their plates are full of pasta. They know that a pasta dinner is high in carbohydrates, the body's major source of energy. During the next day's race, they will need all the energy they can get! Of course, runners are not the only people who need carbohydrates. Everyone needs them.

Carbohydrates are the sugars and starches found in plants and in dairy products. They are made up of carbon, oxygen, and hydrogen. They can be either simple or complex. **Simple carbohydrates** are different forms of sugar. These sugars are found in fruits and vegetables and milk. The most important sugar is glucose. **Glucose** [*GLOO kohs*] is a simple form of sugar that goes directly into the blood stream to provide quick energy. Other sugars must be changed into glucose before the body's cells can use them for energy. The cells use glucose as fuel and to build and repair body tissues. Glucose that is not needed immediately is stored in the body as fat or a form of starch.

Starches are complex carbohydrates. **Complex carbohydrates** are made up of long chains of glucose. The chains must be broken down into single units of glucose. Starches take longer than sugars to break down into glucose. Thus starches provide energy to the body over longer periods of time than do sugars. Foods such as breads, cereals, pasta, and potatoes contain starch. These sources of complex carbohydrates also contain a variety of other nutrients.

Dietary fiber is another complex carbohydrate. Dietary fiber cannot be digested by the human body. It does, however, help strengthen the intestines and aid in digestion. The best sources of dietary fiber are whole-grain cereals, such as wheat, oats, and

Figure 8-1 Some excellent sources of dietary fiber

bran, and the skins of fruits and vegetables, such as those shown in Figure 8-1.

Figure 8-2 lists the percent of carbohydrates found in some common foods. Which two foods are highest in carbohydrates?

Fats

The nutrients that contain the most concentrated forms of energy are **fats.** One ounce of fat provides more than twice as much energy as an ounce of carbohydrate. Fats are chemical substances that are similar to carbohydrates but contain less oxygen. Thus they do not burn off as quickly as carbohydrates.

Fats are an excellent source of energy. Fats carry the flavor of foods, making foods tastier. They also make you feel full. Fats are important as carriers of other nutrients, such as vitamins.

While fats are important nutrients, researchers believe most people in the United States eat more fat than they really need. Most people know about fats found in margarine, butter, and meats. But many other foods provide fats as well. For example, eggs, cheese, and milk products contain fat. See Figure 8-3 on the following page for the percentage of fat found in some common foods.

The major kinds of fats are polyunsaturated, also called mono-unsaturated, and saturated. Most fats that are liquid at room temperature are classified as **polyunsaturated fats.** Fish oils and most vegetable oils, such as corn oil and soybean oil, are sources of this type of fat. In contrast, **saturated fats** remain solid at room temperature. Butter, lard, and other animal fats tend to be highest in saturated fats. But cocunut oil and palm oil also are high in saturated fat.

Some researchers believe polyunsaturated fats lower the body's level of cholesterol. **Cholesterol** is a waxy substance related to

Figure 8-2 Percentage of carbohydrates in some commonly eaten foods

Fruits	
Banana	22%
Grape	16%
Apple	15%
Orange	12%
Peach	10%
Strawberry	8%
Vegetables	
Sweet potato	22%
Potato	17%
Beet	9%
Broccoli	6%
Spinach	4%
Tomato	4%
Lettuce	3%
Legumes	
Dried beans	61%
Green peas, fresh	14%
Green beans	5%
Cereals and Grains	
Flour, all-purpose	76%
Bread, white enriched	50%
Bread, whole wheat	47%
Spaghetti	30%
Rice, cooked	24%

Percentage of Fat in Some Common Foods

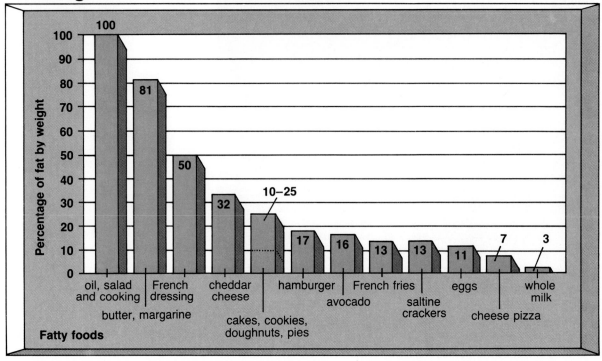

Figure 8-3 Use fatty foods moderately by mixing them with low-fat foods.

fats that helps form nervous tissues. It is found in foods such as butter, eggs, and fatty meats. It is also produced in the liver. Many scientists believe that a diet rich in saturated fats and cholesterol, leading to increased cholesterol levels in the body, increases the risk of heart disease. Some people have an inherited disorder in which the body maintains high levels of cholesterol. Cholesterol tends to build up in the blood vessels and to block the arteries to the heart. Because most people do not need more cholesterol than the body produces, health experts recommend that people eat fewer saturated fats.

Protein

The body needs proteins to build and repair all body tissues. **Proteins** are substances found in every cell of your body. Muscles, skin, and organs such as the lungs and brain all contain protein. Protein is also an important part of red blood cells. Proteins are made up of carbon, hydrogen, oxygen, and nitrogen. The basic units of all proteins are **amino acids.** Some amino acids are components of hormones. These hormones control body functions such as growth and development. Other amino acids are components of antibodies. Antibodies are substances that help the body fight disease.

There are about 20 different amino acids. Nine of them are considered essential. **Essential amino acids** are those amino acids necessary for a healthy body that must be supplied by the foods you eat. Your body cannot manufacture the essential amino acids to meet the body's needs.

Proteins are classified according to whether or not they contain essential amino acids. Foods that contain **complete protein** provide all the essential amino acids needed by the body. Poultry, fish, eggs, meat, milk, and milk products are complete protein foods. An **incomplete protein** lacks some of the essential amino acids. Fruits, vegetables, grains, and legumes are examples of incomplete protein foods. **Legumes** are plants related to peas that bear seeds in pods. Peas, beans, and peanuts are several types of legumes.

Too little of even one essential amino acid can limit your body's use of other amino acids. It is important to get all the essential amino acids daily and in the right amounts. If you eat incomplete proteins, you can still obtain the proper amounts of all the essential amino acids by eating a mix of incomplete protein foods at each meal. A mixture of two or more sources of incomplete protein that provides all the essential amino acids is called a **complementary combination.** Several examples of foods that combine incomplete proteins to make complete protein are black beans and rice, cheese and pasta, cheese pizza, and peanut butter on whole-wheat bread. Figure 8-4 lists several examples of complementary combinations. In Figure 8-4, what is the food listed with lima beans?

Eating the right amount of protein is very important. Too much protein either passes through the body as waste or is stored in the body as fat. The extra protein stored as fat is not needed by most people. Too little protein in the diet causes the body to use its own protein. This condition also occurs when the body does not have enough carbohydrates or fats for energy. In this case, the body changes its own protein into the energy needed. In either case, the body is robbed of protein needed for repairing and maintaining body tissues. This is why diets that are extremely low in carbohydrates are dangerous.

Legumes with Grains
Baked beans and brown bread
Black-eyed peas and rice
Beans and tortilla or corn bread
Beans and barley soup
Lima beans and corn (succotash)
Beans and pasta
Peanut butter sandwich
Refried beans and rice
Peas and rice
Legumes with Seeds
Green beans and almonds
Peanuts and mixed nuts

Figure 8-4 Vegetarians combine plant proteins to get all of the essential amino acids.

Lesson Review

Carbohydrates, fats, and proteins are the nutrients that provide the body with energy. Fats and proteins also affect the body's use of the other four nutrients. Some of each of these nutrients should be included in your daily diet. It is especially important to eat an adequate amount of protein containing the nine essential amino acids. Either too much or too little can be harmful.

1 Which nutrients provide the body with energy?

2 Name two types of complex carbohydrates.

3 Which nutrient provides you with the most Calories per ounce?

4 Give some examples of polyunsaturated fats.

5 Explain what is meant by a complementary combination of proteins.

6 What are some sources of dietary fiber?

Nutrients That Regulate

Vitamins, minerals, and water are not digested by your body as are the other nutrients. They are, however, released from foods and absorbed by the body's tissues. These nutrients maintain bodily functions.

Vitamins

Many years ago it was usual for as many as half the sailors on a long voyage to become very ill with scurvy. Scurvy is a disease in which the gums bleed, teeth become loose, and wounds do not heal. A British navy physician, James Lind, wondered if the illness could be treated by adding something to the sailors' diets. During an experiment, he discovered that he could cure scurvy by feeding the sick sailors citrus fruits such as oranges, lemons, and limes. From that time on, British ships had to carry a supply of limes or other citrus fruits. Ever since then, British sailors have been known as *limeys*.

Experiments in later years revealed that there were other diseases linked to dietary deficiencies. A **deficiency** is having too little of a necessary substance. The term vitamin was introduced to describe the missing substances. Figure 8-5 lists several deficiency diseases. You will notice that other diseases develop because of a lack of vitamins.

Vitamins are found in living things and are needed in small amounts for life and growth. Vitamins help build bones and tissues. They also help change carbohydrates and fats into energy. The body cannot make most vitamins. They must be supplied from the foods you eat.

Vitamins are divided into two groups. **Fat-soluble vitamins** dissolve in fat and can be stored in the body. They are found in oils, vegetables, and organ meats such as liver and kidneys. **Water-soluble vitamins** dissolve in water. Because water-soluble vitamins cannot be stored by the body to any great extent, these vitamins must be eaten more often than fat-soluble vitamins. Fruits and vegetables are good sources of water-soluble vitamins. Figure 8-5 lists the different water-soluble vitamins. It identifies the foods most likely to contain each vitamin and describes how each vitamin functions in your body. Use the information in Figure 8-5 to identify the vitamin that is needed to help with the normal clotting of your blood.

If you are dieting or do not eat certain foods, you may not be getting all the vitamins you need. However, if you eat a variety of healthful foods each day, you should not need to take any type of vitamin supplement. In fact, too much of some vitamins over a long time will harm the body. For example, large amounts of vitamins A and D taken over a long period of time can be toxic to the body. **Toxic** means poisonous. Figure 8-5 lists the symptoms of taking too much of various vitamins. What are the symptoms of vitamin A toxicity?

Figure 8-5 Vitamins: fat-soluble (*blue*) and water-soluble (*green*)

Health History

In 1912, Polish scientist Casimir Funk theorized that food deficiencies cause diseases. He suggested that there must be some unknown substances in food that are necessary for life. Funk coined the term *vitamin* from the Latin word *vita*, meaning *life*.

Vitamin	Sources	Functions in Body	Signs of Toxicity	Signs of Deficiency
Vitamin A	Organ meats, whole milk, cheese, egg yolk, yellow fruits, green vegetables	Maintains healthy eyes, skin, bones, teeth	Liver and nerve dysfunction	Rough skin; fatigue; eye infections
Vitamin D	Milk (fortified), eggs, exposure of skin to sun's ultraviolet rays	Absorbs phosphorus; builds and maintains bones and teeth	Hearing loss	Rickets (poor bone and tooth development)
Vitamin E	Wheat germ, vegetable oils, legumes, nuts, dark green vegetables	Protects red blood cells; functions with certain enzymes	Unknown	Rupture of red blood cells; fat deposits in muscles
Vitamin K	Spinach, kale, cabbage, pork, liver; made by intestinal bacteria	Assists in normal clotting of blood	Unknown	Slow clotting of blood; hemorrhage, especially in newborns

Vitamin	Sources	Functions in Body	Signs of Toxicity	Signs of Deficiency
Thiamine (B₁)	Pork, legumes, whole grain products, organ meats, milk, eggs	Maintains healthy appetite, digestion; function of nerves	Unknown	Beriberi (inflamed nerves, heart failure)
Riboflavin (B₂)	Milk, eggs, whole grains, vegetables, organ meats	Produces energy in cells; healthy appetite; function of nerves	Unknown	Cheilosis (cracking lips, scaling skin, sensitive eyes)
Niacin (Nicotinic Acid)	Red meats, organ meats, fish, enriched breads, green vegetables	Maintains metabolism, normal digestion, nerves and skin	Liver dysfunction	Pellagra (sore mouth, diarrhea, depression)
Vitamin B₆ (Pyridoxine)	Red meats, liver, whole grains, green vegetables	Maintains sodium and phosphorus balance	Dependency	Anemia; inflamed skin; loss of appetite; nausea; nervousness
Pantothenic Acid	Organ meats, eggs, nuts, whole grains, made by intestinal bacteria	Maintains normal blood sugar level; energy release	May contribute to B₁ deficiency	Weakness; nausea; loss of appetite; susceptibility to infection
Biotin	Organ meats, poultry, egg yolk, fish, peas, bananas, melons	Metabolizes carbohydrates and other B vitamins	Unknown	Skin disorders; anemia; muscle pain; poor appetite
Vitamin B₁₂	Organ and muscle meats, milk, cheese, eggs, fish	Metabolism; healthy red blood cells	Unknown	Stunted growth; inflamed nerves; pernicious anemia
Folic Acid (Folacin)	Green vegetables, liver, whole grains, legumes	Produces proteins and red blood cells	Unknown	Inflamed tongue; diarrhea; B₁₂ deficiency
Vitamin C (Ascorbic Acid)	Citrus fruits, melons, green vegetables, potatoes	Keeps teeth firm in gums, healing wounds, iron absorption	Diarrhea, dependency	Scurvy (slow healing wounds, bleeding gums, loose teeth)

Minerals

Substances found in the environment that are essential to the body's functions are **minerals** . Minerals are used to regulate a wide range of body processes, from bone formation to blood clotting. They are also important to the body's structure. Except for iron, the body does not tend to store minerals. Iron tends to be conserved by the body, except when there is blood loss. Most minerals are quickly used or lost in waste products. This means you must eat mineral-rich foods regularly to replenish your supply. Your body uses larger amounts of calcium, phosphorus, and magnesium than of iodine, iron, and zinc.

Calcium keeps the nervous system working well and is needed for blood clotting. Calcium and phosphorous give bones and teeth added strength and hardness. Calcium, together with sodium and potassium, helps you maintain a normal heartbeat. Research indicates that a lack of calcium during the teenage years may result in brittle bones later in life. What are some sources of calcium in the diet listed in Figure 8–7? What is the disease of calcium deficiency that develops in adults?

Iron is an essential part of hemoglobin. **Hemoglobin** [*HEE muh gloh bin*] is a substance in red blood cells that carries oxygen to all parts of the body. Insufficient iron may cause **anemia,** a disease in which the body has either too few red blood cells or too little hemoglobin. As a result, too little oxygen is carried to the cells of the body. People with iron deficiency anemia tend to feel weak and tire quickly, get sick easily, have shortness of breath, or have a hard time concentrating. Dark green vegetables, whole grains, and organ meats are good sources of iron.

Other important minerals include sodium and potassium. One function of these minerals is to help fluids pass into the cells. However, too much sodium in the diet may contribute to high blood pressure. This is a condition in which the arteries become constricted and provide resistance to the flow of the blood. Sodium chloride, or table salt, is a main source of sodium in the diet. Some processed foods, such as canned soups or bologna, also contain large amounts of sodium. Potassium is found in lean meats, milk, citrus fruits, and dark green leafy vegetables. A deficiency of potassium leads to muscle weakness and respiratory failure.

Iodine is needed for the thyroid gland to function properly. The thyroid gland produces substances that control how quickly chemical reactions occur in your body. The primary sources of iodine in the diet are seafoods and iodized table salt. Too little iodine causes the thyroid to become very large, a condition called **goiter,** as shown in Figure 8-6. The primary sources of iodine in the diet are seafoods and iodized table salt.

Manganese, zinc, cobalt, fluorine, and magnesium all play specific roles in the way the body works. Figure 8–7 lists the functions of these and other minerals. The figure also lists the signs of too much or too little of each mineral. The signs of deficiency and toxicity of some minerals, such as sulfur, are unknown.

Figure 8-6 Marie de Medici, who became queen of France in 1610, suffered from goiter. A goiter can be seen at the front of her neck.

Figure 8-7 Essential dietary minerals

Mineral	Sources	Functions in Body	Signs of Toxicity	Signs of Deficiency
Calcium	Milk, broccoli, cabbage, clams, oysters, salmon	Maintains bones and teeth; blood clotting; nerve and heart activity	Extreme fatigue	Slow blood clotting; soft bones; osteoporosis (adults); rickets (children)
Phosphorus	Milk, egg yolk, meat, poultry, fish, whole grain cereals, legumes, nuts	Develops bones and teeth; muscle activity; energy metabolism	Unknown	Fragile bones and teeth; loss of weight and appetite; rickets
Sodium	Table salt, meat, poultry, fish, eggs, milk	Stimulates nerves; water balance outside cells	Hypertension	Nausea; exhaustion; muscle cramps
Potassium	Meat, poultry, fish, cereals, fruits, vegetables	Stimulates nerves; water balance inside cells; heart rhythm	Muscle weakness; irregular heartbeat	Muscle weakness; respiratory failure; abnormal heartbeat
Chlorine	Table salt, meat, milk, eggs	Maintains water balance in body	Unknown	Loss of hair and teeth; poor digestion
Magnesium	Legumes, whole grains, milk, meat, leafy vegetables	Maintains muscles and nerves; energy metabolism; bone composition	Nervous dysfunction	Mental, emotional, muscular disorders
Iron	Organ meats, whole grains, dark green vegetables, legumes, prunes	Forms red blood cells; helps transport oxygen	Liver and pancreas dysfunction	Anemia; fatigue; paleness of skin
Sulfur	Eggs, meat, milk, cheese, nuts, legumes	Forms body tissues; part of amino acids and B vitamins	Unknown	Unknown
Copper	Liver, shellfish, nuts, legumes, whole grains	Forms red blood cells; absorption of iron	Retained in organs and cornea of eyes	Anemia; nerve and bone disorders; skin sores
Manganese	Legumes, nuts, whole grains, vegetables, fruits	Develops bones; enzyme activator	Mental and motor difficulties	Nervousness; muscular excitability
Iodine	Iodized salt, seafood	Assists in function of thyroid gland	Rare	Loss of physical and mental vigor; goiter
Zinc	Seafood, milk, meats, poultry, organ meats, wheat germ	Aids in healing; forms enzymes	Loss of iron and copper from liver	Retarded growth rate; delayed wound healing
Fluorine	Fish, fluoridated water, animal foods	Strengthens bones and teeth	Mottled teeth	Excess dental decay
Selenium	Meat, eggs, milk, seafood, cereals	Complements Vitamin E to prevent cell damage	Unknown	Premature aging; stunted growth

Figure 8-8 Drinking enough water when you exercise in hot weather replaces the water that is lost in perspiration.

Water

Water is the most abundant nutrient in your body. It enables other nutrients to dissolve and be carried to the parts of your body where they are needed. Water is needed for all of your body's functions. These include digesting foods, removing wastes, regulating your temperature, and cushioning sensitive parts of your body, such as your brain.

About 60 percent of your body weight is made up of water. Each day you lose two to three quarts of water. Water is lost when you urinate, perspire, and even as you breathe. If water is not replaced, dehydration will occur. **Dehydration** is the loss of water from body tissues. Dehydration weakens the body and may cause muscle cramps.

Thirst, or the desire to drink fluids, determines your fluid intake. You should drink at least three to six large glasses of water each day. During very hot weather and when you are exercising, you may need to increase your fluid intake to as much as ten large glasses or more.

Lesson Review

Vitamins, minerals, and water are nutrients that do not provide the body with energy. Instead, adequate amounts of these nutrients are necessary to regulate many body functions. Water is the most vital nutrient because it provides the means for all other nutrients to be carried throughout your body.

1 What vitamin is necessary to prevent scurvy?

2 What are the four fat-soluble vitamins?

3 Name two functions of calcium in the body.

4 How does the body use iron?

5 List two ways in which the body uses water.

A Healthy Daily Diet

Good nutrition involves eating a variety of foods in moderation each day. Your diet should provide enough of the six major nutrients and Calories for your growth needs. Moderating how much you eat keeps your Calorie intake at a healthy level.

The Food Groups

Foods are generally divided among five major food groups. Four of these five groups are good sources of nutrients and are often called the Four Food Groups. These are the Vegetable-Fruit group, the Bread-Cereal group, the Milk-Cheese group, and the Meat-Poultry and Fish-Beans group. You need to eat foods from each of these groups every day in order to obtain all the nutrients you need.

Foods containing ingredients from two or more food groups are called **combination foods.** There are many combination foods that provide both Calories and good nutrient value. Chicken chow mein, beef tacos, lasagna, and spaghetti with meat balls are all combination foods that are good nutrient sources.

The Vegetable-Fruit Group
This group provides many nutrients, especially vitamins, minerals, and carbohydrates. Dark green vegetables, such as broccoli or mustard greens, and deep yellow vegetables, such as carrots, are good sources of vitamin A. Dark green vegetables should be eaten at least every other day. Citrus fruits such as grapefruit and oranges provide vitamin C. Potatoes also provide vitamin C. The skins of fruits and vegetables are also a good source of fiber. Teenagers should have four servings from this group each day.

The Bread-Cereal Group
These foods contain products made with whole grains or enriched flour. These include breads, cereals, noodles, spaghetti, and other kinds of pasta such as those pictured in Figure 8–9. Foods in the Bread-Cereal group provide mostly carbohydrates as well as fiber. Other nutrients in this food group include most of the B vitamins, iron, and protein. Teenagers should eat four servings of breads and cereals daily.

The Milk-Cheese Group
This group includes milk and milk products such as yogurt and cheeses. These foods provide the main source of calcium in the diet. These foods also contain protein and vitamins A, B_1, and B_2. Teenagers should eat four servings from this food group daily.

The Meat-Poultry and Fish-Beans Group
Foods in this group include poultry, fish, eggs, red meats such as beef, and organ meats such as liver and kidneys. Legumes, nuts, and seeds are also included in this group. Foods in this group are high in protein, B vitamins, and certain minerals such as magnesium. Zinc is found in red meats and vitamin A is found in liver. Teenagers should eat two servings daily from this food group.

Health History

Did you know that the hamburger originated in Russia? Medieval Tartars enjoyed eating their meat shredded, raw, and seasoned with spices and onion juice. German sailors brought this food back to Hamburg. Finicky Hamburgers chose to broil this seasoned meat rather than eat it raw.

Figure 8-9　The Four Food Groups

The Vegetable-Fruit Group

serving:　½ cup cooked vegetable, fruit, or juice;
1 cup uncooked vegetable or fruit;
1 medium-size vegetable or fruit

recommended number of servings:
child (4), teenager (4), adult (4),
pregnant woman (4)

nutrients:　vitamins A and C, carbohydrate

The Bread-Cereal Group

serving:　1 slice bread; 1 cup dry cereal;
½ cup cooked cereal, pasta, or grits

recommended number of servings:
child (4), teenager (4), adult (4),
pregnant woman (4)

nutrients:　thiamine, niacin, carbohydrate, iron

The Milk-Cheese Group

serving:　1 cup milk, yogurt, or calcium equivalent;
1½ slices (1½ oz.) cheddar cheese;
2 cups cottage cheese;
1 cup pudding

recommended number of servings:
child (3), teenager (4), adult (2),
pregnant woman (4)

nutrients:　riboflavin, calcium, protein

The Meat-Poultry and Fish-Beans Group

serving:　2 oz. cooked lean meat, fish, poultry,
or protein equivalent; 2 eggs;
1 cup legumes (dried peas or beans);
4 tablespoons peanut butter

recommended number of servings:
child (2), teenager (2), adult (2),
pregnant woman (3)

nutrients:　thiamine, niacin, protein

Figure 8-10 Enchiladas are an example of a combination food.

Fats-Sweets Group   Besides the Four Food Groups, nutrition experts identify a fifth group called the Fats-Sweets group. This group contains foods such as candy, pastries, and salad dressings. These foods are high in fat and sugar but low in nutrient value. These foods are not necessary to a healthy diet. In moderation these foods may supplement other foods in the diet. Eating too many foods from this group may fill you up and prevent you from eating enough from the other food groups. As people get older and their Calorie needs decrease, they should further limit their intake of fats and sweets.

The fifth group also includes beverages such as alcohol, coffee, tea, and soft drinks. Some soft drinks contain little more than simple sugars. Coffee, tea, and certain soft drinks contain the stimulant caffeine. A **stimulant** is a drug that speeds up the body's mental or physical activities.

Planning Balanced Meals

Have you ever felt tired or cranky because you skipped a meal or did not have enough to eat? If so, you already know how important it is to eat regular meals. Regular meals help you to feel your best the whole day through.

Breakfast   Start your day off right with a good breakfast, one that provides one fourth to one third of the day's Calories. Since your body has gone 12 to 14 hours without nourishment, breakfast can provide the body with necessary nutrients that will be used throughout the day. It also reduces irritability, decreases nervousness, and increases learning ability. People who miss breakfast lessen their chance of eating an adequate diet.

A well-balanced breakfast might include a glass of orange juice, an egg, toast, and a glass of milk. Remember that each of

Health Bulletin

Did you know that the largest single source of sugar in the American diet is soft drinks? There are ten teaspoons of sugar in a twelve-ounce soft drink. In fact, most people get ten times as much sugar from soft drinks as from candy.

Scientists have shown that eating breakfast really does make a difference. Students who skipped breakfast were proven to be less and less able to do arithmetic problems as the morning wore on.

the Four Food Groups supplies a different group of nutrients. If you miss essential nutrients at one meal, you need to make them up with a well-chosen snack or at the next meal.

Lunch Lunch should make up about one third of your daily Calorie and nutrient needs. Your school cafeteria provides a ready source for selecting nutritious foods. Many school cafeterias provide salad bars. Remember to choose foods from each of the Four Food Groups. A salad, fresh fruit, a glass of milk, and a turkey sandwich make a good food combination.

Dinner For many people, the evening meal is the largest meal of the day. But remember, it should account for one third or less of your daily Calorie intake. It should also make up for nutrients missed at other meals. For example, if lunch did not provide a dark green leafy vegetable, then this should be included in the evening meal.

Snacking Snacks can play an important role in your daily diet, especially during your teenage years when your body has higher energy needs. Select foods that have a large number of nutrients but a low number of Calories. Such foods are considered high in nutrient density. **Nutrient density** is the amount of nutrients in a food as compared to the number of Calories it contains. Some examples of nutrient dense foods include whole-grain breads, rolls, and cereals.

Fruits and raw vegetables are good snack choices because of their low Calories and high nutrient content. Popcorn, nuts, and granola mixtures are also good choices, but if you are watching your Calorie intake, nuts and granola mixtures should be limited. Candy, potato chips, and doughnuts are examples of poor snack choices. These foods have few vitamins and minerals but are high in fats and Calories.

Dietary Guidelines

Many people find it difficult to remember how to select a well-balanced diet from each of the food groups. That is why the United States Department of Agriculture developed the following set of guidelines for eating a balanced diet.

1 Eat a variety of foods.
2 Maintain ideal weight.
3 Avoid too much fat, saturated fat, and cholesterol.
4 Eat foods with adequate starch and fiber.
5 Avoid too much sugar.
6 Avoid too much sodium.
7 If you drink alcohol, do so in moderation.

Most people in the United States need to adjust their diet to fit these guidelines by eating more fruits, vegetables, and whole grains. They should eat less fatty food, sugar, and salt. They also need to cut down on foods high in cholesterol.

Vegetarian Diets

People who choose to eat no meat are **vegetarians.** Some vegetarians eat eggs, milk, and milk products as well as plant foods, but no meat, fish, or poultry. Other vegetarians eat no animal foods of any kind, only plant foods.

A vegetarian diet is healthy as long as it contains all the essential nutrients. Vegetarians need to be careful to eat complementary combinations of protein so that they obtain all the necessary amino acids. They also need to make sure they are eating enough Calories to meet all their energy needs.

To meet their vitamin and mineral needs, vegetarians should eat a variety of vegetables and fruits. Each day should include at least two servings of legumes, nuts, and seeds. Whole-grain and enriched breads and cereals should be eaten at least three times a day. Vegetarians need one or more servings of a vegetable or fruit high in vitamin C. They also should eat two or more servings of vegetables for iron and vitamin A.

Fast Foods

Fast foods are a part of our modern society. Some fast-food restaurants serve only main courses, such as chicken or hamburgers. These meals provide a lot of protein. They are adequate in most B vitamins and iron. Fast-food meals tend to be low in calcium, vitamin A, and folic acid. Many fast foods are deep-fried, and thus are very high in fat. French fries and fried onion rings are also high in sodium. In fact, the sodium content of most fast-food meals is too high.

If you use the information you have learned about nutrition, you can eat a balanced meal at a fast-food restaurant. When ordering, think of getting coleslaw or a salad instead of French fries. Order milk instead of soda. Fill up at the salad bar. No matter where you go, it is possible to eat a well-balanced diet.

Health Bulletin

Did you know that a cheeseburger has about seven times more sodium than French fries? The fries usually taste saltier because the salt sticks to the surface. It's helpful to know that most sodium-processed foods don't taste salty.

Lesson Review

Good nutrition involves selecting foods from the Four Food Groups. It is also important to pay attention to eating a variety of foods at each meal. Busy teenagers may choose high nutrient snacks. Someone who is in a hurry or prefers not to cook at home may choose a meal from a fast-food restaurant. A vegetarian diet can be healthy as long as it contains all of the essential nutrients. It is fine to choose foods that fit your personal tastes, as long as they add up to a well-balanced diet.

1 How many servings should teenagers have each day from the Vegetable-Fruit group?

2 Which of the Four Food Groups requires only two servings each day?

3 Describe the fifth food group.

4 List three snacks that offer good nutrition.

Identifying Nutritious Foods

Taking what you know about nutrition and applying it at the supermarket is not always easy. Food labels can help, but you have to know how to read them. Cost, product freshness, nutrient density, and convenience are just some of the factors to consider when shopping for food.

Food Labeling

Sean wanted a quick breakfast so he bought a box of Honey-Wheat Flakes instant cereal. Wheat is nutritious and honey is better for you than cane sugar, he thought. But when he read the food label at home, he saw that the first ingredient in the cereal was actually sugar. Honey was fourth on the list. The wheat in the cereal was really enriched wheat rather than whole wheat. The cereal did not seem so nutritious after all. Next time, Sean thought, I'll read the label before I buy the product.

One way to find out the nutrients a food contains is to read the labels on packaged foods. The United States Food and Drug Administration (FDA) is a government agency that makes certain that laws regarding food and medicines are followed. This includes laws about food purity. The FDA requires that food labels list four items: the name of the product; the name and address of the manufacturer; the net weight, or weight of the contents without the container; and a list of the ingredients in descending weight order.

Today many manufacturers also list nutritional information on packages. This information is based on the U.S. Recommended Daily Allowance (U.S. RDA). The **U.S. RDA** is a guideline used to determine the amount of nutrients in foods that would be enough to maintain a healthy body. The U.S. RDA was estab-

Figure 8-11 What is the main ingredient of this food?

NUTRITION INFORMATION

SERVING SIZE: 1 OZ. (28.4 g, ABOUT 1 CUP)
PRODUCT ALONE OR WITH ½ CUP VITAMINS A AND D SKIM MILK OR VITAMIN D WHOLE MILK.
SERVINGS PER PACKAGE: 12

common name of product

	CEREAL	WITH SKIM MILK	WITH WHOLE MILK
CALORIES	110	150	180
PROTEIN	2 g	6 g	6 g
CARBOHYDRATE	24 g	30 g	30 g
FAT	0 g	0 g	4 g
CHOLESTEROL	0 mg	0 mg	15 mg
SODIUM	290 mg	350 mg	350 mg
POTASSIUM	35 mg	240 mg	220 mg

list of ingredients by weight

PERCENTAGE OF U.S. RECOMMENDED DAILY ALLOWANCES (U.S. RDA)

	CEREAL	WITH SKIM MILK	WITH WHOLE MILK
PROTEIN	4	15	15
VITAMIN A	100	100	100
VITAMIN C	100	100	100
THIAMIN	100	100	100
RIBOFLAVIN	100	110	110
NIACIN	100	100	100
CALCIUM	*	15	15
IRON	100	100	100
VITAMIN D	50	60	60
VITAMIN E	100	100	100
VITAMIN B$_6$	100	100	100

net weight (usually found on front label)

FOLIC ACID	100	100	100
VITAMIN B$_{12}$	100	110	110
PHOSPHORUS	4	15	15
MAGNESIUM	2	6	6
ZINC	100	100	100
COPPER	2	4	10
PANTOTHENIC ACID	100	100	100

*CONTAINS LESS THAN 2% OF THE U.S. RDA OF THIS NUTRIENT.

INGREDIENTS: CORN; OAT AND WHEAT FLOUR; SUGAR; RICE; SALT; DEFATTED WHEAT GERM; CORN SYRUP; MALT FLAVORING; ANNATTO COLOR;

VITAMINS AND MINERALS: VITAMIN C (SODIUM ASCORBATE AND ASCORBIC ACID); VITAMIN E (ACETATE); VITAMIN B$_3$ (NIACINAMIDE); ZINC (ZINC OXIDE); IRON; CALCIUM PANTOTHENATE; VITAMIN A (PALMITATE, PROTECTED WITH BHT); VITAMIN B$_6$ (PYRIDOXINE HYDROCHLORIDE); VITAMIN B$_2$ (RIBOFLAVIN); VITAMIN B$_1$ (THIAMIN HYDROCHLORIDE); FOLIC ACID; VITAMIN B$_{12}$; AND VITAMIN D.

CARBOHYDRATE INFORMATION

	CEREAL	WITH MILK
STARCH & RELATED CARBOHYDRATES	21 g	21 g
SUCROSE & OTHER SUGARS	3 g	9 g
TOTAL CARBOHYDRATES	24 g	30 g

NET WEIGHT 12 oz. (340 g)

148 Unit 3 Nutrition

lished by the FDA to provide a method of labeling food. The nutrient content is expressed as a percent of the U.S. RDA on food product labels.

Food labels often include the nutrient content per serving and the appropriate U.S. RDA for protein, selected vitamins, and minerals. Look at Figure 8–11. What is the serving or portion size? How many Calories does each serving have? What percentage of the U.S. RDA for proteins is supplied?

Preservatives and Additives When you look at a food label, you may be confused by long chemical names. In most cases, these words are food additives. **Additives** are substances added to food to improve nutritional value and maintain freshness. They may also be used to improve a food's looks, texture, or taste. The most common food additives are sugar, salt, and corn syrup. Others include citric acid, mustard, baking soda, vegetable colors, and pepper. These eight additives make up about 98 percent of those used in the United States.

Preservatives are additives that prevent food from spoiling. Many preservatives stop the growth of bacteria or molds. For example, salt is a preservative added to hams and pickles. Calcium proprionate prevents the growth of mold in bread.

Substances may also be added to enrich or fortify the nutritional value of food. A food is **enriched** when additives are used to help replace nutrients that were lost during processing. Niacin,

 ## Health *Careers*

If you are interested in working with foods, perhaps you should consider a career in the field of nutrition. Dietitians provide nutritional counseling to individuals and groups. They also set up and supervise food services for institutions such as schools and hospitals. Dietitians train by completing a bachelor's degree in foods and nutrition or institutional management.

A dietetic clerk works under the supervision of a dietitian. He or she assists in ordering, receiving, and storing foods for institutions such as schools, nursing homes, and hospitals. Preparing, cooking, and serving food are also responsibilities of the dietetic clerk. Most of the training for this career takes place on the job.

Food processing technicians work in a variety of jobs related to the food industry. Most food processing technicians work in laboratories. Many work for the government. Some work on improving the nutritional value of food. Others develop ways of preventing spoilage or improving the processing of foods. This career requires high school courses in science and mathematics. After high school graduation, food processing technicians train at a two-year technical or vocational school.

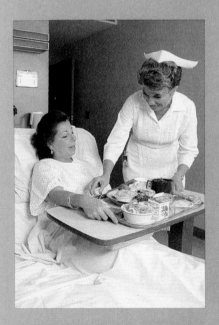

1 What are the duties of a food processing technician?
2 What training is necessary to become a dietitian?

Each year the amount of additives consumed per individual includes over 140 pounds of sweeteners including sucrose (sugar), 15 pounds of sodium chloride (table salt), and 5 to 10 pounds of all others.

thiamine, riboflavin, and iron are added to flours and cereals. A food is **fortified** when vitamins and minerals are added that are not naturally present. For example, milk is usually fortified with vitamin D.

Still other additives are used only to improve the taste, the appearance, or the preparation of foods. **Emulsifiers** are substances that make foods smooth. Ice cream and peanut butter often have emulsifiers added to them. **Leavening agents** are substances such as baking soda, that make breads and cakes rise.

There are over 2800 additives in the United States that have been approved by the FDA. Food additives are carefully controlled today. In most cases, they are not harmful. However, some people may be sensitive to certain chemicals and may have allergic or toxic reactions to additives.

Natural, Organic, and Health Foods Many people believe that foods labeled natural, organic, or health food are better for them than other kinds of food. **Natural foods** contain no additives. They contain no preservatives, artificial coloring, or flavoring. **Organic foods** are those grown on farms that do not use synthetic fertilizers and pesticides. **Health food** is a general term that means only that the food is healthy. These are very general definitions. The government agencies in charge of food labeling have not set up guidelines for the use of these terms. This means that the makers of a cereal can claim it has ''100% Natural Flavor'' even when everything but the flavor is artificial. Growers of organic food can claim a more healthful product. However, organic foods are no more nutritious than those grown with chemical fertilizers.

These labels can therefore be very misleading. Foods labeled natural or organic are often expensive. The important thing to remember when buying foods is to choose a variety of foods from the Four Food Groups. Beware of high cost health foods that may be no more nutritious than other, cheaper brands. Compare nutrient densities when selecting foods for the best buy.

Product Dating Having dates on foods helps the consumer determine the freshness of packaged products. Various forms of product dating are used by food manufacturers. Of most interest to the consumer is the best-if-used-by or the use-by date. The **product date** is the manufacturer's estimate of how long the product will last before it spoils. Most dating systems allow a period of time when the product will be at peak quality, then a period when it will continue to be usable. Foods eaten after the date marked may be dangerous to your health.

Getting the Best Buy After Sean read the label on his cereal, he realized it was not a very good buy after all. He was giving up high nutrient density for convenience, and probably paying more for it. A product's nutrient density and freshness should probably be your most important considerations when comparing two products.

Figure 8-12 Organic farmers use compost, rather than synthetic fertilizers, to grow foods.

Figure 8-13   Which of these items seems to be the best buy?

Cost will determine whether or not you can afford a certain food. However, the cheapest food may not be the best bargain nutritionally, nor is the high-priced brand better because it costs more. That is why comparing labels is important.

Compare product costs by checking the net weight and the unit price. The **unit price** is the cost per unit of measure, usually expressed in pounds or ounces. Refer to Figure 8–13. Compare buying a 16-ounce box of fiber-rich cereal for $0.80 with buying a 12-ounce box of plain cereal for $1.20. What is the cost per ounce of each? Which product is the better buy?

Convenience may also matter in selecting foods. Consider, for example, the choice between fresh, canned, or frozen vegetables. Fresh vegetables provide the greatest nutrient density but take more time to prepare than canned or frozen vegetables.

Lesson Review

Food labels contain important information on the freshness and nutrient density of products. They provide information about the presence of food additives. They also help you make decisions on cost. As a consumer, you have to decide what is most important to you. It may be that you can use a variety of foods and food preparation methods to get a balance of nutritious and easy-to-prepare foods.

1 Identify the four items that must be placed on a food label.

2 Define *preservatives*.

3 What does *enriched* mean?

4 How are organic foods produced?

5 What is a product date?

Chapter Review

Vocabulary

additive	essential amino acid	nutrition
amino acid	fat	organic food
anemia	fat-soluble vitamin	polyunsaturated fat
Calorie	fortified	preservative
carbohydrate	glucose	product date
cholesterol	goiter	protein
combination food	health food	saturated fat
complementary combination	hemoglobin	simple carbohydrate
complete protein	incomplete protein	stimulant
complex carbohydrate	leavening agent	toxic
deficiency	legume	unit price
dehydration	mineral	U.S. RDA
dietary fiber	natural food	vegetarian
emulsifier	nutrient	vitamin
enriched	nutrient density	water-soluble vitamin

Using Vocabulary

Questions 1–10. On a separate sheet of paper, complete each of these sentences with a term from the vocabulary list above.

1 __?__ is a simple sugar that provides cells with energy.

2 Substances in the environment that are essential to the body's functions are __?__.

3 __?__ is the oxygen-carrying substance in red blood cells.

4 Additives that make foods smooth are __?__.

5 __?__ is a blood condition in which the body has either too few red blood cells or too little hemoglobin.

6 __?__ are people who eat no meat of any kind, only plant foods.

7 __?__ is a waxy substance related to fats that helps form nervous tissues.

8 A food is __?__ when vitamins and minerals that are not naturally present are added.

9 __?__ foods are grown in soil that contains no synthetic fertilizers or pesticides.

10 __?__ is a substance that provides all the necessary amino acids.

Interpreting Ideas

1 What are the six main groups of nutrients that your body needs?

2 What is the difference between complex carbohydrates and simple carbohydrates?

3 How do emulsifiers differ from leavening agents?

4 What are two effects of dehydration?

5 How do vegetarians meet their vitamin and mineral needs?

6 Why is it important to drink fluids when you participate in physical activity?

7 What is the difference between saturated and polyunsaturated fats?

8 Which nutrients supply your body with energy?

9 Explain the difference between complete and incomplete proteins. How may incomplete proteins be used to provide you with all the essential amino acids?

10 Why should salt be eliminated from the diet of a person who has high blood pressure?

11 Use Figure 8-5 to identify the vitamin or vitamins in each of the following descriptions: (a) vitamin needed to help with the normal clotting of blood, (b) vitamins that can be toxic when taken over a long period of time, (c) vitamin that helps prevent rickets.

12 How do minerals function in the body? Why must you eat mineral-rich foods regularly?

13 What are the symptoms of iron deficiency anemia? What is the cause?

14 What is the most abundant nutrient in your body? How does it function in the body?

15 Identify the five major food groups and list two foods in each group.

16 List three reasons why additives are used in foods.

17 What are the problems with much of the food served at fast-food restaurants? Is it possible to eat a balanced meal there?

18 What information is listed on all food labels?

19 What is the purpose of the U.S. RDA?

Applying Concepts

1 Use the graph in Figure 8-3 to determine the fat content in each of the following foods: French fries, whole milk, hamburger, cake, margarine.

2 Why is it recommended that your diet contain a greater percentage of carbohydrates than of fats or proteins?

3 If dietary fiber provides little or no nutrition, why is it recommended as a protection against such ailments as constipation, colitis, and colon cancer?

4 Eskimos and natives of Greenland whose diets contain fish, whale, and seal oil rather than butter and lard have a low incidence of heart disease. How might you explain this? Why do some doctors advise against eating more than three eggs per week?

5 Which of the following meals are examples of complementary combinations: macaroni and cheese, a hamburger, a cheese pizza, lentil and pasta salad?

6 It is often said that breakfast is the most important meal of the day. Do you agree with this statement? Why or why not?

7 Compare buying a quarter-pound hamburger at a fast-food restaurant for $1.20 and a pound of lean steak to broil at home for $3.20. What is the cost per ounce of each? Which is the better buy in terms of nutrition?

8 Granola bars, frozen yogurt, and carob-covered raisins are often called natural health foods. Are these foods necessarily healthier or more natural than other snack bars, ice cream, or chocolate-covered raisins? Why or why not?

Projects

1 Keep a log of food choices offered by your school cafeteria over a month's time. Are items available from each of the Four Food Groups? Which foods represent complementary combinations? How would you change the selections offered, in order to achieve higher nutrient density?

2 Set up one platter of snacks that contain preservatives and another platter of the same snacks without preservatives. You might use peanut butter, yogurt, granola, or bread. Have groups of blindfolded students sample the snacks and try to distinguish those that contain preservatives from those that contain no preservatives.

3 To compare the nutritional value of two brands of a particular food, such as white bread or corn flakes, examine the food label of each brand. How many Calories does a serving or portion size of each contain? (Make sure you compare the same size portions.) How many grams each of protein, carbohydrates, and fats are contained in a serving? What is the first item in the list of ingredients? What significance is the order in which ingredients are listed? What percentage of the U.S. RDA for proteins is supplied? Of the U.S. RDA for iron? What preservatives, if any, have been added?

Selecting fresh fruits and vegetables is a wise step in planning a healthy and nutritious diet.

CHAPTER NINE

Planning a
D I E T

Americans today have the choice of a wonderful variety of foods. People can choose from a wide selection of fruits, vegetables, meats, breads, and other foods to meet their nutritional needs. With so many choices, it may not be hard to believe that many people have problems controlling their appetites and weight.

Many people are concerned with special diets to lose weight. Some people work to gain weight. Other people must follow special diets for health reasons. No matter what a person's health needs are, diets should be chosen wisely.

Objectives

- Define *metabolism* and list the factors that affect it.

- Define *overweight, obesity,* and *underweight.*

- Identify safe, healthy ways of controlling body weight.

- Explain why fad diets are unhealthy.

- Describe the eating disorders anorexia nervosa and bulimia.

- Identify three diet needs of athletes.

- Give two reasons that pregnant women should follow healthful eating habits.

- Describe special diets necessary for diabetes, hypoglycemia, high blood pressure, and food allergies.

Controlling Your Weight

Do you have an image of how you would like to look? You probably have heard people talk about their ideal body weight. Different societies often have had different ideas about what the perfect body shape is. But there is no single perfect weight for a particular height and age. The ideal weight for each person depends upon many factors, including bone structure and level of activity.

Trying to reach a perfect weight may be difficult. Your weight should be one at which you feel healthy and comfortable. To control your weight, you need to understand what affects your appetite and what your energy needs really are.

Appetite and Hunger

Do you remember the last time you smelled freshly baked bread, saw a juicy apple, or tasted a beef steak? The senses of smell, sight, and taste all help trigger the appetite. **Appetite** is a desire for food and is a learned response. Learned responses to foods result for many reasons. For example, you eat certain foods at times because it is a social custom, such as having turkey on Thanksgiving Day. You may eat other foods because of a family custom, such as having roast beef every Sunday. Where you live also has an influence on what you eat. If you live near the ocean, you probably eat a lot of seafood. When you are away from the ocean you may have a strong craving for seafood. This is a learned response regarding food.

Hunger is the body's response that alerts you to eat food until you feel full. Some people have little trouble separating feelings of hunger from appetite. They eat when they are hungry, stop when they feel full, and do not eat again until their brain signals them that it is time. In these people, hunger, appetite, and the feeling of fullness work together to help their bodies receive the nutrition they need without extra Calories.

Figure 9-1 You may associate lobster and clam chowder with New England and meat, dairy products, and grains with the Midwest.

Figure 9-2 Most people are a combination of body types rather than one type.

Other people, however, do not pay attention to hunger signals for eating. They may eat too fast, so that their stomach is full before it has a chance to signal the brain that it is time to stop eating. They may also continue eating after their hunger is satisfied because their appetite is stimulated. For example, many people eat dessert even when they are full because it looks so good to them.

People often eat for reasons other than hunger or appetite. Some people eat when they are lonely, bored, or anxious. Others eat because it is a habit connected with an activity, such as always buying popcorn at the movies. Other people eat in order to be sociable, for example, having ice cream at a birthday party. Still others eat when they are under stress, such as right before a big test. One of the first steps in any weight control program is to identify the reasons that you eat. What stimulates your appetite?

Metabolism

The next step in weight control is to understand metabolism. **Metabolism** [*muh TAB uh liz um*] is the process by which your body uses food to release energy and uses the energy to build and repair body tissues. Metabolism involves two processes that work at the same time. One process brings smaller substances together to form larger substances. An example is the growth and repair of cells and tissues. The other process of metabolism involves breaking down larger substances into smaller substances. An example is breaking down complex carbohydrates into simple sugars.

Two main factors determine your energy needs—basal metabolism and physical activity. **Basal metabolism** [*BAY sul*] is the energy used by the body at rest and fasting to carry out basic functions. These functions include maintaining cells, circulating the blood, and breathing.

Basal metabolism varies with age, sex, and body type. Your body type is determined by your basic bone and muscle structure. A muscular person will have a higher basal metabolic rate than a nonmuscular person of the same weight. Figure 9–2 illustrates the three main body types: lean, stocky, and athletic.

The other factor that determines your energy needs is your level of physical activity. A person who is very active, such as a construction worker or professional athlete, will use more energy than a person who works at a desk all day.

How much energy does an adult need to keep the body going? Look at Figure 9–3 and determine the daily activity rating. The values listed are based on various activity levels. You can find out about how many Calories an adult needs every day to maintain weight by using the rating and the following equation.

Daily Activity Rating × Body Weight =

Calories Needed Each Day

Suppose for example, that you are a moderately active adult who weighs 140 pounds. From the chart, you would determine that you have an activity rating of 15. Substitute these values into the equation.

$$15 \times 140 = 2100 \text{ Calories needed per day}$$

Thus, to maintain your current weight, you would need to eat about 2100 Calories each day.

Because teenagers are growing rapidly, they need more Calories than adults. A fifteen-year-old boy may need as many as 3000 Calories each day to be sure that he is getting enough energy. Even though teenage girls are also growing, they are usually smaller than boys. Therefore, they usually need fewer Calories.

Figure 9-3 How many Calories do you need to maintain your weight?

Estimating Calorie Needs

Daily Activity Rating		Activity Level
13		Very light: doing activities while sitting, reading, writing, eating, watching TV, listening to music, personal care
14	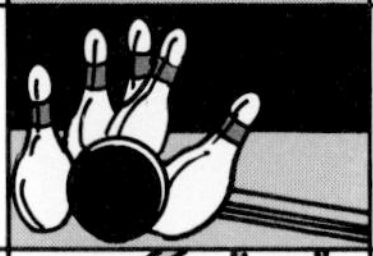	Light: doing assembly work in a factory, walking casually, golfing, bowling, auto repair, carpentry, laying brick
15		Moderate: walking briskly, farming chores (milking cows), gardening, climbing stairs, horseback riding (trotting)
16		Strenuous: doing physical labor (pick and shovel work, moving heavy equipment), vigorous dancing, calisthenics, horseback riding (galloping)
17		Very strenuous: chopping wood, racquetball, swimming, playing football, endurance running, bicycling

Daily Activity Rating × Weight (pounds) = Calories Needed Each Day for an Adult

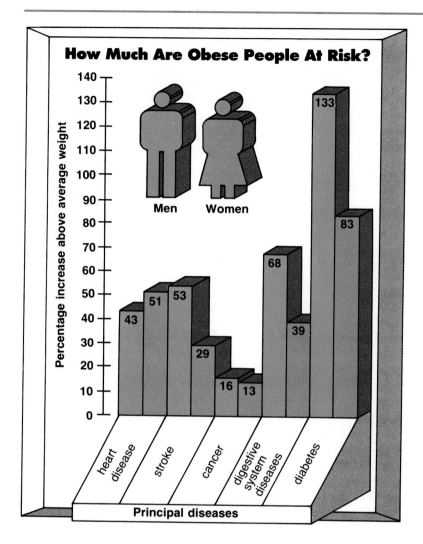

Figure 9-4 Increased health risks associated with obesity

How Much Are Obese People At Risk?

Percentage increase above average weight

Men   Women

heart disease   stroke   cancer   digestive system diseases   diabetes

Principal diseases

Overweight and Obesity

If you eat more Calories than your body can use, it will store the extra energy as fat. If you do this often, you will gain weight. Being more than 10 percent over your comfortable weight is being **overweight. Obesity** is the state at which a person weighs 20 percent more than his or her highest comfortable weight. In some rare cases, obesity is caused by health problems such as an improperly working thyroid gland. This can result in a low rate of metabolism.

Obesity has been linked to many health risks. It is connected to high blood pressure, heart disease, diabetes, breathing difficulties, kidney and gallbladder disease, and problems after surgery. Figure 9–4 shows the increased health risks associated with obesity.

Losing Weight Wisely

Each year about one out of every four people in the United States tries to lose weight. Some succeed, others do not. A successful plan for weight loss usually combines a reduction in Calories with an increase in exercise.

Health Bulletin

Walking fifteen minutes each day for a year will cause the loss of six pounds if nothing else is altered. Walking up one additional flight of stairs for a year will take off ten pounds.

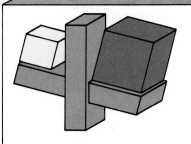
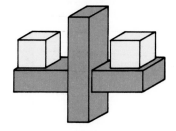
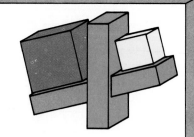

To lose weight:

adjust Calorie input or output

aim to lose 1 pound a week* by eating 500 fewer Calories daily or by using 500 more Calories daily through exercise

To maintain weight:

balance the Calories you eat with the Calories your body uses

if you eat 500 more Calories daily, you should also use 500 Calories daily through exercise

To gain weight:

adjust Calorie input or output

aim to gain 1 pound a week* by eating 500 more Calories daily or by using 500 less Calories daily through exercise

*1 pound = 3500 Calories

Figure 9-5 Counting Calories really does make a difference.

An important first step in any weight control program should be to see your doctor. She or he can help you develop a healthy, safe plan for losing weight and keeping it off.

Your doctor will probably tell you that to lose weight you must eat fewer Calories than your body is using. When this happens, your body will start to use the energy it has stored as fat. On a sound weight-loss program you should lose about one to two pounds each week. One pound of body fat is equal to about 3500 Calories. As shown in Figure 9–5, if you subtract 500 Calories each day from your diet, you should lose about one pound a week. If you also increase your amount of exercise, you will lose weight even more rapidly.

Keep in mind that it is not healthy to lose weight too quickly. If you eat too few Calories, you will not get all of the nutrients that your body needs. Try to set small goals, such as losing five pounds. When you reach that goal, give yourself a reward that is not connected with food. This might include a record, a movie ticket, or some other activity you enjoy.

Figure 9-6 Most successful weight-loss programs include an exercise program.

A wise weight-loss program should focus on food choices and eating patterns rather than Calories. Eat smaller amounts of a wide variety of foods. Choose foods low in fats and sugars and high in fiber. Eat lean meats and foods that are broiled or baked rather than fried. Choose fruit and frozen juice bars over ice cream and candy. Snack on low-Calorie foods such as unbuttered popcorn, rice crackers, and raw vegetables.

Examine your eating patterns to identify the conditions under which you tend to eat too much. If you eat when you are upset or worried, try taking a walk instead. Avoid eating while watching television, reading, or listening to music. Leave the table as soon as you are finished eating so that you are not tempted to take second helpings. Eat your meals at regular times every day. For most people, this means eating three meals a day. However, you may find that your energy needs would be better met with five smaller meals spaced evenly throughout the day. Skipping meals will make you overeat at the next meal.

If you find you have trouble losing weight on your own, consider joining a weight-loss support group, or ask for support from someone who shares your concern about weight. This may provide you with the help you need to lose weight. Remember there is no magic weight-loss plan. Find a program that suits your needs over a long time. Eventually you will find that you are able to accept the changes as part of your daily eating habits.

Fad Diets

There are many health risks associated with fad diets. Every fad diet is nutritionally unbalanced in one way or another. The important thing to remember in considering a fad diet is that if a person eats more Calories than his or her body can use, then that person will gain weight. It does not matter whether those Calories are found in grapefruit, protein powder, or steak. At best, fad diets are good for short-term weight loss. The weight usually returns as soon as you stop following the diet. At worst, fad diets have been known to contribute to high blood pressure, vitamin deficiencies, and even heart failure.

Beware also of pills and other so-called diet aids. Like fad diets, drugs only bring about a short-term weight loss. Some diet aids are habit-forming, so that they are hard to stop taking. Diet pills often make people feel jittery, and some cause a sudden rise in blood pressure. As a rule, if any weight-loss program promises quick results with little effort, it is not worth following. Most people regain their lost weight as soon as they stop dieting.

Gaining Weight Wisely

At fifteen, Jim is tall and thin. He would like to be heavier and more muscular. He tries to gain weight, but it seems that no matter how much he eats, his weight stays the same. He feels embarrassed dressing for gym. His concern about being underweight is beginning to make him moody and withdrawn.

People who are more than 10 percent under their comfortable weight are said to be **underweight.** An underweight person may

Health Bulletin

Exercise keeps muscle mass firm. Dieting alone usually means losing muscle or lean mass as well as fat.

Figure 9-7 Some healthy high-Calorie foods

Food	Serving	Cal.
Lasagna	7 oz.	280
Peanut butter	2 tbsp.	172
Banana	1 large	170
Granola	1 oz.	150
Cream of mushroom soup	7 oz.	149
Lima beans	½ cup	127
Cheddar cheese	1 oz.	112
Avocado	½	190
Cream cheese	2 tbsp.	99
Walnuts	8-15 halves	98
Custard	½ cup	150

have just as much difficulty gaining weight as an overweight person has losing weight. Many factors contribute to being underweight. Teenagers are often underweight because they have grown taller very rapidly and their bodies have not yet filled out. An underweight person's metabolism may be overactive, so that most of the food eaten is used to meet immediate energy needs. Emotional distress may decrease the appetite. Eating patterns established early in life also can contribute to being underweight.

Before you start any program to gain weight, check with a doctor. A doctor will check to be sure there is no medical reason for your being underweight. A doctor can also recommend a sensible way to gain weight.

Your doctor might suggest increased servings at regular mealtimes. It also helps to eat snacks that are high in nutrients and Calories, such as dried fruits and nuts. Look for high-Calorie foods from the carbohydrate and protein groups. An extra sandwich with milk before bedtime or after school should help add pounds. Adding about 500 Calories a day should cause you to gain about one pound a week.

At the same time, continue to exercise on a regular basis. The weight you gain will then become muscle tissue, not just fat. If you are sure to get lots of rest you will store the Calories better. If not, you may use up more Calories than you eat, and you will not gain weight.

Eating Disorders

Carol weighed only 72 pounds when she was admitted to the hospital. She was literally starving to death because of excess dieting. During her stay in the hospital, she became very upset because she was missing her routine of running and exercising three times a day.

Jan is close to her normal weight for her age and size, but she often has a sore throat. Secretly, Jan controls her weight by eating too much and then vomiting. She also takes laxatives.

Carol has anorexia nervosa. **Anorexia nervosa** [*an uh REK see uh nur VOH suh*] is an eating disorder characterized by constant dieting, rapid weight loss, and the feeling of being too fat in spite of the weight loss. Most anorexics are women and girls who view themselves as fat even when their mirror shows a starving body.

The physical signs of anorexia nervosa are loss of body fat, wasting away of muscle tissue, dry skin, and brittle hair. Other signs are dehydration, fainting, and irregular heartbeat. Many anorexics end up in the hospital because of their condition.

Jan suffers from bulimia. **Bulimia** [*byoo LIM ee uh*] is characterized by eating too much food and ridding the body of food through vomiting or the use of laxatives. Some anorexics are also bulimics. Most bulimics are girls or young women who are of average weight or slightly overweight. They tend to gain weight easily and live in constant fear of becoming obese.

Bulimics often have mouth and throat problems due to repeated vomiting. The mouth may have open sores and the throat is often

---

Health **History**

Did you know that anorexia nervosa was first discovered by English physician Richard Morton in 1689?

Figure 9-8 After an eight-year struggle, singer Karen Carpenter died of anorexia nervosa in 1983.

red. The teeth begin to decay because of the constant exposure to acids in the vomit. Like anorexics, bulimics need to be under the care of a doctor.

Anorexics and bulimics have several traits in common. They have trouble feeling good about their bodies no matter how well they may look. Some fear being fat. Others try to be perfect or fear rejection. Some are overachievers. Often, they have trouble identifying and expressing their feelings. A combination of factors contributes to these traits. Some include the person's mental state, family relationships, and cultural background. These conditions require intense medical treatment. If not treated, anorexics and bulimics may die from their illness.

Lesson Review

Your ideal weight should be one at which you feel healthy and comfortable. If a doctor advises you that you are underweight or overweight, you will need to modify two things: your Calorie intake and your level of physical activity. The best way to take off or add pounds is through gradual changes in diet and exercise.

1 What is appetite?

2 Define *metabolism.*

3 What is the difference between being overweight and being obese?

4 Describe a sound way to gain weight.

5 What is *anorexia nervosa?*

Diets for Individual Needs

Nutritional needs vary with the individual. An athlete in training needs more Calories than someone whose only daily exercise is a short walk. A pregnant woman needs extra nutrients to meet her needs as well as her baby's. People with certain diseases must eat carefully controlled diets. This means you should be careful to eat the diet that is best for you, not your best friend.

Diets for Athletes

A high level of physical activity requires more energy. A football player, for example, may need about 15 percent more Calories each day than a less active person of the same age, weight, and body type. Very active teenagers should eat as wide a variety

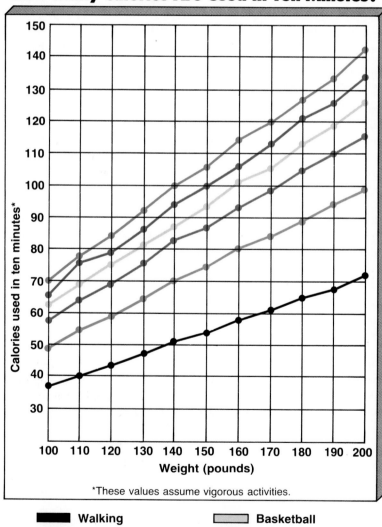

How Many Calories Are Used in Ten Minutes?

*These values assume vigorous activities.

Walking   Basketball
Tennis   Running
Swimming   Bicycling

Figure 9-9 How many Calories do you use in ten minutes of activity?

of foods as nonathletes. But they should eat only in amounts that match their growth and activity level. Remember that complex carbohydrates are a good source of energy.

Drink extra water when exercising. In hot weather, drink two cups of water 15 to 30 minutes before you begin your activity. When you are exercising, replace lost fluids by drinking large amounts of water every 15 to 30 minutes.

You lose some sodium as you perspire. Usually, salt in your diet replaces any sodium lost. Salt tablets should be taken *only* if recommended by a doctor. Excessive perspiration also removes potassium from the body. You can replace this mineral with high-potassium foods such as milk, yogurt, meats, cereals, dried fruits, and vegetables.

Exercise can increase your body's need for thiamine, riboflavin, and niacin. These are the vitamins needed for the release and use of energy. They are found in foods from the Meat-Poultry and Fish-Beans Group and the Milk-Cheese Group.

Diets for Pregnant Women

A woman's nutrition during pregnancy is very important to the health of her baby and herself. The baby is growing very fast and building tissues. To help her child grow well, the mother needs to supply all the baby's nutrients. The need for protein, calcium, phosphorus, magnesium, and folic acid is especially great at this time. An undernourished mother will give birth to a smaller, less healthy baby. She may also harm herself. For example, if she gets too little calcium, the body will use its own calcium to supply the baby. This can weaken the mother's bones and teeth.

An adult woman who already eats a well-balanced diet will need to make only small changes to supply more of these nutrients. Calorie needs increase by 15 percent, or about 300 extra Calories per day. All Calories should come from foods with a high nutrient density, selected from the Four Food Groups.

A pregnant woman should increase liquids by drinking extra water, milk, and fruit and vegetable juices. She should avoid all drugs, including caffeine, alcohol, and aspirin. She usually will need to take a vitamin and mineral supplement, as prescribed by her doctor.

Pregnant teenagers pose a special nutritional problem. The pregnant teenager is still growing herself. She must meet her own growth needs as well as her child's. For this reason, it is important that she be extra careful to eat a variety of nutritional foods. Poor nutrition may permanently damage her health and that of her child.

The nutritional requirements for breast-feeding are the same as for pregnancy, only greater. If a mother chooses to breast-feed her child, she will need to eat about 500 Calories more a day than she did before she became pregnant. She also needs about three quarts of fluid a day, including a quart of milk. Medical authorities including the American Academy of Pediatrics recommend breast milk as the best food for the newborn, provided the mother eats a nutritious diet.

Figure 9-10 Eating a well-balanced diet during pregnancy helps ensure a healthy baby.

Low-Sodium Diets

When blood pressure in the blood vessels is too high, the resulting condition is called **hypertension.** It may lead to heart and kidney disease or stroke. High blood pressure is often associated with too much sodium in the diet. Treatment for hypertension involves reduced sodium intake and, if necessary, medications that will lower blood pressure. Weight loss is recommended for obese patients who have hypertension.

The first step to reducing sodium in the diet is to cut back on added salt. Table salt contains sodium chloride. Take the salt shaker off the kitchen table. When cooking, substitute other spices such as lemon, basil, or garlic. When dining out, ask that foods be prepared without salt. Choose broiled meats or fish, and ask for lemon or lime for seasoning.

These efforts still may not be enough. Most processed foods contain hidden sodium. If you read food labels, you will see that processed foods often contain sodium phosphate, sodium nitrate, and sodium sulfate, as well as sodium chloride. Look for processed foods that say ''no salt added'' or ''low sodium'' on the label. Avoid foods such as processed meats and cheeses, pickles, and salted nuts, pretzels, and potato chips.

Diets for Diabetes

The condition in which the body cannot use carbohydrates, resulting in high blood sugar, is called **diabetes mellitus** [*dy uh BEE tis muh LY tus*]. When most people eat carbohydrates, their body converts the carbohydrates into glucose, a simple sugar. **Insulin** is a substance in the body that transports glucose from the blood into cells. If insulin is present in the right amounts, the body uses glucose for quick energy. Excess glucose is stored for later use.

In diabetes mellitus, the body has little or no natural insulin. With insulin lacking, glucose builds up in the blood. The body expels glucose as waste in the urine, and the cells do not get the glucose they need for energy. If no insulin is available, a diabetic coma may result from a dangerously high blood glucose level.

It is estimated that one in every 1000 people under the age of 17 has diabetes. Adults, especially those who are obese, may also develop diabetes. Diabetes requires close medical supervision. Although no cure has been found yet, daily injections of insulin and a special diet can control this condition in young people. For adults who develop diabetes, treatment usually includes a weight-reduction diet and sometimes medicine.

A good diet for patients with diabetes balances the level of glucose in the blood. The diet should be high in dietary fiber and complex carbohydrates and low in cholesterol and fats. People who have diabetes must avoid eating foods that are high in sugar, which can cause a rapid rise in the level of the blood glucose. Food must be eaten at regular times and in fairly equal amounts. Usually people who have diabetes eat three regular meals, as well as two or three snacks daily. Many diabetics also exercise on a regular basis.

Health History

Insulin was discovered in 1922 by two Canadian scientists, Frederick G. Banting and Charles H. Best. Prior to this, most children with diabetes died before reaching adulthood.

Diets for Hypoglycemia

Hypoglycemia [*hy poh gly SEE mee uh*], or low blood sugar, is a condition caused by too much insulin being produced by the body. Several hours after eating, a hypoglycemic person may feel dizzy, thirsty, hungry, and weak. Foods high in sugar tend to bring on the reaction that occurs several hours after eating the sweets. Eating frequent, small meals and snacks high in protein often controls hypoglycemia. Some doctors also suggest a diet high in complex carbohydrates and dietary fiber.

Food Allergies

Many common foods, such as cow's milk, wheat, eggs, and chocolate, can cause unpleasant reactions for some people. A **food allergy** is a condition in which body cells, in response to certain foods, release certain substances that cause fluid to leak into the surrounding tissues. The substance that causes most of the symptoms of food allergies is called histamine. **Histamine** [*HIS tuh meen*] is a substance that is normally released in small amounts to increase the flow of gastric juices in the stomach and to dilate the walls of small blood vessels. Histamine is found in many cells of the body.

Too much histamine is toxic to the body. The body may react to this distress in many ways. Some people may have skin disorders, such as hives or eczema. Others may have digestive disorders, such as stomach pains and diarrhea, or a breathing disturbance, such as asthma.

Food allergies are sometimes difficult to diagnose. Generally, people can avoid or eliminate certain foods that they suspect cause allergies. If they then eat the food and feel discomfort, they may need to stop eating that food entirely. A substitute for that food may be needed to provide the nutrients that food provides.

Figure 9-11 Snacking on fruits and vegetables is a wise choice for diabetics.

Lesson Review

Different people need to follow different diets to feel healthy and perform at their best. An athlete's nutritional needs differ from those of a diabetic. Pregnant women must have high-calcium diets and should avoid all drugs. People who suffer from high blood pressure, diabetes mellitus, or food allergies must all have special diets. Consider your personal circumstances in order to choose the diet that is best for you.

1 Describe the special nutritional needs of an athlete.

2 Name three nutrients that are particularly important during pregnancy.

3 Define *hypertension*.

4 What is the best way to reduce sodium in the diet?

5 Define *diabetes mellitus*.

6 Define *hypoglycemia*.

Chapter Review

Vocabulary

anorexia nervosa	food allergy	insulin
appetite	histamine	metabolism
basal metabolism	hunger	obesity
bulimia	hypertension	overweight
diabetes mellitus	hypoglycemia	underweight

Using Vocabulary

Questions 1–10. On a separate sheet of paper, write the term from the column on the right that matches the phrase on the left.

1 a substance that transports glucose from the blood to cells
2 process by which the body uses food and energy
3 weighing 20 percent more than your highest comfortable weight
4 energy used by the resting body to carry out basic functions
5 body's response that alerts you to eat food until you feel full
6 condition of high blood sugar
7 eating disorder involving constant dieting and rapid weight loss
8 substance most commonly associated with allergies
9 condition characterized by vomiting or the use of laxatives
10 condition of low blood sugar caused by too much insulin

a metabolism
b diabetes mellitus
c anorexia nervosa
d histamine
e hypoglycemia
f obesity
g bulimia
h hunger
i basal metabolism
j insulin

Questions 11–20. On a separate sheet of paper, write the vocabulary term that correctly completes the sentence.

11 A __?__ is a condition in which body cells release substances that cause fluid to leak into the surrounding tissues.

12 If you are more than 10 percent under your comfortable weight, you are __?__.

13 The condition in which blood pressure in the blood vessels is too high is called __?__.

14 The sight and smell of freshly baked cookies may trigger the __?__, or desire for food.

15 One factor that determines your energy needs is __?__, or the energy that the body uses to maintain cells, breathe, and circulate the blood.

16 If you are more than 10 percent over your comfortable weight, you are __?__.

17 __?__ involves the process of forming larger substances from smaller ones and breaking down larger substances into smaller ones.

18 In the condition known as __?__ people often see themselves as fat even when their bodies are dangerously thin.

19 In __?__ the body has little or no natural insulin.

20 A person who has __?__ often has mouth and throat problems due to repeated vomiting.

Interpreting Ideas

1 Compare what happens in the two processes involved in metabolism.

2 What two factors determine your energy needs?

3 What factors may contribute to being underweight?

4 How is your body type determined? What are the three main body types?

5 Why is it unhealthy to lose weight too quickly? What should be the focus of a wise weight-loss program?

6 If a mother chooses to breast-feed her baby, how would she need to modify her diet?

7 Identify the kinds of food choices and behaviors that will help achieve weight-loss goals.

8 What are the problems of fad diets?

9 How does exercise affect your need for certain vitamins and minerals? How can you get these vitamins and minerals in your diet?

10 How should a woman modify her diet when she becomes pregnant?

11 What problems are associated with the use of pills and other diet aids in weight-loss programs?

12 How may sodium be hidden in the diet? What measures can be taken to lower sodium intake?

13 How may the body react to the presence of too much histamine?

14 What are three diet needs of athletes?

15 Why is it especially important that a pregnant woman follow healthful eating habits? What may happen when the pregnant woman is undernourished?

16 How does insulin function in the body? What happens if the body has little or no natural insulin?

17 Name three reasons other than hunger or appetite that cause people to eat.

18 Why do teenagers need more Calories than most adults? Why do teenage girls generally need fewer Calories per day than teenage boys?

19 What is the relationship between obesity and disease?

20 What are the physical signs of anorexia nervosa? of bulimia? How are the personalities of anorexics and bulimics alike?

Applying Concepts

1 Why is a sound exercise program important in both gaining and losing weight?

2 If a hypoglycemic person has low blood sugar, why do foods high in sugar tend to bring on hypoglycemic symptoms?

3 Why are eating disorders primarily mental health problems and only secondarily nutritional problems?

4 Why does a healthy body weight vary from one individual to another? What factors might influence healthy body weight?

5 Ketosis is a state in which the body begins to use its own protein for energy. In what eating disorder is ketosis likely to occur?

6 Why do you think that anorexia nervosa and bulimia appear more often in girls than in boys?

7 If your comfortable weight is 120 pounds, at what weight would you be considered overweight? obese? underweight?

8 On an exercise program for weight loss, you discover that you are firming and toning muscles but have not actually lost much weight by the scales. How can you explain your observation?

9 What kinds of problems might a person who is allergic to cow's milk anticipate? How can they be avoided?

Projects

1 Collect information about the various weight-loss diets that are currently being advertised. From your findings determine whether these diets contain all the nutrients that the body needs to grow, maintain, and repair itself. If not, suggest an alternate diet plan.

2 Use library materials as well as an interview with a nurse or physician to find out more about diabetes. Is the disease inherited? How is it controlled? Why must some diabetics inject themselves with insulin rather than take insulin by mouth?

3 Aerobic exercise is an efficient method of weight control. Create a classroom mural illustrating categories of aerobic exercise, from the least strenuous (walking or skating) to the most strenuous (jumping rope, jumping jacks, running in place).

A delicious Thanksgiving dinner provides many nutrients. Digestion allows the body to make use of the contents of foods.

CHAPTER TEN

DIGESTION
& EXCRETION

A Thanksgiving dinner provides many of the nutrients your body needs for energy, growth, and repair. Turkey and stuffing contain protein, carbohydrates, and some fat. Side dishes such as sweet potatoes and cranberries are good sources of carbohydrates. Each of these foods also contains some minerals, vitamins, and water. A glass of milk completes the meal, adding protein, fat, and carbohydrates, as well as calcium, riboflavin, and vitamin D.

How is your body able to absorb and use this variety of nutrients? Common sense tells you that your cells need help to obtain nutrients from these foods. Your body must first break foods down into those nutrients that cells can use. The process by which food is broken down is called digestion.

Objectives

- Define *digestion, elimination,* and *excretion.*

- Trace the path of a meal through the digestive system.

- Identify several common digestive disorders, their causes, and treatments.

- Identify the organs of excretion.

- Explain the importance of the kidneys to the body.

- Identify two disorders that affect the urinary system.

The Digestive System

Digestion is the process by which the body breaks down carbo-hydrates, proteins, and fats into substances that cells can absorb and use. There are two kinds of digestion—mechanical and chemical. **Mechanical digestion** is the process of chewing, mashing, and breaking food into smaller pieces. **Chemical digestion** is the process of changing food into simpler substances chiefly through the action of enzymes. **Enzymes** are proteins that speed up the chemical breakdown of complex substances.

Figure 10-1 shows the digestive stystem. The main part of the digestive system is the alimentary canal. The **alimentary canal** is made up of the organs through which food passes. These or-

Figure 10-1 The structure of the digestive system

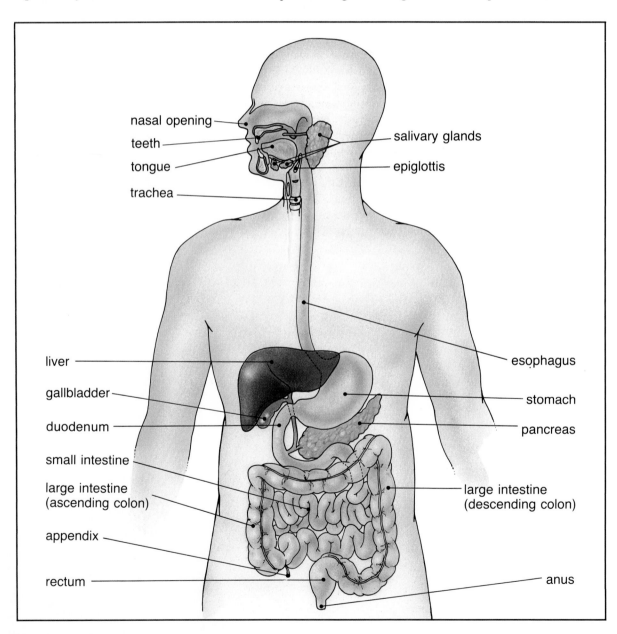

- nasal opening
- teeth
- tongue
- trachea
- salivary glands
- epiglottis
- liver
- gallbladder
- duodenum
- small intestine
- large intestine (ascending colon)
- appendix
- rectum
- esophagus
- stomach
- pancreas
- large intestine (descending colon)
- anus

gans include the mouth, the esophagus, the stomach, the small intestine, and the large intestine. For a more detailed illustration of the digestive system, see Plate Four. Other organs in the digestive system aid in digestion. These organs include the salivary glands, the pancreas, the gallbladder, and the liver. Notice the location of these organs in relation to the alimentary canal. Undigested food never passes through these organs. Instead, they help in digestion by releasing digestive juices into the alimentary canal.

Digestion in the Mouth

The digestion of a meal such as Thanksgiving dinner with turkey and all the trimmings begins as you take your first bite of food. As food enters the mouth, mechanical digestion begins. The teeth tear, grind, and chop food into smaller pieces. The tongue mashes soft food and mixes it with saliva. **Saliva** is a watery, tasteless liquid mixture that moistens chewed food and begins chemical digestion.

The **salivary glands** are the organs that produce saliva. Find the three major salivary glands in Figure 10–1. They are located on the floor and upper back of the mouth. These glands empty saliva into the mouth. Saliva contains amylase. **Amylase** [*AM uh lays*] is an enzyme that begins the chemical digestion of complex carbohydrates, such as the sweet potatoes and stuffing in your Thanksgiving dinner.

Once the food is chewed and softened in the mouth, the tongue rolls it into a ball or **bolus.** The tongue pushes the bolus to the back of the throat to be swallowed. The process of swallowing is shown in Figure 10-2. During swallowing, a small flap of tissue called the **epiglottis** prevents food from entering the windpipe. The food then passes into the esophagus. The **esophagus** [*ih SOF uh gus*] is a muscular tube that connects the mouth to the stomach.

Food moves down the esophagus to the stomach by the action of peristalsis. **Peristalsis** is the wavelike contraction of muscles that moves food through the digestive system. Your turkey dinner passes into the stomach slowly. At the opening of the stomach is a circular muscle, or sphincter [*SFINGK tur*], that opens and closes to keep food from backing up into the esophagus.

Health Bulletin

Scientists indicate that a substance is an enzyme by adding *-ase* to the root word that the enzyme acts upon. Hence, *maltase* is an enzyme that helps to break down maltose. What would be the name of the enzyme that helps to digest sucrose?

Figure 10-2   During swallowing, the epiglottis prevents food from entering the windpipe.

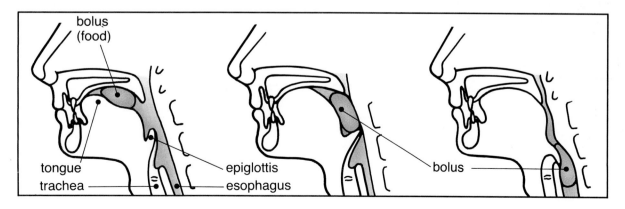

bolus
(food)

tongue
trachea
epiglottis
esophagus
bolus

Digestion in the Stomach

Between the esophagus and the small intestine is the **stomach,** a saclike organ of digestion. The stomach walls are made of three layers of muscle, each arranged on a different angle. As the food enters the stomach, muscle contractions begin to twist, turn, and churn the food. The twisting, turning, and churning of food in the stomach is part of mechanical digestion. The food is mixed with gastric juices. Gastric juices are secreted into the stomach to help liquefy food and break it into simpler forms. Gastric juices contain water, acid, and enzymes.

The chemical digestion of complex carbohydrates begun in the mouth slows down in the stomach. But the gastric juices begin the digestion of proteins and fats. One enzyme in the gastric juices begins the breakdown of proteins, such as those in the turkey from Thanksgiving dinner, into amino acids. Another enzyme begins the digestion of the protein in milk.

Most foods remain in the stomach anywhere from three to four hours. While it is in the stomach, the partially digested food is changed into a thick liquid called chyme. A sphincter at the end of the stomach allows chyme to move into the small intestine a little bit at a time.

Figure 10-3 The enzymes of the digestive system

	Organs or Glands	Secretions and Enzymes	Products of Digestion
Mouth	**Salivary glands**	Salivary amylase	Breaks down starch into dextrins and maltose
Stomach	**Gastric glands**	Pepsin	Breaks down proteins into polypeptides
		Rennin	Digests milk proteins
		Lipase	Breaks down emulsified fats into fatty acids and glycerol
		Hydrochloric acid	Stimulates pepsin to digest protein
Small Intestine	**Pancreas**	Trypsin	Digests certain polypeptides to amino acids
		Lipase	Digests fats to fatty acids and glycerol
		Amylase	Digests starch to maltose
	Intestine	Peptidase	Digests polypeptides to amino acids
		Sucrase	Digests sucrose to glucose and fructose
		Maltase	Digests maltose to two molecules glucose
		Lactase	Digests lactose to galactose and glucose

The Small Intestine

Most chemical digestion and absorption of food occurs in the small intestine. The **small intestine** is a long, coiled organ about one inch in diameter. The stomach connects with the **duodenum** [*doo uh DEE num*], the first part of the small intestine. The duodenum is about a foot long and is shaped like the letter *C*. The major digestion of your Thanksgiving meal begins here. The pancreas and intestinal glands play important roles in completing the breakdown of food. The **pancreas** is a long, soft gland lying behind the stomach that secretes digestive enzymes into the duodenum. The intestinal glands are tiny organs found in the lining of the small intestines. They release digestive enzymes and mucus.

Enzymes from the pancreas and intestinal glands continue the breakdown of proteins. They also change starch into simple sugars and split fats into fatty acids. Many of the enzymes of digestion are listed in Figure 10–3. The body digests and absorbs fat with the help of **bile,** which is a thick yellow-green fluid released by the liver. Bile is stored in the gallbladder and released into the duodenum.

The absorption of nutrients occurs throughout the small intestine. The **villi** [*VIL eye*] are very tiny fingerlike projections lining the walls of the small intestine. Look at Figure 10–4. The many projections of the villi increase the surface area of the small intestine. This increased surface area allows the small intestine to absorb most of the nutrients that enter your body. Inside the villi are blood vessels and vessels containing a fluid called lymph. Fat-soluble vitamins and fatty acids are absorbed into the lymph system. Glucose, amino acids, water-soluble vitamins, and minerals are absorbed into the blood vessels. The blood and lymph then carry the completely digested food throughout the body.

Health Bulletin

If you were to unfold the lining of the small intestines as well as the villi, these organs would completely fill the area of a volleyball court.

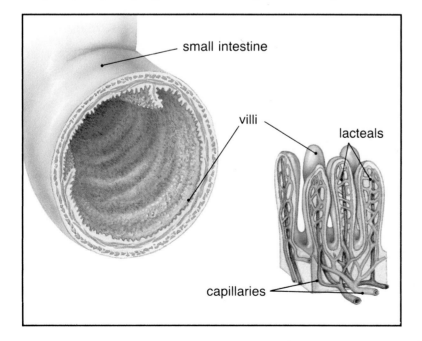

small intestine

villi

lacteals

capillaries

Figure 10-4 Within the villi are complex networks of blood and lymph vessels. Nutrients pass through the villi into the blood and lymphatic system.

The Role of the Liver

Blood containing nutrients travels from the small intestine to the liver. Nutrients in the blood stream are further processed in the liver. The **liver** is a large organ that secretes bile, filters the blood, and stores carbohydrates. In the liver, some digested food is removed from the blood and changed into other forms or stored. Fats are prepared so that they can be combined with proteins. Amino acids are either used to make proteins or stored in the liver until they can be carried by the blood to other parts of the body. Carbohydrates stored in the liver are changed into glucose. Glucose is then released into the blood and carried to all body cells. Excess glucose is stored in the liver as glycogen. **Glycogen** is a starchlike substance used by the body to maintain blood sugar levels between meals.

Elimination of Wastes

Very few nutrients enter the large intestine when well-balanced meals are eaten. Only water, fiber, and foods that the body was unable to break down pass out of the small intestine. From your Thanksgiving dinner, the fiber from the cranberries and carrots will remain undigested.

The **large intestine** is the part of the digestive system that extends from the small intestine to the anus. The large intestine is about five feet long. The major function of the large intestine is to reabsorb the water that was used during digestion. As the water is removed, the wastes become solid. Solid wastes contain bacteria, undigested foods, and cholesterol. Many types of bacteria also line the large intestine. Some bacteria break down some of the undigested materials such as fiber. The remaining solid wastes are called **feces,** or stools.

The last five to six inches of the large intestine make up the rectum. The **rectum** stores solid wastes until the body is ready to expel them. During the process of elimination, solid wastes leave the body through a muscular opening at the end of the rectum called the **anus.**

Lesson Review

As food enters the mouth, mechanical and chemical digestion begin. The chewed and softened food moves down the esophagus to the stomach, where it is changed into chyme. The chyme enters the small intestine, where most of the chemical digestion takes place. The majority of nutrients are absorbed through the villi in the small intestine. The nutrients in the blood and lymphatic systems move to the liver and other parts of the body.

1 What function do enzymes perform?

2 Name five major parts of the alimentary canal.

3 Where is glycogen stored?

4 What is the major function of the large intestine?

Skeletal System

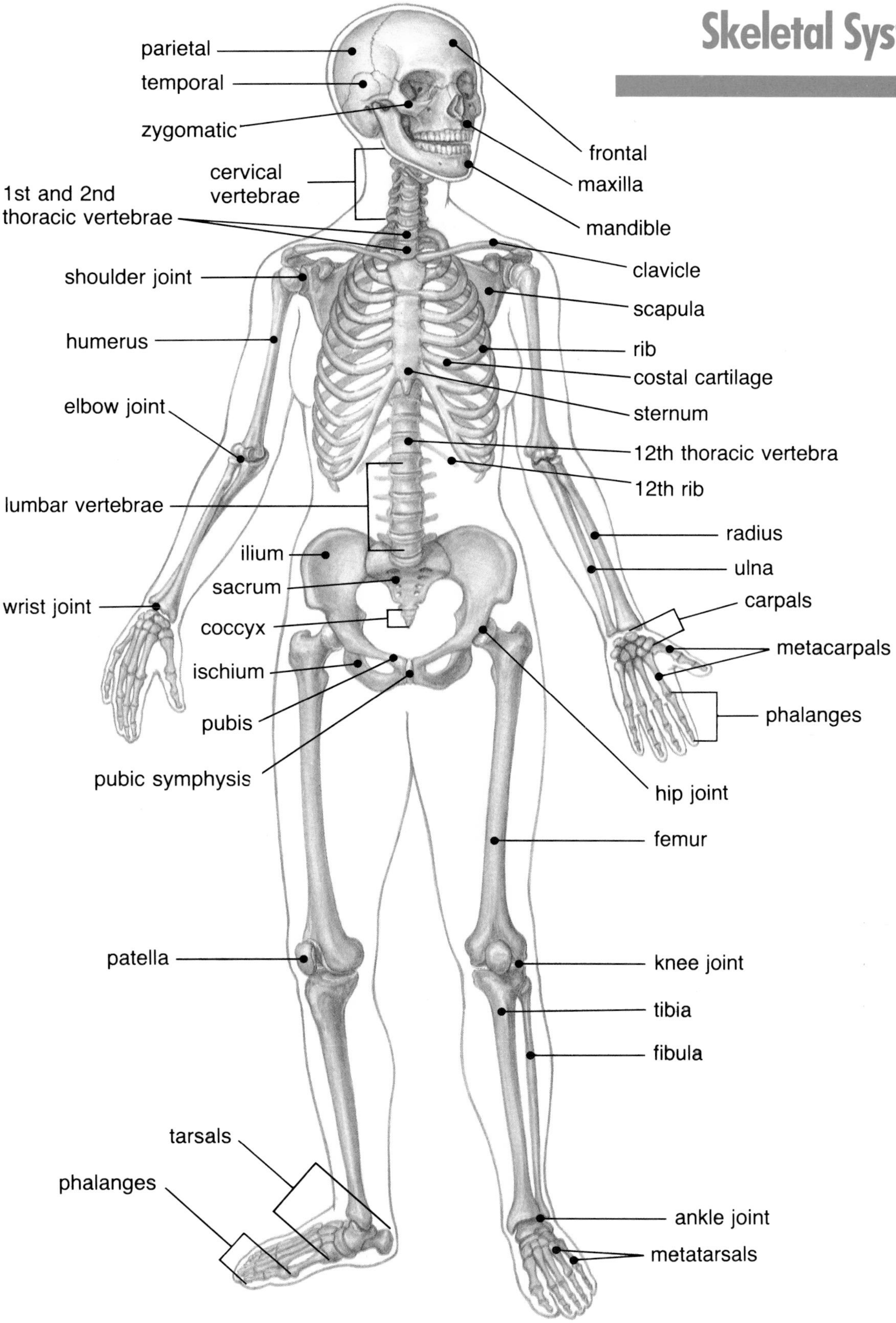

parietal

temporal

zygomatic

cervical vertebrae

1st and 2nd thoracic vertebrae

shoulder joint

humerus

elbow joint

lumbar vertebrae

ilium

sacrum

coccyx

ischium

pubis

wrist joint

pubic symphysis

frontal

maxilla

mandible

clavicle

scapula

rib

costal cartilage

sternum

12th thoracic vertebra

12th rib

radius

ulna

carpals

metacarpals

phalanges

hip joint

femur

patella

knee joint

tibia

fibula

tarsals

phalanges

ankle joint

metatarsals

Muscular System

temporalis

masseter

orbicularis oris

frontalis

orbicularis oculi

sternocleidomastoid

trapezius

pectoralis minor

deltoid

cut edge of
pectoralis major

pectoralis major

latissimus dorsi

ribs

serratus anterior

biceps

triceps

external oblique

extensor carpi
radialis

brachioradialis

flexor carpi radialis

palmaris longus

rectus
abdominis

flexor digitorum

tensor
fascia
lata

iliopsoas

abductor pollicis brevis

pectineus

adductor longus

flexor pollicis brevis

gracilis

adductor pollicis

sartorius

flexor digitorum
tendons

tendon of quadriceps
femoris group

quadriceps femoris group:
vastus lateralis
rectus femoris
vastus medialis

patella

patellar ligament

peroneus longus

gastrocnemius

tibialis anterior

soleus

extensor digitorum longus

tibia

extensor hallucis longus

abductor
hallucis

extensor digitorum tendons

Muscular System

sternocleidomastoid

trapezius

deltoid

triceps

latissimus dorsi

brachioradialis

lumbodorsal fascia

iliac crest

gluteus medius

cut edge of
gluteus maximus

digiti minimi

hamstrings:
  biceps femoris
  semitendinosus
  semimembranosus

soleus

Achilles tendon

splenius capitis

levator scapulae

cut edge of trapezius

infraspinatus

rhomboids

teres minor

teres major

cut edge of latissimus dorsi

scapula

erector spinae

ribs

posterior inferior
serratus

extensor pollicis
longus

external
oblique

extensor digitorum
tendons

extensor
digitorum

tensor fascia lata

gluteus maximus

adductor magnus

gastrocnemius

n

b

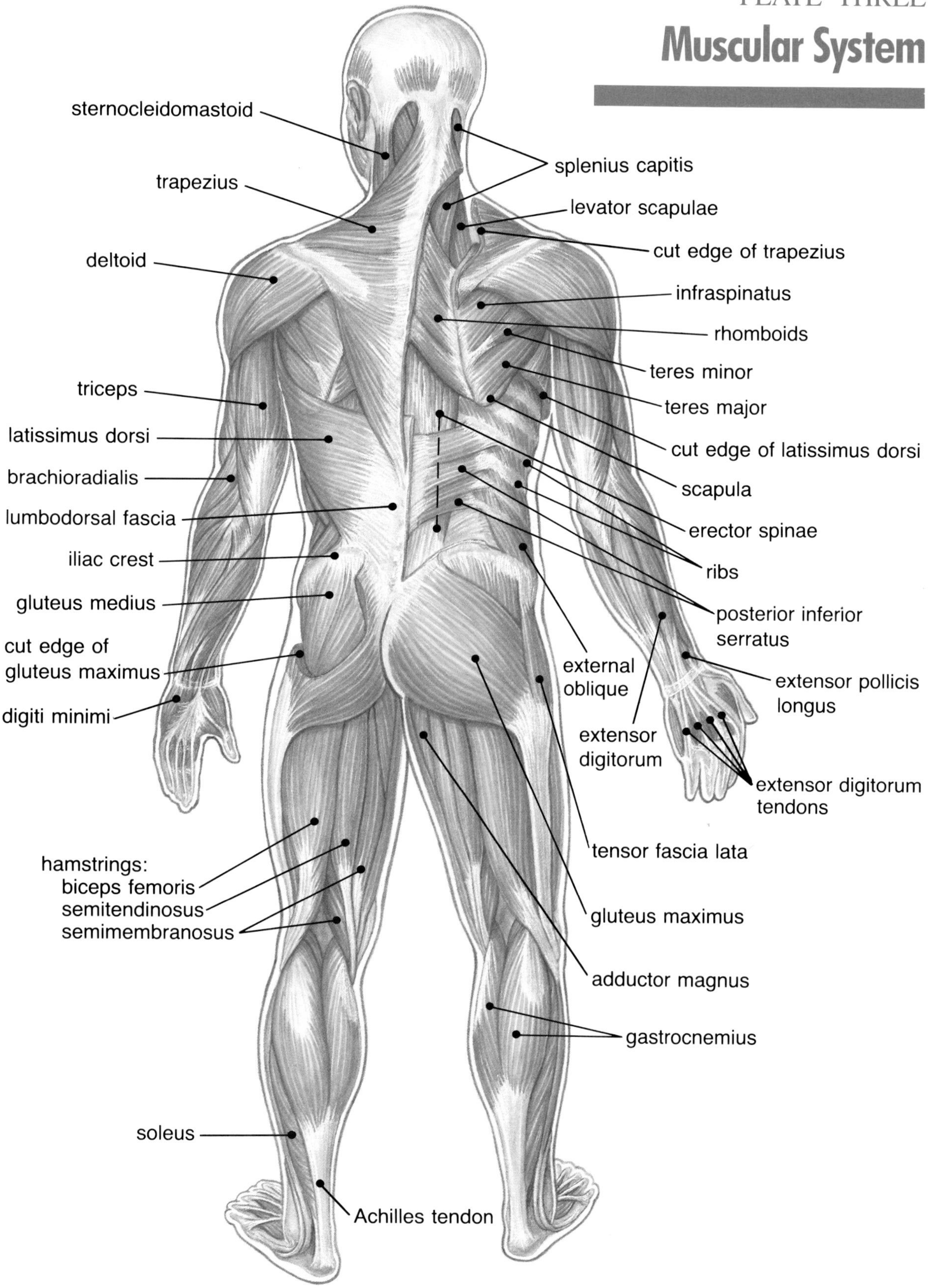

PLATE EIGHT

Nervous System

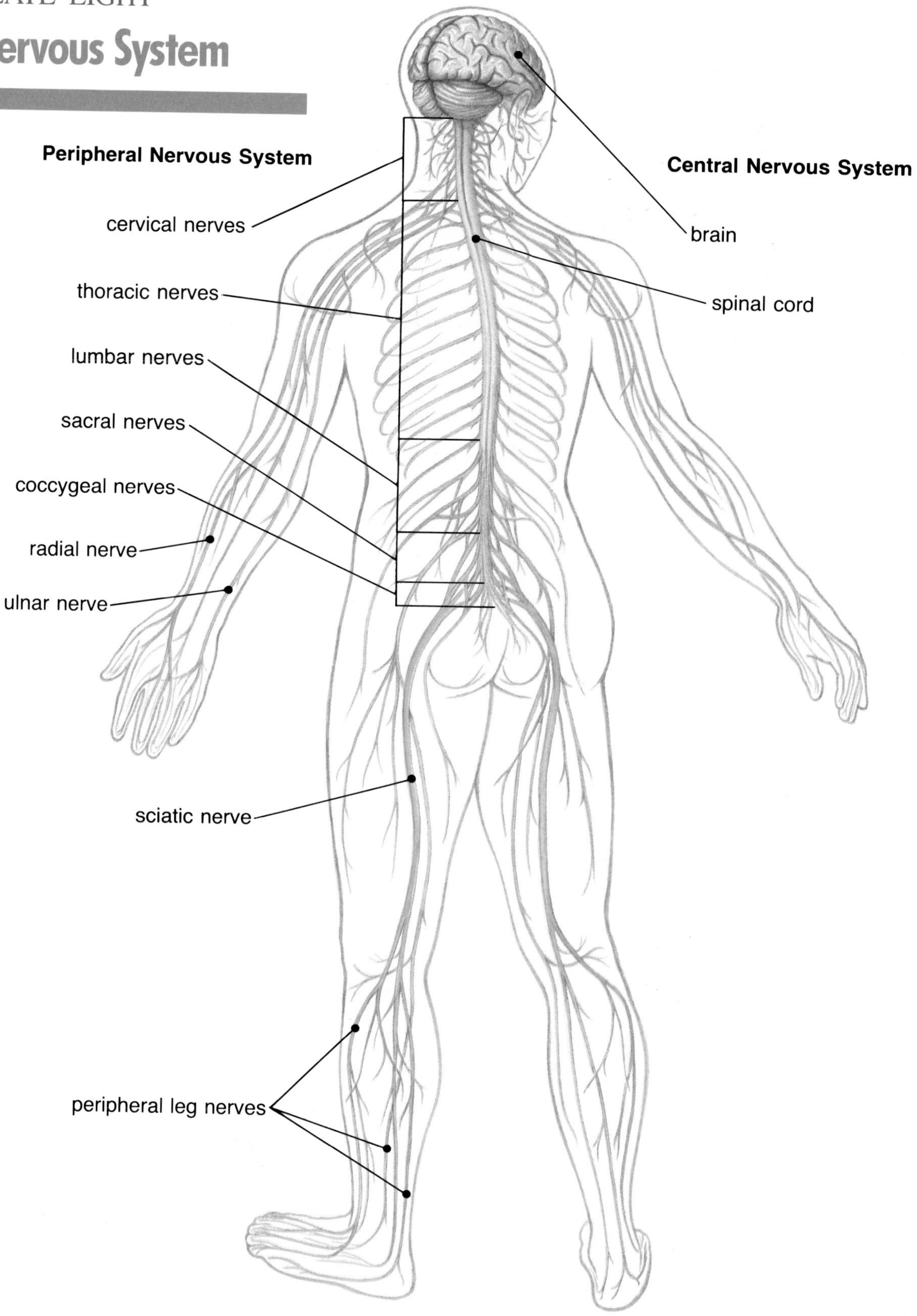

Peripheral Nervous System
cervical nerves
thoracic nerves
lumbar nerves
sacral nerves
coccygeal nerves
radial nerve
ulnar nerve
sciatic nerve
peripheral leg nerves
Central Nervous System
brain
spinal cord

Digestive Disorders

Disorders of the digestive system are often related to eating habits. Overeating or eating foods that the body has trouble digesting can cause problems. Bacteria in food also can upset the digestive system. Trouble with digestion may be a sign of a disease as well. Symptoms of digestive disorders include pains in the chest and abdomen, vomiting, and problems in eliminating wastes. The abdomen is the part of the body that includes the stomach and intestines. If these signs appear often or for long periods of time, you should seek medical help.

Constipation and Diarrhea

Different people have different patterns of waste elimination. Most people have one bowel movement daily. Some people have two or three movements each day and others have only one movement every few days. A change from your usual pattern may be a sign of a disorder.

Constipation is a condition in which the bowel movements are difficult and do not occur often enough. It may be the result of too little exercise, a diet low in fiber, emotional distress, or the misuse of laxatives. A laxative is a medicine that stimulates the process of elimination. If constipation continues for a week or more, it may be a symptom of a more serious condition.

Constipation is best treated by eating high-fiber foods such as whole grains, fresh vegetables and fruits, and beans; drinking

HEALTH + TECHNOLOGY

ARTIFICIAL PANCREAS—Today 10 million people in this country are diabetics. About 1 million diabetics depend on daily insulin shots for survival. Insulin is a hormone that transports simple sugars to cells and tissues. In insulin-dependent diabetes the pancreas produces insufficient insulin.

Recently researchers at the University of Minnesota developed an artificial pancreas in the form of an insulin pump. The insulin pump is a small, circular device that is imbedded beneath the skin. Every two weeks the patient returns to the hospital so the pump can be refilled with insulin from a syringe. A delivery tube connects the pump to a large vein, where insulin is injected continuously into the blood.

Today insulin-dependent diabetics use other artificial organs in the treatment of diabetes. One such device worn by the patient injects insulin through a needle inserted under the skin. The patient receives insulin round the clock. Using this device, patients show excellent control of diabetes after treatment. Thus, artificial organs are effective in eliminating daily insulin shots as well as providing sufficient insulin flow throughout the day.

1 What does an insulin pump do?
2 What condition does the artificial pancreas treat?

plenty of fluids; and exercising regularly. It should not be treated by using laxatives unless recommended by a doctor. Laxatives may help at first, but if taking them becomes a habit, they can upset the regular pattern of waste elimination.

Diarrhea [*dy uh REE uh*] is a condition in which the feces are watery and loose and the bowels move too often. Diarrhea occurs when the large intestine does not reabsorb enough water. Diarrhea may cause great losses of water and other important nutrients. A person with diarrhea should also drink plenty of clear fluids. Diarrhea that continues for more than 48 hours may indicate a serious condition and should not be left untreated. Severe diarrhea may cause dehydration. **Dehydration** is a severe loss of water that may be fatal.

Indigestion

Indigestion is the inability of the body to digest food properly. The signs are usually noticed soon after eating. Some people experience heartburn, or a sharp pain in the chest. Others may experience nausea or cramps in the abdomen. Sometimes indigestion includes flatulence, or an increase in the amount of gas in the intestines. It creates the need to belch or pass gas.

Stress can cause indigestion. Stress often causes people to eat too much, eat too quickly, or eat on the run. When people are in a hurry they tend to swallow too much air, which can cause flatulence. Sometimes gas forms when bacteria in the intestines act on the indigestible remains of foods such as cabbage, beans, or cucumbers. Eating a calm, relaxed meal and avoiding any foods which the body has trouble digesting will help relieve this sort of indigestion. Regular exercise can also help relieve stress-related indigestion.

In some people, not being able to digest lactose (milk sugar) causes indigestion. **Lactose intolerance** is a lack of the enzyme needed to digest milk sugar, or lactose. Lactose intolerance is

Health History

In the 19th century, Sylvester Graham, the father of food reform in the United States, reintroduced many followers to the virtues of whole grains. Graham believed that keeping bran in wheat flour would reduce the incidences of indigestion, a common complaint in those days. What common food did he immortalize?

Figure 10-5   Eating too quickly can often bring on indigestion.

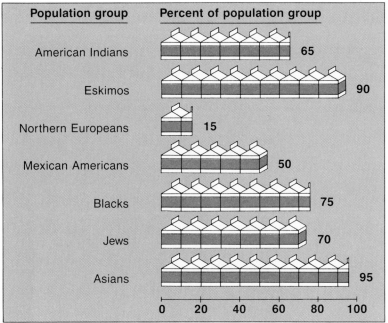

Population group	Percent of population group
American Indians	65
Eskimos	90
Northern Europeans	15
Mexican Americans	50
Blacks	75
Jews	70
Asians	95

0 20 40 60 80 100

Figure 10-6   Lactose intolerance is a hereditary condition that is more common in some ethnic groups than in others.

usually hereditary. As milk sugar builds up in the intestines, it causes a build-up of gas. Many people experience cramps and diarrhea. A person who cannot digest lactose may need to meet his or her calcium requirements with other foods. Some people are able to reduce the problem if they consume milk products less often and in smaller amounts.

Food Poisoning

A serious illness caused by infected food is **food poisoning.** It usually is caused by bacteria in food. The bacteria themselves may be harmful or they may produce poisons that harm the body. The usual signs of food poisoning are severe vomiting, diarrhea, abdominal pains, and fever. The signs usually occur within 24 hours after the infected food was eaten.

Salmonella   *Salmonella* bacteria account for about 25 percent of all confirmed cases of food poisoning. These bacteria, shown in Figure 10–7, grow very fast in human intestines. As the bacteria grow, they cause the usual signs of food poisoning. The infection is rarely fatal, although the body may need extra fluids to replace those lost through vomiting and diarrhea.

Infection from *Salmonella* may be avoided by cleaning hands and cooking utensils well before eating. Raw meat should be kept refrigerated and then cooked well. Thoroughly clean any platters and utensils used in preparing raw meat before further use.

Staphylococcus   Food poisoning may also be caused by *Staphylococcus* bacteria. The signs are similar to those of *Salmonella* infection. *Staphylococcus* bacteria grow in foods such as tuna and chicken salads that are allowed to become warm. They also grow in cream-filled pastries, salted meats, and sausages.

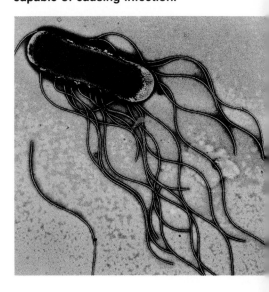

Figure 10-7   There are about 1300 types of *Salmonella*, each capable of causing infection.

Figure 10-8 When preserving acidic foods such as fruits, a boiling water bath is often used to destroy bacteria that may cause botulism.

These foods should be kept as cold as possible before being served. The bacteria are also found in the human body, especially in small cuts, boils, and around the mouth and nose. To avoid infection, wash hands before preparing foods and keep hands away from the face during food preparation.

Botulism A dangerous and often fatal form of food poisoning is **botulism.** Botulism is caused by the poison given off by the *Clostridium botulinum* bacteria. Symptoms include paralysis, double vision, and other signs that the central nervous system has been affected. *Clostridium botulinum* grows in improperly canned foods in the absence of oxygen. This especially includes those with a low acid content such as string beans, corn, and peas. Heating home-canned foods in a pressure cooker is the best means of preventing botulism. If foods are not heated long enough during canning or reheating, the bacteria may not be killed.

Appendicitis

A small pouch located near the junction of the small intestine and the large intestine is the **appendix.** Can you locate it in Figure 10–1? The appendix has no known function. However, if it becomes inflamed, swollen, and filled with pus, a condition called **appendicitis** occurs.

The first sign of appendicitis usually is pain around the navel that moves to the lower right side of the abdomen. Fever, nausea, vomiting, and loss of appetite are usually present as well. If appendicitis is not treated immediately the appendix may burst. Then the pus will move into the abdominal cavity. Treatment for appendicitis involves both surgery and the use of antibiotics to control infection. Figure 10-9 shows the removal of an appendix.

Figure 10-9 Surgery of the appendix. During surgery, the appendix is held away from the surrounding tissue.

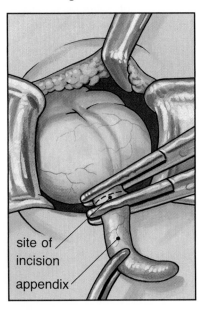

site of incision

appendix

Hemorrhoids

Swollen veins in the anal area are known as **hemorrhoids** [*HEM uh roydz*], or piles. They tend to develop in people who sit a lot or in those who suffer from constipation. Hemorrhoids also occur often in pregnant women and very overweight people.

The signs of hemorrhoids may include itching as well as pain and bleeding. Ointments and hot baths may be used to relieve the pain and itching. In severe cases, surgery may be required. Eating a diet with plenty of fresh fruits, vegetables, and other high-fiber foods is very helpful in preventing hemorrhoids.

Gallstones

One of the most common diseases of the digestive system is the formation of gallstones in the gallbladder. **Gallstones** are hard, stonelike substances that are formed from cholesterol and other substances in the bile. They form because the bile stays in the gallbladder. Gallstones often may be present without causing any trouble unless they get caught in the tube leading from the gallbladder to the small intestine. See Figure 10-10. If the gallstones prevent bile from moving out of the gallbladder, the gallbladder will become inflamed and swollen. This causes severe pain and a fever. Infection may spread to the intestines. Surgical removal of the gallbladder is the usual treatment.

Ulcers

Open sores that form in different parts of the body are called **ulcers.** Sometimes ulcers form in the lining of the stomach. **Peptic ulcers** form in the lining of the duodenum. The main sign of an ulcer is pain caused by digestive juices coming in contact with the ulcer. However, not all ulcers are painful.

Different factors tend to lead to ulcers in different people. Some of these are poor diet, stress, heredity, and too much caffeine, alcohol, tobacco, and aspirin. A peptic ulcer occurs when the stomach makes too much hydrochloric acid and there is a weakening in the protective lining of the stomach or duodenum. Ulcers can cause severe bleeding or blockage of the alimentary canal. As shown in Figure 10–11, ulcers even eat through the wall of the stomach or duodenum.

Several steps can be taken to help ease the pain and allow an ulcer to heal. These include eating regular meals and avoiding cigarettes, alcohol, aspirin, and caffeine. A doctor may prescribe medicines to reduce the amount of acid in the stomach. Some ulcers are treated by surgery.

Crohn's Disease

A chronic disease of the small intestine is **Crohn's disease.** It occurs most frequently in young adults. Yet many cases are reported in children before age 15. The cause of Crohn's disease is unknown. However, research indicates that heredity and the environment play a role in its development. Some symptoms of Crohn's disease include cramps, diarrhea, weight loss, and fever. Often nutrients are not absorbed from the small intestine, and the

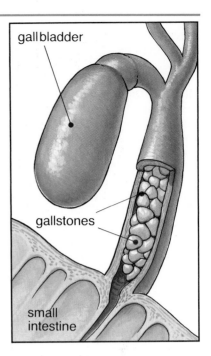

Figure 10-10   Gallstones in the common bile duct.

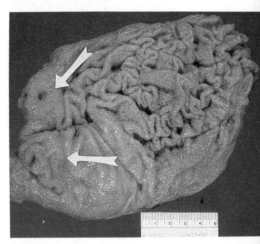

Figure 10-11   Most stomach ulcers occur near the mid-area or back wall of the stomach.

patient suffers from malnutrition. During acute attacks a low-fiber diet is recommended along with vitamin and mineral supplements. As symptoms subside only those foods that aggravate the symptoms are eliminated from the diet.

Ulcerative Colitis

Many adults develop an inflammation of the lining of the colon called **ulcerative colitis** [*UHL suhr uh tihv koh LY tihs*]. The **colon** is the lowest part of the large intestine. Ulcerative colitis is less common than peptic ulcers, and most often affects women and young adults. Some doctors believe that nervous tension may be a factor in ulcerative colitis, although the exact cause is unknown.

Symptoms include pain on the lower left side of the abdomen, diarrhea, fever, and blood in the feces. Doctors may advise a change in diet and medicine. In more serious cases surgery may be needed.

Colon and Stomach Cancer

An uncontrolled growth of cells that invade and destroy neighboring healthy tissue is known as **cancer.** Cancer of the colon and rectum is the third most common type of cancer in the United States. The cancer most often occurs in the lowest part of the colon near the rectum. As the cancer grows larger, it either blocks the colon or causes bleeding, often during elimination. Cancers of this type are slow to spread. Seeking early medical help usually means a good chance for cure. Often adults of middle age or older have yearly tests for hidden blood in the stool.

Cancer of the stomach is much less common than colon and rectum cancer. Early signs may include mild indigestion, vomiting, and loss of appetite. As the cancer grows, pain in the upper abdomen and vomiting increase and weight is lost. Medical care at the early stages improves the chance for cure. Treatment involves removal of all or part of the stomach.

Lesson Review

A number of disorders may affect the digestive system. Disorders related to diet or the body's inability to digest foods include constipation, diarrhea, indigestion, and gallstones. Symptoms for the various disorders are often similar and include a degree of abdominal pain. Because the signs may point to serious disorders, such as food poisoning, appendicitis, and cancer, care by a doctor is important.

1 What are some steps a person can take to control indigestion?

2 What is the function of the appendix?

3 What type of ulcers form in the lining of the duodenum, the first part of the small intestine?

4 What are some of the early symptoms of stomach cancer?

Excretion

The process that removes waste from the blood, tissues, and cells is called **excretion.** The materials that need to be removed are the substances which the body cannot use following metabolism, such as urea. **Urea** [*yoo REE uh*] is a chemical that is the end product of protein digestion. Other wastes include water, carbon dioxide, and salts. The organs of excretion are the skin, the lungs, the liver, the intestines, and most importantly, the kidneys.

The Urinary System

The **kidneys** are located on either side of your spine, behind the intestines, and just above your waist. They are shaped like red kidney beans, but much larger. As you can see in Figure 10-12, the kidneys, the ureters, the bladder, and urethra make up the urinary system. A more detailed illustration of the urinary system is shown on Plate Five.

The kidneys filter wastes from the blood. The main functioning unit of the kidney is the **nephron.** Within each nephron is a network of coiled blood vessels called a **glomerulus.** Each glomerulus is enclosed in a Bowman's capsule. Figure 10–13 shows the flow of blood in a Bowman's capsule.

Water and waste products are drawn from the blood into the nephron, forming urine. **Urine** is a pale yellow solution of urea, water, salts, and other substances. The urine then slowly flows through ureters. **Ureters** are narrow muscular tubes that connect the kidneys to the bladder. The walls of the bladder expand as it fills with urine. The muscle at the neck of the bladder is allowed to relax and urine is squeezed by the muscular bladder through the urethra. The **urethra** is a tube leading from the bladder to the outside of the body.

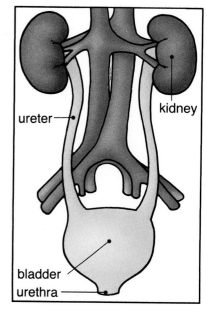

Figure 10-12   The structure of the urinary system

Figure 10-13   The structure of the kidney and a nephron

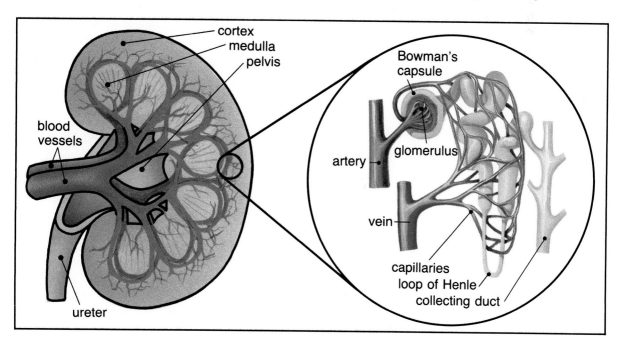

Other Excretory Organs

The liver serves a vital function as an excretory organ. The liver actually begins the process of removing wastes from the blood. As blood passes through the liver, the liver takes out most of the bacteria and other substances that entered the blood from the intestines. The blood then continues to the kidneys where filtering is completed.

The skin also serves as an excretory organ. As you perspire, very small amounts of waste are excreted by the sweat glands. Perspiration contains water, urea, and salts. Thus it serves to both cool your body and to rid it of wastes.

The lungs excrete the gas carbon dioxide, which is a waste that results from metabolism. In the lungs, oxygen is exchanged for carbon dioxide. The carbon dioxide leaves the body through the nose or mouth as you breathe out. The intestines also have a role in excretion. Solid wastes leaving the body contain water, salts, dead cells, and fiber.

Disorders of the Urinary System

The urinary system is vital to your health. When it fails to function well, waste products build up in the body. Serious disorders, and even death, may result.

Bacteria and other disease-causing organisms can enter from outside the body, usually through the urethra. The organisms may enter the kidneys from the blood also. Once inside the urinary system, bacteria can multiply and spread. This causes inflammation and swelling that prevents the normal functioning of the system. Blood or pus in the urine signals an infection or other disorder and should be treated by a doctor.

Kidney stones are the formation of solid material in the kidney. A kidney stone can cause severe pain as it moves out of the kidney if it is not small enough to pass through the ureter. The pain will usually go away as soon as the stone drops into the bladder or is passed out of the body with the urine.

Of the disorders of the urinary system, **kidney failure** causes the most concern. It may be short-term, caused by another disease, a sudden drop in blood pressure, or a blockage in another part of the urinary system. Kidney failure may also develop over a long time and never totally stop the flow of urine. End-stage kidney failure is the most severe condition because wastes are no longer removed from the body.

People with end-stage kidney failure must undergo a regular treatment called **hemodialysis.** Hemodialysis is a common method of filtering directly through the blood stream. The patient's wastes are filtered directly from the blood through a special machine, shown in Figure 10-14.

Many people faced with dialysis elect to have a kidney transplant. In a kidney transplant, the diseased kidney is removed and replaced with a healthy kidney from a close relative or someone with similar body tissue. Most people need only one healthy kidney to sustain life. Kidney transplants are now quite a common and successful procedure.

Figure 10-14 Patients receiving hemodialysis are on the machine at least 12 hours every week. Such treatment is very costly.

Gout is an inherited condition in which the body either overproduces or fails to get rid of uric acid. **Uric acid** is one of the end products of protein digestion. When there is too much uric acid it may be deposited in different parts of the body. The ear lobes, elbows, and in the joints are common places for the deposits. A gout attack often involves the large toe, and is extremely painful. It occurs most often in middle-aged and older men.

An attack of gout tends to be brought on by rapid weight loss, excess food or alcohol, high-fat diets, and certain drugs. Doctors suggest that gout patients eat little meat, eat less fat, drink plenty of fluids, and avoid alcoholic beverages. Doctors may prescribe medicines to lower the amount of uric acid formed in the body.

Cirrhosis [*sih ROH SIS*] of the liver is a scarring of the liver which impairs its functioning. The liver cells are replaced by a harder tissue similar to scar tissue. Cirrhosis of the liver may be caused by infection or poisons in the body, but most commonly by abuse of alcohol. Treatment calls for a diet high in proteins, carbohydrates, and the B-vitamins.

Lesson Review

Excretion is the process that removes the waste products of metabolism from the body. The organs of excretion include the kidneys, the skin, the lungs, the liver, and the intestines. The kidneys filter the blood. The wastes pass through the urinary system and out of the body. The urinary system can be easily infected. If a disorder is suspected, it should not be left untreated.

1 Name the process that removes waste products from the body.

2 Name five organs of excretion.

3 How can disease-causing organisms enter the urinary system?

4 What condition is caused by a build-up of uric acid?

Chapter Review

Vocabulary

alimentary canal	epiglottis	mechanical digestion
amylase	esophagus	nephron
anus	excretion	pancreas
appendicitis	feces	peptic ulcer
appendix	food poisoning	peristalsis
bile	gallstones	rectum
bolus	glomerulus	saliva
botulism	glycogen	salivary gland
cancer	gout	small intestine
chemical digestion	hemodialysis	stomach
cirrhosis	hemorrhoids	ulcerative colitis
colon	indigestion	ulcer
constipation	kidney	urea
Crohn's disease	kidney failure	ureter
dehydration	kidney stone	urethra
diarrhea	lactose intolerance	uric acid
duodenum	large intestine	urine
enzymes	liver	villi

Using Vocabulary

Questions 1–10. On a separate sheet of paper, write the term from the column on the right that matches the phrase on the left.

1 process that removes waste from blood, tissues, and cells
2 wavelike contractions that move food through digestive system
3 open sore that forms in lining of duodenum
4 swollen veins in the anus
5 condition in which bowels move too often
6 severe loss of water that can lead to shock
7 blood-filtering treatment
8 main part of the digestive system
9 lack of enough of the enzyme needed to digest milk sugar
10 condition in which bowel movements are difficult and infrequent

a hemodialysis
b alimentary canal
c lactose intolerance
d hemorrhoids
e excretion
f constipation
g peristalsis
h dehydration
i diarrhea
j peptic ulcer

Interpreting Ideas

1 What is the difference between chemical digestion and mechanical digestion?

2 What are three causes of disorders of the digestive system?

3 What are the functions of the liver?

4 What happens to the food that enters your mouth? Trace the path of the food as it moves through your digestive system. What organs aid in the process of digestion?

5 Why may constipation develop? Describe the best way to treat constipation.

6 What is the cause of food poisoning? What are the symptoms? Identify three kinds of bacteria that cause food poisoning.

7 What are the cause and symptoms of appendicitis? Why is it dangerous to delay treatment?

8 Identify five organs of excretion. What is the role of each of these organs?

9 What is the cause of pain associated with kidney stones?

10 What are the causes of cirrhosis of the liver? What is the treatment for cirrhosis?

11 Why does diarrhea occur? What is the danger of severe diarrhea?

12 What are the signs of indigestion? What can be done to relieve stress-related indigestion?

13 Explain what happens when end-stage kidney failure occurs. Describe the usual treatment for end-stage failure.

14 Describe a peptic ulcer: its location, factors that may lead to its appearance, the cause of the pain it produces, and steps to help ease the pain and encourage healing.

15 List the early symptoms of cancer of the stomach. What is the treatment for stomach cancer?

16 What are the symptoms of botulism? How may it be prevented?

17 What happens in the body to cause the pain of a gout attack? What brings on an attack?

18 How may hemorrhoids be prevented?

19 Identify the products of excretion. What do the products of excretion have in common?

20 Identify and describe the function of the villi.

Applying Concepts

1 How might stress play a role in the development of a peptic ulcer?

2 How do teeth play a role in digestion?

3 Why does your mouth water when you are hungry and smell bread baking?

4 Why does regular exercise help constipation?

5 In each of the following situations, identify the kind of food poisoning likely to occur: (a) chicken salad and cream puffs left in the sun for several hours during a picnic are eaten in the evening; (b) several people share a smoked, uncooked sausage that has very little oxygen inside its skin.

6 Why is a high-fiber diet helpful in preventing hemorrhoids?

7 Why is a low-fiber diet recommended as a treatment for Crohn's disease?

8 Whenever you swallow food, the epiglottis closes over the air passage to the lungs. If there were no epiglottis, what might happen during swallowing?

9 The small intestine contains about 253 inches of coiled, muscular tubing. If food moves through the small intestine at the rate of about 2.8 inches per minute, how long does it take food to move through the entire small intestine?

Projects

1 The appendix has no known function in humans and is therefore referred to as a vestigial organ. Find out more about this organ. Why is appendicitis more common in children than in adults? What long-term effect, if any, may the surgical removal of the appendix have on the health of an individual?

2 In this chapter you learned that saliva contains an enzyme that begins the digestion of complex carbohydrates. What chemical change does a carbohydrate undergo in your mouth? To find out, place a piece of unsalted cracker in your mouth and leave it there for three minutes. After three minutes, how has the taste changed?

3 The Heimlich maneuver is a procedure used to dislodge food that is stuck in the throat. Arrange to have a teacher or a person from the Red Cross demonstrate the procedure and supervise as each student tries it.

4 Prepare a large poster illustrating the organs of the human digestive system. Use bright tempera or poster paints to paint each organ a different color. On sheets of construction paper color-coded to each of the digestive organs, paste lined index cards on which to describe the functions, interesting facts, and possible disorders of the organ. You may want to construct a urinary system poster in the same way.

Critical Thinking

ANALYZING ADVERTISING

"Gain ten pounds of pure muscle in just three weeks!" "Grow more beautiful hair just by drinking our product!" Do these statements sound too good to be true? They should, because they are impossible.

Some advertisements promise more than they can deliver. This is especially true for many ads about diet and physical fitness. Advertisers assume that you will be attracted to their products if you are promised exactly what you want—fantastic results.

An important step in analyzing advertising is deciding whether the data, or information, in an advertisement is adequate to support the advertiser's claim about the product. Having adequate data means having enough information to make a wise decision. For example, if someone tried to sell you a soft drink that could change the color of your hair, you would be suspicious. You would certainly demand more information, or data, before spending your money.

Some advertisements provide a great deal of useful information. For example, consider an advertisement for Cheery Cheddar Cheese that includes the nutritional chart shown above.

Daily Nutrients from One Ounce of Cheery Cheddar Cheese

A one-ounce serving of Cheery Cheddar Cheese will give you all of the following amounts of nutrients* for a low amount of Calories:

Calcium	23.8%
Protein	18.5%
Phosphorus	21.3%
Magnesium	3.0%
Riboflavin	8.3%
Vitamin B_6	1.5%
Vitamin A	9.0%
Vitamin B_{12}	16.7%

*Percentages based on the U.S. RDA for the maintenance of a healthy body.

---

1 Which of the following statements are supported by the nutritional information provided for Cheery Cheddar Cheese?

a One ounce of cheese contains all the nutrients needed daily.

b One ounce of cheese is an excellent source of calcium.

c One ounce of cheese provides more phosphorus than a soft drink.

d One ounce of cheese contains more Calories than one ounce of yogurt.

e Cheddar cheese is low in fat and cholesterol.

2 An advertisement for Cheery Cheddar Cheese also makes the following claims. Which of them are supported by the nutritional information in the chart?

a Eating more cheese is a good way to prevent osteoporosis, or the loss of calcium from bones.

b Cheery Cheddar Cheese is a better buy than beef.

c Cheery Cheddar Cheese is an excellent source of vitamins and minerals.

d Cheery Cheddar Cheese makes a delicious and nutritious snack.

e A weight-reduction diet should include ample portions of Cheery Cheddar Cheese.

3 Based on the information in this advertisement, would you consider buying Cheery Cheddar Cheese? Why or why not?

Although the Cheery Cheddar Cheese advertisement may not answer all of your questions, it does provide solid information on which you could base a decision. Other advertisements, however, present very little information. Some may even be intentionally misleading. For example, look at the advertisement for Meltaway

Candy shown below. This advertisement is similar to ads you might see in a newspaper or popular magazine.

At first glance this advertisement appears to be full of useful data. But look more closely. Does this advertisement really provide enough information for a wise decision?

Consider, for example, the statement that an official advisory panel approves Meltaway Candy. What does this mean? Who was on this advisory panel? What were the qualifications of such advisors? As you can see, the advertisement provides no answers to such questions. Thus

the claims themselves have little meaning.

4 For which of the following statements does the advertisement for Meltaway Candy provide adequate supporting data?

a Medical doctors recommend Meltaway.
b Meltaway Candy is safe and effective for people who need to lose 50 pounds or more.
c Meltaway Candy speeds up the activity of the body's natural fat burners.
d Meltaway Candy is chocolate flavored.
e Meltaway is guaranteed.

5 For each of the unsupported claims that you identified in exercise 4, explain why you think that the claim is unlikely to be true. In writing your answers, use the information you learned in Unit 3 to support your statements.

As you can see by analyzing the advertisement for Meltaway Reducing Candy, not all advertisements provide useful supporting data. Products that promise impossible results are examples of quackery. By looking for supporting data in advertisements, you can protect yourself from quackery and the inflated claims of unethical advertisers.

4

11. **Bones and Muscles**

12. **Circulation and Respiration**

13. **Coordination and Control**

Physical Fitness

14. Lifelong Fitness

Bones and muscles work together to allow mobility. You can walk, run, kick, and jump because muscles pull against bones.

CHAPTER ELEVEN

BONES & **MUSCLES**

Have you ever thought what your body would be like if it had no bones? Would you be able to stand or sit in a chair? Bones are amazing structures. They are as strong as iron but only one fifteenth as heavy. They also repair themselves and change size as the body grows. No other substance is equal to bone as a body-building material.

Attached to bones are muscles. Muscles allow a basketball player to race down the court and a ballet dancer to leap and bend gracefully. Bones and muscles grow stronger with use. If they are not used, they become weak and shrink. Therefore physical exercise is important. Bones and muscles require lifelong care.

Objectives

- Describe the structure and function of bones.

- Describe how bones change with age.

- Identify and give examples of three kinds of joints.

- Compare tendons and ligaments.

- Distinguish between the axial skeleton and the appendicular skeleton.

- Describe symptoms and treatment of common skeletal and muscular problems.

- List three types of muscles and their functions.

- Explain how muscles "pair up" to move bones.

- Explain how diet and exercise may affect bones, muscles, and posture.

Bones—Living Support

Bones are living organs. You may find this hard to believe if you have seen bones at the dinner table. They are made of cells that grow, repair, and replace themselves. Bones also contain minerals, which are nonliving materials.

The bones of the human skeleton differ in size and shape, but in general, they have the same purposes. Bones give structure, protect the internal organs, and supply important minerals to the body. Bones store minerals until other parts of the body need them. They also house tissues that make blood cells.

Structure of Bone

The structure of the kind of bone found in your thigh or upper arm is shown in Figure 11–1. A bone of this sort, with large ends and a narrow middle, is called a **long bone.** The narrow portion of the bone between the bone ends is called the **shaft.**

The outside of the bone is covered with a strong membrane called the **periosteum** [*per ee AHS tee uhm*]. The periosteum, shown in Figure 11–1, covers the entire bone except for the ends. The blood vessels running through the periosteum enter the bone at many points, nourishing the cells of the bone.

Under the periosteum is a layer of tissue called **compact bone.** Compact bone is hard. As the bone grows larger, the compact bone gets thicker. Compact bone covers the entire bone. A network of blood vessels runs through canals in the layer of compact bone. This canal system is called the **Haversian system.**

Look again at Figure 11–1. Notice that the ends of the bone contain **spongy bone.** The cells of spongy bone form many cavities. The arrangement of these cavities provides great strength for bearing weight. Spongy bone acts as a cushion for the rest of the bone by absorbing shocks. Spongy bone contains red bone marrow. **Red bone marrow** is a tissue that makes red blood cells and some white blood cells. Your body makes millions of blood cells every minute.

Figure 11-1 Structure of a long bone. The wedge is taken from the bone shaft below.

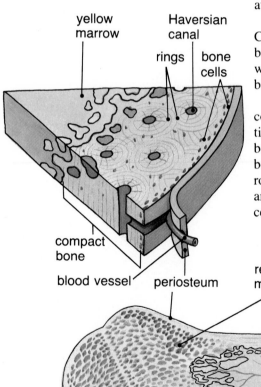

yellow marrow

Haversian canal

rings   bone cells

compact bone

blood vessel   periosteum

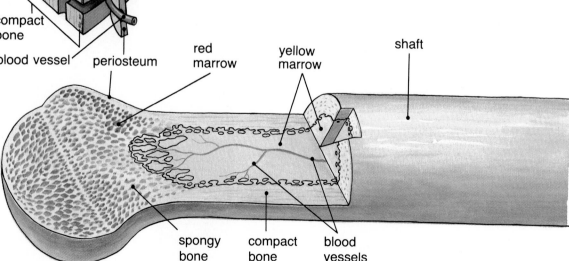

red marrow   yellow marrow   shaft

spongy bone   compact bone   blood vessels

In an adult, there is no red bone marrow under the compact bone in the shaft. Rather, yellow bone marrow fills a cavity that runs the length of the shaft. Yellow bone marrow is mostly fat cells. Yellow bone marrow can, however, make blood cells in certain emergencies, such as after heavy bleeding.

In adults, bones have more nonliving material than living material. You can see the arrangement of material in bone in Figure 11–2. The rings are made of the minerals calcium and phosphorus. Minerals are held together by **collagen,** a strong, flexible material produced by bone cells. The minerals give bone its strength. The lighter-colored core of the rings is filled with blood vessels and nerves. The dark areas between the mineral rings are filled with living bone cells.

How Bones Change

Bones change with age. The bones of a baby are mainly made of cartilage. **Cartilage,** which is mostly collagen, is tough and easy to bend. The bones of babies and children bend easily and seldom break. This is a good thing, since toddlers fall often.

As a baby grows, cartilage cells are replaced by bone cells and by rings of calcium and phosphorus between bone cells. The process of change from cartilage to bone cells and minerals is called **ossification** [ahs uh fih KAY shun]. Ossification continues through childhood into young adult life. As you grow, your bones become heavier and harder, but also less flexible. This means that they are strong but break more easily.

As adults age, they begin to lose minerals and living materials from their bones. The bones become weaker and even more brittle. The elderly suffer more broken bones than middle-aged people. Their bodies also have greater difficulty repairing breaks. However, activity strengthens bones. Exercise helps bones form heavier mineral deposits and thicker layers of compact bone.

Some people develop a bone disorder called osteoporosis. **Osteoporosis** [ahs tee oh puh ROH suhs] is the loss of calcium from bone. The calcium is reabsorbed by the bloodstream. This weakens the bone, allowing it to fracture more readily. Exercise and a proper lifelong diet with lots of calcium and vitamin D may help prevent osteoporosis.

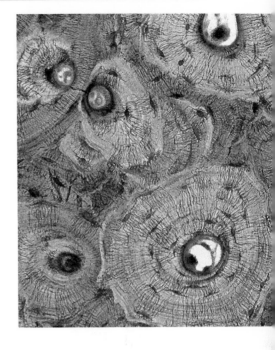

Figure 11-2 Cross-section of bone tissue, magnified

Lesson Review

Bones provide bodies with a living framework that changes throughout life. As children grow, the cartilage in their skeletons is replaced by bone in a process called ossification. Within bones are layers of tissue, including the periosteum, compact bone, spongy bone, and bone marrow. Exercise and a balanced diet with adequate calcium and vitamin D help keep bones strong.

1 What is the name of the membrane that covers the bone?

2 Where are red blood cells produced?

3 What is ossification?

The Human Skeleton

The fully grown human skeleton contains over 200 bones of many shapes, sizes, and functions. A baby is born with more bones. Some of the bones that are separate in a child become fused, or joined, in adults. Bones range in size from the tiny bones of the middle ear, which you learned about in Chapter 3, to the body's largest and strongest bones, the thighbones. Some bones are long and cylindrical like the long bone in Figure 11–1. Others are short, flat, or knobby.

A useful way to study the human skeleton is to examine it divided into two parts: the axial skeleton and the appendicular skeleton. These two parts of the skeleton are shown in Figure 11–3. For a more detailed illustration of the human skeleton, refer to Plate One.

Figure 11-3 The axial skeleton is shown in dark brown; the appendicular skeleton is shown in light brown.

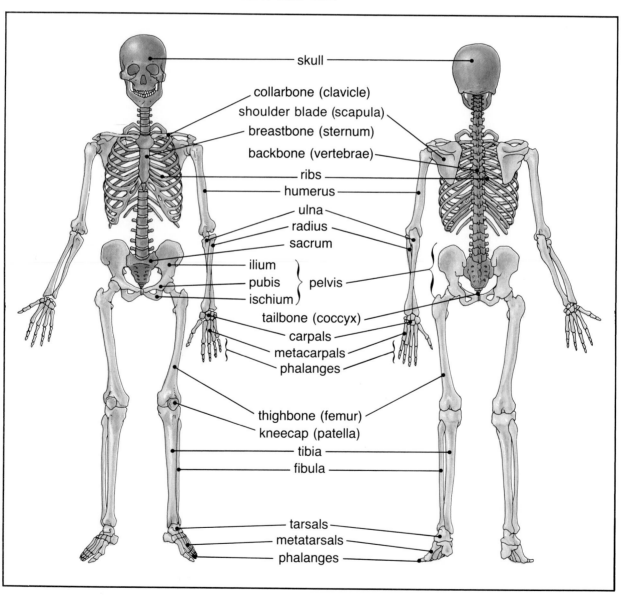

The Axial Skeleton

The bones of the skull, the chest, and the spine make up the **axial skeleton.** The bones of the axial skeleton protect the body's vital organs, namely the brain, spinal cord, heart, and lungs.

Skull   The skull contains 28 bones. Twenty-two of them form the frame of the head. The remaining six bones, three in each ear, carry sound waves from the eardrums to the brain.

The **cranium** is the part of the skull that protects the brain. Eight bones fit together at immovable joints to form the cranium. The zig-zagged shape of the joints makes them stronger than if the joints were straight lines. If you try to feel these joints, you will find that you cannot.

At birth, the bones in the cranium are not joined. There are spaces between them, as you can see in Figure 11–4. During birth these spaces allow the bones to slide under one another so the baby's head can fit through the birth canal. Although some of the bones become joined three months after birth, the cranium does not completely fuse until the child is about two years old. Because there are soft spots between the unfused bones, always protect a baby's head until the cranium closes.

Touch your face. Can you tell, by touch, how many bones are in your face? Six facial bones are fused with immovable joints to create part of the face. Two form the bridge of the nose, two form the cheeks, and two form the upper jaw. A seventh bone, the jawbone, is the only bone in the skull that can move. The jawbone, which is also the largest bone in the skull, moves up, down, and sideways. This range of movement allows you to talk and to chew food.

The **sinuses** are hollow air passages in the skull. They are connected with the nose and throat. The sinuses lighten the weight of the skull. They also act as echo chambers to enhance the sound of the voice. The sinuses are lined with mucous membranes, which help to warm and moisten inhaled air. The sinuses also reabsorb much of the moisture in exhaled air.

Backbone   The backbone, or spinal column, is composed of 33 small bones called the **vertebrae** [*VUR tuh bree*]. The spinal column protects the spinal cord. Run your hand along your vertebrae. Each bump is a separate vertebra. Between the vertebrae, cartilage discs act as cushions to absorb shock.

As you can see in Figure 11–5, the spinal column is divided into regions. The seven **cervical vertebrae** [*SUR vih kuhl*] are found in the neck area and hold up the head. The cervical vertebrae give the neck great flexibility and allow the head to move in many directions. Stretch your head upward or turn it from side to side. Notice how much movement you have. Below the neck, the twelve **thoracic vertebrae** [*thuh RAS ik*] help support the frame of the chest. The five **lumbar vertebrae** [*LUM bur*] are in the lower back, which is the major weight-bearing area of the body. The lower back has the biggest and strongest vertebrae of the spinal column.

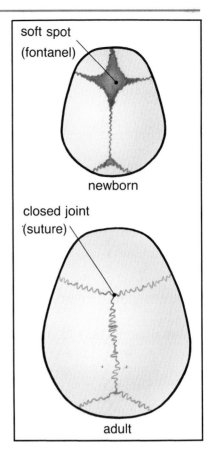

soft spot
(fontanel)

newborn

closed joint
(suture)

adult

Figure 11-4 The bones in the skull are separate at birth. They form strong joints during early childhood.

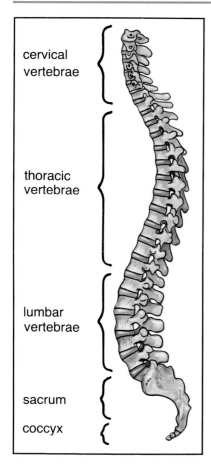

cervical
vertebrae

thoracic
vertebrae

lumbar
vertebrae

sacrum

coccyx

Figure 11-5 The backbone

The five vertebrae of the **sacrum** [*SAY krum*] are fused in the hip area. They are joined to the hip bones on either side. This group of bones—the sacrum and the hip bones—is called the **pelvis.** The sacrum connects the spine to the pelvis. Below the sacrum is the **coccyx** [*KAHK siks*], also called the tailbone. The coccyx has three to five fused vertebrae.

Chest   The bones of the chest form a cage that protects the heart and lungs. This frame expands and contracts as you breathe. Take a breath and notice how your chest expands. Try measuring your chest with a tape measure as you inhale and exhale.

The **sternum,** or breastbone, is a flat bone in the middle and front of the chest. It serves as an anchor for the ribs and for the muscles that help you to breathe. The sternum also protects the heart.

There are twelve pairs of ribs, but they are not all the same. Examine the views of the ribs shown in Figure 11–3. In the back, the ribs connect to the thoracic vertebrae, but in the front their attachments vary. The top seven ribs have cartilage at their ends that connects directly to the sternum. The three pairs of ribs below them are not directly connected to the sternum. These three pairs are connected to cartilage that extends up to the sternum. The bottom two pairs of ribs do not attach to the sternum at all. They are attached only in the back.

The Appendicular Skeleton

The appendages, or limbs, that connect to the axial skeleton make up the **appendicular skeleton** [*ap un DIK yuh lur*]. The 126 bones of the appendicular skeleton include the bones of the hips, legs, and feet plus the bones of the shoulders, arms, and hands. The appendicular skeleton gives the body a wide range of movement.

Pectoral Girdle   On each side of the body a collarbone extends from the top of the sternum to the shoulder blade. Together, the collarbones and the shoulder blades form the **pectoral girdle** [*PEK tur ul*]. The shoulder blade is the large flat bone in the upper part of the back below the shoulder. You can easily feel your collarbones and shoulder blades. The pectoral girdle provides the connecting points for the arms to the axial skeleton.

Arm   Find the bones of the arm and hand in Figure 11-3. You can see that there is only one bone in the upper arm. One end of this bone fits directly into the shoulder blade. The other end meets the two bones of the forearm at the elbow joint. Place one elbow on the desk with the palm facing you. Then use your other hand to feel the bones of your forearm near your wrist. With your palm up, these two bones lie side by side. When you twist your hand over, palm down, the bones criss-cross. Notice how easily this movement occurs. This movement allows the arm and hand to perform many difficult and exact tasks.

Hand The eight small bones of the wrist are angled and arranged in two rows. This group of bones gives the wrist flexibility. The wrist bones connect with five bones in the hand that form the frame of the palm. Each finger has three bones. The thumb, however, has only two bones. All the joints in the fingers and thumb are called knuckles.

The human hand is very special. The joint where the thumb meets the hand allows a wide range of motion. Because of this the tip of the thumb is able to touch the tip of every finger. This enables humans to pick up and hold small objects, such as sewing needles and pencils.

Pelvis The bones of the hip, or pelvis, form a strong ring that balances the weight of the body on the legs. The pelvis also protects most of the abdominal organs, especially the reproductive organs. Although the pelvis contains several bones, they are so tightly fused that they are generally considered as one bone. The hip bones fuse soon after birth.

The structure of the pelvis is different in men and women. Examine Figure 11-6. The female pelvis is broad and shallow, with a large opening that allows a baby to pass through during birth. In contrast, the male pelvis is narrow and deep, with a small opening.

Leg Your thighbones are the biggest, strongest, and heaviest bones in your body. This is because they must support the weight of your upper body while walking, running, or jumping. Each thighbone extends from the pelvis to the knee. Below the knee, two smaller bones share the body's weight. The larger of the two is located on the inside of the leg, while the smaller is on the outside. The larger bone carries most of the weight coming from the thighbone and transfers it to the foot. The smaller bone allows the ankle a wide range of movement.

The kneecap is held in place by tendons from the muscles around it. It protects the knee joint and allows it to bend smoothly. With your leg straight, rest your heel on the floor and relax all your leg muscles. Then gently work the kneecap back and forth with your thumb and forefingers. It should slide around smoothly, with little friction.

Foot The structure of the foot resembles that of the hand, but the foot is stronger and more rigid. Just as in the hand, five bones form a frame for the top of the foot. These bones connect with the bones of the toes. The big toe, like the thumb, has only two bones. The other toes have three bones each, just like the fingers. The large bones of the foot and the smaller bones of the toes absorb the shock of walking.

Joints

The place at which two bones meet is called a **joint.** The construction of a joint varies either to allow the bones at the joint to move, or to prevent movement. Joints are crossed by ligaments

Health **History**
Leonardo da Vinci, the Italian painter who painted the Mona Lisa, was also a scientist. During the fifteenth century, da Vinci drew the first detailed anatomical illustrations.

Figure 11-6 The broader female pelvis can support a developing fetus and allows enough room for childbirth.

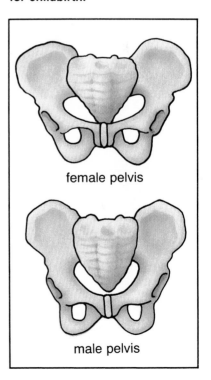

female pelvis

male pelvis

and tendons. **Ligaments** are thick cords of white fibers that bind bones to one another. **Tendons** are bands of white fibers that connect muscles to bones. Both are made of collagen.

There are three kinds of joints: freely movable joints, partially movable joints, and immovable joints. Most of the joints in the body are freely movable joints. There are four kinds of freely movable joints: the hinge joint, the pivot joint, the gliding joint, and the ball-and-socket joint. Examples of each of these types of movable joints are shown in Figure 11-7.

Figure 11-8 illustrates the shoulder, a freely movable joint. The ends of the bones are surrounded by a sac. This sac contains fluid, which acts like oil to lubricate the joint. In addition, a thin layer of cartilage covers the ends of the bones and keeps the bones from rubbing against each other and wearing down. Ligaments surround the sac.

The elbow and the knee joints are examples of **hinge joints,** which swing back and forth like doors on hinges. Where else do you have hinge joints?

The two bones in the forearm meet to form a **pivot joint** at the elbow. In a pivot joint one bone rotates around another. This type of joint lets these bones criss-cross, enabling you to twist a screwdriver or turn a doorknob.

Gliding joints allow bones to slide over one another. The bones in the wrist come together at gliding joints, which permit

Figure 11-7 The six types of joints

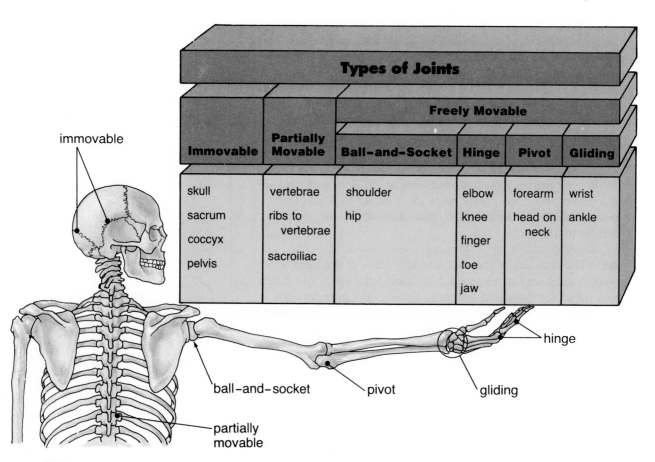

		Types of Joints			
			Freely Movable		
Immovable	**Partially Movable**	**Ball-and-Socket**	**Hinge**	**Pivot**	**Gliding**
skull	vertebrae	shoulder	elbow	forearm	wrist
sacrum	ribs to vertebrae	hip	knee	head on neck	ankle
coccyx	sacroiliac		finger		
pelvis			toe		
			jaw		

immovable

ball-and-socket

partially movable

pivot

gliding

hinge

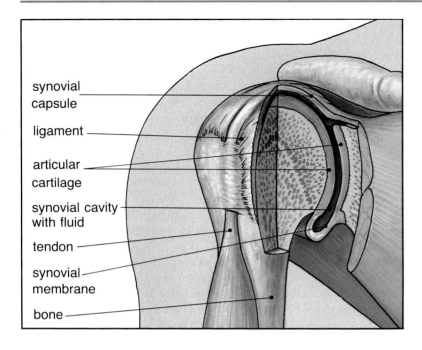

synovial capsule

ligament

articular cartilage

synovial cavity with fluid

tendon

synovial membrane

bone

Figure 11-8 The synovial capsule and articular cartilage protect the bones in a freely movable joint from rubbing on each other.

great overall flexibility. This is also true of the bones in the ankle. A **ball-and-socket joint** is formed when the ball-shaped end of one bone fits into a cup-shaped section of the bone joining it. The shoulder and the hip joints are examples of ball-and-socket joints. Ball-and-socket joints allow movement in almost any direction.

Partially movable and immovable joints are more difficult to notice. The attachment of a rib to the backbone is a partially movable joint. This joint gives strong support but allows the limited movement needed to expand the chest in breathing. The vertebrae also meet at partially movable joints. Look at Figure 11-7. What examples of immovable joints are shown?

Lesson Review

Bones vary in size from the small bones in the ear to the large bones in the legs. Bones meet at joints. Together bones and joints provide a body framework that is strong, durable, and has a wide range of movement. The skeleton also protects vital organs. Joints are classified into three major groupings: freely movable, partially movable, and immovable.

1 Describe the functions of the axial skeleton.

2 How many vertebrae are there?

3 What is the function of the appendicular skeleton?

4 What kind of joints are knuckles?

5 Which bones absorb the shock of walking?

6 Name four kinds of freely movable joints.

Bone and Joint Problems

Because of their function, bones and joints are under constant stress. Sometimes, however, they are pushed beyond their capability. This can happen from overuse, improper use, or from the impact of some outside force. Sports and car accidents are two leading causes of joint and bone injuries in young people.

Fractures

A break in a bone is a **fracture.** The break may be partial or complete. Figure 11-9 illustrates the three main types of fractures. **Greenstick fractures** are partial fractures common in children. Because children's bones are largely cartilage, they are flexible and bend a great deal like green tree twigs. They tend to crack and only break partially.

Simple fractures occur when the bone breaks into two pieces, but the fractured ends do not pierce the skin. In more serious **compound fractures,** the bone ends break through the skin surface. In compound fractures the bone ends are exposed to germs from outside the body, so bone infection is a serious concern.

When a break first occurs, the tissues around the break swell. Then blood rushes to the fracture. A sticky material forms over the break, which helps glue the bones back together. Then the periosteum lays calcium over the break. Gradually, with living cells and minerals, the bone cements itself together. If the broken bone heals properly, the healed portion is actually stronger than the original bone because of the many layers of deposited minerals. If that bone is broken again, it is unlikely it will fracture at the old break.

Bones often need medical aid to heal well. When a complete break occurs, a doctor places the bone ends back into their normal position and applies a cast or brace to hold them in place during healing. If the bone is crushed or fractured into pieces, a steel pin may be surgically inserted into the bone, holding the bone in place.

Health History

During the Middle Ages in Europe, doctors were not allowed to dissect human bodies. To study anatomy, some doctors stole skeletons from gallows and robbed graves.

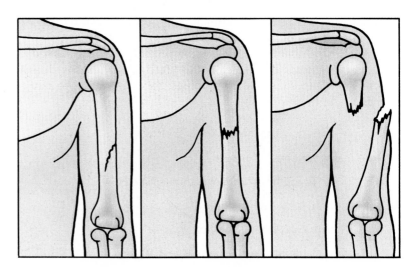

Figure 11-9 The three types of bone fractures are *(left)* greenstick, *(center)* simple, and *(right)* compound.

Doctors have found that running electricity or radio waves through a fractured bone may quicken the healing process. The patient wears a small power pack. Electrical treatment may aid the healing of a fracture that fails to heal by itself.

Injured joints

The most common joint injury is a sprain. A **sprain** occurs when the ligaments and tendons around a joint are stretched. In a severe sprain, these tissues may be torn. A sprain is often accompanied by painful swelling of the joint. The blood vessels and muscles around the joint may also be injured. A sprain results when the joint is moved too far, often from a sudden, unexpected twist or from too much pressure. A twisted ankle is a common example of a sprain. Sprains usually heal by themselves, but slowly. All sprains should be examined by a doctor since some injuries that feel like sprains are actually fractures.

Another type of joint injury is a dislocation. In a **dislocation,** the ends of the bone are pulled out of the joint. The ligaments connected to the joint are severely stretched or torn. Dislocation of the shoulder joint is a common injury. The dislocated bone ends must be placed back into position and held in place with a bandage or cast until the tissues heal.

The cartilage in joints is often damaged. Cartilage can be torn if the joint receives a strong blow. The resulting swelling may not allow free movement in the joint. **Torn cartilage** is a serious condition, usually requiring surgical removal of all or part of the damaged cartilage. Cartilage tears are all too common in

 ## Health *Careers*

If you love playing on a team, you may have dreamed about becoming a coach. A coach is a highly trained man or woman who teaches and directs athletes in individual or group sports. Coaches teach techniques, conduct practice sessions, determine the strategies that will be used, and decide who will play. A coach may work in public and private elementary and secondary schools, colleges and universities, or professionally.

Most coaches begin their career by completing a four-year college degree in health and physical education. A coach then becomes certified as a teacher and becomes a school coach at the elementary or secondary level. Coaches usually teach health and physical education as well as other subjects.

School coaches must have a strong desire to work with young people and possess patience and understanding in assisting students with their problems. Coaches must display strong leadership skills and have the ability to train and motivate all students to develop and perform physically at their maximum potential.

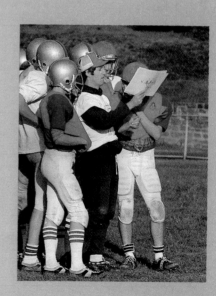

1 What training is necessary to become a coach?
2 Name four types of institutions that hire coaches.

the knees, particularly among football players. Injury occurs when a player's knee is hit while the player's foot is firmly planted on the ground.

Sometimes an injury to the spine causes a ruptured disc. In a **ruptured disc,** the cartilage disc between two vertebrae breaks and the pad inside slips out. The vertebrae or pad may then press on a nerve. This pressure can cause pain and numbness. The discs in the lower back are the most likely to rupture.

Ruptured discs are first treated with bed rest. Sometimes no further treatment is needed. At other times body braces or weights may be used to separate the vertebrae. If disc damage is severe, surgery may be necessary.

Although discs can rupture from an unexpected injury or accident, some disc damage may be preventable. Discs are often damaged as a result of heavy lifting. Disc damage can often be prevented by using proper lifting techniques. Use your legs when lifting. Your leg muscles are the strongest muscles in your body. Practice using the techniques shown in Figure 11–11 to avoid straining your back.

Not all joint problems are caused by an injury. Bursitis is a joint problem that may not be directly related to an injury. **Bursitis** [*bur SY tis*] is the painful inflammation of small sacs

Figure 11-10 More than 55 percent of all sports injuries occur in the four activities shown here.

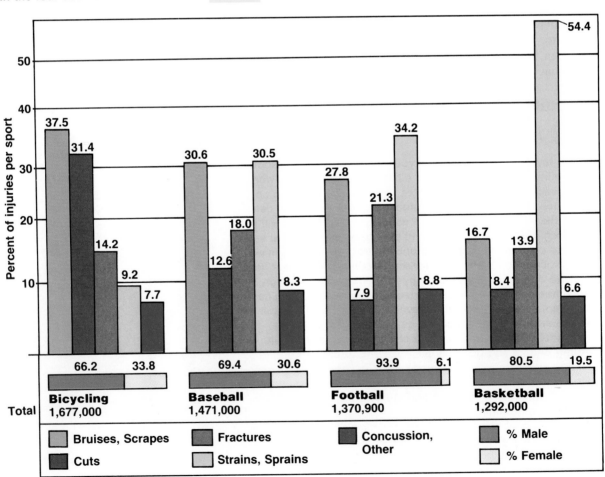

Figure 11-11 When lifting a heavy object, squat as in the left-hand photo, and let your leg muscles do the work. Bending over as in the right-hand photo may injure your back.

located near joints. These sacs, called bursae, lie between tendons or between tendons and bones. Without these sacs, the tendons would rub against each other. After an injury or infection, or because of overuse, the bursae sometimes become inflamed. Bursitis is very common in the shoulder and the knee. Treatment for mild cases includes resting that part of the body, heat, and painkillers. Injections of medicine, or surgery, are sometimes used in more serious cases.

Foot Problems

Every day your feet take tremendous punishment. They must support the weight of your entire body when you stand. In addition, your feet absorb the shock of running and jumping. When you run, your feet hit the ground with enormous force. Obviously, the foot's structure can usually handle this workload, but sometimes a serious problem occurs.

If you stand barefoot on the floor, you may see that part of the middle section of your foot does not touch the floor. This section is called the **arch.** The arch results from the arrangement of bones in your foot and the tension with which the bones are held together by muscles and ligaments. This structure makes your foot act like a spring. When your foot hits the ground, the arch flattens slightly and bounces back. This spring action absorbs shock and uses the energy of the impact to bounce you onto your next step.

Sometimes the arch falls, or becomes flattened. This means the whole bottom part of the foot touches the ground. This throws the body's weight off center. This makes the calf and ankle muscles work harder to keep balance. Pain in the arch, ankle, and calf muscles are often signs of fallen arches. Women who wear high-heeled shoes may develop fallen arches. Wearing low-heeled shoes is a good preventive measure. Shoes with small cushions, called arch supports, can help relieve the pain.

Another painful foot problem is a bunion. A **bunion** is a hard swelling where the big toe joins the foot. Bunions may be caused by arthritis or uneven balance in the foot and leg muscles. They

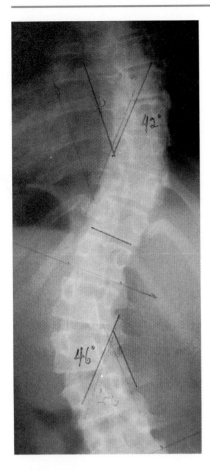

Figure 11-12 Scoliosis can be treated if detected early. Be sure you are tested regularly through your teenage years.

may also be caused by wearing tight shoes that force the toes together. The joint affected in the big toe is a hinge joint which allows the toe to move up and down. Tight shoes squeeze the toes and press this joint from the side. In the early stages of bunion development, wider shoes may help, but surgery may be necessary in advanced cases.

Scoliosis

A lateral, or side-to-side, curvature of the spine is a condition called **scoliosis** [*skoh lee OH sis*]. Abnormal lateral curvature may develop during childhood and adolescence. If not treated early, scoliosis may cause serious deformity later in life.

Teenagers should have regular checkups for scoliosis. The tests are painless and effective. Figure 11–12 shows an x-ray of a person with scoliosis. Other signs of scoliosis are uneven shoulder level, uneven hip level, and an uneven waistline.

Scoliosis is treated with braces that keep the spine from curving further. Electrical stimulation is sometimes used to treat this problem while the person sleeps. Surgery may be required in some instances.

Arthritis

More than a hundred different diseases are given the name **arthritis.** They are characterized by swelling and puffiness of tissues in and around the joints. These diseases affect people of all ages. With some forms of arthritis, the joints may become stiff and may be permanently damaged by the swelling of the joint tissues.

Doctors do not know what causes many types of arthritis. Rest, warmth, diet, and aspirin or similar medications ease some of the pain and swelling. Surgery to replace ball-and-socket joints may relieve stiffness. However, there is no general cure for arthritis.

Lesson Review

Fractures, sprains, and dislocations are the most common injuries of the bones and joints. There are no known cures for some common disorders of the bones and joints, but there are effective treatments and many disorders can be prevented. Learning to use bones and joints in ways that prevent sprains and dislocations is important. To avoid problems, wear shoes that fit properly, use correct lifting techniques, and keep fit with a balanced diet and exercise.

1 What is a greenstick fracture?

2 What is bursitis?

3 What type of treatment can be used to heal fractures that fail to heal by themselves?

4 List four types of treatment that help ease the pain and swelling of arthritis.

Muscles

While bones give the body structure and support, they cannot move by themselves. Muscles produce movement. Walking, lifting, talking, and breathing are all accomplished by muscles. The three main functions of muscles are movement, maintenance of posture, and production of body heat. In addition, muscles help give our body its shape.

Types of Muscles

There are three different types of muscle tissue found in the human body: skeletal muscle, smooth muscle, and cardiac muscle. The **skeletal muscles** are connected to bones. They are also called voluntary because they are under your conscious control. This means that you can make these muscles work when you want them to. The major skeletal muscles of the body are shown on Plates Two and Three.

Skeletal muscle is also called **striated muscle** [*STRY ay tid*] because it looks striped under a microscope, as you can see in Figure 11–13. The stripes are actually individual muscle cells, called muscle fibers. Muscle fibers vary from a fraction of an inch to 16 inches in length. They always occur in groups called bundles.

Unlike skeletal muscle, **smooth muscle** is not consciously controlled. For this reason it is called involuntary. Smooth muscle surrounds many internal organs. Layers of smooth muscle line the digestive tract and automatically push food along during digestion. The walls of blood vessels also contain smooth muscle. This muscle helps control blood pressure. **Cardiac muscle** is a kind of involuntary muscle found only in the heart. Cardiac muscle must work nonstop for a lifetime. At rest, the heart generally beats about 60 to 70 times a minute. Try to imitate the heart by opening and closing your hand once a second for a minute. How quickly does your hand get tired?

Health Bulletin

Muscle fibers are thinner than human hair, and can support up to 1000 times their own weight. There are 6 trillion of them in the body.

Figure 11-13 The three types of muscle tissues are *(left)* skeletal or striated, *(center)* smooth, and *(right)* cardiac.

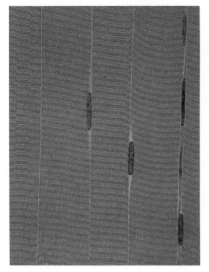
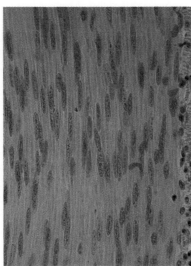
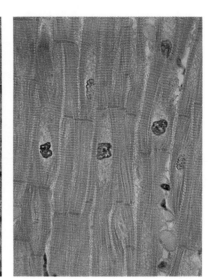

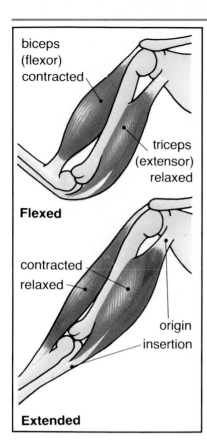

biceps
(flexor)
contracted

triceps
(extensor)
relaxed

Flexed

contracted

relaxed

origin

insertion

Extended

Figure 11-14 A muscle pulls the bone of insertion by contracting. When one muscle contracts, the opposing muscle relaxes.

Muscle Contraction

Skeletal muscles contract, or shorten, to move bones. They can do this because their cells, the muscle fibers, contract. The greater the number of fibers contracting, the stronger the muscle pulls. For example, raise your hand in the air. Now, using the same hand, raise this book in the air. More muscle cells had to contract to lift the book than to lift your arm.

All skeletal movement is the result of muscle pulling bone. One muscle pulls to bend a joint. To straighten the joint again, another muscle must pull the bone back to its original position. Muscles pair up in this manner to create a range of movement. Muscles that bend joints are called **flexors.** They flex, or bend, the joint. Muscles that extend, or straighten, joints are **extensors.** Figure 11–14 shows a familiar muscle pair. The biceps muscle is a flexor. It bends the forearm. The triceps muscle is an extensor. It pulls the forearm straight again. Hold your arm straight out in front of you with your palm up. Bring your hand up toward your shoulder. Watch or feel the biceps bulge. The biceps has contracted and is firm. Feel the triceps. It is loose and relaxed. Now straighten your arm. Feel the biceps relax as the triceps works. In muscle pairs, when one muscle contracts the other relaxes.

At both ends of each muscle are tendons. Tendons attach muscles to bones. One end of a muscle is anchored to a bone to form a stationary attachment called the **origin.** The bone of origin is only an anchor point. It is not moved by the muscle action. At the other end of the muscle, another tendon is connected to the bone the muscle moves. The point at which the muscle is attached to the movable bone is called the **insertion.** Look again at Figure 11–14. Find the points of origin and insertion for the biceps-triceps muscle pair.

Muscles do not usually lie directly on the bone they move. For example, most of the muscles that move the lower leg are found in the thigh; those that move the head are in the neck. Contract your biceps again. This muscle is in your upper arm, but it moves the bones of your lower arm. Can you locate the muscles that move your upper arm?

Figure 11–15 shows the major muscle pairs. What is the muscle that straightens your back? Can you locate it in your body? This muscle works with the abdominal muscles to maintain posture. Your abdominal muscles flex the front of your ribs to your pelvis. The muscle that straightens your back pulls the back of your ribs to the back of your pelvis.

Fuel for Muscles

In order to work, your muscles break down glucose, a form of sugar carried in the blood. Muscles are said to "burn" glucose for energy. This burning requires oxygen, just as in a real fire. When your muscles use glucose, energy becomes available for muscle contraction.

Whenever muscles contract, only part of the energy released is used for contraction. The rest is released as heat, which keeps the body warm. Several waste products are also formed. This is like

Your fingers have no muscles at all—only tendons from muscles in the hand and the forearm.

Major Muscle Pairs

Muscle	Origin	Insertion	Action	Function
Sternocleido-mastoid	Clavicle and top of sternum	Side of cranium	Flexor	Pulls head to shoulder; together pull head to chest
Splenius	Upper vertebrae	Back of cranium	Extensor	Pulls head up and to the side; together raise the head
Rectus abdominis	Front of pelvis	Front of ribs	Flexor	Pulls ribs to pelvis; important for posture
Erector spinae	Lower vertebrae and top of pelvis	Back of ribs and thoracic vertebrae	Extensor	Straightens back
Trapezius	Back of cranium and upper vertebrae	Clavicle and scapula	Flexor	Raises shoulder
Serratus anterior	Side of ribs	Scapula	Extensor	Pulls shoulder down
Biceps	Side of scapula	Upper radius	Flexor	Flexes forearm
Triceps	Side of scapula and back of humerus	Upper ulna	Extensor	Straightens forearm
Flexor carpi	Lower humerus	Metacarpals	Flexors	Close hand and fingers
Extensor carpi	Lower humerus	Metacarpals	Extensors	Open hand and fingers
Hamstring	Pelvis and upper femur	Upper tibia and fibula	Flexor	Pulls lower leg back
Quadriceps femoris	Femur and top of pelvis	Upper front of tibia	Extensor	Straightens lower leg
Tibialis anterior	Upper side of tibia	Metatarsal	Flexor	Raises foot
Gastrocnemius	Lower back of femur	Heel bone	Extensor	Points foot down

burning wood. When wood burns, heat and light are produced and gases and ash are left over. The waste products from the breakdown of glucose are carbon dioxide and water. These wastes are removed from muscle cells and carried in the blood until they can be removed from the body. Carbon dioxide and water vapor are exhaled by the lungs. Water also leaves the body as urine.

The amount of glucose used varies according to your activity. When you are sitting at your desk, your muscles use little glucose. When you exercise vigorously, your muscles demand a lot

Figure 11-15 Find some of these muscles in your body. Can you trace them from origin to insertion, and identify their actions?

of energy and use a great deal more glucose. You breathe more deeply and more rapidly during exercise. This supplies more oxygen to break down glucose. It also helps to get rid of the carbon dioxide produced by the muscular activity.

Sometimes during exhausting exercise, your blood cannot supply enough oxygen to burn all the glucose your muscles need. Your muscles then break down a form of stored glucose without using oxygen. This produces **lactic acid,** another waste product. A build-up of lactic acid may cause your muscles to ache and feel tired. You may have noticed that after vigorous exercise, you continue breathing deeply for a while. The additional oxygen from this breathing helps convert the lactic acid back into stored glucose.

Posture and Muscle Tone

With good posture, the parts of your body are in balance with one another. Figure 11–16 shows proper posture. When you stand, your neck, shoulders, lower back, and pelvis and hip joints should be in a straight line. When you sit, your hips and the back of your thighs should support your weight and your feet should be flat on the floor. The back of the chair should support your lower back. Poor posture makes the body's muscles work harder because the body is out of balance. Bones, ligaments, and joints have to bear a greater load over time. This can cause pain in the lower back area.

Good posture depends on muscle tone. **Muscle tone** is the slight but constant contraction maintained by all muscles. Only a few muscle fibers in any one muscle contract at a time. The fibers alternate contracting and relaxing. One group contracts while the others relax. Muscle tone also keeps the internal organs in place. Muscle tone of the abdominal muscles helps support body weight. Weak abdominal muscles place additional strain on the lower back vertebrae, increasing the likelihood of lower back pain and disc rupture. Exercise and stretching help keep muscles in tone.

Muscle Injuries and Disorders

Muscle injuries are common. You have probably overworked or overstretched your muscles at times. Although muscles can suffer damage, they usually heal themselves.

A common muscular problem is a cramp. A **cramp** is a prolonged muscle contraction causing pain. Muscles may cramp when overworked. Massaging and gently stretching against the pull of the muscle may help relieve the cramp.

Muscle strain, or a pulled muscle, may result from severely overworking the muscle. Lifting too much weight can cause muscle strain. Do not confuse a strain, which is a muscle injury, with a sprain, which is an injury of the ligaments and tendons in a joint. Usually no permanent damage results from a strain, although the muscle may continue to be sore for some time. Strains commonly occur to large muscles, such as the thigh and calf muscles. Ice packs will relieve some of the pain of muscle strains and

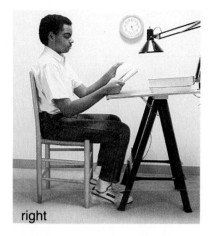

right

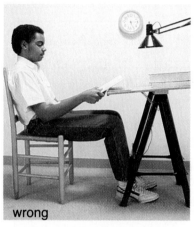

wrong

Figure 11-16 Strong abdominal muscles provide good posture, by keeping the back straight.

Health Bulletin

Humans have 30 facial muscles—more than any other animal. Smiling alone uses 17 muscles.

keep swelling down. After 48 hours heat may be applied. Allowing the muscle to rest aids in healing.

A more serious injury is a torn muscle. A **torn muscle** is a rip of the muscle fiber. It can result from heavy lifting or a sudden force or pull. Sometimes tendons rupture or are pulled loose from the bone. Treatment for torn muscles is similar to that for muscle strain. Ice, then heat and rest, may relieve some of the discomfort. Since this is a severe injury, it may take a long time for the muscle to repair itself.

Tendons may also be damaged by overwork or injury. The condition in which a tendon becomes irritated and swollen is called **tendonitis** [*ten duh NY tis*]. Tennis elbow, which produces a distinctive pain in the area of the elbow, is one example of this injury. Tendonitis can be a troublesome condition since it may recur. It also heals slowly. Rest seems to be the only cure.

A **hernia** [*HUR nee uh*] occurs when a portion of the intestine pushes itself through the layer of skeletal muscle in the abdomen or groin. Hernias are most frequent in naturally-occurring weak spots in this layer of muscle. Hernias usually occur when a person lifts too much weight, but they can happen when a person coughs or sneezes violently. People who have little strength and muscle tone most often develop hernias. With the aid of a support, the intestine may slip back into place, allowing the muscle to heal by itself. However, surgical correction of the condition is often necessary.

The causes of some muscular diseases are unknown. One such disease is **muscular dystrophy** [*MUHS kyuh lur DIS truh fee*], a hereditary disease that slowly destroys muscle fibers. Its victims gradually lose control of their muscles until they are unable to move. Death occurs from paralysis of the muscles that control breathing or from failure of the cardiac muscle. There is no known cure for this disease.

Figure 11-17 Ice packs applied during the first 48 hours decrease swelling in a muscle strain or tear.

Lesson Review

Muscles help bodies move, maintain posture, and produce heat. People can voluntarily control some muscles. Other muscles work involuntarily. Skeletal muscles work in pairs, contracting to move bones. A body sugar called glucose supplies the fuel for muscles to contract. Exercise is important to keep muscles in tone. Muscle tone contributes to good posture and helps prevent muscle injuries such as cramps, strains, and torn muscles.

1 What are the voluntary muscles called?

2 Describe the cardiac muscle.

3 What are flexors?

4 Name three common muscle injuries.

5 What is a hernia?

Chapter Review

Vocabulary

appendicular skeleton	gliding joint	pivot joint
arch	greenstick fracture	red bone marrow
arthritis	Haversian system	ruptured disc
axial skeleton	hernia	sacrum
ball-and-socket joint	hinge joint	scoliosis
bunion	insertion	shaft
bursitis	joint	simple fracture
cardiac muscle	lactic acid	sinus
cartilage	ligament	skeletal muscle
cervical vertebra	long bone	smooth muscle
coccyx	lumbar vertebra	spongy bone
collagen	muscle strain	sprain
compact bone	muscle tone	sternum
compound fracture	muscular dystrophy	striated muscle
cramp	origin	tendon
cranium	ossification	tendonitis
dislocation	osteoporosis	thoracic vertebra
extensor	pectoral girdle	torn cartilage
flexor	pelvis	torn muscle
fracture	periosteum	vertebra

Using Vocabulary

Questions 1–10. On a separate sheet of paper, write the name of the muscle, joint, or bone disorder described in each clue.

1 disease characterized by swelling and puffiness of tissues in and around joints

2 side-to-side curvature of the spine

3 hereditary disease that destroys muscle fiber

4 inflammation of the sacs between tendons or between tendons and bones

5 disorder involving the loss of calcium from bone

6 condition that occurs when the intestine pushes itself through the muscle layer in the abdomen or groin

7 hard swelling where the big toe joins the foot

8 prolonged muscle contraction causing pain

9 disorder in which a bone is pulled out of its joint

10 break in a bone

Interpreting Ideas

1 What are the functions of the bones in the human skeleton?

2 Identify and describe the two main groups of bones of the human skeleton.

3 Why do babies very rarely break a bone? How does the content of bone change with age?

4 Identify and describe the classifications of fractures.

5 What is the difference between a ligament and a tendon?

6 Compare the function and location of red bone marrow and yellow bone marrow.

7 Identify and list the function of the three types of human muscle tissue. Classify each as voluntary muscle or involuntary muscle.

8 What is the relationship between exercise and bone strength?

9 Why is it important to have good posture?

10 Identify the three major types of joints found in the human body. Give an example of each.

11 What happens when your body is not able to supply enough oxygen to break down the glucose needed during vigorous exercise?

12 Describe what happens when a sprain occurs. Why should a sprain be examined by a doctor?

13 How is electrical treatment being used to heal fractures?

14 What are the three functions of muscles?

15 What is the source of energy for muscle contraction? What are the waste products that result from this process? How are they removed?

16 What treatments are used to heal ruptured discs? How may disc damage be prevented?

17 Compare the causes and treatment of muscle strain and a torn muscle.

18 Explain how skeletal muscles work in pairs. Cite an example of a muscle pair.

19 Why is it important to protect a baby's head?

20 What is the function of each of the following bones or groups of bones: sternum, kneecap, cranium, spinal column?

Applying Concepts

1 If humans are supposed to have just over 200 bones, how is it possible that a newborn baby has over 300 bones? How would you explain how an adult could have an extra bone in the arch of the foot?

2 Why is the cranium referred to as the brain's "crash helmet"?

3 At fourteen, Jim ate a diet that consisted mainly of fast foods, starches, and sweets. To ensure healthy bone formation, what kind of diet do you think Jim should have?

4 What is unique about the cells that make up muscle tissue?

5 How can you explain the soft spot on a baby's head? Why might a baby's head be somewhat misshapen just after birth?

6 Most ossification has been completed by age 20 in humans. Why, then, is it important to continue to have a diet rich in calcium after age 20? What effect does exercise have on bone health once ossification is complete?

7 Many of your bones are hollow. What functions does this quality serve?

8 Recently Karen's family had noticed that she carried one of her shoulders lower than the other. Karen realized her hips had become uneven. In a routine exam in gym class, the school nurse discovered the problem. What do you suspect the diagnosis was?

9 What kinds of problems might result from poor muscle tone?

Projects

1 In the stories of the Trojan War, Achilles was the greatest warrior of the Greek army. According to one tale, he was invulnerable except for a certain tendon in his body. Find out the location of this tendon and how Achilles' tendon became vulnerable. Then find your own Achilles tendon, one of the largest tendons in your body. It should feel like a thick, stiff rope.

2 The opposable thumb makes it possible to pick up and hold small objects. Only people, apes, and some monkeys can do this. To illustrate the importance of the opposable thumb, try the following activity. Fold both thumbs under and ask a classmate to tape them to your palms. Then try to tie your shoelaces, write, or pick up a book and turn its pages.

Active sports, such as swimming, are excellent activities for both the circulatory and respiratory systems.

CHAPTER TWELVE

CIRCULATION
& Respiration

Whether you are running or swimming toward the finish
line, your body responds to its need to take in oxygen and
get rid of other gases. When you exercise, your heart beats faster.
Your breathing rate speeds up. As your heart rate increases, it
speeds the flow of blood to your muscles and other tissues. The
blood ensures that these tissues get enough nutrients and
oxygen. At the same time, the blood picks up wastes from
your cells and carries them to the kidneys, the lungs,
and the other organs of excretion. The blood also helps
keep your body temperature constant. Thus your circulatory
and respiratory systems work together to help you enjoy
an active life.

Objectives

- Trace the pathway of blood through
  the four chambers of the heart.

- List the functions of pulmonary circulation
  and systemic circulation.

- Describe how blood clots.

- Name the major functions of red and white
  blood cells.

- Name two important functions of the
  lymphatic system.

- List the major parts of the upper and
  lower respiratory tract.

- Name two gases that are exchanged
  between air sacs and capillaries.

- List disorders or diseases that affect the
  circulatory and respiratory systems.

- Identify behaviors that help maintain
  healthy circulatory and respiratory systems.

The Circulatory System

In ancient times, it was thought that the heart was the seat of all emotions. People believed that the heart controlled life's fortunes and determined whether a person fell in love. Today the heart is still used as a symbol of love. However, now scientists know that the heart is one of the most powerful organs in the body. Your heart and branching network of large and small blood vessels make up your **circulatory system.** It is also called your cardiovascular system. A detailed illustration of the circulatory system can be seen on Plate Six. Your circulatory system carries life-sustaining nutrients to all your cells. At the same time, it picks up and removes wastes.

The Structure of the Heart

The muscular pump that lies in the center of your upper chest cavity between your lungs is your **heart.** It is about the size of your clenched fist. It sends blood through the blood vessels of your body by beating constantly, about 60 to 80 times every minute when you are at rest.

The heart is a double pump. The right side of the heart receives oxygen-poor blood from the body and pumps it to your lungs. The left side of the heart receives oxygen-rich blood from the lungs and pumps it to your body.

An inner wall of muscles separates your heart into a right and a left side. Normally, this wall has no openings. As you can see in Figure 12-1, the wall prevents the blood on each side of the heart from mixing.

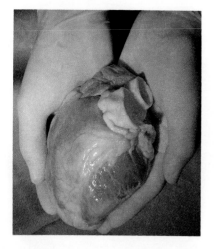

Figure 12-1   The heart *(above)* **is about the size of a large clenched fist. Its internal structure is shown at right.**

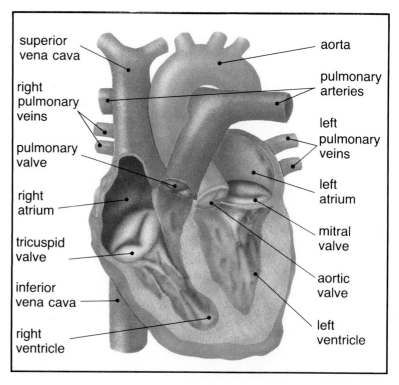

superior
vena cava

right
pulmonary
veins

pulmonary
valve

right
atrium

tricuspid
valve

inferior
vena cava

right
ventricle

aorta

pulmonary
arteries

left
pulmonary
veins

left
atrium

mitral
valve

aortic
valve

left
ventricle

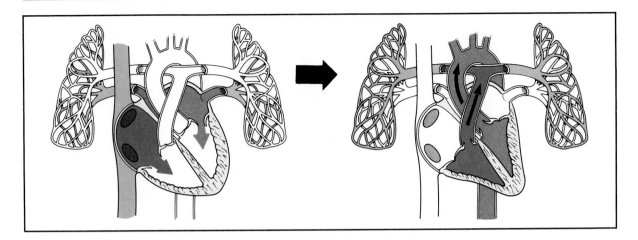

Each side of your heart is further divided into two chambers, one on top of the other. The two chambers are connected by a one-way valve. An upper chamber in the heart is known as an **atrium** [*AY tree um*]. A lower chamber in the heart is called a **ventricle** [*VEN trih kul*]. On the right side of the heart, the atrium receives oxygen-poor blood from the body. This blood is let through the valve to the lower chamber, the right ventricle. The right ventricle pumps the oxygen-poor blood to the lungs.

Like the right side of the heart, the left side of the heart is divided into an atrium on top and a ventricle beneath. The left atrium is a little larger than the right atrium. Its job is to receive oxygen-rich blood from the lungs. The blood then passes through the valve to the left ventricle. The wall of the left ventricle is thicker and more muscular than that of the right ventricle. The left ventricle is larger than the right ventricle because it pumps the oxygen-rich blood to the body.

Figure 12-2 shows the flow of blood through the chambers of the heart. As you can see, both atria pump at the same time and both ventricles pump at the same time. The sound of the heartbeat is actually the alternating closing of the valves in the atria and ventricles.

Figure 12-2 Atria pump blood into the ventricles *(left)*. Ventricles pump blood to the lungs and the body *(right)*.

The Circulatory Vessels

Your circulatory system is a closed system. This means that, except when a part of the system is injured or opened, all of the blood remains trapped in the system. Your blood follows the same paths over and over again throughout your body.

There are five kinds of blood vessels. They are the arteries, veins, arterioles, capillaries, and venules. The largest blood vessels are arteries and veins. **Arteries** are blood vessels that carry blood away from your heart. Arteries have thick muscular walls. The **aorta** [*ay AWR tuh*] is the largest artery. Oxygen-rich blood from the left ventricle passes through the aorta to the rest of the body through a branching system of increasingly smaller arteries. **Veins** are blood vessels that carry blood to your heart. Veins have thinner walls than arteries. As shown in Figure 12-3, veins have valves that keep the blood from backing up.

Figure 12-3 Blood flowing through a vein towards the heart opens the valve *(left)*. When blood backs up in the vein, the valve closes *(right)*.

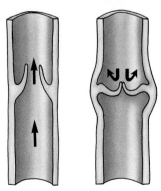

Figure 12-4   Cross-section of an arteriole *(right)* **and a venule** *(left).* **The layers of muscle and elastic tissue are much thicker in the arteriole.**

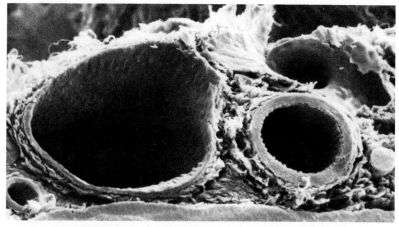

Photo above from *Tissues and Organs: A Text-Atlas of Scanning Electron Microscopy* by Richard G. Kessel & Randy H. Kardon, W.H. Freeman and Co. ©1979.

Figure 12-5   The circulatory system is traditionally illustrated with red arteries and blue veins. The blood in veins is actually a dull blue-red.

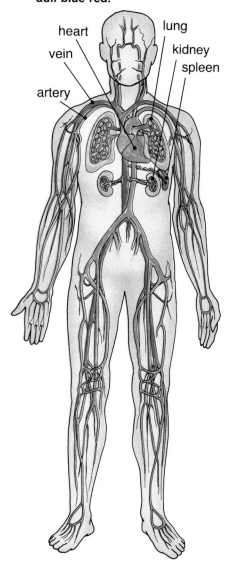

heart
lung
vein
kidney
spleen
artery

The arteries branch into smaller blood vessels that are called **arterioles** [*ahr TEER ee ohlz*]. These small tubes have muscular walls. The muscles allow the arterioles to expand and contract to control the flow of blood into the capillaries.

The smallest blood vessels are the capillaries. **Capillaries** are microscopic blood vessels with extremely thin walls. Gases and nutrients can pass in or out of the circulatory system through these thin walls. Capillaries branch out from the arterioles and they connect with tiny veins. The blood enters the capillaries from the arterioles. Then materials are exchanged between the blood in the capillaries and surrounding cells.

After the materials have been exchanged, the blood flows from the capillaries into venules. **Venules** [*VEN yoolz*] are small vessels that lead from capillaries to veins. In the venules, the blood begins its journey back to the heart. The venules connect with increasingly larger veins.

Pulmonary Circulation

From your heart, blood travels through one of two subsystems of the circulatory system. In one of the subsystems, blood passes to the lungs, where it gives off carbon dioxide and takes the oxygen your cells need to release energy. In the other subsystem, blood travels through your body, carrying oxygen to the cells and picking up waste materials, including carbon dioxide.

The pathway of blood from the heart through the lungs is called **pulmonary circulation.** In this pathway, blood from the right ventricle travels through the pulmonary arteries to a network of blood vessels in your lungs. The vessels become thinner and thinner as they travel past the tiny air compartments of your lungs. The thin walls of the vessels and air sacs allow carbon dioxide to pass out of the vessels and oxygen to pass in. The vessels leading from the lungs widen as they near the heart. Blood flows from the lungs into the left atrium. In the pulmonary circulation, blood in the arteries is oxygen-poor. Blood in the pulmonary veins is oxygen-rich. Remember that arteries carry blood away from the heart, while veins carry blood to the heart.

Systemic Circulation

The subsystem that moves oxygen-rich blood to all parts of the body other than the lungs is called the **systemic circulation.** In the systemic circulation, arteries carry oxygen-rich blood and veins carry oxygen-poor blood. Three of the most important blood pathways within this system carry blood to and from the walls of the heart, the kidneys, and the liver.

Coronary Circulation   Because the muscles of the heart work constantly, they need a constant supply of oxygen and nutrients. Contrary to what you might expect, the blood passing through the chambers of your heart does not nourish the heart muscle. Instead, **coronary arteries** are the blood vessels that deliver nutrients and oxygen to the heart muscle. These arteries are the first branches coming from the aorta. They divide into many smaller branches that end in capillaries. After passing through the capillaries, blood returns to the right atrium of the heart through a system of veins.

Renal Circulation   The circulation of blood to and from the kidneys is especially important because the kidneys help to remove wastes from the blood. One fifth of the blood that leaves the heart travels to the kidneys. **Renal arteries** bring blood to the kidneys from the aorta. Veins from the kidneys empty into a large, central vein, which returns the blood to the heart.

Portal Circulation   As you learned in Chapter 10, blood from the stomach, spleen, pancreas, gallbladder, and intestines is full of many nutrients and materials that have entered the body. Substances that might harm the body must be removed before this blood can be passed to the heart for recirculation. This blood is moved to the liver for cleansing. The vessel that carries blood to the liver for cleansing is the **portal vein.** The liver's tissues are fed by blood from arteries.

The liver removes toxic substances from the blood before returning it to the heart. The blood then flows into the veins that return it to the heart. You can see these veins on Plate Six.

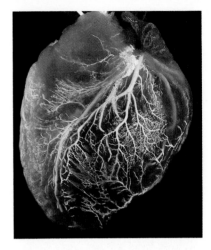

Figure 12-6   The coronary arteries branch directly from the aorta, supplying the heart with highly oxygenated blood.

Health Bulletin

Five percent of the blood that leaves the left ventricle goes through the coronary arteries to feed the heart muscle. Except for the brain, no other organ requires as much blood.

Lesson Review

Blood carries nutrients and other materials to and from the cells of the body. The heart powers the system. When the heart is pumping efficiently, other major organs of the body receive adequate blood supplies.

1 List the four chambers of the heart.

2 List the two largest kinds of blood vessels and explain their functions.

3 What is *pulmonary circulation?*

4 What vessels carry blood to the kidneys?

Regulating Circulation

In a system as complex as the circulatory system, it is important that all of the organs and blood vessels work together smoothly. This involves regulating the rate of the heartbeat and the force of the blood as it flows through the vessels.

Heartbeat and the Pacemaker

Your nervous system regulates your heart's pumping rate. At the back of the right atrium is a control center called the pacemaker. The **pacemaker** is a small mass of nerve and muscle cells that starts each heartbeat. This tissue releases nervous impulses that flow swiftly along nerve fibers in the heart muscle. The impulses move downward and across to the left atrium. The impulses trigger another mass of nerve tissue between the ventricles, which carries impulses to the outer walls of the ventricles. This system allows the atria to contract first. Then the ventricles contract, forcing blood into the arteries.

When you are at rest, the impulses signal the heart to contract at a slow pace. But when you are exercising, your muscle cells send impulses to the brain. These impulses tell the brain that the body needs more oxygen and nutrients. The brain sends this message to the heart by way of the pacemaker. The heartbeat quickens, thus moving the blood through the body more rapidly. In this way the pacemaker, which automatically keeps the heart beating, speeds up or slows down according to the body's needs.

Blood Pressure

The force with which blood pushes against the vessel walls as it travels the circulatory system is called **blood pressure.** If the force is too great, too much pressure could be put on the system. The system could be damaged.

Having your blood pressure checked is a routine part of a physical checkup. The pressure of the blood in an artery is measured as the amount of pressure needed to raise a column of mercury. Blood pressure is recorded in millimeters of mercury (Hg).

Two kinds of blood pressure readings are taken. One is called systolic pressure and the other one is called diastolic pressure. **Systolic pressure** [*sis TAHL ik*] is the force of the blood pushing against the walls of the arteries when the ventricles of the heart contract. This is normally about 110 to 120 millimeters of Hg in young adults. **Diastolic pressure** [*dy uh STAHL ik*] is the force of the blood between beats, when the ventricles of the heart relax. This is normally about 70 to 80 millimeters of Hg in young adults. Blood pressure is recorded with the systolic reading written over the diastolic reading. Thus a blood pressure between 110/70 and 120/80 is considered normal for young people, although some healthy people have lower blood pressures.

Your blood pressure varies from place to place in your circulatory system. Your blood pressure also changes during the day, as your level of activity changes.

Health Bulletin

An adult's heart at rest pumps almost 1½ gallons of blood every minute, or 2100 gallons each day. A 74-year-old's heart has pumped more than 56 million gallons of blood.

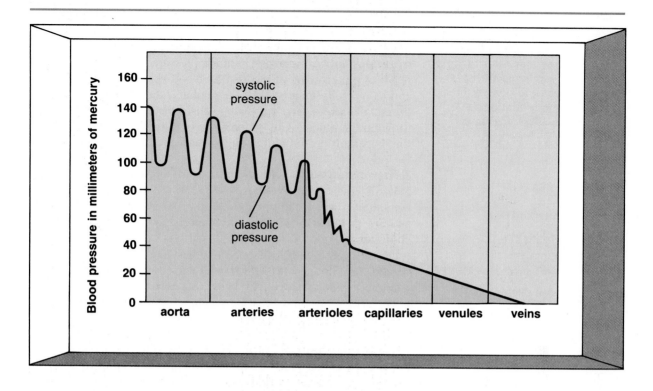

Figure 12-7 The arterioles absorb much blood pressure, thus protecting the capillaries from bursting. Pressure is measured in millimeters of mercury (Hg).

Heart Disorders and Diseases

Your heart must be healthy and fit if it is to pump blood through your circulatory system. When the heart cannot pump effectively, or the blood cannot flow smoothly, serious problems are likely to develop. There are several kinds of heart disorders, including congenital heart disorders, rheumatic heart disease, hypertension, coronary heart disease, and heart attack.

Congenital Heart Disorders Not all people begin life with a healthy heart. Some infants are born with irregularities in the way the heart is formed, called **congenital heart disorders.** Valves in the heart that regulate blood flow may not function properly. There may be a hole between the two sides of the heart. These disorders and others can limit growth and activity or even cause death. Some types of disorders heal by themselves, because the heart tissue continues to grow. In other cases, surgery may be able to correct the disorder.

Rheumatic Heart Disease Until recently, a common cause of heart disease among children and young adults was rheumatic fever. **Rheumatic fever** [*roo MAT ik*] is a disease caused by strep bacteria that can result in inflammation of the heart valves and muscle tissue. This swelling can damage and scar the heart valves. The damage may disturb the flow of blood through the heart and cause rheumatic heart disease in later years. The first sign of strep infection is often a sore throat. Treating the initial strep infection with antibiotics prevents heart damage from developing.

Hypertension   High blood pressure is also strongly linked to heart disease and stroke. High blood pressure is called **hypertension.** An increase in blood pressure is believed to be the result of a narrowing of the smaller blood vessels. Why this occurs is not fully understood. But smoking, diet, stress, and heredity are all factors. The narrowing causes the heart to beat harder to pump the blood. A blood pressure of 140/90 represents borderline hypertension for adults. Higher pressure may be more serious.

Atherosclerosis   Many other heart problems are caused by atherosclerosis. **Atherosclerosis** [*ath uh roh skluh ROH sis*] is a condition in which fatty material builds up on the walls of arteries and blocks blood flow. This fatty material is largely made of **cholesterol** [*kuh LES tuh rawl*]. If the blockage is noted in time, it can be treated with medicine or surgery. If the blockage is not treated, the coronary blood flow will decrease and damage the heart and vessels. **Coronary heart disease,** also called coronary artery disease, occurs when the coronary arteries become clogged from atherosclerosis. All people should have their cholesterol levels tested. A high level can be lowered with a low-fat diet.

Long-term coronary heart disease can lead to a heart attack. A **heart attack** is a sudden, life-threatening event during which the heart muscles do not receive enough blood. Portions of the heart muscle die. More than 1.5 million Americans each year suffer a heart attack.

Preventing Heart Disease

Coronary heart disease and heart attacks are the leading causes of death in the United States. However, you can reduce your chances of developing these heart problems with a careful diet, regular exercise, and medical checkups. Diet is especially important. Avoiding foods that are high in cholesterol and other animal fats is important. Reducing the amount of salt you eat can help too. Salt contributes to hypertension, which greatly increases the risk of heart attack. Regular exercise is very important in preventing heart disease. Because the heart is largely made up of muscle tissue, it grows stronger with regular exercise.

Lesson Review

The pacemaker and blood pressure are two ways your body regulates the heart and the circulatory system. There are many disorders that can affect the proper functioning of the heart. However, exercise and a good diet can help the circulatory system function and prevent blockages that can lead to heart damage.

1 Explain the function of the pacemaker.

2 What are the two measurements of blood pressure?

3 List three kinds of heart disorders.

4 Explain how regular exercise can prevent heart disease.

Blood and Lymph

Every time you run or dance, cut grass or shovel snow, you depend on blood to nourish each cell of your body. Blood carries nutrients to the cells and picks up wastes. Blood is more than just a collection of cells in liquid. It is an organized system that can carry materials, protect itself, and guard the body against infection. Blood is made up of four main parts: plasma, platelets, red blood cells, and white blood cells.

Plasma and Blood Clotting

Blood cells are contained in a watery substance called plasma. **Plasma** is the liquid part of the blood that makes up a little more than one half of the circulating blood. When separated from whole blood, plasma appears yellowish. Plasma is about 90 percent water and 10 percent dissolved substances. Many of these dissolved substances, such as hormones, nutrients, and plasma proteins, are vital to the healthy functioning of your body.

Among the nutrients in plasma are fats, amino acids, and glucose. Other substances in plasma are sodium, potassium, and calcium salts. A proper amount and distribution of these salts is important to all body functions. For example, these salts are necessary in the sending of nerve messages throughout the body.

The plasma also contains several different proteins, including fibrinogen. **Fibrinogen** [*fy BRIN uh jun*] is a blood protein that plays an important role in blood clotting. When an injury tears open a blood vessel, small disklike structures in the blood called **blood platelets** stick to the wall of the broken vessel. Fibrinogen gathers on the platelets and changes into a tangled network of fine threads, as you can see in Figure 12-8. The platelets and fibrinogen together form a clot, which in turn catches more platelets and blood cells. The clot closes the vessel walls and stops the bleeding. On the skin, a dried clot is called a scab.

Red Blood Cells

The blood parts that carry oxygen from the lungs to the body tissues and waste carbon dioxide from the body tissues to the lungs are the **red blood cells.** They are the most numerous kind of blood cells. Healthy red blood cells look like tiny red saucers, as shown in Figure 12-8. Their coloring comes from a substance called hemoglobin. **Hemoglobin** [*HEE muh gloh bin*] is an iron-containing substance that readily attaches to oxygen in the blood. The combination of hemoglobin and oxygen gives blood a bright red color. After red blood cells give up oxygen to cells of the body, the blood returns to a dull red coloring. Oxygen-poor blood is never blue, although it appears blue in the veins seen through your skin.

A red blood cell lives about 120 days. Your body must constantly replace the red blood cells that die. As you learned in Chapter 11, red bone marrow produces new red blood cells. Each day of your life, your red marrow forms new red blood cells to replace those that die.

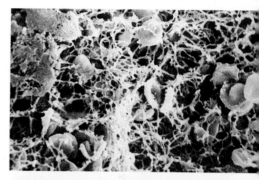
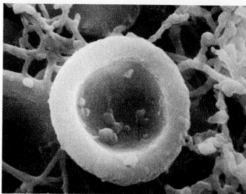
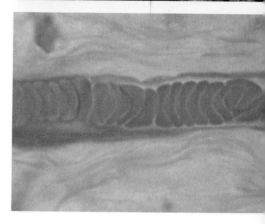

Figure 12-8 A blood clot *(top)* traps red blood cells *(center)*. Red blood cells move in single file through a capillary *(bottom)*.

Figure 12-9 The formed elements in blood include red blood cells, several types of white blood cells, and blood platelets.

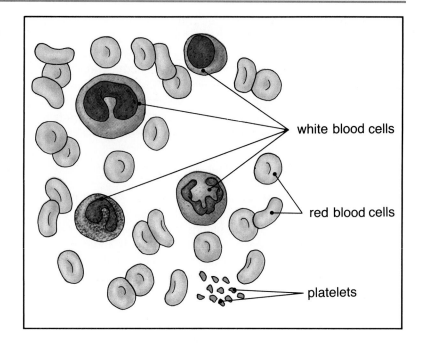

white blood cells

red blood cells

platelets

White Blood Cells

The blood cells that guard the body against disease and infection are the **white blood cells.** They are larger than red blood cells. There are normally fewer white than red blood cells in the body. The production of white blood cells increases when the body has an infection. White blood cells generally stay in the bloodstream for less than 12 hours.

White blood cells fight infections in two ways. One is by forming substances called antibodies. **Antibodies** are proteins that destroy disease-causing organisms by attaching to them. Then white blood cells can attack the organisms. White blood cells attack with their second method of fighting infections. They surround and digest the bacteria. While fighting infections, some white blood cells are killed as well as the bacteria. Some of the surrounding tissue cells are also killed. These dead cells plus tissue fluids and living white blood cells form pus.

The Lymphatic System

There are several kinds of white blood cells. Most are formed in the red bone marrow. Others are formed in the lymphatic system. The plasma that seeps out of capillaries and fills the spaces between the cells is called **lymph** [*limf*]. It is collected by your lymphatic system, shown in Figure 12-10. The **lymphatic system** returns fluid from body tissues to the blood stream and acts as one of the body's defenses against infection. It consists of the lymphatic vessels and the lymph nodes. The **lymphatic vessels** are tubes that resemble small veins and capillaries. They are widely distributed throughout the body. Lymph is pushed through these vessels by the action of the body's muscles. The large

Health Bulletin

One small drop of blood from a pin prick may contain over 5 million red blood cells. In your body, about 8 million red blood cells die and are replaced every second.

lymphatic vessels have one-way valves that prevent lymph from backing up in the system. Lymph traveling in the lymphatic system eventually drains into large veins in the neck region.

All lymph also must pass through lymph nodes. **Lymph nodes** are tissues containing special cells, including white blood cells, that trap and filter out disease-causing agents. These nodes vary in size. Some are as small as a pinhead. Others are as large as a thimble. These nodes may swell when the body is fighting an infection. Lymph nodes are located in the neck, armpits, and groin.

In addition to fighting infection, lymph carries nutrients, especially fats. Lymph also can absorb waste substances and other materials that cannot be absorbed by the blood capillaries.

Blood Types and Blood Banks

A healthy person has about five quarts of blood. When people lose blood, as in a severe accident, they may need blood to save their lives or speed their recoveries. Other people need extra blood to make up for a deficiency, or lack of a vital substance, in their blood. This requires getting the extra blood from other people. Taking blood from one person and putting it into the circulatory system of another person is called a **blood transfusion.**

A **blood donor** is the person who gives the blood for another person to use. Donating blood is not difficult or painful. It does not harm the donor because the donor's blood supply is renewed. Donated blood is taken from one person through a sterile, or germ-free, needle inserted into a vein in the arm. Blood flows into a collection bag. In the bag the blood is mixed with a preservative. The blood then is cooled to help it stay fresh longer. Later, the blood may be separated into red blood cells, white blood cells, platelets, and plasma or blood serum. **Blood serum** is blood plasma without the clotting agents.

Donated blood is collected and stored by hospitals and health organizations throughout the country. This blood is used by patients and is ready in the event of a large community disaster.

Before a transfusion can be performed, a doctor must determine the patient's blood type. Not all blood is the same. If blood that is transfused does not match the patient's own blood, the new blood may cause the red blood cells to clump together. If these clumps pass through the heart or brain, they may kill the patient. A system of **blood types** is used to classify blood according to the presence of substances on the red blood cells that cause clumping. The four major blood types are O, A, B, and AB. A donor's blood type must match that of the person receiving it.

Doctors must also consider the presence or absence of the Rh factor. The **Rh factor** is a substance found on the red blood cells of some people. About 85 to 95 percent of the population have the Rh factor in their blood. People who have the Rh factor are termed Rh positive. The 5 to 15 percent of the population who lack this substance are referred to as Rh negative. When an Rh negative person receives Rh positive blood, the receiver may produce antibodies against the Rh factor. This can cause several

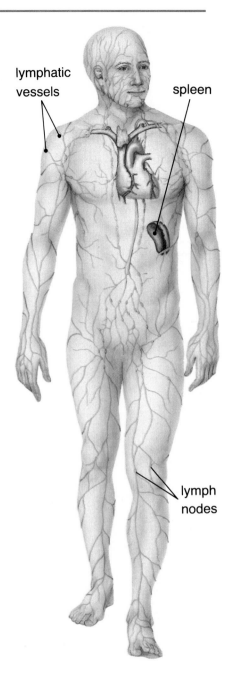

lymphatic vessels

spleen

lymph nodes

Figure 12-10   The lymphatic system extends throughout the body.

Blood group	Donates to	Receives from
O	O, A, B, AB	O
A	A, AB	O, A
B	B, AB	O, B
AB	AB	O, A, B, AB

Figure 12-11 Learn your blood type. To which types can you donate blood?

problems, including clumping of the blood the next time that person receives Rh positive blood.

In addition to testing for blood type and Rh factor, donated blood is also tested to make sure that no diseases are passed on to the person receiving the blood. Hepatitis and AIDS are two diseases for which blood is tested.

Blood Disorders

Blood tests are some of the most common ways to get concrete information about your health. When you have a physical checkup, you may be asked to give a blood sample. This sample is much smaller than the amount donated for a transfusion. More than 30 tests may be conducted on this one sample of blood. A health problem in other parts of the body may show up in the blood tests. Other problems may concern the blood itself.

Diseases of the blood are sometimes life-threatening, but more often reduce the ability to lead an active life. For example, some people suffer from anemia. **Anemia** [*uh NEE mee uh*] is a disorder in which the blood does not have enough red blood cells or there is not enough hemoglobin to carry an adequate supply of oxygen. Anemia may be caused by a vitamin or iron deficiency, destruction of red blood cells, or an inherited defect. The result is that the anemic person is weak, pale, and easily tired. Because women lose blood naturally through menstruation, they are more susceptible to iron-deficiency anemia. Iron-deficiency anemia can often be treated successfully with iron supplements in the diet.

Sickle-cell disease is a type of anemia in which abnormal hemoglobin in the red blood cells inhibits the carrying of oxygen. The red blood cells are not round, but sickle-shaped. These cells have shortened life spans, and cannot go through capillaries well. The disease is inherited and occurs most often in people of Black ancestry. It can be very painful and life-threatening. There is no cure, but blood tests can detect it.

Lesson Review

Your blood and lymph provide a system of transportation within your body and help guard your body against infection. Red blood cells carry oxygen to your cells. White blood cells and lymph nodes trap and fight infectious agents. Platelets and fibrinogen are important in the process of blood clotting. If a large amount of blood is lost, such as during an accident or because of surgery, donated blood from another person can be added.

1 Explain how blood clots.

2 What is the function of red blood cells?

3 What are the two main functions of the lymphatic system?

4 Explain the importance of the blood being matched in any blood transfusion.

5 List two disorders of the blood.

The Respiratory System

Whether you are running after a bus, singing in a chorus, or talking with a friend, your respiratory system is very important to you. Your **respiratory system** is made up of your lungs and air passages. These organs carry out the process of respiration, or taking in oxygen from the air and releasing carbon dioxide. **Carbon dioxide** is a waste product that your cells produce when breaking down glucose for energy. All of the cells in your body need oxygen to carry out their functions. Your respiratory system works closely with your circulatory system to ensure that your body receives enough oxygen.

The Upper Respiratory Tract

The organs of the respiratory system are grouped by location. The **upper respiratory tract** extends from the nose to the opening of the windpipe. The **lower respiratory tract** extends from the windpipe to the lungs. Figure 12-12 shows the organs of the respiratory system. A detailed illustration of the respiratory system is also shown on Plate Seven.

The area that lies between the roof of the mouth and the floor of the brain cavity is the **nasal cavity.** Air enters the body through the nasal cavity. As you breathe in, air enters your nose

Health **History**

The importance of air for life was recognized by the ancient Greeks. They believed that air was the source of life, and that the body renewed its life energy with each breath.

Figure 12-12   The respiratory system and a detail of alveoli

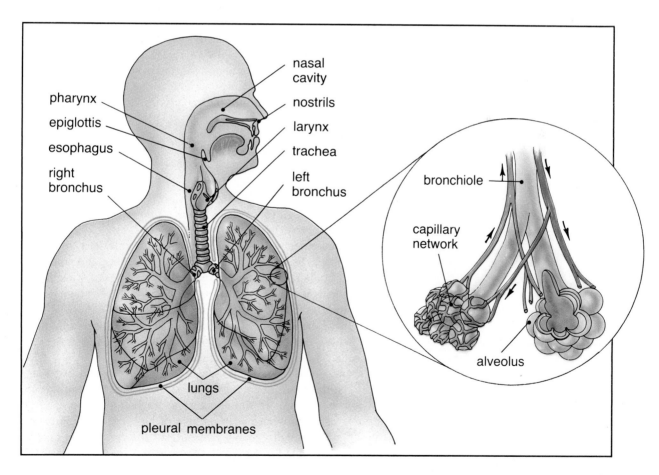

pharynx
epiglottis
esophagus
right bronchus

nasal cavity
nostrils
larynx
trachea
left bronchus

bronchiole
capillary network
alveolus

lungs
pleural membranes

through the nostrils. The nostrils and the rest of the nasal cavity are lined with mucous membrane. **Mucous membrane** is tissue that helps warm and moisten the air before it enters the lungs. The mucous membrane also filters out bacteria to help protect the lungs from infection. Mucus and cilia in the nose trap most particles from the air before they can infect the lung tissue. **Cilia** are hairlike structures in the mucous membrane that keep the lungs clean by trapping dust and foreign matter.

At the back of the mouth are reddish masses of lymphatic tissue called the **tonsils.** The tonsils trap and destroy bacteria that enter the throat and mouth. From the mouth and nasal cavity, air passes into the upper part of your throat. Your throat opens into your windpipe and esophagus. Air passes down the throat through an opening that leads to the windpipe. Food and liquids pass down the throat through another opening into the esophagus. Normally, you cannot breathe and swallow at the same time. When you swallow, the soft palate is raised to keep food or liquids from entering your nasal cavities. At the same time, the epiglottis covers the entrance to the windpipe. When food goes down the wrong pipe, the food or liquid goes into your windpipe by mistake and you gag or cough.

The Lower Respiratory Tract

The opening to the windpipe is known as the **larynx.** The larynx lies at the base of the tongue, just below and in front of the lowest part of the throat. The larynx is known commonly as the voice box because it serves as the voice organ. The mucous membrane of the larynx helps remove harmful particles from the incoming air. It functions in a way similar to the mucous membrane in the nasal cavity to filter out these particles. It also warms and moistens the air.

The windpipe, including the larynx, is made up of muscle with rings of cartilage. The section of the windpipe below the larynx is called the **trachea** [*TRAY kee uh*]. The rings of cartilage keep the trachea firm and open for the passage of air to and from the lungs.

The lower end of the windpipe divides into two large air tubes that are called **bronchi** [*BRAHNG ky*]. Each tube is a bronchus. One bronchus enters each lung. The bronchi divide into smaller branches. These branches in turn divide into smaller and smaller tubes. The smallest tubes end in clusters of tiny air sacs inside the lungs. When you inhale, air passes through the upper respiratory tract and the bronchi before flowing into the lungs.

The pair of organs that carry out the major breathing function are the **lungs.** They lie in the upper chest cavity. Cilia in the lungs protect them from dust particles.

Air moves in and out of the lungs because of differences in air pressure. Simply put, air moves from areas of high pressure to areas of lower pressure. If you puncture an air balloon, you can see the effects of air moving out of an area of high pressure. Pressure in the lungs continually changes because of the contraction and relaxation of the diaphragm. The **diaphragm** [*DY uh fram*] is the

Health Bulletin

Keeping irritants out of the lungs is so important that a person will automatically cough when any foreign matter or too much mucus enters the windpipe. Unconscious people who cannot cough can often be saved from choking by simply turning them on their front.

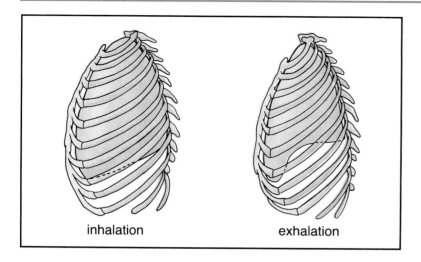

Figure 12-13 The chest expands during inhalation, when the diaphragm contracts and the ribs spread apart.

large muscle that stretches across the base of the chest cavity and separates the chest from the abdomen. It is the chief muscle used in breathing. When you inhale, the diaphragm moves downward. The chest cavity then becomes larger. When the chest cavity expands, the air pressure within it drops. Pressure outside is greater. To equalize the pressure, air moves into the lungs.

When you exhale, the process is reversed. To move air out of the lungs, the diaphragm relaxes and curves upward. This decreases the size of the chest cavity. Air pressure inside the chest cavity then increases. Air is driven out of the lungs. Figure 12-13 illustrates this process.

The lungs are filled with tiny air sacs called **alveoli** [*al VEE uh ly*]. These air sacs branch out of the smallest air tubes into the lungs. There are about 300 million alveoli in the lungs. These tiny air sacs are surrounded by capillaries. Only the thin walls of the air sacs and the capillaries separate air in the lungs from the blood in the capillaries. When you breathe in, oxygen enters these air sacs. Oxygen from the air sacs then passes through these thin walls and enters the red blood cells. At the same time, carbon dioxide moves from the capillaries into the air sacs. When you exhale, carbon dioxide is thus breathed out into the air. Oxygen is passed into the cells as carbon dioxide is passed out.

Respiratory Disorders

When you are at rest, the amount of air exchanged with each breath is about 500 milliliters, or about one-half quart of air. This amount may increase by up to five or six times when you exercise. It is important, then, that your respiratory organs be healthy to handle the increased exchange of gases during exercise.

Respiratory diseases may affect the nose, throat, or lungs. Regular exercise, a good diet, enough rest, and good hygiene may help you avoid some of these common respiratory disorders.

Pneumonia   Several different lung infections are classified under the general term pneumonia. **Pneumonia** is an infection that causes an inflammation of the lung tissue. The infection may

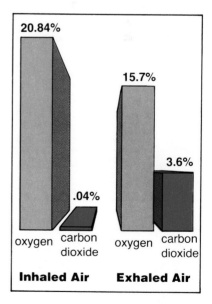

Figure 12-14 Oxygen and carbon dioxide levels in inhaled and exhaled air

Health Bulletin

The involuntary rate of breathing is controlled by the concentration of carbon dioxide in the blood. Heavy exercise produces very high concentrations of carbon dioxide, which trigger rapid breathing.

be caused by bacteria or viruses. With pneumonia, fluid can collect in the lungs, making breathing difficult. The signs of pneumonia are most often fever and coughing. Treatment depends on the type of infection present. Physicians generally advise drinking lots of fluids, resting, and taking a prescribed antibiotic.

Bacterial pneumonia can result in death, especially among older people. It must be treated carefully. A vaccine protects against some bacterial pneumonias. While viral pneumonia is also a serious disease, it generally is not as life-threatening.

Bronchitis   An inflammation of the mucous membrane of the bronchi is called **bronchitis** . Bronchitis may be caused by bacteria, viruses, or irritants. Fluid gathers in the bronchi, resulting in a thick mucus build-up. Dust particles or new bacteria or viruses can further irritate the condition. Bronchitis may start out like a cold. Hoarseness and coughing are common signs of the disease. Bronchitis may last for only a few days or a week.

Bronchitis caused by bacteria can be treated with antibiotics. The infection can severely weaken the body and lower resistance to other infections. If not treated properly, the disease can persist for a year or more. Bronchitis is very difficult to treat once the infection is well-established. People who smoke or who are exposed to harmful substances in the air increase their risk of developing bronchitis.

Asthma   Some respiratory diseases are chronic, or long lasting. They recur regularly and require continued treatment. One such disease is asthma. **Asthma** is a respiratory disorder characterized by shortness of breath, wheezing, and coughing. Usually, asthma is triggered by a substance that is breathed in or eaten. This results in a narrowing or spasm of the smooth muscle in the bronchial tubes. A swelling of the mucous membrane also occurs. Asthma attacks can be relieved with drugs that relax the bronchial muscles and open up the air passages.

Figure 12-15   Asthma attacks are often triggered by these four common factors.

Do not keep or handle pets to which you react. Such allergies often worsen over time.

Keep your house as dust-free as possible. Many people are allergic to house dust.

If you react to feathers, avoid feather-filled pillows, quilts, clothing, and cushions.

Pollen allergies occur when the flowers bloom. Avoid exposure however you can.

Emphysema Another chronic respiratory problem, more common in middle-aged or older people, is **emphysema.** Emphysema is a respiratory disease caused by a weakening of lung tissue and characterized by a serious shortness of breath. Emphysema usually develops over many years. The air sacs of the lungs are stretched thin and gradually destroyed, causing the lung tissue to lose its elasticity. This makes it very difficult for a person with emphysema to exhale. This hampers the exchange of gases. Treatment of this disease is very limited because the lung damage is permanent. This disease is most common among smokers. Disability and death are the outcomes from this lung disease.

The Air You Breathe

Unclean air can harm the respiratory system. The contamination of the air you breathe is called **air pollution.** Polluted air may contain substances that can cause inflammation in the respiratory tract. Smoke from factories and chemicals from spray cans are examples of pollutants that can harm your body. Certain pollutants tend to harm the linings of the bronchial airways. They slow down or stop the action of the cilia lining the airways. When this happens, mucus filled with dust or bacteria cannot be removed from the airways. Irritants may then clog the air passages and cause swelling. A respiratory infection may result. Air pollution may also worsen many respiratory disorders and diseases.

Smokers tend to suffer more respiratory problems and diseases than those who do not smoke. The air that smokers breathe is continually polluted with their own tobacco smoke. Some common short-term effects of smoking are bronchitis, a chronic cough, scratchy throat, and hoarse voice. Emphysema and different forms of cancer also are linked to prolonged cigarette smoking. Fortunately, through education, many more people are beginning to understand that smoking can cause serious health problems, and they can choose not to smoke.

Figure 12-16 Workers in certain industries must use filters to protect their respiratory systems from pollutants.

Lesson Review

Your respiratory system provides oxygen for every cell of your body. It also rids your body of waste carbon dioxide. The respiratory system helps your body guard against infection. However, the respiratory system itself can be injured by infections. Smoking can severely damage the respiratory system. You can help protect your respiratory system by not smoking.

1 Where is the upper respiratory tract located?

2 What are the bronchi?

3 What is the chief muscle used in breathing?

4 List two chronic respiratory diseases.

5 Explain why smokers are more likely to suffer from respiratory disease than nonsmokers.

Chapter Review

Vocabulary

air pollution	cilia	nasal cavity
alveolus	circulatory system	pacemaker
anemia	congenital heart disorder	plasma
antibody	coronary artery	pneumonia
aorta	coronary heart disease	portal vein
artery	diaphragm	pulmonary circulation
arteriole	diastolic pressure	red blood cell
asthma	emphysema	renal artery
atherosclerosis	fibrinogen	respiratory system
atrium	heart	rheumatic fever
blood donor	heart attack	Rh factor
blood platelet	hemoglobin	sickle-cell disease
blood pressure	hypertension	systemic circulation
blood serum	larynx	systolic pressure
blood transfusion	lower respiratory tract	tonsil
blood type	lung	trachea
bronchus	lymph	upper respiratory tract
bronchitis	lymph node	vein
capillary	lymphatic system	ventricle
carbon dioxide	lymphatic vessel	venule
cholesterol	mucous membrane	white blood cell

Using Vocabulary

Questions 1–15. On a separate sheet of paper, write the term from the column on the right that matches the phrase on the left.

1 muscular pump in the center of the upper chest cavity
2 proteins formed by white blood cells; used to fight infections
3 lungs and air passages
4 condition in which fatty material blocks the arteries
5 largest artery
6 blood vessels that carry blood to the heart
7 small mass of nerves and muscle cells that starts each heartbeat
8 microscopic blood vessels with extremely thin walls
9 waste product released by cells when they break down glucose for energy
10 heart and branching network of large and small blood vessels
11 respiratory disorder characterized by shortness of breath, wheezing, and coughing
12 substance found on the red blood cells of some people
13 force of blood against the walls of vessels
14 infection that causes an inflammation of the lung tissue
15 large muscle that stretches across the base of the chest cavity

a circulatory system
b carbon dioxide
c aorta
d Rh factor
e respiratory system
f pneumonia
g heart
h capillaries
i blood pressure
j antibodies
k pacemaker
l diaphragm
m atherosclerosis
n asthma
o veins

Interpreting Ideas

1 What is the difference between systolic pressure and diastolic pressure?

2 In what sense is the heart a double pump? How are its chambers arranged? Describe the function of each of the four chambers of the heart.

3 What is the chief muscle used in breathing? How is it involved in inhalation? in exhalation?

4 Compare the purposes of the pulmonary and systemic circulation.

5 Describe three circulatory system diseases.

6 What are the four main parts of blood? As a system, what are two functions of blood?

7 What two gases are exchanged between the air sacs and the capillaries in the lungs?

8 Compare the causes of pneumonia and emphysema.

9 What gases do red blood cells carry?

10 What are the two main functions of the lymphatic system?

11 Why do smokers tend to have more respiratory problems than those who do not smoke? List three short-term effects of smoking.

12 List the parts of the respiratory system in the order with which air travels through them.

13 Describe what may happen when Rh positive blood is donated to an Rh negative person.

14 Describe the ways that you can reduce your chances of developing heart disease.

15 Identify the organs that help clean the blood.

16 How does blood clot?

17 How can air pollution lead to a respiratory disease?

18 Describe hypertension: what it is, the factors that may cause it, and its treatment.

Applying Concepts

1 Why do children with strep throat need immediate medical attention?

2 In what sense is the cardiovascular system a transport system and a cleansing system?

3 Why are blood tests taken when you are ill?

4 Why do you think there are 500 times as many red blood cells as white blood cells? When does your body make extra white blood cells?

5 The tonsils are lymph nodes. In the past, it was common to remove the tonsils when children had frequent tonsillitis, colds, or ear infections. Why do doctors today think differently about removing this tissue?

6 When you take your own pulse, why do you use your second or third finger rather than your thumb? Try taking your pulse with a thumb, and then a finger. You may feel the difference.

7 If you go out on an extremely cold day and take a quick deep breath you will feel a sudden discomfort. What can you do to avoid this discomfort? What tissue and structures help you to avoid discomfort and lung infection?

8 Why do you think that the left ventricle is more muscular than the other chambers in the heart? Which other chamber contracts at the same time as the left ventricle?

Projects

1 Construct a simple stethoscope to listen to the sound your heart makes. Attach a foot of rubber tubing to a metal kitchen funnel. Then press the funnel against your chest and listen through the tubing. What information can a doctor obtain by listening to your heart? What causes the lub'dub, lub'dub sound that your heart makes?

2 At your school or local library, find out more about the various blood types and the Rh factor. Why can't a blood transfusion involve just any two persons' blood? How did the Rh factor get its name? How can the Rh factor affect a mother and her unborn child? What are the names of some other blood types?

The nervous system is the most complex system of the body. It helps this wind surfer coordinate many physical and mental tasks.

CHAPTER THIRTEEN

Coordination and Control

Every day you perform thousands of actions. They begin the moment you open your eyes and swing your legs out of bed. On a typical day, you may run, walk, and play sports. You will breathe and blink your eyes. You will probably hold a pencil, read a book, and eat. What other actions do you do each day?

Every day you also think hundreds of thousands of thoughts. You think about your schoolwork, your friends, and whatever else is on your mind. You react to the world around you. You make decisions. You feel happy or sad or angry.

You are a complex person who can perform a great many actions and think a variety of thoughts. Yet as different and varied as they may be, all your thoughts, feelings, and actions are controlled by one part of your body—the nervous system.

Objectives

- Describe the structures and functions of the two major parts of the nervous system.

- Describe the functions of the two parts of the autonomic nervous system.

- Define *reflexes*.

- Describe the types, parts, and functions of neurons.

- Describe the stages of sleep, sleep problems, and ways to get a good night's sleep.

- Describe four nervous system disorders and their causes.

The Nervous System

The complex group of organs and nerves that control all your actions and thoughts is your **nervous system.** A detailed illustration of the human nervous system is shown on Plate Eight. The brain is the control center of the nervous system. Nerve cells in the brain receive messages from every part of the body. The brain processes these messages and sends a response back to other parts of the body through other nerve cells. Most of the messages travel through the spinal cord.

Your nervous system allows you to respond to changes in your environment. Your nervous system stores information to be used days, months, or even years later. It also is in charge of your body's voluntary and involuntary muscle movements. It makes your muscles contract and relax. Your nervous system can do all this because of billions of nerve cells throughout your body. The nerve cells send signals to each other and to muscles.

Nerve Cells

The basic unit of the nervous system is the **neuron.** It is commonly called a nerve cell. Neurons carry messages from one part of your body to another. These messages of sensation and information are called **impulses.** Neurons form the communication system that controls the body's many functions and stores information. Although there are different types of neurons, there are certain features that are similar in all types.

Structure of Nerves A neuron has a cell body with fibers leading to and from it as shown in Figure 13-1. The nerve fibers consist of one axon and one or more dendrites.

The **axon** is a long fiber that carries impulses away from the cell body to other neurons. Axons that reach through your body to distant neurons may be over one yard long. A nerve is actually a bundle of axons from many neurons. One nerve may have more than 1000 axons bound together. Each axon acts independently of the others.

The **dendrites** are fibers like tiny trees that receive impulses and send them to the cell body. They are too small to be seen without a microscope. Because dendrites have many branches, one neuron can receive messages from hundreds of other neurons.

Figure 13-1   Neuron structure

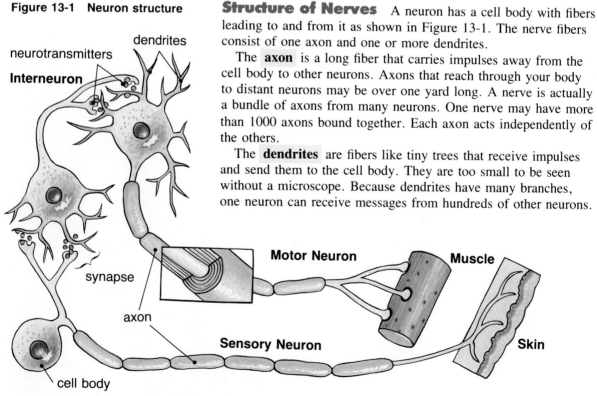

neurotransmitters

dendrites

Interneuron

synapse

axon

cell body

Motor Neuron

Muscle

Sensory Neuron

Skin

Nerve Impulses The impulse that travels along a neuron is similar to a tiny electrical charge. Nerve impulses may travel as fast as 360 feet per second along an axon. At that speed, an impulse could cover the length of a football field in less than one second.

Between the end of the axon of one neuron and the dendrite of another is a space called a **synapse** [*SIN aps*]. As an impulse reaches the end of an axon, it is passed to a dendrite of the next neuron by neurotransmitters. **Neurotransmitters** [*nur oh TRANS mit urz*] are chemicals that pass across a synapse from an axon to a dendrite. Neurotransmitters trigger an impulse, which travels down the dendrite to the cell body and out along the axon.

Kinds of Neurons There are three kinds of neurons. Figure 13-1 illustrates the relationships among the kinds of neurons. **Sensory neurons** are the neurons that detect changes in the environment, both outside and inside you. They carry nerve impulses from the sense organs, the skin, the muscles, and the internal organs to the spinal cord or brain. For example, when you touch an ice cube, the neurons that sense cold send this message to your brain.

The **interneurons** are neurons that receive sensory messages and send responses. They are found only in the brain and spinal cord. In the example above, many interneurons in your brain act together to form an awareness that you are touching an ice cube. They then send messages to motor neurons to produce actions.

The **motor neurons** are neurons that carry a response from the interneurons to the muscles, glands, and internal organs of the body. Every movement of the body, from a blink of the eyes to a jump through the air, is controlled by messages carried by motor neurons to the muscles. In the example of the ice cube, the message being carried by the motor neurons might be to stimulate the hand's muscles to pick up the ice cube and place it in a glass.

The Central Nervous System

People once thought that the heart controlled the body. Scientists now know that the brain is the master control unit for the body. The ability of this three-pound mass of spongy tissue to receive, store, and send information is fascinating, but is still not fully understood. The brain and spinal cord together make up the **central nervous system.** The brain and the spinal cord have many parts, each with a role in central nervous system functions.

Protective Coverings Because the brain and spinal cord are so vital, they have several protective coverings. The outer covering is bone. The skull surrounds and protects the brain. The vertebrae cover the spinal cord. Under the skull and vertebrae, three membranes provide even more protection. In addition, a substance called **cerebrospinal fluid** [*ser uh broh SPY nul*] fills the spaces between the middle and inner membranes and certain spaces within the brain. This fluid cushions the brain and spinal cord in the event of an impact or a sudden change of direction.

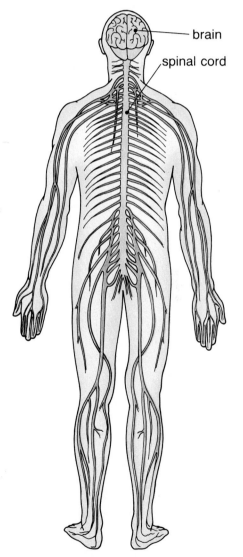

brain

spinal cord

Figure 13-2 The central nervous system *(yellow)* and the peripheral nervous system *(brown)*

Figure 13-3 **The structure of the brain** *(right),* **and a cross section of a cerebellum** *(top)*

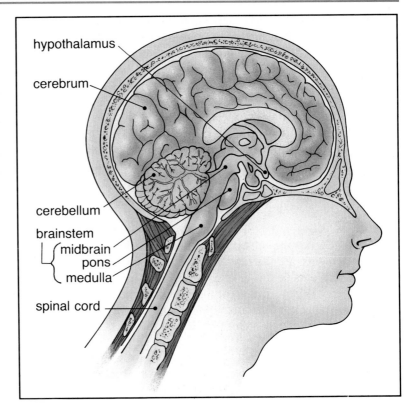

hypothalamus
cerebrum
cerebellum
brainstem
    midbrain
    pons
    medulla
spinal cord

Health Bulletin

During a 70-year lifetime, a person's memory stores at least 100 trillion bits of information. That is as many bits as 500,000 copies of an encyclopedia and more than 500 times the number of stars in the Milky Way Galaxy.

The Cerebrum The largest and uppermost part of the brain, which regulates your thoughts and actions, is the **cerebrum** [*SER uh brum*]. The cerebrum is responsible for the highly developed intelligence of human beings. As you can see in Figure 13-4, the surface of the cerebrum looks like a wrinkled walnut with many grooves. These grooves follow a pattern in normal brains. The patterns are used to identify specific regions of the brain. Some regions receive messages about what you see, hear, and smell, or how you move. Other parts control your ability to think, write, talk, and express emotions. Figure 13-4 identifies different regions of the brain.

The outer layer of the cerebrum is called the **cerebral cortex** [*suh REE brul*]. It is made up of interneuron cell bodies. About three fourths of all the nerve cell bodies in your nervous system are here. Since the nerve cell bodies of the cerebral cortex are gray in color, it is called the **gray matter.** The layer of the cerebrum below the cortex is called the **white matter.** The white matter contains billions of axons running to and from the cortex. Buried deep within the cerebrum are the thalamus and the hypothalamus. The **thalamus** is the part of the brain that relays sensory impulses to the cerebral cortex. The **hypothalamus** is the part of the brain that regulates some of the body's most basic needs, such as body temperature, sleep, digestion, and the release of hormones. You can see these structures in Figure 13-3.

The cerebrum is divided in half from front to back. The two halves of the cerebrum control opposite sides of the body. The right side of the brain actually controls the muscles of the left side of the body. The left side of the brain controls the muscles of the right side of the body.

The Cerebellum   The part of the brain that coordinates the muscles that you use for action, such as running and walking, is the **cerebellum** [*sehr uh BEL um*]. The cerebellum is under and behind the cerebrum, and coordinates a constant flow of nerve impulses from the body and cerebrum. The cerebellum puts this information together to help your muscles perform the way you want. It also helps control your balance and maintain posture.

The Brainstem   The structure that connects the cerebrum with the spinal cord is the **brainstem.** The three divisions that form this stem are shown in Figure 13-3. The midbrain is at the top of the stem, followed by the pons and the medulla.

The medulla is found just above the spinal cord. The **medulla** [*muh DUL uh*] is the center that controls some of the most important functions of life, such as breathing, blood pressure, heart rate, and swallowing. When you get excited or frightened, you breathe harder and your heart beats more rapidly. Your sense organs and emotional centers of the brain stimulate the medulla.

The **pons** is a bundle of nerve fibers that link the cerebrum with the cerebellum and the right side of the brain with the left side of the brain. The pons helps control eye movements and regulates breathing. The **midbrain** is a group of nerves that control certain involuntary actions such as pupil size and eye movements.

The Spinal Cord   Within the vertebral column is the main nerve trunk of the body, the **spinal cord.** It extends from the medulla to just below the ribs. The nerve fibers in the spinal cord reach out to all parts of the body, connecting all of the nerves in

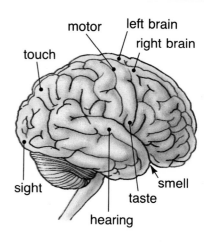

Figure 13-4   Control centers of the brain

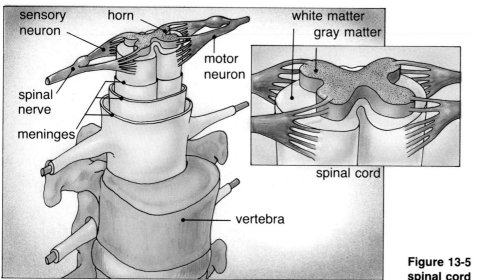

Figure 13-5   Structure of the spinal cord

your body to the central nervous system. If the spinal cord is damaged, the body may be unable to feel or move from the point of injury downward.

Figure 13-5 shows a cross section of the spinal cord and the arrangement of its protective coverings. As you can see, the gray matter is on the inside of the spinal cord.

The Peripheral Nervous System

The system that carries messages between the body and the central nervous system is the **peripheral nervous system.** Impulses constantly travel between the two nervous systems. This happens through 31 pairs of large nerves branching from the spinal cord and 12 pairs of nerves branching from the brain. These nerves contain thousands of sensory and motor nerve fibers that reach to all parts of the body. Part of the peripheral nervous system carries sensory information. This includes sensations of

Figure 13-6 Actions of the autonomic nervous system

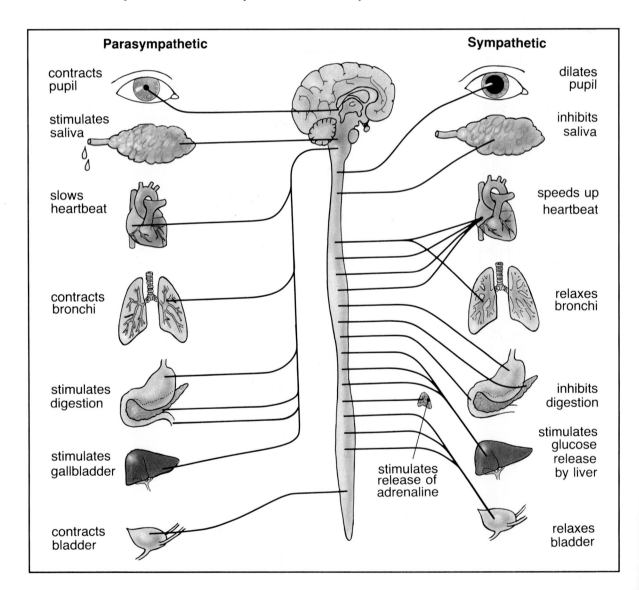

Parasympathetic

contracts pupil

stimulates saliva

slows heartbeat

contracts bronchi

stimulates digestion

stimulates gallbladder

contracts bladder

Sympathetic

dilates pupil

inhibits saliva

speeds up heartbeat

relaxes bronchi

inhibits digestion

stimulates glucose release by liver

stimulates release of adrenaline

relaxes bladder

which you are aware, such as touch. It also carries sensations of which you are not aware, such as the pressure on your tendons. Part of the peripheral nervous system carries motor impulses that control voluntary action.

The part of the peripheral nervous system that controls involuntary responses is called the **autonomic nervous system** [*aw tuh NAHM ik*]. For example, your breathing and digestion are controlled by involuntary responses. The autonomic nervous system is made up largely of motor nerves.

The autonomic nervous system affects many organs. These include the heart, lungs, stomach, intestines, liver, kidneys, sweat glands, salivary glands, and pupils of the eye. The autonomic nervous system consists of two parts. The two parts of the autonomic nervous system reach and affect the same organs, but produce opposite effects. The **parasympathetic nervous system** is the part of the autonomic nervous system that generally slows down the body's functions. For example, when you are sleeping, it slows the heartbeat and rate of breathing. It is most active when you are resting.

The **sympathetic nervous system** is the part of the autonomic nervous system that works when you are active or under emotional stress. As you read this, you are probably calm and sitting still. Parasympathetic impulses are regulating your heart rate, keeping it slow and steady. If something were to excite you or if you were to move quickly, your sympathetic nervous system would take a stronger role. Your heart rate would speed up and your breathing rate would increase. Blood flow would decrease in organs such as the stomach and the intestines. At the same time, blood flow would increase to active muscles. This interplay between the two parts of the autonomic nervous system keeps your body working properly in all situations. It is done without your conscious control. Figure 13-6 illustrates the relationship of the sympathetic and parasympathetic nervous systems.

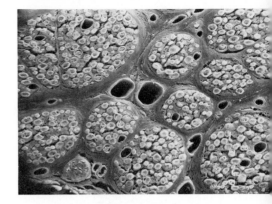

Figure 13-7 Each nerve is a bundle of sensory and motor nerve fibers.

Photo above from *Tissues and Organs: A Text-Atlas of Scanning Electron Microscopy* by Richard G. Kessel & Randy H. Kardon, W.H. Freeman and Co. ©1979.

Health Health

The first electrical experiments on the brain were carried out by medical officers in 1870. They found that stimulation of one side of the brain produced movement on the opposite side of the body.

Lesson Review

Your nervous system is a complex group of organs and nerves that control all of your actions and thoughts. The two main parts of the nervous system work together to send impulses to all parts of the body. The body's control center, the brain, coordinates your muscles, balance, posture, and other important body functions as well as your intellectual thoughts.

1 What is a synapse?

2 Name three kinds of neurons.

3 Define *gray matter*.

4 Where would you find the medulla, pons, and midbrain?

5 Which part of the autonomic nervous system has a stronger role in responding to emotional stress?

Coordination

Every day, you perform many activities. You brush your teeth, comb your hair, and tie your shoes. Most of the time you do not even think when you perform these activities. It is almost as if your body is carrying out these tasks without your conscious thought. What controls the routine movements of your body?

Reflexes

A rapid, automatic response to the environment that occurs without action from the brain is called a **reflex.** You were born with reflexes. Reflexes are involuntary, although you can sometimes overrule them. Most reflexes protect you from harm. For example, coughing and sneezing are reflexes that help to remove objects from your throat and air passages. Blinking is a reflex that helps protect your eyes.

You may have had your reflexes tested during a medical examination. The knee jerk is a common test to determine whether your nerves are working properly. When your knee is tapped, the leg reacts by jerking upward. This involuntary jerking is called a **reflex action.** When your knee is tapped, nerve endings send a message through a sensory neuron to the spinal cord. Here the impulse passes by way of an interneuron to a motor neuron. The motor neuron, in turn, passes the impulse along its axon to muscles in the leg, which tighten to make the leg move. This entire reflex response takes less than 1/50 of a second.

The route the impulses travel during a reflex action is called a **reflex arc.** This reflex arc is illustrated in Figure 13-8. The reflex arc is the simplest response pattern in the body. This kind of response does not involve the brain. It involves only the coordination of sensory and motor neurons. Because a reflex is not processed by the brain, it can happen quickly.

When you accidentally touch a hot pan, your muscles quickly pull your arm away from the heat. The reflex for moving your hand travels to the spinal cord and then back to the muscles. This prevents the hand from being as badly burned as it would have been if the impulses had traveled first to the brain and then back

Health **History**

Descartes, the great seventeenth century philosopher, developed the idea of reflex action. He mistakenly believed, though, that nerves were fluid-filled tubes that ballooned with liquid to make muscles contract.

Figure 13-8   The knee-jerk reflex arc involves only three neurons.

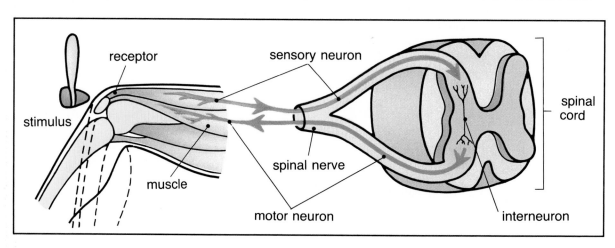

stimulus · receptor · sensory neuron · spinal cord · spinal nerve · motor neuron · interneuron · muscle

to the arm muscles. At the same time, your hand sends messages of pain to the brain. By the time the pain signal reaches the brain and you feel pain, you have already let go of the hot pan.

Voluntary Body Movements

Simple muscular movements blended together to achieve a desired response are called **voluntary body movements.** Your nervous system coordinates these movements in several ways, each as simple or complex as the movement itself. Your spinal cord, brainstem, cerebellum, and cerebrum each play a role in that control.

Your body is always in motion. When you sit still or sleep, many parts of your body are moving. Your nervous system does more than control all of your individual movements. It causes them to work together smoothly. The ability to make many movements work together smoothly is called **coordination.** As you read this, your nervous system coordinates the movement of your eyes so that they both focus to see the page as one image.

Think of all the different ways you use your fingers during the day. Buttoning a shirt, eating with a fork, turning a doorknob, and throwing a ball all require different kinds of coordination. In addition, your body movements must adjust to varying demands. For example, eating with a fork or spoon requires a more delicate control than throwing a ball as far as you can.

Balance and Smooth Movement

Much of your muscle control occurs without your conscious direction. When you walk down the stairs, you do not think about which muscles to contract to keep your balance. Two parts of the brain control your balance and the smoothness of your movements. These are the brainstem and the cerebellum. Impulses from your inner ear constantly go to the brainstem. The brainstem sends impulses to your muscles, making them tighten just enough to keep you balanced. When you are standing or sitting, the muscles in your legs, abdomen, and back receive signals. The constant slight contractions of these muscles keep you upright.

Your cerebellum perfects all of your movements. Special sensory neurons are located in your muscles, tendons, and joints. These neurons send impulses to your cerebellum and tell it how much your muscles are contracting and the angle of each joint. Your cerebellum combines this information with signals from your inner ears and eyes to coordinate your movements.

Your cerebellum uses this information to make sure that you move the way you want. Although the cerebellum does not start actions, it receives messages from the rest of the central nervous system whenever an action is started. The cerebellum compares the command with the resulting action. Then it sends its own signals to the muscle to correct any errors. Thus the cerebellum might direct the triceps muscles to contract slightly to slow down the action of the biceps. It might also send a message to the biceps that would decrease the biceps contractions. Such controls occur whenever you move.

Figure 13-9 The axon of a motor neuron ends at a motor end plate. Neurotransmitters at the motor end plate bring the nerve impulse to the muscle fiber.

Figure 13-10 The cerebellum and brainstem make even difficult balancing possible.

Figure 13-11 Practice allows mastery of difficult movements.

Developing Skilled Movements

You can learn many tasks by practicing the motions involved over and over. Learning to tie your shoes is a simple example. Once you mastered the task, you could tie your shoes without thinking. You had developed memories of the different motions needed to tie your shoes. Your brain remembers the way to perform a task in a special code called an **engram.** An engram is like a computer program. It records a pattern of skilled movements. When activated, the engram orders the body to repeat the exact pattern. Now when you want to tie your shoes, you call forth an engram that sets the proper motor nerves into action. Sensory nerves let your brain know how the body is actually moving. The sensations are compared to the engram commands, and minor adjustments are made as needed.

During your life, many engrams are developed and stored in your cerebrum. You can call on these to perform thousands of complex motions. Playing a musical instrument, writing, and playing sports require many engrams. Throughout your life, you can form patterns for new skills. To develop enough engrams to become an expert, you need to practice a skill over and over. You then perform the movements with little conscious thought.

Lesson Review

Coordination is the ability to make many movements work together smoothly. Coordination is largely controlled by the brainstem and the cerebellum. Skilled movements can be learned by practicing the motions over and over again, until a pattern of movements is recorded in an engram.

1 What term describes a rapid, automatic response to the environment that occurs without the action of the brain?

2 What two parts of the brain control your balance?

3 Describe an engram.

Brain Activity and Sleep

No matter what you are doing, neurons in your brain are constantly transmitting and receiving impulses. Changes in the electrical activity of the brain can be recorded as **brain waves.** Brain waves can be recorded by a special instrument called an **electroencephalograph** [*ih lek troh en SEF uh luh graf*], or EEG. An EEG gives a visual record of brain impulses. When you are thinking hard, the waves occur more often and do not vary in height very much. During sleep, the waves occur more slowly but vary greatly in height. In certain types of brain disorders the waves show other changes. Your brain activity varies, depending upon the kind of activity in which you are involved.

Sleep

In an average day, you go from a low-level awareness of the world around you to a state of alertness. After you are awake for a while you go back to sleep. Sleep is a type of unconsciousness. **Unconsciousness** is a state of being unaware of the world.

Sleep is essential to good health. Sleep refreshes the body and mind. People feel and work better if they get a regular amount of sleep every night. However, the reasons for this need are not yet well understood.

Recorded brain waves have helped in the study of the different stages of sleep. These studies indicate that there are four stages of sleep occurring in cycles. Each cycle lasts about 90 minutes. When you first fall asleep, your brain waves slow down. They get slower in the second and third stages of sleep as you relax. In

Health Bulletin

Total lack of sleep will cause death in about 10 days—sooner than death caused by starvation.

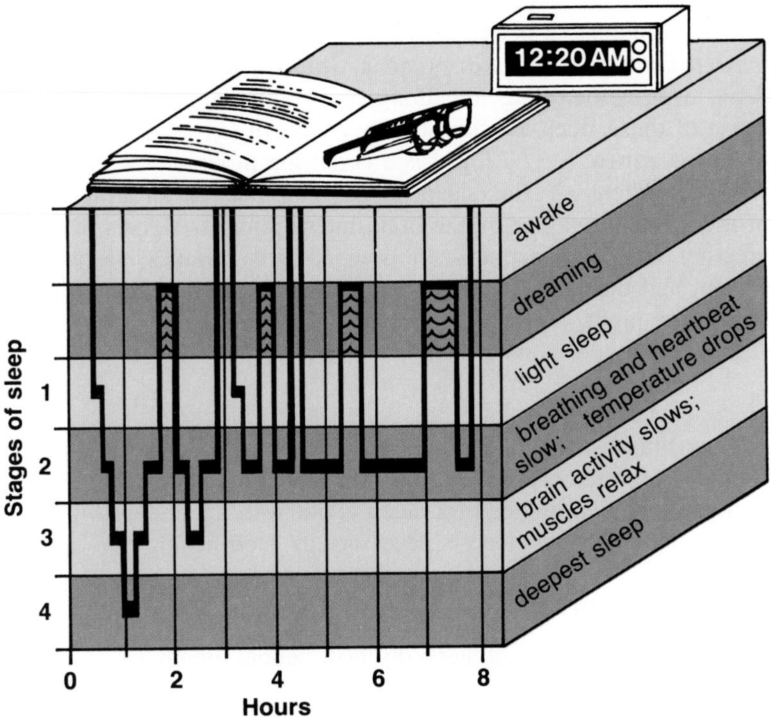

Figure 13-12 Brain wave activity goes through several stages during a night of sleep. Muscle relaxation is greatest during dreaming sleep.

Figure 13-13   The need for sleep decreases with age. This infant may sleep as much as 16–20 hours a day. His grandparents may need only 5–6 hours of sleep a night.

these stages, you become even more unaware of the world outside. The fourth stage is the deepest stage in the cycle.

After this sleep, you drift into a lighter sleep. This is the time when most people dream. **Rapid eye movement,** or REM sleep, is the dream stage. REM is indicated by the back-and-forth movement of your eyes under your eyelids. After ten or more minutes of REM sleep, the sleep cycle repeats three or four times.

Dreaming is good for your health. People who are kept from dreaming often show signs of mental illness. Although you may not remember your dreams, it is thought that everyone dreams. People are most likely to remember their dreams when they wake up during REM sleep.

Sleep Problems

Most people sleep seven to eight hours a day. The normal amount of sleep varies from person to person. The inability to sleep your usual amount is called **insomnia** [*in SAHM nee uh*]. Insomnia is a problem for an estimated 75 million Americans.

Often to get a good night's sleep, doctors advise avoiding foods or medications that keep you awake. These include many drinks that contain caffeine, such as coffee, chocolate, and cola drinks. Exercise during the day often helps people sleep better. Establish a regular bedtime and go to bed only when you are tired. If you just cannot sleep one night, get up and read a book or do work on some project. Remember that not being able to sleep well occasionally happens to everyone. Constant insomnia is serious and should be treated by a doctor. It can be a sign of a physical or mental illness.

Some people may have problems staying awake during the day, even though they get a full night's sleep. Extreme daytime sleepiness may indicate a disorder called narcolepsy. **Narcolepsy** [*NAHR kuh lep see*] is a disorder in which people fall asleep suddenly even while doing something such as talking or driving. The cause of these sleep attacks is often unknown.

Sleep apnea [*ap NEE uh*] is a condition in which breathing stops periodically during sleep. It may stop because of a blockage of the upper airway or by the brain interrupting its signals to breathe. When this happens, the sleeper partly awakes, gasps for breath, and then falls back to sleep. This may happen many times during the night, leaving the person feeling very tired by day.

Lesson Review

Your brain gives off impulses that can be recorded as brain waves. Brain activity varies, depending on whether you are asleep or awake. While the need for sleep is not well understood, it is known that adequate sleep is necessary to good health.

1 Define *unconsciousness*.

2 During which stage of sleep do most people dream?

3 List three sleeping problems.

Nervous System Disorders

The nervous system is subject to many disorders. Signs of a nervous system disorder may include pain, numbness in the limbs, or slurred speech. However, these symptoms may also be caused by other body ailments. Because the nervous system controls and receives input from all parts of the body, it can give a warning of many disorders. For example, a numbness in the jaw that runs down the left arm is often a symptom of a heart problem. Other pains may be symptoms of other problems.

Disorders that affect the nervous system itself range from the common headache to life-threatening conditions.

Headaches

Headaches are among the most common pains affecting people. They may be caused by stress, eyestrain, allergies, colds, and infected sinuses. Headaches also may be caused by a brain tumor, disease, or head injury. Few headaches are caused by problems in the nervous system, even though the pain of a headache is felt through the nervous system. Since the brain does not have sensory neurons for feeling pain, headaches are not perceived in the brain, but in the muscles and other tissues surrounding it.

Tension is probably the major cause of headaches. A tension headache can happen when the muscles of the face, neck, or scalp tighten. This causes a dull, squeezing pain in the forehead, jaws, and back of the head and neck. This sort of headache may also be due to a physical problem such as poor eyesight or holding the head in an awkward position for a long time. This type of headache is best treated by removing the cause of the strain or tension. Any headache that lasts for several days should get medical attention.

A **migraine** [*MY grayn*] is a severe headache caused by a narrowing of blood vessels in the brain followed by an enlargement of these vessels. Before the pain begins, some people see bright spots or feel tingling sensations in their legs and arms. This is followed by intense pain, sensitivity to light, and often nausea. As the early symptoms fade away, an intense throbbing headache follows. A migraine comes on quickly and may last a day or two. It may occur repeatedly or very rarely.

There seem to be many causes of migraines. This type of headache may be brought on by stress, drinking alcohol, smoking, particular foods or chemicals, or changes in the daily routine. A tendency toward having migraines may be passed on through families. Many medicines have been used to relieve these headaches, with some success. At present there is no cure.

Head Injuries

Any blow to the head or serious fall can cause an injury to the nervous system. A hard blow to the head that causes unconsciousness is called a **concussion** [*kun KUSH un*]. Rest usually brings recovery. A very hard blow to the head may result in a contusion. A **contusion** [*kun TOO zhun*] is a bruise. A contusion of the

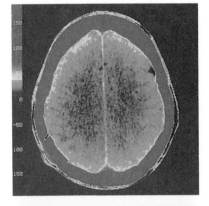
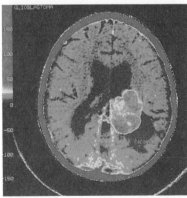

Figure 13-14 Today computerized scanning devices can detect many structural problems of the brain. Compare the scan of a normal brain *(top)* with one of a brain that has an abnormal growth *(bottom)*.

Figure 13-15   Protective head-gear can prevent serious injury of the brain.

brain tissue is much more serious than a concussion. It may cause a coma that lasts for days or weeks. A **coma** [*KOH muh*] is a deep unconsciousness from which a person cannot be awakened. If a blow to the head cracks the skull, the fracture will usually heal with bed rest. However, when a skull fracture results in a contusion, the person may be in serious danger. Blood from the contusion may cause a clot in the brain. Surgery may be necessary to remove the blood clot.

Protect yourself against head injuries by wearing protective headgear during sports, when bike riding, and when working in dangerous places. Wear a safety belt when driving. Be careful also when swimming or diving. Do not dive into shallow water, or where the bottom is rocky. Proper first aid and medical attention should be given in any situation where an injury might have occurred. When providing first aid for a person who has had a serious fall, be sure not to move the person until trained medical workers arrive. If the injury has not caused nerve damage, movement may cause it. Since neurons seldom regrow, nerve damage can have permanent effects.

Other causes of coma include drug overdose, alcohol and carbon monoxide poisoning, and disease. If an injured person's heart stops beating or if he or she stops breathing, brain cells may begin to die from a lack of oxygen. Without the brain functioning, a person is unable to survive without artificial means.

When the cells of the cerebral cortex and the brainstem are dead, an EEG will show no brain waves. When the brain cells die and the person's central nervous system stops functioning, that person is called **brain dead.** Machines and medical staff can sometimes keep the heart and kidneys working, and provide nutrition. However, a patient who is brain dead will not be aware of any sensations, and will not be able to think.

Spinal Cord Injuries

An injury to the spinal cord may cause permanent paralysis. **Paralysis** [*puh RAL ih sis*] is a loss of the ability to move a part of the body due to nerve or muscle damage. It may affect one little muscle or most of the body. **Paraplegia** [*par uh PLEE jee uh*] is the paralysis of the lower body and legs. **Quadriplegia** [*kwahd ruh PLEE jee uh*] is the paralysis of the body from the neck down.

Accidents are the most common cause of injuries to the spinal cord. Many injuries result from auto and work-related accidents. You may prevent some of these injuries by wearing a safety belt, driving safely, and following safety rules at work.

Much has been done to help paraplegics and quadriplegics in leading productive lives. Exercise therapy may help them learn to function independently despite their injuries. With improved construction of wheelchairs, the paralyzed have increased mobility. People confined to wheelchairs often play basketball or take part in races. Scientists are developing computerized devices that stimulate muscles and help the paralyzed person move without the use of a wheelchair.

Health Bulletin

About 12,000 serious spinal cord injuries occur in the U.S. each year. Three quarters of them result from automobile accidents.

Nervous System Inflammations

Infections of the nerves are less common than are infections of other systems of the body. Unlike the lungs and skin, the brain and spinal cord are well protected from the outside environment. Bacteria and viruses can reach the nervous system only through the blood stream, air spaces in the sinuses and ears, or through fractures of the skull. The tissues of the nervous system are, however, subject to a variety of inflammations. These swellings usually have causes other than infection.

A wide range of disorders that affect the nerves are referred to as neuritis. Inflammation of the nerves is called **neuritis** [*noo RY tis*]. This inflammation is often due to injury or overuse, and rarely to infection. Diabetes or alcohol abuse can also lead to neuritis in the limbs.

An inflammation of the membranes around the brain and spinal cord is called **meningitis** [*men in JY tis*]. It may be caused by a bacterial or viral infection. Some types spread from person to person, usually children and teenagers. The signs are fever, severe headache, nausea, and vomiting. Other key signs are a stiff neck and being bothered by bright lights. Although most children recover, sometimes meningitis can cause deafness, mental retardation, and death. Bacterial infections are treated by antibiotics. When left untreated, meningitis from a bacterial infection may be fatal.

HEALTH + Technology

ELECTRICAL MUSCLE STIMULATION—At least 20 times a day someone in the United States becomes paralyzed by a spinal cord injury. Electrical stimulation of paralyzed limbs may someday restore their freedom of movement. Functional neuromuscular stimulation (FNS) is a method of using computer-controlled electrodes to stimulate muscles, thus artificially controlling and coordinating movement.

Using FNS, paraplegic patients have been able to walk short distances with walkers and crutches. Some have even walked up and down stairs using railings for support. Several quadriplegics have managed to feed themselves, comb their hair, and brush their teeth.

The system you see in the photograph is under development at Wright State University in Dayton, Ohio. The walking system is computer controlled and is operated by a wrist switch. A brace and a walker or canes provide additional support.

Researchers face two major challenges: finding ways to stimulate many small muscle bundles, and developing sensors that will give more complete information on the positions of the limbs. Even the most highly developed systems use only about 50 electrodes, while the body has thousands of motor neurons. Sensors used so far provide only rough information to the computer.

1 What is FNS?
2 What two challenges do researchers face?

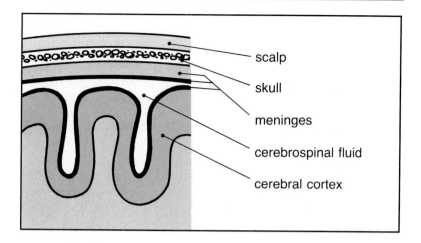

Figure 13-16 The brain's protective membranes, called the meninges, become inflamed in meningitis.

A vaccine is now available to protect against one form of bacterial meningitis. It is recommended for every child who has reached two years of age. Except for some older people, most adults are immune to this infection. For that reason adults seldom receive the vaccine.

An inflammation of the brain cells is called **encephalitis** [*en sef uh LY tis*]. It may be caused by infections, drugs, or diseases that spread from other parts of the body. In mild cases, the common signs are a headache, fever, loss of energy, and a stiff neck. In severe cases, victims feel drowsy, weak, may run a high fever, and may become unconscious. Brain function may be permanently affected, even after recovery.

Other Nervous System Disorders

The causes of several nervous system disorders are unknown or only partly understood. These disorders may have long-lasting effects. In some cases they do not progress very far. In other cases they become disabling. Fortunately, these disorders affect relatively few people. Medication and other forms of aid frequently help these patients.

A disease in which the tissue that surrounds and protects many nerve fibers is destroyed is called **multiple sclerosis** [*skluh ROH sis*]. It causes the patients to gradually lose nervous system control over much of the body, especially the muscles. Patients develop trouble walking, talking, and seeing. Symptoms may disappear and never return, or they may return years later. The cause of this condition is unknown.

Although there is no known cure for multiple sclerosis, its symptoms may be helped by exercise therapy to keep muscle tone. Certain medicines and lots of rest are also helpful to some people. Most people with multiple sclerosis are able to carry out normal activities.

A general term for various disorders that result from brain injury during birth is **cerebral palsy** [*suh REE brul PAWL zee*]. Infections suffered by the mother or toxic substances in her blood during the baby's development may also cause this disabling condition.

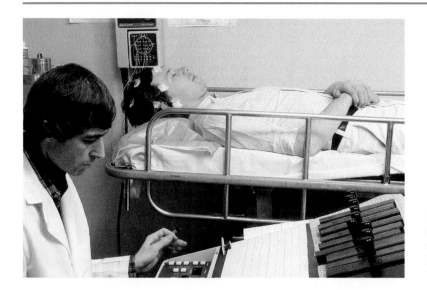

normal EEG

EEG during an epileptic seizure

Figure 13-17   An EEG records changes in the brain's electrical activity. Compare the graph of normal brain activity with one of an epileptic seizure.

The effects of cerebral palsy range from a slight problem in coordinating the muscles to major handicaps. The symptoms may range from jerky movements to poor balance and speech problems. Special exercises help some people overcome the disability to some extent. In severe cases, braces and other supportive devices are often helpful.

A disorder marked by sudden surges of electrical impulses in the brain is called **epilepsy** [*EP uh lep see*]. An attack of epilepsy is called a **seizure.** Some surges may cause violent body shaking and loss of consciousness. Others may cause just a brief clouding of consciousness, such as staring into space.

There are many causes of epilepsy. These might be a chemical imbalance, an infection, a brain injury, a very high fever, or a tumor in the brain. In some cases, the cause is never known. Certain medicines control the seizures and allow most epileptics to lead normal lives. Epilepsy in children is often a mild form of the disorder. It usually ends by adolescence.

Health **History**

Epilepsy was known in ancient Greece. The disease was called "the sacred disease," because people believed that it was a gift from the gods.

Lesson Review

Because the nervous system controls and receives input from the entire body, it often sounds the warning signal for many disorders. Disorders in the nervous system itself range from minor to major problems. Major disorders may be permanent, since neurons seldom regrow. The nervous system should be guarded as much as possible against injury and infection.

1 What is the major cause of headaches?

2 Define *migraine*.

3 What is a contusion?

4 List two inflammations of the nervous system.

5 List two of the symptoms of cerebral palsy.

Chapter Review

Vocabulary

autonomic nervous system
axon
brain dead
brainstem
brain wave
central nervous system
cerebellum
cerebral cortex
cerebral palsy
cerebrospinal fluid
cerebrum
concussion
coma
contusion
coordination
dendrite
electroencephalograph
encephalitis
engram

epilepsy
gray matter
hypothalamus
impulse
insomnia
interneuron
medulla
meningitis
midbrain
migraine
motor neuron
multiple sclerosis
narcolepsy
nervous system
neuritis
neuron
neurotransmitter
paralysis
paraplegia

parasympathetic nervous system
peripheral nervous system
pons
quadriplegia
rapid eye movement
reflex
reflex action
reflex arc
seizure
sensory neuron
sleep apnea
spinal cord
sympathetic nervous system
synapse
thalamus
unconsciousness
voluntary body movement
white matter

Using Vocabulary

Questions 1–13. On a separate sheet of paper, write the term from the column on the right that matches the phrase on the left.

1 message of sensation and information
2 period of sleep when most people dream
3 hard blow to the head that causes unconsciousness
4 fiber that carries impulses away from the cell body
5 part of the brain that controls balance and maintains posture
6 inability to sleep
7 group of organs and nerves that control your thoughts and actions
8 basic unit of the nervous system
9 term for disorders that result from brain injury during birth
10 automatic response to a change in the environment that occurs without action from the brain
11 disorder marked by surges of electrical impulses in the brain
12 brain center that controls breathing, heart rate, and swallowing
13 changes in the electrical activity of the brain

a cerebral palsy
b reflex
c nervous system
d epilepsy
e rapid eye movement
f brain waves
g cerebellum
h medulla
i neuron
j axon
k insomnia
l impulse
m concussion

Interpreting Ideas

1 What part of the body is affected in a case of paraplegia? of quadriplegia?

2 Compare and contrast neuritis, meningitis, and encephalitis.

3 Describe the stages of sleep. How many cycles of sleep usually occur in one night?

4 Describe the functions of each of the three divisions of the brainstem.

5 Identify and briefly describe the two major parts of the nervous system.

6 Describe a neuron—its parts, its function, and its importance in the body.

7 Describe two kinds of headaches and list their causes.

8 Identify the two main parts of the central nervous system. How are both parts protected?

9 What steps can you take to get a good night's sleep?

10 Describe the condition known as sleep apnea—what causes it and why a person with this condition feels tired during the day.

11 Describe the three types of neurons.

12 What is the difference between a concussion and a contusion?

13 Why is the cerebral cortex also called the gray matter?

14 What are some causes of epilepsy? How can the seizures be controlled?

15 If neurons do not actually touch one another, how does an impulse get from the axon of one neuron to the dendrite of the next neuron?

16 What is the function of cerebrospinal fluid?

17 Identify and describe the two parts of the autonomic nervous system.

18 What is the function of most reflexes? How does a reflex happen so quickly?

Applying Concepts

1 Bob accidentally touched a hot baking dish on the stove. He quickly moved his hand away from the dish. (a) Was Bob's action voluntary or involuntary? (b) Did Bob feel pain before pulling his hand away? (c) What happened in his central nervous system that allowed Bob to act so quickly?

2 How can a person be blind even though there is nothing wrong with his or her eyes?

3 What changes occur in your brain when you practice a piano piece over and over? How are your senses involved?

4 How are the central and peripheral nervous systems like a telephone system?

5 Identify the part of the autonomic nervous system that is more active in each of the following activities: (a) sleeping restfully, (b) running in a marathon, (c) saving a drowning victim, (d) reading a book in a hammock.

6 Why is the medulla vital to life?

7 What part of the brain might be damaged if a person is suffering from loss of speech and memory? loss of balance and coordination? loss of control of eye movements?

8 If you wanted to remember your dreams, during which part of the sleep cycle would it be best for you to wake up?

9 Use the information in each of the following examples to suggest a diagnosis: (a) Frank began to experience double vision and unsteadiness in walking at age 35. Two years after these symptoms cleared up, he became paralyzed. (b) Since the age of 10, 15-year-old Jane suffered momentary lapses of awareness and periods of violent shaking. (c) Three-year-old Aaron woke with fever and a stiff neck. His parents noticed later that day that he was sensitive to bright lights.

Projects

1 Find out more about the two halves of the brain: what functions each side is specialized to perform and how the sides communicate with each other.

2 Find out how optical illusions trick the brain. Create several optical illusions on poster board and put on an optical illusion magic show.

3 Invite the school nurse or other trained professional to do a simple neurological test of a student's reflexes. Ask the nurse to explain as he or she goes through each of the following tests: the knee-jerk reflex, the reflex reaction of the pupils of the eyes, and the Babinski reflex test for both infants and adults.

Proper exercise throughout life can help you remain active during later years.

◆ LIFELONG ◆
F I T N E S S

Being physically active is as natural and necessary as eating and sleeping. The need for exercise is not new. Many years ago, most people had to use physical labor in their daily lives. Today much of this work is done by machines. But the body still needs exercise.

Being fit makes it easier to carry out your everyday activities. A fit person has energy to study long hours, play in a band, or perhaps meet the demands of a part-time job after school. In addition, the physically fit person can enjoy many activities such as swimming, biking, and canoeing with friends and family. Physically fit people look good, stay at a healthy weight, and feel better about themselves. Set yourself goals of increased physical fitness and explore the many activities that can help you attain these goals. After reaching your overall fitness goal, it is important to make exercise a regular part of your life.

Objectives

- List the benefits of physical fitness.

- List the five components of fitness and the ways to test for them.

- Identify four factors to consider when developing an exercise plan.

- Describe how to check heart rate during a workout and calculate maximal heart rate and target heart rate.

- Describe the three stages of a physical fitness workout.

- Identify three safety considerations in planning a physical fitness program.

Test Your Fitness Level

Ken wants to build his muscles so that he can make the football team next year. Tara wants to be able to run the 100-yard dash fast enough to beat a rival at another school. Yukio is looking for an exercise to trim her body and help her lose some extra weight. David gets winded after five minutes in a neighborhood basketball game and would like to increase his playing time.

Do you recognize yourself in one of these four people? Physical fitness is a personal matter. Your interests and abilities differ from those of other people, yet improved physical fitness will increase your enjoyment of any activity you choose. Understanding the health benefits of physical fitness will also give you good reasons to get in top condition.

Benefits of Fitness

The ability of your heart, blood vessels, lungs, and muscles to work their best is called **physical fitness.** To be physically fit, you need a regular program of exercise. Exercise makes your muscles and bones strong. It works your circulatory and respiratory systems so that they deliver needed amounts of fuel and oxygen to your cells with less effort. Exercise also improves your coordination. In addition, it burns Calories and aids the digestive system. Fitness helps you look better, manage your weight, and have more energy. Overall, people who are physically fit tend to be more healthy. They usually have lower blood pressure, fewer cases of heart disease, and increased resistance to disease.

Fitness Tests and Ratings

Testing for physical fitness is a good way to identify your physical strengths and weaknesses. The tests that follow measure different components of fitness. Each one shows how well certain parts of your body are working. You can be fit in one component and be unfit in others. Overall fitness requires a well-rounded approach to developing all the components. These tests will give you an idea of how fit you are overall. The tests are easy to take and need little equipment. If you test yourself, work with a partner. It is safer, and more fun. It also may be easier for someone else to measure your time and other factors.

Each test has a rating chart. The ratings range from poor to excellent. The ratings are based on performance. Keep in mind that these ratings give only a rough idea of your fitness. A *good* rating is within the reach of most young people who are free from physical disability.

Do not worry about how you rate against others, since comparisons may not be very helpful. For example, if a 125-pound person can do eight pull-ups and a 175-pound person can do only six, who is stronger? The heavier person does fewer pull-ups but is lifting an extra 50 pounds. Such a comparison is not very useful. Rather, use the tests to help you set the goals that work best for you. After a time of working to meet your goals, you may want to retest yourself to see how well you have progressed.

Improved Appearance
Maintains good muscle tone
Keeps off excess fat
Maintains posture

Improved Body Functions
Strengthens bones and ligaments
Provides strength and muscular endurance
Keeps muscles and joints flexible
Improves digestive and excretory functions
Sharpens nervous control
Reduces chances of injury
Provides greater energy

Improved Health
Reduces backaches
Enhances cardiorespiratory efficiency
Lowers blood pressure
Increases resistance to disease
Reduces the risks of heart disease

Improved Mental, Social, and Emotional Well-being
Improves self-image
Reduces stress
Improves alertness
Enhances quality of sleep
Increases social involvement
Relieves depression

Figure 14–1   Some benefits of physical fitness

Cardiorespiratory Endurance

The ability of the heart, lungs, and blood vessels to send fuel and oxygen to the body's tissues during long periods of vigorous activity is called **cardiorespiratory endurance** [*kahr dee oh RES pur uh tawr ee*]. It is the single most important component of fitness because it greatly affects your overall health. High endurance shows that your heart, lungs, and muscles can work efficiently for a long time without tiring. A person with high cardiorespiratory endurance has more energy and ''wind.'' Such a person tends to have a slower, stronger heartbeat than a less fit person. This is true when the person is at rest as well as when the person is active.

You can get a good idea of your cardiorespiratory fitness from taking certain tests. One test is the time it takes to run a distance of one mile. The higher your endurance, the more quickly you will be able to run the distance. Figure 14-3 provides standards for a one-mile run test. If you have not been active recently, do not take the test immediately. Instead, wait and take the test after you follow an exercise program for a while.

To take the one-mile run test, use an area where distance has been measured and marked out, such as a track or athletic field. Find out the number of laps it will take to complete a mile. For example, it will take you four laps to complete one mile on a 440-yard track. You may want to practice for a few days so that you can give it your best. Before taking the test, be sure to warm up your muscles by stretching and walking quickly for about five minutes. For the test, use a watch to time yourself, and go as quickly as you can. You may only be able to run a short distance at a time. If so, take turns running and walking, but keep going as quickly as you can for the whole distance. Your score is the time it takes to cover one mile.

Figure 14–2 One-mile run test

	One-Mile Run		Step Test
	Girls	Boys	Pulse rate (30 seconds)
Outstanding	under 7:30	under 6:30	50 or less
Excellent	7:31–8:00	6:31–7:00	51–55
Good	8:01–8:30	7:01–7:30	56–60
Average	8:31–9:00	7:31–8:00	61–65
Fair	9:01–9:30	8:01–8:30	66–70
Low	9:31–10:00	8:31–9:00	71–75
Poor	10:01 plus	9:01 plus	76 plus

Figure 14–3 This table gives ratings for cardiorespiratory endurance tests. Times are given in minutes and seconds.

  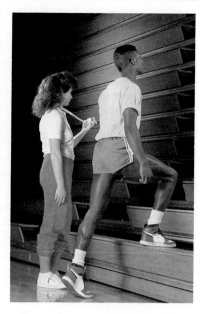

Figure 14–4   Step test

You may choose to try the three-minute step test instead of the one-mile run. This test shows how your heart recovers after a period of stepping on and off a bench. Although it is not the best measure of cardiorespiratory fitness, it does show how your heart responds to exercise. A person who is physically fit will recover faster than a person who is less fit. All you need to take the test is a steady bench or chair that measures about 16 inches high. The first row of a bleacher makes a good stepping bench.

To take the test, step up and down off the bench 30 times a minute for three minutes. Step up with one foot, then bring up your other foot. Then put the first foot down, the other following. Be sure to straighten your knees when you are up on the bench. You must stand with both feet on the bench before you step down. Have a partner there to catch you if you lose your balance. Stop if you become very tired, have trouble breathing, or feel pain. See Figure 14-4 for the correct order of steps. Complete a full set of up-and-down steps every two seconds.

After three minutes of stepping, sit down and find your pulse. Place the two fingers of one hand on the wrist of the other hand just before the base of the thumb. Do not check your pulse with your thumb. The thumb has a pulse which could confuse you. After sitting quietly for one minute, count your pulse for 30 seconds. Do not count your pulse for a full minute, since your heart rate is still going down. A pulse rate of 50 or less in 30 seconds shows a very high level of physical fitness. Refer to Figure 14-3 to find your rating.

Strength and Muscular Endurance

The ability of a muscle to exert force is called **strength.** Lifting a weight and pushing against a wall are acts of strength. The greater weight a muscle can lift, the greater its strength. You gain strength when you overload your muscles, or push them to do more than they already can.

Muscular endurance is the ability to apply strength over a period of time. This includes the ability of a muscle to work over and over again. It is also the ability to hold a contraction over a period of time. Many day-to-day activities require endurance. For example, keeping a firm grip on a screwdriver while putting up shelves requires muscular endurance.

The upper body, abdominal area, and legs are most often tested for strength and endurance. Sit-ups test the abdominal area. To do sit-ups, lie on your back with your hands clasped loosely behind your neck. Draw your feet back, bending your knees until your feet are flat on the floor. Sit-ups should never be done with the legs straight. If you do sit-ups with your legs straight, your hip muscles, rather than your abdominal muscles, do most of the work of curling your body up. Your lower legs should be at a right angle to your thighs, and your lower back should be flat against the floor. For the purpose of testing, you may have a partner place one knee between your feet and hold both of your ankles, as in Figure 14-5. However, with such support, you also tend to use the hip muscles more than the abdominals and is only suggested for testing. To do a sit-up, curl your body up until your elbows reach past your knees. Gently return to the floor. Be sure to curl your back, rather than coming up with a straight or arched back. Do not pull yourself up with your hands, or let yourself fall back heavily. Either could cause an injury.

Your score is the number of sit-ups you do in one minute. You may rest during the test, but only on your back with your hands and legs in the proper positions. Only complete sit-ups with the hands behind the head should be counted.

Pull-ups measure upper-body strength and endurance. For pull-ups, start by grasping an overhead bar with your palms facing away from you. Hang with your arms straight. Pull yourself up until your chin clears the top of the bar. Then lower yourself to the starting position, with your arms straight. Do as many pull-

Health Bulletin

During endurance competition, such as running a marathon, muscle tissue may use up all of its stored glucose. The muscles then can no longer contract, and the runner stops moving. This is known as "hitting the wall."

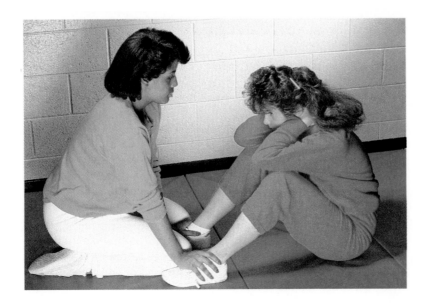

Figure 14-5 Sit-ups must be done carefully to avoid injury.

Figure 14–6 Pull-ups and the flexed-arm hang use the same upper body position. Author Bud Getchell shows the proper way to spot a person during this test.

ups as you can. There is no time limit. Score only those in which your chin clears the bar, as shown in Figure 14-6. You must also return to a "dead hang," with your elbows straight, between pull-ups. Have a partner help you count and hold you if you start to slip.

The flexed-arm hang is an alternative test for those unable to do a pull-up. As in a pull-up, grasp an overhead bar with your palms away from you. Raise yourself until your chin is above the bar and your elbows are flexed as in a pull-up. You may use a ladder or have help to get into the flexed position. When you are in position and no one is supporting you, have someone start timing you. Your time ends when you can no longer hold the position. Your score is the number of seconds your chin stays above the bar. Use Figure 14-7 to see how you rate on these tests.

Figure 14–7 These tables give ratings for the muscular strength and endurance tests. Use the flexed-arm hang if you cannot do one pull-up.

Flexed-arm hang Seconds	
30 plus	Should be able to do one or more pull-ups; try again
15–29	May be able to do a pull-up; keep working on upper body
up to 14	Need more work

	Sit-ups		Pull-ups	
	Girls	Boys	Girls	Boys
Outstanding	40 plus	45 plus	5 plus	8 plus
Excellent	35–39	40–44	4	7
Good	30–34	35–39	3	6
Average	25–29	30–34	2	5
Fair	20–24	25–29	1	3–4
Low	15–19	20–24	0	2
Poor	up to 14	up to 19	0	0–1

Flexibility

The ability to bend joints and stretch muscles through a full range of motion is called **flexibility.** All movements require some degree of flexibility. Joints and muscles that are not flexible limit movement and add to the risk of injury. When you increase your flexibility, you help prevent muscle strains and other problems, such as backache. Flexibility is especially important in activities such as gymnastics and dance.

Since flexibility involves all of your muscles and joints, no single test can measure your overall flexibility. The following test, the sit-and-reach test, is an example of one flexibility test. It tests your ability to stretch the major muscles in your lower back and the back of your legs. These muscles are often the first to tighten up, so their flexibility helps show your general flexibility. Figure 14-8 provides you with a rating scale for this test.

Sit with your legs straight and the bottoms of your feet flat against something solid, as shown in Figure 14-9. Do not wear shoes. Stretch your arms forward as far as they will go without pain. Hold this position for a count of three. Do not bend your knees. Do not bounce forward and back, as this can injure muscles and tendons. Have someone measure the number of inches between your fingertips and the soles of your feet. If you are not able to reach your toes, the distance is a negative score. If you can reach beyond your toes, the distance is a positive score.

Motor Skills

Overall coordination involves the use of a range of motor skills. **Motor skills** are skills of balance and control of movement. Such motor skills bring together all the other elements of fitness. You see well-developed motor skills in action when you watch great athletes or dancers.

Different activities, such as sprints, walking, balance beam, and various jumps, use different motor skills. Thus any one test cannot measure all the skills used in motor activities. However,

	Sit-and-Reach Test	
	Girls	Boys
Excellent	+5 to +8 in.	+4 to +6 in.
Good	+2 to +4 in.	+1 to +3 in.
Average	+2 in.	+1 in.
Fair	−1 to +2 in.	−3 to +1 in.
Low	−4 to −2 in.	−6 to −3 in.

Figure 14–8 This table gives ratings for the sit-and-reach test. Distance reached beyond toes is plus (+); distance short of toes is minus (−).

Health History

The greatest standing jump athlete was Ray Ewry of the United States, who won every gold medal in three events during four Olympic Games. Born in 1873, Ewry contracted polio as a child and lost the ability to walk. He trained himself to become a world-class athlete.

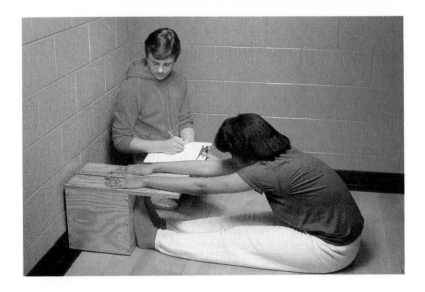

Figure 14–9 Sit-and-reach test

Figure 14–10 Standing broad jump

the standing broad jump and an agility test can give you information about your abilities in these areas. These two tests also serve as a general test of your motor skills.

The standing broad jump is a measure of coordination and the body's power. Stand behind a line on the floor. Bend your knees, and swing your arms backward as in Figure 14-10. Then jump forward as far as you can. Swing your arms forward during the jump to help yourself go farther. Mark the spot where your back heel lands. Try a few times, and use your best jump as your score. An average jump is a distance equal to your height. Figure 14-11 presents ratings for this test and the agility test.

The agility test measures your ability to change direction quickly. To take the agility test, first place two parallel strips of tape on the floor eight feet apart and a third halfway between them.

	Standing Broad Jump		Agility Test
	Girls	Boys	Times crossed middle line
Outstanding	80 in. or more	90 in. or more	20 or more
Excellent	73–79 in.	83–89 in.	18–19
Good	66–72 in.	76–82 in.	16–17
Average	59–65 in.	69–75 in.	15
Fair	52–58 in.	62–68 in.	13–14
Low	45–51 in.	55–61 in.	11–12
Poor	38–44 in.	48–54 in.	up to 10

Figure 14–11 This table gives ratings for motor skills tests.

Stand with one foot on each side of the middle line, as shown in Figure 14-12. With someone timing you, sidestep to the left until your left foot crosses over the left line. Then sidestep back to the right, until your right foot crosses the right line. Keep sidestepping to the left and right. Your score is the number of times both feet cross the center line in 20 seconds. If your feet cross each other the test will not count. You must face forward during the whole test. Wear rubber-soled shoes. Leather and other nongripping soles may cause you to slip.

Body Composition

The amount of fat tissue relative to the other tissue in your body is called **body composition.** Your body composition is based not on how much you weigh, but on how much of your weight is fat. You can have a heavy, athletic build and have very little fat, or be slim but have poor muscle development and relatively more fat. A **skinfold caliper** is a simple tool used to measure the amount of fat on the body. It will help you estimate the proportion of non-fat body weight to fat weight in your body.

You will probably want to perform this test in privacy. You will need someone experienced with calipers to measure your skinfolds. Skinfolds are usually measured on the body's right side. Generally two or three measurements are made at each site. Use the average of the readings as the skinfold measurement for the place measured. Two sites are measured, to give an average reading of total body fat.

For girls, the sites to be measured are the triceps and side of the waist. Measure the triceps skinfold midway between the shoulder and elbow joints, on the back of the upper arm. For the side of the waist, measure just above the hipbone. For boys, the measurements should be taken at the bottom of the shoulder blade and the front of the thigh. The thigh measurement should be taken on the front of the leg, midway between the hip and knee.

To measure a skinfold, grasp the skin between the thumb and forefinger, pulling the fold away from the underlying muscle. Apply the caliper pincers one-half inch below the finger pinch, as shown in Figure 14-13.

Figure 14–12 Agility test

Figure 14–13 The skinfold test requires the use of calipers. With practice you will be able to take accurate measurements.

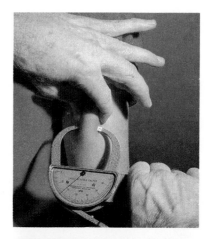

Chapter 14 Lifelong Fitness **263**

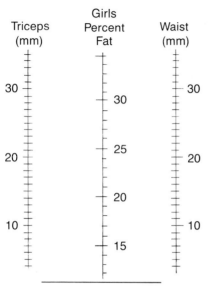

Triceps (mm) · Girls Percent Fat · Waist (mm)

Shoulder Blade (mm) · Boys · Thigh (mm) · Percent Fat

	Percent Fat in Total Body Weight	
	Girls	Boys
Very low	16–18	7–10
Low	18–20	10–13
Average	20–24	13–17
Above average	24–29	17–22
Very high	29–35	22–30
Obese	35 or more	30 or more

Your percentage of fat can be quickly determined from Figure 14-14. Lay a ruler across the points where your two skinfold values lie on those scales. The point at which the ruler crosses the percent fat scale is your percent fat value. For instance, a girl with skinfold values of 20 millimeters each has a body composition of 24 percent fat. A boy with skinfold values of 20 millimeters each has a body composition of 20 percent fat.

Your sex, heredity, and age account for the distribution of fat on your body. The pattern of stored fat on your body is called **body fat distribution.** Women tend to store fat on their legs, hips, and upper arms. Men tend to store fat around the abdomen. When your fat tissues grow, they do so in a pattern that is particularly yours. When you lose fat, it comes from all of your fat tissue. You cannot exercise to lose fat from particular spots, but you can do exercises to tighten up the underlying muscle in a certain area. You also cannot perspire fat away. Perspiration is simply water and other fluids.

Remember, the best way to lose fat and keep it off is to combine exercise with a moderate diet. Your fat tissues grow when the energy in the foods you eat is not used up during your daily activities. Any sort of food can be stored as fat.

Lesson Review

Being physically fit helps you stay healthy and carry out your daily activities. Physical fitness is made up of cardiorespiratory endurance, muscular strength and endurance, flexibility, motor skills, and body composition.

1 What is physical fitness?

2 What is cardiorespiratory endurance?

3 What distance would an average standing broad jump cover?

4 What are the five components of fitness?

Exercise Guidelines

By now you should have an idea of how fit you are. Do not be discouraged if you did not score well in some areas. Instead, use the information to set fitness goals for yourself. Different people have different fitness goals. Some people exercise because they want to compete in athletic events. Others enjoy the chance to be involved with a group. Many people exercise because they are concerned about how they look.

Set goals that are reasonable for you so that you can have the satisfaction of reaching them. Whatever your goals, there are four factors to consider in selecting exercises. These factors are intensity, duration, frequency, and type of activity.

Exercise Intensity

How hard you exercise is called the **exercise intensity.** To improve your physical fitness, you must work your muscular and cardiorespiratory systems at higher-than-normal levels. You do this by imposing a stress that is greater than normal on the body or muscle. This will produce a quicker heartbeat, an increased blood flow, and deeper breathing.

During exercise, your heart must pump enough blood to meet the needs of your muscles. The harder your body works, the faster your heart pumps. Of course, your heart has a top speed. Your **maximal heart rate,** or HRmax, is the highest heart rate at which you can exercise safely. It is your heart rate at exhaustion. At rest, the average person's heart beats about 70 times each minute. The average HRmax for a young person ranges from 180 to 200 beats per minute. The difference between the rate of heartbeat at rest and the rate of heartbeat at exhaustion is the **heart rate reserve.** For the average person, the heart rate reserve will therefore be the range between 70 and 200. The rate at which you must exercise your heart to improve your cardiorespiratory fitness is called your **target heart rate.** The target heart rate is the sum of your resting heart rate and 70 percent of your heart rate reserve. As you become more fit, your target heart rate will probably change because the range of your heart rate reserve will change.

Exercising at too low an intensity does not overload your heart enough to improve your fitness. But exercising at too high an intensity is not necessary to improve your fitness. Too much exercise can lead to fatigue and injuries. When you become too tired, your judgment and muscle control decrease, which may cause an injury. Most injuries are the result of doing too much too soon. Your heart, lungs, and muscles need time to adjust to the increased demands you are making on them. Prolonged fatigue for one hour or more after you exercise is another sign that your activity was too demanding.

You can check your exercise intensity by counting your pulse rate immediately after exercise. You can find your pulse in several places. A **pulse point** is a place at which you can feel your pulse easily. A pulse point on your neck and another on your

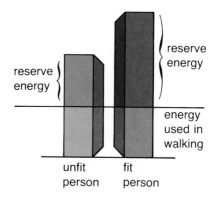

Figure 14–15 A physically fit person has more reserve energy.

Figure 14–16 Fitness gains require exertion, but not to the point of exhaustion. You should be able to talk comfortably during exercise.

wrist are usually the easiest to find. Use whichever one works best for you. Both pulse points are shown in Figure 14-17.

Practice taking your pulse at rest. Use a watch or clock with a second hand. Count your pulse for 30 seconds, and multiply the number of pulses by 2 to find your pulse rate per minute. Your pulse rate is equal to your heart rate, since each pulse is produced by one heartbeat.

When checking your heart rate during a workout, take your pulse within five seconds after you stop exercising. Count the beats for ten seconds. Then multiply your ten-second pulse rate by six to determine your pulse in beats per minute. This is your exercising rate. It is important to check your pulse quickly after exercise, since it slows down rapidly once you stop moving.

Figure your target heart rate by completing the following steps:

1 Take your heart rate at rest.

2 Subtract your resting rate from 200, the average HRmax. This will give your heart rate reserve.

3 Multiply your heart rate reserve by 0.70.

4 Add the result to your resting rate. This number is your target heart rate.

For example, suppose your resting heart rate is 70 beats per minute. Subtract 70 from 200 to get 130, your heart rate reserve. Multiply 130 times .70, which equals 91. Add 91 to 70 to obtain 161. Your target heart rate would be 161 beats per minute. Thus the rate at which you must exercise to improve your cardiorespiratory fitness is 161. Because this formula includes the resting heart rate, the result is a more exact figure—one that considers individual differences in fitness levels.

Exercise Duration and Frequency

The length of time given to an exercise is known as the **exercise duration.** You will get the greatest cardiorespiratory benefit if you exercise at your target heart rate for a period of 20 to 30 minutes. For a beginning program, however, you may be unable to exercise for 20 minutes at this level. At the start, limit your workout to a session of 10 to 15 minutes. Include several one-minute recovery periods between periods of heavy activity. The recovery periods should involve mild exercise such as brisk walking, rather than complete rest. Such mild activity helps you rid your blood stream of waste products more readily. Recovery periods allow you to stretch your workout over a longer period of time, allowing your heart to pump at a high rate without exhaustion. Eventually you will be able to exercise continuously at your target heart rate for longer periods.

Your **exercise frequency** is the number of times you exercise over a given period. Even though you must exercise regularly if you are to reach and maintain a good level of fitness, daily workouts are not needed. Regular workouts three to five times a week will give you above-average physical fitness. In fact, you should take a day off after two or three days of exercising to give your body a rest.

Figure 14–17 Practice finding and counting your pulse immediately after exercising.

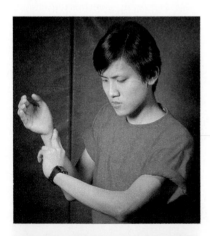

Type of Activity

Not all activities have the same results. Some benefit the cardiorespiratory system, while others increase strength, muscular endurance, flexibility, agility, or motor skills. Activities may differ in both intensity and duration.

Vigorous and continuous exercise is necessary to produce cardiorespiratory fitness. Such exercise includes brisk walking, running, swimming, and continuous dancing. These activities are often called aerobic exercise if they are done for at least 12 minutes. They move the entire body. They raise the heartbeat to a high enough rate for a long enough time to strengthen the heart.

Although cardiorespiratory endurance is the most important part of physical fitness for your health, strength and muscular endurance are also important. They are increased through activities that use isotonic and isometric exercises. **Isotonic** [*eye suh TAHN ik*] exercises contract the muscles and move the limbs. They include calisthenics and weight training, in addition to the exercises listed above. **Calisthenics** [*kal is THEN iks*] are gymnastic exercises designed to develop muscle tone. When done quickly and continuously for at least 12 minutes, calisthenics may also increase cardiorespiratory endurance.

Weight training involves repeating the lifting of barbells, dumbbells, or machines. Through a properly supervised plan, weight training can improve muscular strength and endurance in both boys and girls. Some weight machines are designed to provide maximum resistance to the muscles throughout their full range of movement. Therefore they increase flexibility as well. Weight training usually is not continuous or prolonged. Thus it appears to have little effect on cardiorespiratory fitness. To prevent injury, weight training should be supervised. Movements should be slow and smooth, not abrupt or jerky.

Another form of exercise is isometric exercise. **Isometric** [*eye suh MET rik*] exercise is the contraction of muscle without moving the limbs. Isometric exercise can include pushing against an immovable object such as a wall or the floor, or the pushing of muscle against muscle as in arm wrestling. Isometric exercise is a good way to develop strength without the use of equipment.

Figure 14–18 Low intensity sports often develop motor skills and flexibility, but do not build cardiorespiratory endurance.

Health History

In the 19th century, Eadweard Muybridge of Great Britain pioneered the photographic study of human and animal movement. He photographed the sequence of movements involved in many activities, by using a series of cameras set up along the line of action.

Lesson Review

When you plan an exercise program, you need to consider four factors. These are the exercise's intensity, duration, frequency, and type. A healthy exercise program is one in which you exercise at your target heart rate for 20 to 30 minutes. Frequency should be about three to five times a week. Vigorous and continous activity increases cardiovascular fitness. Isotonic and isometric exercises increase muscular strength and endurance.

1 Define *target heart rate*.

2 How can you check your exercise intensity during a workout?

3 Name three activities that provide cardiorespiratory benefits.

Your Workout Plan

Your workout should be designed to meet your immediate goals and work toward a healthy life. Do not worry about keeping up with your friends and classmates. Remember, you are working with your own body, not theirs. Your fitness will increase in time, but you must work within your present abilities, starting from your present level of fitness. Whatever type of activity you choose, follow intensity, duration, and frequency guidelines to get the best results.

Your health teacher or physical education instructor can probably help you develop a plan and start to follow it. When the class ends, though, the responsibility to exercise rests with you. If you can stay with your program for a few weeks, you will be well on your way to making exercise a regular part of your life. Do not assume that your recreational activities will keep you fit. Often they do not provide enough exercise. You may have to adapt your fitness program as your life changes. But the habit of including exercise in your life is just as important as the habit of a healthy diet.

Preparing to Work Out

When planning a fitness program, you should consider health precautions. It is good to begin planning your program with a complete medical checkup. Individuals who are very overweight or who have medical problems may need to start out with low-intensity activities. If that is true in your case, exercise for longer periods of time at a slower pace. Walking briskly for 45 to 60 minutes is a good exercise. You will gain cardiorespiratory benefits even if your heartbeat does not reach your target rate. Eventually, you will be able to do more intense exercise.

Figure 14–19 Proper instruction reduces safety risks.

Low back pain is a common problem for many people. Many back problems are caused by a lack of muscular strength and poor flexibility. Some back problems and muscle and joint strains, however, can be caused by improper exercise technique. Be sure to do the exercises as instructed. If you have a heart problem, weak back, knee problem, or any other condition that may limit your physical activity, discuss your problem with your doctor when planning an exercise program.

Finally, sufficient rest every day will help ensure your safety. Rest helps to restore strength after periods of activity. It gives your muscles and tissues time to build. You do not need to work out each day, but you do need enough rest.

Workout Stages

Doing your workout in stages will ensure that you exercise safely. Your physical fitness workout should consist of three stages: a warm-up, a vigorous conditioning period, and a cool-down. All three are essential for an effective program.

Warm-up   Increasing circulation to the muscles through slow, fluid motions is called a **warm-up.** Warming up properly before each workout prepares your body for the stressful activity to follow. You will avoid unnecessary injuries and muscle soreness if you warm up first. A complete warm-up gradually builds up the heart rate and blood flow to the muscles. It also raises muscle temperature. It stretches the muscles and tendons in preparation for more forceful movements.

The warm-up should last between five and ten minutes. Cool weather requires longer warm-ups. During your warm-up you should stretch and tone key muscle groups. The exercises shown on the following pages are popular examples.

Conditioning   Exercise that develops cardiorespiratory endurance or muscular strength and endurance is **conditioning.** If you are working on cardiorespiratory endurance, pace your activity so that your average heart rate is at your target level. If you alternate periods of vigorous exercise with exercise of lower intensity, your heart rate can range between 10 or 15 percent above and below your target rate. This will average out at the target level. Conditioning should last between 20 and 30 minutes.

Cool-down   A tapering-off period after completion of the main workout is called a **cool-down.** You cool down to allow slow muscle contractions to pump blood from your limbs back to your heart. If you do not take time to cool down, blood may pool in your muscles and keep other parts of your body from receiving enough blood. Keep moving until your breathing and heart rate return to near normal. Generally, recovery takes about five minutes. Walking is the most common cool-down activity. You should also repeat the stretches you used during warm-up. If you are cycling, cool down with easy slow pedaling. If you swim, do some stretching in the water or on the deck.

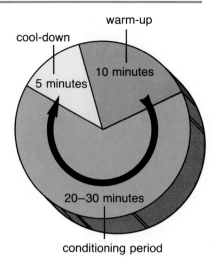

Figure 14–20   A workout should have these three stages.

Warm-up Exercises

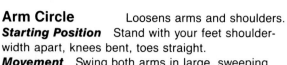

Arm Circle   Loosens arms and shoulders.
Starting Position   Stand with your feet shoulder-width apart, knees bent, toes straight.
Movement   Swing both arms in large, sweeping circles inward across your body, upward across your face, out and back down. Keep your elbows straight and swing your arms from the shoulders.
Repetitions   Start with 10 and build up to 20.

Trunk Twist   Loosens back and shoulders.
Starting Position   Stand with your feet shoulder-width apart, knees bent, toes straight. Hold your arms out at your sides.
Movement   With your heels flat, twist your trunk slowly as far as you can, first to one side and then to the other. Move smoothly; do not bounce.
Repetitions   Start with 6 and build up to 12.

Side Stretch   Loosens back and shoulders.
Starting Position   Stand with your feet shoulder-width apart, knees bent, toes straight. Extend one arm over your head and keep the other down at your side, with both palms inward.
Movement   Bend sideways in the direction of your lower hand. Stretch your other hand over your head in the direction of your bend, keeping your arm straight. Go as far as you can comfortably, then repeat on the other side.
Repetitions   Start with 6 and build up to 12.

Leg Over   Loosens lower back and hips.
Starting Position   Lie on your back with your legs straight, arms out straight, palms up.
Movement   Raise one leg straight up, with toes pointed. Keep your arms on the floor and lower your leg across your body to the floor. Then raise your leg back up, return to the starting position, and repeat with your other leg.
Repetitions   Start with 4 and build up to 8.

Side Leg Raise

Loosens hips.

Starting Position   Lie on one side with your legs straight, head on your hand, upper arm along your thigh.

Movement   Raise your upper leg as high as you can, keeping it straight. Do the repetitions for one side, then repeat on your other side.

Repetitions   Start with 10 and build up to 20.

Low-Back Stretch   Loosens lower back and hips.

Starting Position   Lie on your back with your legs straight.

Movement   Bring one knee to your chest. Grasp the leg just below the knee, and pull the knee toward your chest. Hold for 5 seconds. Curl your shoulders and head toward your knee. Hold for 5 more seconds. Repeat with the other leg.

Repetitions   Start with 4 and build up to 8.

Hamstring Stretch

Loosens back of thighs.

Starting Position   Sit on the floor with one leg straight in front of you, toes pointing up, and the other foot tucked against your extended thigh.

Movement   Lean forward and slide your hands down your straightened leg, until you feel a stretch. Hold for 5 seconds. Do not reach so far that it hurts. Repeat with the other leg.

Repetitions   Start with 2 and build up to 6.

Achilles and Calf Stretch

Loosens calves.

Starting Position   Stand facing a wall an arm's length away, with hands resting on the wall, feet shoulder-width apart, knees and toes straight.

Movement   Lean forward, bending your elbows down slowly. Keep your legs and body straight and your heels on the floor. Do not lean so far that it hurts. Hold for 10 seconds and return to the starting position.

Repetitions   Start with 2 and build up to 6.

All photos were taken at the Indiana University Natatorium, Indianapolis, Indiana.

Workout Choices

The types of exercise you choose will depend on several considerations. Your fitness goals along with your present condition are two important ones. Others are the available facilities, what activities your friends are engaged in, what activities you enjoy, and the cost of equipment. For example, do not choose to play tennis if there are no tennis courts nearby. You will probably find you do not want to travel a long distance to exercise.

Each exercise activity has something different to offer: the speed of bicycling, the floating sensation of swimming; the joy of moving to music in dance; the brisk pace of walking. Whatever you do, be sure to build up gradually. Also remember that the most important part of your workout is increasing your cardiorespiratory endurance.

Figure 14–21 Any sport must be played at a steady, vigorous rate to produce fitness benefits.

Playing sports can provide much enjoyment. Some sports also help build and maintain your physical fitness. You often have to get in shape to enjoy playing your sport. Most sports require

Sport	Cardiorespiratory Endurance	Muscular Strength	Muscular Endurance	Flexibility
Aerobic dancing	G to E	G	G	G
Baseball/Softball	F	F	F	F
Basketball	G	F	G	F
Bicycling (at least 10 mph)	E	G	E	F
Bowling	P	F	P	F
Calisthenics	G	G to E	G to E	G to E
Canoeing	F to G	G	G	F
Football	F to G	F	F	F
Golf	P	F	P	F to G
Gymnastics	F to G	G	G	E
Handball	G	F to G	G	F to G
Hockey	F to G	F to G	F to G	F
Horseback riding	F	F	F	G
Jogging/Running (at least 6 mph)	G to E	F	G	F
Judo/Karate	F	G	F	G to E
Racquetball	F to G	F	G	F to G
Rowing	G to E	G	G to E	F to G
Skating (ice, roller)	F to G	F	F to G	F to G
Skiing (cross-country)	G to E	G	G to E	G
Skiing (downhill)	F	F to G	F to G	G
Soccer	G to E	G	G	G
Swimming	G to E	G	G	G to E
Tennis	F to G	F	G	F to G
Volleyball	F to G	F to G	G	F to G
Walking (at least 3 mph)	F to G	F	G	F to G
Weight training	P	G to E	G to E	G
Wrestling	G to E	F to G	G to E	G to E

Rating scale: P=Poor F=Fair G=Good E=Excellent

Step	Rating from Figure 14–3	One set is:		Start with:	Add 1 set at a time up to:	Approximate distance run:
		Run	**Walk**			
1	Poor	30–45 sec.	30 sec.	8 sets	12 sets	½–¾ mile
2	Low	1–1½ min.	30 sec.	6 sets	12 sets	¾–1½ miles
3	Fair	2–3 min.	30–45 sec.	6 sets	10 sets	1½–2½ miles
4	Average	4–6 min.	30–45 sec.	4 sets	6 sets for two days	2–3 miles
5	Good	8–12 min.	1–2 min.	2 sets	4 sets	2–4 miles
6	Excellent	12–16 min.	2–3 min.	1 set	2 sets	3 miles or more
7	Outstanding	20–40 min.	5 min. or more	Run continuously, then walk until cooled down.		2–4 miles

Figure 14–22 In following this run-walk-run program, run at a target heart rate of 75% heart rate reserve.

some basic conditioning to obtain the fitness needed to enjoy play. This basic conditioning can be part of your fitness plan.

Often people limit themselves in their sports selection. There are a wide variety of activities that can open up new possibilities for a lifetime of enjoyable participation. Try many different activities so that you are not dependent on weather, facilities, or other people for your exercise. Do not shy away from a sport in which you have no experience. Give it a try.

It is important to build exercise habits while you are young to get an idea of the range of activities you may be able to continue at a later stage in life. Figure 14-21 lists many common activities and shows their value in building cardiorespiratory endurance, strength, muscular endurance, and flexibility. Select activities according to your interests and skills.

The run-walk-run plan in Figure 14-22 is designed to take you from your present fitness level and gradually increase your workouts until you can exercise at your target heart rate for 30 minutes or more. Check how you rated on the cardiorespiratory test. For example, if you scored *fair* on the step test or on the one-mile run, start with Step 3. If you rated *good,* start with Step 5.

You may have difficulty starting the run-walk-run program at your rating level. If you have not been running lately, your body will need time to become accustomed to the demands of that form of exercise.

Walking is a natural and healthy form of exercise. It is less stressful than running. Many people think that walking is even more healthful than running. To avoid injury, use a program of walking with gradual increases in distance and vigor. Start out walking at your normal easy gait. Keep a steady pace. At first, cover a mile if you can. Then, as you get used to walking, try to

Figure 14–23   Many people use indoor equipment, a convenient way to raise their fitness level.

increase the distance each day until you can walk two miles. Be sure to check your pulse rate but do not be concerned if you are not at your target heart rate.

Once you can walk for two miles, speed up your pace. This will cause a higher heart rate. As you become accustomed to walking briskly, gradually increase your walks to three miles in 45 to 50 minutes. At this point, providing you have no muscle and joint soreness or any other health limitations, you can consider starting at Step 1 of the run-walk-run program.

Other forms of exercise can help you in your fitness program. Some have advantages over others. Cycling for fitness requires more exertion than a leisurely ride. As a general guideline, you have to ride at twice the speed you jog or run to get the same fitness benefits. For example, running one mile in 10 minutes is equivalent to cycling one mile in only 5 minutes. Alternate high-intensity and low-intensity exercise as in the run-walk-run program and increase the duration and frequency of your high-intensity segments as you are able. Use the steps in Figure 14-22, and cycle at your target heart rate during the "run" segments of your workout. For example, at Step 3, ride a bike vigorously for two to three minutes. Then cycle slowly for 30 to 45 seconds. Start at a level that is easy, and move up at a comfortable rate.

Swimming is an excellent exercise for overall fitness. Swimming one half mile is equivalent to running two miles. In addition, people with joint problems or some types of disability can benefit from swimming because the water supports the weight of the body. Thus no stress is placed on the joints. You can follow the program in Figure 14-22 for swimming as well as running and biking.

Aerobic dancing and similar programs set continuous calisthenics to music. These forms of exercise have good fitness benefits when done properly. Muscle strength, endurance, and tone can be improved throughout the body if the intensity meets the guideline standards. Follow duration guidelines as well. To avoid injury and gain proper fitness benefits, enroll in a program run by a qualified exercise specialist.

Indoor fitness equipment, such as stationary bicycles, rowing machines, and treadmills, are regularly used for cardiorespiratory exercise. Such equipment can provide the heart rate needed to improve fitness. However, be sure you are using the machines safely and correctly.

Sensible Planning

With sensible planning, you can lower your risk of injury or illness from exercise. The extent to which you exercise, the place and weather in which you exercise, and your clothing and equipment all need to be carefully considered. Plan an exercise program that you will enjoy following. Schedule regular times in which you can exercise without rushing. Sensible precautions can help you get the most health benefits and enjoyment from your exercise program.

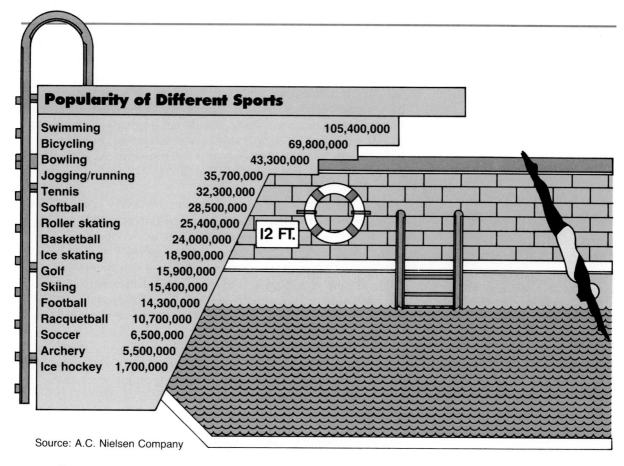

Popularity of Different Sports

Sport	Number
Swimming	105,400,000
Bicycling	69,800,000
Bowling	43,300,000
Jogging/running	35,700,000
Tennis	32,300,000
Softball	28,500,000
Roller skating	25,400,000
Basketball	24,000,000
Ice skating	18,900,000
Golf	15,900,000
Skiing	15,400,000
Football	14,300,000
Racquetball	10,700,000
Soccer	6,500,000
Archery	5,500,000
Ice hockey	1,700,000

12 FT.

Source: A.C. Nielsen Company

Muscle Soreness Many people believe that if exercise does not hurt, it will not help. That is not true. If you feel pain while you are exercising, you are either working too hard or you have not warmed up adequately. It is also common to experience muscle soreness about one day after exercising. This soreness usually disappears after a few days. Muscle soreness is usually due to either muscle strains, lactic acid build-up, or muscle cramps. Chapter 11 covers these subjects in greater detail.

Soreness either during or after exercise can usually be prevented. The best prevention is stretching. Stretch before and after exercising, and any other time you feel sore. Building up gradually will also help prevent soreness. Warm up slowly during each exercise session. Also, start your exercise program at an easy level of intensity. Build up your workouts over time.

One common type of soreness, especially among runners, is a shin splint. A **shin splint** is an aching pain on the front of the lower leg, usually caused by a muscle strain. It happens mainly when the legs are out of shape. As with other strains, treatment includes ice packs for 48 hours followed by heat, and a week of rest with frequent stretching.

If you experience joint tenderness or an inflammation of a tendon, rest for a few days. If the problem continues after a few days, seek professional help. You may have a more serious injury and need medical treatment.

Figure 14–24   The number of people in the United States who participate regularly in several different sports

Where to Exercise

Where to Exercise   Finding a place to exercise can be a problem. Fortunately, many communities now have places for people to work out, such as gyms and indoor swimming pools. School gyms and pools often schedule open hours as well. You may want to consider exercising outdoors. However, remember to take safety precautions. These include not jogging or working out in isolated places. You will also have increased security if you have friends join you. Not only is it safer to work out with others in case of injury, but it is also more fun.

When to Exercise   If you exercise outdoors, you also have to consider the weather. Exercising in the rain or cold is safe as long as you use good judgment. You may enjoy jogging in the rain, but do not go out during a cold downpour. If you exercise during a cold rain, there is a danger that you will become too cold, causing your body temperature to fall dangerously. During freezing weather, you should also keep your hands and ears covered for protection from frostbite. Winter exercise also holds the risk of a serious fall on icy surfaces.

With proper precautions you can avoid the dangers of exercising on hot and humid days. When the body is not used to hot and humid weather, it may overheat, causing illness or even death. Be sure to drink plenty of liquids in hot weather, whether exercising or not. It is important to replace the fluids lost through perspiration. In warm climates and during summer months, an early morning workout is safer. Swimming may be your best exercise choice during the warmer months. See the First Aid Manual for care of problems related to exposure to cold and heat.

You may decide to exercise in the morning, afternoon, or evening. You should not, however, exercise during the hour immediately after a meal. Just after you eat, your digestive system requires an increased supply of blood. Since your muscles need extra blood during exercise, it is best to wait at least two hours after eating before working out. You may also find that exercising late at night makes it difficult for you to fall asleep.

Clothing and Equipment   Your final consideration is proper clothing and equipment. Proper clothing can make a difference in your comfort and safety. Padding will protect your body against the bumps and falls common in many sports. Proper footwear will help protect you from foot and leg injuries.

Choose the right equipment for the activity. For example, running shoes should not be used for basketball; cycling shoes are not suited for tennis. You do not need two pairs of socks unless you are making sudden shifts in direction, as in basketball. Seek advice on footwear from experienced athletes, teachers, and friends.

In general, clothing should be light and loose-fitting for most activities. Cotton shorts and shirts are good for warm weather. Do not wear nylon or rubber clothing in the heat, as it could cause you to overheat. In cold weather, be sure to wear mittens or gloves and a warm hat. Keep your upper body warm with several

---

Health Bulletin

Heat exhaustion is a common illness due to hot weather. It develops as a result of water and salt loss, and is most likely during exercise. People who are not used to hot weather or are not physically fit are most likely to develop heat exhaustion.

Figure 14–25 Do not let the weather keep you from exercising. With proper clothing and safety precautions, you can enjoy the outdoors all year long.

thin layers of clothing, such as a cotton turtleneck sweater and a sweatshirt. You can then peel off or replace layers as you warm up or cool down. The outer layer should be a light windbreaker. Wear reflective clothing when exercising outdoors at night. With proper clothing you can join the many people who enjoy jogging, walking, and cross-country skiing all winter long.

Lesson Review

Keeping fit for a lifetime means choosing a well-balanced program that will build and maintain your overall fitness. Choose a variety of activities that will increase your cardiorespiratory endurance, muscular strength and endurance, and flexibility. When exercising, be sure to consider your safety. Avoid unnecessary injury by warming up and cooling down and by not doing too much too soon. If you exercise outdoors, take sensible safety precautions and watch weather conditions. At different stages in your life you may have to adapt your exercise program.

1 What are the three essential stages that make up a physical fitness workout?

2 What is a good exercise that can be performed even by people with joint problems?

3 Name two types of indoor fitness equipment that can help you improve physical fitness.

4 Why should you keep your hands and ears protected in freezing weather?

5 How long after eating is it best to wait before exercising?

Chapter Review

Vocabulary

body composition
body fat distribution
calisthenics
cardiorespiratory endurance
conditioning
cool-down
exercise duration
exercise frequency

exercise intensity
flexibility
heart rate reserve
isometric
isotonic
maximal heart rate
motor skill
muscular endurance

physical fitness
pulse point
shin splint
skinfold caliper
strength
target heart rate
warm-up

Using Vocabulary

Questions 1-15. On a separate sheet of paper, write the term from the column on the right that matches the phrase on the left.

1 contraction of muscle without moving the limbs
2 exercise that contracts the muscles and moves the limbs
3 ability of a muscle to exert force
4 pattern of stored fat on the body
5 skills of balance and control of movement
6 act of increasing circulation to the muscles through slow, fluid motions
7 ability to bend and stretch through a full range of motion
8 ability of heart, blood vessels, lungs, and muscles to work at their best
9 tapering-off period after completion of the main workout
10 simple tool used to measure the amount of fat on the body
11 ability to apply strength over a period of time
12 measure of how hard a person exercises
13 exercise that develops cardiorespiratory endurance or muscular strength and endurance
14 gymnastic exercises designed to develop muscle tone
15 amount of fat tissue relative to the other tissue in the body

a physical fitness
b motor skills
c muscular endurance
d flexibility
e skinfold caliper
f isometric exercise
g body composition
h isotonic exercise
i calisthenics
j strength
k exercise intensity
l body fat distribution
m conditioning
n cool-down
o warm-up

Interpreting Ideas

1 What is the difference between exercise frequency and exercise duration?

2 List three ways in which exercise can improve your mental, social, and emotional well-being.

3 What are the three stages of a physical fitness workout? What does each stage accomplish?

4 Compare heart rate reserve with maximal heart rate. Is it safe to exercise above the HR max?

5 Describe how the standing broad jump is done. What does it measure?

6 What factors determine body fat distribution?

7 What are the results of working your muscular and cardiorespiratory systems at levels that are higher than normal?

8 What exercise frequency will give you above-average physical fitness?

9 Describe the three-minute step test. What is it designed to show? For which test of cardiorespiratory fitness may the three-minute step test be substituted?

10 Describe the procedure for checking your heart rate during a workout.

11 What are the advantages of increasing your flexibility?

12 What makes fat tissues grow? What is the best way to lose fat and keep it off?

13 Describe the four factors that you should consider in selecting exercises.

14 What is target heart rate? How can you determine your target heart rate?

15 Why is it best to wait at least two hours after eating before working out?

16 In planning your physical fitness program, what safety guidelines should you consider?

17 What does each of the following tests measure: (a) agility test, (b) one-mile run test, (c) sit-ups, (d) pull-ups, (e) flexed-arm hang, (f) sit-and-reach test?

18 Both isotonic and isometric exercises build strength. Which can also build endurance?

19 When you begin an exercise program, why should you include several recovery periods?

20 List four examples of aerobic exercise. How does aerobic exercise affect the body?

Applying Concepts

1 At 14, Dave was thin and unmuscular. What type of exercise might benefit Dave?

2 When she first started an exercise program, Gina had a body composition of 26 percent fat. After six months of aerobic exercise, Gina had a body composition of 23 percent fat. She had lost inches off her waist and hips. When she weighed herself, however, she had gained 5 pounds. How can you explain this weight gain?

3 Andrew's resting heart rate is 72 beats per minute. His HRmax is 200 beats per minute. What is Andrew's target heart rate?

4 When you do sit-ups, why is it important to curl your back up rather than coming up with a straight or arched back?

5 Tracy, who is 5 feet 3 inches tall, was tested with the standing broad jump. How far would an average jump be?

6 If it takes four laps to complete one mile on a 440-yard track, how many miles did Ann complete when she ran 10 laps? How many laps must she run to complete five miles?

7 Explain why the following statement is false: If you wear a sweatsuit or a heated belt while exercising, you will increase the rate at which you burn fat.

8 Which of the following are aerobic exercises? (a) jumping rope, (b) cross-country skiing, (c) weight lifting, (d) golf, (e) cycling, (f) running in place, (g) tennis, (h) roller skating, (i) rowing. Remember that an exercise must be done continuously for at least 12 minutes to be considered aerobic.

9 Julio wants to keep in shape during the winter to be ready for baseball practice in the spring. What safety precautions should he take during the icy conditions of winter?

Projects

1 Sponsor a Physical Fitness Day at your school. Ask the school nurse or doctor to show students how to take their pulse, use a skinfold caliper, and measure their blood pressure. Have a gym teacher or trainer administer the tests for cardiorespiratory endurance, strength and muscular endurance, flexibility, and motor skills. Arrange for a podiatrist or a doctor whose specialty is sports medicine to give a presentation on running.

2 Do a survey of a particular kind of exercise equipment. For example, you might investigate stationary bikes, rowing machines, or weights. Compare four or five different brands for price, special features, and relative quality.

3 With several classmates, put together a series of skits that humorously illustrate some common mistakes a person may make before or during exercise. Ask the audience to guess what mistake is being illustrated.

ANALYZING ADVERTISING

The mission of advertising can be described in three words: persuade, persuade, persuade. Advertising tries to win you over by appealing to your wants or needs.

The heart of an advertisement is its argument. An advertisement's argument is not a quarrel, but the persuasive reasons an advertiser uses to sell a product. The argument is the central message of the advertisement.

Sometimes the reasons for buying a product are clearly stated. For example, consider this slogan: "Heckle's basketball is the best value for the price." In this case, the argument for buying the product is clearly stated—it is the best value.

In other advertisements, the central argument is unstated. For example, consider this slogan: "Jeckle's basketball—play with a champion." Notice that no reasons for buying the basketball are stated. Instead, the Jeckle Company associates their product with the word *champion*. Their appeal is to the flattering image of you as a champion.

The main appeal of an advertisement may not be immediately obvious. It may be hidden by eye-catching pictures or persuasive words. In some ads, the central

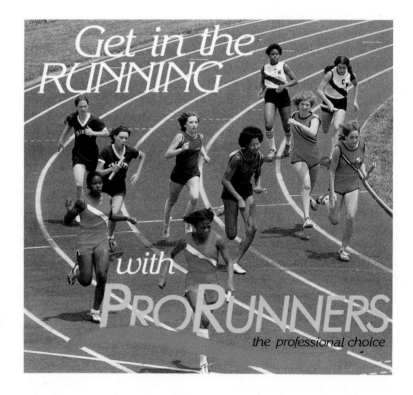

Get in the RUNNING with PRORUNNERS
the professional choice

message tricks or flatters the consumer into wanting the product. Some of the more common types of advertising appeals are described below. You can probably quote the slogans of products that use each of these different forms of appeal.

Pleasure Appeal Ads with this appeal show people having a good time. These people may be at parties or playing games. They appear happy and active. The

central message of such advertising is that using the product will bring you fun and friends.

Snob Appeal Everyone wants to feel successful. That is why some ads feature well-known, successful people. Such ads show well-dressed people in their plush offices or fancy homes. The central message in these advertisements is that if you wish to show that you are successful, you should purchase the product.

Individualism Appeal This technique is a variation of the snob appeal. Do you want people to think of you as your own person—tough and independent? Ads appealing to this desire may show ranchers, mountain climbers, or skydivers—men and women who appear independent. These people seem very sure of themselves. The central message of these ads is that using the product will make you stand out from the crowd.

Bandwagon Appeal Sometimes people just want to be a part of the gang. In this appeal, advertisers imply that everyone is using their product. The central message is that if the product is that popular, maybe you should be using it, too.

Romance Appeal Countless products, from perfume to toothpaste, are sold using romantic images in their advertisements. These ads may show an attractive couple at a candlelit table. The central message of these ads is that using the product will make you more attractive and bring you love and romance.

In the following examples, identify the form of appeal. Then write a sentence that describes the central message presented by the advertisement.

1 A shoe company makes these statements in an advertisement for new running shoes: "Run only in Pro-Runners. Their aerodynamic design increases your speed. These shoes set you apart from the pack."

2 An advertisement for membership in a health club makes the following statement: "Belonging to the Diamond Health Club is a luxury that not everyone can afford. But believe me, baby, you deserve it."

3 A bowling alley develops a radio commercial with the following statement: "Last year over 10 thousand families visited our lanes. Bowling is a great sport for family togetherness!"

4 The manufacturers of a beverage called Awesome Energizer make the following statement:

"Are you building muscles of steel? When you're working for a stronger body, you need more fuel to help renew your body. Drinking Awesome Energizer repairs muscles quickly. It makes your workouts more effective, and helps make a more attractive you."

the shoe that sets you APART from the pack

ProRUNNERS

Becoming physically fit does not require expensive equipment, clothes, or diets. It can be achieved by following the principles presented in this book. If you want to buy things for your physical fitness activities, remember to think critically about advertisements for these products by identifying their central message.

a Luxury you Deserve

DIAMOND HEALTH CLUB

5

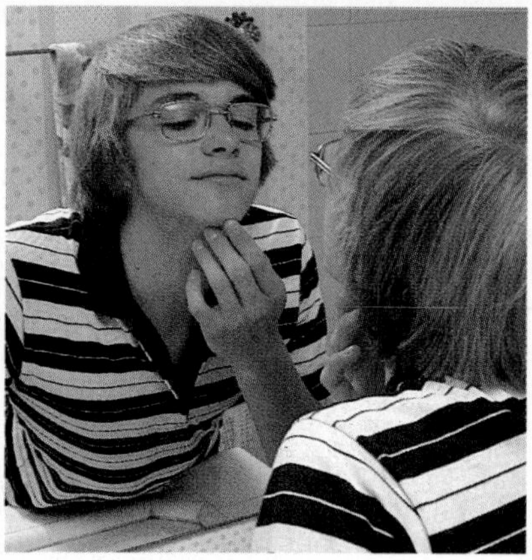

16. Growth and Development

15. Family Life

Human **D**evelopment

17. Reproduction and Heredity

Though the average size of the American family has changed through the years, the family remains the center of American social life.

CHAPTER FIFTEEN

Family LIFE

How would you like to be a member of an exclusive club? One that helped provide your food, clothing, shelter, and education. A club that is very concerned about your health, your happiness, and your future. Its members encourage you to develop your mental, social, and emotional skills. This club would help you plan your future and reach your goals. Wouldn't that kind of club have a new-member waiting list a mile long? Almost impossible to get in? As you have probably already guessed, you are already a prized member. The club is your family.

Objectives

- Describe four different types of families.
- Describe the responsibilities of parents.
- Define *contraception* and list the advantages of family planning.
- Identify three stages in the development of interest in the opposite sex.
- List eight questions to ask when deciding about marriage.
- Explain what happens in a divorce.
- Identify four kinds of help available in times of family crisis.
- Define *child abuse* and *child neglect.*

The Family Unit

If you had been born 100 years ago, your family might have been very different from your family today. Your family would probably have been large with many brothers and sisters. You may have lived with grandparents and cousins. It is likely that you would have lived on a farm. Many families grew their own food, raised their own animals, and made their own clothes.

Since then, there have been many changes in society and in the family. But parents still teach their children responsibility and help them develop values.

Family Structure

Today in this country there are several different types of families. These are the nuclear family, the extended family, the blended family, and the single-parent family. The development of these different types is related to social and economic reasons.

A family consisting of a mother and father and their children is a **nuclear family.** The traditional American family, in which the father was the primary wage-earner and the mother cared for the children at home, was a form of nuclear family. Today, however, the roles of the father and mother are changing. Both may earn wages outside the home, as well as share the responsibility for the home and the children.

A household that contains relatives who are not part of the nuclear family is an **extended family.** Extended families can include grandparents, aunts, uncles or cousins, and also grown-up children living at home.

Extended families may form for many reasons. Grandparents may come to live with children and grandchildren after they retire. The death of a spouse or a parent may leave a relative without a home or without enough money to manage alone.

Many grown-up children live at home before and after marriage. The cost of housing may be too much for a young married couple. They may live with their in-laws until they can save

Figure 15-1   The basic unit of the family—father, mother, and children—has withstood the test of time.

enough money for housing. Single parents gain from the additional benefit of help with the children.

One fifth of the families in this country are **single-parent families.** A single-parent family is a household in which only one parent lives with a child or children. Today in this country, divorce is the major cause of single-parent families. Single-parent families are also created after the death of a parent or when parents fail to get married. Many teenage mothers, for example, do not get married.

Over 90 percent of single-parent families are headed by women. This is because mothers are usually awarded custody of the children in a divorce. **Custody** is the legal right of guardianship over someone. In some divorce settlements, however, the father wins custody of the children. In other cases, divorced parents have joint custody, or equal responsibility for rearing children.

Single-parent families have the same responsibilities and problems as two-parent families. However, the single parent must manage the family alone. This places extra stress on the single parent, who may already have problems dealing with a failed marriage or the death of a spouse. Financial problems are often a major concern in a single-parent family. One parent, usually the father, is required to provide the child with financial support. However, in many cases, these payments are very low, or are not made regularly.

When single parents remarry, they create a **blended family.** A blended family is made up of the natural father or mother, a stepmother or stepfather, and the children of one or both of the parents. The prefix *step* indicates a family relationship by marriage and not by blood. If the new couple have children, these children will be half brothers or half sisters of the other children. The prefix *half* indicates that children are related to each other by blood through only one parent.

Figure 15-2 Loving parents are essential to a child's development.

Family Responsibilities

Providing love and support for one another is one important family function. Another important and difficult job in most families is rearing children. Our society requires that all children be cared for by adults.

Not all children live with their natural parents. Some children are orphaned. Others come from families that are unable to care for them adequately. Such children may be adopted by couples who cannot have children of their own or who simply want a bigger family and would like to give a home to a child who needs one. Children can become a part of a family through the legal process of **adoption.** Sometimes relatives or stepparents decide to adopt children for whom they are responsible. Other couples may decide to adopt a child by applying to an adoption agency. The agency interviews the family and tries to match the family with a child to best meet the needs of both the child and the family. Children may be adopted at any age.

Not all children who cannot live with their natural families are adopted. **Foster children** are children who receive parental care

Figure 15-3 Parents often share with their children the joys of success and achievement.

Figure 15-4 Day care centers play an important role in child care while parents work.

from people without being related to or legally adopted by them. **Wards of state** are children who have been placed under the care of a guardian or the courts. This is usually done for children whose parents are not considered capable of taking care of them. Other children whose parents find difficulty in caring for them may live with relatives, either temporarily or permanently.

Parents' Responsibilities Adults who act as parents must provide food, clothing, and shelter to the children. Parents must also care for children when they are sick. Parents have a legal responsibility to provide these basic physical needs. Working parents also have the responsibility to find loving care and a healthy environment for their children while they are at work. This may involve placing a child in a day care center, or in the care of another family.

Parental care involves more than providing for basic needs. Children need many other things from their family besides food, clothing, shelter, and care when they are sick. Parents should help prepare the child to become a responsible, healthy adult. Parents are responsible for much of the education of their children. Many families pay for all or part of college expenses for children, or help their children start a business or trade. Throughout the life of a child, parents try to give their children love and guidance in helping with the problems of growing up. This involves providing a stimulating environment and using discipline when necessary.

Children's Responsibilities Children also have responsibilities within a family. The child's role in the family changes as the child grows. Young children learn to obey rules and cooperate with other family members. For example, children are often expected to do simple chores and to do well in school. Completing chores and taking schoolwork seriously are signs that children are becoming more mature.

During the teenage years, children begin to take on more adult responsibilities. Teenagers often help care for younger brothers and sisters and may help care for elderly relatives. Teenagers also learn to carry out more important household chores. Many teenagers get jobs to earn money for personal expenses. Other teenagers are expected to earn money to help support the family. Problems often arise between teenagers and their parents over how much freedom the children should have. Teenagers usually want to date, spend more time away from the house with their friends, and drive a car. Each of these activities involves the responsibility of obeying the family's rules. This requires calm, serious discussions between parents and children. Families who successfully work out these issues have succeeded in acting responsibly towards each other.

Responsibilities to Older Family Members An important family responsibility is the concern and care for other relatives as they get older or face serious problems. This responsibility stems from family ties rather than legal obligations. While most adults prefer to be independent, they may need financial help. Longer lifespans and the high cost of hospitalization have increased the numbers of older relatives living with their families.

Communication Honest communication is often listed as the number one factor that makes family life function smoothly. Communication is important between husband and wife, between brother and sister, and between parent and child. Sometimes family members find it difficult to talk about problems. They are afraid people will not listen or that arguments will result. Arguments are a normal part of communication, and do not mean that people have stopped loving one another. Some families find it helpful to set aside certain times for discussion of problems. This means that everyone will be heard and that problems will be treated seriously.

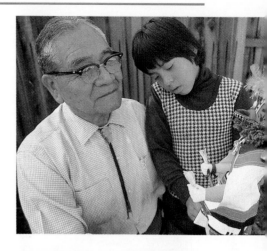

Figure 15-5 In the past, grandparents often lived with families. Today it is not at all uncommon to have grandparents, aunts, or uncles living in families.

Lesson Review

Each member of a family has responsibilities that help the family operate smoothly. Parents provide food, clothing, shelter, love, and discipline for their children. As children grow older, they learn cooperation and take more responsibility for their own behavior. Other family responsibilities include care and concern for older relatives.

1 What are four different kinds of family structure?

2 What is a half sister?

3 What are two important functions that most families fulfill for their members?

4 What are two responsibilities teenagers might have within a family?

Dating and Marriage

Over 90 percent of you will probably marry before the age of 45. You will have had your first date long before that. Dating helps young people learn more about themselves and the responsibilities of developing new friendships. This helps in making decisions about getting married and having children.

Attraction to Other People

Children usually develop an interest in members of the opposite sex during adolescence. There is no one "right" age for this attraction to begin. Boys and girls often feel shy around the opposite sex. Talking to a member of the opposite sex or going places together is a big step for most young people.

Normally in adolescence boys and girls will also develop strong friendships with members of the same sex. Later on, attraction for the opposite sex usually replaces these feelings.

When feelings of interest in the opposite sex begin, they often take the form of crushes or infatuations. An **infatuation** is a short-lived burst of interest in a person. Sometimes teenagers become infatuated with someone they do not know, such as a popular rock star. This brief period of interest usually has no long-lasting results. Infatuations are a sign that a person is developing the ability to form strong attachments.

During adolescence, most people develop an interest in members of the opposite sex. People who are attracted to members of the other sex are said to be **heterosexual.** Some people, however, develop an attraction toward members of their own sex. People who are attracted to members of their own sex are said to be **homosexual.** The reasons for a person's sexual preference are not fully understood. Physical or personal characteristics do not determine sexual preference. Friendships also do not necessarily indicate sexual preference. Most people form friendships, both with members of the same sex and opposite sex, throughout their lives.

Figure 15-6 Infatuations usually happen very rapidly and present an unrealistic view of love. This brief period of interest usually has no long-lasting results.

Figure 15-7 Attending activities with other people helps you to develop friendships with the opposite sex.

Dating

Dating can help young people learn about themselves and others. Dating is also a way to develop responsibility. Agreeing on rules with parents, observing curfews, and showing courtesy to a date are all parts of responsible behavior.

Dating usually begins during adolescence, but all people do not become interested in dating at the same age. A person may be more interested in sports, playing in a band, school activities, or other projects. Shyness may also delay dating.

Dating often begins as a group activity. Attending sports events, dances, parties, or movies with other individuals of both sexes is a form of group dating. Many young people feel more comfortable in this group type of setting.

Surveys show that most young people prefer to date several different individuals before picking out one special partner. But sooner or later, many young people choose one person for a special relationship and go steady. Going steady means that each person will date only the other person. Couples can develop a strong friendship and sense of loyalty to each other. However, steady relationships may develop problems.

Steve and Anne have been going steady for about a year. Steve has left for college in another state. He does not want Anne, a high school senior, to date others. But Anne is feeling lonely and would like to start dating other boys.

Jim and Michelle, both juniors, have been going steady since they were 15. Lately, Jim has been trying to talk Michelle into having a sexual relationship. Michelle wants to continue seeing Jim but she feels that her personal values are being challenged.

How has going steady helped create these problems? Both of these situations call for the people involved to be mature and responsible. Sometimes going steady for a long time can force young people into decisions they are not yet prepared to make. Dating can help people learn more about themselves. Dating helps you value other people and their goals. Couples also have to learn to work out differences. It usually takes years to develop these skills and attitudes, so individuals are more likely to have successful relationships if they do not rush them.

Figure 15-8   Dating different people helps you to learn more about yourself and others.

Teenage Pregnancy

Teenagers have the physical ability to create new life. This fact means that sexual responsibility in a dating relationship is very important. Most teenagers are able to stick to their own personal standards and learn to respect the standards of others. However, statistics show that many teenagers fail to handle this responsibility. One out of every seven births in this country is to an unwed teenager. The number of births to younger and younger girls is increasing. Figure 15-9 compares teenage pregnancy in the United States to that in other developed countries. Pregnancy for a teenager, especially under the age of 18, can be a serious health problem for the mother and her baby. This places a heavy burden of responsibility on both the mother and the father.

Health Bulletin

The teenage pregnancy rate in the United States is the highest in the developed world. It is twice as great as Canada's and seven times greater than that of the Netherlands.

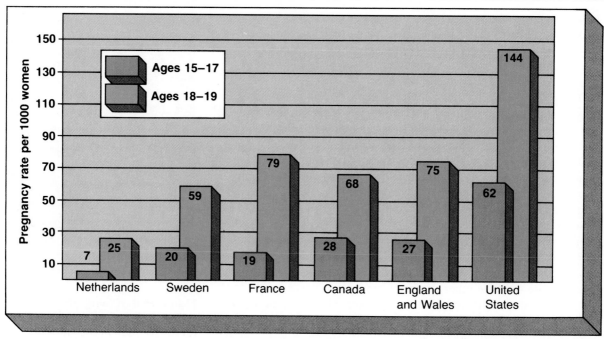

Source: The Alan Guttmacher Institute

Figure 15-9 The United States has the highest rate of teenage pregnancy of all developed countries.

Teenage pregnancy often occurs because teenagers have not given serious thought to the consequences of sexual behavior. Feelings of sexual attraction to a member of the opposite sex are normal. These feelings may occur almost immediately in a relationship or develop over a long period of time. Thinking ahead about how to deal with these feelings is important. Making decisions at the last minute often results in confusion, anger, and strong guilt feelings. An unwanted pregnancy can be the outcome. Setting ground rules for sexual behavior in a relationship is a sign that you are ready for serious, responsible dating.

Teenage pregnancy can also occur because young women feel they are grown-up enough to have a baby. Some girls think that having a baby will make their boyfriends marry them. Some feel a baby will provide them with love and give their life some purpose. These reasons are usually tragically wrong.

Most teenagers who have babies believe they made a mistake in getting pregnant. They realize that they are not ready to care for a baby 24 hours a day. Instead of giving their life a purpose, the responsibility of the baby usually overwhelms them, and they feel trapped. Teenage mothers usually have little money and must drop out of school to take care of their babies.

Teenage fathers are rarely present to help the mother. Despite the hopes of the young woman or the promises of the father, teenage couples with children rarely marry. The father is rarely able to provide his family with any financial support. Even if the mother and father do marry, the marriage is not likely to last. Teen marriages are more likely to end in divorce than the marriages of older couples. These are other signs that teenagers are seldom ready for the responsibilities of parenthood.

Thinking About Marriage

Surveys show that most teenagers plan to marry between the ages of 21 and 25. These plans probably will come true. Ninety percent of the population marries before age 45, and most people marry between the ages of 20 and 24. However, in recent years, the divorce rate has increased greatly. There are over one million divorces each year, and nearly one-half of all marriages now end in divorce. Obviously, many people are marrying before they are ready or for the wrong reasons.

When two people begin to think about marriage, it should be because a strong love has developed. The romantic, head-over-heels feeling should have grown into a more mature, steady relationship. Couples should know each other well and have seen their partners at their best and at their worst. A couple who has never argued has probably not been honest with each other.

The following list of questions are important when thinking about marriage. Think carefully as you answer each.

1 Are your cultural and religious backgrounds similar?
2 Do you have many common interests?
3 Do you have similar goals?
4 How will you support yourselves?
5 Where will you live?
6 Do you want children? If so, how many?
7 Are there advantages in delaying the marriage for a while?
8 Do you get along with each other's family?

There is no clear right or wrong answer to these questions. Some may be more important to you than others. Major disagreements on just one of these questions can lead to serious problems. That does not mean that you should not get married, but it does indicate that you will have to compromise. **Compromise** is the process by which opposing sides settle differences by both sides giving in a little bit. Successful couples can learn to handle conflicts and make changes.

Having similar backgrounds and educational experiences can contribute to the success of a marriage. Decisions about social activities, rearing children, and religious practices are easier to make when couples have similar backgrounds. Although marriages of individuals with widely different backgrounds can succeed, it usually takes more discussion and compromise.

One of the most important questions on the list above deals with money. Problems are sure to develop when a couple does not have enough money. The couple's attitude toward money is just as important as how much money they have. For example, a wife may want to save a larger share of the family income while the husband wants to spend it remodeling the house. Both goals may be important, but someone has to give in if there is not enough money to do both. The couple must agree on financial concerns and work together to reach their goals.

Marriage may not be the right choice for everybody. Some people like to live alone or feel their circle of friends satisfies their need for companionship.

Figure 15-10   A marriage means a lifetime of sharing between two people. While love is important, emotional maturity and shared values and interests contribute to its success.

Health History

The concept of marrying for love is relatively new in the world. For most of history, marriages were arranged by parents. Consideration was usually given to the financial and social status of the bride's and bridegroom's families, rather than to the feelings of the young couple.

Housing	$1678
Transportation	$801
Food	$712
Medical care	$281
Clothing	$186
Other	$550
Total costs	$4208

Source: U.S. Department of Agriculture

Figure 15-11 The cost of rearing a child for one year. Additional costs of day care range from $1200 to $5000 per year.

Figure 15-12 A family doctor or clinic can provide information about family planning.

Having Children

The decision whether or not to have children is one of the most important decisions a married couple makes. Both parents should help make the decision. Children bring great joy, but they also bring a great deal of responsibility. Children demand a great deal of time. Sometimes both parents give up some activities to help rear their children. Children also represent an added expense. From the hospital costs of delivering a baby to clothes and food, a new child is a big addition to the family budget.

Deciding when to have children and how many to have are matters of family planning. Family planning helps a family avoid having children before it is ready and to have only the number of children it wants. By using family planning, couples can be prepared financially and emotionally for a new child.

Family planning involves birth control. Preventing pregnancy, usually by preventing the union of the egg and sperm, is called **contraception.** Some means of contraception are safer than others and some are more effective than others. In addition, some types of contraception are forbidden by certain religions. Before using contraception, it is important to consult a doctor or health clinic for information.

Sometimes, despite family planning, unwanted pregnancies do occur. Unwanted pregnancies bring a great deal of stress. Support and assistance from the family are especially important at this time. Decisions about what to do should be made thoughtfully and with the advice of trusted counselors, family members, and doctors. Both parents must consider that choices are available.

There are many people who wish to adopt babies. If the natural parents are unable to cope with bringing up the baby, a responsible adoption agency will find a loving home for their baby.

Another choice for some people may be abortion. **Abortion** is the ending of a pregnancy. Abortions performed in hospitals or health clinics pose little physical risk for a woman as long as they are performed early in pregnancy. However, abortions performed by someone without medical training can be very dangerous. Abortion is different from contraception since abortion occurs after the woman is pregnant. Many people believe that it is morally wrong to take the life of a fetus.

Lesson Review

Dating requires an increased awareness of social responsibility, including responsibility for sexual behavior. When marriage is being considered, there is a wide range of questions about interests and goals that can help a couple in this decision. Family planning can help a couple prepare for children.

1 Define *infatuation*.

2 Name three common, severe problems of teenage pregnancy.

3 What is the term for the prevention of pregnancy?

Family in Crisis

The family can be a source of comfort and love. But any family can experience serious problems. Sometimes these problems are temporary and can be solved with the help of friends and counselors. At other times, the problems are more serious. Parents who cannot get along break up the family by getting a divorce. Physical violence, neglect, and alcoholism can also threaten the family. Crisis in the family places a great stress on all family members, but children are often the most seriously affected.

Separation and Divorce

Allan and Janice had been married for eight years. They had two children and nearly everyone thought they were happily married. But Janice did not think so. Allan often became violent with her and the children after he had been drinking alcohol. She could not trust him with the children and often he spent all of the family's money on liquor. Janice felt she had to have some time to herself to sort out the problems. Their marriage counselor suggested Allan and Janice live apart for a few weeks.

Allan and Janice agreed to a separation. A **separation** is an act in which husband and wife agree to live apart while they try to work out their differences. In many cases, a separation gives a couple time to sort out their feelings and see what must be done to save the marriage. At other times, a couple may decide that they are happier living separately.

Children often go through the stages of grieving when their parents separate. These stages include denial, anger, bargaining, depression, and acceptance. Children may fear that they are going to be abandoned or that they are going to lose the love and support of one or both parents. Many children blame themselves for the separation. This is rarely true. Marriages break up because two adults cannot get along, not because of what their children do.

Allan and Janice may decide to get a divorce. A **divorce** is the legal ending of a marriage. Divorce involves splitting up a household, including deciding who will receive the things the couple owns. It also involves determining who will gain custody of the children. Divorce agreements usually require that the person who does not have custody of the child pay child support to the parent with the children. **Child support** is money given to the parent who cares for the child for that care. In most cases, the father will pay the mother money to help pay for the children's expenses. The courts require this because even if the father does not live with the children, he still has a responsibility for their upbringing. Child support payments usually continue until the child reaches 18.

Divorces usually represent a final break. Only a small percentage of divorced people later remarry one another. Children often hope that their family can get back together. Parents need to explain to children that this is not likely. However, children can still go on loving both parents. Family counselors can often help children deal with their feelings.

Figure 15-13 Today juggling a job and family places a great challenge on single parents.

Figure 15-14 **Medical professionals are required by law to report cases of child abuse to the proper authorities.**

Violence in the Family

John appeared to be a loving husband and father. No one suspected that at times he lost his temper and beat his wife and children. Peggy was a loving mother. But there were times when she hit her baby because she could not stand to hear it cry.

Violence can easily lead to the injury of a family member and destroy family unity. Violent behavior can appear in any member of a family. Frustration and anger can flare up and cause a person to strike out, even at the closest relative. A father, for example, may feel under a lot of stress because of his job. If the stress becomes too hard to manage, he may take it out on a family member. The physical or emotional maltreatment of children is **child abuse.** It is estimated that more than 100,000 children are severely beaten each year. Many wives are also victims of beatings, and even some husbands are attacked.

Family members are often too afraid or embarrassed to report acts of violence. Signs of physical abuse may include bruises, black eyes, or other noticeable signs. Children often need medical attention for their injuries and parents frequently lie about how the child was hurt. Children sometimes believe that their parents are not doing anything wrong when they hurt them. Children can confuse reasonable discipline with child abuse.

Another aspect of mistreatment of children is child neglect. **Child neglect** is not providing children with proper care. Parents may fail to give their children enough food, warm clothes, or even a home. Parents can also neglect their children by failing to give them emotional support and love.

Parents who are guilty of such treatment obviously need help in dealing with this problem. In some cases, it may be necessary to call the police to stop the violence and get help. In severe situations, the state may remove the child from its home to prevent further harm. In many cities, family crisis centers offer counseling and help for the victims of violence. Parents Anonymous is a group that parents can use if they are abusers of their children. This group works with parents to help them understand and stop their abusive behavior. Children may find it useful to tell friends, teachers, doctors, or youth group leaders about the problem.

Sexual Abuse

Another form of child abuse is sexual abuse. **Sexual abuse** is inappropriate sexual activity between an adult and a child. In some cases of sexual abuse, a father, a close male relative, or an older brother has sexual activity with a female child. Sexual abuse can involve boys, too, if an adult has sexual relations with them. Incidents of sexual abuse are much more difficult to spot than physical abuse or child neglect. But for the victim of sexual abuse, the emotional harm can be great and long-lasting.

Like physical violence, family members are often afraid or embarrassed to talk about the problem or to seek help. Family members need to realize that sexual abuse is not a normal situation and that the abuser should receive help for the problem. The problem of sexual abuse in families has become more publicized in recent years. Many communities now have sexual abuse programs and counselors. Many school counselors are also trained to deal with this problem.

Alcoholism and Drug Abuse

One common cause of family crises is alcoholism. **Alcoholism** is a disease characterized by psychological and physical dependence on alcohol and the inability to control drinking. Alcoholics may easily lose control of their actions. Alcoholics often cause economic problems for the family. They have trouble keeping jobs and use a great deal of the family money for alcohol.

One program designed to help teenagers who have an alcoholic in the family is Alateen. Led by a group discussion leader, teens discuss family problems such as divorce, unemployment, and abuse that are linked with alcoholism. Alateen can help a teenager understand that he or she is not alone.

Family problems can also develop if a family member is an abuser of drugs other than alcohol. Drug habits cause behavior that is not logical and often require huge sums of money. A drug user may turn to crime for the money to support a habit. Family members are often innocent victims.

Runaways

It is not surprising that some children want to run away from a family in crisis. Many runaways leave home because they are being abused by their parents or another relative. Running away may get a child away from the immediate problem, but it usually leads to much worse problems. Without a family to provide food and shelter, runaways often turn to crime to support themselves. Others become the victims of crime.

Many areas of the country have a special telephone number to a Runaway Switchboard. This number connects runaways to a counselor who can answer questions and provide help. The counselors have experience dealing with runaway children and know the problems they face. An operator can give the number of the Runaway Switchboard or other agencies that offer help.

Figure 15-15   Each year over 100,000 runaways are reported in this country.

Lesson Review

Family crises cause great stress for children and other family members. Separation and divorce often result in children being confused about their family situation. Violence and sexual abuse also present serious family problems. Faced with a family crisis, some teenagers choose to run away. Running away usually causes more problems than it solves.

1 What is a separation?

2 Define *child support*.

3 Name three kinds of help people can get if they suffer from child abuse or neglect.

Chapter Review

Vocabulary

abortion	compromise	homosexual
adoption	contraception	infatuation
alcoholism	custody	nuclear family
blended family	divorce	separation
child abuse	extended family	sexual abuse
child neglect	foster children	single-parent family
child support	heterosexual	wards of state

Using Vocabulary

Questions 1–13. On a separate sheet of paper, write the term from the column on the right that matches the phrase on the left.

1 failure to provide children with proper care
2 people who are attracted to members of the same sex
3 ending of a pregnancy
4 process by which opposing sides settle differences by both sides giving in a little bit
5 children placed under the care of a guardian or the courts
6 agreement between husband and wife to live apart while they try to work out their differences
7 children who receive parental care from people without being related to or legally adopted by them
8 household in which only one parent lives with a child or children
9 disease of psychological and physical dependence on alcohol and the inability to control drinking
10 household that contains relatives who are not part of the nuclear family
11 legal ending of a marriage
12 physical violence or emotional pressure directed at children
13 legal right of guardianship over someone

a separation
b child abuse
c alcoholism
d homosexual
e divorce
f compromise
g foster children
h child neglect
i abortion
j wards of state
k custody
l extended family
m single-parent family

Interpreting Ideas

1 Identify and describe four family structures.

2 Describe three stages in the development of interest in the opposite sex.

3 What is one of the main reasons children run away? What problems do runaways face?

4 What are the advantages of family planning?

5 What do infatuations mean in a person's development?

6 What are some sources of help for teenagers who must deal with sexual abuse in the family? For teenagers whose parents are alcoholics?

7 Compare child abuse and child neglect.

8 List three things that must be decided or arranged when a divorce occurs.

9 What is the difference between a stepbrother and a half brother?

10 Describe joint custody.

11 Describe some of the problems teenagers face when they have a baby.

12 What basic physical needs must parents provide their children? What other responsibilities do parents have toward their children?

13 What help is available to parents who are guilty of mistreatment of children?

14 Describe the advantages and disadvantages of going steady.

15 What are the stages of grieving that children may go through when their parents separate?

16 What problems may develop if a family member is an abuser of drugs other than alcohol?

17 What are some of the reasons for the formation of an extended family?

18 How do similar backgrounds and educational experiences contribute to marital success?

Applying Concepts

1 Why do you think that the divorce rate has recently increased to the highest point in history?

2 Why does compromise play such an important role in the success of a marriage?

3 A 17-year-old friend is thinking of quitting school and getting married. When she comes to you for advice about her plan, what will you say to her?

4 Recently Mark confided that his parents were getting a divorce. Not only did Mark feel sad that his family would be splitting up; he also recalled how his parents had frequently argued over him and his brother, and he somehow blamed himself for his parents' decision. Is Mark's thinking on target? How would you talk with Mark about what has happened between his parents?

5 What are some of the advantages of the extended family structure in today's world? Some of the drawbacks?

6 In the last month or so Janet has been acting more reserved than usual and, you notice, even a bit sad. At school last week there were several large bruises on her arms and a cut, partially covered with makeup, just above her left eye. She recently mentioned that her father had lost his job and her mother had begun to work three nights a week. What do you think may be happening in Janet's home? What should you do?

7 How can children benefit from their fathers' taking a more active role in their upbringing?

8 Your best friend has just told you that a close family member, whom she would not identify, has been sexually abusing her for over a year. The abuser has threatened her if she reveals his identity or tries to get help. Under these circumstances, how can you help your friend?

9 What arguments would you use to convince someone not to run away from home? What alternatives might a teenager consider?

Projects

1 Write a series of humorous skits illustrating stages of interest in the opposite sex. Ask several classmates to perform the skits and have the audience guess which stage is being illustrated in each skit.

2 Investigate the agencies and services in your community that are set up to help solve family problems. You may wish to interview a psychiatric social worker about how his or her agency assists families in times of crisis. You may also want to attend a meeting of Alcoholics Anonymous or Alateen to get an idea of how such groups help families struggling with the effects of an alcoholic family member. Other sources of information include a police officer, a school counselor, and a lawyer who handles divorce.

3 Plan a budget for a newly wed family. In your plan include essentials, such as rent or house payment, utilities, food, clothing, insurance, and transportation, and non-essentials such as entertainment and vacations. What are the weekly, monthly, and yearly financial requirements? Who should be responsible for planning the budget? What are some additional expenses that may arise?

4 Spend some time at a nursing home or a senior recreation center talking with some elderly people. Ask them about how they spend their time now and what they plan for their future. What would they do if they were your age? Can the elderly people help you with their advice?

The endocrine system helps to regulate the day-to-day functions of the body as well as coordinate long-term growth.

CHAPTER SIXTEEN

GROWTH
AND DEVELOPMENT

E very moment of your life, chemical messengers are circulating through your blood stream. These chemicals regulate the activity of all your organs. They affect the rate at which you breathe and the amount of energy available to your cells. Chemical regulators in your blood help you respond to stress and influence your emotions.

The chemicals in your blood also send signals that cause your body to grow and change. Every teenager has a particular timetable for development. Some people start growing sooner than others. In any high school class, some students will be fully grown by age 15, while others may not be fully mature until they are 18 or 19. This results in boys and girls of the same age having reached quite different stages of development. Never again in your lifetime will people who are your age have such great physical differences.

Objectives

- Describe the endocrine glands and their functions.

- Describe the major disorders of the endocrine system.

- Describe how the adrenal glands control your body's fight or flight response.

- Describe the changes that occur in puberty.

- Identify the male and female reproductive organs and secondary sex characteristics.

- Describe the process of menstruation.

- Name the common disorders of the female reproductive system.

- Name the common disorders of the male reproductive system.

The Endocrine System

You have already experienced many changes in growth in your life. When you were an infant you could not even sit up. As you entered childhood, you grew stronger and heavier, and began to run and climb. As a teenager, the same organs that caused your rapid development from a helpless baby to a curious toddler continue to play a major role in your growth. Sometime between the ages of 10 and 14 both girls and boys go through the change called puberty. **Puberty** [*PYOO bur tee*] is the stage of development in which the reproductive system matures. Puberty marks the beginning of adolescence, which ends at adulthood.

Your growth during childhood and the changes during puberty are controlled by your endocrine system. The **endocrine system** [*EN duh krin*] is the body's network of organs that control the chemical messengers in the body. The chemical messengers maintain bodily functions and promote growth.

Glands and Hormones

The endocrine system is made up of a set of organs called **endocrine glands** that produce and release hormones. The major glands of the endocrine system are shown in Figure 16-1. **Hormones** are chemical substances that are released into the blood stream and travel to other organs and tissues, where they stimulate growth and regulate activity. Hormones control many functions, ranging from matters as routine as food digestion to long-lasting changes in appearance and size.

Some endocrine glands release their hormones almost continuously. Other glands release their hormones at a specific time. When hormones are released from the glands, they travel through the blood stream carrying chemical messages throughout the body. Some hormones carry messages for only certain cells. Other hormones seem to affect nearly every cell. Some hormones work together to control the changes in your body. Figure 16-5 lists some of the hormones that are produced and released by the endocrine system.

Endocrine Glands in the Brain

The hypothalamus and pituitary glands are located in the brain. The hypothalamus and the pituitary glands are connected by blood vessels and nerves and work together to control the activity of many other glands of the body. The **hypothalamus** [*hy poh THAL uh mus*] is the part of the brain that controls automatic functions, such as breathing, heartbeat, thirst, and appetite. The hypothalamus could also be called the master gland, because it controls the pituitary gland and therefore many other glands. The hypothalamus monitors the levels of hormones in the blood stream. When it senses low levels of hormones, it sends **releasing hormones** to the pituitary gland. These releasing hormones stimulate the pituitary gland to release specific hormones.

The **pituitary gland** [*pih TOO ih tehr ee*] is the gland that produces hormones that regulate growth rate and influence the

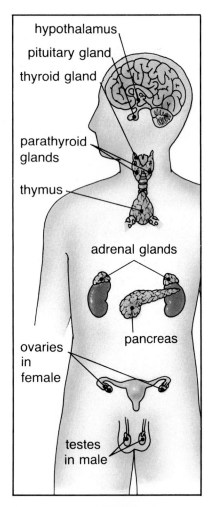

Figure 16-1 The endocrine system. Some people classify the thymus as an endocrine gland since it regulates the immune system. However, it produces antibodies, not hormones.

actions of other glands. The pituitary gland is about the size of a pea. It is located at the base of the brain and is well protected by the hard bones of the skull.

As shown in Figure 16-2, the front part of the pituitary gland is called the **anterior lobe.** The anterior lobe produces several hormones, including a growth hormone that regulates the development of long bones and muscles in the body. It causes growth throughout childhood and adolescence and helps your body reach its adult size. Other hormones influence the growth and hormone production of the reproductive glands. This part of the pituitary is actually controlled by the hypothalamus.

The rear section of the pituitary gland, or the **posterior lobe,** does not produce its own hormones. Instead it stores hormones produced by the hypothalamus that help regulate the body's water balance. It also keeps the kidneys from removing too much water from the blood.

When, in rare cases, the pituitary gland fails to function properly, serious health problems can result. If the pituitary gland does not produce enough growth hormone, a person may be very short but have a normally proportioned body. If too much growth hormone is released during childhood or adolescence, the person may be extremely tall. If too much growth hormone is released during adulthood, the bones of the hands and feet may enlarge. Disorders of the pituitary do not affect mental development.

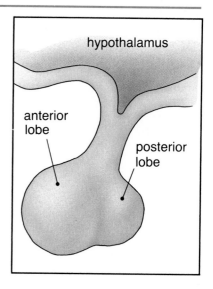

Figure 16-2   The pituitary gland

The Thyroid Gland

At the front of the neck is a large gland that helps control the rate of chemical activity in your body. This gland, shown in Figure 16-3, is the **thyroid gland** [*THY royd*]. The thyroid is shaped like a butterfly and fits around your windpipe. Two hormones released by the thyroid gland control your metabolism. As you recall from Chapter 9, metabolism is the rate at which cells break down nutrients and release energy.

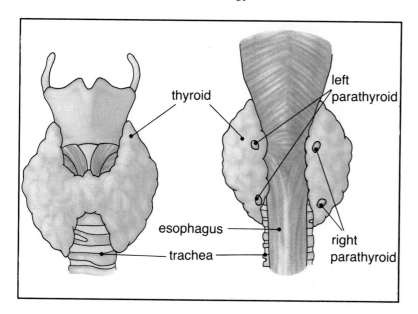

Figure 16-3   The thyroid gland is at the front of the throat (left). The parathyroid glands are firmly fixed in the rear of the thyroid gland (right).

Health **History**

The great physicist Albert Einstein once commented on the influence of the endocrine system. "Even our destiny is determined by the endocrine glands," he said.

The hormones that affect metabolism are made from iodine circulating in your body. Iodine is a mineral found in seafoods and enriched table salt. Some people have diets that do not contain enough iodine. Often the thyroid will respond to the lack of iodine by growing large. An enlarged thyroid is called a **goiter.**

Other problems with the thyroid occur when the thyroid releases its hormones at the wrong rate. An overactive thyroid causes metabolism to speed up. Body cells produce more energy, the heart rate increases, and body temperature and blood pressure rise. These changes may cause nervousness, sweating, difficulty in sleeping, and weight loss. Without treatment, an overactive thyroid can cause damage to the heart.

An underactive thyroid causes the metabolism to slow down. Body cells produce less energy, heart rate decreases, and nervous system activity is reduced. Fatigue, dry skin, weight gain, mental changes, and hoarseness are symptoms. Problems with the thyroid gland are usually treated with medicine and surgery.

The Parathyroid Glands

Four glands that control the levels of calcium and phosophorus in your body are called the **parathyroid glands.** They are attached to the thyroid gland, as shown in Figure 16-3. Calcium and phosphorus are minerals required for healthy bone growth and muscle contraction. A hormone from the parathyroids causes bones to release calcium into the blood stream.

Overactive parathyroid glands cause too much calcium to circulate through the blood. Muscle weakness, weight loss, fatigue, and kidney stones can result. Underactive parathyroid glands lead to low levels of calcium in the blood and usually cause painful muscle spasms.

The Adrenal Glands

Located at the top of each kidney is an **adrenal gland** [*uh DREE nul*] that produces many hormones, including adrenaline and cortisol. **Adrenaline** [*uh DREN uh lin*] is the hormone that

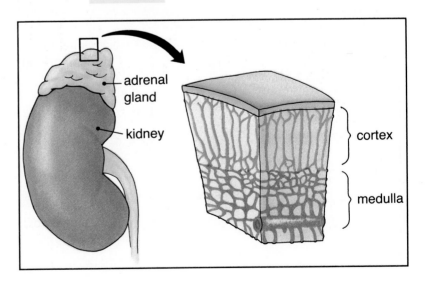

adrenal gland

kidney

cortex

medulla

Figure 16-4   An adrenal gland

Endocrine Glands

Gland	Hormone	Function
Pituitary anterior lobe	Growth hormone	Controls growth of bones and skeleton
	ACTH	Stimulates secretion of adrenal cortex hormones
	Thyroid stimulating	Regulates body metabolism and the size of the thyroid gland
	Prolactin	Influences mammary glands to secrete milk
	Luteinizing	Induces production and growth of corpus luteum
	Follicle stimulating	Stimulates development of eggs in ovaries
Hypothalamus	Oxytocin	Stimulates muscle contractions of uterus and milk production in mammary glands
	Antidiuretic	Controls reabsorption of water in kidney
Thyroid	Thyroxin	Controls body's metabolic rate
	Calcitonin	Prevents bones from releasing calcium
Parathyroids	Parathyroid	Controls calcium and phosphorus metabolism
Adrenal cortex	Aldosterone	Prevents excess sodium and water loss into urine
	Cortisol	Controls protein metabolism and the production of glucose by the liver Regulates connective tissue structure and the amount of sodium and potassium in body tissues
Medulla	Adrenaline	Constricts blood vessels in liver, heart, and skeletal muscles Elevates blood pressure and respiratory rate Converts glycogen to glucose
Pancreas	Glucagon	Converts glycogen to glucose
	Insulin	Regulates glucose metabolism in liver and body tissues
Testes	Testosterone	Produces male secondary sex characteristics
Ovaries	Estrogen	Produces female secondary sex characteristics
	Progesterone	Maintains uterine lining

Figure 16-5   The endocrine glands and their hormones

is released when you are angry, frightened, excited, or under stress. As you read in Chapter 6, the preparation of your body for quick action is called the fight or flight response. Adrenaline makes your heart beat faster and stronger, increasing blood flow to vital organs to give your body a surge in power.

Adrenaline, which is also called epinephrine, is produced in the medulla. The **medulla** [*muh DUL uh*] is the central core of cells in the adrenal glands. The tissue in the adrenal glands that surrounds the medulla is called the **cortex.** The cortex produces several hormones, including cortisol. **Cortisol** is a hormone that regulates the storage of starch in the liver and the production of glucose from protein.

The adrenal glands may produce too much adrenaline. This may be caused by prolonged worry and stress. It may also be caused by the reaction of the adrenal glands to other chemical imbalances in the body.

Disorders of Endocrine Glands

Gland	Hormone	Underproduction	Overproduction
Pituitary anterior lobe	Growth hormone	Dwarfism (childhood): stunted bone growth, impaired sexual development, normal mental development	Giantism (childhood): advanced bone growth, normal body proportions, normal mental development Acromegaly (adulthood): enlarged bones of face, hands and feet; mental processes not affected
Thyroid	Thyroxin	Hypothyroidism (adulthood): weight gain, puffy skin, slowed down mental activity and metabolism Cretinism (infancy): dwarflike body, mental retardation	Hyperthyroidism: increased nervousness, irritability, heart beat, blood pressure; protruding eyes, goiter, loss of weight
Adrenal cortex	Aldosterone Cortisol	Addison's disease: abnormal blood glucose level, weight loss, sluggish activity, skin pigmentation	Cushing's disease: excess fatty deposits in face, red and moon-shaped face; weakness and tiredness
Pancreas	Glucagon	Lower than normal levels of blood sugar	Higher than normal levels of blood sugar
	Insulin	Diabetes: weight loss, high blood sugar level, frequent thirst and urination	Insulin shock: lowered blood sugar level, weakness, nervousness, excess perspiration, unconsciousness, death, if untreated

Figure 16-6   Some common disorders of the endocrine system

The Pancreas

Just below the stomach is a gland that is part of both the digestive system and the endocrine system. This is the **pancreas** [*PANG kree us*]. As a part of the digestive system, the pancreas releases digestive juices into the small intestine. As a part of the endocrine system, the pancreas produces several hormones, including insulin and glucagon. **Insulin** is a hormone that regulates the metabolism of sugar in the body. Insulin stimulates cells to take glucose, or blood sugar, from the blood. Insulin also speeds up the changing of glucose into glycogen. **Glycogen** [*GLY kuh jun*] is a starch stored in the liver that maintains blood sugar levels between meals.

If the body does not get enough insulin, or if the cells fail to use insulin, the amount of sugar in the blood increases, producing a condition called diabetes mellitus. In the most serious form of diabetes, the body does not make enough insulin. Daily insulin shots and a special diet are necessary to treat this form of diabetes, which is known as insulin-dependent diabetes. If the pancreas produces too much insulin, the amount of sugar in the blood decreases. Low blood sugar can cause headaches and weakness.

The Reproductive Glands

In women the organs that produce egg cells and release sex hormones are called **ovaries.** The ovaries are located on each side of the womb in the pelvic region. One hormone produced by the ovaries is **estrogen** [*ES truh jun*], which stimulates many of the physical changes young women go through during puberty.

Men have endocrine glands called **testes** [*TES teez*], which hang in a small outer pouch below the pelvis. The testes release hormones that lead to many of the physical changes young men experience during puberty. The testes produce the male sex hormone **testosterone** [*TES tahs tuh rohn*]. Since small quantities of sex hormones are produced by the adrenal cortex, adult men have some female hormones and adult women have some male hormones circulating in their blood.

Lesson Review

The endocrine system releases hormones into the blood stream. Hormones affect many bodily functions, including growth of bones and muscles, metabolism, the nervous system, digestion, and sexual development. Many disorders can be caused by the overproduction or underproduction of hormones.

1 Name two endocrine glands located in the brain.

2 How are the functions of the hypothalamus and the pituitary glands related?

3 Which gland produces insulin?

4 List a hormone produced by the ovaries and a hormone produced by the testes.

Female Development

The maturation of the female reproductive system begins when the pituitary gland releases hormones that activate the ovaries. The ovaries begin to produce estrogen. During the next few years, girls begin to develop the physical characteristics of women. Puberty generally begins earlier in girls than in boys.

Changes During Puberty

The development of secondary sex characteristics marks the beginning of puberty. **Secondary sex characteristics** are the physical traits that develop during puberty and distinguish adults from children. In girls, these changes include the growth of breasts, increased body hair, and other changes in appearance. The changes vary widely and usually depend on heredity.

One of the first signs that puberty is occurring in a girl is the growth of breasts. It usually takes several years for the breasts to reach their full size. Another early sign that puberty has begun is the growth of pubic hair. Pubic hair is the coarse hair that grows around the external sex organs. Hair also begins to grow under the arms and on the legs.

Other changes during puberty include a widening of the hips and a change in the tone of voice. The skin also changes. Pores become larger and oil glands in the skin produce more oils. This can cause acne, which is common during puberty. Scalp hair also becomes oilier, making it necessary to shampoo more often. Body odor increases, and many girls begin using deodorant.

Female Reproductive System

Important changes also occur inside the body during puberty. The reproductive organs reach maturity. The female reproductive organs are shown in Figure 16-8. The largest sex organ is the **uterus** [*YOO tur us*], which has the function of protecting and

Figure 16-7 The development of secondary sex characteristics in girls usually occurs between the ages of 11 and 17.

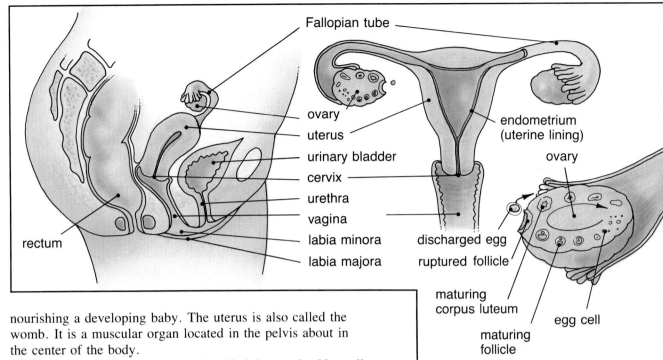

Fallopian tube

ovary
uterus
urinary bladder
cervix
urethra
vagina
labia minora
labia majora

rectum

endometrium
(uterine lining)

ovary

discharged egg
ruptured follicle

maturing
corpus luteum

egg cell

maturing
follicle

**Figure 16-8   The female repro-
ductive system**

nourishing a developing baby. The uterus is also called the
womb. It is a muscular organ located in the pelvis about in
the center of the body.

The bottom third of the uterus is called the cervix. Normally
the opening to the cervix is smaller than a zero in this book.
When a baby is born, the cervix stretches to allow for the size of
the baby. The cervix opens into the vagina. The **vagina** is a hollow tube that connects the uterus to the outside opening of the
body. The vagina is also called the birth canal. It serves as a passageway for the baby during childbirth.

The two ovaries are located on each side of the uterus. The
ovaries release hormones that help control growth and development. The ovaries also contain thousands of reproductive
cells. These female reproductive cells are called **ova,** or egg
cells. These ova are present at birth and are stored in the ovaries.
Approximately once a month, an egg cell is released by an ovary.
This monthly release of an egg is called **ovulation.** When an egg
cell is released from the ovary, it travels to the uterus through a
tiny tube. The narrow tube that carries the egg cell is called the
Fallopian tube [*fuh LOH pee un*]. There are two Fallopian tubes,
one for each ovary. Tiny hairs in the Fallopian tubes, called
cilia, sweep the egg along, moving it toward the uterus.

The Menstrual Cycle

Another signal that a girl's reproductive system is maturing is
the beginning of menstruation. **Menstruation** [*men stroo AY
shun*] is the monthly process in which an unfertilized egg cell and
the inner lining of the uterus are discharged from a woman's
body. It occurs in women who are in their childbearing years.
While most young girls usually begin to menstruate around the
age of 12, some may mature earlier or later than this. Menstruation may begin any time between the ages of 10 and 16 and still
be considered normal.

The ovaries release one egg cell about every 28 days. Menstruation occurs about two weeks after the ovary releases an egg cell. This means that menstruation, or a period as it is commonly called, will occur about once a month. However, during the first few years it is very common for young women to experience periods more or less often than this.

After the egg leaves the ovary and travels through the Fallopian tube to the uterus, it attaches itself to the lining of the uterus, called the **endometrium** [*en doh MEE tree um*]. The endometrium is spongy tissue that thickens to give nourishment to the egg. If a woman becomes pregnant, the egg will remain attached to the endometrium and develop into a baby. If the woman does not be-

Figure 16-9 The stages of the menstrual cycle

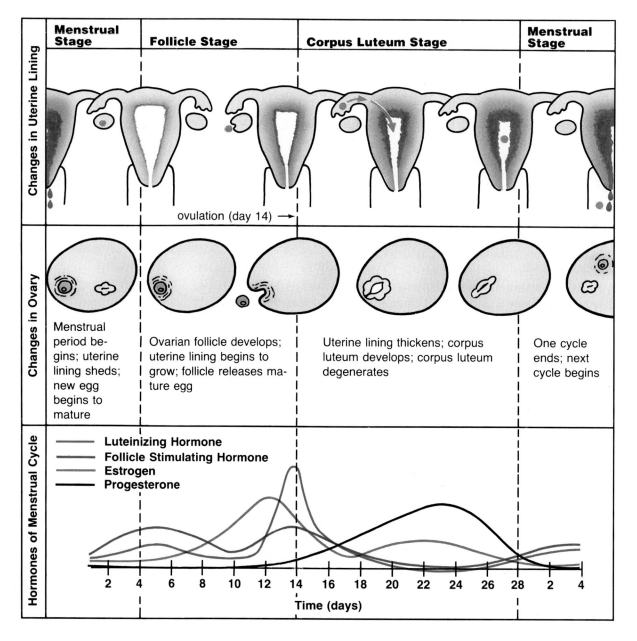

come pregnant in a few days, the endometrium begins to change into a fluid. This fluid also contains blood. The fluid from the endometrium flows from the uterus and out the body through the vagina. A menstrual period usually lasts from three to seven days. Women wear sanitary pads or tampons to absorb the fluid from menstruation. Both pads and tampons must be removed every few hours so that bacteria will not grow.

Menstruation usually occurs each month for as long as a woman has a healthy reproductive system or until she reaches the age of 45 to 55. Around this time, the ovaries stop producing the hormone that controls menstruation. After a while, the ovaries stop releasing eggs and menstruation ends. The time of life when a woman stops menstruation is called **menopause.** After menopause a woman can no longer bear children.

Female Reproductive Disorders

Women may experience different symptoms as a result of menstruation and changing hormone levels. Some women feel little discomfort during menstruation. A few, though, suffer cramps in the abdomen and back, headaches, soreness in the breasts, and a swollen or bloated feeling. Heating pads, rest, and exercise can help reduce the pain from cramps. Despite the uncomfortable feelings that sometimes accompany menstruation, women can stay involved in any activities they feel like doing. Swimming or other forms of strenuous exercise will not harm them during this time.

 ## Health *Careers*

The primary source of health care for most families is the family physician. A family physician is a medical doctor who provides comprehensive medical care with emphasis on the family unit. Family physicians treat internal disorders, infectious diseases, and mental illness. They are also qualified to provide medical care during pregnancy and birth, to handle the health problems of children, and to prepare patients for surgery. To become a family physician, an individual must graduate from college and then train in a medical school. After medical school, the doctor must study in a three-year program that stresses the medical care of the family. A family physician must pass regular examinations for certification throughout his or her career.

A family physician may work with a medical assistant. Medical assistants conduct medical procedures such as taking medical histories and caring for minor wounds. They may be trained to take blood samples and prepare blood reports. Medical assistants may train on the job or by attending a training program in a junior college or vocational school.

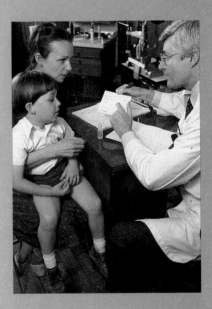

1. What kind of doctor is specialized to provide general medical treatment for all the members of a family?
2. What training is necessary to be a medical assistant?

One common disorder that sometimes occurs before menstruation is premenstrual syndrome. **Premenstrual syndrome,** or PMS, is a feeling of depression that occurs several days to two weeks before a period begins. Other symptoms may include nausea, weight gain, and the inability to sleep or concentrate. The cause of PMS is not known for certain but it is believed that wide ranges of hormone levels may be responsible.

A rare but serious illness associated with the use of tampons is **toxic shock syndrome.** It is characterized by a sudden, high fever and vomiting, a rash, faintness, and sometimes diarrhea. A woman should contact a doctor at once if she has these symptoms. The cause of toxic shock syndrome is not completely understood, but it is believed to be caused by a toxic substance produced by a particular kind of bacteria. If not treated, this illness may cause death. Removing a tampon every few hours will prevent the growth of bacteria that may lead to toxic shock syndrome.

Another reproductive disorder that is fairly common among women is ovarian cysts. An **ovarian cyst** is a fluid-filled sac that may grow on the ovaries. Small cysts may occur as a result of regular changes in hormone levels and may disappear without treatment. Cysts that are large may cause severe pain in the abdomen. Sometimes surgery may be necessary to remove large, painful cysts.

Cancer is the most serious disease that can affect the female reproductive system. Cancer is the uncontrolled growth of abnormal cells. Cells that grow wildly in this way may invade many sites of the reproductive system. The uterus and cervix are the most common sites. Cancers of this type may be detected early through regular pelvic checkups. A Pap test is part of this checkup. A **Pap test** is an examination in which a doctor takes a smear of cells from the cervix and vagina. The cells are then studied for any sign of cancer. If detected early, these kinds of cancer have cure rates of 80 percent or higher. Breast cancer is another common form of cancer. All women should examine their breasts for lumps that could be cancerous immediately after their monthly period.

Health Bulletin

The female reproductive system is very efficient at conceiving. Ninety percent of women who are sexually active become pregnant within one year.

Lesson Review

During adolescence, girls reach sexual maturity and menstruation begins. Menstruation continues until menopause, when the ovaries stop producing eggs and a woman's childbearing years are over. Many disorders of the female reproductive system can be prevented and cured.

1 List three physical signs of puberty in girls.

2 What is the organ that nourishes and protects a developing baby?

3 Define *menstruation*.

4 What is the endometrium?

5 What disease can be detected by a Pap test?

Male Development

Puberty usually begins a year or two later for boys than girls. Male development generally occurs between the ages of 11 and 15. When the testes begin to release testosterone, many physical signs of puberty begin to appear.

Changes During Puberty

During the adolescent years, boys grow taller and gain weight just as girls do. The arms and legs grow faster than the rest of the body, which sometimes causes a person to be awkward and clumsy. As the rest of the body catches up, coordination improves. Boys differ greatly in body sizes, depending largely on heredity. There is no one right size or shape. By age 20, most boys will have reached their adult size. In some cases, though, growth continues into the twenties. Testosterone also provides for the development of muscular strength. Thus boys become stronger during puberty.

One of the first signs of sexual development in boys is the growth of pubic hair. Body hair also grows under the arms. Hair grows on the legs, arms, and sometimes the chest. The amount of hair on the body differs greatly from one boy to another. Boys also grow facial hair. As with all other aspects of puberty, boys develop facial hair at different ages. Some boys begin to shave by the time they are in their mid-teens. Others do not start until their late teens.

During puberty, a boy's voice becomes much deeper. The change happens slowly, over many months. During the time the voice is becoming deeper, it is common for voices to "crack," or to switch back to high tones.

Boys also experience an increased production of oil from the oil glands in the skin during puberty. Acne may also be a problem at this time. Regular shampooing, daily bathing, and the use of a deodorant become very important during puberty.

Figure 16-10 Beginning to shave is a sign of puberty.

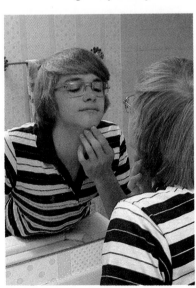

Male Reproductive System

The male reproductive system reaches maturity during puberty. The male reproductive organs are mostly external organs. The different organs are pictured in Figure 16-12. The **penis,** shaped like a cylinder, grows larger during puberty. The testes produce and store sperm cells. **Sperm** are tiny cells that fertilize the female egg in the first step of creating new life. Each sperm has a head, body, and a long whiplike tail.

Just before or shortly after a boy is born, the testes, which are formed inside the body, descend into the scrotum. The **scrotum** [SKROH tum] is a pouch of loose skin that houses the testes. The external location of the testes allows sperm to develop. Sperm cannot develop at the normal body temperature of 98.6°F. They require a lower temperature, and the temperature in the scrotum is approximately 1.8°F lower than body temperature. The testes begin to produce sperm cells during puberty and continue to do so throughout a man's life.

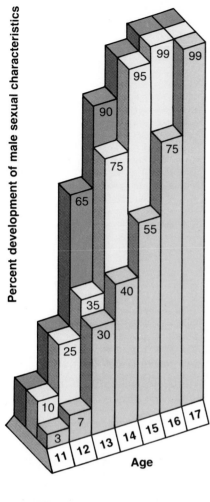

Percent development of male sexual characteristics

99   99
95
90   75
75
65   55
40
35   30
25
10
7
3
11 12 13 14 15 16 17

Age

■ Nocturnal Emission

□ Pubic Hair

■ Voice Change

Figure 16-11 The rate of physical development varies greatly among adolescent boys.

Once sperm cells are released, they travel along a tube called the vas deferens. The **vas deferens** [*vas DEF ur unz*] is the tube that connects the testes to the urethra. The **urethra** [*YOO ree thruh*] is the passageway for urine and sperm out of the body. The urethra is enclosed in the penis. As the sperm move toward the urethra, they combine with fluids from other sex glands, forming semen. A thin white fluid that makes up most of the liquid in the semen is produced by the **prostate gland.** The prostate is located near the bladder, and is about the size of a walnut. The sperm eventually make their way through the vas deferens and into the urethra. The urethra never carries both urine and semen at the same time.

At the tip of the penis is the opening for the urethra. Normally, the penis hangs limp. However, when extra blood fills the spongy tissue and blood vessels of the penis, an erection will occur. An **erection** is a stiffening of the penis that causes it to point up and away from the body.

After puberty begins, sperm cells are produced in great numbers, up to 300 million cells per day. Occasionally young men experience **nocturnal emissions,** or wet dreams. A nocturnal emission is the process by which semen is released from the body during sleep. Nocturnal emissions are normal and harmless. Sperm leave the body in a process called ejaculation. **Ejaculation** [*ih jak yuh LAY shun*] occurs when muscle contractions push the semen through the urethra and out of the penis.

At birth, the end of the penis is covered by a flap of skin called **foreskin.** This flap is often removed shortly after birth. The removal of the foreskin by surgery is called **circumcision.**

Circumcision is performed for social or religious reasons. The decision to have a baby circumcised is up to the parents. Some parents decide not to have their baby circumcised. If the penis is not circumcised, it is important to clean around the foreskin regularly. Otherwise, a build-up of fluid from small glands in the foreskin will develop and may cause infection.

Male Reproductive Disorders

Two common disorders may occur when the testes enter the scrotum. Once the testes descend into the scrotum shortly after birth, the opening they travel through usually closes. This opening is inside the body between the abdomen and the scrotum. If this opening does not close properly, the boy may develop a hernia later in life. An **inguinal hernia** [*IHNG gwuh nuhl*] is a condition in which tissue is pushed through the opening between the abdomen and the scrotum. Sometimes an inguinal hernia is caused by a weakness in the abdominal muscles. This type of hernia can be corrected with surgery.

When one or both testes fail to descend into the scrotum shortly after birth, a disorder called **undescended testes** results. This may be caused by a failure in the endocrine system. In this case, doctors may try to correct the problem by giving the boy more pituitary hormones. Surgery may also be used to correct an undescended testis if it is caused by a physical barrier.

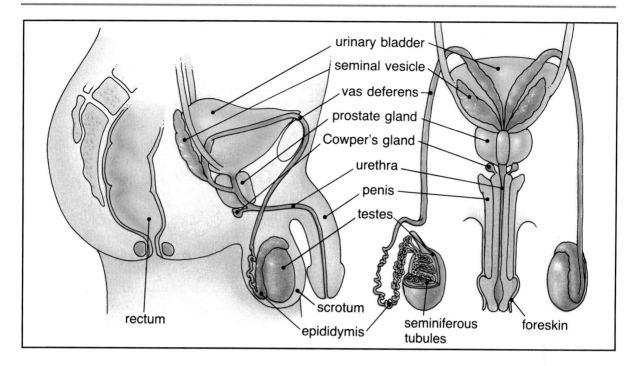

urinary bladder
seminal vesicle
vas deferens
prostate gland
Cowper's gland
urethra
penis
testes
scrotum
rectum
epididymis
seminiferous tubules
foreskin

Another common disorder occurs when older men develop an enlargement of the prostate gland. The enlargement of this gland may block urination. If the blockage is not treated, infection of the bladder and kidneys may occur. Surgery is often necessary to correct this problem.

Cancer may develop in the prostate gland or the testes. Men should examine their testes monthly for lumps that could be cancerous. Prostate cancer develops most often in men over the age of 60. If detected early, the cure rate is very high. Regular checkups of the prostate gland can help detect this disease.

Figure 16-12 The male reproductive system (above); sperm cells (below)

Lesson Review

Male development usually occurs somewhat later than female development. Secondary sex characteristics develop, including a deepening of the voice and the growth of pubic, body, and facial hair. Boys also grow taller, stronger, and gain weight. Sexual organs, including the testes and penis, reach maturity. Many disorders of the male reproductive system can be prevented or cured. Regular medical checkups can help detect a serious disease such as cancer.

1 List three physical signs of puberty in boys.

2 Define *sperm*.

3 Describe the path of the sperm through the male reproductive system.

4 List three disorders of the male reproductive system.

5 Define *inguinal hernia*.

Chapter Review

Vocabulary

adrenal gland	hormone	posterior lobe
adrenaline	hypothalamus	premenstrual syndrome
anterior lobe	inguinal hernia	prostate gland
cilia	insulin	puberty
circumcision	medulla	releasing hormones
cortex	menopause	scrotum
cortisol	menstruation	secondary sex characteristic
ejaculation	nocturnal emission	sperm
endocrine gland	ova	testes
endocrine system	ovarian cyst	testosterone
endometrium	ovary	thyroid gland
erection	ovulation	toxic shock syndrome
estrogen	pancreas	undescended testes
Fallopian tube	Pap test	urethra
foreskin	parathyroid gland	uterus
glycogen	penis	vagina
goiter	pituitary gland	vas deferens

Using Vocabulary

Questions 1–12. On a separate sheet of paper, write the term from the column on the right that matches the phrase on the left.

1 time of life when a woman stops menstruating
2 organs that produce egg cells and release sex hormones
3 tiny cells that fertilize the egg
4 network of organs that control the body's chemical messengers
5 chemical substances that stimulate growth and activity in the cells of tissues and organs
6 pouch of loose skin that houses the testes
7 physical traits that develop during puberty and distinguish men from women
8 narrow tube that carries the egg cell
9 male endocrine glands
10 hormone that regulates metabolism of sugar in the body
11 stage of development in which the reproductive system matures
12 passageway for urine and sperm out of the body

a testes
b urethra
c insulin
d Fallopian tube
e puberty
f ovaries
g secondary sex characteristics
h endocrine system
i menopause
j scrotum
k sperm
l hormones

Interpreting Ideas

1 Describe the functions of the hormones produced by the pituitary gland.

2 How do the adrenal glands control your body's fight or flight response?

3 Identify and describe two disorders of the female reproductive system and two disorders of the male reproductive system.

4 Identify and describe the function of the female endocrine glands and the male endocrine glands.

5 Identify and describe the function of the two endocrine glands located in the brain.

6 Describe the thyroid gland—its shape, its location, and the function of its hormones.

7 Describe the process of menstruation. What happens to the egg and the endometrium when a woman becomes pregnant?

8 Describe the examination called a Pap test. Why is this test performed?

9 Define a *nocturnal emission.*

10 What is the function of the parathyroid glands? What may happen if the parathyroids are overactive? underactive?

11 Identify the hormones that are produced by the adrenal glands.

12 What are the major hormones produced by the pancreas? What are their functions?

13 What may be the cause of acne during puberty?

14 What event generally signifies that a girl has become capable of bearing children?

15 Identify and describe the organs of the female reproductive system and of the male reproductive system.

16 What happens when the body does not get enough insulin? when the body produces too much insulin?

17 What may happen when the adrenal glands produce too much adrenaline? when they produce too little adrenaline?

18 What is the role of the hypothalamus?

19 Why do doctors recommend that men perform monthly testicular self-examinations?

Applying Concepts

1 How are the changes that occur during puberty similar for girls and boys?

2 Why can't a woman become pregnant after she has gone through menopause?

3 In what sense does the thyroid gland serve as the body's thermostat?

4 What kind of hormone imbalance may cause dwarfism or gigantism?

5 How is blood calcium level regulated?

6 Why is the hypothalamus sometimes called the ''master gland''?

7 Identify the hormone being described in each of the following examples: (a) has an influence on the growth and functioning of bones and muscles; (b) causes a rise in blood pressure and rate of respiration; (c) produces female secondary sex characteristics; (d) stimulates the deepening of a boy's voice at puberty.

8 The statements that follow describe a hormone imbalance. Determine which hormones are involved and whether there is an undersecretion or oversecretion: (a) an abnormally high level of blood glucose; (b) low blood calcium and muscle spasms; (c) impaired growth and abnormally small stature for a person's age.

9 Why do you think that puberty is regarded as a more difficult life stage to pass through than some of the other life stages?

Projects

1 At your school or local library research the new ways that hormones, both natural and synthetic, are being used in the medical field.

2 Create a bulletin board in which you illustrate the location and describe the functions of each of the endocrine glands in the human body.

3 The pineal gland may have a role in regulating the body's daily rhythms and produces a hormone that may affect the functions of the sex glands. At your school or local library research the pineal gland. Where is it located? What hormone does the pineal gland secrete, and what are its functions?

4 Invite a medical professional to discuss some aspect of the endocrine system or the reproductive system. You might ask an endocrinologist to talk about recent developments in the treatment of endocrine system disorders, such as dwarfism, diabetes, and acromegaly. A nurse practitioner might discuss pre-menstrual syndrome (theories about its causes and measures used to treat it), toxic shock syndrome, or infertility. An internist might answer questions, which you and your classmates have prepared ahead of time, about problems related to the sexually maturing body.

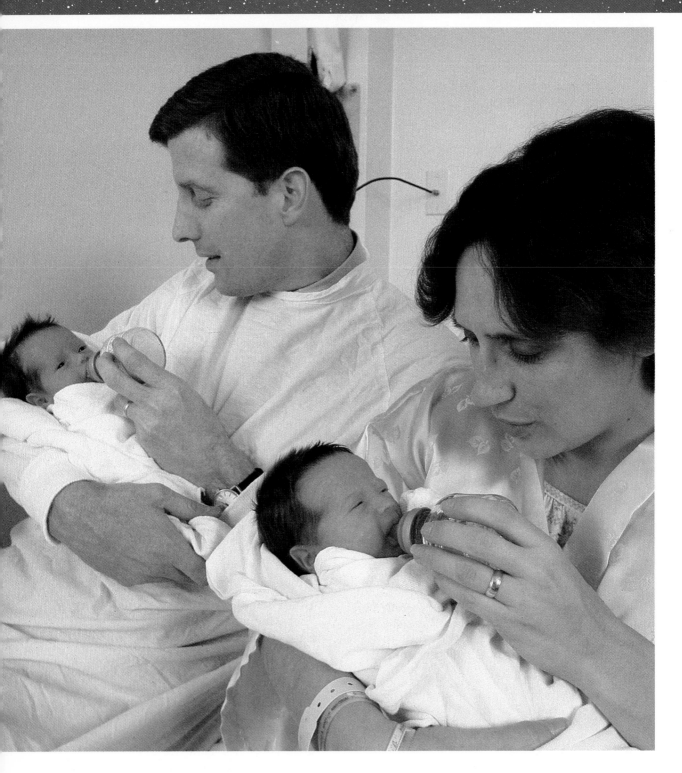

The birth of any child is a special event, but the birth of twins is quite unusual. Twins occur about once in every 80 births.

CHAPTER SEVENTEEN

Reproduction & HEREDITY

When you were born, your parents probably compared you to themselves or to members of their family. Each may have pointed to you and said, "She has your eyes," or "He has grandfather's dimple." They were looking for signs of physical likeness, or inherited physical traits. Your height, hair texture, and even the length of your toes are all inherited characteristics. You are the unique combination of traits inherited from your parents.

You are unique genetically, that is, unless you have an identical twin. Although identical twins may have very different personalities, their genetic information is exactly the same.

Objectives

- Describe the development of a baby from fertilization to a newborn.

- Describe the stages of labor.

- List two complications of pregnancy and of birth.

- Identify three birth defects and their possible causes.

- Explain the process by which traits are inherited.

- Describe two forms of genetic disorders.

- Explain why genetic counseling is important.

- List two ways to detect birth disorders.

- Describe how a mother's decisions can affect the health of her baby.

Beginning of Life

The development of a new individual begins when a sperm and egg cell unite. Even though these tiny cells are much smaller than a period on this page, they contain all the information needed to make a new person.

Fertilization

The joining of an egg and a sperm is called **fertilization** [*fur til ih ZAY shun*]. Fertilization takes place in the mother's Fallopian tubes. Three conditions are necessary for fertilization to occur. First, an egg must be present in the Fallopian tube. The egg will be in the Fallopian tube for approximately two days after ovulation. Second, sperm must also be in the Fallopian tube. Sperm swim into the Fallopian tube after they have been deposited in the woman's vagina.

The third event that actually leads to fertilization is the joining of the egg and the sperm. Millions of sperm surround the thin wall of tissue that covers the egg, trying to break through to the egg. Only one sperm can succeed. If one sperm enters the egg, fertilization occurs. Immediately the fertilized cell begins to grow. The egg splits into two cells. These two cells divide into four, these four become eight, these eight become sixteen, and so on. What starts as one fertilized cell grows in nine months into a baby made of 200 billion cells. However, if fertilization should not occur, the egg disintegrates in the uterus.

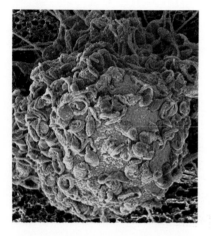

Figure 17–1   Sperm cells surrounding an egg cell (*above*). The fertilized egg implants itself in the endometrium (*below*).

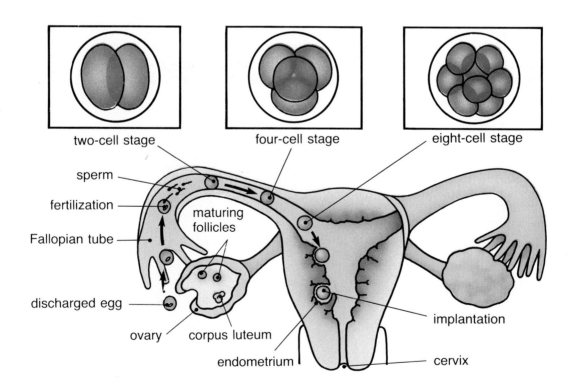

two-cell stage

four-cell stage

eight-cell stage

sperm

fertilization

maturing follicles

Fallopian tube

discharged egg

ovary

corpus luteum

endometrium

implantation

cervix

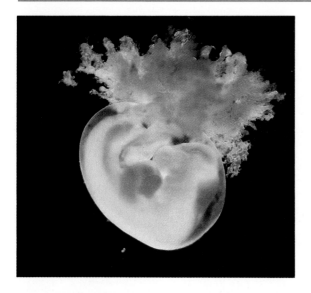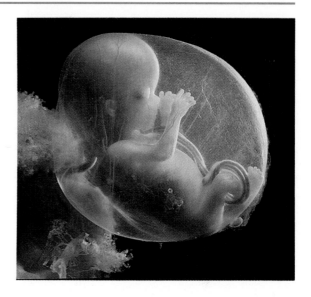

The Embryo

The fertilized egg begins growing in the Fallopian tube. Soon it reaches the uterus, where the fertilized egg attaches to the lining of the uterus wall. At this point, the fertilized egg has 200 cells and is about the size of the period at the end of this sentence. During its first two months the fertilized egg is called an **embryo** [*EM bree oh*].

Early on, the embryo consists of several layers of cells. The inside layers grow into muscles, bones, heart, brain, and other organs. The outside layer of cells forms a special organ called the **placenta** [*pluh SEN tuh*], which soon surrounds the embryo. The placenta is connected to the embryo by a thick cord called the **umbilical cord** [*um BIL ih kul*]. The placenta absorbs nutrients and oxygen from the mother and passes them through the umbilical cord to the embryo. The placenta also receives the waste products from the embryo and passes them through the umbilical cord into the mother's blood stream. Although substances may pass from the mother to the embryo through the placenta, notice that the mother and the embryo have two separate circulatory systems.

The placenta produces several hormones that control most of the changes in the woman's body during pregnancy. These hormones control the build-up of a milk supply in the breasts, the growth of the uterus, and have a role in the birth process.

The embryo is wrapped in a protective covering called the **amniotic sac** [*am nee AHT ik*]. The amniotic sac is filled with fluid that helps protect the embryo from jolts and bumps.

A five-week old embryo is shown in Figure 17-2. During the first two months, the embryo grows rapidly. The placenta and amniotic sac grow along with it. After four weeks, the tiny heart begins to beat. By the seventh week, the eyes, the ears, and the mouth have developed, and limbs are beginning to grow. At this stage, the largest part of the embryo is the head, which is curved over the stomach. The embryo is about one inch long.

Figure 17-2   An embryo at 5 weeks (*left*), and a fetus at 3 months (*right*)

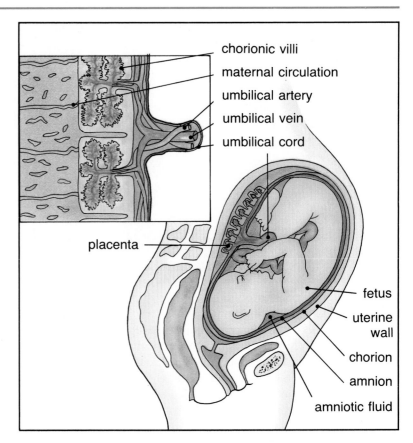

chorionic villi
maternal circulation
umbilical artery
umbilical vein
umbilical cord
placenta
fetus
uterine wall
chorion
amnion
amniotic fluid

Figure 17-3   Villi within the placenta transfer nutrients from the mother's blood to the fetus.

Health Bulletin

At eight weeks, the eyes, ears, nose, and mouth of the fetus are identifiable. By this stage the fingers, toes, and even fingerprints are formed. Although the fingernails do not appear until the eighth month, the fingerprints will remain unique throughout the baby's life.

The Fetus

From the third month until birth, the embryo is called a **fetus** [*FEE tus*]. Its rapid growth continues, and bone starts to replace the cartilage in its skeleton. The fetus begins to use its muscles, and the mother can feel it stretching and rolling. The fetus may suck its thumb or even have hiccups. By the end of the sixth month, the fetus is about one foot long and weighs about two pounds. It is beginning to look like a newborn baby.

In the final three months of pregnancy, the skin of the fetus becomes thicker and tougher. A soft covering of hair appears over much of the fetus, but disappears before the baby is born. The fetus grows plump. At birth, the average baby weighs more than 7 pounds and is about 20 inches long.

In the final weeks of pregnancy, the fetus may change position several times. At birth, it usually faces down toward the birth canal. The bulge in the mother's abdomen, which has grown bigger and bigger during the past few months, sinks lower. The head of the fetus rests against the cervix, ready for birth to begin.

Birth

Approximately 40 weeks after fertilization, the baby is ready to be born. Birth occurs in three stages, as shown in Figure 17-4. The process of birth is called **labor.** The term *labor* is appropriate, for it is hard work for the mother to deliver the baby. The first stage of labor is usually mild muscle contractions in the mother's abdomen. These contractions are caused as muscles in the uterus begin to push the baby out through the cervix. The pushing gradually causes the cervix to dilate, or open.

At first, the contractions, called labor pains, occur about every 15 to 20 minutes and only last a few seconds. As labor continues, the contractions occur every few minutes and are much stronger. Just before birth, the pains come every minute and are stronger still. The first stage of labor ends when the cervix is completely stretched so that the baby can move into the birth canal.

During the second stage of labor, the baby passes through the cervix and moves into the birth canal. The head appears first, pushing its way through the opening of the birth canal. The baby turns slightly and its shoulders and the rest of its body slip out.

The final stage of labor occurs after the baby is born. The muscles of the uterus continue to contract, causing the placenta to separate from the lining of the uterus. The delivery of the placenta, now called the afterbirth, takes between 5 and 10 minutes. On the average, the entire birth process takes about 14 hours for the first baby and 8 hours for second and third births. However, labor can last more than a day or less than an hour.

The Newborn Infant

Several important events occur immediately after the baby is born. The baby's lungs fill with air and the baby takes its first breath. This first breath is accompanied by a loud cry and is a healthy sign that the lungs are working.

Since the baby no longer needs the umbilical cord, it is cut by the doctor. There are no nerves in the umbilical cord, so this procedure is painless. The spot on the infant's abdomen where the umbilical cord is attached will become its navel. Drops that protect against eye infections are placed in the baby's eyes. Finally, the baby is weighed and examined to make sure it is healthy.

At birth, the baby has several natural reflexes, or involuntary responses to a stimulus. The stimulus could be pressure or light. For example, touching the bottom of the foot will cause the baby's toes to curl. The baby will grab a finger placed in its palm. All these reflexes are signs that the baby is alert and that its nervous system is working properly.

The infant soon wants food and is able to suck from a bottle or its mother's nipple immediately after birth. The best food for a newborn baby is milk from its mother's breast. For some women, bottle feeding is more convenient, and formulas provide many needed nutrients. If possible, doctors encourage mothers to breast-feed their infants. Breast-feeding is also called nursing.

By the end of pregnancy, the mother's breasts are ready to produce milk. This milk is ideal for the new baby. It provides nutrition as well as immunity from certain diseases, including colds. Breast-feeding also has benefits for the mother. Nursing contracts the muscles of the uterus, helping it return to its normal size.

Women who breast-feed must eat an extra 500 Calories a day and drink extra fluids. They must also be available to feed their babies on a regular basis each day.

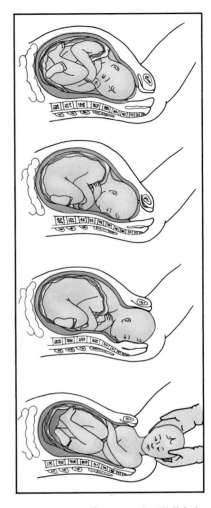

Figure 17-4   Stages of childbirth

Multiple Births

Women usually give birth to just one baby at a time. Multiple births do occur, of course, and twins are the most common form of multiple births.

Multiple births happen in one of two ways. Both of these ways are shown in Figure 17-5. The first type of multiple birth occurs when the small group of cells that make up the embryo split into two or more groups. Each group grows into a complete embryo and then into a fetus. The fetuses share the same placenta, although they have separate amniotic sacs. Since the fetuses develop from the same egg and sperm, the twins will be the same sex and will look almost exactly alike. Twins that develop from the same embryo are called **identical twins.** If the embryo splits into three groups, the babies will be identical triplets.

A second type of multiple birth occurs when an ovary releases more than one egg at one time. Each egg is fertilized by a different sperm and develops as a separate embryo in the uterus. Each fetus has its own placenta. The babies will be no more alike or different than brothers and sisters, except they will be the same age. Twins that develop at the same time but from different embryos are called **fraternal twins.**

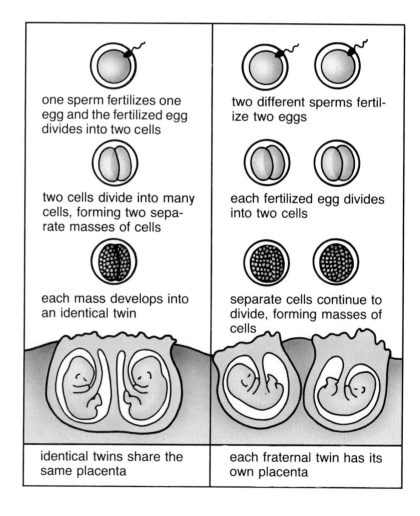

one sperm fertilizes one egg and the fertilized egg divides into two cells

two different sperms fertilize two eggs

two cells divide into many cells, forming two separate masses of cells

each fertilized egg divides into two cells

each mass develops into an identical twin

separate cells continue to divide, forming masses of cells

identical twins share the same placenta

each fraternal twin has its own placenta

Figure 17-5 Identical twins (*left*); fraternal twins (*right*)

Figure 17-6   Identical twins develop from a single embryo.

Multiple births often cause problems for some of the babies. There may not be enough room in the uterus for the fetuses to grow normally. The babies can be small and not fully developed.

Problems of Delivery

With every birth, there is the chance of something going wrong. Most births are normal, but the presence of a trained doctor or professional is necessary to help the mother have a smooth delivery and to take quick action if there are problems. One problem is the failure of the baby to turn head down before delivery. This results in a breech birth. A **breech birth** is one in which the feet or buttocks of the baby enter the birth canal first. Doctors check to see if the baby will be born in the breech position. If so, they then work to protect the baby from injury.

Sometimes a woman cannot deliver a baby safely through the birth canal. Doctors then make an incision in the abdomen and uterus, and lift the baby out. This method of delivery is called a **Caesarean section.**

Health **History**

The name Caesarean section comes from the Roman emperor Julius Caesar, who was reportedly born in this manner over 2000 years ago.

Lesson Review

The process of reproduction begins with an egg and a sperm cell. As the cells grow from a fertilized egg to an embryo to a fetus, a human life takes shape. Immediately after birth, the newborn baby can respond to many different stimuli. These responses are taken as signs that the baby is healthy.

1 Define *fertilization*.

2 What is the developing baby called during the first two months of pregnancy?

3 What happens in the first stage of labor?

4 Name a reflex an infant has at birth.

5 Distinguish between identical and fraternal twins.

Prenatal Care

Beginning a new life is not without risks, for both mother and child. However, proper medical care during pregnancy, called **prenatal care,** helps increase the chance that a baby will be born healthy and that the mother will have no serious health problems.

Care During Pregnancy

The best time to see a doctor is before becoming pregnant. The medical histories of both parents can be reviewed for any likely problems. Routine tests can determine if any diseases may be passed on from parent to child. Medical checkups can also make sure that the parents are in good physical condition.

One of the signs of pregnancy is a missed menstrual period. Other signs include swollen and tender breasts, nausea, fatigue, and more frequent urination. As soon as a woman believes she is pregnant, she should see a doctor for a pregnancy test. Most doctors recommend that a pregnancy test be given if a period is more than two weeks late. A simple, inexpensive test of the woman's urine or blood will determine whether she is pregnant. Tests can be given in a doctor's office, a hospital, or a health clinic.

If the woman is pregnant, her doctor will usually recommend a change in her diet to provide extra protein, calcium, and certain vitamins. Under normal conditions, a woman will gain between 20 and 25 pounds during pregnancy. This extra weight includes the weight of the baby and the placenta. The doctor may also recommend an exercise program.

Doctor's visits are normally scheduled once a month for the first seven months. After that, visits occur more often. The doctor checks the mother's urine, blood pressure, and weight. After the fifth month, the doctor also checks the heartbeat of the fetus.

Figure 17-7 Exercising regularly helps tone muscles for the hard work of labor.

One important test a doctor performs early in the pregnancy determines the Rh factor in the mother's blood. Blood that contains a certain group of proteins is called **Rh positive.** About 85 percent of the population is Rh positive. The remaining 15 percent of the population lacks these proteins. Blood without these proteins is called **Rh negative** blood. If a pregnant mother is Rh negative and the father is Rh positive, the fetus will likely be Rh positive. Since the blood of the mother and fetus are different, the mother's blood will respond to the fetus' blood as a foreign substance and build up antibodies against it. This will not affect her first baby. But if the woman has another child, the antibodies she developed against Rh positive blood will attack and destroy the red blood cells of the new fetus. The baby will need a blood transfusion at birth. A woman who knows she is Rh negative can be vaccinated after her first baby to prevent antibodies from forming.

A pregnant woman should try to avoid people with infectious diseases. Some diseases, such as rubella (German measles), may not cause serious health problems for the mother, but they can be very dangerous to the fetus. Rubella is caused by a virus that can cross the placenta. This infection can harm the fetus, and may result in deafness, blindness, or mental retardation.

Problems of Pregnancy

Most women experience many discomforts during pregnancy. Some of these, such as nausea in the morning, usually disappear after a few months. Other common problems last longer but are not threatening to the pregnancy. These include headaches and trouble with digestion and bowel movements.

Another problem that develops chiefly in women under 16, older women, and women in their first pregnancy is **toxemia** [*tahk SEE mee uh*]. This condition is characterized by swelling, rapid weight gain, high blood pressure, protein in the urine, and stomach pain. Convulsions or coma may occur. Toxemia requires hospital care. It can threaten the lives of both mother and baby.

Some pregnant women have too little iron in their blood, a condition called **anemia** [*uh NEE mee uh*]. Anemia can occur because the fetus takes iron from the mother's blood stream to make its own red blood cells. An expecting mother who suffers from anemia will feel tired and weak during the pregnancy. Iron pills are usually prescribed.

Miscarriage and Stillbirth

Sometimes a pregnancy can end unsuccessfully. The egg or sperm may have been defective. The fertilized egg may not have attached itself properly to the uterus. The embryo may not have been healthy from the beginning. When the pregnancy is not developing normally, the mother's body may end it. When the muscles of the uterus contract and force the nonliving embryo from the body, it is called a **miscarriage.** About one third of all pregnancies end in miscarriages. These usually occur in the first three months of pregnancy and often occur so early that the woman may not know she was pregnant. The risk of miscarriage increases for women who do not receive regular prenatal care.

Sometimes the mother is pregnant for the entire nine months, but the fetus dies just before birth. When a fetus is born dead, it is called a **stillbirth.**

Premature Births

Babies who are born before they are fully developed are said to be **premature** [*pree muh TYOOR*]. Premature babies are born before the thirty-seventh week of pregnancy. Premature births can occur for many reasons. The fetus may not be developing normally in the uterus. The uterus itself may not be functioning as it should. The mother may be addicted to drugs or have high blood pressure. In some cases, doctors will cause a premature birth by starting labor early because they have found some problem with the fetus that needs immediate care.

Premature babies are almost always smaller than the average baby, generally weighing less than five pounds. They are usually placed in an incubator. An **incubator** [*IN kyuh bay tur*] is a special container that keeps the baby warm and protects it from disease. The baby is fed on a regular schedule and the hospital staff watches closely for any problems. Protected in the incubator, the baby can develop and grow strong until it can go home.

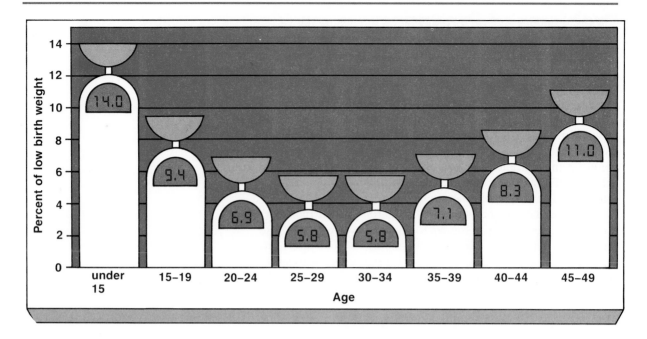

Figure 17-8 Teenage girls are more likely to have low birth weight babies than adult women.

Teenage Pregnancy

This year in the United States, over one-half million women will have a baby before the age of 20. Yet, a young woman is still growing. Her bones and muscles may not be ready for the physical stress of pregnancy. She may not be emotionally prepared. Many people consider teenage pregnancy one of the country's most serious health problems.

Statistics show that 25 percent of the babies born to teenage mothers are born prematurely. Even when a pregnancy lasts a full nine months, most babies of teenage mothers have a low birth weight. Low weight babies are 20 times more likely to die than babies born at normal weight.

Many of the medical problems related to teenage pregnancy can be avoided by going to a doctor early. However, many girls put off a visit to a doctor because they are afraid. Many teenagers feel they cannot turn to their parents or friends for support. Teenage mothers rarely receive any emotional or financial support from the baby's father. Most do not get married. As a result, the mother and the fetus often do not receive good health care.

Many communities now offer programs for helping teens think more carefully about teenage pregnancy. They offer suggestions for avoiding pregnancy and counseling for teenagers who feel they need someone to talk to. If a teenager is already pregnant, the programs offer prenatal care and classes on childbirth and parenting. Classes for teenage fathers may also be offered.

Medicines and Drugs

Nearly everything that a mother-to-be takes into her body can be absorbed through the placenta. When a pregnant woman smokes, drinks, uses drugs, or takes medicine that has not been prescribed by a doctor, she threatens the health of her fetus.

Pregnant women who smoke have more premature deliveries and more underweight babies. Women who smoke also suffer twice as many miscarriages as women who do not smoke.

When a pregnant woman drinks an alcoholic beverage, the fetus also receives the alcohol. The presence of too much alcohol can affect the fetus by causing birth defects. A **birth defect** is damage to the fetus, such as mental retardation or an unusual physical characteristic. A birth defect caused by too much alcohol is called **Fetal Alcohol Syndrome** (FAS). FAS causes mental retardation, low birth weight, and unusual fetal characteristics.

Other addictive drugs, such as heroin, can seriously harm the fetus. The fetus may actually become addicted to the drug just as the mother is, and suffer withdrawal from the drug after birth. Drug withdrawal is very hard physically for an adult and can be fatal for a newborn baby.

Pregnant women should consult a doctor before taking any medicine, even something as common as aspirin. Nearly all non-prescription drugs carry this warning: "As with any drug, if you are pregnant or nursing a baby, seek the advice of a health professional before using this product."

Other Birth Defects

Birth defects can also occur as a result of accidents, certain infectious diseases, exposure to x-rays, injury at birth, or for unknown reasons. Babies may be born with a heart defect that prevents the blood from carrying enough oxygen. The baby's skin appears blue due to the lack of oxygen, leading to the term "blue baby." Surgery may be able to correct this heart defect.

Cerebral palsy [*suh REE brul PAWL zee*] is the result of brain damage that occurs either before, during, or soon after birth. This defect occurs when there is a lack of oxygen to the brain. Brain damage can result from the poor diet of the mother, from injuries to the baby during childbirth, and from many other causes. Victims usually have poor muscle control, unclear speech, and vision and hearing problems. Cerebral palsy cannot be cured, although victims can improve their muscle coordination with physical therapy. Braces and walkers can also help.

Lesson Review

A growing fetus makes great demands on the mother's body. The risks of pregnancy range from occasional nausea to life-threatening conditions that require medical treatment. Even under a doctor's care, pregnancies may end in miscarriage or in premature birth. To be sure that her baby has the best chance of being born healthy, a pregnant woman should refrain from the use of tobacco, drugs, or alcohol.

1 When should a woman have a pregnancy test?

2 How may a mother's decision to smoke affect her baby?

3 List three problems associated with teenage pregnancy.

Heredity

Every baby is born with its own special characteristics. Physical traits, such as skin, hair, and eye color, are determined largely by heredity. Mental traits, such as intelligence and personality, are also influenced by heredity.

Chromosomes and Heredity

Within almost every cell of the body are tiny threadlike structures called **chromosomes** [*KROH muh sohmz*]. Chromosomes carry the hereditary information from generation to generation. Chromosomes are made of a chemical substance called deoxyribonucleic acid, or **DNA.**

Most cells in the body contain 23 pairs of chromosomes, or a total of 46 chromosomes. But the sex cells, the egg and the sperm, contain only one chromosome from each of the 23 pairs, or a total of 23 chromosomes. When an egg and sperm cell unite, the fertilized egg receives 23 chromosomes from the egg and 23 from the sperm. Thus the fertilized egg has 46 chromosomes, or a complete set. Half of the chromosomes come from the mother and half from the father. Thus each individual inherits information from both its father and its mother.

The sex of the new child is determined by its chromosomes. Each egg contains one female chromosome, which is called an **X chromosome.** About half of the sperm cells also contain an X chromosome. The other half of the sperm contain a male chromosome, called a **Y chromosome.** If the egg is fertilized by a sperm carrying an X chromosome, it will contain two X chromosomes, and thus be female. If the egg is fertilized by a sperm carrying a Y chromosome, it will contain one X chromosome and one Y chromosome, making it a male. Thus the sex of the baby is determined by the chromosomes carried in the sperm.

Dominant and Recessive Genes

The chromosomes contain the basic units of heredity called **genes.** Genes determine the physical characteristics of each individual, including hair and eye color, body shape and height, and other physical traits.

Like the chromosomes on which they are located, genes occur in pairs. Each gene in a pair is inherited from a different parent. When the egg and sperm cells unite, they bring together genetic information from two different people. The mother may have blue eyes and curly hair. The father may have brown eyes and straight hair. What determines how the baby will look?

Some genes are expressed whenever they are present. Such genes are said to be **dominant.** Other genes, which are expressed only if the dominant gene is not present, are said to be **recessive.** For example, curly hair is a dominant trait and straight hair is a recessive trait. If a baby receives a gene for curly hair from its mother and a gene for straight hair from its father, it will have curly hair. Only if the baby receives two genes for straight hair will its hair be straight.

Figure 17-9 The way that people look is largely determined by their heredity.

Genetic Disorders

Sometimes children inherit genetic disorders. Fortunately, most genetic disorders are recessive, so a child will only express the disorder if it inherits the trait from both parents. Figure 17-10 illustrates how the genes for albinism can be inherited. **Albinism** is a recessive genetic condition in which the body does not produce the pigment melanin. Albinos have very pale hair, eyes, and skin. Notice from the diagrams that two parents who appear normal may have a child who is an albino.

Sickle-cell disease is a recessive genetic disease that causes the red blood cells to have a long, curved shape as shown in Figure 17-11. These abnormal blood cells clog up tiny blood vessels and cut off oxygen to certain tissues. Muscle pains, poor vision,

Figure 17-10   Inheritance of albinism, a recessive trait

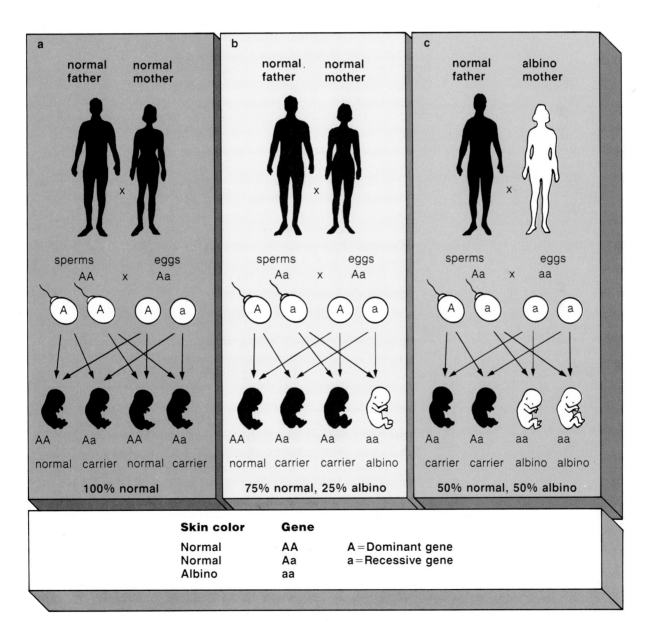

	a			b			c	
normal father	normal mother		normal father	normal mother		normal father	albino mother	
sperms AA	x	eggs Aa	sperms Aa	x	eggs Aa	sperms Aa	x	eggs aa
A A		A a	A a		A a	A a		a a
AA	Aa	AA	Aa	AA	Aa	Aa	aa	Aa	Aa	aa	aa
normal	carrier	normal	carrier	normal	carrier	carrier	albino	carrier	carrier	albino	albino
100% normal			**75% normal, 25% albino**			**50% normal, 50% albino**		

Skin color	Gene	
Normal	AA	A = Dominant gene
Normal	Aa	a = Recessive gene
Albino	aa	

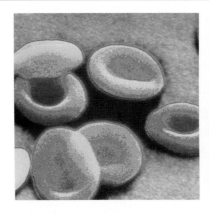

Figure 17-11 Normal red blood cells (*left*); the red blood cells of a person who has sickle-cell disease (*right*)

general tiredness, slow growth, and even death can result from sickle-cell disease.

Sickle-cell disease is found primarily in people of African descent. The gene that causes sickle-cell disease is passed from one generation to another. A person who has only one sickle-cell gene will not suffer the severe symptoms of sickle-cell disease. However, this person can pass the gene on to his or her child. If the child inherits two defective genes, one from the mother and one from the father, sickle-cell disease results.

Another genetic disease that tends to affect only a limited population is Tay-Sachs disease. **Tay-Sachs disease** is a condition caused by the lack of a certain substance that leads to fatal brain damage. It affects some children of Eastern European and Jewish descent. A child with this disease appears healthy until the age of six months. Then the nervous system stops functioning normally. The child dies by age three or four. Like sickle-cell disease, a child will suffer from Tay-Sachs disease only if it inherits the trait from both parents. Tay-Sachs disease affects about 50 children a year in the United States.

Cystic fibrosis [*SIS tik fy BROH sis*] is a recessive disease that affects the mucus-secreting glands. It causes the bronchial tube glands to release a thick mucus that damages the tubes in the lungs. The digestive glands also release too much mucus. This causes diarrhea and poor digestion. Children usually suffer from breathing problems and do not grow or gain weight as they should. Special breathing exercises and physical therapy can help the lungs function more normally. Most victims can reach adulthood with proper medical treatment. Approximately one in 1500 babies inherits cystic fibrosis.

Phenylketonuria [*fehn ul keet uh NOOR ee uh*], or PKU, is a genetic disease characterized by the inability to break down phenylalanine, an amino acid that is common in many foods. Because phenylalanine cannot be broken down, it builds up in the body. High levels of phenylalanine can poison the brain and cause severe mental retardation. Children suffering from PKU also may develop skin disorders and epileptic seizures. Although PKU is a serious disorder, it can be treated successfully. New-born infants are routinely tested for PKU. Babies with the disease are fed a special diet lacking phenylalanine. Once the brain has

Health Bulletin

Although sickle-cell disease is a very serious condition, people who carry a single gene for this trait may actually be at an advantage in certain situations. A single gene for this trait makes individuals less susceptible to malaria. This probably explains why many people whose ancestors came from tropical regions where malaria is common carry this trait.

fully developed, the build-up of phenylalanine will no longer cause retardation. For this reason, children may need to stay on the special diet only until puberty. PKU is a rare disease, present in only about one out of every 10,000 births.

Sex-Linked Traits

The inheritance of most traits is not influenced by the individual's sex. The genes for some traits, however, are located on the X chromosome. Because women have two X chromosomes, a recessive trait on only one X chromosome will not be expressed. In contrast, men have only one X chromosome, so they will always express a trait on the X chromosome. Genetic disorders passed on by the X chromosome are called **sex-linked disorders.** Men suffer from these disorders more often than women.

One common sex-linked disorder is **colorblindness.** Colorblindness is a condition in which a person cannot distinguish certain colors, usually red and green. Women are rarely colorblind, but the condition is much more frequent in men. Women can, however, pass this trait on to their sons and daughters. All sons who receive the gene will be colorblind. Daughters will not be colorblind unless they also inherit the gene from their father.

A more serious sex-linked disorder is hemophilia. **Hemophilia** [*hee muh FIL ee uh*] is a condition in which the blood lacks a substance that is necessary for blood to clot properly. The smallest cut or bruise can be very dangerous since the blood will not stop flowing. In an extreme case, the person with hemophilia can bleed to death from a very minor injury. Hemophilia is treated by transfusions of blood plasma or injections of the substance that helps blood clot.

Figure 17-12   Nicholas II, the last czar of Russia, and his family in 1917. His son, Grand Duke Alexis, inherited hemophilia from his great-grandmother, Queen Victoria of England.

HEALTH + Technology

RECOMBINANT DNA—Pituitary dwarfism is a rare genetic disorder that results from a deficiency of growth hormone in childhood. If left untreated, the affected child will not grow to a normal height. Treatment usually involves injections of human growth hormone until the child reaches adulthood.

Until recently, human growth hormone was available only from cadavers. Today, however, human growth hormone can be mass produced using recombinant DNA. In this technique, scientists use enzymes to extract the gene that produces growth hormone from a human cell. Next, they reinsert this gene into the DNA of bacteria. Bacteria containing recombinant DNA are grown in big vats, from which large quantities of growth hormone are harvested.

This sophisticated technique now produces several other human proteins, including insulin, cortisol, and anti-hemophilia protein. In the future, DNA research is likely to play an important role in treating not only genetic disorders, but also cancer.

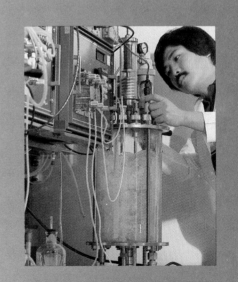

1. How is recombinant DNA technique performed?
2. What human proteins have been produced?

Chromosomal Disorders

Some genetic disorders occur when an entire chromosome or parts of a chromosome are defective. A person may be born with too many chromosomes, too few chromosomes, or defects in the structure of certain chromosomes. The most common chromosomal disorder is Down syndrome. **Down syndrome** is a chromosomal disorder that usually causes mental retardation and slowed physical development. It occurs when a person has 47 instead of the normal 46 chromosomes. About one out of every 1000 children is born with this condition.

Down syndrome is the leading cause of mental retardation in the world. Individuals with this syndrome are usually mildly to moderately retarded, but there is a wide range of abilities among people with this condition. In addition to mental retardation, these individuals tend to be shorter and stockier than others. They often have poor muscle development and breathing and heart problems.

Down syndrome children are more frequently born to mothers who are over 35 years old than to younger women. The condition may also be related to viral infections, x-rays, or other influences on the mother. It is suggested that women who have suffered from viral hepatitis may be at risk and should avoid pregnancy for several months after recovering from the disease.

Figure 17-13   Mental abilities, behavior, and development vary widely among children with Down syndrome.

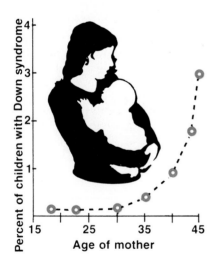

Figure 17-14   Older women have a greater risk of giving birth to a child with Down syndrome than younger women.

Genetic Counseling

Genetic disorders usually have no cure. For some disorders there is not even a successful treatment. For this reason, couples who want to become parents should always consider genetic counseling before having a child. Genetic counseling usually can help couples understand their risk of having a child with a genetic disorder.

Genetic counseling is very important for couples in high-risk groups. For example, a person with a history of genetic disorders in the family is in a high-risk group. People who come from families whose members have had cystic fibrosis, hemophilia, sickle-cell disease, or other genetic diseases may be carrying these traits. Other high-risk groups include couples who have already had one child with a genetic disorder, women who have had several miscarriages, and women who are over 35.

Prenatal Diagnosis

Many birth disorders can be identified by tests on the unborn fetus. About 100 kinds of genetic disorders can be found by testing samples of the amniotic fluid surrounding the fetus. This fluid contains cells from the fetus. Testing the amniotic fluid is called **amniocentesis** [am nee oh sen TEE sus]. Amniocentesis can be performed after about the sixteenth week of pregnancy. The information from the test can be used to prepare parents for any problems and to help doctors start whatever treatments are possible. The sex of the baby can also be determined at this time.

Another method of testing the unborn fetus is called ultrasound. **Ultrasound** is a technique that uses sound waves to make an image of certain areas of the body on a screen. The sound waves are

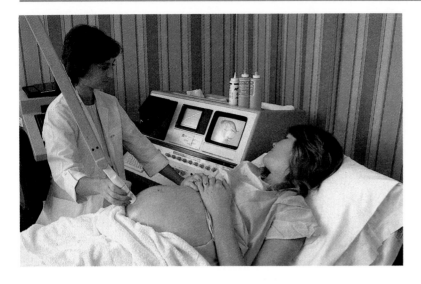

Figure 17-15 Ultrasound provides valuable information on fetal development.

above the range of human hearing. An ultrasound machine can direct sound waves at the fetus and produce an image of the fetus. Doctors study the images for any signs of genetic disorders and possible birth defects. Ultrasound is similar to an x-ray, but is safer because it does not produce radiation.

A very recent test for birth disorders is a chorionic villus biopsy. A **chorionic villus biopsy** [*kawr ee AHN ik VIL us*] is a test in which a sample is taken from the wall of the amniotic sac. This test allows doctors to detect birth disorders as early as the sixth or eighth week of pregnancy.

Recent advances in medicine now allow doctors not only to detect problems, but also to treat them before birth. Doctors have given injections and even performed surgery while the fetus was still in its mother's uterus.

Lesson Review

When the genetic material carried by the egg and the sperm unite, the chromosomes in each determine the characteristics of the baby. Chromosomes carry genes for dominant and recessive traits. Genetic counselors can help couples understand their risks of having a child with a genetic disorder. Doctors can now detect and sometimes treat birth defects before the child is born. Continued advances in these areas will increase the number of babies who are born healthy.

1 How many chromosomes does each egg or sperm carry?

2 Name two sex-linked genetic disorders. Are these conditions more common in men or in women?

3 Name a disorder caused by having an extra chromosome.

4 What is amniocentesis?

5 Who should receive genetic counseling?

Health Bulletin

Ultrasound not only allows doctors to diagnose health problems of the developing baby, but it also reveals the actions of the baby within its mother's uterus. Ultrasound pictures have shown babies kicking, stretching, and even sucking their thumbs.

Chapter Review

Vocabulary

albinism	Down syndrome	premature
amniocentesis	embryo	prenatal care
amniotic sac	fertilization	recessive
anemia	Fetal Alcohol Syndrome	Rh negative
birth defect	fetus	Rh positive
breech birth	fraternal twin	sex-linked disorder
Caesarean section	gene	sickle-cell disease
cerebral palsy	hemophilia	stillbirth
chorionic villus biopsy	identical twin	Tay-Sachs disease
chromosome	incubator	toxemia
colorblindness	labor	ultrasound
cystic fibrosis	miscarriage	umbilical cord
DNA	phenylketonuria	X chromosome
dominant	placenta	Y chromosome

Using Vocabulary

Questions 1–12. On a separate sheet of paper, complete each of these sentences with a term from the vocabulary list above.

1 The medical care that a woman receives during pregnancy is called __?__.

2 The __?__ is the thick cord that connects the placenta to the embryo.

3 __?__ is the term applied to the developing baby from the third month until birth.

4 A condition in which there is too little iron in the blood is called __?__.

5 __?__ is a recessive genetic disease that affects the mucus-secreting glands.

6 __?__ is a technique that uses sound waves to make an image of areas of the body on a screen. It is often used to observe a fetus.

7 The __?__ is the organ that surrounds and nourishes the embryo.

8 __?__ is a chemical substance from which chromosomes are made.

9 A condition in which the blood lacks a substance necessary to clot properly is __?__.

10 A recessive genetic condition in which the body does not produce the pigment melanin is __?__.

11 __?__ is a test in which a sample is taken from the wall of the amniotic sac.

12 __?__ is a serious complication of pregnancy characterized by high blood pressure and protein in the urine.

Interpreting Ideas

1 What are the three conditions necessary for fertilization to occur?

2 Identify and describe three birth defects.

3 Describe three situations in which genetic counseling is important.

4 What sort of special treatment should premature infants receive?

5 Describe the three stages of labor.

6 Describe three ways that prenatal birth disorders can be diagnosed.

7 What are the functions of the placenta?

8 Explain why men are much more likely to be colorblind than women.

9 How can phenylketonuria be treated?

10 What are two complications of pregnancy? of birth and delivery?

11 If a woman smokes, how may her fetus be affected? How is smoking linked to birth weight and premature delivery?

12 How does breast-feeding benefit both mother and baby?

13 Explain how it is possible for two parents who have brown eyes to have a child with blue eyes.

14 Describe four events or procedures that occur immediately after the baby is born.

15 What are two medical problems related to teenage pregnancy?

16 How do community programs help teenagers who are already pregnant?

17 How does the father's sperm determine whether the baby is a girl or a boy?

18 Identify five possible causes of birth defects.

19 How does the amniotic sac protect the embryo?

20 Compare the cause of Down syndrome with the way in which sickle-cell disease or cystic fibrosis is inherited.

Applying Concepts

1 How can the behavior of a pregnant woman influence the health of her baby? Describe four positive steps a pregnant woman can take to ensure the health of her child.

2 Why may miscarriage occur?

3 Why is it important that a pregnant woman's blood pressure be closely monitored?

4 Although colorblindness is a sex-linked trait, there are women who are colorblind. Explain what set of genes would cause a woman to be colorblind. Was her father colorblind? Was her mother?

5 If the baby weighs only six to eight pounds, why should a pregnant woman gain 20 to 25 pounds during her pregnancy?

6 What measures should a couple consider if the woman has Rh negative blood?

7 In what sense does the father determine the sex of a child?

8 If a mother is Rh negative and the father is Rh positive, their child is more likely to be Rh positive than negative. Based on this information, do you think Rh positive is a dominant or recessive trait? Explain why.

9 In what sense are an egg cell and a sperm cell incomplete cells? How may these cells become complete?

10 When she was two months pregnant, Laura was having severe morning sickness, which caused her to be away from her job a significant amount of time each week. However, Laura's obstetrician was not willing to prescribe an anti-nausea medication. Why do you think that Laura's doctor was unwilling to prescribe medicine to relieve her symptoms?

Projects

1 Find out about the Apgar scale, a test done immediately after birth and again, five minutes later, to rate a newborn's condition. What points are tested? How are they scored?

2 Plan a three-day menu of nutritious meals for a woman in her last few weeks of pregnancy. Include information about supplementary vitamins and minerals as well as suggestions for appropriate snacks.

3 Research the use of fertility drugs. How are these drugs related to the incidence of multiple births?

4 Investigate the various programs in your community that are designed to help teenagers think more carefully about pregnancy. Are the programs free? Do they offer classes on prenatal care, childbirth, and parenting? Are there classes for teenage fathers as well? Is there a counselor on staff with whom a teenager can talk? Report your findings to your classmates.

5 Collect information about organizations in your community that assist parents of children with the following disorders: Down syndrome, Tay-Sachs disease, and sickle-cell disease.

6

18. Tobacco

19. Alcohol

Substance Abuse

20. Preventing Drug Abuse

Playing a flute or trumpet requires healthy lungs. The best way to preserve the health of your lungs is to avoid smoking.

CHAPTER EIGHTEEN

TOBACCO

If the Surgeon General—the government's chief doctor—is successful, the United States will be a smokeless society by the year 2000. Students in the twenty-first century may see no-smoking signs only in antique stores. They may read about "the smoking habit" and wonder why people ever wanted to practice this strange custom.

At present almost 350,000 people die each year from diseases related to smoking tobacco. Even so, one third of American adults—about 55 million people—still smoke. Most smokers would love to quit. But tobacco is habit-forming. Once people start smoking, it is hard to stop. Smokeless forms of tobacco, such as snuff and chewing tobacco, are also harmful. In all its forms, tobacco is a dangerous enemy.

Objectives

- Explain how the use of tobacco became popular in Europe.
- Identify the major reasons why people start smoking.
- Describe the stages of nicotine addiction.
- Describe the body's response to tobacco.
- Identify the long-term risks of smoking.
- Describe the effects of tobacco smoke on nonsmokers.
- Discuss ways to quit smoking and the benefits of quitting.
- List healthy and unhealthy alternatives to smoking.
- List the factors that affect the extent of damage from tobacco use.

The Tobacco Habit

The way tobacco is used has changed over the years. Pipes, cigars, chewing tobacco, cigarettes, and snuff have been in fashion at different times in history. The leaves of the tobacco plant are dried and crumbled. The crumbled tobacco is used in pipes, cigars, and cigarettes, which are smoked. **Snuff** is tobacco ground into a fine powder that is inhaled through the nostrils or held against the gums. **Chewing tobacco** is made of poor-quality leaves mixed with honey or molasses. It is chewed, and then the leaves and juices are spat out.

People have started to smoke for different reasons. Sometimes they are urged to do so by friends. Sometimes they wish to appear more grown up, at ease, or attractive. But the more a person smokes, the harder it is to stop.

Tobacco in History

Tobacco use was unknown to Europeans until Columbus reached America. The American Indians used tobacco in their religious ceremonies. They smoked it in pipes and chewed it. They also used snuff. Columbus returned to Europe with tobacco samples, but few people there used tobacco until 1580. In that year, Sir Walter Raleigh started a smoking fad in Europe. Raleigh, pictured in Figure 18-1, was a very popular person in Queen Elizabeth I's court. When he started smoking, many people copied him. Smoking soon spread to other European countries and to England's colonies in Africa and Asia.

Tobacco is one of the oldest industries in the United States. Tobacco's popularity in Europe helped the English colony in Jamestown, Virginia, survive. Jamestown was nearly abandoned in 1614. But tobacco crops that were sold to England soon brought prosperity.

Cigarettes became popular only after the cigarette manufacturing machine was invented in 1881. Growing public disgust at tobacco spitting also made people change to cigarettes. The cigarettes rolled out by the new machine were easy to keep lit up and came in handy packages. Cigarettes became more popular in the 1920's when large numbers of women began smoking. Until that time, it was not socially acceptable for women to smoke. The major increase of women smokers, however, began during World War II.

Smoking's popularity was at its height in 1964, when 42 percent of all adults in the United States smoked. In that year, the *Surgeon General's Report on Smoking and Health* linked smoking to heart disease, lung cancer, and other lung diseases. Since this 1964 report, the percentage of smokers over 17 years of age has declined to 33 percent today. In 1964, about one half of all men smoked whereas only 38 percent do so today. There has been a slight drop since 1964 in the percentage of women smokers to 28 percent today. Since 1965 each cigarette smoker, on average, has smoked fewer cigarettes or cigars. It is worth noting that well over one half the doctors, dentists, and pharmacists in the United States who once smoked have quit.

Figure 18-1 While Sir Walter Raleigh was smoking a pipe of tobacco, his servant dashed him with water, thinking he was on fire.

A setback to this trend is that a greater number of teenage girls are smoking today. About 13 percent of the girls between the ages of 12 and 19 smoke regularly. Only about 11 percent of the boys in the same age group smoke, but chewing tobacco and snuff have recently become more popular among them.

Tobacco in the United States is still a giant business that employs hundreds of thousands of people. The sale of tobacco products, 95 percent of them cigarettes, brings in billions of dollars a year. Tobacco sales supply the federal, state, and local governments with billions of dollars in taxes. The federal government gives the tobacco industry millions of dollars each year to control prices and to study how best to grow tobacco.

On the other hand, the government pays millions for scientists to study the dangers of smoking. It also spends large amounts of money for medical care and Social Security benefits for people with diseases caused by smoking. Private industry and people who pay for their own health insurance pay higher premiums because of illnesses caused by tobacco.

Why People Start Smoking

Raleigh's popularity helped spread the smoking habit in the sixteenth century. Nowadays, too, people often start to smoke because of social pressures. They smoke to be like someone they admire. This might be a friend, a parent, a public figure, or a figure in an advertisement.

Often, people who feel they have personal weaknesses are more likely to give in to the social pressures. For example, people who are shy may think smoking gives them something to do with their hands. Some may use offering a cigarette as a way of starting a conversation. Others may think of smoking as a good way to eat less or to stop biting their nails.

Peer and Family Pressures   During the teenage years, almost everyone pushes to leave childhood behind and to gain the social skills and rights of adulthood. Young people often view

Health **History**

In 1945, cuspidors were banned from U.S. Federal buildings. Cuspidors are the containers used to catch the tobacco juice spat out by tobacco chewers.

Figure 18-2   A teenager who does not want to smoke must resist peer influences.

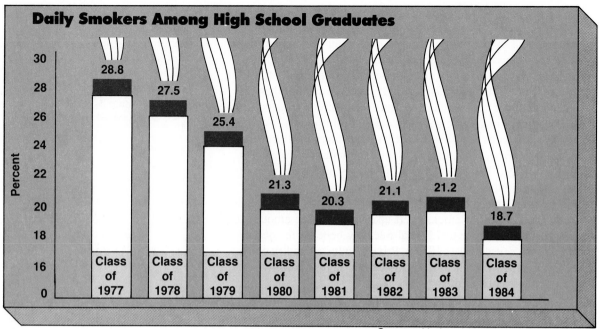

Daily Smokers Among High School Graduates

	Class of 1977	Class of 1978	Class of 1979	Class of 1980	Class of 1981	Class of 1982	Class of 1983	Class of 1984
Percent	28.8	27.5	25.4	21.3	20.3	21.1	21.2	18.7

Source: National Institute on Drug Abuse

Figure 18-3   Today teenage smoking is declining.

Figure 18-4   The appeal of successful film stars helped smoking appear glamorous. But the late actor Yul Brynner regretted his smoking habit.

smoking as one of the signs of adulthood. Many of them think that smoking will make them appear sophisticated, or in control of situations.

Most young smokers learn to smoke from their friends. Peer pressure is a very strong force. If your friends smoke, it may seem hard to say *no*. Parents who smoke also influence their children's behavior. Smokers are three times more likely than non-smokers to have parents who smoke. Many people do not think to question something they see every day. It is often easy for children of smokers to assume they will smoke also. But sometimes the children of parents who do not smoke try to prove their independence by smoking.

Three fourths of the people who smoke started before they were 21 years old. The average age at which people become regular smokers is 16. This means that the decision to acquire a smoking habit is usually made at a time when the risks may not be clearly understood.

Glamorous Images   Young people may also copy film stars who smoke or sports heroes who chew tobacco. Before the health hazards of smoking were known, films were full of glamorous stars, such as Yul Brynner, smoking cigarettes. Successful people portrayed in films were often shown offering their friends the most expensive cigars.

Advertising is another powerful social force. Although there are more people who do not smoke than who do, advertising presents a picture that makes you think everyone would like to smoke. Cigarette advertising shows smokers as happy, exciting, and attractive people. These images try to make you think that you will be like these people if you smoke cigarettes. The message is that you will somehow gain freedom, glamour, sophistication, and success. Advertising does not show nervous, coughing smokers with discolored teeth, wrinkled skin, and yellow-stained fingers. Some tobacco manufacturers even deny that there is a connection between smoking and poor health.

After research proved there is a definite connection, the United States government banned cigarette, cigar, and pipe advertising from television and radio. Newspapers, magazines, and billboard owners now receive most of the tobacco industry's multibillion dollar advertising budget. Cigarette manufacturers also sponsor entertainment and sports events to associate cigarettes with health and "the good life."

Soon after the 1964 Surgeon General's report, cigarette manufacturers were required by the federal government to clearly label all cigarette packages with: "Warning: The Surgeon General Has Determined That Cigarette Smoking Is Dangerous to Your Health." In 1984, the United States Congress, reacting to pressure from doctors and public interest groups, passed a bill requiring cigarette packages to bear the stronger warnings shown in Figure 18-5.

Figure 18-5 Federal law requires that cigarette manufacturers alternate these four warnings on cigarette packages.

How People Become Addicted

People who try smoking usually have bad memories of their first cigarette. The smoke makes them cough and forces tears to their eyes. Many even become nauseated. Many people never touch another cigarette. Others keep trying until their bodies become used to the ill effects.

Most regular smokers experience a lift after inhaling a few puffs. The lift comes from chemical changes in the body caused by nicotine. **Nicotine** is a habit-forming drug found only in tobacco. The lift is short-lived. Since the body builds up a **tolerance,** or resistance, to the drug, more and more cigarettes are needed to achieve the same feeling. The smoker passes through stages of increased need. At each stage the smoker becomes more dependent on nicotine. Because all forms of tobacco contain nicotine, users of other forms of tobacco go through similar stages.

The Pleasure Smoker A person at this stage has overcome the first unpleasant effects of nicotine. This person is a social smoker. The person likes the taste, the lift, and the relaxation provided by cigarettes. Cigarette smoking is still not a habit, and the smoker has little trouble quitting. The pleasure smoker has not yet taken in enough nicotine to cause dependence.

The Negative Effect Smoker Such a person now reaches for cigarettes when not at a party or with friends. For this person, smoking seems to be a way of relieving stress. A short time of freedom from worry is the major pleasure for this smoker. At this stage, the smoker has become psychologically dependent. **Psychological dependence** means being dependent on something to the point of becoming emotionally upset without it.

Health Bulletin

People smoke rather than swallow nicotine because the liver destroys any nicotine absorbed from the stomach or intestine.

Figure 18-6 Long-term smoking increases facial wrinkles.

The Habitual Smoker This person smokes without thinking and desires cigarettes when they are not available. A habitual smoker cannot start the day without a cigarette and is not at peace unless cigarettes are available. This person must make a strong effort to quit. Now the smoker is addicted. **Addiction** means that a person's body has become dependent upon a chemical to function normally. Addiction is also called **physical dependence.**

The Heavy Smoker By now the smoker chain smokes to keep enough nicotine in the blood system. Nicotine addiction is the main reason most smokers who quit start again. This smoker may sleep poorly and have to get up at night to smoke because of nicotine withdrawal. **Withdrawal** is the discomfort and sickness that people suffer when they stop taking a drug to which they are addicted. Signs of nicotine withdrawal may include being irritable, nervous, tired, weak, and having headaches.

Lesson Review

The use of tobacco, which started hundreds of years ago, grew steadily until 20 years ago. The discovery of the harmful effects of tobacco has sharply reduced tobacco use in the United States. However, there are still many young people who start smoking. They may believe smoking will help them appear glamorous or sophisticated. If young people allow smoking to become a social crutch, they usually become addicted.

1 What important report on smoking came out in 1964?

2 Why do some people start smoking?

3 What is the average age at which regular smoking begins?

4 What is the name of the addictive drug in tobacco?

5 List the stages of cigarette addiction.

Tobacco's Immediate Effects

For hundreds of years, people did not agree about the harm of tobacco. But in the last 30 years, medical research has proved that tobacco has many harmful effects. It is harmful to the human body both immediately and in the long run.

In its pure form, nicotine is a fatal poison. Heavy smokers absorb enough nicotine in a day to kill them if it were injected into their blood streams all at once. Fortunately, nicotine does not stay in the body long enough to be fatal because the body excretes it in urine. Tobacco smoke contains more than 3000 different chemicals. About 1200 of them are poisonous. The poisons are different in cigarette, pipe, and cigar smoke. The differences depend on the mix of the tobacco, the chemicals used by farmers on the plants, and the amount of heat generated. But no matter what form tobacco is in, or whether it is smoked or used as smokeless tobacco, tobacco is harmful to the body.

Cigarettes

Cigarette smokers absorb nicotine more quickly than pipe and cigar smokers or those who chew tobacco or use snuff. This is because most cigarette smokers inhale, which is the fastest way of getting nicotine to the brain. New smokers often experience nicotine poisoning. Nicotine poisoning causes dizziness, faintness, clammy skin, and sometimes vomiting and diarrhea. Any smoker may suffer from nicotine poisoning by smoking too many cigarettes too quickly. Most of the poisons become concentrated at the filter end of a cigarette as it is smoked. Smoking down to the filter means that the poisons will surely get into the lungs.

From the first puff, cigarette smoke keeps the body from working properly. Nicotine makes certain glands release adrenaline. **Adrenaline** is the hormone that prepares your body to fight danger or flee from it. Usually only an emergency releases adrenaline into the blood stream. When a person smokes, however, adrenaline pours into the blood constantly. The smoker then may feel nervous and tense for no obvious reason.

Adrenaline speeds up the heart rate. Sometimes it causes an uneven heartbeat. Besides increasing the heart rate, adrenaline makes the blood vessels narrower. This causes the heart to beat faster to push enough blood through narrower veins and arteries. As a result, the blood pressure rises. The narrower blood vessels prevent the blood from flowing easily to the skin, hands, and feet.

Poison also exists in cigarette smoke in many forms, including carbon monoxide. Carbon monoxide is a dangerous gas that drives oxygen out of the body's red blood cells. Cigarette smoke also contains other harmful chemicals such as ammonia, hydrogen cyanide, and nitrogen oxide.

Air flow to the lungs is reduced as well because of the tar and resins which cling to bits of matter in the cigarette smoke. **Tar** is a dark oily mixture consisting mainly of carbon and hydrogen. This compound is formed as tobacco burns. **Resin** is a clear or

Health Bulletin

Nicotine is a poison that is often used in insecticides.

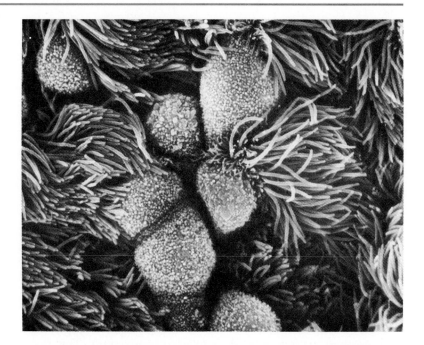

Figure 18-7 Healthy cilia help capture and expel dust and foreign particles from air passages.

yellow-brown plant material. Tars, resins, and heat irritate the mucous membranes that line the air passages of the respiratory system. The irritated membranes restrict the flow of air in the lungs. This makes it hard for smokers to breathe. They often complain of a loss of wind.

The air passages are lined with cilia. **Cilia** [*SIL ee uh*], shown in Figure 18-7, are microscopic hairlike structures that keep the lungs clean by capturing dust and foreign matter. The chemicals in smoke paralyze the cilia and eventually kill the cells. Without the action of cilia, mucus builds up in the air passages. A persistent cough, often called smoker's hack, may develop. This coughing is the body's attempt to clear the lungs and bronchi of mucus and foreign matter. The **bronchi** are the tubes that lead from the windpipe into the rest of the lungs.

Cigarette smoke interferes with the body's use of food. Some scientists believe smokers need additional vitamin C. Smoking may also reduce the smoker's appetite.

Low Tar, Low Nicotine Cigarettes

In an attempt to cut down the health hazards of smoking, the tobacco industry created what are called **low tar, low nicotine cigarettes.** These have special filters to reduce the amount of tar and nicotine in the smoke. Smokers who are addicted to nicotine, however, may smoke a larger number of these cigarettes and inhale the smoke more deeply to avoid withdrawal. Thus they still have a high intake of tar, nicotine, and carbon monoxide.

Herbal Cigarettes

Cigarettes made with the leaves of herbs, such as cloves, are called **herbal cigarettes.** Contrary to what many people think, herbal cigarettes usually contain tobacco. Clove cigarettes contain about 60 percent of a low-grade to-

Figure 18-8 The tars and resins of cigarettes irritate the membranes of respiratory passages.

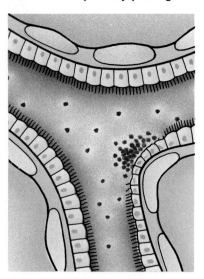

bacco that has a high level of poison gases and tar. These cigarettes are more harmful than regular cigarettes.

Clove cigarettes have an extra danger as well. Cloves contain a natural painkiller. When this painkiller is inhaled, it dulls the reaction of the throat and windpipe to irritation. This weakens the body's defenses against foreign substances and serious infections. Clove cigarettes, even with very little use, have been linked directly to severe illness and death in some otherwise healthy young adults.

Herbal cigarettes have recently become popular among young people. An informal survey by the American Lung Association gave two main reasons for the popularity of these cigarettes. One was that users mistakenly think these cigarettes are safer than normal cigarettes. The other was that clove cigarettes smell like marijuana, so the user feels daring.

Pipes and Cigars

Little cigars contain more tar and nicotine than cigarettes. Thus they are more harmful if their smoke is inhaled. In general, pipe and cigar smokers do not inhale the smoke deeply.

Some cigarette smokers believe switching to pipes or cigars will be better for them. However, research shows that cigarette smokers tend to have a fixed smoking pattern. They are likely to continue inhaling the smoke of pipes and cigars, which is hotter and more irritating. This takes away whatever benefits they had hoped to gain.

Smokeless Tobacco

The use of snuff or chewing tobacco is increasingly common among teenage boys. Some advertisements hint that these smokeless habits are safer than smoking.

When snuff is put in the nose, the nicotine is absorbed through the membranes of the nose and thus into the blood stream. When

Figure 18-9 Cigarettes are the main cause of fatal fires in the United States. Careless smoking habits account for about 18,000 deaths each year.

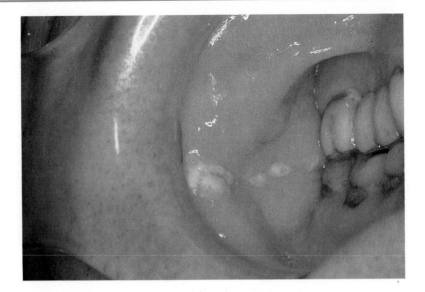

Figure 18-10 Some celebrity athletes have helped popularize chewing tobacco, which can irritate the gums and cheeks and cause oral cancer.

tobacco is chewed or snuff is placed in the mouth, the nicotine is absorbed through the membranes of the mouth.

Although smokeless tobacco may be used as an alternative to smoking, it is not a safe one. Chewing tobacco and snuff are still tobacco. The nicotine they contain has the same physical and addictive effects as any other tobacco. In addition, tobacco juices irritate the gums and cheeks, often creating long-lasting changes in the mouth that may lead to cancer. These changes are often in the form of leathery white patches called **leukoplakia** [*loo kuh PLAY kee uh*]. Tobacco juice also increases the heart rate and affects the blood vessels. Chewing tobacco contains sand and grit, which wear away surfaces of the teeth. Chewers and snuff users lose their sense of taste and smell. They also have discolored teeth, just as smokers do.

Lesson Review

Nicotine is a poison that acts immediately on the body. The nicotine, smoke, and tars and resins in tobacco products all cause harm. A number of factors affect how much tobacco use damages health. The younger a person starts smoking, the worse the damage. People who smoke daily are at greater risk than those who smoke only once in a while. The number of puffs taken and how deeply the smoker inhales are important factors. The public still has some mistaken beliefs that there are safe uses of tobacco products. All consumption of tobacco is harmful.

1 What hormone does nicotine stimulate the body to release?

2 What poisonous gas does cigarette smoke contain?

3 What do cilia do in the lungs?

4 Why are clove cigarettes so dangerous?

5 What is leukoplakia?

Tobacco's Long-term Risks

The immediate effects of tobacco use worsen and multiply over time. These effects are dangerous to both smokers and nonsmokers. Several diseases and health risks have been linked to tobacco use.

Risks for Smokers

Hundreds of thousands of people in the United States die early because they smoke. Smokers have higher risks of getting certain diseases. They also need to receive hospital care more often than nonsmokers. Medical bills for diseases tied to smoking are estimated at $50 billion a year.

Heart Disease Each year, about 125,000 Americans die from heart disease brought on by smoking cigarettes. Women in general have a lower risk of heart disease than men. But there has been a rise in the rate of heart disease among women. This is because more of them are smoking.

Nicotine and carbon monoxide are believed to be major factors in heart disease. Nicotine causes the heart to beat faster and raises blood pressure. Carbon monoxide decreases oxygen in blood. These factors place a great strain on the heart and increase the risk of heart disease. Heredity, stress, diet, and exercise habits all play a part in whether a person has a healthy heart. But the U.S. Surgeon General has called smoking the most controllable risk factor of heart disease.

Lung Cancer Cigarette smoking is the leading cause of deaths due to cancer in this country. In fact, more than 80 percent of all lung cancer deaths are tied to cigarette smoking. Cancer of the lung is a major cause of death among men and women. Among women lung cancer has tripled in the last twenty years. This is a result of the added number of women who now smoke.

Cancer is an uncontrollable growth of cells that invade and destroy neighboring healthy cells. Some cancers spread to parts of the body far from where they begin. Substances that cause cancer are called **carcinogens** [*kahr SIN uh junz*]. **Benzopyrine** [*ben zoh PY reen*] is a deadly carcinogen, found in cigarette smoke and coal tar. Researchers studying cancer cells use benzopyrine to cause cancer in laboratory rats. Tars and resins also contain promoters. **Promoters** are substances that do not start cancer, but help cancer cells grow faster.

Often the first sign of lung cancer comes after it has spread. Some people, however, will develop increased shortness of breath, and will cough up mucus and sometimes blood. These symptoms are so similar to the usual problems smokers have that most smokers ignore them. Eventually, the victim loses strength and body weight. Only 10 percent of the people found to have lung cancer are alive after five years. Lung cancer may be cured in the early stages. Treatment involves removing the diseased lung by surgery and using anticancer drugs.

Health Bulletin

According to the American Cancer Society, the average life span of a 30-year-old nonsmoker is 74 years, as compared to a two-pack-a-day smoker, who will live only 66 years.

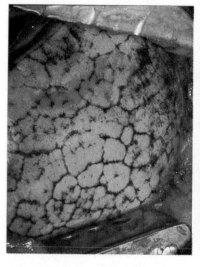

Figure 18-11 What differences do you notice between the lungs of a nonsmoker *(right)* and a smoker *(left)*?

Cigarettes multiply the effects of other carcinogens. Nonsmokers who work with asbestos, for example, are eight times more likely to get cancer than other nonsmokers. But asbestos workers who smoke are 92 times more likely to get lung cancer than nonsmokers who do not work with asbestos.

Other Forms of Cancer Smoking makes cancer of the voice box, esophagus, and bladder more likely. Smokers are twice as likely to die of bladder cancer as nonsmokers. The poisons from tobacco that collect in the bladder promote cancer.

Oral cancer is cancer of the mouth or throat area. People who smoke, chew tobacco, or take snuff are most likely to develop oral cancer. The cancers form where tobacco has touched the person's lips, mouth, and throat tissues and created leukoplakia. Smokers who also drink alcohol have an even higher risk of developing oral cancer.

Chronic Lung Diseases Cigarette smoking is the major cause of chronic lung disease in the United States. Chronic diseases are those that remain for a very long time. Smoking greatly adds to the chances of developing lung disease.

Asthma is a disease often caused by allergies that narrows the airways in the lungs. Sudden contraction of smooth muscles that encircle the air passages causes them to become so narrow that little air can reach the lungs.

Bronchitis is a redness and swelling of the linings of the air passages. When bronchitis occurs, the cilia are destroyed. Dust has gotten past the bronchi, invading the tiny air passages of the lungs. This dust often consists of matter from cigarette smoke. The air passages become irritated and then become clogged with mucus and dust. This can lead to infections.

Smoking can also cause emphysema. **Emphysema** [*em fih SEE muh*] is a disease in which the lungs lose their normal structure. Therefore the lungs do not exchange carbon dioxide for oxy-

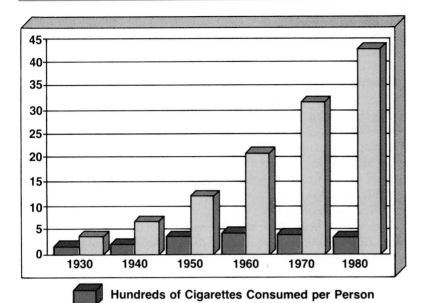

Hundreds of Cigarettes Consumed per Person

Lung Cancer Deaths per 100,000 People

Figure 18-12 Cigarette smoking is decreasing, but lung cancer takes so long to develop that lung cancer deaths are still going up.

gen well. For a person with emphysema, the work of just breathing is immense, and the smallest effort causes shortness of breath. Quitting the smoking habit will keep the disease from getting worse, but the damage that has already been done is permanent.

Other Health Problems Smokers in general are in worse health than nonsmokers. This is because smoking damages the parts of the body that protect a person from disease. Smoking also triggers allergies and may lead to sinusitis. **Sinusitis** is the redness and swelling of the sinuses. Sinusitis causes nagging headaches, a constantly stuffy nose, and a sore throat. Smokers suffer more with the common cold because of irritated mouth and throat tissues. Smokers are also more likely to get infectious lung diseases, such as influenza and pneumonia.

Smokers have a 50 percent greater chance of developing peptic ulcers than nonsmokers. **Peptic ulcers** are open sores in the lining of the stomach or small intestine. Smoking makes ulcers difficult to treat. Habits that often go with smoking, such as drinking coffee, make ulcers worse and harder to heal.

Cigarette smoking promotes noncancerous oral diseases that affect the gums and bones of the mouth. Smoking contributes to loss of teeth and delays healing after dental surgery.

Risks to Nonsmokers

A nonsmoker sharing the same air with a smoker is called a **passive smoker.** Nonsmokers who are near heavy smokers can "smoke" the equivalent of one to ten cigarettes a day. The Environmental Protection Agency has estimated that 500 to 5000 deaths a year are caused by passive smoking. This makes cigarette smoke the most dangerous airborne carcinogen known.

Health Bulletin

A smoke-filled room can have levels of carbon monoxide and other pollutants as high as the level of an air pollution "emergency." This causes eye irritation, headaches, coughing, and serious allergic reactions in the nonsmoker.

Sidestream Smoke   There are two types of cigarette smoke. Smoke that has been inhaled and then exhaled by the smoker is called **mainstream smoke.** The smoker's lungs trap much of the matter and poisons in mainstream smoke. **Sidestream smoke** comes directly from the burning end of a cigarette. Sidestream smoke has not been inhaled or exhaled by a smoker or changed by a cigarette filter. So it is more harmful to the passive smoker than mainstream smoke. It contains twice the amount of tar and nicotine, three times the amount of benzopyrine, three times the carbon monoxide, and seventy times the ammonia of mainstream smoke.

Children of smoking parents especially suffer as passive smokers. The lungs of children whose parents smoke tend to grow at a slower rate. These children suffer more infections, miss more time from school, and need more days of hospital care than the children of nonsmokers.

Pregnancy and Smoking   The unborn baby of a pregnant woman who smokes is a passive smoker. Since carbon monoxide competes with oxygen, smoking reduces the oxygen supply to the baby. A woman who smokes two packs a day cuts her baby's oxygen supply by 40 percent. Nicotine increases the baby's heart rate and blood pressure. It also upsets chemical balances, interferes with vitamin use, and reduces nourishment to the baby's developing body.

Pregnant women who smoke double their chances of miscarriage. They have more stillbirths (the baby is born dead) and more premature births than nonsmokers. Babies born to mothers who smoke weigh less than those born to women who do not smoke. They also have a higher chance of having malformed organs and have a lower survival rate. Nicotine is excreted in breast milk, so a baby can receive nicotine by nursing.

Figure 18-13   Smoking is harmful to both the mother and her unborn child.

Lesson Review

Heart disease and cancer are the two major causes of death in the United States today. The use of tobacco greatly increases the risk of developing these illnesses. Smokers suffer from these and other diseases on a much greater scale than nonsmokers. Nonsmokers who live and work around smokers also suffer the harmful effects of smoke. Pregnant women who smoke may harm their unborn children.

1 What is a carcinogen?

2 What is a promoter?

3 Name two deadly diseases that smokers are more likely to get than nonsmokers.

4 What is sidestream smoke?

5 What are the risks to an unborn child if the pregnant mother smokes?

Reducing Tobacco Use

If the United States is going to be a tobacco-free society by the year 2000, many young people will have to quit using it. Fortunately, social pressure against smoking is increasing. Because of information about the harmful effects of tobacco, most people no longer consider smoking to be a glamorous habit. Laws against public smoking are also making the habit more inconvenient. These changing attitudes discourage people from starting. They also support smokers who are trying the difficult task of quitting.

Laws That Help

As the harmful effects of tobacco have become known, citizens have begun to see the need to protect nonsmokers from harm. Just as people in the past claimed their right to use tobacco products, now nonsmokers claim the right to clean air.

A number of state and local governments have passed laws protecting the rights of nonsmokers. The 1973 Minnesota Clean Indoor Air Act was the first such law in the United States. It made smoking illegal inside all public buildings except in specific areas. Previous laws had set aside only small nonsmoking areas. A recent count showed that more than 40 states have laws that limit public smoking. Most states also prohibit the sale of cigarettes to people under the age of 16.

Giving Up the Habit

Quitting the smoking habit may not be easy, but it is possible. About 95 percent of successful quitters stop smoking without the aid of hypnosis, gadgets, or gimmicks. Often, understanding the benefits of quitting helps get people started.

Reasons to Quit   Many people are not aware of the positive side of quitting. Much of the damage to the body caused by smoking begins to reverse almost immediately. When a person stops smoking, the cells lining the bronchi gradually return to normal and the cilia are renewed. Smoker's hack disappears. The lungs slowly clear and breathing is easier. Colds and other lung infections occur less often. Sinusitis clears up. Peptic ulcers and oral disease are more likely to heal.

Even some of the damage of heart disease can be overcome. High blood pressure may decrease. The amount of oxygen in the blood increases. Within five to ten years, the risk of heart disease is no greater than that of a nonsmoker.

People who quit smoking soon discover that food tastes better, and that their sense of smell improves. The bad taste in their mouth disappears. Many people believe that if they quit smoking they will gain weight. But weight gain depends on your eating and exercise habits. In general, one third of quitters gain weight, one third lose weight, and one third stay the same.

Quitting improves a person's appearance in many ways. Teeth, fingers, and fingernails will not be stained. The breath will be much fresher. Skin will have a much more healthy appearance.

A person will sleep more soundly, and look and feel rested. Clothes will not carry an odor of stale smoke or have holes or scorch marks on them. The cost of smoking is also a factor to think about. A lot of money that is now spent on tobacco will be available to use on other things. Finally, a person who quits will have the satisfaction of controlling his or her own life.

Quitting Trying to stop smoking gradually rarely works. The gradual method takes months. The quitter is constantly suffering from nicotine withdrawal. In contrast, smokers who stop suddenly experience withdrawal for a much shorter period. For most people, quitting suddenly, or "cold turkey," is the easiest way to quit. Figure 18-14 lists some tips on quitting.

Three or four days after quitting, the nicotine will be gone from the body. Once it is gone, physical dependence is broken. But the psychological dependence may continue. The hardest time in quitting occurs seven to ten days after the last cigarette. Some smokers give up and begin smoking again at this time. If so, the reasons for starting the habit again should be examined. Is the smoker using cigarettes as a crutch to overcome shyness or to relieve tension? Finding another way to relieve tension or shyness will allow the smoker to work on the smoking habit.

Quitting the Habit

1 Set a quitting date: Choose a date 30 days ahead and mark it on your calendar. During this time period, motivate yourself by listing all the reasons you want to quit. Reviewing this chapter may help you. Also remind yourself you can save hundreds of dollars a year if you now smoke one to two packs a day.

2 Prepare to quit: Count down to quitting day on your calendar. Read your list of reasons to yourself out loud before going to bed each night. Begin breaking the habits you associate with smoking. Get up from the table immediately after eating and take a walk. Postpone the first cigarette of the day by 15 minutes on the first day and by an additional five minutes each day thereafter. Don't give in to craving right away. Distract yourself with exercise, a conversation, or imagining yourself doing your favorite activity. Create nonsmoking hours and gradually extend them.

A few techniques to remind yourself of your smoking habits are: smoke with the hand you normally don't use, save all your butts in a jar for a month, leave ashtrays full.

3 Quit: Be determined. Focus on the positive aspects. You will soon notice that you feel better physically. Reward yourself with the cigarette money you have saved. Avoid situations that you associate with smoking. Keep your hands busy. Keep a calendar and cross each day off for three months. If you weaken, take a few deep breaths, light a match, and slowly blow it out. Crush the match as you would a cigarette.

If you fail, quit again immediately. Developing will power is like a sport—practice makes perfect.

Figure 18-14 Quitting the habit

Figure 18-15 People who quit smoking become healthier and more attractive.

Many workshops are available to help people quit smoking. Some of these workshops are sponsored by national health organizations, such as the American Lung Association and American Cancer Society. Smokers who choose to attend workshops should avoid ones that seem to make impossible claims. They should also avoid groups that will not give a direct answer to the question, "How much does it cost?" It is important that the workshop leaders be trained in health sciences or counseling.

For people who smoke very heavily and who experience intense withdrawal, there may be help from a new product. This product is nicotine chewing gum. **Nicotine gum** cannot be bought without a doctor's prescription. Because it contains nicotine, the gum itself is addictive. The gum does allow heavy smokers to switch their addiction from cigarettes to the gum. Although the body is still abused by nicotine, it is no longer harmed by the smoke. Nicotine gum is most effective in helping smokers who are not able to change their habits that lead to smoking. In such cases, professional counseling may be needed. Eventually, though, the person must go through nicotine withdrawal in order to quit using the gum.

Lesson Review

Smokers and nonsmokers in the United States have become much more aware of the need to reduce tobacco use. The right of nonsmokers to clean air is increasingly being protected by law and by changing social attitudes. Smokers who quit can undo much of the harm done to their bodies. Many organizations now exist to help them in this task.

1 Which was the first law to protect the rights of nonsmokers to clean air?

2 List three possible improvements in health that a smoker can expect after quitting.

3 Why does it rarely work to quit smoking gradually?

Chapter Review

Vocabulary

addiction	emphysema	physical dependence
adrenaline	herbal cigarette	promoter
asthma	leukoplakia	psychological dependence
benzopyrine	low tar, low nicotine cigarette	resin
bronchi	mainstream smoke	sidestream smoke
bronchitis	nicotine	sinusitis
cancer	nicotine gum	snuff
carcinogen	oral cancer	tar
chewing tobacco	passive smoker	tolerance
cilia	peptic ulcer	withdrawal

Using Vocabulary

Questions 1-10. On a separate sheet of paper, write the term from the column on the right that matches the phrase on the left.

1 drug found only in tobacco
2 tobacco in powder form that is inhaled or held against the gums
3 deadly carcinogen found in cigarette smoke and coal tar
4 leathery white patches inside the mouth
5 cancer-causing substances
6 disease in which the lungs lose the ability to breathe in fresh air and push out stale air
7 hairlike structures that capture foreign matter in the lungs
8 disease that narrows the airways in the lungs
9 tubes that lead from the windpipe to the lungs
10 substances that help cancer cells grow faster

a cilia
b promoters
c carcinogens
d asthma
e bronchi
f leukoplakia
g nicotine
h emphysema
i benzopyrine
j snuff

Questions 11-20. On a separate sheet of paper, write the term that most correctly completes the sentence.

11 In 1964, the United States Surgeon General first linked smoking to __?__. (lung disease, ulcers, emotional problems, infertility)

12 The inhalation of nicotine causes certain glands to release __?__ into the blood stream. (resin, tar, adrenaline, benzopyrine)

13 When a person's body has become dependent on a chemical to function normally, the person experiences __?__. (tolerance, addiction, withdrawal, nicotine poisoning)

14 In its pure form, __?__ is a fatal poison. (nicotine, resin, tar, adrenaline)

15 __?__ are hairlike structures that keep the lungs clean. (bronchi, alveoli, capillaries, cilia)

16 A redness and swelling of the linings of the air passages is called __?__. (emphysema, sinusitis, asthma, bronchitis)

17 __?__ is made of poor-quality tobacco leaves mixed with honey or molasses. (snuff, chewing tobacco, cigarettes, cigars)

18 A hormone that prepares your body to fight danger or flee from it is __?__. (insulin, carbon monoxide, adrenaline, benzopyrine)

19 __?__ is smoke that has been inhaled, then exhaled by the smoker. (smog, mainstream smoke, sidestream smoke, passive smoke)

20 __?__ do not start cancer but help cancer cells to grow. (activators, carcinogens, promoters)

Interpreting Ideas

1 Identify and describe several ways to quit the smoking habit.

2 What is the difference between physical and psychological dependence?

3 Explain the difference between sidestream and mainstream smoke. In terms of its effect on the body, which is more dangerous?

4 Explain how cigarette smoke affects the air passages.

5 How may nicotine gum help a smoker who is trying to quit?

6 Identify and describe the stages (smoker types) that lead to addiction to nicotine.

7 Identify some healthy alternatives to smoking.

8 Explain why the gradual method of quitting a smoking habit is less effective than the cold-turkey method.

9 Why may some women be taking a greater risk than men in smoking cigarettes?

10 Why do people start smoking?

11 How did the use of tobacco become popular in Europe?

12 How does smoking cigarettes affect the appearance of the smoker?

13 Identify and describe the chronic lung diseases that may be developed from smoking.

14 How might children who grow up in a home where at least one parent smokes be affected?

15 What are the symptoms of nicotine poisoning? Why does it occur?

16 What factors affect the extent to which tobacco use damages health?

17 Why is smokeless tobacco not a safe alternative to smoking?

18 Identify and describe the forms of cancer that have been linked to the use of tobacco.

19 Why are herbal cigarettes so popular? Why are clove cigarettes a particularly dangerous kind of herbal cigarette?

20 What are the benefits of quitting smoking?

Applying Concepts

1 How can you explain the decline in the percentage of smokers since 1964?

2 What arguments would you use to convince a friend to stop smoking?

3 Why are smokers with high blood pressure told to quit?

4 Predict the effect of smoking on people who exercise on a regular basis.

5 Imagine that you have become a passive smoker in a poorly ventilated office building with a heavy smoker across from you. What suggestions would you make in order to reduce the risks of sidestream smoke?

6 What is the source of the nervousness and tension that a smoker experiences? Given these and other responses to nicotine, why do you think that a person continues to smoke?

Projects

1 Wage a campaign to eliminate smoking by designing eye-catching posters or bulletin boards that show the contents of cigarettes, describe the effects of smoking, or present profiles of the four categories of smokers.

2 Record the pulses of several smokers before and after each has smoked a cigarette. Then note whether the heart rate speeded up after smoking. Explain any change in the pulse.

3 Calculate the cost of smoking one pack of cigarettes each day for a year.

4 Debate whether or not cigarette smoking should be banned in public places.

5 Hypnosis is a method sometimes used to stop smoking. Find out how this method is performed and how effective a method it is.

At Alateen meetings, teenagers learn to cope with the problems that alcohol abuse creates within the family.

CHAPTER NINETEEN

ALCOHOL

Alcohol is a powerful drug. Alcohol abuse is the nation's greatest drug problem. Since drinking alcoholic beverages is legal and is a common habit among many adults, alcohol abuse may not be noticed until it has already begun to ruin the drinker's life.

Over 14 million people in the United States—from baseball players to lawyers, from factory workers to nurses, and from teenagers to the aged—are in deep trouble from drinking. Many innocent people on the road, on the job, and in the home feel the effects of alcohol as well. In response to the problems of alcohol abuse, many organizations have been formed to help alcoholics and their families. One such group is Alateen. Alateen helps teenagers cope with the problems caused by alcohol abuse by a family member.

Objectives

- Describe the different types of alcohol.
- List three reasons why people start to drink.
- Identify the immediate effects of intoxication.
- List three factors that affect the level of alcoholic intoxication.
- Identify the long-term effects of alcohol abuse.
- Describe alcoholism and the types of treatment available for alcoholics.
- Describe how alcohol affects driving ability.
- Name and describe the goals of three organizations that help alcoholics and their families.
- Describe how alcoholism affects the family.

Alcohol, The Problem Drink

People have been drinking alcoholic beverages for 6000 years or longer. These beverages contain varying amounts of alcohol. People begin to drink for a number of reasons. Most often, they drink to relax, to celebrate, to avoid bad situations, or to get a short-lived feeling of well-being.

What Is Alcohol?

There are many types of alcohol. **Ethanol** [*ETH uh nawl*] is the kind of alcohol found in alcoholic drinks and the only alcohol that is safe to drink in small quantities. In large doses it is poisonous. Alcohols other than ethanol are poisonous in any amount. Some of these, such as methanol and rubbing alcohol, are found around the house in paint products, antiseptics, and shaving lotions. Even breathing in some of these alcohols can make you blind; swallowing them may cause death.

Different alcoholic drinks contain varying amounts of ethanol. The total alcoholic content can range from 2 percent to more than 55 percent. The ethanol in alcoholic beverages is produced by fermentation. **Fermentation** is the process by which yeast changes sugar into carbon dioxide and alcohol. Alcoholic beverages with higher alcohol content than beer or wine are produced by distillation of the fermented juices. In **distillation,** wines or beers are evaporated to gases and then cooled back to liquids, after allowing some of the water vapor to escape. The resulting liquor has a greater percentage of alcohol than beer or wine.

Most beers and wines are labeled with the percentage of their alcohol content. Stronger alcoholic drinks such as whiskey, gin, and brandy are generally labeled by proof. **Proof** is a measurement of the alcohol content of beverages. The proof is equal to twice the percentage of alcohol. Thus whiskey that is labeled 80 proof contains 40 percent alcohol.

Why People Drink

About one third of American adults do not drink at all. There are many reasons that people choose not to drink. Some people do not like the taste of alcohol. Others do not drink alcohol because of religious beliefs or social customs. People who are

Figure 19-1   Wine is made from fermented grapes *(left)*. Beer comes from fermented grain and hops *(center)*. Liquors are produced by fermentation and distillation *(right).*

© 1982 John McGrail, all rights reserved

watching their weight sometimes do not drink alcohol because it is fattening. Some people do not feel the need for alcohol, or simply like their natural self better than the person they become when they use a drug.

Other American adults drink at least once in a while. People may drink alcohol together to share friendship and good wishes or to mark happy events. Alcohol in small amounts increases the flow of digestive juices, thus improving the appetite. Because of this, many people enjoy having wine with their meals.

Once people begin drinking regularly, they may continue for several reasons. Some people use alcohol to escape bad times and feelings. Some people may feel that they need to drink to deal with stress or to appear happy. A few people also drink to get a short lift.

Social pressure may encourage people to drink. Alcohol usually makes people talk and joke more. Therefore, alcohol is often served when strangers gather at parties or business meetings. Some people like to offer expensive wines or whiskey as a sign of their success in life.

Many young people first discover alcohol in family settings. Adults in the family may drink at meals, or sitting around the home, or at parties and weddings. Some children view drinking as part of growing up, just like going to work. Some people first notice the use of alcohol, usually wine, in religious services. However, peer pressure is still regarded by many as the main reason young people start drinking. Recent studies suggest that the majority of young people who drink had their first drink by the time they were thirteen.

Advertising also promotes drinking. Advertising shows drinkers as glamorous and successful. When television and movie actors use beer bottles, wine glasses, and drinks as props on the screen, alcohol gets free advertising. Even a magazine advertisement for lawn chairs may show someone sitting with a drink in hand.

Health History

The habit of drinking wine and beer with meals began when clean drinking water was scarce. Today in many parts of the world, wine and beer contain fewer germs than available drinking water.

Lesson Review

The only type of alcohol that humans can drink at all safely is ethanol. Alcoholic drinks contain varying amounts of ethanol. Although one third of the adult population does not drink, many people drink at least occasionally. People begin to drink for reasons that range from celebrating to escaping unpleasant feelings.

1 Name a household product containing a type of alcohol that is poisonous even in small amounts.

2 What is the process in which yeast changes sugar into carbon dioxide and alcohol?

3 What is the measurement used for the alcoholic content of distilled alcoholic drinks?

4 Give three reasons why people may start to drink.

5 List two ways that advertising promotes the use of alcohol.

Intoxication

Alcohol is toxic. **Toxic** [*TAHK sik*] means poisonous. **Intoxication** is the set of bad effects that alcohol has on the body and mind. Intoxication begins with one drink. It affects the drinker's personality, mind, and body.

Many things influence how people respond to alcohol. Intoxication can make people relaxed and friendly. But it can also make them unpleasant and rough. Because drinking is so common, people often forget that alcohol is really a drug. Most people who drink do not truly understand what alcohol does to them.

Effects on the Body

The brain is the first organ affected by alcohol. This makes people more relaxed and more talkative for a while. However, alcohol is really a depressant. A **depressant** slows down important nerve activity. Alcohol slows down nerve activity in the brain and spinal cord. This affects the area of the brain that controls inhibitions, attention, and memory. **Inhibitions** [*in huh BISH unz*] are checks on the emotions. With inhibitions weakened by alcohol, people have less self-control. Buried feelings may come out, sometimes in sudden bursts of anger. While drinking, people may not be able to judge what is a dangerous act.

Alcohol slows the body's reflexes by interfering with nerve signals. **Reflexes** are automatic muscle responses to pain or danger. You depend on them to pull your hand away from a hot stove or to jam on the brakes of your bike or car. Thus alcohol affects muscle coordination. The drinker becomes clumsy and may have difficulty walking. Beverage glasses somehow get broken and things get knocked over.

Figure 19-2 Consumption of alcohol affects coordination.

1. **Drinking alcohol affects areas of the cerebrum that control behavior, memory, speech, personality, and judgment.**

2. **When intoxication depresses the motor centers of the brain, coordination is impaired and reflexes become sluggish.**

3. **Severe intoxication depresses the areas of the brainstem that control breathing and heartbeat. Coma and death may occur.**

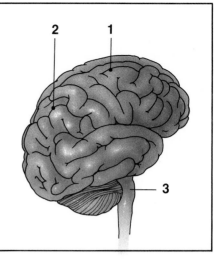

Figure 19-3 Alcohol depresses the functions of the central nervous system.

If drinking continues, the part of the brain that controls speech and eye muscles is affected. Speech and vision get worse. The drinker may see double. The person cannot judge distance or see to the sides when looking straight ahead. Alcohol can also cause colorblindness for a short time.

When intoxication gets this bad, the part of the brain that holds the automatic nerve controls for breathing and heartbeat is affected. What is the name of this part of the brain? See Figure 19-3. If alcohol slows down those controls enough, the heartbeat becomes uneven and breathing stops. This results in death by alcohol poisoning. Drinking contests present a huge risk of death by alcohol poisoning.

Usually people pass out before they are able to drink themselves to death. Sometimes, however, a drinker swallows a fatal drink just before passing out. A fifth, a quart, or a liter of drinks with a large amount of alcohol drunk in a short time may cause death.

Heavy drinkers may suffer blackouts, or periods of time that they cannot remember. Other people may remember seeing the drinker walking, talking, or performing some activity, but the drinker cannot remember anything. Heavy drinkers often wake up wondering what happened the night before.

Once alcohol gets into the blood, it causes the blood vessels to relax. This makes more blood flow near the skin's surface. This action causes a feeling of warmth for a short time as the face flushes and eyes become bloodshot, but the body's inside temperature drops. The blood near the skin's surface allows body heat to escape outside. Thus drinking to stay warm in winter does not work. In fact, in very cold weather it can be dangerous.

Alcohol prevents the release of the hormone that regulates how much urine is made. Without the braking action of this hormone, urine is made in the kidneys continuously. As a result, the drinker's body fluids are reduced. Not only does he or she become very thirsty, but the person also loses fluids that are necessary for the body to function.

Measuring Intoxication

The level of alcohol intoxication is measured by the **blood alcohol content** (BAC). BAC measures the number of milligrams of ethanol in each milliliter of blood. It is expressed as a percentage of total blood content. The higher the BAC, the greater the alcohol's effect on body and mind.

A BAC of 0.1 percent means that 0.001, or 1/1000 of the fluid in the blood, is alcohol. A BAC of 0.1 percent seriously slows muscle control and reflex reaction time. It also affects a person's ability to make wise decisions.

Intoxication of 0.1 percent may be reached if a 150-pound person drinks about three ounces of alcohol in an hour or less. This is three to four shots of whiskey, three to four glasses of wine, or four to five bottles of beer. Figure 19-4 shows how various levels of BAC work on the mind and the body.

Many people drink themselves sick. Too much alcohol in the stomach causes vomiting. At this point vomiting may occur as a defense against alcohol poisoning. Vomiting decreases the amount of alcohol in the body before it can enter the blood stream. Thus the BAC is lowered.

Effects of Alcohol

BAC	Effects
0.1	Dulls intelligence, sensory perceptions, and motor skills Lowers inhibitions Increases talkativeness and activity Encourages false confidence and bravado
0.2	Inhibits clear thinking, impairs memory, slows movement Encourages bursts of anger, weeping, or excitement Inhibits balance; walking a straight line becomes difficult
0.3	Impairs function of all sense organs; slurs speech; may cause double vision and staggering Inhibits judgment of distances Encourages sudden and exaggerated mood shifts
0.4	Severely reduces nervous and mental functions Greatly inhibits control of body movements Stimulates uncontrolled vomiting and urination May lead to unconsciousness
0.5	Usually causes unconsciousness; little or no reflexes Severely reduces blood pressure, breathing, and heartbeat Inactivates brain function
over 0.5	Usually causes death

Figure 19-4   The level of alcoholic intoxication is measured as a percentage of total blood content. The higher the blood alcohol content (BAC), the greater the risk of accident or death.

Factors Influencing Intoxication

For reasons not completely understood, intoxication shows in some people more than in others. There are a number of factors that cause the differences.

The Drinker   The body weight of a drinker is important to BAC. The heavier the person, the more alcohol he or she can drink without showing signs of intoxication. Lighter people have less blood and fewer tissues, so their BAC levels rise faster. Younger people are usually lighter than middle-aged people and are therefore more affected by alcohol.

The emotions and state of health of drinkers can also change their intoxication level. A person who is worn out emotionally or has recently been ill will be hit harder by alcohol.

As with many drugs, the effects of alcohol may become less obvious as people get used to drinking. However, this seeming ability to handle alcohol can suddenly break down in long-term drinkers. Sometimes one drink can completely intoxicate them.

Some long-term drinkers even learn to hide the fact that they have been drinking. But this trick does not mean they can deal with alcohol. Instead, it gives the drinker false confidence. The drinker may be legally drunk and simply not show it.

Concentration of Alcohol   Eating before drinking also affects levels of intoxication. The amount of food in the stomach changes the rate at which alcohol is passed from the stomach into the intestines and is then absorbed into the blood stream. Food can slow down the rate at which alcohol enters the blood stream. Foods that have fats and proteins in them especially slow down the amount of alcohol taken in. Milk, which contains much fat and protein, does this very well.

The stronger the alcohol in the drink, the faster it enters the blood stream. Because of this, the alcohol from one shot of whiskey reaches the blood stream faster than the alcohol from one glass of wine, even though they both contain the same amount of alcohol.

Beer and wine contain carbohydrates, minerals, and vitamins. These substances slow alcohol absorption. Carbonation speeds up the absorption. Carbonated beverages contain carbon dioxide to make them bubble. Such beverages include beer, champagne, and any mixed drink made with a carbonated mixer. Mixers include sparkling water and soft drinks, such as colas and ginger ale.

Many people believe that drinking different types of drinks has an effect on intoxication. This is not true. Only the amount of alcohol taken in matters.

Rate of Drinking   The liver changes alcohol into water and carbon dioxide, releasing energy in the process. This process reduces the BAC by about 0.015 percent per hour. If the drinker takes in alcohol faster than the liver can get rid of it, the BAC rises. After drinking six beers, a person who weighs between 150 and 180 pounds will take six to twelve hours to become sober.

Figure 19-5   Beer and wine can be just as dangerous as hard liquor. The amount of alcohol in a 12-ounce mug of beer, a 5-ounce glass of wine, and 1.5 ounces of whiskey is nearly the same. All contain about 0.5 ounces of alcohol.

Property of the STATE OF ILLINOIS MARILLAC HIGH SCHOOL NORTHFIELD, ILLINOIS 60093

Recovering From Intoxication

The liver removes about 95 percent of the alcohol from the blood. The other 5 percent of the alcohol in the blood stream leaves the body in urine, in perspiration, and in breath. Alcohol shows up on the breath even in low doses. Tests can be used by the police to detect alcohol and to prove intoxication. When a person breathes into a special machine, the BAC of the breath is quickly measured. As long as alcohol is present in the blood stream some intoxication remains. None of the supposed cures for drunkenness—black coffee, cold showers, hard exercise, or walks in the fresh air—work. These "cures" do not stop the physical and mental effects of alcohol either. A person's coordination, reaction time, and reasoning ability return only as the liver reduces the BAC.

A **hangover** is the unpleasant physical effects following the heavy use of alcohol. A hangover may include stomach upsets, headaches, tiredness, dizziness, thirst, and feelings of anger. Drinkers often suffer from worry, sadness, and guilt, particularly if they cannot remember how they behaved when they were drinking. On the other hand, sometimes the drinker wishes he or she could forget!

Intoxication and Other Drugs

Since intoxication begins with one drink, it is very dangerous for a person who has had even one drink to take other drugs or medicines during the same time. For example, some medicines taken for allergies or to dry up a stuffy nose can change the way alcohol affects people.

Alcohol and tranquilizers (drugs used to calm a person down) are a deadly combination. Both are depressants. They multiply each other's effects, and may even cause breathing to stop. Many accidental deaths have occurred when these two drugs were used together. Alcohol and some medicines used to treat sexually transmitted diseases can also cause serious reactions.

Lesson Review

Drinking begins a process of intoxication, which dangerously affects the mind and the body. Some people become intoxicated more quickly than others, but there is a level of intoxication that brings death to anyone. At any level of intoxication, even after one drink, it is extremely dangerous to take any medications or other drugs.

1 What do a 12-ounce glass of beer, a 5-ounce glass of wine, and a 1.5-ounce shot of whiskey have in common?

2 Name two ways alcohol may affect your vision.

3 What do the initials BAC stand for?

4 What can happen if someone drinks alcohol and takes some other drugs at the same time?

Long-Term Effects

The damaging effects of intoxication on the body multiply with the long-term use of alcohol. Some effects vary with the type of drinker. Other damaging effects occur with even light or moderate alcohol use. For those people who experience problems with drinking and wish to recover, medical treatment and support from different organizations are available.

Types of Drinkers

There are basically three terms commonly used to identify drinkers—social drinkers, problem drinkers, and alcoholics. Although there is much disagreement as to when someone actually becomes alcoholic, most alcoholics were once social drinkers. Today ten percent of those who drink consume 50 percent of the alcoholic beverages sold in the United States.

Social drinkers are people who have certain times when alcohol fits into their social life and who can stop drinking without any trouble. They connect drinking with pleasant occasions. Generally they drink only at meals and special events.

Problem drinkers are heavy, regular drinkers who are psychologically dependent on alcohol. They use alcohol as a social crutch. They drink to handle stress, worry, and unhappiness. They are able to stop drinking if they have a very strong reason. For example, they may stop if they wish to improve their health, get a job, or please someone important to them.

Alcoholics are psychologically and physically dependent on alcohol and cannot control their drinking. Drinking is the most important part of their life. It is more important than family, friends, job, or health. Alcoholics go through withdrawal when they cannot get alcohol. **Delirium tremens,** or the D.T.'s, may be described as the uncontrollable trembling that alcoholics suffer during withdrawal. Delirium tremens is a life-threatening reaction

Figure 19-6   One out of ten people who drink becomes an alcoholic.

Symptoms of Problem Drinking and Alcoholism

The Problem Drinker	The Alcoholic
Drinks often	May not drink often, but drinks without stopping
Drinks alone	Drinks alone
Drinks in the morning	Is physically addicted to alcohol
Goes to work or school drunk	Absent often from work or school
Has brief blackouts or loss of memory	Loses memory for hours, days, or weeks
Hides bottle and frequently sneaks drinks	Cannot hide drinking problem
Finds reasons to continue drinking habit	May blame drinking problem on others
Promises to quit drinking but cannot	Suffers painful withdrawal symptoms when denied alcohol

Figure 19-7   The difference between a problem drinker and an alcoholic is not clear-cut.

of the central nervous system. Alcoholics also **hallucinate** [*huh LOO suh nayt*] during withdrawal. To hallucinate is to see, smell, or feel things that are not real. Often, alcoholics ''see'' large insects or other animals. Figure 19-7 shows signs that may help identify problem drinkers and alcoholics.

An alcoholic is often thought of as a person who lives on the streets and wears ragged clothes. Only 5 percent of alcoholics fit this description. The other 95 percent work in all kinds of jobs, are all ages, and come from all kinds of backgrounds.

Alcoholics also include women. Until recently, the majority of known heavy drinkers were men. Today drinking problems among women are almost equal to those among men. This may stem from causes such as promotional campaigns directed at women and from a greater social acceptance of women's drinking.

Damage to the Body

Generally, moderate drinking does not cause a lot of damage to the body or mind. But pregnant women who drink at all risk damaging the health of their unborn babies. Problem drinkers and alcoholics cannot escape damaging their own bodies. Their life expectancy is ten to twelve years shorter than average.

Brain   Heavy drinking permanently damages the brain. Memory and intelligence damaged by alcohol abuse can never be fully recovered. Heavy drinking has been linked with some forms of mental illness, such as depression.

Health Bulletin

Heavy drinking can lower levels of the male hormone and feminize the male body, causing development of breasts.

Mouth and Throat   Strong alcoholic drinks harm the delicate tissues of the mouth and throat. The throat of a heavy drinker is nearly always red and swollen. This makes cancer more likely, particularly if the drinker smokes cigarettes. Drinkers who smoke are ten times more likely to get oral cancer than nondrinkers who do not smoke. In very heavy drinkers, blood vessels in the esophagus become enlarged and can bleed heavily. As a result, drinkers run a higher risk of cancer of the esophagus.

Digestive System and Heart   Long-term alcohol use increases the risk of cancer of the stomach, pancreas, and colon. Large amounts of alcohol cause the stomach to produce too much stomach acid. This causes indigestion and worsens ulcers. Although alcohol does contain food energy, it should not be thought of as a food. It has more Calories per ounce than sugar, but no body-building nutrients or vitamins. When the body gets more Calories than it can use, it stores the extra as fat. Heavy drinkers may gain weight, but their bodies starve for protein, minerals, and vitamins. This is because a drinker may fill up on alcohol and not feel the need for more nutritional foods. Thus many alcoholics suffer from poor nutrition.

Poor nutrition greatly affects the heart. When there is a lack of vitamin B_1, people get beriberi. Beriberi is a deficiency disease that leads to an enlarged heart and heart failure. A lack of protein also damages other muscles. When the body needs more protein

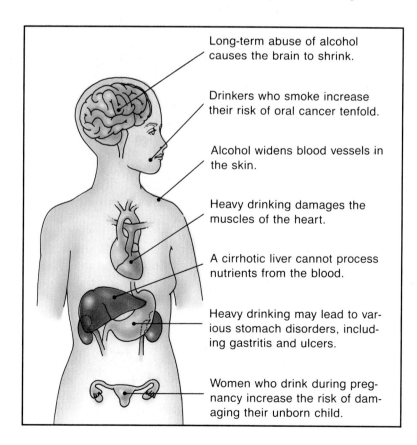

Long-term abuse of alcohol causes the brain to shrink.

Drinkers who smoke increase their risk of oral cancer tenfold.

Alcohol widens blood vessels in the skin.

Heavy drinking damages the muscles of the heart.

A cirrhotic liver cannot process nutrients from the blood.

Heavy drinking may lead to various stomach disorders, including gastritis and ulcers.

Women who drink during pregnancy increase the risk of damaging their unborn child.

Figure 19-8   Alcohol abuse may lead to a number of serious long-term diseases.

Figure 19-9 A healthy liver *(left)* contains smooth, even tissue. The liver of a heavy drinker may be fatty *(center)* or contain non-functioning scar tissue *(right).*

Health Bulletin

Heavy drinking among young people can cause brain damage before permanent liver damage occurs.

than it receives from food, it removes it from body tissues and muscles. The heart muscle is also weakened by the toxic effect of alcohol, which causes scar tissue to build up between the small fibers of heart muscle.

Liver   Next to the brain, the liver suffers most from alcohol. Alcohol keeps the liver from breaking down fats as well as it should. Fats collect in the livers of even moderate drinkers. Too much fat in the liver and high levels of alcohol appear to cause the cells to die. Scar tissue grows in place of living cells. Scarring of the liver is called **cirrhosis** [*sih ROH sis*]. With fewer functioning cells, the liver begins to fail. Many heavy drinkers have cirrhosis of the liver, the leading cause of death among alcoholics. If cirrhosis is detected early, however, the liver can repair itself. Cirrhosis is painless in the early stages and often progresses undetected. But there is now a blood test that can detect the disease at a very early stage.

Heavy drinkers are also likely to contract a form of hepatitis. **Hepatitis** [*hep uh TY tis*] is an inflammation of the liver caused by infection or toxic agents. The toxic effects of alcoholic drinks can cause alcoholic hepatitis. The victim has little energy because important chemical activity controlled by the liver does not take place. Liver cancer, too, is more common among heavy drinkers than among other people.

Unborn Babies   **Fetal Alcohol Syndrome,** or FAS, is a group of birth defects caused by a pregnant woman's drinking alcohol. *Fetal* refers to an unborn baby. Alcohol enters the unborn baby's blood stream from the blood stream of the mother. Some studies show that the fetal BAC is ten times greater than that of the mother. FAS is the third most common cause of mental retardation. **Mental retardation** is a condition in which people never develop the full mental abilities of their age group. Alcohol can also cause other birth defects, such as stunted growth and damaged organs and limbs.

Studies have proven that if a pregnant woman has one or two drinks a day, there is a 14 percent risk that her baby will be deformed. With six or more drinks a day, she increases the risk of FAS to 75 percent. Just one bout of heavy drinking during the important early stages of fetal development can cause birth defects. Not drinking at all is the only safe course for an expectant mother. Unfortunately, many women may drink and cause damage before they even know they are pregnant.

Alcoholism

Individuals who have a psychological and physical dependence on alcohol and are unable to control drinking are said to suffer from the disease of **alcoholism.** About one in ten alcohol users becomes an alcoholic. It is difficult to tell the difference between the signs of intoxication in an occasional drinker and the signs of intoxication in someone who is in the early stages of alcoholism. Thus alcoholism is a hard problem to identify.

Theories of Alcohol Addiction
The causes of alcoholism are not clear. Several different theories explain alcoholism in physical, psychological, and social terms.

A large number of children of alcoholics become alcoholics themselves, even when they are reared by adoptive parents. This fact makes some researchers conclude that the tendency to become an alcoholic is biologically passed from parent to child. Although many children of alcoholics do not become alcoholics, they may face a higher risk of alcoholism than other children.

Drinking patterns of parents and children living together are clearly connected. Parents who drink moderately tend to raise children who drink moderately. Heavy drinkers raise children who tend to drink heavily. The children of nondrinking parents often tend to extremes. Either they become nondrinkers or, if they turn against their parents, they may become problem drinkers.

Researchers often seek a personality trait common to all alcoholics. None has been found. The only fact many scientists agree upon is that most problem drinkers and alcoholics suffer greater stress in their everyday lives than other people.

High-Risk Groups
Anyone who drinks runs the risk of becoming an alcoholic. But studies suggest that beginning the drinking habit as a teenager increases that risk. Addiction may occur rather quickly after only a few times of drinking.

Old people are more likely to become alcoholics than young or middle-aged adults. This higher risk for older people may be due to an increased amount of time for social events. It may also be

HEALTH + TECHNOLOGY

BREATHALYZER—As a result of nationwide campaigns to crack down on intoxicated motorists, the deaths of drunk drivers have decreased by nearly a third since 1980. A major weapon in this campaign has been the breathalyzer. The breathalyzer, or breath analyzer, is an instrument that measures the amount of alcohol present in the air exhaled from the lungs. The amount of alcohol in the breath gives an accurate indication of the amount of alcohol circulating in the blood stream. Using chemicals, infrared techniques, or other methods, the breathalyzer quickly estimates the approximate concentration of alcohol in the blood. By government standards, blood alcohol concentrations of 0.1 percent or more are considered to be proof of intoxication.

At one time, breathalyzers were used only by law enforcement officers. Today, though, drinkers may voluntarily check their own levels of blood alcohol using coin-operated machines. People who use these machines realize that it is wiser and safer to spend a few cents for prevention than to risk injury or death by driving while intoxicated.

1 What does a breathalyzer measure?
2 How may a breathalyzer be used to prevent drunk driving?

from the stress of losing loved ones or a need to escape from health problems. It is also possible that alcohol affects the aged more because of changes in their nervous system.

Recovery From Alcoholism

Recovering from alcoholism is difficult. The alcoholic's state of mind is what counts most. Alcoholics must first understand that they have a problem. Then they must be determined to stop drinking and be willing to accept help. Often it takes an unhappy event to shock the alcoholic into wanting to change. This might be losing a job, getting into trouble with the police, or being left by their families.

Alcoholism is never cured. Alcoholics can recover, though, by not ever drinking alcohol again. If they do drink again, alcohol will take over and physical addiction will return. Fortunately, there are ways to help alcoholics recover. Many organizations offer medical care, general help, and moral support.

Detoxification For the seriously addicted person, the physical damage of alcoholism must be treated before the behavior patterns causing the problem can be changed. The addicted drinker must undergo detoxification. **Detoxification** is the removal of all alcohol from the body. Drugs are given to make withdrawal less dangerous. Withdrawal usually lasts about three or four days. This treatment needs medical supervision and perhaps hospital care. Delirium tremens can cause hallucinations, fits, and in about 10 percent of cases, death.

After detoxification, many alcoholics move to other places of treatment, which offer continued care and counseling. These places try to help the alcoholic adjust to the normal pace and stress of everyday life.

Figure 19-10 Alcoholics may suffer the uncontrolled trembling and frightful hallucinations of delirium tremens during withdrawal from alcohol.

Psychotherapy The treatment of mental, emotional, and nervous disorders is **psychotherapy** [*sy koh THEH ruh pee*]. A specially trained person works with alcoholics to help them overcome alcoholism. The alcoholic may begin to understand behavior patterns that cause alcoholism and learn to change them.

Drug Therapy Doctors sometimes give alcoholics drugs to stop their drinking. For example, people who take a drug called Antabuse become very ill if they drink. Drugs are also used in aversion therapy. **Aversion therapy** [*uh VUR zhun*] is treatment that changes behavior by connecting it with unpleasant feelings. A sickness-causing drug is given to the alcoholic at the same time as alcohol. With this method, alcoholics connect alcohol with sickness. They stop drinking to avoid nausea. Drug therapy works best when combined with psychotherapy.

Supportive Organizations Many churches, family service organizations, community programs, health agencies, and private organizations offer help to alcoholics. Some groups have offices throughout the country. Alcoholics Anonymous (AA) is a

Figure 19-11 Various organizations are willing to help in the reform of an alcoholic.

group of people who help alcoholics stop drinking and remain sober. The members are either recovered alcoholics or alcoholics who wish to stop drinking. AA was formed in 1935 when two alcoholics, a doctor and a businessman, decided to try the buddy system in quitting.

AA is a totally volunteer organization. The organization gets money only from members and none need give any. The only rule is that members must want to stop drinking. AA members meet daily or weekly in local groups and talk about the day-to-day challenges and rewards of living a life free from alcohol. Friendship and group help have been very effective in fighting alcoholism. AA has 38,000 groups in the United States.

Lesson Review

Drinkers may be classified according to how much alcohol they drink and how it affects them. Many people become physically and psychologically dependent upon alcohol. Heavy drinkers risk long-term physical and mental damage, and, sometimes, death. Recovery is difficult for alcoholics, but help through medical treatment and support organizations is available. Such help has proven effective, especially if the alcoholic is determined.

1 Name three diseases of the liver related to alcohol abuse.

2 What condition caused by alcohol is designated by the letters *FAS?*

3 What is the uncontrollable trembling that alcoholics suffer in withdrawal?

4 What is required of a member of AA?

Alcohol and Society

The 14 million problem drinkers in the United States harm not only themselves but many others as well. Even people who are mildly intoxicated can bring hardship to others on the roads, on the job, at school, or at home. Alcohol abuse causes accidents, increases medical costs, and creates a need for social services to treat alcoholism.

In the Home

A recent poll found that 38 percent of the nation's households experience problems that are related to alcohol abuse. Alcoholism, the "family disease," destroys one of the most important parts of family life—trust. The alcoholic thinks only about the need to drink and cannot be depended on as a parent, husband, or wife. Alcoholics often use money meant for food, rent, clothing, or medical expenses to buy alcohol. Family members live in constant fear of the alcoholic's sudden and angry mood changes. Alcohol abuse is often cited as one of the main causes of spouse beatings and other forms of violence in homes.

Alcohol abuse is involved in two thirds of all child abuse cases. Abuse may be in the form of neglect when the children are not adequately fed or cared for. Children in such a home feel helpless and often have behavior problems in school and in their social life. In some cases the abuse is violent and involves great physical and mental harm to the child. The mental harm can last into adulthood.

Family members often feel shame because of the alcoholic's public behavior. This shame can turn into feelings of guilt because the family no longer respects the alcoholic. Separation and divorce are common in families of alcoholics. Many families keep away from their friends and try to hide the problem. Family members begin to lie and make excuses for the alcoholic. But this behavior only make things worse. Rather than being protected by excuses, alcoholics must see that they are responsible for their own actions.

Teenagers

Teenagers use alcohol more than they use any other drug. About three fourths of all high school students drink alcoholic drinks once in a while. One third drink them regularly. Almost one in ten will one day become an alcoholic.

Psychologists believe that teenagers are more likely to develop alcohol problems than adults are. Teenagers have fewer experiences with alcohol than adults, and they often do not understand how powerful its effects are. They think they will be able to handle it but they cannot.

Psychologists believe that the use of alcohol slows social development. Young people are learning about social relations and emotional control. If they use a drug every time they are under stress, they may never be able to develop their social and emotional abilities.

Figure 19-12 Many teenagers underestimate the powerful effects of alcohol.

Figure 19-13 Alcohol-related automobile accidents kill thousands of people each year.

On the Job and in the Classroom

Alcohol use at work or in school leads to days away from work and school, poor work, and accidents. Almost one half of all deaths caused by accidents on the job are connected with alcohol. Whether the drinkers drink before or during school or work, they do less work. Heavy drinkers often lose their jobs. Many companies have faced the problem and now offer their workers treatment programs.

On the Road

In one half of all traffic deaths in the United States, the driver has been drinking. One third of pedestrians struck and killed by cars were drunk. **Driving while intoxicated,** or DWI, is illegal in every state. In most states, it is illegal to drive a car if the BAC is 0.1 percent or greater. In most states, it is illegal to drink alcohol while driving. In some, it is against the law to have an open container of any alcoholic drink in the car.

In truth, anyone planning to drive should not drink at all. Signs of intoxication can appear at a BAC as low as 0.02 or 0.03 percent. Studies show that even one drink harms vision and reactions. A driver with a BAC of 0.05 percent, even though he or she is within the legal limit, is twice as likely to have an accident as a nondrinking driver. A BAC of 0.1 percent increases the risk of being in an accident by seven times. At BAC 0.15 percent, the risk is ten times greater.

Intoxication can cause accidents in several ways. Intoxicated drivers cannot concentrate on driving as well, and drinking may make them take careless risks. At a BAC of 0.05, reflex time is only three fourths of its normal speed. Visual sharpness is reduced by one third, which is the same as wearing sunglasses at night. The eyes move more slowly and are slow to recover from headlight glare at night. At higher levels of intoxication, the driver may not be able to read signs because of blurred vision.

Health **History**

From 1961 to 1971, about 274,000 U.S. citizens died in alcohol-related driving accidents. This figure is about five times the fatality of U.S. soldiers in Vietnam.

Health Bulletin

Many countries have strict drunk driving laws. In the United Kingdom, Sweden, and Finland, drunk drivers are jailed for one year. In Turkey, they are taken 20 miles from town and made to walk back under police escort.

Drunken driving can be a horrible offense. Thirty thousand people a year are killed and another one half million are hurt. Figure 19-14 shows that drunk drivers aged 18–24 cause more fatal accidents than any other age group. Car accidents in which the drivers have been drinking are also the chief cause of death for teenagers and young adults up to the age of 24. Disturbing numbers such as these have led to greater awareness of the problem by society. Organizations such as Mothers Against Drunk Driving (M.A.D.D.) and Students Against Driving Drunk (S.A.D.D.) have also helped to bring about changes. Pressure from such groups and society in general has led to stricter penalities in every state for drinking and driving.

Drinking and the Law   Due to recent social pressure against drunk driving, new laws now control the sale of alcohol. Many states now outlaw "happy hours," in which bars offer lower prices on drinks to encourage people to drink after work. In many states bartenders are held responsible for damage done by a drunk driver who has been drinking at their bars. People who have parties in their homes are also considered responsible for their guests. The law also forbids bartenders and friends from giving drinks to someone already drunk.

Since 1987, the legal drinking age in every state is 21. In several states, any person under the legal drinking age who is caught driving while intoxicated (DWI) can have his or her driver's license taken away on the spot. It is illegal in most states for minors, or those under the age of 21, to buy an alcoholic beverage or to pretend they are older than the drinking age. The law also puts part of the burden on the adults. It is illegal for a person to sell an alcoholic drink to a minor.

Figure 19-14   Most of these fatal accidents are caused by young drivers.

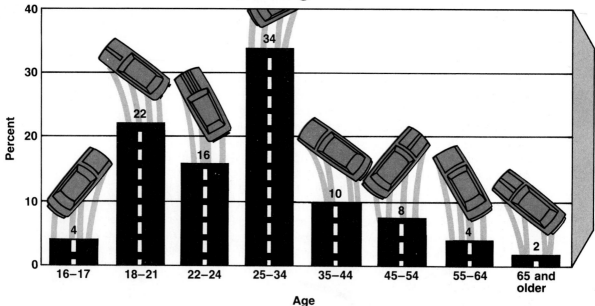

Fatal Accidents Caused by Driving Drunk

Percent

Age	Percent
16–17	4
18–21	22
22–24	16
25–34	34
35–44	10
45–54	8
55–64	4
65 and older	2

Age

New Drinking Habits

In recent years, drinking has been viewed less favorably than in the past. This is partly due to campaigns against drunk driving. Also, attitudes towards health, fitness, and self-image have changed.

Because of public pressure, prime-time television has cut back on showing alcohol use on the screen. Owners of sports arenas now have family sections where drinking is not allowed. Public tolerance of intoxication is decreasing, so people have cut back on drinking. Consumption of alcoholic beverages is at its lowest level in 30 years. The alcohol industry has brought out new lines of light beers and wines with low alcohol content. Nonalcoholic fruit drinks and carbonated waters now satisfy many people's thirst at parties, lunches, and celebrations.

The Choice Is Yours

Many teenagers and adults choose not to drink. If this is your choice, stick by it. Do not let others decide for you. If you do choose to drink, respect the opinion of others who choose not to drink. More and more, young people are learning to socialize without alcohol. People are also learning to deal with stress through healthy activity or by changing their behavior.

If you must deal with alcoholism in your family, help is available. Al-Anon is an organization that helps the families of alcoholics cope with their situations. It encourages family members to seek help for themselves and not to wait until the alcoholic decides to seek help. Al-Anon reminds the family members not to accept the guilt the alcoholic may try to place on them.

Alateen is an organization of and for teenagers who live with alcoholics. The organization of Alateen is similar to that of Al-Anon. Teenagers come together not to treat family members, but to deal with their own problems. Membership is open to young people who wish to discuss, share, and learn to deal with their own situations.

Lesson Review

The harmful effects of alcohol spread throughout society. People pay a high price for these harmful effects. The high costs are seen in alcohol-related deaths, diseases, and loss of work. Drinkers continue to make life difficult for their workmates and families. Many organizations exist to help family members of alcoholics, particularly teenagers with alcoholic parents. There are other groups that work especially against drunk driving. Tougher laws may help reduce the number of drunk driving accidents.

1 What is DWI?

2 To what age will states have to raise their legal drinking age by 1987 in order to receive federal highway funds?

3 What is the name of an organization of and for teenagers who live with alcoholics?

Chapter Review

Vocabulary

alcoholic	driving while intoxicated	intoxication
alcoholism	ethanol	mental retardation
aversion therapy	fermentation	problem drinker
blood alcohol content	Fetal Alcohol Syndrome	proof
cirrhosis	hangover	psychotherapy
delirium tremens	hallucinate	reflex
depressant	hepatitis	social drinker
detoxification	inhibition	toxic
distillation		

Using Vocabulary

Questions 1-10. On a separate sheet of paper, write the term that most correctly completes the sentence.

1 __?__ are checks on the emotions. (reflexes, inhibitions, depressants, toxins)

2 The uncontrollable trembling that alcoholics suffer during withdrawal is known as __?__. (hallucinations, delirium tremens, sublimation, displacement)

3 The leading cause of death among alcoholics is __?__. (cirrhosis of the liver, mental retardation, Fetal Alcohol Syndrome, hepatitis)

4 __?__ is the treatment of mental, emotional, and nervous disorders. (aversion therapy, chiropractic, detoxification, psychotherapy)

5 __?__ is an inflammation of the liver caused by infectious or toxic agents. (arteriosclerosis, cancer, hepatitis, FAS)

6 __?__ measures the number of milligrams of ethanol in each milliliter of blood. (BAC, FAS, proof, D.T.)

7 A __?__ may include stomach upsets, headaches, dizziness, and angry feelings. (hangover, hallucination, depressant, concussion)

8 Alcohol is __?__, or poisonous. (a stimulant, harmless, an inhibitor, toxic)

9 __?__ is illegal in every state. (DWI, failure to wear seat belts, FAS, BAC)

10 When alcoholics __?__, they may "see" animals or large insects. (become intoxicated, undergo psychotherapy, drive while intoxicated, hallucinate)

Interpreting Ideas

1 Explain why drinking contests are a dangerous activity.

2 Why does alcohol consumption cause more damage to the liver than any other organ except the brain?

3 Why do children in families where there is an alcoholic often develop behavior problems in school?

4 What types of treatment are available to help alcoholics?

5 How do family members sometimes contribute to the alcoholic's problem?

6 Why should someone expecting to drive not drink at all?

7 Compare the objectives of Alcoholics Anonymous, Al-Anon, and Alateen.

8 How does drinking affect vision? How could these changes influence driving?

9 What birth defects may be caused by alcohol?

10 What are the factors that affect the level of alcohol intoxication?

11 Identify the parts of the body that are adversely affected by heavy habitual drinking.

12 Why should alcohol and tranquilizers never be combined?

13 List five good reasons for deciding not to drink at all.

14 Identify and describe the three basic types of drinkers.

15 How is proof used on the labels of alcoholic beverages?

16 Identify four reasons why people drink alcohol.

17 Why does alcohol make a drinker thirsty?

18 Identify the immediate effects of intoxication.

19 Why may drinking be an especially difficult problem for teenagers?

20 Why may women's drinking problems have begun to match those of men?

Applying Concepts

1 If alcohol is very fattening, how can a diet high in ethanol lead to malnutrition?

2 At a party Bob had three shots of whiskey and Ed had three glasses of wine. Predict who is likely to become intoxicated more quickly. Why? Who do you think should drive home from the party?

3 Why are alcoholics frequently depicted with a large red nose?

4 Suppose you are trying to convince a friend who is drunk not to drive home from a party. What arguments would you use to convince him or her not to drive?

5 Is it likely that teenagers who use alcohol in family celebrations will become alcoholics? Why or why not?

6 In your opinion, what is the biggest "cost" of alcohol abuse? Give several reasons for your answer.

7 If ethanol makes people more active and talkative, why is it considered a depressant?

8 Why does carbonation of beverages speed up alcohol absorption?

9 What is the link between alcohol and crime?

10 Predict what may happen in each of the following cases: (a) After the party, John, who had a BAC of 0.1 percent, began driving home; (b) Karen combined her three alcoholic drinks with two tranquilizers; (c) Before the champagne wedding reception, Ben had a light supper of cheese, bread, and milk.

Projects

1 Find out more about organizations such as Alcoholics Anonymous and Alateen whose purpose is to give information and support to alcoholics and members of their families. You may wish to get permission to attend a meeting of one of these organizations. What are the goals of the people who attend the meetings? What happens at the meetings?

2 Write a profile of a likely candidate for alcoholism. The profile should include a description of the person's personality and family background.

3 Write for brochures and other materials about driving drunk from organizations such as MADD and SADD. Use the information in these materials to write radio or television ads to convince the public not to drive if they are drinking.

4 Construct a life-size cardboard model of a man or a woman. On the model highlight the internal organs that are affected by alcohol consumption. Color code each organ to a card that contains an explanation of the specific effect(s) of alcohol on that organ.

5 Before a school dance or prom, wage a campaign against driving drunk. You and other classmates may wish to use this chapter to prepare fact sheets about the costs of alcohol abuse, then distribute the sheets to the entire student body. You may also want to create posters on drunk driving for display in the corridors and cafeteria. For example, a humorous poster entitled "Things to Do Instead of Drinking" might illustrate activities such as dancing, swimming, and camping.

Although various hotlines can help drug abusers with their problems, simply saying *no* to drug abuse is the best solution.

CHAPTER TWENTY

PREVENTING

DRUG ABUSE

Today drug education is helping many teens to say *no* to drugs. Even so, drug abuse is still a great problem in society. Drug abuse has ruined the lives of not only the abusers, but also many innocent people.

Some people turn to drugs because they think that drugs are a quick, easy way of improving their moods. This abuse of drugs can easily get out of hand and may lead to dependence on drugs. Teenagers can help themselves and others by learning to recognize early signs of drug abuse. Hot lines throughout the country provide help to people suffering from drug-related problems. Hospital programs and community groups also have been established to treat drug dependence.

Objectives

- Distinguish between legal and illegal drugs.

- State several reasons why someone might start taking drugs.

- Compare physical and psychological dependence on drugs.

- Describe the short-term and long-term effects of commonly abused drugs.

- Identify the commonly abused drugs.

- List three problems associated with drug dependence.

- Describe withdrawal symptoms.

- Identify the signs of drug abuse.

- Name three types of programs that offer help to drug abusers.

- Describe the legal consequences of drug abuse.

Legal and Illegal Drugs

A chemical that causes changes in the body or the mind, and sometimes both, is called a **drug.** Drugs may be swallowed, inhaled, applied to the skin, or injected. Medicines are drugs used to treat or prevent illness.

The use of a drug for other than medical purposes is called **drug abuse.** Drug abusers are generally seeking some form of mental escape when they start abusing drugs. A mind-altering drug is called a **psychoactive drug** [*sy koh AK tiv*]. After a while the continued use of psychoactive drugs may become a habit. Users continue because they are dependent on the drug.

The Nature of Drugs

Chemicals that make up drugs originally came from plants, animals, or minerals. Today these chemicals can also be created artificially. A **synthetic drug** is a drug created in a laboratory by combining other chemicals.

The Food and Drug Administration of the federal government regulates the sale of drugs. **Legal drugs** are those that are considered useful enough to be available for sale. Most legal drugs, except caffeine, alcohol, and tobacco, contain a chemical or chemicals designed to treat medical problems. There are two kinds of legal drugs. Drugs that may be purchased without a doctor's permission are called **over-the-counter drugs.** Over-the-counter drugs include such items as mild pain relievers, motion sickness pills, cough syrups, diet pills, and sleep aids. Although it is legal to sell these drugs to anyone, they are safe only when the instructions on the labels are followed.

Drugs available from drugstores only with a doctor's written permission are called **prescription drugs.** Laws regulate their manufacture and sale. These drugs are controlled more closely than over-the-counter drugs because they have more dangerous effects if misused. A doctor must consider the particular person and the particular medical problem in deciding on the correct dosage of these drugs. Prescription drugs sometimes are misused when someone takes them for other than medical reasons or takes too much of them. Taking enough of a drug to cause shock, coma, or death is called an **overdose.** Prescription drugs can be abused when taken by someone other than the person for whom they were prescribed. If doctors or pharmacists prescribe or sell drugs to persons who do not medically need them, they are acting illegally. All drugs are potentially dangerous. In fact, more Americans suffer medical emergencies or die from incorrect use of prescription drugs than from the abuse of illegal drugs.

The possession and sale of **illegal drugs** are forbidden by law because their harmful effects outweigh any useful purposes the drugs may have. In spite of government efforts, illegal drugs continue to be supplied by international and national criminal networks. Many drugs are grown or made out of the country and smuggled in. Some drugs are grown secretly and then processed. Others are created from chemicals in secret laboratories.

Figure 20-1 Most drugs are manufactured for constructive medical purposes.

Figure 20-2 People involved in the illegal sale of drugs risk a 15-year prison sentence.

Causes of Drug Abuse

If you interviewed ten different drug abusers, each might give a different reason for starting to use drugs. Some might say that they first took drugs to be popular with their friends. Others might explain that they wanted to forget their problems. Still others may have wanted to seek thrills or appear grown up. Reasons for drug abuse are complex. There is no one single cause, and reasons for abusing drugs overlap and interact.

Many young people take drugs because they find it hard to resist peer pressure. Peer pressure is a fact of teenage life. As teenagers try to depend less on their parents, they depend more on their friends. If there is peer pressure to take drugs, teenagers may be persuaded that drugs are a way to escape from their problems. Those who lack self-esteem or feel cut off from others may feel that drug taking will get them friends.

Acceptance by friends is very important. But it can also cause problems. Teenagers almost always experiment with drugs in groups, usually at the suggestion of a friend or relative. Some teenagers are easily influenced by peer pressure to use drugs. More independent teenagers find it easier to say *no*.

People with personal or family problems are more likely to respond to pressures to turn to drugs. Taking drugs will not solve their problems, though. Instead, their personal problems usually increase once they start taking drugs. Their ties with other people weaken, and they become more and more dependent upon drugs. Thus they have entered a hard-to-break cycle.

Many drug abusers start to take drugs to escape from problems. For some people, drugs create a sense of euphoria. **Euphoria** [*yoo FAWR ee uh*] is a feeling of great happiness or well-being. Other people take drugs to forget reality.

People who believe they have little chance to achieve their goals may become drug abusers. They feel cut off from the rest of society. Some of them are poor and see no way to escape from

Figure 20-3   Drug abuse has ended the careers and lives of many popular performers, such as John Belushi.

their poverty. Others do badly in school and see no reason to stay. These people have little chance of employment. They may turn to drugs to ease their sense of hopelessness.

People living in comfortable surroundings may seem to have less reason to use drugs. But anyone, including successful people in business, athletics, medicine, and the arts, can abuse and become dependent upon drugs. Some of these abusers may be trying to relieve stress related to their job or their personal life. Others are thrill seekers, simply looking for new experiences.

Teenagers who have money are particularly likely to be pressured by peers. Drug pushers make sure that drugs are easily available to young people who can afford to pay for increasing amounts of drugs if they become addicted.

Family life also greatly affects drug use. Parental attitudes and behavior are important factors. Some parents use sleeping pills regularly or abuse alcohol. Some parents tolerate a small amount of drug abuse and do not think it will get out of hand. Studies show that the children in such families are more likely to use illegal drugs than those in stricter families. Teenagers may follow the example of a brother or sister who abuses drugs. On the other hand, some teenagers avoid drugs because of the damage that drugs have done to a family member.

Some teenagers turn to drugs to escape from families where they are neglected or abused, or from families who have difficulty talking to each other or do not have time for each other. Teenagers who do not learn how to make decisions for themselves or to develop a sense of responsibility may find it hard to resist peer pressure to try drugs.

Whatever the reason for starting, once people begin abusing drugs, other reasons take over. Drugs cause problems that may make it difficult to quit. As problems become worse, the abuser may depend more and more upon the drug to escape reality. But abusing drugs will never solve personal problems—instead, the drugs themselves become a problem.

Lesson Review

Drug abuse includes the improper use of legal over-the-counter and prescription drugs as well as the use of illegal drugs. Causes of drug abuse are usually problems in people's personal lives. These problems make it more likely for some teenagers to turn to drugs when they feel pressure from their peers.

1 Define a *psychoactive drug.*

2 Why are prescription drugs available only with a doctor's written permission?

3 What term describes a false sense of well-being induced by drugs?

4 Why are some drugs illegal?

5 State three reasons why teenagers may begin abusing drugs.

Dangers of Drug Abuse

The dangerous nature of drugs has been widely publicized. Drug education has helped people realize that when taking any drug, they take risks. These risks include dangerous side effects as well as addiction. Drug abuse can bring physical suffering. The drug abuser's ties with family and society are usually broken, and many drug abusers turn to crime to support their habits.

Side Effects

The human body maintains a delicate chemical balance. Drugs rarely affect one part of the body without affecting others. A drug's **chief effect** is the physical or mental change for which it is taken. A different, unknown, or undesirable reaction to a drug is called a **side effect.** For example, two persons may take aspirin for their headaches. The chief effect for both will be relief from pain. One person, however, may suffer a side effect of an upset stomach. The upset stomach may be the result of irritation of the lining of the stomach.

Not all side effects can be predicted. Some drugs that were originally developed as mild anxiety relievers turned out unexpectedly to be habit-forming. Others have caused birth defects. Similar discoveries may be made in the future about drugs currently thought to be safe. Long-term effects of many new drugs are not known yet. The side effects of a particular drug may vary from person to person.

A common effect of many drugs is the development of tolerance. **Tolerance** occurs when the body develops a resistance to the effects of a drug. This often occurs during regular drug use. As a result, the drug user must take larger doses of the drug to achieve the same effect.

Dependence and Addiction

Nearly all illegal drugs and some prescription drugs can cause dependence. They can cause psychological or physical dependence, or both. As you learned in Chapter 18, physical dependence, or addiction, occurs after a drug has been taken regularly for some time. The amount of time required varies according to the drug and to the individual. Usually the body undergoes a chemical change and then requires the drug to function normally. Figure 20-4 shows the stages of drug abuse leading to addiction.

Psychological dependence occurs when a person develops a craving for a drug, based on a need to reach euphoria or to escape from problems. This is also called habituation. Because the drug's effects are temporary and often become harder to achieve the longer a drug is used, psychological dependence can become as powerful as physical dependence. A person's problems, on the other hand, are not so temporary.

Drug dependence has many related dangers. Some drug addicts starve themselves because eating seems less important than the use of drugs. Many abusers contract hepatitis, AIDS, or other infectious diseases from using dirty needles. Their habit places drug

Health Bulletin

Drug overdoses were once treated by pumping out the stomach. Now artificial kidneys and medication to increase the production of urine cause the drugs to be eliminated from the body four times as fast. For this to be successful, however, the victim must be treated in time.

Stages of Drug Abuse

Experimental	User is more curious about the drug's effects than the dangers, expects to use the drug once or twice and then quit.
Occasional Use	User associates drug use with social events. Peer approval or disapproval is influential.
Regular Use	User takes the drug only to feel the effect of the drug, begins to use the drug while alone. Psychological dependence has occurred, although the user will deny it. The drug interferes with normal activities.
Addiction	User continues abuse to avoid the discomfort of withdrawal. A person in this state will steal money to buy more of the drug. Withdrawal must usually be accomplished under medical supervision.

Figure 20-4 Drug abuse may progress through certain stages.

abusers in the power of people who may harm or even kill them. A drug habit may affect more than just the drug abuser. Women who abuse drugs increase their risk of having children with birth defects. Babies born to drug addicts may begin life with painful withdrawal symptoms.

Withdrawal

People who stop taking a drug to which they are addicted experience withdrawal. Withdrawal symptoms vary from drug to drug. They include nervousness, irritability, and sudden mood changes. Others are nausea, vomiting, sweating, and increased heart rate. Some abusers hallucinate; some have stomach and muscle cramps. Some abusers suffer delirium tremens. Certain cases of withdrawal are severe enough to cause death.

Mixing Drugs

Mixing drugs can cause unexpected effects. Alcohol mixed with prescription sleeping pills, for example, can be deadly. Mixing drugs also increases the possibility of addiction.

One of the chief dangers of illegal drugs is that they are often mixed and the mixture is not known. Thus no user can really know what the effects will be. Whether a drug was made in an illegal laboratory or smuggled in, the story is the same. Smugglers and amateur chemists make more money when they cut, or dilute, their drugs. Sometimes another drug or sugar is used in the cutting process. Then these drugs are sold to distributors.

Distributors cut the drug again before selling to drug dealers. Dealers also want to make money and so they cut the drug again. As a result, drug abusers never know how strong the drug really is, so they can never be sure of the dosage. Abusers also do not know exactly which drugs have been mixed together. Each time they purchase drugs, drug abusers are risking an overdose or a dangerous mixture.

Figure 20-5 Drug abusers risk arrest, overdose, and death.

Damage to Social Relationships

Since an abuser's life is dominated by the need to obtain drugs, other concerns such as family, friends, career, and community may no longer count. Family life is often harmed because the addict prefers to be alone or with other drug abusers. The abuser may be unable to keep a job or to fulfill family responsibilities. Addicts may lose interest in giving or receiving affection. They may become violent and insulting, both under the influence of drugs and during withdrawal.

Drug abusers may lie, cheat, steal, or use violence to obtain their drugs. Robbery and mugging are often the only way they can get money to buy drugs. There is also a lot of violence between drug dealers in which innocent people get hurt.

Lesson Review

Drug abusers risk physical and psychological dependence. Dangerous side effects may be multiplied by mixing drugs. Illegal drugs are especially dangerous because they are often mixed with other drugs. Because the mixture of illegal drugs is not known, abusers risk death by overdose. Addiction to drugs causes great mental and physical damage. The pain of withdrawal prevents many addicts from being able to give up their habit.

1 What is the name of a different, unknown, or undesirable reaction to a drug?

2 What are three common dangers related to a physical dependence on drugs?

3 What are four withdrawal symptoms suffered by addicts?

4 Name three ways in which drug abuse is a problem to society.

Commonly Abused Drugs

Many different drugs are abused. The main classifications of abused drugs are stimulants, depressants, hallucinogens, marijuana, and narcotics, although other drugs are also abused. Most of these drugs can cause physical and psychological dependence. Their risks to health are shown in Figure 20-7.

Stimulants

Drugs that speed up the body's processes are called stimulants. **Stimulants** increase the heart rate, blood pressure, and rate of breathing. These drugs make people seem more awake and hide tiredness. Thus the users seem nervous and jumpy. Some stimulants are fairly weak. Others are much stronger and much more dangerous.

Caffeine is a legal psychoactive drug that is found in coffee, soft drinks, and cocoa. Many over-the-counter drugs sold to relieve tiredness contain caffeine. Although caffeine can help overcome muscle tiredness, it may also damage the user's stomach or make ulcers worse. Overuse can cause a person to be irritable and to have an irregular heart rate. It may also keep a person from sleeping well. Physical and psychological dependence are possible results of the regular use of caffeine.

Amphetamines [am FET uh meenz] are a group of very strong stimulants. Doctors sometimes prescribe small doses of amphetamines to reduce appetite or to treat sleep disorders. Doctors also give small doses of amphetamines to hyperactive children. For some unknown reason, amphetamines affect hyperactive children differently from adults. Amphetamines slow these children down instead of speeding them up.

Amphetamines are sometimes called "speed." They are sold illegally in the forms of pills, white powder, or shots. Amphetamines are also called "uppers," because they cause euphoria. This promise of euphoria makes uppers popular. However, their effects quickly wear off and abusers feel suddenly depressed, or "crash." Feeling tired and depressed, they take more drugs. Thus the use of these drugs becomes a vicious cycle.

The use of amphetamines can destroy the abuser's body very quickly. Because they lose interest in food, abusers often suffer from poor nutrition. They seem to be on edge and aggressive. They also lose interest in their appearance, lose touch with reality, and distrust others. Often, they become infected from dirty needles. Amphetamines cause psychological dependence, depression, mental illness, nervous aggression, seizures, and even coma and death.

Cocaine is a painkiller used in ear, nose, and throat surgery. When used illegally, this strong stimulant is inhaled or put into a vein with a needle. Illegal cocaine is also called "coke" or "snow." Cocaine causes psychological and physical dependence, seizures, stomach disorders, and liver damage. Repeated sniffing of cocaine can form a permanent hole in the nasal septum, the wall separating the two nasal cavities.

Figure 20-6   Cocaine is extracted from the leaves of the coca plant.

Abusers of cocaine frequently hallucinate and feel that others want to harm them. Abusers often use depressants to calm themselves down from the high of cocaine. They then take more cocaine or amphetamines to get high again. This mixing of stimulants and depressants can cause death.

A very dangerous way of using cocaine is called freebasing. This involves smoking or injecting a paste form of cocaine. Freebasing brings about stronger effects for a shorter time. It is likely to produce bad mental effects very quickly. Another highly dangerous form of cocaine is called "crack."

Crack is a rocklike substance that is smoked rather than sniffed. Crack can cause convulsions, respiratory failure, or heart attack. Addiction to crack occurs more rapidly than any other form of drug addiction.

Depressants

Drugs that slow down the processes of the body are called **depressants.** They slow brain and body reactions. This means a lower blood pressure, body temperature, muscle action, and heart rate. Depressants are used to calm people down.

Doctors used to treat people suffering from prolonged anxiety with barbiturates. **Barbiturates** [*bahr BICH ur its*] are strong depressants made from barbituric acid. These help people relax. Barbiturates are also prescribed to help people sleep. Used illegally, the effects of barbiturates or "downers" vary from one person to the next. Abusers stagger and slur their speech. Their sight becomes unclear and their reaction time slows down. As their tolerance increases, abusers cannot sleep without barbiturates. Psychological and physical dependence follow.

Early on, withdrawal from barbiturates includes anxiety, shaking, and raised pulse rate and temperature. These last up to two weeks. Days after withdrawal, abusers imagine sights and sounds, feel fearful, and show signs of serious mental disease. Sudden withdrawal can be fatal. Since the drugs affect memory, many users accidentally take overdoses.

Doctors treat anxious patients with tranquilizers. **Tranquilizers** [*TRAN kwuh lyz urz*] are drugs that slow down nerve activity, relax muscle tension, lower alertness, and cause drowsiness. Tranquilizers can produce physical and psychological dependence. Abusers turn to these tranquilizers whenever they face stress. They can suffer seizures when they try to stop using them. Abusers who try to withdraw from these drugs without medical help may die. Abuse of tranquilizers during pregnancy can also lead to birth defects in the user's children.

Methaqualone [*meth uh KWAY lohn*] is a tranquilizer with effects similar to those of barbiturates. Methaqualone is also referred to as "ludes." Other nicknames include "714s" and "sopors." Taking a little of this drug creates a feeling of calmness. A large dose gives a feeling of euphoria. The side effects include headaches, nosebleeds, dizziness, and diarrhea. Methaqualone causes psychological and physical dependence. When mixed with alcohol, it can cause death.

Figure 20-7 Risks of drug abuse

	Drug	Short-term Risks	Long-term Risks	Risk of Dependence	Withdrawal Symptoms
Stimulants	Amphetamines (Benzedrine, Dexedrine, Methedrine, Preludin)	Excitation, restlessness, rapid speech, irritability, convulsions	Insomnia, excitability, hallucinations, severe mental disorders, malnutrition	Heavy psychological dependence; some physical dependence	Withdrawal after prolonged use at high dosage may include extreme fatigue and mental depression, irritability, hyperactivity, and changes in brain waves during sleep.
	Antidepressants (Elavil, Ritalin, Tofranil)	Nausea, hypertension, loss of weight, insomnia	Stupor, coma, convulsions, heart failure, damage to liver and white blood cells, death	Moderate psychological dependence	
	Cocaine ("Crack")	Irritability, depression, hallucinations, increased heart and breathing rate	Damage to nose and stomach, severe mental disorders, seizures, death	Heavy psychological dependence	
	Nicotine	Headache, loss of appetite, nausea	Difficulty in breathing, heart and lung diseases	Heavy psychological dependence; some physical dependence	
Depressants	Alcohol (beer, wine, liquor)	Decreased alertness, depression, stupor, nausea, unconsciousness, death	Obesity, malnutrition, fetal alcohol syndrome, impotence, severe mental disorders, ulcers, brain damage, delirium tremens, liver damage	Heavy psychological dependence; some physical dependence	Withdrawal may include tremors, convulsions, delirium, anxiety, restlessness, or death.
	Barbiturates (Nembutal, Seconal, Phenobarbital, Quaalude, Sopor)	Decreased alertness, drowsiness, poor coordination	Confusion, irritability, sleepiness	Heavy psychological dependence; some physical dependence	
	Tranquilizers (Valium, Librium, Thorazine)	Drowsiness, blurred vision, dizziness, slurred speech	Destruction of blood cells, jaundice, coma	Moderate to heavy psychological dependence	

Category	Drug	Possible Effects	Long-Term/Health Effects	Dependence	Withdrawal Symptoms
Hallucinogens	Mescaline; Psilocybin; PCP (Sernylan); LSD, DMT, STP	Changes in perception, anxiety, hallucinations, vomiting, panic, mental disorders	Delusions, increased panic, severe mental disorders	Moderate psychological dependence	Withdrawal symptoms are unconfirmed or unknown.
Cannabis	Marijuana; Hashish	Reduction of inhibitions, panic, loss of memory, stupor, changes in perception, delusions, paranoia	Lung damage, possible sterility	Moderate to heavy psychological dependence	Withdrawal symptoms are unconfirmed or unknown.
Narcotics	Opium (Dover's powder, Paregoric)	Decreased alertness, hallucinations, stupor, nausea, vomiting, unconsciousness, death	Constipation, sluggish speech, temporary sterility and impotence, convulsions, coma, death	Heavy psychological and physical dependence	Withdrawal may include excessive sweating, fever, chills, restlessness, depression, tremors, abdominal cramps, involuntary twitching and kicking, anorexia, vomiting, and diarrhea.
Narcotics	Methadone (Dolophine, Methadose)	Decreased alertness, hallucinations, stupor, nausea, vomiting, unconsciousness, death	Constipation, sluggish speech, temporary sterility and impotence, convulsions, coma, death	Heavy psychological and physical dependence	
Narcotics	Meperidine (Demerol, Pethadol); Morphine; Codeine; Heroin; Percodan	Decreased alertness, hallucinations, stupor, nausea, vomiting, unconsciousness, death	Constipation, sluggish speech, temporary sterility and impotence, convulsions, coma, death	Heavy psychological and physical dependence	
Inhalants	Airplane glue; Amyl nitrite; Nitrous oxide	Poor coordination, stupor, unconsciousness, death	Hallucinations; damage to liver, kidney, bone marrow, and brain	Heavy psychological dependence	Withdrawal symptoms are unconfirmed or unknown.
Steroids	Anadrol; Winstrol; Anavar	Excessive muscle building, acne, nausea, vomiting, diarrhea, excitation, insomnia, chills, impotence	Sterility, baldness, irreversible hairiness, iron-deficiency anemia, premature maturation of bone, deeper voice, coma, death	Psychological dependence	Withdrawal symptoms are unconfirmed or unknown.

Hallucinogens

Drugs that cause abusers to see, hear, and feel things that do not exist are called **hallucinogens** [*huh LOO suh nuh juhnz*]. Objects seem farther away or closer than they are. The abuser loses the proper sense of time and space. These drugs are illegal and have no value as medicine. No one knows exactly how hallucinogens work. The mental state of the abuser influences the mind altering effect of these drugs. Not much is known yet about their long-term effects.

A very powerful hallucinogen is **LSD** (lysergic acid diethylamide). LSD has no smell or color. It is usually placed on foods such as sugar cubes or gelatin and eaten. Only a few particles of LSD cause intoxication. One common nickname for LSD is "acid." LSD abusers say that taking LSD or "dropping acid" makes their senses sharper. They see strange shapes and pictures. Ideas flow through their minds, but users cannot act on them. Side effects of LSD include tension, chills, fever, trembling, loss of appetite, and nausea.

A LSD "trip" can be long—from six to eight hours. During a "bad trip," abusers may become terrified. They fear they are in danger. LSD can increase anxiety a person already feels and cause a mental breakdown. Abusers may feel depressed, anxious, and unreal for days after a trip. Some have "flashbacks," or moments when the drug's effect returns, days or months later. LSD causes psychological dependence.

PCP (phencyclidine) is a depressant and a hallucinogen originally developed as a tranquilizer and anesthetic for animals. Use of PCP by humans is illegal because of its dangerous and unpredictable side effects. PCP, or "angel dust," can be sniffed, swallowed, or injected. Low doses make some people feel drunk and fearful. They may have frightful images and thoughts of death. Large doses cause violent rages, mental illness, a dazed look, seizures, coma, or death. Abusers seem awake but cannot talk. PCP rages have caused some abusers to injure themselves and commit suicide or murder. PCP's effects remain long after the drug leaves the body.

Peyote [*pay OH tee*] is a hallucinogenic cactus grown in the Southwest and Mexico. **Mescaline** is the chemical in peyote that causes hallucinations. The effects of mescaline are similar to LSD

Figure 20-8 The fungus ergot *(left)* contains a chemical that may be used to produce LSD. The buttons of the peyote cactus *(right)* contain mescaline.

but milder. Psychological dependence is possible. Peyote can be used legally only during ceremonies of the Native American Church. Users see imagined figures and patterns. Dried peyote is very bitter whether chewed or drunk as a tea. Peyote causes vomiting, after which a user will begin 4 to 12 hours of intoxication. Stomach cramps and excess sweating may occur.

Psilocybin [*sil uh SY bin*] and **psilocin** are two psychoactive chemicals found in certain mushrooms. The effects and dangers of these illegal chemicals are similar to LSD but milder. The Aztecs first used these mushrooms in religious services. Today some Mexican Indians still use them in religious services. Nicknames for them include "magic mushrooms" and "ghrooms." Psychological dependence is possible.

Marijuana

The drug with the widest illegal use in the United States is marijuana. **Marijuana,** which comes from the leaves and flowers of the Indian hemp plant, is a stimulant, depressant, and hallucinogen. It causes psychological dependence. Doctors have been trying out marijuana as a treatment for glaucoma, an eye disorder. It is also used by some cancer patients after chemotherapy. Marijuana eases the nausea resulting from these treatments.

The scientific name of the marijuana plant is *Cannabis sativa.* Marijuana's many nicknames include "pot," "grass," "dope," "weed," "joints," "mary jane," and "sinsemilla." Marijuana is usually smoked; it can also be eaten. When smoked, it increases heart rate and blood pressure and lowers body temperature. Just as with tobacco, tars and resins from marijuana smoke are damaging. Smokers inhale more deeply than cigarette smokers. They also hold the smoke in their lungs longer. The damage caused by marijuana smoke is still being studied.

Abusers believe that a low dose of marijuana makes them more fun to be around. Some abusers feel light-headed and giddy. Others feel friendly and peaceful. However, many smokers smoke alone and become silent and withdrawn during intoxication. Abusers' eyes become bloodshot; their mouths dry out. Unlike many drugs, marijuana makes people want to eat. Marijuana also changes people's ability to move, see, and think. Memory and learning abilities are affected by use of this drug. It can reduce sperm production. There is some concern that mood and mental changes brought on by the drug may last forever.

Some new users become very anxious after smoking marijuana. This anxiety can turn into severe mental illness needing hospital care for several days. High doses act as hallucinogens. Some abusers find that after a while they need to smoke less to achieve the same effect. Eventually, though, smokers develop tolerance and require more of the drug. Crossness is the major result of withdrawal. Marijuana's psychoactive chemicals remain in the body for many days.

Hashish is a purified extract taken from the marijuana plant. It can be smoked, chewed, or drunk. Hashish is a stronger drug than marijuana.

Figure 20-9 Marijuana comes from the leaves of the Indian hemp plant, *Cannabis sativa.*

Figure 20-10 The seed pod of the opium poppy is the source of most narcotics.

Narcotics

Strong painkillers that cause sleepiness are called **narcotics.** They are sometimes called opiates because most come from the seed pods of the opium poppy. Narcotics include some of the most dangerous drugs, such as morphine and heroin. Weaker and less dangerous painkillers are codeine and opium. All narcotics are very addictive, both physically and psychologically.

Codeine is a weak pain reliever and can be used to check coughing. Codeine is often abused for the euphoria it produces. A nickname for codeine is ''school boy.'' Long-term effects can include constipation and losing the desire to eat. Although codeine is the least habit-forming narcotic, it can cause dependence.

Opium is a narcotic doctors can use to ease pain and diarrhea. When used illegally, it is mixed with tobacco and smoked. Two nicknames for opium are ''blue velvet'' and ''black stuff.'' Opium reduces breathing and heart rates. For several hours it causes sleep filled with colorful dreams. Side effects include excess perspiration, constipation, and lowered temperature. Opium also lowers mental abilities and appetite. Opium causes mental and physical dependence and severe withdrawal symptoms.

Morphine is a painkiller ten times stronger than opium. It is one of the strongest painkillers known to medicine. Because it is so addictive, its medical use is limited. Patients who have painful heart attacks or who are dying of cancer may be given morphine to ease their pain. Many persons abuse morphine for its euphoric effect. They soon become addicted. Morphine can be inhaled, smoked, or injected. Some nicknames for the drug are ''white stuff'' and ''morf.'' Morphine causes psychological and physical dependence. As with other narcotics, withdrawal from morphine addiction is difficult and very painful.

The most widely abused narcotic in the United States is heroin. Made from morphine, **heroin** is two or three times stronger than morphine. In the United States it is illegal to use heroin as a medicine because it is so addictive. Heroin, or ''horse,'' ''junk,'' or ''smack,'' can be inhaled, smoked, or injected. Injecting an illegal drug into a vein is called mainlining.

Heroin dulls the senses and eases the abuser's fears and worries. Abusers usually first take heroin for the sense of intense euphoria. Later they take heroin to avoid sickness from withdrawal. Heroin users appear to be in a daze that lasts for hours. Abusers are careless about their health and frequently suffer from poor nutrition. They also get infections by using dirty needles.

Physical addiction to heroin develops quickly. Abusers may be hooked after daily use for two weeks. Withdrawal symptoms begin 12 to 16 hours after drug use. They include sweating, shaking, chills, nausea, diarrhea, and cramps. To avoid these symptoms, addicts take the drug daily. Later they have to take it several times daily. Accidental overdoses that result in death are common. Dealers mix heroin with other drugs and materials. Because of this, the amount of heroin is different in each ''fix.'' A fix with pure heroin becomes a deadly overdose. Sometimes the cutting substance also contributes to the overdose.

Health **History**

During the Civil War, many soldiers who had been wounded were given morphine to relieve their pain. Many of these soldiers became addicted. Heroin was first developed to help them overcome their morphine addiction. Unfortunately, heroin proved to be even more addictive than morphine.

Inhalants

Drugs inhaled through the nose are called **inhalants** [*ihn HAY lahnts*]. Inhaled drugs quickly pass through the mucous membrane into the blood stream. People inhale drugs to get a quick lift. This method of taking drugs is sometimes called "snorting." Inhalants are sometimes legal drugs, which may be over-the-counter or prescription drugs, or household products.

Amyl nitrite [*AM ul NY tryt*] is a legal prescription drug used to lower blood pressure. An illegal drug that is similar to amyl nitrite is **butyl nitrite.** Nicknames for these two drugs include "locker room," "rush," and "poppers." They make healthy people feel relaxed, light-headed, and sometimes more energetic. Abuse can cause strokes and heart attacks. Both forms of nitrite can cause psychological dependence.

An inhalant that is used by dentists as a mild painkiller is **nitrous oxide** [*NY trus AHK syd*]. This drug's nicknames include "whippitts," "laughing gas," and "peppermint gas," due to its smell. This gas causes relaxation and giddiness. Other effects include dizziness and ringing in the ears. Long-term effects can include damage to the liver, kidneys, or bone marrow. Nitrous oxide can cause psychological dependence.

Many household products contain poisonous chemicals that affect the body and mind. Most come in containers with a warning to use them in a well-ventilated area. Some of the poisons, such as those in nail polish, some glues, paint thinner, and varnishes and shellacs, are addictive. Once inhaled, these chemicals produce a strange, violent intoxication. Effects include dizziness, loss of muscle coordination, and slurred speech. Blurred vision, imaginary sights and sounds, upset stomach, and depression also occur. These effects last 15 minutes to one hour. They may be followed by an hour of sleepiness or nausea.

Heavier poisoning by these chemicals causes seizures, unconsciousness, and perhaps death. Glue sniffers also develop webs of glue in their noses and lungs. Sniffers do not usually measure how much they take in, so getting an overdose is very easy. Frequent use damages the liver, the kidneys, the bones, and the nerves. Long-term use can damage mental abilities and physical coordination. These poisons can cause psychological dependence.

Steroids

One group of drugs that is abused for physical rather than mental effects is steroids. **Steroids** [*STEHR oydz*] are synthetic drugs that are like the male hormone testosterone. All their short- and long-term effects are not yet known. Of great concern today is the increase in steroid abuse among high school-age males hoping to make themselves more physically attractive.

Some athletes take steroids to make their bodies stronger, but this is very dangerous. Steroids can damage their hearts and bones and cause ulcers and diabetes. Young people taking steroids also face dangers that stem from the wrong amount of hormone, such as irregular growth. Because of the dangers, steroids are allowed by law to be given only on doctors' orders.

Drug Abuse Among High School Seniors

Drug	Ever Used Class of		Daily Users Class of	
	1979	1984	1979	1984
Marijuana	60%	55%	10.3%	5.0%
Inhalants	13	14	0.0	0.1
Amyl & Butyl Nitrites	11	8	0.0	0.1
Hallucinogens	14	11	0.1	0.1
LSD	10	8	0.0	0.1
PCP	13	5	0.1	0.1
Cocaine	15	16	0.2	0.2
Heroin	1	1	0.0	0.0
Barbiturates	12	10	0.0	0.0
Methaqualone	8	8	0.0	0.0
Tranquilizers	16	12	0.1	0.1
Alcohol	93	93	6.9	4.8
Cigarettes	74	70	25.4	18.7

Source: National Institute on Drug Abuse.

Figure 20-11 Although drug abuse among high school seniors may be declining, it remains a major problem.

Synthetic Drugs

All of the drugs described so far are regulated by state and federal laws. You will notice in Figure 20-11 that abuse of most of these drugs is declining among high school students. But chemists today are able to develop new, synthetic drugs, also called designer drugs, that are not controlled. These new drugs are often very similar to drugs that are regulated, such as heroin or cocaine. Synthetic drugs are potentially very dangerous. In California alone they have caused over 100 deaths from overdose, and have caused irreversible brain damage in many other people. Recently three of the most popular of these drugs—ecstasy, MPPP, and PEPAP— were outlawed. Unfortunately, other drugs can be developed easily and cheaply. The potential for harm from these drugs is very great, and the risks are unknown.

Lesson Review

The major classifications of abused drugs are stimulants, depressants, hallucinogens, marijuana, and narcotics. Inhalants and steroids may also be abused. Abuse of many of these drugs may lead to physical and psychological dependence. Abusers may die from overdose, withdrawal, poor nutrition, or infections related to drug abuse.

1 Name three short-term effects of inhaling poisonous household products.

2 What are the symptoms of withdrawal from barbiturates?

3 Name a stimulant that is frequently inhaled or smoked.

4 Why do some people abuse steroids?

5 What is the most commonly abused narcotic?

Handling the Problem

Drug abuse among teenagers is a major concern. But the decision to use or avoid drugs begins with individuals. Education about drugs is helping people make healthy choices. Recognizing signs of drug abuse early is very important in helping someone with a drug problem. There are many forms of treatment available for drug dependence. The effectiveness of treatment depends on many factors, but mostly on the will of the abusers to change their lives.

Preventing Drug Abuse

Prevention is the best possible way of handling the problem of drug abuse. By selecting friends and activities that will not expose you to drug use, you can reduce problems of peer pressure. The availability of drugs often leads to experimentation. Most experimenters try drugs just because the drugs are offered or are easy to get. Very few people will work hard to try to find drugs. If you avoid settings where drugs can be found, such as unsupervised parties and out-of-the-way hangouts, you can have fun without being faced with drug use. Attend drug-free activities and dances instead.

Make a commitment to yourself, or perhaps to some friends, not to use or abuse drugs. Peer pressure can work in a positive way to help you in your determination to stay away from drugs. Development of interests that include other people and demand concentration may help some young people who are tempted by drugs. Mixing with drug-free classmates may remove the peer pressure to use drugs.

Finding other ways to reduce stress can also help people turn away from drugs. Developing relaxing interests, and learning positive ways to handle stress, such as those covered in Chapter 6, can help reduce the pressure to abuse drugs.

Figure 20-12 The social pressure technique uses peer or adult pressure to show that drug abuse is unpopular.

Legal Prevention

Because of the dangers of drug abuse to individuals and society as a whole, the federal government has passed laws to protect the public. One law is the 1970 Drug Abuse Prevention and Control Act. It covers the manufacture, distribution, possession, use, and sale of drugs. Under this law, making or selling drugs can lead to a 15-year prison sentence and a $25,000 fine. Possession of some drugs can mean a year in jail and a $5000 fine. Second offenses and sales to minors carry stronger penalties.

State laws about making, possessing, using, and selling drugs vary greatly. When drug trafficking across state lines occurs, the federal government also becomes involved. The defendant is prosecuted under both federal and state laws.

Being found guilty of violating drug laws can often ruin a life. Even if no jail sentence is involved, the user may be punished in many different ways. Depending on the specific offense and the state, individuals convicted of drug-related offenses may lose their jobs, their driver's licenses, and their right to vote. Colleges may

Figure 20-13 Eliminating the source and traffic of drugs is one way of decreasing the temptation to abuse drugs.

deny them scholarships or entrance to law school or medical school. They may not be allowed to run for political office or to become officers in the armed forces. They may also be denied national security clearances, which are required for certain jobs.

Laws against drug abuse are intended not only to protect the public but also to protect drug abusers from themselves and each other. The legal punishments are meant to discourage people from starting to use drugs as well as to prevent people from continuing to use them. There are particularly strong laws against selling drugs to minors in order to prevent the spread of drug abuse among those too young to know all the dangers of drug addiction.

Signs of Drug Abuse

How can you tell if a friend is abusing drugs? How can you help a friend avoid addiction and trouble with the law? Drug abuse leads to certain types of social behavior. One sign alone does not prove drug abuse, but many together are a warning that someone needs help. Figure 20-14 lists several signs of drug abuse. For example, drug abusers may suddenly do badly in school. They may stay away from home or school for days or weeks. They may no longer care about school or grades, only drugs. This sudden lack of caring also may show up in the way they dress, the state of their room, lack of personal hygiene, and disregard for former friends and family.

Abusers' personalities may seem to change suddenly. They may become confused, cross, and absent-minded. They may appear drunk and slur words when they speak. At times they may become very talkative or restless. They might develop extreme forms of attention-getting behavior. At other times, they may withdraw from people. They may distrust people, fearing others will harm them. Drug abusers may take refuge in a fantasy world where they can do impossible things. They will probably be unre-

Poor school performance

Cutting classes or school

Antisocial behavior: lying, stealing, cheating

Aggression

Theft

Irresponsible driving

Delinquency

Sexual promiscuity

Figure 20-14 Behavior problems that may be signs of drug abuse

alistic and deny that they have a drug problem. They may say, and perhaps truly believe, "I can stop any time." Statistics prove they cannot.

If you know people who are experimenting with drugs and need counseling or help for drug abuse, suggest that they use a drug hot line. Drug abusers can aid the counseling by being honest about their problem. Most hot lines are open 24 hours a day. The calls are kept strictly confidential. Sympathetic, knowledgeable people will give practical help and information. Hot lines are listed in the yellow pages of the phone book under drug abuse.

Treating Addiction

Once hooked on a drug, abusers continue taking it for two chief reasons. First, to avoid the physical and psychological pain of withdrawal. Second, to continue to escape reality. To overcome drug dependence, abusers must change their thinking, desires, and goals. This change may not come until they face a personal crisis, death, or physical harm.

Complete recovery from heavy drug use is possible, but very difficult. Once abusers quit, they must survive the pain of withdrawal. Then they have to change their habits and adopt a drug-free life. They must be able to conquer the environment that led them into drug abuse. Recovery, however, hinges on one factor: the abuser's determination to change. Many abusers do not possess the willpower to break their dependence. Sometimes a breakdown in health, a police arrest, or the guilt of using violence to get drugs may shock an abuser into seeking help.

 Health **Careers**

Illegal traffic in drugs is a nationwide problem. Among those fighting the battle against this problem are the special agents of the U.S. Drug Enforcement Administration. The job of a special agent is to enforce the federal drug abuse prevention and control laws. Special agents carry out criminal investigations, infiltrate drug rings, apprehend drug traffickers, and confiscate illegal drug supplies. They also give sworn testimony in court cases and work with other law enforcement officials at the local and state levels. Because their duties are frequently dangerous, special agents are authorized to carry firearms.

To interview to become a special agent, you must be in excellent physical condition, have good eyesight, a valid driver's license, and be willing to relocate to another part of the United States. Most special agents have a college degree and at least one year of experience conducting criminal investigations, often for a local police force.

1. For which agency do the special agents who enforce the federal drug abuse and prevention laws work?
2. What type of work experience is helpful in applying to become a special agent?

Figure 20-15 **The world is full of many exciting alternatives to drug abuse. Constructive adventure provides a lasting improvement of self-esteem.**

Detoxification Detoxification is usually the first step in treating drug abusers. Many addicts may have to return to detoxification programs several times. However, detoxification is a necessary start before drug abusers can really work on their dependence. Programs include medical care that helps make withdrawal safer and less painful.

Detoxification should be followed by counseling to conquer psychological dependence. Abusers need to learn why they turned to drugs. Psychotherapy helps them find different ways to solve their problems. With teenage abusers, therapy frequently involves their families. The therapist teaches family members new ways of handling problems. Together, they try to overcome the situations that led to drug abuse.

Therapeutic Communities Highly structured, drug-free residential programs are called **therapeutic communities** [*theh ruh PYOO tik*]. Hospitals, community organizations, and private drug treatment centers often sponsor such aid. Since abusers often suffer from very poor health, it is often helpful for them to enter a residential program where proper diet, hygiene, and rest are available. A change from the environment that led to drug abuse is also achieved by residential programs. Treating all forms of drug abuse, the communities may house from a dozen to hundreds of residents. The programs offer many types of support: an extended family, peer support, jobs, counseling, and sometimes job training.

When abusers enter a residential program, they have to stop using drugs. They are given simple jobs. As they prove their trustworthiness, they are given greater responsibilities. Each week they participate in group therapy. Group therapy forces people to examine their own faults. Each member must attempt to change for the better. If they do not try to change, other members remind them.

Membership in these communities is usually voluntary. Members can come and go as they please. Because recovery from dependence is difficult, one out of three abusers drops out within the first two weeks. Once members return to their old environments, their drug habits may recur. A year after leaving the program, about two out of three exmembers use drugs sometimes. Generally, the longer a person stays in a program, the greater the chance of success. In some states, addicts who are arrested must choose between entering prison or a drug program.

Outpatient Maintenance Programs Some hospitals operate drug recovery programs for patients who do not stay there. **Outpatient recovery programs** allow drug abusers to live at home and visit the hospital for treatment. During hospital visits, abusers also receive counseling.

Some hospitals and organizations also offer maintenance programs. In **drug maintenance programs,** narcotic abusers receive a legal drug to replace their illegal drug. The most common one is methadone. **Methadone** [*METH uh dohn*] is a synthetic narcotic taken by mouth and used to spare addicts from the pains of withdrawal. In small doses, it does not cause intoxication. In addition to chemical therapy, patients in maintenance programs undergo counseling.

Like all narcotics, methadone is addictive. Methadone treatment replaces one addictive drug with another. However, since it does not make addicts high, they can hold jobs and function normally. Methadone is not a cure for addiction. In large doses it does cause intoxication. Addicts must end addiction through their own efforts and determination to break the habit.

Figure 20-16 Only one in 20 addicts in methadone treatment succeeds in breaking the habit.

Lesson Review

Drug abuse is a serious problem, especially among young people. The best way to handle the problem of drug abuse is through prevention. Prevention efforts include early education and laws restricting the use of drugs. But in cases of abuse, there are various forms of treatment available.

1 Name three ways to avoid pressure to abuse drugs.

2 Describe four signs of drug abuse.

3 What is a drug hot line?

4 List three kinds of places where a drug abuser can turn for help.

5 What synthetic narcotic may be used to spare addicts the pain of withdrawal?

Chapter Review

Vocabulary

amphetamine	heroin	over-the-counter drug
amyl nitrite	illegal drug	PCP
barbiturate	inhalant	peyote
butyl nitrite	legal drug	prescription drug
caffeine	LSD	psilocin
chief effect	marijuana	psilocybin
cocaine	mescaline	psychoactive drug
codeine	methadone	side effect
depressant	methaqualone	steroid
drug	morphine	stimulant
drug abuse	narcotic	synthetic drug
drug maintenance program	nitrous oxide	therapeutic community
euphoria	opium	tolerance
hallucinogen	outpatient recovery program	tranquilizer
hashish	overdose	

Using Vocabulary

Questions 1-15. On a separate sheet of paper, write the term from the column on the right that matches the phrase on the left.

1 synthetic narcotic used to spare addicts the pains of withdrawal
2 drug that slows brain and body reactions
3 feeling of great happiness or well-being
4 mind-altering chemical
5 hallucinogenic cactus grown in the Southwest and Mexico
6 chemical that causes changes in the body and/or the mind
7 plant that is a stimulant, depressant, and hallucinogen
8 use of any drug for other than medical purposes
9 drug that slows down nerve activity and relaxes muscle tension
10 term applied to taking enough of a drug to cause death
11 different, unknown, or undesirable reaction to a drug
12 drug that is a purified extract of marijuana
13 highly structured, drug-free residential program
14 mild painkiller used by dentists; called laughing gas
15 drug drawn into the body through the nose

a hashish
b drug
c side effect
d methadone
e overdose
f marijuana
g therapeutic community
h depressant
i euphoria
j drug abuse
k inhalant
l peyote
m nitrous oxide
n tranquilizer
o psychoactive drug

Interpreting Ideas

1 Explain how legal and illegal drugs differ.

2 Identify five commonly abused drugs by their nicknames.

3 What are four signs of drug abuse?

4 Identify three places where drug abusers can seek help.

5 Identify the two categories of legal drugs. How may each category of drugs be misused?

6 List three reasons why people become drug abusers.

7 What are three problems of addiction for the drug addict?

8 What are the short-term and long-term effects of using butyl nitrite, using codeine, and using LSD?

9 Describe heroin. Tell how it may be taken into the body, how it is made (materials used to make it), and why it may be abused.

10 How does physical dependence differ from psychological dependence?

11 Many household products contain chemicals that cause intoxication when they are inhaled. What are some effects of inhalation of these poisonous chemicals?

12 What is a ''flashback''?

13 What products contain caffeine? What are some signs of its overuse?

14 What are the broad provisions of the 1970 Drug Abuse Prevention and Control Act? List four consequences of illegal drug use.

15 What are the medical uses of marijuana?

16 How do people develop tolerance for a drug? Why is tolerance a problem?

17 Although withdrawal symptoms vary from drug to drug, what are eight common withdrawal symptoms?

18 How do drug abusers affect the lives of others?

19 Compare the effects of stimulants and those of depressants.

20 How may violence play a role in the life of the drug addict?

Applying Concepts

1 In each of the following examples, explain what may have happened: (a) Over the weekend Joan suffered a painful swollen ankle from a running injury. To relieve the pain, she took a friend's prescription drug containing codeine. Soon Joan experienced nausea. (b) A person who drinks heavily at a party takes two sleeping pills when he returns home. The next day he is found unconscious in his bed.

2 How may the use of marijuana produce infertility in couples?

3 A friend who is very concerned about getting into the college of her choice confides in you that she is taking increasingly greater amounts of speed to allow her to study more hours. What course of action, if any, would you take in order to help your friend?

4 If the use of drugs such as steroids does not result in physical dependence, why would you try to talk a friend out of experimenting with them?

5 Why is caffeine added to many over-the-counter painkillers?

6 Lately Adam's parents were aware that he had tremendous bursts of energy and then would sleep as much as 15 hours at a time. Adam had frequent mood swings—from talkative and cheerful to hostile and irritable. His nose, they noticed, was often red, inflamed, and runny. One day Adam's mother discovered a box filled with small white crystals, a pocket mirror, and some straws that had been cut in half. What has happened to Adam? How can he get the help he needs?

7 The use of marijuana in grades six to eight is on the rise. Over 500,000, or about 6%, of the students in these grades smoke marijuana. How can you account for this alarming increase among younger students? What do you think should be done to solve this problem?

8 Why should you throw out leftover prescription drugs?

Projects

1 Draw an original cartoon or create a poster that illustrates reasons teenagers begin using drugs.

2 In a campaign to reduce the number of drug users among young people, write a public television or radio announcement that describes the physical and emotional dangers of drug abuse.

3 Debate whether marijuana should be legalized.

4 Prepare a pamphlet for school-wide distribution that describes different types of drugs, ways that any drug may be misused, the physical and emotional dangers of drug abuse, and the treatment for various types of drug abuse.

Critical Thinking

RESISTING PEER PRESSURE

There are times when you have to say *no* to friends. Being able to refuse tobacco, alcohol, or drugs is a major challenge in your resistance to peer pressure. Being smart enough to say *no* may risk friendships, especially with those who ask you to join in unhealthy or illegal activities. It is better to end a false friendship than to let peers pressure you.

Your friends may have a number of ways to persuade you to accept their view of things. Sometimes it seems as if your friends have all sorts of good reasons why you should join in.

These methods of persuasion are similar to the ways that advertisers sell products. Repetition, emotional words, testimonials, and bandwagon appeal are several different forms of persuasion. Recognizing these different persuasive techniques will give you a clearer understanding of how people are trying to influence you. Below are descriptions of common advertising techniques.

Repetition Advertisers often repeat the product's name over and over. Sometimes it is the only information presented in the advertisement. Often the product's name is repeated several times in a small space. By constantly re-peating the name of the product, the advertiser hopes that consumers will recall the product's name.

Emotional Words Some words call to mind strong emotions. On a travel brochure, for example, you might read the words "cool breeze," "sail away," "vacation," and "relaxing." These words conjure up pleasant feelings. They create a sort of glow around the product, although they actually provide very little information.

Emotional words can be positive or negative. For example, name-calling is a way of using emotional words for a negative effect.

Testimonial A testimonial uses famous people or experts to tell you about a certain product. Sports heroes and movie stars are most often used in this kind of advertisement. These famous people are being paid to represent the product. By showing a product with a famous person's picture or recommendation, the advertiser is hoping that the reputation and glamour of the personality will come to be associated with the product being endorsed. For example, if a famous model endorses a line of clothing, people may buy the clothing with the expectation of looking like the model.

The testimonial technique is also used among peers, but it is not as obvious. Of course, your peers are not being paid to provide testimonials. But when people who are popular recommend an idea or use a product, other people often imitate them.

Bandwagon Before the automobile was invented, people running for public office used to travel through town on horse-drawn wagons carrying bands. Supporters of the politician would show their support by climbing on the wagon. "Getting on the bandwagon" came to mean doing what everyone else was doing.

Advertisers, too, realize the power of this technique. No one wants to feel left out. By telling consumers that everyone else is using their product, advertisers hope to convince more customers to jump on the bandwagon.

Your friends use many of these advertising techniques to persuade you to join in their behavior. Are you able to recognize their methods of persuasion?

To practice, read the following story. Then write the numbers 1 through 6 on a separate sheet of paper. Next to each number, write the name of the persuasive technique being used in the paragraph with that number.

Ramon and his family had just moved to a new town. Ramon had attended his new school for several weeks, but was still feeling lonely. The boys who rode his school bus invited him to go to a party with them on Friday night. Nervous but happy to be included, Ramon went to the party. Ramon was having a good time until one of the boys pulled a bottle of liquor from his coat pocket.

1 "Come on Ramon, lighten up. Join the party! Everybody's going to have a good time tonight!"

2 Another boy lit a cigarette. "Hey, Ramon, have a cigarette," he offered. "Yeah, Ramon, smoke a cigarette," the other boys chimed in. "Go ahead, light up and smoke a cigarette."

3 "All the kids are trying it. Come on, Ramon, give it a try. Just try it so you can tell everyone you had some, too."

4 Another boy offered Ramon some chewing tobacco. "You should try some of this," he said. "It will make you look really tough. Like a real man. Why not treat yourself?"

When Ramon hesitated, the other boys laughed. With a lump in his throat, Ramon left the party feeling like a coward.

5 When he got on the bus Monday morning, Ramon heard the other boys clucking like hens. "You sure chickened out last Friday. Chicken! That's the only thing to call you, a chicken. Chickens cluck, heroes chug." By the time Ramon got to school, he was so embarrassed that he felt like crawling inside his locker and never coming out.

That afternoon before civics class, Ramon talked with Nina, a popular girl whom Ramon admired. Ramon told Nina about the party.

"I guess I was pretty stupid," said Ramon. "Where I come from, none of my friends drank liquor or smoked cigarettes. You must think I'm a loser."

6 "No, I don't," said Nina. "In fact, most of the popular kids here don't do those things, either. For example, the captain of the football team is the president of Students Against Driving Drunk."

"The boys on your bus think they're tough," continued Nina. "But none of them has many friends or does well in school. They're the losers, Ramon, not you."

7

22. Noninfectious Diseases

21. Infectious Diseases

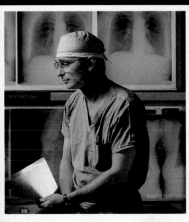

23. Selecting Health Care

24. Public Health

Modern Health Problems

25. Personal Safety

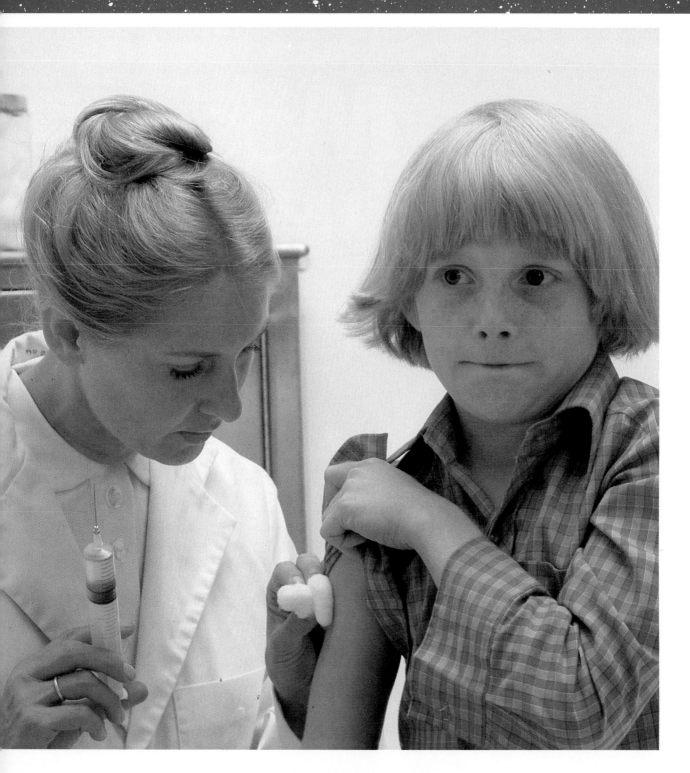

Many infectious diseases may be prevented with a simple vaccination.

CHAPTER TWENTY-ONE

INFECTIOUS
DISEASES

For thousands of years, people have fought against a mysterious and dangerous enemy—infectious disease. In the 1300s, a disease known as the Black Death spread across Europe, killing more than 25 million people. In 1918 and 1919, a new and serious type of flu led to the deaths of more than 20 million people around the world.

Fortunately, doctors and scientists have made many discoveries that have helped stop the spread of many infectious diseases. One disease, smallpox, has been completely wiped out. In the meantime, vaccinations, such as the one this young child is receiving, help stop the spread of others. Such advances are made possible by increasing knowledge of what causes diseases and how the body responds to them. This knowledge has encouraged people to use good health habits in fighting infectious diseases.

Objectives

- Identify five kinds of pathogens.
- Describe four ways in which diseases may be spread.
- Describe the body's structural and cellular defenses against pathogens.
- Describe the immune system and immune deficiency.
- Explain how vaccination works.
- List the stages of disease.
- Identify and describe the most common infectious diseases.
- Describe the symptoms and treatment of sexually transmitted diseases.

Causes Of Disease

Diseases that are caused by organisms and are passed from one person to another are **infectious diseases.** The common cold is an example. Nearly everyone has had a cold, and many people suffer from two to three colds each year.

Scientists have worked for hundreds of years to learn what causes colds and other diseases. They have tried many ways to cure them. Fortunately, today we understand what causes infectious diseases. This understanding allows us to prevent many infectious diseases and to treat diseases when they occur.

Pathogens

Infectious diseases are caused by living organisms. Organisms that cause disease are called **pathogens** [*PATH uh junz*]. You may have used the more common term germs. A person infected with a disease can spread pathogens to a person who does not have the disease. The small living organisms that cause infectious diseases belong to five groups—bacteria, viruses, fungi, protists, and animal parasites. Most pathogens are so small that they can be seen only with a microscope.

Bacteria   One group of pathogens is the bacteria. **Bacteria** are one-celled organisms made up of a very small amount of living matter surrounded by a thin cell wall. As shown in Figure 21-1, bacteria can be classified by the shape of their cells.

After bacteria reach full size, they multiply by dividing in half. Under good conditions, many bacteria can double every 30 minutes. Bacteria grow nearly everywhere. They have been found 7 miles deep in the ocean and floating 40 miles above the earth. Most bacteria do not cause disease. In fact, they help people in many ways. Some bacteria are used to make cheese. Others live in people's bodies and aid body functions, such as digestion.

Some bacteria are dangerous. They produce toxins, which cause disease. **Toxins** are poisons. Some toxins attack specific cells. For example, **tetanus** is a disease caused by bacteria that make toxins that affect the nerve cells. Bacteria cause many diseases. Most of these diseases can now be treated and controlled by medicines.

Figure 21-1   Three groups of bacteria: *(left)* coccus, *(center)* bacillus, and *(right)* spirillum

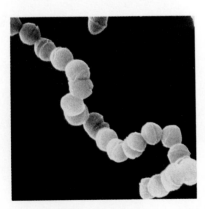
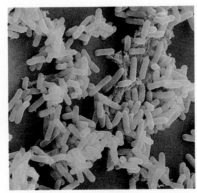
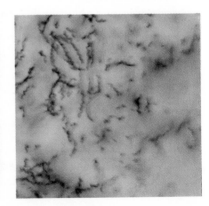

Viruses Viruses also cause disease. A **virus** is a single unit of genetic material in a protein shell. See Figure 21-2. Viruses are the smallest of the pathogens, and can only be seen with a special microscope. If a red blood cell were the size of a frisbee, a virus would be smaller than a period on this page. Unlike bacteria, viruses can live and multiply only inside living cells.

Their size allows viruses to enter other cells easily. Once inside the cell, the virus uses parts of the cell to multiply itself. The cell it has invaded may die. Then the new viruses attack other cells.

Viruses cause the common cold and many other diseases. Successful treatments for many of these have not yet been found. Fortunately, the body's defenses overcome most viruses.

Fungi Another group that includes pathogens is the fungi. **Fungi** are small plantlike organisms. Some fungi, such as mushrooms, are easy to see. Other fungi can only be seen with a microscope. Microscopic fungi cause such skin diseases as athlete's foot, shown in Figure 21-2. Fungal pathogens are sometimes hard to control, but they hardly ever cause death.

Protists One-celled organisms with specialized internal structures are called **protists.** They are usually larger than bacteria. They include different types of amoeba. Others move about by using a whiplike structure. Diseases caused by protists are much more common in tropical countries than in the United States.

Animal Parasites Some human diseases are caused by animals that are parasites. **Parasites** are organisms that live by feeding on or in another animal. Animal parasites are usually visible without a microscope. These animals can enter the body in infected food and water and often live in the intestines. They include many kinds of worms. One serious disease caused by parasitic worms is trichinosis. **Trichinosis** [*trik uh NOH sis*] is a disease usually caused by eating infected pork. If pork from an infected pig is not fully cooked, the worms may not be killed. When a person eats the undercooked pork, the worms are released. They spread through the body, causing stomach upsets, muscle pain, and fever. Trichinosis, as well as most other diseases caused by parasitic animals, can be treated with medication.

Figure 21-2 Pathogens range in size from a tiny influenza virus (left), to athlete's foot fungus (center), and up to a tapeworm (right), which may grow to 30 feet in length.

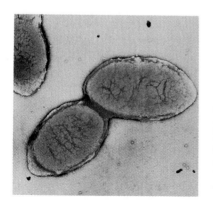
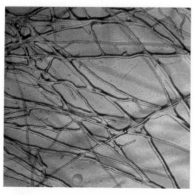

Disease Transmission

Diseases may be spread in a number of ways. You can catch a disease by direct or indirect contact with a person who is already infected. One way disease is spread is through the air. An infected person can send pathogens into the air through a sneeze or cough. When you breathe in this air the pathogens enter your respiratory system. Colds and other viral diseases are often transmitted this way. People can help prevent the spread of pathogens by covering their mouths when they cough or sneeze.

Figure 21-3 Hats, gloves, and clean equipment avoid the spread of disease in food packaging.

The foods you eat can also carry pathogens. Sometimes this is because they have not been cooked enough, as in the case of pork infected with trichinosis. Another practice that prevents the spread of disease is the pasteurization of milk. **Pasteurization** is the process of heating liquids to kill germs.

Some bacterial diseases may be spread if untreated sewage gets into lakes, wells, or rivers that supply drinking water. Pathogens can also be carried on objects you touch. Drinking fountains, plates, silverware, coins, and other familiar objects can spread disease if they have been touched by an infected person.

Some infectious diseases can be spread through blood transfusions. An infected person can give blood, perhaps not knowing that the blood may contain pathogens. However, special blood tests can now tell when blood carries disease. Blood transfusions are safe when the proper tests are used.

Direct bodily contact spreads some diseases. Direct contact includes touching, kissing, and sexual contact. People with colds, for example, may spread germs with their hands. Syphilis and gonorrhea are examples of diseases spread by sexual contact.

Some infectious diseases are spread by animals. Rabies, for example, is spread through the bite of an infected dog, bat, or other mammal. Rocky Mountain spotted fever is carried by ticks.

One reason infectious diseases are hard to control is that people can be carriers of a disease but not develop any symptoms. Typhoid fever is a disease that can be spread indirectly, usually by an infected person touching water or food. The first known carrier of typhoid fever in the United States was a cook named Mary Mallon. Through her contact with food she infected more than 50 people. This earned her the nickname ''Typhoid Mary.''

Lesson Review

Infectious diseases are diseases that are spread from one person to another by pathogens. They are passed by direct or indirect contact with an already infected person or animal. Good personal hygiene can help reduce the spread of infectious diseases.

1 List five kinds of pathogens.

2 What disease can be caused by eating undercooked pork?

3 What is the process that milk goes through to rid it of germs?

4 How is Rocky Mountain spotted fever spread?

Fighting Infections

As you read this page, you are surrounded by millions of tiny organisms. Although many of them are pathogens, it is unlikely that any of them will be able to infect your body and cause a disease. This is because your body is always hard at work fighting against disease. Your body's defenses are also helped by the products of medical science. You are thus exposed to far more diseases than you ever catch.

Structural Defenses

The body's defenses are shown in Figure 21-4. The **structural defenses** are the defenses that the body has because of its physical form. The first defense against pathogens is the skin. Unless the skin is broken by a wound, it usually stops pathogens from entering the body. Body oils and perspiration also destroy pathogens. Tears wash pathogens from the eyes, and saliva kills bacteria. Inside your body, acid in your stomach destroys bacteria that enter with food.

Pathogens that enter the body through a natural opening, such as the mouth or nose, face a tough defense in the mucous membranes. **Mucous membranes** are the layers of tissue that line the respiratory, digestive, and reproductive systems. In some areas, these membranes contain cilia. **Cilia** [*SIL ee uh*] are tiny hairlike structures that keep the lungs and other areas of the body clean by trapping dust and foreign matter. Cilia in the respiratory tract trap pathogens in the air and use a wavelike motion to push them to the throat. Here the pathogens are coughed out or swallowed and destroyed by the digestive system. Glands in the mucous membranes secrete **mucus,** a thick liquid coating. When the mucous membranes become irritated, they produce more mucus. Mucus is swept outward by the cilia, and is sneezed or coughed up, forcing pathogens out of the body. This ongoing action protects the lungs.

Cellular Defenses

Sometimes pathogens get by the structural defenses and enter the body. Your body quickly identifies the pathogens and your cellular defenses begin to fight back. **Cellular defenses** are cells within the body that destroy pathogens. Special kinds of white blood cells are able to identify pathogens. **Phagocytes** [*FAG uh syts*] are white blood cells that surround pathogens and destroy them, as shown in Figure 21-5.

When they are under attack from pathogens, your cells release chemicals that cause nearby small blood vessels to widen. This brings many more phagocytes to the area and causes inflammation. **Inflammation** is the redness, swelling, and tenderness in an infected area. This is a natural stage of healing. An inflammation often contains pus, a mixture of living and dead phagocytes and pathogens.

Another sign that your body is fighting an infection is a fever. Your body's cells can best fight against an infection in temperatures a little higher than the normal body temperature of 98.6° F.

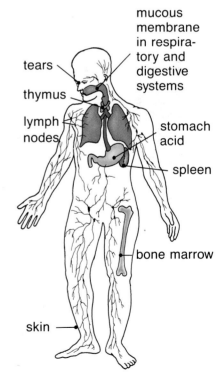

Figure 21-4   Your body's defenses against pathogens

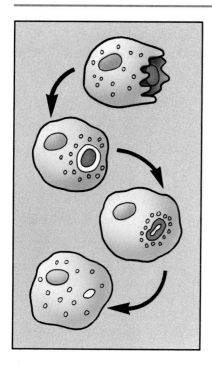

Figure 21-5   A phagocyte engulfing a bacterium

Many pathogens also multiply more slowly at higher temperatures. When infection-fighting cells find a pathogen, they send a message to the brain to raise the body's temperature. Aches and pains are felt when your body sends some of the energy stored in muscle to help fight the infection. Your muscles ache from the waste products of the process, but your cells have more energy to fight the infection.

The Immune System

When an infection spreads too fast for the phagocytes to control it, another line of defense comes into action. **Helper T cells** are special white blood cells that identify the infection. The helper T cells take their message to the lymphatic system.

As you learned in Chapter 12, the lymphatic system carries lymph fluid, which contains white blood cells. The lymphatic system has vessels alongside the veins and arteries, and contains lymph nodes. The **lymph nodes** are small cell factories. When the helper T cells arrive at a lymph node, the lymph node makes special new T cells called killer T cells. Killer T cells enter the blood stream at once and race to the area of the infection. They help keep the infection from spreading.

The lymph nodes also begin to make a second kind of special cell, called a B cell. **B cells** are cells that form chemical weapons called antibodies. **Antibodies** are proteins in the blood that produce resistance against pathogens or their toxins. The antibodies enter the blood stream and join the fight against the infection.

Once the infection is beaten, many of the killer T cells and B cells that were formed may remain in the blood stream. These cells, called **memory cells,** retain the ability to produce antibodies against a pathogen they have fought. If that infection returns, the memory cells will give you a head start in the new battle.

Memory cells give you immunity to a disease. **Immunity** is an inherited or acquired resistance to a specific pathogen. For example, if you have had the measles, your immunity will prevent you from getting it again. Unfortunately, not all illnesses result in immunity.

Babies also receive some immunity from their mothers. The antibodies produced by a mother against diseases she had and recovered from are passed from her blood to her baby's blood before birth. Antibodies may also be passed on to breast-fed infants in their mother's milk. These antibodies eventually break down.

Vaccinations

On May 14, 1796, an English doctor named Edward Jenner treated a woman for a disease called cowpox. Jenner knew that cowpox was like smallpox, but that cowpox was not nearly as dangerous. Smallpox killed millions of people each year.

Jenner drew some pus from a cowpox scab. He then scratched a bit of the cowpox into the arm of an eight-year-old boy. In a few days, the boy developed a mild form of cowpox. He soon recovered. Jenner then scratched the boy's arm with pus taken from a smallpox scab. The boy did not get sick.

Jenner's experiment had worked. He was able to stop the spread of smallpox by first giving a patient a small dose of cowpox. Jenner called his method of preventing disease vaccination, from the Latin word *vacca*, meaning cow. **Vaccination** is a treatment in which the body is given a small dose of a disease, causing the body to build up an immunity against it. Since Jenner's first vaccination almost 200 years ago, smallpox has disappeared from the earth.

Jenner's vaccination was successful because the cowpox virus and the smallpox virus were almost exactly the same. The body could not tell them apart. When the body fought the infection of cowpox, it created memory cells that also worked against smallpox. When the smallpox virus entered the body after a person had cowpox, the body's immune system was ready. T cells and B cells reacted to the virus, even though it was smallpox and not cowpox.

In 1885, the method of vaccination was further developed by the French scientist Louis Pasteur in his work with rabies. Pasteur found a way to weaken the rabies virus. He then gave the weakened rabies virus to animals. When he later gave the same animals the full-strength rabies virus, the animals did not contract the disease.

In the middle of this century, polio vaccinations were developed by the American scientists Jonas Salk and Albert Sabin. Polio, or poliomyletis, was once a common disease that often left its victims paralyzed. Most victims were children, although adults, including former President Franklin D. Roosevelt, were struck with polio. Salk's vaccine was made up of weak polio viruses. It was successfully tested in 1954. In 1961, Sabin developed an oral vaccine that was easier to give. The two vaccines have done their

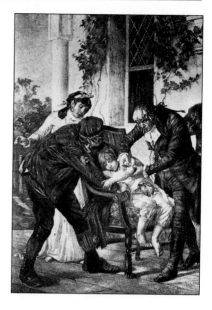

Figure 21-6 Edward Jenner tested the first vaccine in 1796, before pathogens had been identified as the source of infectious diseases.

Age	Type of Immunization
2 months	Diphtheria-tetanus-pertussis (whooping cough) vaccine (DTP), oral polio vaccine
4 months	DTP, oral polio vaccine
6 months	DTP, oral polio vaccine
1 year	Tuberculin test
15 months	Measles-mumps-rubella
18 months	DTP, oral polio vaccine
24 months	Haemophilus influenza type b
4 to 6 years	DTP, oral polio vaccine
14 to 16 years	Tetanus-diphtheria
every 10 years	Tetanus-diphtheria booster
when recommended	Influenza, pneumococcus, hepatitis B

Figure 21-7 Are your immunizations up-to-date?

© 1982 John McGrail, all rights reserved

Health **History**

The eighteenth-century Italian physician Giovanni Morgagni began the practice of examining bodies after death. Morgagni's work created a new definition of disease in terms of changes in internal organs.

work so well that polio has disappeared from many areas of the world. However, unless young children continue to receive polio vaccinations, the disease could spread again.

All vaccinations work in the same way. Weakened pathogens in the vaccine trigger the body's defenses. T cells and B cells are produced to fight the infection. Because the vaccination is a weak form of the disease, you do not get sick. However, the memory cells remain to fight the disease if it enters the body again.

Children usually receive a number of vaccinations. Most children receive a series of DTP vaccines beginning at the age of two months. These vaccines protect against diphtheria, tetanus, and pertussis, or whooping cough. Figure 21-7 lists vaccinations and when they should be given. At what age is the measles shot required? Since many vaccinations are only good for a certain period of time, it is sometimes important to get more shots later.

Since many infectious diseases do not occur in the United States, travelers should be vaccinated when they go to places where these diseases are common. Adults should also receive tetanus booster shots every 10 years, or if they receive a puncture wound more than five years after their last tetanus shot.

Medicines

There are times when your body's defenses fail to protect you. If you catch a serious infectious disease you will need medical attention. For example, strep throat needs to be treated or it may develop into rheumatic fever, which damages the heart. Flu and colds may leave you more susceptible to pneumonia.

A doctor will examine you and give you medicine to cure the disease or to relieve the symptoms. In some cases, doctors may prescribe an antibiotic. **Antibiotics** are medicines that fight disease-causing bacteria. They are made from fungi or bacteria. Penicillin is one of the most helpful antibiotics. Penicillin was discovered in 1929, and is used against such diseases as scarlet fever and syphilis. Streptomycin is an antibiotic used against tuberculosis. Antibiotics are not useful against viruses.

A new medicine that scientists hope to use in the fight against viruses is interferon. **Interferon** is a protein that is produced by the body to protect cells from viruses. Scientists are now learning to produce interferon in laboratories.

AIDS

Diseases sometimes occur in which the body does not produce enough defenses such as antibodies or B cells and T cells. Without adequate defenses, the person has decreased resistance to infections. Immune-deficiency diseases result in frequent illnesses. Even minor infections can become life-threatening. Some people are born with such diseases. Others acquire, or develop, them.

Acquired immune-deficiency syndrome, or AIDS, is a fatal disease of the immune system. AIDS is caused by a virus that destroys many of the T cells so that they cannot do their normal job. The infected person is unable to fight off infections. The AIDS virus itself does not kill people. AIDS victims die from

Figure 21-8 Interferon is produced in small quantities in cells. New methods make it possible to produce large quantities in laboratories.

other infections that would normally not be fatal, but that their impaired immune systems cannot fight off. More than half of all AIDS-victims die from pneumonia. Other killers are rare cancers and viruses, and a parasite.

In the 1970s, AIDS was almost unknown in the United States. By 1987, an estimated one and a half million people had been infected with the AIDS virus. Only 5 to 30 percent of these people are expected to develop the disease. Another 10 percent will develop a milder condition. The rest are carriers.

AIDS is passed from person to person by sexual contact, by drug injections from infected needles, or by receiving blood transfusions of infected blood. The first groups in the United States to be affected by the disease were homosexual men, drug users who injected drugs with infected needles, and people who received infected blood in blood transfusions. However, people outside these groups are now getting AIDS and there is concern that AIDS may spread to the general population. Pregnant women who have AIDS pass the disease to their unborn children.

Preventive measures for AIDS include abstaining from sex until marriage. If neither you nor your spouse ever has sex with anyone else or uses intravenous drugs, you will not get AIDS.

If you are sexually active, always use a condom and contraceptive foam. Always avoid intravenous drug use and sexual contact with people who inject drugs. Also avoid sexual contact with prostitutes or other promiscuous people.

Currently there is no cure for AIDS; all victims eventually die. The United States Government is spending millions of dollars on AIDS research. A public health measure that helps limit the spread of AIDS is the screening of all blood donors for the presence of antibodies to the AIDS virus. AIDS has become one of the most serious public health problems in the 1980s.

Figure 21-9 This baby receives care for AIDS, which she contracted from her mother.

Lesson Review

Your body has defenses against infectious diseases. Structural defenses keep pathogens out of the body, or destroy them after they enter the body. If pathogens do succeed in invading the body, your cellular defenses take up the fight against infection. Your immune system provides special cells that attack pathogens and often provide future immunity after the infection is overcome. Your immune system is also activated by vaccinations.

1 What are the white cells that surround and destroy pathogens?

2 How do the lymph nodes fight disease?

3 What kinds of cells act as memory cells to help the body fight a disease the second time?

4 What treatment helps the body build immunity to a disease?

5 What are antibiotics?

Common Infectious Diseases

Many infectious diseases, such as the common cold and flu, affect millions of people each year. Cures for these and other infectious diseases have not yet been found. But the fight against some infectious diseases has been more successful. In this country only a few cases of mumps, measles, and malaria are reported each year. There are almost no more cases of polio and diphtheria. These are no longer common diseases in the United States. However, the pathogens that cause these diseases still remain. Outbreaks can occur again. The threat of an outbreak of measles at colleges recently led thousands of students to get measles vaccinations.

Measles and other diseases could once again become widespread if the public fails to follow vaccination guidelines. The best defense against infectious diseases is knowledge of what they are and how they develop. With this knowledge, they can be kept from spreading.

Stages of Disease

Infectious diseases can pass through several stages. There are different paths that a disease can follow through these stages. These are shown in Figure 21-10. Note that a disease sometimes goes through just two stages, sometimes more.

The beginning of any infectious disease is incubation. The **incubation stage** is the time between entry of the pathogen and the time when the first symptoms appear. The pathogen multiplies during this time until it overcomes your body's defenses. If your body fights off the pathogen during the incubation stage, you may never become ill. The incubation period may be as short as several hours or as long as months or years. Most last between two

Figure 21-10 The stages and paths of disease

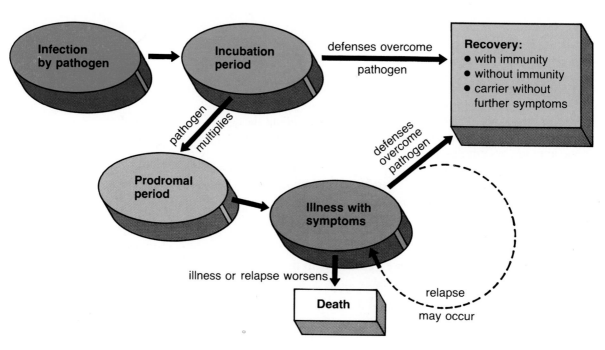

days and two weeks. If you have influenza, for example, the incubation period lasts from one to three days.

The **prodromal stage** is the time during which the earliest symptoms appear but have not fully developed. It is a very infectious time because you do not yet feel very sick and to most people you do not appear sick. However, pathogens are winning the battle against your body's defenses. Some may be passed to other people. During this period of influenza you may have many of the signs of a mild cold.

The **illness stage** is the stage when a disease is fully developed. Your case of the flu is now complete with fever, aches and pains, stuffy nose, coughing, and other symptoms. Now that you know you have the flu, you should take extra care not to give it to others.

The **recovery stage** is when a disease is finally overcome by the body's defenses. Influenza, for example, will end after several days. A **relapse** may also occur, in which a person recovers partially and then becomes ill again. A relapse can be dangerous because the body is already weakened from fighting the disease.

Illness sometimes ends in death. People are more likely to die after a relapse than during the first illness stage.

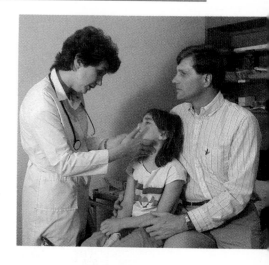

Figure 21-11   Swollen lymph glands are a common sign that the body is fighting infection.

The Common Cold and the Flu

Colds are the most widespread of all infectious diseases. The **common cold** is caused by many different kinds of viruses that cause a runny nose, sore throat, coughing, and headaches. Colds are spread through the air by coughs and sneezes. Anyone who then breathes this air will inhale a cold virus, thus running the risk of catching a cold. Colds are also commonly spread by hand contact. Colds spread rapidly in public places and among friends and family members.

The incubation period of a cold is short, lasting from 18 to 48 hours. A cold usually lasts less than a week. If you have a cold, stay away from people during the first few days of the cold when you are most infectious. For your own health, you should stay away from a person who has just come down with a cold.

There is no cure for the common cold. Scientists have only recently been able to identify the viruses that cause colds. Because there are so many different kinds, people do not build up immunity to colds. Fortunately, colds generally clear up on their own in a few days. Keeping in good physical condition, getting plenty of rest, and eating a healthy diet should help keep down your chances of catching a cold. Not smoking will help as well, since smokers tend to have more respiratory infections. Taking care of yourself once you have a cold will help you prevent a more serious illness from developing.

Influenza is an infectious disease caused by many different kinds of viruses, all of which bring on fever, aches, coughing, and a tired feeling. Some patients even feel depressed. The flu is very infectious. It is spread from person to person in much the same way as the cold. Most doctors recommend bed rest, fluids, and some medicine to ease muscle aches. Older flu patients, or

Health **History**

The flu epidemic of 1918–19 killed more people than all those killed in World War I. It infected at least one fifth of the total human population.

Figure 21-12 Bed rest is an important part of treating many common diseases.

Health **History**

The rubella vaccine became available in 1969. Since then, cases of rubella have dropped by 98 percent.

patients who are not in good health, may suffer more serious illnesses after getting the flu. Vaccines and other medicine help high-risk people avoid the flu.

Mononucleosis

People between the ages of 15 and 24 are the most common victims of mononucleosis. **Mononucleosis** is a viral disease causing a sore throat and the swelling of the lymph glands and spleen, the largest organ in the lymphatic system. Doctors are not sure how it spreads, although the virus may be spread by kissing. It does not appear to be spread by ordinary contact since it is rare for more than one person in a household to have the disease.

The first signs of mononucleosis are similar to a cold. Doctors can tell if you have mononucleosis from a simple blood test. Bed rest is often the prescribed treatment. The illness usually lasts from three to six weeks. A tired feeling often continues during the recovery stage, which may last from days to months.

Chicken Pox

An itchy skin rash and blisters that form scabs characterize **chicken pox.** The incubation period of this viral disease is from 14 to 21 days. The first sign of the disease is the skin rash, followed by aching muscles and fever.

Once a person gets chicken pox, nothing can be done to stop the disease from running its course. When it is over, the scabs fall off and the skin returns to normal. However, if the patient scratches the skin, infection and scars can result. Patients build up immunity to chicken pox and rarely get the disease again.

Chicken pox usually affects young children. It is a milder disease in young children than it is in teenagers and adults. The same virus also causes shingles in older people. **Shingles** occurs when the chicken pox virus becomes active again after a period of inactivity in a nerve root. The skin reached by that nerve becomes very sensitive and a rash and blisters appear. Although the skin clears up in a few weeks, the pain can go on for many months. A vaccine being developed may prevent chicken pox and shingles.

Rubella

German measles, or **rubella,** is a viral disease characterized by a skin rash, mild fever, sore throat, and a runny nose. It is most often caught in childhood. It is usually spread by an infected person coughing or sneezing.

The incubation period is about 14 to 21 days. A person is infectious from about one week before the rash develops until about five days after it appears. There is no cure for rubella. While the disease runs its course the patient should be kept comfortable.

Rubella is not a dangerous disease unless a woman gets it early in pregnancy. In that case the baby may be born with severe birth defects. Doctors now recommend vaccination against rubella when a child is about 15 months old. A woman should not be vaccinated from three months before she becomes pregnant until the end of her pregnancy, or the baby may be harmed.

Disease	Pathogen	Method of Transmission	Usual Entry Area	Preventive Practice
Chicken Pox	Virus	Direct or indirect contact; airborne	Skin, respiratory tract, mouth	Avoid contact
Common Cold	Viruses (more than 120)	Direct or indirect contact; airborne	Nose, throat, mouth	Avoid contact
Diphtheria	Bacteria	Direct contact	Nose, throat, mouth	Immunization; avoid contact
Hepatitis A	Virus	Direct contact; food and water	Mouth, intestinal tract	Avoid contact; practice good hygiene
Hepatitis B	Virus	Blood transfusions; dirty hypodermic needles; sexual contact	Site of needle entry	Screen blood donors; avoid using unsterilized needles
Influenza	Viruses (more than 100)	Direct and indirect contact; airborne	Mouth, nose, throat	Immunization; avoid contact
Measles	Virus	Throat or nose discharge; airborne	Mouth, nose, throat	Immunization; avoid contact
Mono-nucleosis	Virus	Direct contact	Mouth, throat	Avoid contact
Mumps	Virus	Direct or indirect contact	Mouth, throat, nose	Immunization; avoid contact
Polio-myelitis	Virus	Direct and indirect contact	Mouth, throat	Immunization
Rabies	Virus	Saliva from bite of infected animals, including dogs, cats, skunks, raccoons, bats	Site of bite	Immunization of pets; avoid contact with wild animals
Rubella (German Measles)	Virus	Throat or nose discharge; airborne	Mouth, nose, throat	Immunization; avoid contact
Strep Throat	Bacteria	Throat discharge	Mouth, throat	Avoid contact
Tetanus	Bacteria	Puncture wounds; soil and animal feces	Site of puncture	Immunization
Whooping Cough	Bacteria	Direct and indirect contact; airborne	Mouth, nose, throat	Immunization; avoid contact

Figure 21-13   With prevention, you can avoid most diseases.

Hepatitis

Another viral disease is hepatitis. **Hepatitis** [*hep uh TY tis*] infects and enlarges the liver, causing jaundice (yellowing of the skin), nausea, fever, and pain in the abdomen. Hepatitis is a serious disease and can lead to other health problems. People who get better may carry the disease in their blood for years and can infect others. Hepatitis is one of the few infectious diseases that is increasing, especially among young adults. There are two main types of hepatitis — hepatitis A and hepatitis B.

Hepatitis A usually results from contact with infected food or water. The incubation period is from 3 to 6 weeks after infection. The first signs of the disease occur when the skin begins to turn yellow. Doctors prescribe bed rest, and the recovery period is very slow, usually taking several weeks.

Hepatitis B is thought to spread primarily through the blood, by sexual contact with an infected person, or through the use of dirty needles to inject drugs. The first symptoms are similar to those of hepatitis A. It is the more dangerous type of the disease and may even cause death. The incubation period for hepatitis B is from 6 to 12 weeks.

All hepatitis patients are very infectious. Careful handling of wastes and food and water is important to keep either kind from spreading.

Figure 21-14 Contaminated shellfish are a common source of hepatitis A infection.

Tuberculosis

At one time one of the major infectious diseases in this country was tuberculosis. **Tuberculosis,** or TB, is caused by bacteria that first attack the lungs. People who had tuberculosis often spent many years in special TB hospitals, and were kept away from other people. The first symptoms of TB may be long coughing spells. At a later point, the victim may cough up blood, develop a fever, and lose weight. TB is also called consumption.

A simple skin test can determine if you have been exposed to TB. Medicines are used to fight the disease, but the cure can take as long as two years. Today TB is far less of a risk because it can be treated with medicines, but TB is still a health problem. Over 25,000 new cases of TB are discovered each year in the United States, and about 2000 people die from it.

Lesson Review

An infection passes through several stages. Most of the infectious diseases that are still common in this country are caused by viruses. Because people are often infected before they know it, it is hard to control the spread of these diseases.

1 What are five main stages of disease in a body?

2 How are cold viruses spread?

3 When is rubella particularly dangerous?

4 List two forms of hepatitis.

Sexually Transmitted Diseases

Diseases that are passed from one person to another during a sexual act are called **sexually transmitted diseases** (STDs). They are a serious and sometimes deadly group of infectious diseases. There are about 20 identified STDs, and it is possible to be infected by more than one disease at the same time. Even though the number of cases of STDs is increasing, most STDs can be controlled or cured.

Controlling the Spread of STDs

The number of cases of STDs has been increasing for several years. Two reasons for the increase in STDs are increased sexual activity among young people and two fairly new diseases, herpes type II and AIDS. The result is that more and more people, especially young adults, have STDs. STDs were once thought of as infecting only those people who had many sexual partners or who did not practice good health habits. This is no longer true. Anyone who is sexually active must be alert to the dangers of STDs and be ready to seek treatment immediately.

Public health laws have attempted to help control the spread of STDs. One law requires doctors to report certain STDs to local public health officials. Records are strictly confidential. These records provide information helpful in controlling the disease. Reporting STDs to health officials is only one step in stopping them from spreading. Infected individuals must also refrain from sexual contact until they are treated and cured. They should also inform previous sexual partners so that everyone who has been exposed to the disease can be treated. STDs are highly infectious.

Gonorrhea

One of the most common STDs is gonorrhea. **Gonorrhea** [*gahn uh REE uh*] is caused by bacteria and most often transmitted by sexual contact. An infected person can pass the disease to other individuals within two to nine days after getting the disease.

Health Bulletin

Estimates of yearly new cases of STDs in the United States are 3 to 4 million cases of chlamydia, 2 million cases of gonorrhea, 1 million cases of genital warts, and ½ million cases of herpes type II.

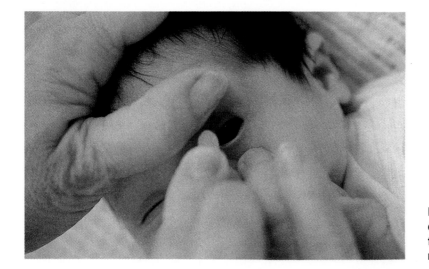

Figure 21-15 Silver nitrate eye drops protect newborn babies from blindness caused by gonorrhea bacteria.

The signs of gonorrhea are different in men than in women. Men will usually experience an unusual discharge from the penis, and an intense burning when passing urine. A few infected males may not have symptoms. A large number of women with cervical gonorrhea have no obvious symptoms. Sometimes, though, there is an unusual discharge or burning during urination.

Both men and women should seek medical attention if there is any reason to suspect they have been exposed to the disease. This is important because even when there are no obvious symptoms, an infected person can still pass along the disease. Gonorrhea continues to be infectious until the disease has been medically treated and cured.

Untreated gonorrhea can lead to major complications. In men, it can lead to difficulty in passing urine, inflammation of the prostate gland, swelling of the testicles, and sterility. In women, untreated gonorrhea usually causes severe inflammation of the pelvic cavity. This can make it difficult or impossible for a woman to become pregnant. An untreated gonorrhea infection may also infect the joints.

Gonorrhea is treated with an antibiotic. The treatment is usually successful. If an infected woman is pregnant, her baby may be born with gonorrhea. Hospitals place silver nitrate or antibiotic eyedrops in the eyes of all newborn babies to prevent blindness that may be caused by the gonorrhea bacteria.

Syphilis

Syphilis is also widespread, although it is not as common as gonorrhea. **Syphilis** is an STD caused by bacteria and characterized by an open sore or rash. The disease spreads when a noninfected person comes in contact with the discharge from the sore or rash. The newly infected person will develop symptoms within ten days to ten weeks, but usually about three weeks after being exposed to the disease. Syphilis also can be passed by an infected pregnant woman to an unborn infant. Syphilis seriously affects the development of the baby after birth.

Health Bulletin

Americans spend more than $2 billion annually on STD-related health care.

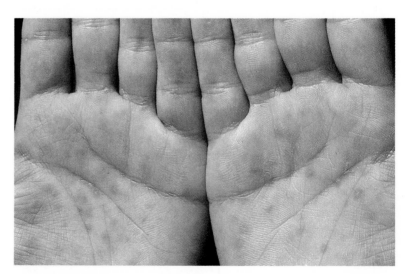

Figure 21-16   This body rash is a symptom of the secondary stage of syphilis.

Syphilis has four distinct stages: primary, secondary, latent, and late. In the primary stage, a chancre appears on the skin or mucous membrane where the pathogen entered the body. A **chancre** [*SHANG kur*] is an open sore. The chancre is firm and rounded with a ragged edge. The chancre is painless and can be either quite small or as large as a dime. Regardless of its size, if a chancre is present the disease is highly contagious. If syphilis is not treated at this stage, it will seem to disappear in two to six weeks. However, the disease is still present, and the victim will develop more serious problems.

If there has been no medical treatment, the secondary stage begins from one month to several months after the primary stage ends. This stage may include many symptoms. These include body rashes, white patches on the mucous membranes of the mouth or throat, low-grade fever, headache, swollen lymph glands, large moist sores around the mouth or genital area, red eyes, pain in the joints, and even patches of hair falling out. At this stage the disease can be spread through touching the open sores or rashes.

The third stage, latent syphilis, may last from one to forty years. The bacteria keep on attacking different organs in the body, including the heart and brain, but there are no obvious symptoms. In the final stage, or late syphilis, a victim may experience heart damage, blindness, paralysis, and mental disorders.

As frightening as this disease sounds, treatment is simple and very effective during the first two stages. Doctors use tests to tell syphilis from diseases it may look like or to discover its presence during the latent stage.

Herpes Type II

Herpes type II is a very common STD. Many public health workers think it is more widespread than gonorrhea, because it is highly infectious and there is no known cure for the disease. **Herpes type II** is caused by a virus and is characterized by painful blisters and sores in the genital area.

Herpes type II is usually transmitted during sexual contact. The incubation period for herpes is from two to ten days. It is most infectious when open sores are present. Even during active periods, the sores may not be visible. For example, they may be on a woman's cervix. The virus may also be present in saliva, semen, or vaginal secretions. Anyone who has had herpes in the past is likely to be infectious even if there are no obvious signs of the disease. Active cases of herpes type II in pregnant women can threaten the lives of their babies. Women who have herpes may also face an increased risk of cervical cancer.

Unlike most STDs, which can be easily and successfully treated, herpes type II currently has no cure. Some people have several outbreaks during a year. Many treatments have been attempted without success. These include ointments, vaccines, exposure to light, and the use of ultrasonic waves and laser beam therapy. One new medicine offers hope. It is effective with the first outbreak, and can shorten the repeated outbreaks.

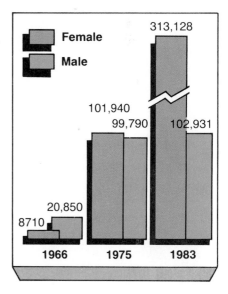

Figure 21-17 Genital herpes is a fast-growing problem. Visits to doctors for this incurable disease have risen sharply.

Chlamydia

There are several similar diseases grouped under the heading chlamydia. **Chlamydia** [*kluh MID ee uh*] is a common STD that causes inflammation of the urethra in men and of the vagina in women. While this group of diseases is not as serious as gonorrhea, it is a major health problem because of the complications caused when victims do not seek medical treatment.

Chlamydia is transmitted by direct sexual contact and can also be carried on the hands to the eyes. Incubation is from five to twelve days after contact with any infected person.

The symptoms of these diseases are similar to those of gonorrhea. Men may experience pain during urination. They may also have a discharge from the penis, which often goes undetected. The discharge is not as heavy as that of gonorrhea. Most women have no obvious symptoms. However, some may have a white vaginal discharge and vaginal itching.

In men, prolonged and untreated chlamydia may lead to inflammation of the penis and testicles. In women, the untreated disease may cause serious health problems much like gonorrhea. In the newborn child, the risks of catching pneumonia and developing eye infections are quite high when the mother has chlamydia.

Chlamydia is easily treated with antibiotics. The cures are very successful. As with other STDs, both sexual partners must be treated or the nontreated partner can reinfect the cured partner.

Vaginitis

A general inflammation of the vagina is called **vaginitis.** There are several types of vaginitis, including one caused by a yeast and one caused by a protist. In many cases, vaginitis can occur without sexual contact. The yeast infection often results from the use of antibiotics or from hormonal changes. The protist infection can be spread by sexual contact as an STD. It is also possible to pass on these diseases through contact with infected articles such as clothing and towels. Vaginitis is very infectious when there is inflammation.

Women usually have vaginal soreness, discharges, and annoying itching. Men may have similar genital problems, except the itching is less severe. The complications of these diseases are more annoying than harmful. As in other STDs, unborn and newborn babies may be infected by their mothers. Vaginitis is easily treated. Both sexual partners must be treated to prevent the cured partner from becoming infected again.

Chancroid

A bacterial STD in which the symptoms in males are similar to those of syphilis is **chancroid** [*SHANG kroyd*]. The incubation period usually lasts from three to five days. Chancroid is very infectious if active open sores are present.

Chancroid is not very common, but is important because of the similarity between its symptoms and those of syphilis in males. A chancre appears on the penis or in the genital area. It differs from the syphilitic chancre in that it is painful. Touching the chancres

Figure 21-18 Help for dealing with STDs is widely available. If you suspect you might have an STD, see a doctor right away.

causes them to bleed. If they are not cleansed and treated, they will destroy surrounding tissue. The lymph nodes near the chancre accumulate large amounts of pus and may rupture at the slightest pressure. Women may have similar signs. In over one half of the cases, though, women do not have obvious signs since the sores may be on the cervix.

Doctors identify the disease by taking a sample smear of the discharged pus of a chancre. Treatment and control of chancroid are fairly simple.

Genital Warts

One STD that is becoming more common is genital warts. **Genital warts** are caused by a virus and are transmitted only through sexual contact. The condition has a fairly long incubation time, about one to six months. Genital warts are very infectious, even when they are not yet visible. Warts can be small, or they may grow together and look like small cauliflowers.

Doctors may take a scraping from the warts to make sure they are not cancerous. Often the warts are left untreated unless they begin to grow, or their presence becomes annoying.

Pubic Lice

Lice that feed on blood and the skin of the genital region are called **pubic lice.** Pubic lice, or crab lice, are fairly common animal parasites. Pubic lice are most often transmitted through sexual contact. They can also be spread on infected clothing, bed linens, bath towels, or other similar items.

The female lice attach eggs to the pubic hair. The eggs hatch in six to nine days. The hatched lice mature in about 14 to 21 days. The disease is infectious throughout the life cycle of the lice. Symptoms include severe itching in the genital area. The treatment for pubic lice is rather simple. The infected area is cleansed with soap and warm water and medication is applied.

Figure 21-19 Pubic lice have curved claws with which they hold on to hair.

Lesson Review

While most infectious diseases are less common today, the number of cases of STDs has been increasing. Anyone who is sexually active may get one or more STDs at the same time. Early medical attention will usually clear up most of these infections. However, there are some STDs for which no cure has been found. Medical help at the first sign of any infectious disease in either sexual partner is very important. Some people may be embarassed to report STDs, but doctors, school nurses, and clinics will provide confidential help.

1 List two reasons why the cases of STDs are increasing.

2 Why must gonorrhea be medically treated?

3 Name the four stages of syphilis.

4 What is vaginitis?

Chapter Review

Vocabulary

acquired immune-deficiency
  syndrome
antibody
antibiotic
B cell
bacteria
cellular defense
chancre
chancroid
chicken pox
chlamydia
cilia
common cold
fungi
genital warts
gonorrhea
helper T cell
hepatitis

hepatitis A
hepatitis B
herpes type II
illness stage
immunity
incubation stage
infectious disease
inflammation
influenza
interferon
lymph node
memory cell
mononucleosis
mucous membrane
mucus
parasite
pasteurization
pathogen

phagocyte
prodromal stage
protist
pubic lice
recovery stage
relapse
rubella
sexually transmitted disease
shingles
structural defense
syphilis
tetanus
toxin
trichinosis
tuberculosis
vaccination
vaginitis
virus

Using Vocabulary

Questions 1-18. On a separate sheet of paper, write the name of the disease or pathogen that correctly completes the sentence.

1 A __?__ is a single unit of genetic material in a protein shell.

2 Many-celled organisms that live by feeding on or in other animals are called __?__.

3 __?__ is a new, fatal disease of the immune system that attacks the T cells.

4 A viral disease that causes a sore throat and swelling of lymph glands is __?__.

5 Aches, coughing, and fever are symptoms of __?__, a disease caused by different viruses.

6 An incurable STD caused by a virus and characterized by genital sores is __?__.

7 A group of STDs with symptoms similar to those of gonorrhea is __?__.

8 __?__ is an uncommon STD that causes symptoms in men similar to those of syphilis.

9 A disease that occurs when the chicken pox virus becomes active in a nerve root is __?__.

10 __?__ is a dangerous viral disease that is spread through the blood and causes jaundice.

11 __?__ are one-celled organisms with specialized internal structures.

12 __?__ is an STD caused by an animal parasite.

13 A disease usually transmitted by eating infected pork is __?__. It is caused by a parasitic worm.

14 __?__ is a viral disease characterized by a skin rash of itchy blisters.

15 A bacterially-caused disease, also called consumption, that first attacks the lungs is __?__.

16 The most widespread of all infectious diseases is __?__. It is caused by different viruses.

17 __?__ are microscopic plantlike organisms that cause such skin diseases as athlete's foot.

18 One-celled organisms made up of a small amount of living matter surrounded by a thin cell wall are called __?__.

Interpreting Ideas

1 Describe four ways that diseases may be spread. How is pasteurization used to combat the spread of pathogens?

2 Identify and describe the body's structural defenses against pathogens.

3 How does the body gain immunity to disease?

4 Describe the stages of infectious diseases.

5 Describe the course of mononucleosis—its cause, symptoms, treatment, and duration.

6 How does a vaccination work in the body?

7 When is herpes type II most infectious?

8 Why is it a good idea not to scratch your skin when you have chicken pox? How are chicken pox and shingles related?

9 How do cilia help prevent infection?

10 Compare the actions of T cells and B cells.

11 Describe the prodromal stage of disease.

12 Describe rubella—its symptoms, how it is spread, and its incubation period. What danger does rubella present to pregnant women?

13 What is the role of phagocytes?

14 How does hepatitis affect the body? What is the difference between hepatitis A and hepatitis B?

15 How can the AIDS virus be transmitted? Identify two preventive measures against AIDS.

16 How do the symptoms of gonorrhea differ in men and in women? What are the complications of untreated gonorrhea in men and women?

17 Describe the four stages of syphilis.

18 Why has the number of cases of STDs been increasing in recent years?

19 Compare recovery from disease with and without a relapse. What are the risks in a relapse?

20 What is the function of a memory cell?

Applying Concepts

1 Joe received a puncture wound when he stepped on a rusty nail with his bare foot. The skin was broken on Maria's arm when her friend's cat scratched her. How should each of these injuries be treated?

2 Why do many doctors not recommend giving children aspirin or other medicines to reduce fever unless the temperature is over 103°F?

3 Why are antibiotics not used to treat the common cold?

4 Someone who has mumps will not get the virus again. Why is this true?

5 A person who has mononucleosis often has an elevated white blood cell count. Why do you think this is so?

6 For each of the following diseases, use the table in Figure 21-13 to identify the pathogen and methods of prevention: (a) diphtheria, (b) whooping cough, (c) mumps, (d) hepatitis B.

Projects

1 Write a public service announcement urging people to have their young children vaccinated against diphtheria, whooping cough, and polio. In your message, tell the public where they can go for free immunizations and describe the relatively simple procedure involved in receiving a vaccine. (One of the polio vaccines, for example, can be taken orally.) Warn that diseases such as diphtheria and polio could spread again unless young children continue to be vaccinated against these diseases.

2 Investigate the progress in the development of vaccines for hepatitis, AIDS, and the common cold. What problems have thwarted the development of a vaccine for each of these diseases?

3 Find out more about the antiviral protein interferon. Under what conditions is it produced? How has it been used experimentally? How can interferon be useful if it does not directly inhibit the production of viruses?

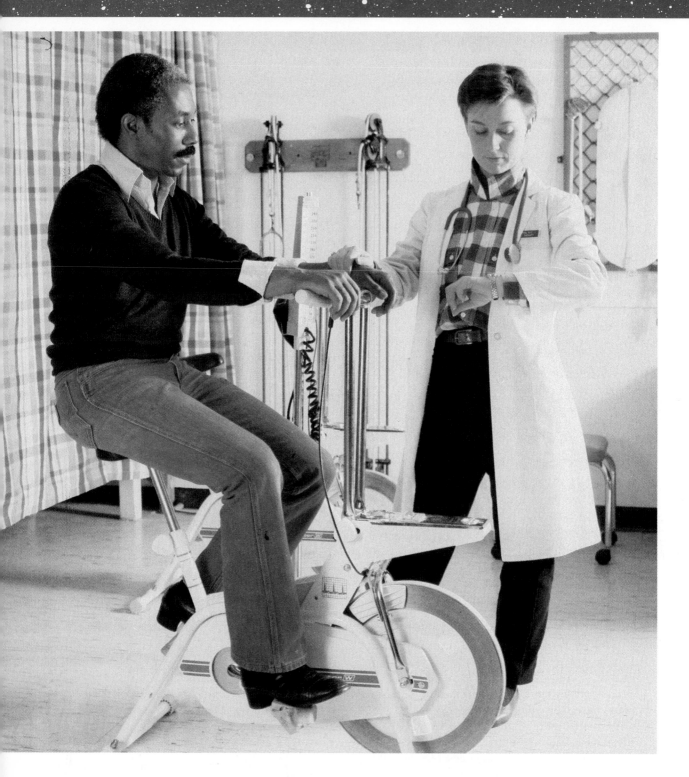

Physical therapy and controlled exercises help speed the recovery of many heart attack and stroke victims.

CHAPTER TWENTY-TWO

NONINFECTIOUS DISEASES

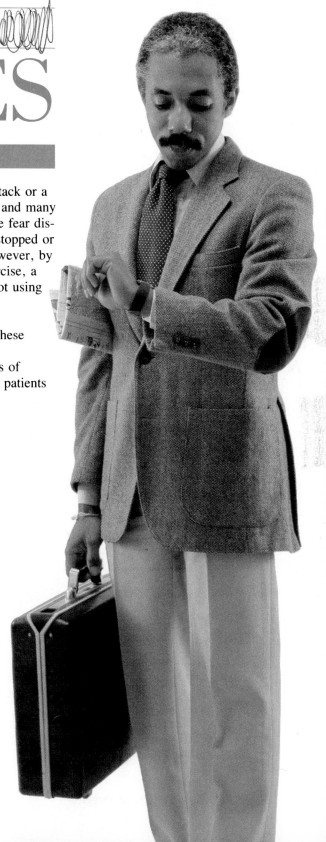

You probably know someone who has had a heart attack or a stroke, or perhaps is fighting against cancer. These and many other diseases are not caused by pathogens. Many people fear diseases that develop slowly, thinking that they cannot by stopped or overcome. Many of these diseases can be prevented, however, by the practice of good personal health habits. Regular exercise, a proper diet, healthful ways of dealing with stress, and not using tobacco can reduce your risk of developing the diseases described in this chapter.

In addition, proper care and self-help can often keep these diseases from disabling their victims. Physical therapy, careful exercise, and a controlled diet are important parts of treatment. Combined with medical care, they help many patients recover or slow the development of disease.

Objectives

- Describe five cardiovascular diseases.
- Describe three causes of a stroke.
- List four kinds of treatment for cardio-vascular diseases.
- State the seven warning signs of cancer.
- Describe three types of cancer.
- Describe the process by which cancer grows.
- Identify three types of cancer treatment.
- Describe three noninfectious diseases other than cardiovascular disease and cancer.
- List four ways to help prevent noninfectious diseases.

Cardiovascular Diseases

Those diseases that are not caused by pathogens are called **noninfectious diseases.** Two forms of noninfectious diseases are cancer and cardiovascular diseases. **Cardiovascular diseases** [*kahr dee oh VAS kyuh lur*] are diseases of the heart and the blood vessels. When the heart and blood vessels are healthy, blood flows smoothly throughout the body. But sometimes the circulatory system fails to work properly. Blood may not flow properly through the arteries and veins. Serious health problems can then result. Some people are born with cardiovascular problems. But most cardiovascular diseases take years to develop. Cardiovascular diseases cause more deaths in the United States then all other causes combined.

Hypertension

Under normal conditions, your blood vessels are smooth and elastic. They expand and contract as your blood pumps through them. The force with which the blood pushes against the walls of the vessels as it travels through the cardiovascular system is called **blood pressure.** High blood pressure is also known as **hypertension.** Hypertension is a very common cardiovascular disease, affecting about one in five Americans. It is thought to result from a narrowing of the small blood vessels. The narrowing causes the heart to beat harder to pump the blood. Over many years, this extra pressure can damage the blood vessels and the heart.

In most cases, the cause of hypertension is unknown, but the condition has a clear link with several factors. Weighing too much, a diet heavy in salt, smoking, and a family history of the disease are all connected to high blood pressure. People who are overweight when young seem to be at higher risk of high blood pressure when they reach middle age. Doctors estimate that in this country about 35 million adults have hypertension that should be controlled with medicine. Another estimated 25 million adults have high blood pressure that needs to be watched closely, but does not require medicine.

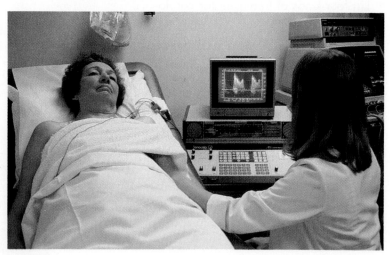

Figure 22–1   An echogram monitors and records heart function by examining the sound of the heart at work.

Many people do not know they have hypertension because there are rarely any symptoms until their blood pressure is extremely high. Because of its lack of symptoms, hypertension is often called the "silent killer." People most often discover they have hypertension during a routine physical checkup. You can have your blood pressure checked easily by a doctor or nurse.

Diseases of the Arteries

A condition in which the arteries become hard is called **arteriosclerosis** [*ahr teer ee oh skluh ROH sis*]. Arteriosclerosis is often called hardening of the arteries. In this condition, calcium often builds up in the artery walls. Less blood can move through the hardened arteries, because the walls thicken and the passageways narrow.

Arteriosclerosis slows the flow of blood to the parts of the body fed by the affected arteries. Arteries leading to the legs and brain are most often affected. People who suffer from arteriosclerosis may first notice an aching in their legs and feet, especially during physical activity. If the arteries to the brain are affected, victims may get dizzy or suffer temporary loss of sight.

The most important form of arteriosclerosis is atherosclerosis. **Atherosclerosis** [*ath uh roh skluh ROH sis*] is a disease caused by the build-up of fatty masses in the walls of the arteries, as shown in Figure 22-3. If the build-up is too great, the flow of blood can be reduced to a trickle or even stopped. When blockage occurs in the arteries feeding the heart muscle, the disease can lead to heart damage.

The major fatty substance that blocks the arteries is **cholesterol** [*kuh LES tuh rawl*]. Cholesterol is needed by the body to help form vitamin D and certain hormones. It is produced in the liver and also is found in many foods, including dairy products and meat. However, people who eat foods high in saturated fats may build up more cholesterol than they need, and increase their chances of developing atherosclerosis. In a push to lower heart disease, the National Institutes of Health now recommend that everyone be tested for high blood cholesterol. If your cholesterol level is high during your teens, you will have an increased risk of heart disease when you are older.

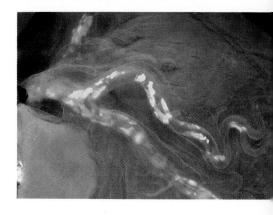

Figure 22–2 Fatty build-up in a blocked coronary artery, marked with a special dye

Figure 22–3 As atherosclerosis progresses, a normal healthy artery *(left)* becomes more and more clogged *(center and right).*

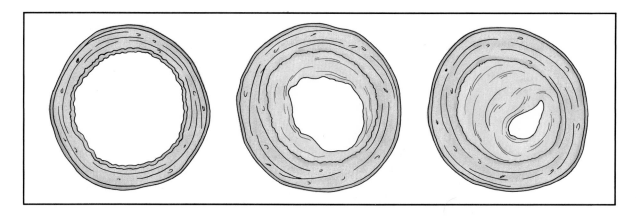

Figure 22–4 High blood pressure forces the heart to pump harder, thus straining the blood vessels.

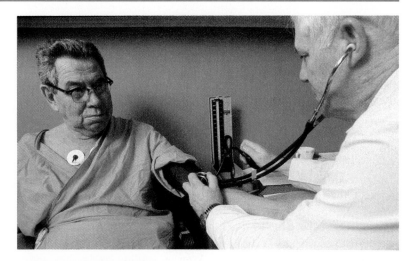

Heart Attack

For the heart to remain in good health, it requires oxygen and nutrients carried by the blood. A **heart attack** is a sudden, life-threatening malfunction of the heart muscle. A heart attack occurs when one or more of the arteries supplying blood to the heart muscles becomes blocked. Part of the heart then dies from the lack of oxygen.

Some injuries to the heart are more serious and long-lasting than others. The site of the blockage determines how serious the attack will be. If the blockage is in a major artery, a large section of the heart may be damaged, causing immediate death. If the blockage is in a smaller artery, the heart can often continue to beat. The chances of recovery are good.

A temporary lack of oxygen in the heart muscle causes a feeling of suffocation and chest pain called **angina pectoris** [*an JY nuh PEK tur is*]. Angina is a symptom rather than a disease. Attacks of angina usually occur during periods of heavy physical or emotional stress. They generally last only as long as the stress continues. People who suffer from angina may never have a heart attack. But angina does indicate that there is some blockage in the coronary arteries.

The symptoms of a heart attack are different from those of angina. The pain of a heart attack may be as mild as a case of indigestion. In other cases, a heart attack feels as if there is a very heavy weight on the victim's chest. The pain may spread to the jaw and arms, and it does not stop with rest. Nausea and sweating often accompany the pain.

Heart Failure

Years of high blood pressure, arteriosclerosis, and other cardiovascular problems can lead to a general weakening of the heart. **Heart failure** is a condition in which the heart is no longer able to pump a normal amount of blood. Heart failure may affect one or both sides of the heart. In either case, blood backs up in the veins leading to that side of the heart. The legs or lung tissue may then swell.

Heart failure does not mean that the heart will stop pumping. People can live for many years by taking medicines that help the heart beat more efficiently. The heart then does not work as hard. Diets that are low in sodium help people who have this sort of heart problem. High levels of sodium cause the body to hold water, which increases swelling and makes the heart work harder.

Stroke

Just as a drop in blood supply to the heart causes a heart attack, a drop in blood supply to the brain causes a stroke. A **stroke** occurs when a blockage or rupture of a blood vessel in the brain causes a part of the brain to be damaged. There are three types of strokes—cerebral hemorrhage, thrombosis, and embolism. All three usually result from hypertension or atherosclerosis.

Long periods of hypertension can weaken blood vessel walls. This can lead to a hemorrhage, or bleeding from a broken blood vessel. When a hemorrhage occurs in the brain, it is called a **cerebral hemorrhage.** The weak wall of an artery can hemorrhage and allow blood to seep out into the brain. The pressure of this blood collecting in the brain damages brain tissues.

A second cause of stroke is thrombosis. **Thrombosis** is a process in which a blood clot blocks an artery. It usually occurs in an artery that has been narrowed by atherosclerosis.

A third cause of stroke is an embolism. An **embolism** occurs when an artery in the brain is blocked by a moving blood clot or piece of cholesterol. Usually the clot causing an embolism has broken off from a site of atherosclerosis or a blood clot elsewhere in the body.

When a blockage occurs in the brain, cells fed by the affected artery die. The type of damage that results depends on which area of the brain dies. For example, if the blood vessels leading to the speech center in the brain are blocked, the person's speech may be slurred. If the blockage is in an area of the brain that controls muscles, paralysis may result.

It is common for victims of stroke to suffer speech problems, paralysis, and loss of memory. Patients may also suffer from depression and rapid shifts in mood.

The loss of physical and mental abilities may be temporary if large areas of the brain are not damaged. A patient may even enjoy a full recovery. Often the recovery involves physical therapy. Physical therapy includes the use of exercises that help the patient learn how to reuse the affected limbs. In other cases, though, the stroke victim may never regain mental functions or the full use of limbs. A very severe stroke can result in death.

Treating Cardiovascular Disease

Death from cardiovascular disease can often be prevented if the disease is detected and treatment is started early enough. However, early diagnosis can be made only if the patient tells the doctor of any warning signs. There are several tests and operations that can determine the nature of the problem and help the patient recover from the disease.

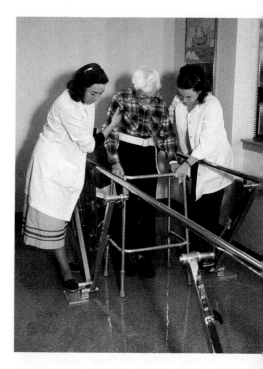

Figure 22–5 Stroke victims often need physical therapy to recover the use of their limbs.

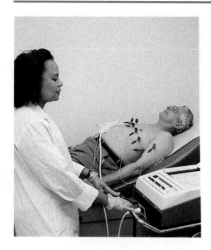

Figure 22–6 The electrocardiogram records the electrical activity of the heart.

Electrocardiogram Each beat of the heart is caused by a small jolt of electricity. Doctors study heart action from a graph of the electrical impulses, called an **electrocardiogram** or ECG. A normal heart produces a certain pattern of peaks and valleys on the graph. A damaged or diseased heart produces an ECG that differs from the usual pattern. Thus ECGs can be used to determine if a person has a heart disease.

Medication Cardiovascular diseases can sometimes be controlled with medicines. Some medications act directly on the heart, while others affect only the blood and blood vessels. Some medicines increase the heart's oxygen supply by expanding narrow cardiac arteries. One such medication is nitroglycerine, which is used to relieve angina. Medicines that stimulate the heart help sluggish hearts beat stronger and faster. Other medicines calm rapid and uncontrolled heartbeats.

Medicines that lower blood pressure are sometimes used to treat hypertension and prevent strokes. Some help lower blood pressure by reducing the amount of salt in the body. Others lower blood pressure by relaxing the arteries. Medicines that prevent blood clots are used to reduce the risk of heart attack and stroke.

Surgery Some cardiovascular diseases may be treated by surgery. For example, defects in the heart that are present at birth can often be corrected. Damaged valves can be replaced with substitutes. A small electric device called a **pacemaker** can be placed under the skin to help keep the heart beating regularly. The heart beats on its own, but the pacemaker, which runs on batteries, keeps the beats at a steady pace.

Another surgical treatment clears clogged arteries. In this procedure, a doctor inserts a small, flexible tube into an artery. The build-up in the artery is then flattened against the artery walls by a balloon inflated at the end of the tube.

The most frequently performed type of heart surgery is a coronary artery bypass. A **coronary artery bypass** is a procedure in which doctors build a bypass around a blocked artery to the heart. In this procedure, a large vein is taken from the patient's leg and grafted onto the heart artery. Blood then flows into the heart through the new blood vessel.

In cases in which a patient's heart is badly damaged, doctors may remove the weak heart. A **heart transplant** is a procedure in which a healthy heart is removed from a person who has recently died and placed in the body of the patient. Scientists are also developing artificial hearts.

Preventing Heart Disease

Many of the problems that cause cardiovascular disease begin early in life. You can lower your risk of heart disease later in life if you start to practice good health habits now. A healthy diet, regular exercise, reducing stress, and not smoking can greatly reduce your risk of a heart attack. These health habits are especially important if someone in your family has had a heart attack.

Health Bulletin

One new technique for clearing clogged arteries uses laser technology. A tiny hollow tube is passed inside an artery to the blockage. Laser light travels along the tube and vaporizes blood clots and fatty build-up.

Exercise is one way to keep the heart and circulatory system healthy. Physical activity makes the heart muscle strong, and a strong heart does not have to work as hard as a weak one to keep pumping blood. The exercises that do your heart the most good are aerobic exercises. As you learned in Chapter 14, aerobic exercises increase the heartbeat for a period that is long enough to strengthen the heart. A regular program of aerobic exercise could include swimming, jogging, or dancing.

A diet of too much food or the wrong kinds of food can also increase your risk of heart attack. The risk of developing hypertension increases in people who are overweight. People with diets high in sodium and fats are also at high risk of developing high blood pressure. The most important dietary factors are eating less cholesterol and eating polyunsaturated fats instead of saturated fats. By controlling what and how much you eat, you can reduce your risk of developing cardiovascular diseases.

Smoking is another threat to the health of your cardiovascular system. Smoking affects your entire body, but it harms the lungs and heart most of all. Smoking just one cigarette increases your heart rate and raises your blood pressure. Substances in smoke reduce the blood's ability to carry oxygen and encourage the buildup of fatty deposits in the arteries. The more you smoke and the longer you smoke, the greater your chances of having a heart attack. If you already smoke, quitting will allow your body to begin repairing itself almost immediately. By quitting, you can prevent further damage and increase your chances of good health as you get older.

Mental and emotional stress can also damage your heart. Stress causes the heart rate, blood pressure, and cholesterol level to increase. If this continues over time, your health may suffer. If your cardiovascular system is diseased, stress may bring on a heart attack.

Figure 22–7 Aerobic exercise, such as swimming, strengthens the heart and stimulates the growth of new blood vessels.

Lesson Review

Hypertension, arteriosclerosis, and atherosclerosis are common diseases of the blood vessels. They develop slowly over many years and can lead to angina, heart attacks, and strokes. Several treatments, including medication and surgery, have been developed to treat cardiovascular diseases. The risk of cardiovascular diseases can be greatly reduced by exercising regularly, eating a well-balanced diet, and avoiding or quitting smoking.

1 List two factors linked with hypertension.

2 Describe both arteriosclerosis and atherosclerosis. What is their relationship?

3 List two common effects of a stroke.

4 Describe an electrocardiogram.

5 What changes in diet can reduce the risk of heart attack?

Cancer

Several different diseases characterized by the uncontrolled growth of cells are known as **cancer.** Cancer can affect any part of the body and occur in people of any age. Although cancer is feared as a killer, new medical treatments now cure one third of all cancer patients in the United States. Even more lives could be saved if people avoided cancer risks and sought medical help at the first sign of something wrong.

How Cancer Grows

Normally, your body replaces worn out and injured cells by the multiplication of healthy cells. Sometimes, though, something goes wrong with the control of cell multiplication. Cells may begin to grow very rapidly and form a mass of tissue called a tumor. A tumor that does not spread is called a **benign tumor** [*bih NYN*]. Benign tumors are usually harmless, but they can cause pressure on vital organs and often must be removed by surgery.

If the tumor has uncontrolled growth, it is considered cancerous and is called a **malignant tumor** [*muh LIG nunt*]. A malignant tumor is more serious than a benign tumor because the cancer cells take the nourishment that regular cells need. In addition, malignant tumors can spread cancer cells to other parts of the body. The cancer cells break off from the first tumor and spread through the blood stream or the lymphatic system to other parts of the body, as shown in Figure 22-8. New tumors can begin to grow. The process by which cancer cells spread throughout the body is called **metastasis** [*muh TAS tuh sis*]. If a malignant tumor can be detected before metastasis occurs, doctors may be able to successfully treat the cancer.

Causes of Cancer

No single cause has been found to account for all forms of cancer. Instead, several different factors have been linked to cancer. Because people in the same family tend to develop the same kinds of cancer, researchers believe people can inherit a tendency to develop certain cancers. Factors in the environment, such as smoke and radiation, may also cause cancer. Any chemical, organism, or type of radiation that causes cancer is a **carcinogen** [*kahr SIN uh jin*]. Some chemical carcinogens are present in factory smoke, automobile exhaust, cigarette smoke, and dust from asbestos insulation.

Although they have not yet been linked with human cancers, certain viruses, bacteria, and parasites have been found to cause cancers in laboratory animals. Radiation can also act as a carcinogen. For example, the ultraviolet radiation in sunlight is the greatest single cause of skin cancer.

Recent research suggests that all people have genes in their cells that can cause cancerous growth. The genes that can make the cells grow without control are called **oncogenes** [*AHN koh jeenz*]. Oncogenes regulate normal cell growth, and may cause cancerous growth when they are changed by carcinogens.

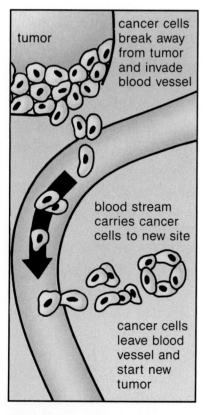

Figure 22–8 How a malignant tumor metastasizes

tumor

cancer cells break away from tumor and invade blood vessel

blood stream carries cancer cells to new site

cancer cells leave blood vessel and start new tumor

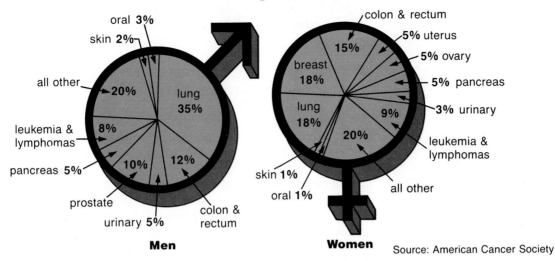

Cancer Deaths by Site and Sex

Men

oral **3%**
skin **2%**
all other **20%**
leukemia & lymphomas **8%**
pancreas **5%**
prostate **10%**
urinary **5%**
colon & rectum **12%**
lung **35%**

Women

colon & rectum **15%**
5% uterus
5% ovary
5% pancreas
3% urinary
leukemia & lymphomas **9%**
all other **20%**
breast **18%**
lung **18%**
skin **1%**
oral **1%**

Source: American Cancer Society

Figure 22–9   Not all cancers are equally deadly.

Exposure to a large amount of a carcinogen may cause cancer. In small amounts, however, a carcinogen acts as an initiator. An **initiator** activates an oncogene, but not enough to make the cell grow more quickly. A second step is needed to cause cancer. The cell must be exposed to another substance, called a promoter. A **promoter** causes cells already activated by an initiator to become cancerous. After exposure to an initiator, repeated exposure to a promoter may produce cancer. Fortunately, cells often repair the damage done by a promoter.

Research suggests that strong immune systems may kill young cancer cells. When the immune system is weak, cancer cells may grow and spread. Once these cells are established in the body, the immune system cannot destroy them.

Types of Cancer

Any body tissue or organ can develop cancerous cells. While these cells may spread to many locations, cancers are always named after their site of origin. For example, a cancer could begin in a lung and then spread elsewhere in the body. This cancer would always be referred to as lung cancer. The death rates from some common types of cancer are shown in Figure 22-9.

Lung Cancer   More people in the United States suffer from lung cancer than from any other type of cancer. Yet lung cancer, which is usually fatal, is the most preventable form of cancer. Smoking tobacco is linked with between 80 and 85 percent of all cases. Lung cancer among women is increasing since more and more women have taken up smoking over the past 30 years. One recent study showed that lung cancer has replaced breast cancer as the leading form of cancer among women. The early signs of lung cancer include a nagging cough, shortness of breath, chest pains, and coughing up mucus or blood. As the cancer continues to grow, the person loses weight and strength. Lung cancer can be

Figure 22–10 A small T cell attacks a large tumor cell. The blisters on the tumor cell may protect it from the attack.

Health **History**

In 1775, the Englishman Sir Percival Pott discovered the first link between a chemical agent and cancer. He connected the high frequency of cancer in chimney sweeps to their exposure to soot and coal tar. It took 140 years for his idea to be tested.

cured only in its very early stages. When it is discovered early, surgery to remove the cancer is the usual treatment. Unfortunately, lung cancer is usually well established before there are any symptoms.

Skin Cancer There are three kinds of skin cancer. One type is a small growth that may spread to surrounding tissues but does not spread to other parts of the body. This kind of cancer is easy to cure. The second type is a lump that may spread to other areas of the body. The third and most deadly type, called malignant **melanoma,** usually begins as a dark mole. This kind of cancer can spread throughout the body very quickly.

Skin cancer is almost always connected with overexposure to the sun. People who are fair-skinned are more likely to develop skin cancer than dark-skinned people. The risk of developing skin cancer increases with age and the length of exposure to the sun.

Oral Cancer Cancerous growths on the lips, gums, throat, and larynx are called **oral cancers.** Oral cancers are strongly connected with smoking and tobacco. Warning signs include a nagging sore throat or hoarseness, difficulty swallowing, and a sore in the mouth. Most cases of oral cancer are curable if they are treated early.

Colon and Rectal Cancer Cancer of the colon or rectum is one of the most common forms of cancer in the United States. It affects men and women in equal numbers. A high-fat, low-fiber diet may contribute to its development. Early detection could reduce the death rate by one half. Blood in the stools is one symptom of cancer of the colon or rectum.

Breast Cancer Breast cancer strikes more than 100,000 women in this country each year and takes the lives of one third of them. It accounts for nearly one fifth of all cancers among women. Women over 40 are at the greatest risk.

As with many other types of cancers, early detection could prevent many deaths. Every woman should examine her breasts monthly. A simple self-exam is shown in Figure 22-11. A self-exam of the breast can reveal unusual lumps. Anything unusual should be reported to a doctor. Most lumps are not cancerous, but women should not put off a doctor's visit if they discover a lump. A doctor will follow up with a more thorough examination to determine the location and nature of the lump. If breast cancer is diagnosed, part or all of the breast may be removed in an operation called a **mastectomy.**

Uterine and Cervical Cancer A cancerous growth in the uterus is called uterine cancer. Cancer of the opening of the uterus, or the cervix, is called **cervical cancer.** Cervical cancer was once a leading cause of death among women. Early detection through regular pelvic examinations has reduced the death rate from these kinds of cancer.

1 In the Shower

With fingers flat, examine gently every part of each breast. Use the right hand for the left breast, and the left hand for the right breast. Check carefully for any lump, hard knot, or thickening.

2 Before a Mirror

Examine each breast with arms at the sides, then raise your arms high overhead. Look closely for any changes in shape of each breast, swelling, dimpling of skin, or changes in the nipple.

Next, with palms on hips, press down firmly to flex the chest muscles. Check carefully again.

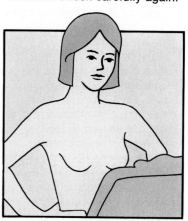

3 Lying Down

Place a pillow or folded towel under the right shoulder. Place right hand behind the head. With the fingers of left hand flat, press gently in small circular motions around an imaginary clock face. Begin at the outermost top, or 12

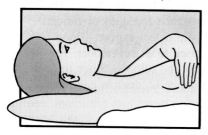

o'clock, position of your right breast, then move to 1 o'clock, and so on around the circle back to 12 o'clock. A ridge in the lower curve of each breast is normal. Move the hand in an inch, toward the nipple. Keep circling to examine every

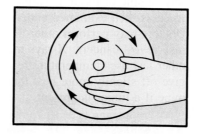

part of the breast, including the nipple. Repeat the procedure for the left breast. Finally, squeeze the nipple of each breast gently between the thumb and index finger. Any discharge should be reported to a doctor immediately.

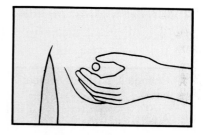

Part of the pelvic examination is the Pap test. A **Pap test** is an exam in which a doctor takes cell samples from the cervix and vagina. These cells are examined for any sign of cancer. Women should have a Pap test yearly. If discovered early, over 80 percent of cases of cervical cancer and 90 percent of cases of uterine cancer are curable.

Figure 22–11 The three-step breast exam

Prostate and Testicular Cancer Cancerous growth in the prostate gland is rare in young men. The chance of developing this disease increases with age. Prostate cancer is the second most common cancer in men over 70 years old, and accounts for almost 10 percent of male cancer deaths. Difficulty in urinating or frequent urination at night are its chief symptoms. Prostate cancer is often detected during a rectal exam.

Cancerous growth in the testes is called **testicular cancer.** Testicular cancer usually appears between the ages of 15 and 35.

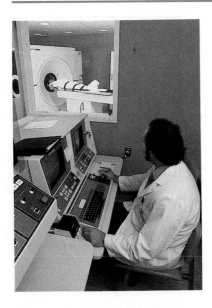

Figure 22–14 Tools such as the CAT scan help doctors confirm the presence of cancer.

Scientists hope one chemical manufactured by the immune system itself may prove useful against cancer. Interferon is a substance naturally produced by cells to ward off damage from invading viruses. Some patients do not produce enough interferon. Artificially produced interferon may become useful in fighting some forms of cancer.

Reducing Cancer Risks

You may have inherited a tendency to develop certain forms of cancer. Some cancer risk factors, such as age and family history, cannot be changed. But you can control other risk factors, such as your diet and use of known carcinogens. The following guidelines are ways you can lower your chances of developing cancer.

1 Avoid all forms of tobacco, including cigarettes, snuff, and chewing tobacco. Most lung cancer patients are smokers. Chewing tobacco and snuff have been linked to cancer of the mouth, throat, and larynx.

2 Limit your intake of alcohol. Heavy drinking increases the risk of developing cancers of the mouth, throat, and larynx.

3 Eat properly balanced meals. Almost four out of ten cancer deaths are estimated to be related to diet. A low-fat, high-fiber diet reduces the risk of developing cancer of the colon. Try to eat more fresh fruits and vegetables. Cut down on fats, eggs, and charcoal-broiled and smoked foods.

4 Avoid overexposure to the sun. Suntanning, once thought to be a healthy activity, can lead to skin cancer. If you cannot avoid long periods of time in the sun, use a sunscreen to block out the sun's harmful rays.

5 Keep informed. When new carcinogens are discovered, avoid them as much as possible.

6 Know your body and recognize the warning signs of cancer if they develop. Visit your doctor immediately if you suspect a problem. Early detection is important in curing many cancers.

Lesson Review

The death rate from cancer in the United States has increased dramatically during the twentieth century. However, new methods of detection and treatment have raised the cure rates for many types of cancer. About one third of all cancer patients can now be cured. Many factors, such as the environment, heredity, and viruses, have been linked to the development of certain cancers. Many kinds of cancer can be prevented by avoiding known carcinogens and practicing good health habits.

1 Distinguish between a benign and a malignant tumor.

2 Define *carcinogen*.

3 What genetic factor may make cells grow uncontrollably?

4 List two methods of detecting cancer.

Other Diseases

Some noninfectious diseases are not as well known as heart disease and cancer, but they affect millions of Americans each year. Some of these diseases strike young people and become more serious over time. Other diseases result from the body's aging process. Most of the diseases resulting from aging have no cure, but many can be controlled through proper medical care. Scientists continue to look for cures for these diseases.

Diabetes

Over 10 million people in the United States suffer from diabetes mellitus, often called simply diabetes. **Diabetes mellitus** [*dy uh BEE tis muh LY tus*] is a condition in which the body does not produce or properly use insulin. Insulin is the hormone that carries glucose, or blood sugar, from the blood into the cells. Thus insulin is needed for the body to convert starches and sugars into energy.

Left untreated, diabetes can lead to very serious problems. High levels of sugar in the blood can cause poor circulation and nerve damage. These conditions may lead to severe pain in the limbs, blindness, kidney failure, and death. Small injuries may cause tissue death, which may require the amputation of a limb. Diabetes also increases the risk of developing atherosclerosis.

There are two types of diabetes—insulin-dependent diabetes and noninsulin-dependent diabetes. **Insulin-dependent diabetes** is the more serious but less common form. This form is probably hereditary. Insulin-dependent diabetes, which is also called juvenile-onset diabetes, usually begins in childhood and occurs when the pancreas does not make enough insulin. Without enough insulin, glucose builds up in the blood and the cells do not get the glucose they need. Symptoms of insulin-dependent diabetes include frequent urination accompanied by a very high level of thirst, fatigue, and rapid weight loss. Patients must receive insulin through injections, which they usually administer themselves.

Before insulin was discovered in 1921, almost all of these diabetics died from the disease. Now people with insulin-dependent diabetes can lead a long life by receiving injections of insulin and eating a proper diet. In addition, this disease may soon be cured with pancreas transplants.

Insulin-dependent diabetics often have difficulty balancing the levels of sugar and insulin in their bodies. For example, illness, physical activity, or even excitement may cause the body to use too much blood sugar. This leaves the patient with low blood sugar and too much insulin. A very low level of blood sugar and a high level of insulin can bring on **insulin shock.** The symptoms of insulin shock include dizziness, rapid pulse, excessive sweating, and paleness. This condition can be treated quickly by eating or drinking high-sugar foods such as orange juice.

An opposite condition occurs when there is too much sugar in the blood. A **diabetic coma** is a state of partial or complete unconsciousness brought on when the blood sugar level is very high

Figure 22–15 Patients with diabetes can monitor their blood sugar levels with meters such as this one.

and the insulin level is low. The person's pulse is weak and rapid, the skin is very dry, and large amounts of sugar are excreted in the urine. Without immediate medical attention, a diabetic coma may be fatal.

Noninsulin-dependent diabetes, or mature-onset diabetes, usually appears in adults. In this form of diabetes, the pancreas produces enough insulin, but the cells cannot take in glucose. This form of diabetes is most common among those who are obese. Obesity affects the cells so they do not take in glucose. People can inherit a tendency to develop noninsulin-dependent diabetes. The symptoms of noninsulin-dependent diabetes include blurred vision, fatigue, frequent infections, frequent urination, and increased thirst. This type of diabetes can usually be controlled by diet, exercise, and medicines. If not treated, the glucose level can build up and cause a diabetic coma.

Arthritis

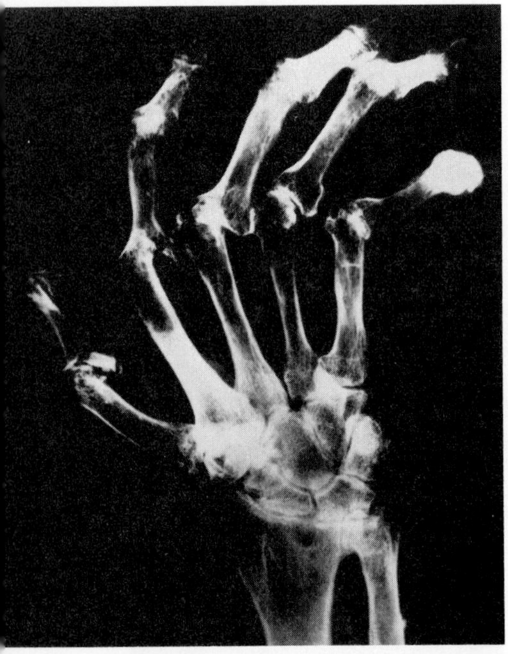

Most people develop some form of arthritis during their lifetime. Although few people die from it, arthritis affects more people than any other chronic disease. **Arthritis** is a family of diseases in which the joints in the body become swollen and sore. The general symptoms include pain and stiffness in the joints. Forms of arthritis may develop in both children and adults.

Osteoarthritis [*ahs tee oh ahr THRY tis*] is a disease in which the smooth layers of cartilage at the ends of the bones become rough. Normal joint movement becomes painful and difficult. Bony deposits may build up and make the affected joints appear knobby. Joints of the knees, hips, and spine are most commonly affected. Because osteoarthritis results from natural wear and tear, it most often affects older people. Osteoarthritis is the most common of all joint disorders.

Rheumatoid arthritis [*ROO muh toyd*] is a disease in which the membranes in the joints become swollen. It occurs in younger people, and is most common in the joints of the hands and feet. It also occurs in the wrists, ankles, knees, and neck. In addition to painful swollen joints, patients may experience fatigue, fever, muscle weakness, and weight loss. In many cases the disease causes inflammation in the heart muscle and blood vessels. While this disease may seem very serious, only one in ten patients becomes disabled by it.

Aspirin and other medicines can reduce some of the pain and swelling of arthritis. Special diets, heat, and physical therapy can also help. Surgery to replace badly diseased joints is an option for some patients with osteoarthritis. Daily activity will help prevent arthritis and minimize the symptoms after the disease develops.

Figure 22–16 This x-ray shows joint dislocation in the fingers caused by rheumatoid arthritis. The knobby joint in the thumb is caused by osteoarthritis.

The Aging Process and Disease

The aging process does not keep most older people from leading active lives. Many older Americans participate in regular athletic activities, travel, and continue to work in their seventies. Aging cannot be avoided, but good health habits, a well-balanced diet, and regular exercise can help reduce the health risks of aging. Continued physical activity and mental involvement actually slow down the aging process.

The aging process, however, does weaken many parts of the body. People who live into their sixties and beyond often suffer some problems that come with growing older. Among the most common problems of aging are failing eyesight and hearing, and loss of muscle tone and endurance.

As the heart, lungs, and kidneys age, they do not work as well. The lungs take in less oxygen, the heart pumps less blood, and the kidneys cannot rid the body of wastes as quickly as they once did. Body temperature is more difficult to regulate and older people often feel uncomfortable in the heat and cold. Two specific diseases that are often connected with aging are Parkinson's disease and senile dementia.

Parkinson's disease is a malfunction of the nervous system that causes muscle stiffness and tremors in the body. In this disease, certain nerve centers in the brain stop working correctly. It usually affects people over 50. Medicines are often successful in controlling the symptoms, but the disease cannot be cured.

Senile dementia is a group of disorders in which an older person becomes severely forgetful, confused, and out of touch with the surroundings. Symptoms include the loss of memory, the loss of thinking ability, the loss of certain physical movements, and a change in personality. Senility, as this condition is commonly known, is sometimes caused by arteriosclerosis in arteries that feed the brain. However, the most common cause of senility is **Alzheimer's disease,** a disorder resulting from increased loss of brain cells. More than 100,000 people die of Alzheimer's disease every year. There is no cure. Although most victims are older than 65, Alzheimer's disease may strike people in their forties and fifties.

The brain damage caused by senility cannot be reversed. Senile patients need almost constant care, as well as emotional support from their families. Not all old people who are confused or forgetful have senile dementia. Other treatable diseases sometimes produce similar symptoms.

Figure 22–17   People who keep active increase their chances of maintaining good health well into old age.

Lesson Review

Long-lasting diseases and diseases resulting from aging affect millions of Americans. Diseases of aging involve the gradual breakdown of the body's organs. Medical research continues to seek a better understanding of these diseases.

1 What is the cause of insulin shock?

2 What kind of arthritis produces swollen membranes in the joints?

3 List two symptoms of Parkinson's disease.

4 Define *senile dementia*.

Chapter Review

Vocabulary

Alzheimer's disease
angina pectoris
arteriosclerosis
arthritis
atherosclerosis
benign tumor
biopsy
blood pressure
cancer
carcinogen
cardiovascular disease
cerebral hemorrhage
cervical cancer
chemotherapy
cholesterol
coronary artery bypass
diabetes mellitus

diabetic coma
electrocardiogram
embolism
heart attack
heart failure
heart transplant
Hodgkin's disease
hypertension
immunotherapy
initiator
insulin-dependent diabetes
insulin shock
leukemia
malignant tumor
mastectomy
melanoma

metastasis
noninfectious disease
noninsulin-dependent diabetes
oncogene
oral cancer
osteoarthritis
pacemaker
Pap test
Parkinson's disease
promoter
radiation therapy
rheumatoid arthritis
senile dementia
stroke
testicular cancer
thrombosis

Using Vocabulary

Questions 1–11. On a separate sheet of paper, write the term from the column on the right that matches the phrase on the left.

1 cancer of the lymph nodes
2 deadly skin cancer that begins as a dark mole
3 substance or type of radiation that causes cancer
4 cancer of the bone marrow
5 blockage or rupture of a blood vessel in the brain
6 checkup in which the doctor takes cells from the cervix and vagina to examine for signs of cancer
7 gene that can make cells grow without control
8 record of the electrical impulses used to study heart action
9 blockage of an artery in the brain by a blood clot that has moved to the brain through the blood stream
10 group of diseases characterized by uncontrolled cell growth
11 test in which a tiny sample of tissue is surgically removed from the body

a stroke
b biopsy
c electrocardiogram
d embolism
e Hodgkin's disease
f melanoma
g carcinogen
h Pap test
i cancer
j leukemia
k oncogene

Interpreting Ideas

1 Describe five cardiovascular diseases, including their causes and symptoms.

2 Describe a stroke—what it is, what causes it, what its effects are, and what treatment is used.

3 What is the difference between a thrombosis and an embolism?

4 Describe three kinds of treatment for cancer.

5 Why are low-sodium diets prescribed for people who have heart failure?

6 What test can a doctor use to determine whether or not a person has a heart disease?

7 Describe the three types of skin cancer.

8 What are the warning signs of oral cancer?

9 What kind of diet may lead to the development of rectal and colon cancer? What is one symptom of this kind of cancer?

10 What role do oncogenes play in the development of cancer?

11 Compare the causes and symptoms of rheumatoid arthritis with those of osteoarthritis.

12 What are the symptoms of Parkinson's disease? What causes the disease?

13 Describe the two forms of diabetes.

14 List four ways to reduce your risk of developing cancer.

15 How do an initiator and a promoter work together to produce cancer?

16 What are the early signs of lung cancer?

17 Describe the most frequently performed type of heart surgery.

18 Describe four ways that medicines are used to control cardiovascular diseases.

19 Compare the symptoms of a heart attack with those of angina pectoris.

20 List four ways to reduce your risk of cardiovascular diseases.

Applying Concepts

1 Of the following foods, state which you would reduce or eliminate from your diet in order to protect yourself against heart disease: chicken, carrots, butter, steak, broccoli, cereal with added sugar, salt, fish, processed meats.

2 Why may stroke victims suffer from depression and shifts in mood?

3 How do cancer cells differ from normal cells?

4 A 45-year-old woman who has smoked for 27 years has developed a deep smoker's hack, shortness of breath, and chest pains. Given the woman's medical history, what disease might you suspect?

5 If you ate no cholesterol, but had a diet high in saturated fats, would you be in danger of developing atherosclerosis? Why or why not?

6 If you were exposed to low levels of a carcinogen and to few promoters, would you have a high or low risk of developing cancer? Why?

7 Name two serious diseases that might result if an older patient develops arteriosclerosis in the arteries that feed the brain.

8 Lately, when playing actively with his children, Jose's father has had sharp chest pains and felt as though he couldn't breathe. What might Jose's father be experiencing, and what should he do about it?

9 Why do you think that cardiovascular diseases are now the leading causes of death?

10 At age 23, Lynn experienced an unexplained weight loss accompanied by joint pain and stiffness. What disease might Lynn have?

Projects

1 Some research suggests that there is a Type C, or cancer-prone, personality. Find out the traits that characterize this personality.

2 Learn about several cultures around the world that have low rates of heart disease. Research their diets, and make menus of representative foods and meals that are low in saturated fats and sodium. Then prepare a meal of a range of dishes from your menus.

3 Invite an oncologist (cancer specialist) or a radiologist to discuss the latest methods of detecting and treating cancer or the status of current research aimed at eradicating cancer.

4 Create a bulletin board that illustrates each of the guidelines for lowering your chances of developing cancer. You may include the anti-cancer diet recommendations put out by a committee of the National Academy of Sciences, as well as the guidelines of the American Cancer Society.

5 The cause of Alzheimer's disease is not known. At your school or local library, research this disease. What suspected causes are under investigation? What are the effects of the disease? What parts of the brain are affected by the disease? Is treatment available for the disease?

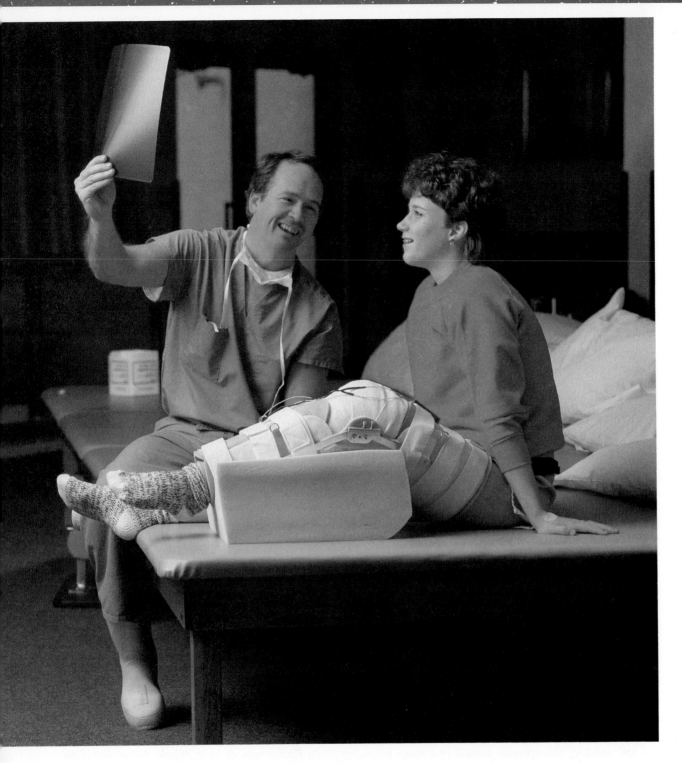

Clear and open communication is the key to receiving good health care.

CHAPTER TWENTY-THREE

◆ SELECTING ◆

Health Care

Can you talk comfortably with your doctor? Do you discuss your condition, the results of your medical exams, and prescribed treatments? When you are ill or injured, do you know where to go for help? If you answered *no* to any of these questions, you are not getting everything you need from your health care services.

You are a consumer of health care services and products. Your health behaviors are important in maintaining good health. Health care providers can also help keep you healthy. To receive good care, you need to communicate with your health care providers. You also need to know who they are and what services they can provide. You can help yourself receive the health care you need.

Objectives

- List the rights of patients.

- Describe how to choose a doctor and how to prepare for a physical examination.

- List sudden and long-term symptoms for which you should seek medical help.

- Name four health professionals other than medical doctors.

- Describe four health care settings.

- Describe a health maintenance organization and major medical insurance.

- Compare two medical insurance programs sponsored by the federal government.

- Explain the difference between prescription medicines and over-the-counter medicines.

- Explain how to prevent accidents with medicines.

- Describe how to avoid medical quackery.

You and Your Doctor

Your great-grandparents were probably born at home. When they or their children were sick, the family doctor probably visited them at home. Today most babies are born in hospitals. You probably see your doctor at an office or clinic. One thing has remained constant through the years, however. A trusting relationship with your doctor is still an important part of a personal health plan.

Choosing a Doctor

Generally, the term *doctor* refers to a medical doctor or physician. A **medical doctor** is someone who has earned either the degree of doctor of medicine (M.D.) or doctor of osteopathy (D.O.). To practice medicine, a doctor must be licensed by his or her state. The requirements include the degree of M.D. or D.O., a year of study working in a hospital as an intern, and passing a test. A license allows a doctor to identify diseases, write prescriptions, and treat patients. Your doctor should have diplomas, a medical license, and certificates of any special training displayed in his or her office.

The best time to choose a doctor is while you are well. In choosing a doctor, consider the doctor's background, training, and personality. Choosing a doctor with whom you feel comfortable will help establish good communication and trust. State or local medical societies and hospitals can give you a list of qualified doctors. People you know may also make recommendations.

When you compare doctors, you will find that doctors have different types of practices. If the doctor is not on the staff of an organization such as a hospital, he or she is in **private practice.** A doctor in private practice may work alone or in a group. Some patients like knowing that the same doctor will provide treatment during each visit, and prefer a doctor working alone. Other patients prefer going to a group, because they know that one of the doctors is always available. Even though they may not always see the same doctor, the patients feel confident of receiving care.

The Rights of Patients

As a health consumer, you have rights and responsibilities. Patients have the right to open communication with their doctors. However, all communication and records of medical care should be kept confidential. Only the patient and the patient's parents or guardians should be given information about a patient.

Patients have a right to know the results of their doctor's evaluation. The doctor should explain any symptoms, the treatment, and the diagnosis. A **diagnosis** [*dy ug NOH sis*] is the identification of a medical condition. If the doctor uses terms you do not understand, ask for a simpler explanation.

If the doctor prescribes a treatment, you have the right and the responsibility to know why you need the treatment, how much it will cost, what risks are involved, and what your choices are. If the doctor prescribes surgery or other major forms of treatment, you will probably want to go to another doctor to get a second

Figure 23–1   As a patient you have the right to receive proper treatment and information.

Rights of Patients
Confidentiality
Good communication
Ethical treatment
Second opinion
Trust
Knowledge of:
alternative treatments
cost of treatment
results of evaluations
risks of procedures

opinion. A good doctor will not be offended if you want a second opinion. In fact, many encourage it and supply patients with the names of consulting physicians.

If you feel that your doctor has treated you unethically, discuss the situation with him or her. Many problems can be worked out between a doctor and patient. If you still have a problem, you can take action. You can contact your local medical society, state licensing board, or Better Business Bureau. You have a right to quality medical care and ethical treatment.

The Physical Examination

An important part of preventive medicine is a regular physical examination. A physical exam may reveal medical problems. Your doctor may also discover effects of a poor diet or other unhealthy habits that may lead to problems later. In general, teenagers with no major health problems should be examined every two years. Teenagers who are active in sports should be examined every year. The frequency may increase in later adulthood, depending on the individual's condition.

You can prepare for a physical examination. The first part of an examination is usually the preparation of a medical history. A **medical history** is a record of the medical problems and events of you and your family. You will be asked many questions about your physical condition, and the problems and diseases of family members. In preparation, you should know about past illnesses, allergies, injuries, surgery, and immunizations. The history provides background information needed for the doctor to understand your health care needs.

When you visit your doctor, be as detailed as possible in describing any symptoms you have. Tell your doctor all your symptoms, not just the ones that you think are important. You can help by knowing your body well enough to notice changes that may be symptoms of a problem. Some of the conditions that require a doctor's attention are listed in Figure 23-2.

If you think your illness or injury may be life-threatening, never hesitate to go to a medical emergency room. Always notify your parents or guardians if you are seeking medical help. You may need their permission.

Sudden Symptoms	
	severe pain
	high fever
	continued vomiting or diarrhea
	difficulty breathing
	sudden vision problems
	a serious accident
	broken bones
	animal bites and swelling bee stings
	blood in the phlegm
	blood in the stools or urine
Long-term Symptoms	
	a mysterious rash
	unusual weight gain or loss
	frequent or painful urination
	long-lasting fatigue
	long-lasting headaches
	continued depression
	slow-healing cuts
	a mole that bleeds

Figure 23–2   See a doctor if you have any of these sudden or long-term symptoms.

Lesson Review

It is important to find a doctor with whom you feel comfortable. A doctor should respect your rights to honest communication and confidentiality, to know your diagnosis, and to ethical treatment. You can work effectively with your doctor by paying attention to changes in your physical condition.

1 What are three rights of patients?

2 What are three sudden symptoms that require a doctor's immediate attention?

3 What types of information make up a medical history?

The Physical Examination

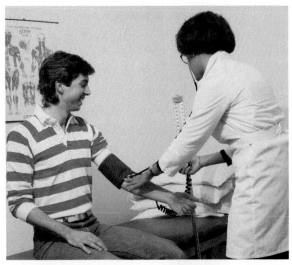

Blood Pressure   A physical exam usually begins after you have given your medical history. The order of the exam varies from doctor to doctor, and different exams may include different tests.

Many physicians begin with a blood pressure reading. The doctor wraps a rubber cuff around your upper arm and listens to your pulse with a stethoscope. Then the doctor pumps air into the cuff to tighten it until no blood can pass through the arteries and there is no pulse. To read your systolic pressure, the doctor releases air from the cuff until your heartbeat pushes blood past the cuff. This produces a pulse. To read your diastolic pressure, your doctor releases more air until your blood pushes through your arteries continuously.

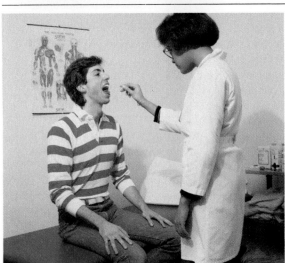

Eyes, Ears, Nose, Throat   Doctors usually check these organs as a group. To test your vision you may be asked to read an eye chart. Your doctor shines a light into your eyes to examine the optic nerves and the blood vessels in the retinas. Your doctor also looks into your ear canals and checks your eardrums. A middle ear infection changes the shape of the eardrum.

By holding your tongue down with a tongue depressor, your doctor can look into your throat. When you open your mouth and say "ahh," your doctor is looking at your teeth, tongue, throat, and tonsils. Swollen or red tonsils are signs that you are fighting an infection. Your doctor also feels the lymph nodes in your neck to see if they are swollen.

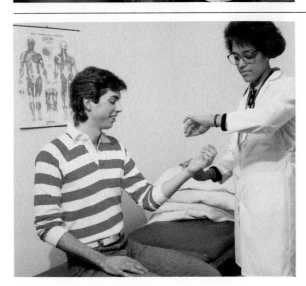

Heart and Pulse   Your doctor gets information about your heart by observing you breathe, feeling your heartbeat, and tapping your chest. These simple tests tell the doctor about the rhythm and rate of the heartbeat, and any problem in the structure of the heart or aorta. With a stethoscope the doctor can listen to the heart valves opening and closing, and can also hear any disturbance in the heartbeats.

A doctor or nurse checks your pulse while you are relaxed. Your doctor may ask you to run in place for a minute or two and check your pulse again. Then your doctor may check the time it takes your pulse to return to its resting rate.

Lungs Your doctor taps on your chest and back and listens to your lungs with a stethoscope to check for any problems. Healthy lungs produce sounds that are different from those produced by scarred or diseased lungs. Signs of problems include wheezing, hollow thuds, and a rasping breath. Such sounds may indicate blockage or moisture in the airways, or inflamed lung tissue. Your doctor may check your lung capacity by asking you to breathe deeply or by having you blow steadily into a tube for as long as possible. If these tests reveal any problems, your doctor may order a chest x-ray.

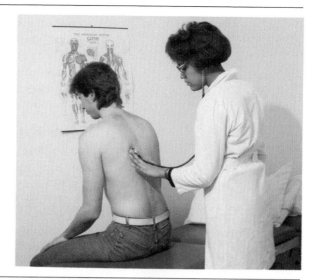

Abdomen, Rectum Your doctor can feel the position, size, and general condition of several abdominal organs when you are relaxed. The doctor checks for unusual lumps on the organs, and any tenderness or pain in this area. Your doctor may also use a gloved finger to examine your rectum. This may reveal growths, hemorrhoids, or irregularities in nearby organs.

A doctor examines male reproductive organs visually and by gentle manipulation. To check for a hernia, a doctor may ask a boy to stand up and cough. In examining female reproductive organs, a doctor uses gloved fingers and an instrument that holds the walls of the vagina apart. The doctor can then see the cervix.

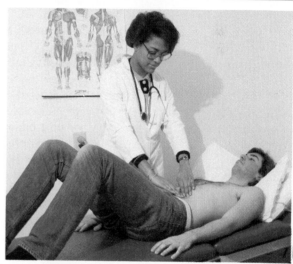

Nervous System, Skeletal System, Muscles Your doctor may end the exam with a few basic tests of your nervous system and muscles. The most familiar of these is a test of the knee-jerk reflex. Your doctor taps lightly with a rubber hammer just below your kneecap, and watches for the proper reflex action. Your doctor also checks as you flex your arms and legs, bend at the waist, and perform other movements. The doctor or nurse will weigh you, and your doctor will note any weight problem.

During the exam, your doctor will have checked your skin for rashes, bruises, moles, and signs of infection. If any problems have been revealed during the examination, your doctor may order laboratory tests of your blood or urine.

Selecting Health Services

Until the middle of this century, most physicians received only general training, and there were few types of health care providers. Today, the rapid advances in medical knowledge and technology often require special training. Now if you become ill, many people may help with your treatment. Each of these people will be specially prepared to provide part of your medical care.

The Health Care Team

Your family physician can take care of most of your medical problems. When he or she faces a problem that is in another specialty, your physician may work with other specialists. Your doctor may ask for advice, or ask another doctor to take over treating you for the particular condition. Usually, you will continue to see your family doctor for any other problems.

There are many specialties. One example is psychiatry. A psychiatrist is a specialist who deals with mental illness and emotional disorders. Figure 23-3 lists several medical specialties.

Nurses   No matter where you go for medical care, you will probably deal with a nurse. Nurses are specially trained and licensed health professionals who work in hospitals, doctor's offices, schools, factories, and community health agencies. They have various levels of training and responsibility. Some work very closely with one doctor, while others work in busy hospitals or visit patients in their homes.

Registered nurses (R.N.'s) are graduates of two-year or three-year hospital programs or college nursing programs, and are licensed by their states. Most R.N.'s work in hospitals. They are needed in all forms of health care, from the nursery to the operating room. **Nurse practitioners** are R.N.'s who have had further training in a specialty. Nurse practitioners perform many tasks that were once done only by doctors. They usually work in clinics or with doctors in private practice.

Licensed practical nurses (L.P.N.'s) complete one-year or two-year programs. L.P.N.'s help registered nurses in all health care settings. They are often responsible for patients' basic needs, such as feeding and bathing.

Other Team Members   Modern medicine has created the need for many specialists other than doctors. Each branch of health care has its own specialties. This includes dental care and mental health as well as care of the whole body. Dental care is covered in more detail in Chapter 2. Mental health is covered in Unit 2.

Physician's assistants are people who work with physicians to provide certain types of health care once given only by doctors. This includes certain types of physical examinations and treatments done in the doctor's office.

Physical therapists, occupational therapists, and speech therapists are trained to help patients with disabilities. Very often, dis-

Figure 23-3   Medical specialties

Anesthesiologist
Administers anesthetics

Cardiologist
Heart disease

Dermatologist
Skin, hair, and scalp

Family Practitioner/Internist
The whole body

Gynecologist
Female reproductive organs

Neurologist
Brain, spine, and nerves

Obstetrician
Pregnant women and delivery of babies

Pediatrician
Infants and children

Psychiatrist
Emotional and mental disorders

Radiologist
Diagnosis and treatment using x-rays and isotopes

Urologist
Male and female urinary systems and male reproductive organs

abilities are caused by strokes, accidents, or other conditions. These therapists may work in a variety of health care settings. Technicians work in laboratories, x-ray departments, and elsewhere to do tests and other diagnostic procedures.

On a visit to the dentist you will probably be seen by other dental professionals as well. A **dental hygienist** (*hy JEE nist*) is a health care specialist who has learned how to treat tooth and gum disease in a four-year college program. A **dental assistant** is a person usually trained in a technical school to examine teeth and gums, take x-rays, and clean teeth.

A **psychologist** (*sy KAHL uh jist*) is a person who has earned a master's degree or a doctor of philosophy (Ph.D.) in psychology and is qualified to diagnose and work with people who have emotional problems. Although psychologists have the title of doctor, they are not physicians.

Professionals without doctorates who help people with mental or emotional problems are **mental health counselors** and **social workers.** Some counselors and social workers specialize in one area, such as drug or alcohol abuse. Many have master's degrees in counseling or social work.

Figure 23–4 An x-ray technician knows how to position the body so that the internal organs photograph properly.

Health Care Settings

Medical care from prevention through treatment can be classified as primary or secondary care. **Primary care** is preventive medicine, routine checkups, and the diagnosis and treatment of common medical problems. It can be given at a doctor's office, clinic, or an independent health center. **Secondary care** is treatment of medical problems in hospitals.

HEALTH + Technology

COMPUTERIZED MEDICAL RECORDS—Computers are playing new roles in hospitals. They are helping diagnose and treat patients. At one hospital, intensive care patients have bedside monitors that record their blood pressure, heart rate, temperature, and brain pressure. The information is displayed as graphs on computer screens. At another hospital, surgically inserted monitors measure stomach acid in patients who suffer from high acid levels. The monitors feed into a computer that displays charts on the patients' conditions.

Doctors also are beginning to use computers from the first step of diagnosis. For instance, one computer system developed for hospitals contains a huge library of medical information. Each patient's medical history is added. In an examination a doctor types in the patient's symptoms. The computer then identifies disorders that fit the symptoms and recommends further tests. Test results are fed back to the computer, which also lists medications and surgical procedures for each diagnosed disorder. Of course, the doctor still selects treatment.

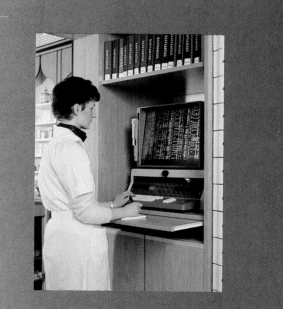

1 What new roles are computers playing in hospitals?
2 How does one system help in the first step of diagnosis?

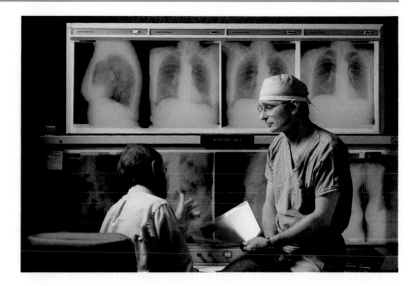

Figure 23–5 The x-ray department serves an essential role in most hospitals.

Hospitals and Clinics Today, the modern hospital is a place to diagnose and treat many kinds of illnesses and injuries. The care provided by all hospitals is reviewed by a special commission on hospitals. Most hospitals treat a range of problems. Some hospitals treat only one kind of problem, such as cancer, ear and eye problems, and mental illness.

Medical centers contain groups of hospital services that can treat almost any medical problem. These centers have separate sections that deal with specific medical problems.

You may have been to a hospital or medical center emergency room. An **emergency room** receives victims of accidents and people with sudden illnesses. You should visit an emergency room only if you have a medical emergency. Illnesses and injuries are classified into one of three catagories—emergency, serious but stable, or not serious. If you go with a problem that is not serious, you may have to wait while others are treated.

Parts of hospitals that treat medical problems that are not emergencies are called **hospital clinics.** These clinics often arrange for follow-up care. Patients are seen as outpatients. **Outpatient care** is medical attention given only at an office or a special section of a hospital or clinic. Outpatients do not stay overnight in the hospital. Medical care given to a patient staying overnight in a hospital is called **inpatient care.**

Low-cost and free walk-in clinics are health care options that offer general medical care for people who have low incomes. Sometimes they treat young adults with special concerns, such as family planning or sexually transmitted diseases.

Independent clinics that provide primary care and treat minor medical emergencies are called **episodic treatment centers** [*ep ih SAHD ik*]. These centers were first established in the 1970s. You do not need an appointment for a visit. There is no membership requirement and most are open seven days a week. They often do not have the variety of doctors or the equipment to treat serious health problems.

Health **History**

The first health care institution in the United States to be called a *hospital* was founded in Philadelphia in 1752.

Nursing Homes   Because of medical problems, many people require continuous care. **Nursing homes** are health care centers that provide long-term care for those who are chronically ill. Nursing homes today house over one million Americans. Most of these people are elderly. The patients cannot care for themselves. They may receive help eating, bathing, getting dressed, or taking medicines. If medical problems become more serious, they are treated at a hospital.

Care in the Home   Many people who need some medical care live in private homes but receive the help of a visiting nurse. A **visiting nurse** is a health care specialist who visits people who are ill or recuperating in their homes. The nurse helps them take medicines, eat, bathe, and care for their general health. Tasks that do not require a nurse's training may be handled by an aide. Without a visiting nurse, many people would have to stay in a hospital or nursing home to receive basic care that could safely be provided at home.

Hospice   A growing number of people who know they are dying choose a type of care provided by a hospice. A **hospice** [*HAHS pis*] is a system of medical care intended to make a dying patient more comfortable. Hospices provide pain control, spiritual care, and programs about grief for the family. The hospice philosophy is that the dying patient should be made as comfortable as possible, and the surviving family members should be helped to adjust to their loss. Hospice care is provided at home when possible. Some hospices have inpatient facilities as well. Family members, pets, and personal possessions are welcomed at all hours. Most hospices are separate from hospitals. Others are special units within hospitals. Hospices may be staffed by doctors, nurses, social workers, chaplains, and others who can provide special services to dying patients. Family members are also trained to help care for the patient.

Figure 23–6   Dr. Elisabeth Kübler-Ross pioneered the hospice movement in the United States and helped change medical views on death and dying.

Lesson Review

You have many choices about the types of health care you receive. Medical advances have led to an increase in the number of health care specialists who detect and treat illnesses. All of these health care options offer you the opportunity to receive the type of care you need.

1 Name three specialists who help patients with disabilities.

2 List two health professionals who care for teeth and gums.

3 What type of care includes overnight stays in a hospital?

4 List four health care settings.

5 What type of nurse goes to patients' homes to help care for them there?

Selecting Health Insurance

Americans spend billions of dollars each year on health care. A ten-minute visit to your family doctor may cost $25, and an organ transplant could cost $100,000 or more. Why does health care cost so much? Think of all the medical staff and modern equipment needed for checkups, hospital stays, and surgery. The cost of a night in any hospital often is four times as much as the cost of a night in a hotel. The left-hand pie chart in Figure 23-7 shows why this is so. Your hospital payments go toward many salaries and the cost of running very expensive equipment, in addition to the cost of your food and lodging.

Because medical costs can be so high, about 85 percent of Americans have health insurance. **Insurance** divides the possible health costs of all the insured people among them. If you have insurance, you pay the insurance company a steady amount. When you receive medical care, your insurance company pays most or all of the cost. The right-hand pie chart in Figure 23-7 shows how much of hospital expenses patients pay directly. As you can see, even though patient costs are high, they actually cover only a small portion of the costs of running hospitals. What part of hospital costs are covered by insurance payments?

You probably are covered by your parents' insurance now. Most adults either buy health insurance for themselves or receive health insurance as a benefit of employment.

Figure 23–7 Where the typical patient's dollar goes *(left),* **and a breakdown of the sources of hospital funding** *(right)*

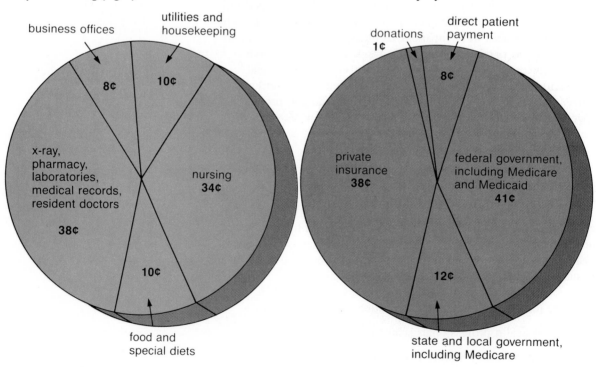

Source: Massachusetts General Hospital

Source: American Hospital Association
Health Care Financing Administration

Understanding Insurance Terms

Anyone buying health insurance pays a premium. A **premium** is a set amount of money paid each year to cover the cost of health care received during the year. The premium generally covers health care for three areas: hospital care, physicians' charges, and other charges such as outpatient medicines and ambulances.

Your insurance agreement will explain that these three types of coverage may apply only to a certain number of days in the hospital or only for part of a doctor's fees. If you do not have full coverage, you will have to pay the part of the hospital or doctors' fees not paid by the insurance company.

Major medical insurance is a plan that offers more protection by paying large costs not usually covered by other kinds of health insurance. When you are injured or ill, you pay a deductible. A **deductible** is a flat fee you pay subtracted from the insurance company's payment. It usually ranges between $100 and $500. Your major medical insurance usually covers 80 percent of the balance of the bill. In addition to the deductible, you pay the remaining 20 percent of the bill. Thus, with a $1000 medical bill, you might pay a $500 deductible and $100 of the balance.

Before buying insurance, you should read several policies. An **insurance policy** is a contract offering certain services in return for certain premiums. Check your policy. What are the limits to its coverage? Is there a deductible? What percentage of the bill will you have to pay? Make sure your policy covers the kinds of care you might need. Most policies do not cover the costs of services meant to prevent illness.

Health Maintenance Organizations

A medical group that provides a variety of medical services only for its members is a **health maintenance organization,** or HMO. Services may be provided at an HMO center or in the offices of member doctors. HMOs usually put more emphasis on preventive medicine. **Preventive medicine** is the use of practices by both patients and health care workers that promote health and help avoid medical problems. If hospital care is needed, you may be asked to go to an institution that has a contract with the HMO. Those who operate HMOs hope that preventive medicine will keep their patients healthy and out of the hospital. This will keep the cost of the patients' care low.

Because their low costs are passed on to the patients, HMOs have become very popular. The HMOs can be convenient because a single agency provides all services. Some HMOs operate like clinics, in which a patient may see a different doctor in each visit. Other HMOs allow patients to select a primary care physician.

A variation of the HMO is the preferred provider organization. A **preferred provider organization,** or PPO, is a plan that pays for medical costs if patients use doctors who are part of the organization. PPOs often provide a range of services similar to those at an HMO, and allow patients to choose their doctors. Some PPOs will pay all doctors' fees if the doctors are part of the PPO, or only a portion if the doctor is not a PPO member.

Medical care costs in 1965 were 2½ times larger than they were 30 years before. In the 20 years from 1965 to 1985, however, medical costs rose by 4½ times.

Figure 23–8 People who are 65 or older can receive health care through Medicare regardless of their incomes.

Medicaid and Medicare

Even people who cannot afford to buy health insurance on their own, or who cannot get these benefits from an employer, have choices in health care. In 1965, the United States Congress established two public health insurance programs. One is for people who cannot afford the cost of health insurance, and the other is for older people regardless of income. As you can see in Figure 23-7, the federal government pays for a large portion of the nation's medical bills.

Medicaid is a public health insurance program that pays for the health care of people who have low incomes. It also covers families whose children depend on government aid for food and housing. Medicaid is paid for by federal, state, and local taxes. It covers many medical costs for both inpatient and outpatient care. The range of services for which Medicaid pays varies from state to state. People eligible for Medicaid can apply at their local welfare office.

Medicare is a federal health insurance plan for people 65 or older and others who receive Social Security benefits, such as those who are disabled. It pays for part of the cost of hospital care and some follow-up care. Senior citizens who pay an extra amount can get assistance in paying for doctors' services.

The government reimburses hospitals for their Medicare patients in a new, controversial way. Payment is based on diagnosis related groups (DRGs). A DRG is a category of diagnoses for which any hospital gets the same reimbursement. For example, one DRG includes heart failure. All hospitals receive the same reimbursement for each patient with heart failure. If a hospital spends more money on the patient than the DRG rate, the reimbursement will not cover costs. If a hospital spends less than the DRG rate, it makes money on the reimbursement. Some insurance companies are also adopting the DRG system.

Lesson Review

If you are ill or injured, the cost of your treatment could create financial problems. To prevent these kinds of problems, many people buy medical insurance. This insurance covers the cost of most hospital care, surgery, and doctors' fees. People now have several choices about their insurance. Many of these focus on preventive care. The government also provides insurance for those who cannot afford treatment.

1 What is an insurance premium?

2 What is the name for a flat fee you pay subtracted from the insurance company's payment?

3 What document should you read before you buy insurance?

4 Who receives medical services from an HMO?

5 Which government insurance plan pays for hospital care for people who receive Social Security benefits?

Using Medicines Wisely

A substance used to treat medical problems or diseases is a **medicine.** Today, with so many medicines and health products available, people must learn how to choose them wisely and use them safely. Agencies also exist to review product safety, provide public information, and help pass laws that protect the public from faulty products.

Medicines and Their Labels

A medicine that cannot be bought without a doctor's permission is called a **prescription medicine.** Prescription medicines are prepared and given out by a pharmacist. A **pharmacist** is a health care specialist who has studied the use of medicines in treating diseases and has learned how to prepare medications. A pharmacist usually has a college degree and a state license to prepare and sell medicines.

Your doctor writes the prescription for the pharmacist, usually using medical terms and abbreviations. The pharmacist prepares the medicine and types up the label for the container based on the prescription. Sometimes the doctor's abbreviations appear on the label. More often, the pharmacist translates them into more common language, as in Figure 23-9. Pharmacists are excellent sources of information about prescription and nonprescription medicines. If you want to know more about any medication, ask your pharmacist.

Medicines are sold under different brand names, created by the manufacturers. Many medicines are also sold under the generic name. The **generic name** [*juh NEHR ik*] is the common name of the substance and is established by health professionals. For example, *tetracycline* is the generic name for one type of antibiotic. Several companies make tetracycline, each sold with its own brand name. Ask your doctor about writing a prescription for the generic name of the medicine. Generic medicines are usually cheaper than those sold under brand names, but they may not have undergone the same tests for effectiveness. Your doctor may specify the brand name at times.

Figure 23–9 Make sure you read your prescription medicine labels carefully. A mistake in reading a label could have serious results.

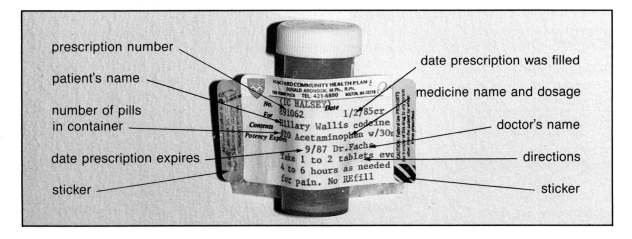

prescription number

patient's name

number of pills in container

date prescription expires

sticker

date prescription was filled

medicine name and dosage

doctor's name

directions

sticker

| Read the label carefully. |
| Ask the pharmacist if you have questions about the medicine, the label, or the directions. |
| Follow directions completely. |
| Take the medicine for the length of time suggested by the doctor, even if you are feeling better. |
| Call your doctor immediately if you notice any unusual reaction after taking the medicine. |
| Keep medicines in their original containers. |
| Store medicines in a cool, dry, dark place away from food products. |
| Do not take anyone else's medicine, even though your symptoms may seem similar. |
| Destroy medicines when the expiration date has passed. |
| Do not use alcohol or other drugs while taking medication. |

Figure 23–10 Guidelines for using prescription medicines

When your doctor prescribes a medicine, he or she should tell you what the medicine should do for you, exactly how you should take it, and how long you should take it. You also should be told about possible side effects. A **side effect** is an unexpected or undesirable reaction to a medicine. Many medicines, for example, may cause side effects of drowsiness or an upset stomach. People who have side effects from any substance should tell their doctors. If you get a prescription from your doctor, be sure both your doctor and pharmacist know about any other medicines you are taking. Some combinations of medicines may also cause side effects. Pharmacists often keep records of all the medicines prescribed for patients, so that they can check for potentially harmful combinations. If your doctor does not tell you about your medicines, be sure to ask.

Many medicines can be purchased without asking a doctor. Medicines that can be bought without a prescription are called **over-the-counter medicines.** Hundreds of medicines for colds, headaches, and other medical problems are found in supermarkets and on the drugstore shelf.

Whether you are taking prescription medicines or over-the-counter medicines, you should follow label directions and warnings very carefully. All medicine labels should list the name of the medicine and directions for taking it. All medicines should carry any necessary warnings, such as ''Do not take with food or milk.'' Labels on over-the-counter medicines will list possible side effects and other product safety information. Never take medications with alcohol or other drugs. Prescription medicines will list the name of the patient, the prescription date, how often to take the medicine, how many refills you may get, and an expiration date. The **expiration date** is the date after which the medicine may no longer be fresh or useful.

You can help prevent accidents with medicines if you keep your medicine storage up to date. Check the contents once a month. Destroy medicines if their expiration date has passed.

Health Bulletin

Taking some medicines with carbonated soft drinks or acid fruit juices causes them to dissolve quickly in the stomach. They are absorbed into the blood stream more slowly there than in the intestines. Taken with a full glass of water, medicines are carried quickly to the intestines.

Get rid of prescription medicines that you are no longer taking under a doctor's care. Destroy any medicines that have changed in color or odor.

Many doctors recommend against keeping medicines in a bathroom medicine cabinet. Small children can climb on the sink and get into the cabinet. Humidity can also harm some medicines. Medicines should be kept in a cool, dry place.

Safeguarding Against Quackery

A few people in every field claim to have products that work wonders, but are actually frauds. Probably none does so much harm as the medical quack. **Quackery** is selling products as cures when they have little or no healing power. The quack is the person who promotes the use of these worthless medical products.

Many years ago, quacks traveled by horse-pulled wagons from town to town performing medicine shows. They were entertaining, and the quacks claimed to have a fast cure for diseases and injuries. This kind of show does not exist today, but medical quacks still do. Useless products are sold through the mail, by telephone, and door-to-door. Quacks take advantage of fads, and they profit from the despair and fears of others. Quacks often prey on people who seek help for conditions and diseases that have no current cure. These problems range from baldness to arthritis and some forms of cancer.

How can you avoid becoming a victim of medical quackery? Do not believe guarantees. Beware of secret remedies or people who try to scare you into using a product. Ask questions. Talk to your doctor. Every product should have been tested for safety and usefulness through scientific studies.

Government, business, and private groups have been formed to prevent quackery and encourage proper product testing. The U.S. Food and Drug Administration (FDA) is an agency of the federal government that reviews research on food and medical products before they can be sold. This makes sure that they meet certain quality standards. Contact the FDA if you suspect medical quackery. You can also contact your area Better Business Bureau or, if the mail is involved, the U.S. Postal Service.

Figure 23–11 **In the past, medicines sold by quacks were advertized in colorful and inviting ways. The overblown claims convinced many people to buy the often useless preparations.**

Lesson Review

Some medicines are prepared especially for you by a pharmacist following a doctor's order. You can buy other medicines without a doctor's order. When taking any medicine, you should read and follow the advice on the label. Your doctor or pharmacist can also help you become a wise buyer of health care.

1 How are prescription medicines different from over-the-counter medicines?

2 Define *expiration date*.

3 Give two examples of conditions or diseases that quacks claim to cure.

Chapter Review

Vocabulary

deductible	licensed practical nurse	physician's assistant
dental assistant	major medical insurance	preferred provider organization
dental hygienist	Medicaid	premium
diagnosis	medical center	prescription medicine
emergency room	medical doctor	preventive medicine
episodic treatment center	medical history	primary care
expiration date	Medicare	private practice
generic name	medicine	psychologist
health maintenance organization	mental health counselor	quackery
hospice	nurse practitioner	registered nurse
hospital clinic	nursing home	secondary care
inpatient care	outpatient care	side effect
insurance	over-the-counter medicine	social worker
insurance policy	pharmacist	visiting nurse

Using Vocabulary

Questions 1–14. On a separate sheet of paper, write the term from the column on the right that identifies the phrase on the left.

1 the use of practices that promote health and help avoid medical problems
2 medical care to make a dying patient more comfortable
3 common name of a substance; established by health professionals
4 record of past and present medical problems
5 medical attention given only at an office or clinic
6 health care specialist who prepares medicines
7 identification of a medical problem
8 parts of hospitals that treat problems other than emergencies
9 nurse who is highly trained to provide specialized care
10 preventive medicine, routine checkups, and the diagnosis and treatment of common medical problems
11 fraud, or selling products as cures when they have little or no healing power
12 health care specialist who has learned how to treat tooth and gum disease in a four-year college program
13 unexpected or undesirable reaction to a medicine
14 the practice of a doctor who is not on the staff of an organization such as a hospital

a medical history
b quackery
c private practice
d nurse practitioner
e dental hygienist
f preventive medicine
g hospice
h pharmacist
i primary care
j hospital clinic
k generic name
l diagnosis
m outpatient care
n side effect

Interpreting Ideas

1 How can you prepare for a medical history?

2 From the patient's point of view, what is one advantage of a doctor in private practice working alone? in a group?

3 List five symptoms for which you should seek medical help.

4 Describe four settings where people can seek health care.

5 Where could you receive primary care? secondary care?

6 Describe the work of four health professionals other than medical doctors.

7 What is the difference between a prescription medicine and an over-the-counter medicine?

8 Describe the hospice philosophy. What does a hospice provide for the patient and the family?

9 Describe two medical insurance programs sponsored by the federal government.

10 Under what conditions might the care of a visiting nurse be preferred to staying in a nursing home?

11 What is an HMO? Why have HMOs become very popular?

12 What can you do to avoid becoming a victim of medical quackery?

13 What is the principal difference between an HMO and a PPO?

14 As buyers of medical services, patients have certain rights. List three of them.

15 List three ways you can help prevent accidents with medicines.

16 What is one function of the Food and Drug Administration?

17 When your doctor prescribes a medicine, what should he or she tell you about it?

18 What areas of health care are generally covered by the insurance premium?

19 When might you want to ask another doctor for a second opinion?

20 Why is the best time to choose a doctor when you are well?

Applying Concepts

1 You receive a sports-related injury and believe that you may have broken a bone. Which of the specialists listed in Figure 23-3 might you see for diagnosis?

2 A 45-year-old woman with two children and a limited income becomes disabled from a work-related injury. For what public health insurance program(s) might she be eligible?

3 What is the advantage of a hospice over a traditional hospital setting in caring for terminally ill patients?

4 If you had a choice between buying major medical insurance and joining an HMO, which would you choose? Why?

5 Your medical treatment for a brief illness cost $800. Your insurance plan covered 80 percent of the balance of your bill after you had paid a deductible of $100. How much of your bill was paid by your insurance? How much did you have to pay in all?

6 Some people have been critical of certain aspects of HMOs. In terms of staffing and quality of care, what problems may an HMO have?

7 Why is it helpful to know the generic name of a medicine prescribed by your doctor?

8 Samantha and Don have the same illness. They have been prescribed similar medicines by their doctors. Samantha left her medicine home one day. Should she take Don's medicine? Why or why not?

9 How can you help prevent accidents with medicines if there are young children in the house?

10 If you were choosing a doctor, what personal and professional characteristics would you consider important?

Projects

1 Debate whether or not the federal government should institute national health insurance.

2 Research the departments of a nearby hospital or medical center. Find out what departments and clinics it has, and arrange for a field trip to tour the facility.

3 Make an informal survey of advertisers' claims. Collect newspaper and magazine ads for products such as health foods and tonics, diet aids, and over-the-counter painkillers. Which claims do you consider to be quackery? How would you go about checking them out?

Proper use will help preserve natural environments, such as this mountain lake, for many future generations.

CHAPTER TWENTY-FOUR

PUBLIC
HEALTH

Keeping yourself in good health is a big job. You have to practice good health habits, be aware of threats to your health, and visit a doctor regularly for checkups.

Now try to imagine keeping your entire city, state, country, or the world healthy! This is the difficult, but important job of public health agencies. Public health involves the protection of the health of all the people in an area, not just the health of one individual or family. Public health programs work to control the spread of infectious diseases. They also work toward protecting the environment from harmful chemicals and pollution. Because the same health problems can affect people worldwide, many public health officials also work with people and organizations in other nations.

Objectives

- Explain the functions of various public health agencies.
- Define *pollution* and *pollutants*.
- Name four areas of environmental pollution.
- Identify the major sources of pollution today.
- List the dangers of exposure to radiation.
- Name eight ways people can work to protect the environment.

Preventing Disease

The effort to protect and improve the health of a group of people is called **public health.** It may involve a small town, a large nation, or the world. Methods used to protect and improve the health of people range from vaccination programs to checking the safety of water and food supplies.

Public Health at Work

The fight against a mysterious, deadly disease that struck parts of the United States in 1976 shows how public health agencies work to keep people healthy. In the summer of 1976, several Pennsylvania residents became seriously ill with a disease that had many of the symptoms of pneumonia. Doctors who first treated these people found many patients did not respond to treatment. Within a few days, 11 people had died.

As more cases of this unknown disease were reported, public health officials began to notice a pattern. Most of the victims were people who had just attended a meeting of the American Legion in Philadelphia. A few other victims had not been at the meeting, but had walked by the hotel where the Legionnaires stayed. In the next few days, the death toll rose to 29 and over 180 other cases of the disease had been reported.

In Atlanta, Georgia, officials of the national office of the Centers for Disease Control (CDC) began to study the facts. The CDC is the agency of the United States government that is chiefly responsible for investigating and controlling epidemics. An **epidemic** is the rapid spread of an infectious disease. The CDC scientists wondered what had caused the disease. Why did it seem to be centered in the hotel in Philadelphia? Could the disease spread and become a serious national epidemic? Should they quarantine the victims? A **quarantine** is a restriction that separates sick people from others to keep an infectious disease from spreading.

Fortunately, the disease, now called Legionnaires' disease, did not seem to be spreading quickly. The CDC focused its attention on discovering what caused Legionnaires' disease. Victims' families were interviewed. Scientists studied blood and urine samples from the victims. Scientists spent hundreds of hours looking at samples under a microscope. Finally, after five months, scientists identified the bacteria that caused Legionnaires' disease.

Scientists still did not know how the disease spread. New cases of Legionnaires' disease were discovered in other states. Like the Philadelphia outbreak, these new cases involved people who had stayed in hotels or worked in large buildings. Scientists finally discovered that the bacteria grew in the water in air-conditioning units. Scientists found the bacteria could be controlled by putting chlorine in the air-conditioning systems.

As part of the public health system of the United States, the scientists at the CDC helped to keep a serious disease from spreading. Public health agencies at all levels of government work every day to keep our cities, states, and nation free of disease.

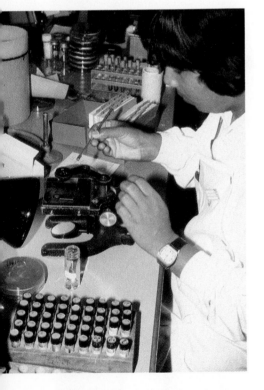

Figure 24–1   A health department technician prepares samples for testing.

History of Public Health

Public health began as a concern for preventing the spread of infectious disease when people began living together in large cities. People had to work together to try to prevent disease. One of the first written public health codes is over 3500 years old. It can be found in the Bible in the Book of Leviticus.

During the nineteenth century, scientists discovered that diseases can be spread by infected food and water. Therefore, governments passed laws to keep food and water clean. Milk, meat, and other foods had to be inspected before they could be sold. Since wells were often unsafe, many cities built water systems to bring clean water into every home and business. Cities also built better sewer systems to prevent the spread of disease. Vaccination programs were required for certain diseases. Hospitals had to follow strict rules of cleanliness.

The success of public health measures in helping control the spread of infectious disease has been dramatic. For example, in 1900, the leading causes of death in the United States were infectious diseases such as pneumonia, influenza, and tuberculosis. Today, infectious diseases rank far down the list. One result of the efforts of public health agencies has been to help the average person live longer. From 1900 to 1985, the average life span of Americans increased by over 25 years.

Local and State Governments

State and local health departments help control the spread of infectious disease. One important service involves keeping the water in your community free of disease. Diseases that can be spread by infected water include cholera, typhoid, and dysentery.

The local water company is responsible for keeping drinking water safe. This typically involves filtering the water and adding chlorine, which kills most disease-causing pathogens. The sewage department is responsible for treating waste water so that it does not spread disease. Waste water from toilets and drains in homes and businesses is usually cleaned in sewage treatment plants. Once the water is free of disease, it is then released into a stream, river, lake, or ocean.

Another important health service performed by your city, county, or state government is inspecting places that sell or serve food. Restaurants, grocery stores, and your school cafeteria must meet certain health standards. Hotels, motels, and other public buildings are also inspected to see that sheets, towels, and bathrooms are kept clean. Most city governments also provide services to pick up trash and stray or dead animals.

Local or state health departments often sponsor health centers or clinics for the needy. State agencies license doctors and other health care professionals.

State or county governments are usually responsible for collecting and analyzing important health information, called vital health statistics. Vital health statistics are figures on births, deaths, and marriages. Figure 24-3 on the following page lists some of the functions of local, state, and national public health agencies.

Figure 24–2   Sewage treatment plants provide safe disposal and treatment of sewage by killing bacteria.

Health History

In 1850, Samuel Shattuck, chairman of the Massachusetts Sanitary Commission, suggested that state and local agencies be developed to deal with public health issues. The result was the first state board of health, established in 1869 in Massachusetts. Now all states have health boards.

Figure 24–3   Typical services of
a local public health department

Vital Statistics	Births, deaths, records, charts
Communicable Disease Control	Immunization, laboratory testing, quarantine, home instruction
Sanitation	Water and sewage: inspection/enforcement, laboratory control Air pollution: inspection/enforcement Food and drug: handling of food, inspecting food in restaurants and hotels, drug and laboratory control Milk: dairy inspection, pasteurization, laboratory testing Housing: rodent and insect control, garbage disposal
Industrial Hygiene	Inspection/enforcement, safety, detection of poisons
Maternal and Child Care	Clinics, nursing Education: infant hygiene, nutrition, dental hygiene, mental health

National Government

The national government agency most responsible for public health is the Department of Health and Human Services. It includes the Centers for Disease Control (CDC), the Public Health Service, and several agencies. The head of the Public Health Service is the Surgeon General of the United States. The Surgeon General has become well known for placing health warnings on cigarettes. In addition to the CDC, the Public Health Service runs other programs that research and control infectious disease. Finding a cure for acquired immune deficiency syndrome (AIDS) is a major research effort in the 1980s. In 1985, the National Institutes of Health, a part of the Public Health Service, along with researchers from the Pasteur Institute in France, discovered the virus that causes AIDS.

The federal government also is responsible for inspecting food and medicines. Before the U.S. Food and Drug Administration (FDA) was formed, it was not unusual for some food companies to sell spoiled food or to prepare food in unsanitary places. Food labels also contained false information. The FDA has made the packaging of food much safer. Food preparation areas have also been cleaned up. Food labels now have to be truthful. Any chemicals added to food have to be safe.

In addition, the FDA requires that all new medicines be tested before they can be sold. In the 1960s, the FDA refused to allow a new medicine for sickness during pregnancy, called thalidomide, to be sold in the United States until it had been proven safe. Even though the medicine was being sold in Europe and Canada, the FDA wanted to run more tests. Before the FDA tests were complete, a number of Canadian and European women who had taken

Health History

During the 13th century, King Henry III of England set punishments for adding impurities to food. In 1634 the penalties were broadened to include the sale of any "musty or corrupted meal."

thalidomide gave birth to children with serious physical defects. When the tragic effects of thalidomide were discovered, the FDA banned the sale of thalidomide in the United States.

Another agency, the Occupational Safety and Health Administration (OSHA), is responsible for safety and health standards at the work site. Thousands of accidents occur each year in the work place. Many of these cause death or serious injury. OSHA works with businesses to try to make work places safer. For example, you may have heard a loud beeper on a work vehicle when it is backing up. This beeper is required by OSHA as a safety precaution so that workers or passersby will not be run over. OSHA also requires workers on certain jobs to wear hard hats, safety glasses, and other protective devices.

The federal government is also active in helping communities recover from natural disasters, such as tornadoes, hurricanes, or floods. Since natural disasters can wreck a city's water system or create other health problems, the federal government provides funds and other assistance to help prevent the spread of disease.

To protect people from health-threatening illegal drugs, the federal Drug Enforcement Administration (DEA) was established in 1973. The DEA investigates drug abuse and arrests suspected offenders. It also investigates the smuggling of dangerous drugs into the United States and coordinates its work with state and local agencies. The DEA also works with agencies in other nations to stop the worldwide traffic of drugs.

International Health Organizations

An epidemic does not stop at the border of a country. It can spread as people, animals, or water move from place to place. Countries frequently work together to help solve health problems. One way they combine their efforts is through the United Nations. The United Nations is an organization of 157 nations that works for peace, health, and good living conditions worldwide.

Figure 24–4 To prevent accidents, OSHA requires workers to wear protective clothing.

Figure 24–5 The Mexican Red Cross searched for victims and provided care for survivors after the earthquake in Mexico City.

One of the most dramatic victories over disease was the worldwide elimination of smallpox. This battle involved people working together in many different nations under the leadership of a United Nations agency called the World Health Organization (WHO). By the 1950s, the use of vaccination and quarantine had caused smallpox to disappear from many countries, including the United States, but smallpox was still a serious problem in some Asian and African nations. Helped by CDC, WHO finally eliminated smallpox in 1975.

WHO has also helped set up family planning programs in overpopulated countries. Family planning involves counseling and providing birth control methods to parents. These programs help parents prepare financially and emotionally for a family.

Another agency of the United Nations is the International Children's Emergency Fund, or UNICEF. UNICEF helps mothers and young children by sponsoring nutrition, education, and disease prevention programs. As a child, you may have gone trick-or-treating for UNICEF during Halloween to help raise money.

United Nations agencies such as the Food and Agriculture Organization (FAO) provide help in growing food and building better water and sewer systems. During a famine, FAO and many other international organizations send food and doctors to the area. A **famine** is an extreme shortage of food. In the early 1980s, millions of dollars worth of food and supplies were shipped to people suffering from famine in Africa. Other agencies of the United Nations help refugees from Southeast Asia and Arab countries with food, medicine, and shelter. **Refugees** are people who flee to another country for protection or safety.

Independent organizations, such as OXFAM (Oxford Committee for Famine Relief), organize food relief programs to famine areas. The International Red Cross is composed of organizations in 120 nations that work to relieve suffering worldwide. The International Red Cross is especially well known for its work during war and natural disasters. Many religious organizations also provide medical assistance and famine relief.

Lesson Review

Public health began as an effort to prevent the spread of infectious diseases. Today, local, state, and national governments are still involved in that effort and other health services. International agencies also help prevent the spread of disease and work to improve the health and well-being of people around the world.

1 What federal agency investigates and controls epidemics?

2 What is the purpose of a quarantine?

3 What are three ways local and state governments work to protect public health?

4 What two things does the FDA monitor?

5 Name two international public health organizations.

Environmental Health

Infectious diseases are only one type of health threat. During the last 25 years, citizens have become more aware of health problems in the environment. The **environment** is made up of all the living and nonliving things surrounding an individual or a community. Environmental health problems are often caused by pollution. **Pollution** is the dirtying of the air, water, or soil by chemicals, disease, or waste products. Many forms of pollution have been linked with serious diseases, including cancer. Since the 1960s, local, state, and national governments have passed many laws to clean up and protect the environment. Despite much progress, pollution continues to be a health problem today.

A Delicate Balance

Nearly everyone wants a clean, healthy environment. However, cleaning up the environment is difficult. One reason is that many of the things people make, use, and do every day cause pollution. Actions and things that cause pollution are called **pollutants.** Such a common event as driving a car causes pollution.

People often do not even understand how their actions affect the environment. For example, thousands of new chemicals are invented each year. Some are used to make new products. Some are used to help farmers grow crops. The chemicals may prove to be safe in tests, but what will happen over many years of use?

One example of a dangerous chemical that passed early safety tests is DDT (dichloro-diphenyl-trichloroethane). DDT was first used in the 1940s to help kill insect pests. Farmers put millions of pounds of DDT on their fields every year. DDT was sprayed on swamps to kill mosquitoes that transmitted malaria. DDT was so successful that the scientists who developed it won the Nobel Prize. But within 30 years, DDT was found to be unsafe. Traces of DDT were found in food. Over the years, people who had eaten food from farms treated with DDT had high levels of DDT in their bodies. DDT was suspected of causing cancer. DDT was too powerful for the delicate balance needed in the environment. In 1972, the United States government put a stop to the general use of DDT. Public health agencies now test all new chemicals thoroughly, and continue to keep testing them after they are in use.

Air Pollution

The air has become a dump site for many different wastes produced by automobiles, factories, and machines. High levels of certain waste products in the air can cause health problems. Figure 24-6 shows the major sources of air pollution. Most air pollution comes from the burning of fossil fuels. Fossil fuels, which were formed millions of years ago from the remains of plants and animals, include coal, petroleum, and natural gas. These fuels are used to heat homes and businesses, to make electricity, and to run motor vehicles. All fossil fuels can release dangerous pollutants into the air.

Figure 24–6   Several sources of air pollution

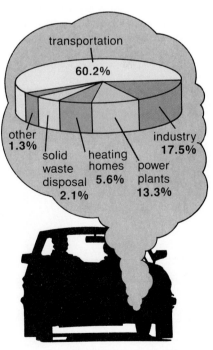

Source: *Air Pollution Primer*, American Lung Association

Particulates are one type of pollutant produced by burning fossil fuels and other materials. Particulates are tiny specks of dust, dirt, ash, and other solid materials. Particulates can irritate the eyes, nose, throat, and lungs. **Sulfur oxides** are a second type of pollutant. Sulfur oxides are foul-smelling gases released by the burning of coal and oil in factories and power plants. They are also irritating to the eyes, throat, and lungs. They may cause bronchitis and aggravate asthma and other lung diseases.

One form of air pollutant released from the burning of gasoline is carbon monoxide. **Carbon monoxide** is a highly poisonous gas that has no odor or color. It can cause brain damage and even death if it is inhaled in great amounts. Hydrocarbons are another group of pollutants produced by cars and trucks. **Hydrocarbons** are chemical compounds that contain both hydrogen and carbon. One type of hydrocarbon, benzene, can cause leukemia. A third type of pollutant released by cars is lead. **Lead** is a poisonous metal added to some gasolines. About 80 percent of the lead found in the air comes from the burning of leaded gasoline. High levels of lead can harm the mental development of children.

In many large cities, air pollution can become serious enough to cause health emergencies. The emergencies can result from a temperature inversion. A **temperature inversion** is a condition that occurs when a layer of cool air becomes trapped under a layer of warm air. Pollution from cars also becomes trapped and builds up. As rays from the sun hit the pollution, they change some chemicals into additional pollutants. The result is smog. **Smog,** a combination of the words smoke and fog, is a term used to describe the brown haze caused by the action of sunlight on air pollution.

To warn people of an air pollution problem, scientists now use a smog index. A **smog index** is a measure of the amount of pollution in the air. If the smog index rises too high, public health

Figure 24–7 A temperature inversion traps pollutants near the ground *(left)*. **When cool air is trapped under a layer of warmer air, pollutants build up to high levels** *(center)*. **Hot air rises under normal conditions** *(right)*.

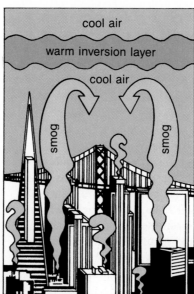
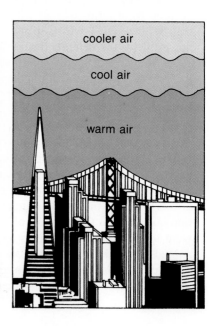

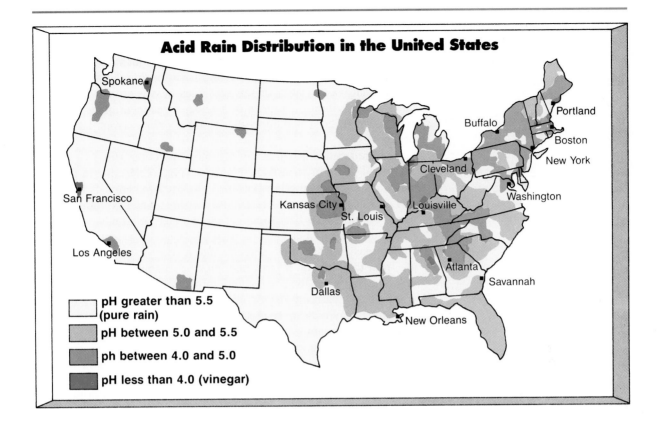

Acid Rain Distribution in the United States

Spokane
San Francisco
Los Angeles
Buffalo
Portland
Boston
New York
Cleveland
Washington
Kansas City
St. Louis
Louisville
Atlanta
Savannah
Dallas
New Orleans

pH greater than 5.5
(pure rain)

pH between 5.0 and 5.5

ph between 4.0 and 5.0

pH less than 4.0 (vinegar)

officials issue a smog alert. A **smog alert** is a warning that the level of air pollution may cause serious health problems, especially for older people and people with breathing problems.

Another air pollution problem is acid rain. **Acid rain** is moisture in the form of rain, snow, fog, and dew that carries air pollution back to the ground. As shown in Figure 24-8, acid rain is a serious problem in many areas of the United States. The acid in the moisture can kill fish and plants and harm the soil. Over time, acid rain can kill forest trees and make it hard to grow crops. It also damages many buildings, monuments, and statues. Acid rain is a very difficult problem to control since the wind blows pollutants hundreds of miles before moisture returns them to the earth. This makes it hard to know just where the air pollutants came from in the first place. Acid rain is not only a local problem but a national concern.

The federal government and most states and large cities have passed air pollution laws. The U.S. Environmental Protection Agency, or the EPA, is a government agency that was set up in 1970 to help protect the nation from all types of pollution. The EPA has made strict rules for the burning of gasoline, coal, oil, and natural gas. For example, most cars must now use a type of gasoline that has less lead in it. In the future, gasoline may have no lead at all. At the time the EPA began its work, air pollution was so bad that the air was unhealthy in the average city about 70 days a year. By the mid-1980s, there were only about 35 serious air pollution days each year.

Figure 24–8 Air pollutants travel many miles before acid rain returns them to earth *(above)*. Acid rain has greatly damaged many buildings, monuments, and statues *(below)*.

Health Bulletin

Some studies estimate that by the 1990s, 350,000 of the nation's service stations will be leaking gasoline into our water system because of corroded underground tanks. A leak of only 1½ cups an hour can contaminate 1,000,000 gallons of ground water a day.

Water Pollution

In the United States each person uses about 75 gallons of water every day for drinking, cooking, cleaning, and many other purposes. After the water is used, it is flushed or drained away. Where that waste water, or sewage, goes next is critical to good health. In most cities, it goes to a sewage treatment plant where it is cleaned. Then it is dumped back into a stream, river, lake, or ocean.

Sewage treatment plants can kill most infectious diseases that are found in water. But these plants are not so effective in getting rid of chemicals and other poisons. The use of chemicals in factories and in growing crops has caused serious water pollution problems. Figure 24-10 lists some common water pollutants.

Not all waste water goes through a sewage treatment plant. In some areas, sewage flows directly into a river or lake. For example, rain that falls on a farm may pick up chemicals used to kill insects. The water then seeps underground and flows slowly toward a river, carrying the chemicals with it. Snow melting on a city street may pick up road salt and other particles and run directly into a stream.

In many communities, public health officials test the water to see if it is safe for swimming or fishing. Drinking polluted water or eating seafood from polluted areas can cause serious health problems. In the 1970s, many people living in a Japanese fishing village suffered severe health problems after eating fish from a polluted bay. The bay and the fish contained particles of mercury dumped into the bay by a factory. Some of the women who had high levels of mercury in their bodies gave birth to children with severe deformities.

To avoid such tragedies, the EPA sets safety standards for the nation's water as well as the air. The EPA and local and state agencies have been successful in cleaning up many lakes and rivers. Many areas of the Great Lakes, for example, were once unsafe for fishing or swimming. Because of the efforts to clean the waters, in recent years long-closed beaches have opened and fish

Figure 24–9 Volunteers clean up after an oil spill.

Figure 24-10 Major forms of
water pollutants

Pollutant	Source	Environmental effects
Industrial chemicals, polychlorinated biphenyls (PCBs)	Industrial and chemical plants	Poisonous to humans and wildlife
Pesticides	Insect control for crops	Poisonous to humans and wildlife
Inorganic salts	By-products of industry and irrigation	Dangerous to sea life and crops
Phosphates and nitrates	Waste water, detergents, and fertilizers	Overproduction of algae
Oil	Spills	Poisonous to sea life, soils seashores
Mercury substances	Manufacture of chemicals and paper	Poisonous to humans and wildlife

are now safe to eat. In the future, the EPA hopes to find ways to
stop pollution coming from mines, farms, and underground
sources. Before swimming or fishing in any stream, check with
local officials to make sure the water is safe.

Toxic Wastes

Each year the average American produces up to one ton of
waste material. Most of the waste produced is not harmful. However, some of the waste, especially materials produced by factories, is toxic. **Toxic** is a term that means deadly or poisonous.

For many years, toxic wastes were just buried in the ground in
dumps around the country. Often they were not even put in protective containers. Some of these wastes have leaked into the soil
and into water supplies. Some of the toxic wastes that were stored
in containers have begun to leak out. In the 1970s, people living
near the Love Canal in Niagara Falls, New York, found out how
dangerous toxic wastes could be. Toxic wastes that had been
dumped in the Love Canal leaked into the ground and into the
community's water supply. People became sick. Some of the
waste seems to have been mutagenic. A **mutagenic substance**
[*myoo tuh JEN ik*] is one that causes changes in genes leading to
birth defects or miscarriages. In 1979, only two of the twelve babies born to women living near the Love Canal were normal.
People had to move from their homes to avoid further poisoning.
Despite efforts to clean up the toxic wastes, some of the poison
remains in the water supply.

Figure 24–11 The use of nuclear energy requires many safety precautions to prevent harm from radiation.

Chemicals found in toxic waste can cause many health problems. Many are carcinogenic, or cause cancers. Scientists and public health officials are working to find safer ways of getting rid of toxic wastes. Cleaning up the most dangerous of the old dumps will also be necessary. The EPA estimates that it will cost over 11 billion dollars to clean up 2000 of the worst toxic waste dumps in the United States.

Radiation

One invisible form of energy is **nuclear radiation.** Radiation occurs naturally in space and in certain minerals on earth. It also can be made artificially. Sources of artificial radiation include nuclear bombs and nuclear power plants. Natural radiation does not pose as serious a health problem because most people receive small dosages of it. Artificial radiation can be a more serious problem. It can be a carcinogen or a mutagen, but it has no smell or taste and it cannot be felt or heard. Its presence may not be noticed until after its damage has been done.

A major danger from radiation is **radiation sickness.** Radiation sickness is a condition that occurs when a person has been exposed to radiation over a long period of time. Leukemia, a form of cancer, can be a result of radiation sickness. The federal government has established safety regulations to protect employees who work with radiation in factories, mines, or research. For example, people who work around radiation are required to wear special tags that monitor their exposure.

Another health problem results from the disposal of radioactive wastes. **Radioactive wastes** are wastes that give off radiation. Radioactive wastes from nuclear power plants, for example, are very difficult to dispose of safely because the radiation will last for thousands of years. Scientists are continuing to look for safe ways to dispose of radioactive wastes.

Figure 24–12 Water pollution often carries human and industrial wastes *(left)*. With careful planning, we can restore the beauty of our waterways *(right)*.

What Can You Do?

Public health officials have the major job of finding ways to lower the risks from pollution. But protecting the environment is everyone's job. Here are some steps you can take to help make the environment better.

1 Cut down on your use of electricity. Electric power plants are some of the biggest polluters.

2 Walk or ride your bicycle more often. Combine many errands into one trip. By using cars more wisely, you will burn less gasoline and cause less pollution.

3 Learn what threats to health exist in your community. Some areas are more likely to have serious air pollution problems; other areas may have lakes or rivers that are unsafe. Find out how you can work with others in your community to solve these problems.

4 Stay informed. Newly discovered health problems and solutions are reported in magazines and newspapers. For example, people may be warned of problems with the water supply, the quality of the air, or certain foods.

5 Have your water tested if it comes from a well. Ask that it be checked for petroleum products in particular.

6 If you work with dangerous chemicals, make sure that you and others follow proper safety procedures in disposing of these materials.

7 Recycle glass, paper, and metals when possible. Reusing materials reduces the need to mine or manufacture new goods. Many communities even burn trash to generate electricity.

8 If you see signs of a pollution problem, report it. For example, if you suspect there may be toxic wastes in your area, contact a local public health agency, the EPA, or your local newspaper, radio, or television station.

Lesson Review

Maintaining a safe environment is very important to everyone's health. Because many substances and actions pollute the environment, pollution is a difficult problem to solve. However, there are laws and organizations that are helping improve the health of the environment. If everyone works to fight pollution, solutions can be found to our current environmental problems.

1 What is the source of most air pollution?

2 What is a measure of the amount of pollution in the air?

3 Which federal agency is responsible for keeping the air and water clean?

4 Why is artificial radiation dangerous?

Chapter Review

Vocabulary

acid rain	nuclear radiation	refugee
carbon monoxide	particulate	smog
environment	public health	smog alert
epidemic	pollutant	smog index
famine	pollution	sulfur oxide
hydrocarbon	quarantine	temperature inversion
lead	radiation sickness	toxic
mutagenic substance	radioactive waste	

Using Vocabulary

Questions 1–10. On a separate sheet of paper, write the term from the right that matches the phrase on the left.

1 highly poisonous gas that has no odor or color
2 tiny bits of dust and ash; given off by burning some fossil fuels and other materials
3 effort to protect and improve the health of a group of people
4 substance that causes changes in genes leading to birth defects or miscarriages
5 restriction that separates sick people from others to keep a disease from spreading
6 condition that occurs when a person has been exposed to radiation over a long period of time
7 condition that occurs when a layer of cool air becomes trapped under a layer of warm air
8 invisible form of energy; occurs naturally in space and in certain minerals on earth
9 warning that the air pollution level may cause serious health problems
10 foul-smelling gas released by the burning of oil and coal in factories and power plants

a radiation sickness
b temperature inversion
c sulfur oxide
d public health
e nuclear radiation
f carbon monoxide
g particulates
h mutagenic substance
i smog alert
j quarantine

Interpreting Ideas

1 Identify five types of pollutants produced from burning fossil fuels.

2 What are the dangers of exposure to radiation?

3 List eight ways that you can work to protect the environment.

4 What is the purpose of the Environmental Protection Agency? How has the EPA brought about positive change?

5 What is the function of the Centers for Disease Control?

6 Describe pollution: (a) its causes, (b) the four broad categories of environmental pollution, and (c) health problems linked with pollution.

7 What diseases can be spread by infected water? How do local water companies keep drinking water safe?

8 Describe the responsibilities of each of the following agencies of the Department of Health and Human Services: FDA, OSHA, and DEA.

9 Identify and describe the work of two independent health organizations.

10 How does artificial radiation pose a serious health problem?

11 List the health services provided by most state or local governments.

12 What are the problems associated with the disposal of toxic wastes?

13 How has the World Health Organization been involved in working for good health?

14 Describe the practices by food companies before the FDA was formed. What changes occurred under the direction of the FDA?

15 Identify three air pollutants released by cars. What health problem is associated with each pollutant?

16 Describe what happens during a temperature inversion. How does smog form? What does a smog index measure? How is the index used?

17 How are particulates and sulfur oxides classified? Describe their effects on people.

18 Why was DDT used in the 1940s? Why is it no longer used in this country?

Applying Concepts

1 Some people believe that a quarantine is a violation of personal freedom. How can you justify such an action?

2 Identify some acts of "progress" that have since been associated with polluting the environment.

3 How can factories in one part of the country cause pollution in another?

4 Several women who lived within a few blocks of a toxic waste dump site gave birth to babies with various types of disorders. How might this situation be explained?

5 Which of the following pollutants would be especially dangerous to a patient with emphysema: hydrocarbons, sulfur oxides, carbon monoxide, particulates, lead?

6 Who should be responsible for maintaining the quality of the environment: individuals, industry, local government, or national agencies? Why?

7 Why is it not possible for the EPA to simply ban the use of all pesticides?

8 How is pollution an international problem?

Projects

1 In 1906, Upton Sinclair's book *The Jungle* aroused public indignation at the quality of processed meat, thereby helping to bring about the passage of food inspection laws. In 1962, Rachel Carson's book *Silent Spring* created a worldwide awareness of the dangers of environmental pollution. Read one or both of these important works. Report to your class the findings of Sinclair or Carson. How would you plan a book reporting the use of pesticides and additives in the production of food today?

2 Create a bulletin board that uses graphics and photographs to illustrate ways that you can help make the environment better. You might entitle the bulletin board "Cleaning Up the Environment Is Everybody's Business."

3 What happens to waste water from the toilet and drains in your home? What happens to your garbage? Arrange to visit the local sewage disposal facility and sanitary landfill area.

4 Find out whether there is a recycling program in your community and, if so, how your class can participate in it. If there is no communitywide recycling program, enlist the help of classmates to wage a campaign to "Clean Up by Recycling" in your school. Arrange convenient drop-off barrels for bottles and cans in the corridors, in the cafeteria, and on the school grounds.

5 Ask a local public health official to visit your class to discuss the various forms of pollution in your community and how each is being handled. Before the visit, ask your classmates to help you prepare a set of questions for the health official: What is the source of our community's water supply? Does our community have noise abatement laws? What are the health standards that must be met by our day care centers, restaurants, grocery stores, and school cafeterias? What services are sponsored by our local public health department?

Even when relaxing at the beach, you are responsible for making wise decisions about your own safety and that of others.

CHAPTER TWENTY-FIVE

Personal Safety

Many people enjoy spending a day at the beach. The sun, the sand, the waves—all combine to provide a setting for fun and relaxation. Yet going to the beach and swimming involve risk. The lifeguard is on duty to help ensure that you follow safety rules and to assist you if an accident occurs.

Safety rules are enforced by a number of people, such as the police, the fire department, and community leaders. However, there are many occasions when you must rely on your own judgment to keep yourself safe. Everything you do carries some risk. But you can decide to remove as many of the causes of accidents from your life as possible.

Objectives

- Identify three human factors that may cause accidents.

- Describe ways to avoid accidental poisonings and falls in the home.

- Describe five ways to guard against fires and burns.

- Explain how you can help to prevent electrocution.

- Explain how pedestrians and drivers can avoid accidents.

- List ways to prevent drowning, boating accidents, and firearm injuries.

- Describe a neighborhood crime watch.

- Identify five ways to prevent assault or rape.

- Describe three ways to prepare for severe weather.

- Describe how to protect yourself during some natural disasters.

Safety at Home and Work

Accidents are the major cause of death for people between the ages of 1 and 44. An **accident** is an unplanned, sudden event. Current statistics indicate that every 10 minutes in the United States, 2 people are killed and 170 people suffer disabling injuries in accidents. Figure 25-1 shows the numbers of deaths caused by various types of accidents.

Preventing Accidents

Claudia was replacing a mirror in her bathroom when the glass started to slide from her hands. As she moved to catch it, she slipped and fell. When she came to, she found herself kneeling in a heap of broken glass and a pool of blood.

Accidents are unexpected events, but they are not just caused by bad luck. Most accidents can be prevented when the causes are identified and eliminated. But since accidents happen suddenly, the steps to prevent them must be thought about in advance.

The steps should become safety habits that result from careful decision-making. Decision-making is a process that includes looking at risks and choosing among different ways of acting to achieve a goal. After you have chosen the safest ways to act to prevent accidents, those ways of acting should be repeated often so that they become habits.

Decisions about ways to prevent accidents should be based on three human factors that are likely to contribute to accidents. One of the most important factors is a person's emotional and mental state. People who are under stress, get upset, or lose their tempers are more likely to have accidents than people who stay calm. When you are in a hurry, you do not concentrate well. Being drunk or sleepy may be dangerous also. In such situations your

Figure 25–1 In a typical year, more people die in motor vehicle accidents than in all other types of accidents combined.

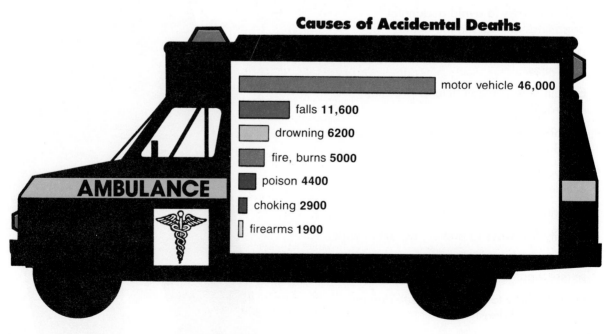

Causes of Accidental Deaths

motor vehicle **46,000**

falls **11,600**

drowning **6200**

fire, burns **5000**

poison **4400**

choking **2900**

firearms **1900**

judgment is impaired, and you cannot always make wise decisions and perform tasks well. Many automobile accidents result from drivers who have had too much to drink or who fall asleep at the wheel.

A second factor in accidents is physical ability. When a person is not able to meet the demands of a particular situation, an accident is likely to occur. For example, people with a poor sense of balance are more likely to fall. Young children do not have the ability to perform many activities without the help of an adult.

The third factor involves acting to keep surroundings safe and equipment in good repair. Accidents can be prevented by identifying hazardous situations and eliminating the hazards.

Understanding these three factors can help you develop good safety habits. Knowledge about how accidents are caused can help you prevent many of them. Being alert to hazards, wherever you are, could save your life.

Health Bulletin

Ninety percent of all accidents are directly attributed to something a person does or does not do. Only 6 percent of accidents result from equipment malfunction or failure, and only 4 percent from adverse environmental factors such as hurricanes.

Safety at Home

More than 24 million injuries occur at home each year. Thousands of people die, and many more are injured, from falls, fires and burns, poisoning, and contact with electrical current. Many of these accidents could be prevented by having good safety habits and by removing possible hazards. Figure 25-2 on the next page shows many areas in the home where safety hazards can occur.

Falls Falls account for one third of all injuries and deaths at home. Many young children do not have the balance to go up and down stairs safely. Families with young children should put a gate at the bottom and top of any staircases, and keep cellar doors locked. Falls often result in serious injuries for some elderly people because their vision may be dimmed or their reflexes slowed. They may also suffer from osteoporosis and therefore be more fragile. Osteoporosis is a thinning of the bones that makes them break more easily.

Some falls are caused by unsteady ladders and stepladders. Many falls are caused by polished floors and other slippery surfaces. To make your home safe, put nonskid padding under throw rugs. Wet floors are particularly dangerous. In the bathroom, use nonslip bathmats and rugs. Families with elderly members may want to consider installing grab bars in the shower and tub area, a seat for the tub, and an elevated toilet seat. Provide a clear path between the bedroom and the bathroom. When not in use, toys should be put away to keep people from tripping on them.

Poisoning Poisoning is the most frequent cause of home accidents among teenagers. Home poisonings include abuse of medicines and use of illegal drugs. To prevent accidental poisonings in your home, keep medicines and cleaning products in their own containers and out of the reach of children. Buy products with child-resistant caps. If you cannot use these caps, lock up medicines and poisons. Read the directions for their use. Teach children to ask first before taking any medicine, and never refer to medicine as candy. Avoid taking medicines in front of children. Dispose of all old medicines by flushing them down the toilet.

Keep the number of the nearest poison control center next to the telephone. **Poison control centers** are places where information and help can be obtained when someone has taken poison. If an accidental poisoning occurs, call the poison control center immediately. To help in treatment, be sure to say what poison was taken and how much. You may be told to use syrup of ipecac to make the victim vomit. You can obtain a standard dose from your local pharmacy.

Fire and Burns Most burn deaths in homes are caused by the careless use of matches, cigarettes, or cigars. Cooking accidents and faulty heaters and furnaces also cause home fires and burns. If you have central heating, it should be checked each year to be sure the furnace is working safely. If you have a working fireplace, the chimney should be inspected and cleaned at least once a year. Be sure your fireplace has a screen around it. Do not leave paper, fabrics, paints, wood, or anything that could catch fire near a fireplace. Never use a liquid that burns easily, such as kerosene, to start any fire, indoors or outdoors. Never store gasoline or other such liquids indoors.

In the kitchen, guard against fires and burns by avoiding clutter in the area where you cook. Always keep the handles of pots and

Figure 25–2 Prevention of accidents in the home is the whole family's responsibility. What could you do to help make your home safer?

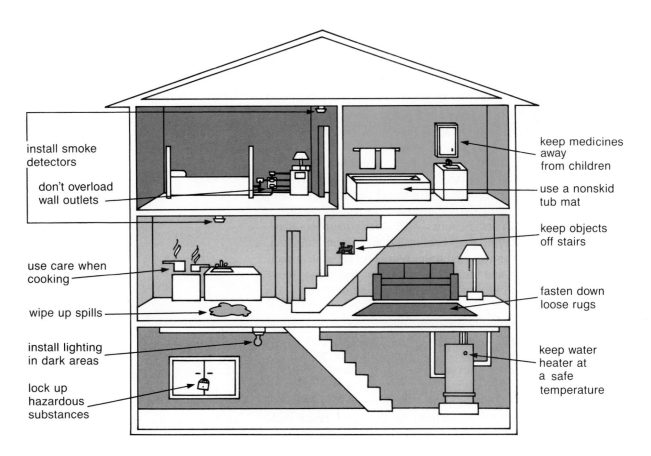

install smoke detectors

don't overload wall outlets

keep medicines away from children

use a nonskid tub mat

keep objects off stairs

use care when cooking

wipe up spills

fasten down loose rugs

install lighting in dark areas

lock up hazardous substances

keep water heater at a safe temperature

pans turned sideways so you won't knock them off the stove top and so small children can't pull them down. Remove the knobs on gas stoves if there are toddlers in the house so that they cannot turn on the gas. Be sure to use dry pot holders or mitts, as wet ones do not protect you properly against the heat. If you have a microwave oven, be sure to follow the proper instructions for its use. Never throw a glowing match or cigarette into the garbage.

Fire Drills   If a fire does start in your home, early detection is your best prevention against harm. Most home fire deaths happen at night when the victims are sleeping. Smoke detectors give your family the warning it needs to get safely out of the house. Smoke detectors should be placed between the sleeping areas and the rest of the house on each floor. Once in place they should be tested regularly. Also keep a small fire extinguisher in the kitchen.

Every family should have regular fire drills. In the event of fire, get everyone out of the house. Have a specific place to meet, so that you can quickly notice if anyone is missing. Call the fire department from a neighbor's house. Never go back into a burning house to save pets or possessions.

Electrical Hazards   Fires may result from faulty wiring, damaged cords, or using too many appliances at once. Any of these situations may also cause electrocution if the faulty appliance or cord is touched. **Electrocution** is death caused by an electric shock.

Never use appliances in wet areas. For example, you should never plug in a hair dryer with wet hands or while in the tub. Also, do not mow wet grass with an electric mower. Children should be taught not to fly kites or climb trees near power lines. In houses where there are young children, electrical sockets should be covered up with safety caps.

Using Tools Safely   Wherever you use tools, use them correctly. Keep all machinery, tools, and other equipment in good condition. Use the safety devices that are provided for machinery, and wear goggles or safety glasses when working with tools or chemicals that require eye protection. These include hammers, saws, lawn mowers, sprayers, and other tools. Do not wear jewelry or loose-fitting clothes that might catch in a machine. Also keep long hair covered up. Turn off the power before adjusting or fixing tools and machinery.

Never allow children to operate or play on power equipment, and do not climb on or around machinery yourself when it is operating. Store tools in the same place every time, out of the reach of children. Check your tools often to make sure they are working properly. Hammers and ax heads should be securely on the handle. Many tools have safety warnings printed on the handles. Read and follow them carefully.

If you are not sure how to do something, try to find a neighbor, friend, or professional who does. The money saved doing a home repair is not worth it if you injure yourself in the process.

Figure 25–3   One way of avoiding electrical hazards is to be sure every electrical appliance you use has an Underwriter's Laboratory label.

Figure 25–4   Always follow proper safety precautions when using tools.

Figure 25–5 On-the-job accidents can be avoided through the use of safety equipment.

Safety At Work

Accidents at work affect both the worker and the employer. The employer loses a worker who often has special skills, experience, and knowledge. But the worker is the real victim. He or she may be disabled for life.

Employer's Responsibility   Since 1912, accidental deaths in work settings have been reduced by more than 75 percent. Injuries on the job have been cut by getting rid of health dangers wherever possible. The use of protective headgear and clothing has also helped. Many plants have started safety education programs for their workers.

Companies that use heavy equipment, such as manufacturing and construction companies, usually have a higher accident rate than service or trading companies. Some workers are exposed to toxic substances or radiation. The harmful effects may take several years to appear. Several states require that workers be informed about the dangers of the materials with which they work.

Worker's Responsibility   As much as the employer can do to safeguard workers, it is up to each person to be careful on the job. If you suspect a health hazard in the area where you work, tell your supervisor. If you do not get a response, contact the Occupational Safety and Health Administration (OSHA), the government agency responsible for enforcing safety regulations.

If all else fails, you may want to consider looking for another job. Your health is too important to be put in danger.

Farm Safety   Since they work for themselves, farmers must enforce their own safety rules. Many farm accidents are caused by the special machinery used in farming. Tractors, corn pickers, and other machines should be operated at a safe, slow speed. As with all machines, farm machines should be turned off before you reach into the moving parts.

The farmyard should be kept clear of tools and rubbish, and water tanks and wells should be enclosed by fences. Avoid storing loose materials in enclosed overhead areas, as these areas may overheat and catch fire.

Lesson Review

Developing good safety habits and making your surroundings as safe as possible are the best ways to prevent accidents. Try to be in a safe mental and physical state when involved in any activity. Try also to make your home and work areas safe.

1 Name four personal conditions that will make you more likely to have an accident.

2 Why are falls particularly dangerous for elderly people?

3 Name four types of accidents that may happen in the home.

4 List three safety precautions that farm families should follow.

Vehicle Safety

More people in the United States have died from automobile accidents than have died in all the wars this country has ever fought. Most safety experts say that many of the automobile deaths and injuries could have been prevented. Prevention depends on each person, community, and manufacturer taking a good look at the factors that cause these accidents.

Driving Conditions

The driver's condition is a very important factor in vehicular accidents. Alcohol is involved in nearly half of the fatal accidents. Safe driving means *never* driving when under the influence of alcohol or drugs. For instance, medicines for colds and allergies often cause dizziness or sleepiness, which can slow reflexes and weaken judgment. In addition, if you need eyeglasses when you are driving, never drive without them.

You should also keep your car in good order. Tire blowouts, stalled vehicles, or failed brakes are just some of the problems that cause accidents. Heavy rainstorms, icy roads, bad visibility, and roads in poor repair cut down on safe travel. It is better to pull over to the side of the road or try to find another route rather than risk an accident.

Driving Safely

People between 15 and 24 years old are the most likely to have an automobile accident. Yet this is the age group with probably the best health and coordination. Teenagers and young adults could have a good safety record if they followed the rules for driving safely.

Driving safely begins with taking a driver's education class to learn the rules of the road. In many cases, this will also lower your insurance rates. Have a valid license and never encourage

Figure 25–6 The frequency of automobile accidents increases during bad weather. If you must drive in severe weather, be even more careful than usual.

Health Bulletin

A recent study of 15,000 accidents by the National Highway Safety Administration indicates that a lap belt can reduce injuries in an accident by 31 percent. A lap–shoulder belt reduces injuries by 57 percent.

anyone without a valid license to drive. Learn to be a defensive driver. A **defensive driver** is one who is always prepared for poor driving on the part of others and for poor road conditions. Keep a margin of safety between your car and the cars around you. Don't tailgate. **Tailgating** is driving so closely behind the car in front of you that you cannot stop or swerve in an emergency. Obey traffic signs and do not exceed the speed limit.

While you are driving, you are responsible for the safety of everyone in your car. Do not let other passengers or the radio or tape deck distract you. If you stop paying attention for even a second, you could be involved in an accident.

Safety Restraints

Do you wear a safety belt every time you are in a motor vehicle? If you do not wear a safety belt, see if you recognize yourself in one of the following people.

Tomas only wears a safety belt on the highway, not on short trips around the city. Edith does not wear a safety belt at all because she is afraid she will get trapped in the car. Francine says that if she were in an accident she could brace herself with her hands. Jesse only wears his safety belt when he is in the front seat, because he thinks rear seat passengers do not need belts.

Are any of these people right? The answer is *no*. Many more accidents happen on city streets than on highways. A crash at speeds as low as 12 miles per hour can kill. People who are thrown free may scrape along the ground for yards before landing, or even be crushed by their own cars. In almost any accident, safety belts help people avoid injury. They can quickly unbuckle the belt and escape if necessary. The force caused by an accident is so great and so sudden that nobody can control the movements of his or her body. Rear seat passengers usually are thrown into the front seat. Front seat passengers usually are thrown against the dashboard or through the windshield. Wearing a safety belt can help the driver maintain control of the vehicle, thereby reducing the severity of an accident.

As a driver, you have a special responsibility to make sure all your passengers wear their safety belts. Studies show that most people are willing to put on their belts if asked by the driver. Keeping children secured in a safety belt or child safety seat is safer not only for the children, but also keeps them from distracting the driver.

Motorcycle and Bicycle Safety

Motorcycles, mopeds, and bicycles are low-cost forms of transportation. Unfortunately, they are also very dangerous if not ridden carefully. Motorcyclists are eight times more likely to be injured or killed in an accident than someone in a more protected vehicle. Any two-wheel vehicle is less stable than those with more wheels.

The rules for safe motorcycle and bicycle travel are similar to those any defensive driver follows. Cyclists should know how to operate their vehicles and keep them in good shape. Nearly 20

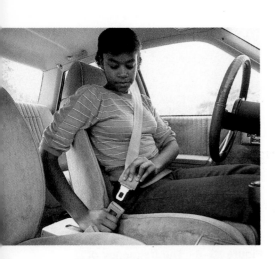

Figure 25–7 Buckling up is a quick and easy way of reducing the risk of serious injury in an automobile accident.

percent of all bicycle accidents are caused by problems such as brake failure or by riding too large a bike.

When on a bicycle, ride single file on the right side of the road and obey traffic laws. All cyclists should be careful at intersections and use hand or turn signals. Bicyclists must also follow the same traffic laws as motorists, including stopping at stop signs. More than half of all bicycle–car accidents occur at intersections. Watch out for doors opening on parked cars. Do not ride with two or more people on a bike or play games in traffic. Hitching a ride on another vehicle is extremely dangerous as it may stop suddenly and crush you. Watch out for holes in the road that may cause falls, and report them to your local government.

Many states have helmet laws to protect motorcyclists from falls. Helmets have also prevented fatal injuries to bicyclists. Always wear reflective clothing or strips, especially when traveling at night. Make sure you have front and back bicycle lights.

Driving or riding in an all-terrain vehicle (ATV) can be fun but can also be dangerous. Never ride with two people on an ATV. You should observe precautions listed on the device, including speed, sharp turns, and safe terrains. Do not operate an ATV on the streets or highways. It is a good idea to always wear a helmet when riding.

Figure 25–8 Never ride a motorcycle without wearing a helmet and protective gear.

Safety on Foot

People who travel on foot are called **pedestrians.** The first safety rule for pedestrians is to know the laws governing traffic. As a pedestrian you are especially at risk when crossing or entering the street. Use crosswalks and always look both ways before you cross. Do not assume that drivers will see you. If there is no sidewalk, walk on the left side of the road so that you can watch for oncoming traffic. When walking at night, you should try to wear light-colored clothing or carry a flashlight. Joggers should wear reflective clothing or strips.

Lesson Review

The major cause of vehicular accidents is alcohol and drug use while driving. Other causes include disobeying traffic laws, faulty equipment, and poor driving conditions. Whether driving, biking, or walking, assume that the other person may do the unexpected. Try to concentrate and pay attention at all times, so that if something should happen, you will be alert enough to handle it in a safe manner.

1 Name three personal conditions in which you should not drive.

2 Name two types of weather that may cause dangerous road conditions.

3 What are three myths that may prevent people from using safety belts?

4 Name three safety precautions for pedestrians.

Recreational Safety

Recreation and sports activities are fun. They also provide exercise and a way to relax after school or work. However, every year more people get hurt during recreational activities. Many of these accidents could be prevented. A little common sense plus some safety knowledge can keep recreation fun.

Learn the necessary skills and safety rules for your particular sport, and follow them. When doing any hard physical activity, remember to warm up and cool down gradually. You should also be sure you have the proper equipment. During any recreational activity, it is helpful to know basic first aid procedures.

Water Safety

Swimming, fishing, boating, and water skiing are favorite forms of recreation for many people. However, any water activity carries with it the risk of drowning. A great many of those drowned every year are teenagers, mostly teenage boys. About one third of these deaths result from swimming or playing in water. The other two thirds happen after people fall into the water from bridges, docks, or boats. Recent studies show that about 35 percent of recreational boating deaths are connected to alcohol. About two thirds of all drowning victims have drunk alcohol before entering the water. Never mix alcohol and water activities.

One of the best ways to prevent drowning is to learn how to swim. Many drowning deaths occur 50 feet or less from shore. Even if you do know how to swim, always swim with another person who could run for help if necessary. Never jump or dive into unknown waters; there could be a hidden rock or current you do not know about. Swim only at supervised beaches and pools.

Many drownings could be avoided if people knew a technique called drownproofing. **Drownproofing** is a system of rhythmic breathing and vertical floating that helps you save energy in a water emergency. A person can use this technique for hours without

Figure 25–9   The steps of drownproofing. Float with your face in the water, legs slightly tucked (*a*). When you need to breathe, slowly raise your arms and stretch out your legs and exhale into the water (*b*). Raise your head just far enough to take a breath through your mouth (*c*). Slowly return to the resting position (*d*).

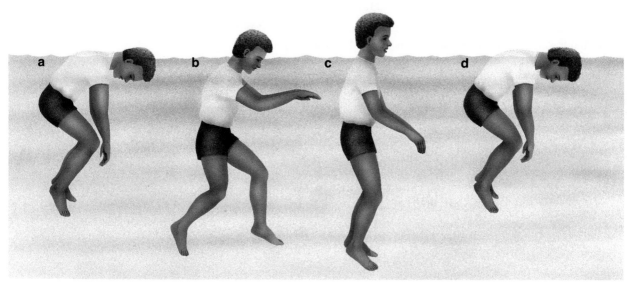

getting tired. It is not necessary to remove your clothing, since it adds to your ability to stay afloat and also keeps in body heat. Whatever your swimming ability, you can master the technique of drownproofing.

When boating, check the weather and the condition of the boat before leaving shore. Have an approved life preserver aboard for each passenger and carry a fire extinguisher. Learn to handle the boat by practicing near the shore. Remember to slow down when passing other boats or when near beaches. Never carry more passengers than the boat allows, and enter and move about on the boat one at a time.

When water skiing, wear a life jacket and know how to swim well. Never ski at night or in shallow water. If you fall down, you should hold up a ski as a signal for other boaters. The boat driver should stop the boat while assisting the skier back into the boat. The law requires that there be another person in addition to the driver on board to watch the water skier at all times.

Figure 25–10 Red Cross approved water safety lessons are a good way to ensure safety at the beach or a pool.

Safe Use of Firearms

Every year about 100,000 people are injured because of the improper use of firearms, one fourth in recreational activities including hunting, and three fourths in the home. About 2000 of the victims die. People under the age of 24 are most likely to be involved in accidents with firearms.

Everyone in a household should be taught to respect and follow firearm safety rules. Always treat a gun as if it were loaded. Never point a gun at anyone. Guns should be stored unloaded and locked up, out of the reach of children. Store ammunition separately from guns. When you are carrying a gun, keep the gun barrel pointed down. Never lean the gun against a tree, wall, or vehicle. When traveling, carry your guns unloaded until you are ready to begin hunting or target practice. Keep the safety catch on until you are ready to shoot.

These same rules should be followed for every type of gun, including air rifles, BB guns, and pea shooters. Even a stray BB can put an eye out. Any person who uses a gun should be trained in the correct way to use it. Inexperienced firearm users may harm or kill an innocent person. It is also important to know and obey the laws for hunting in your state.

Lesson Review

Recreational activities can be both safe and fun. However, if proper safety rules are not followed many sports can lead to deadly accidents. Use the proper equipment for each activity, and make sure to check it each time before you use it. Always wear protective clothing and gear if the activity requires it.

1 What is drownproofing?

2 What are two safety rules to remember when boating?

3 Give four rules for the safe use of firearms.

Crime Prevention

Some injuries and deaths are caused by crimes of violence. Crime affects young people because they are most often both the victims and the criminals. For example, murder is the second leading cause of death among people aged 15 to 24. Police are not the only people who can prevent crime. Individuals can help protect themselves and others against violence.

Community Watch

Concern about crime has caused some communities to work more closely with their police officers to cut down on crime. Neighborhood crime watch areas have been established. A **neighborhood crime watch** is a group of people who look out for unusual activities or people in their area. The group asks the local police or sheriff's department to help them set up the program. Neighbors are taught to observe and report suspicious activity to the authorities.

Preventing Assault

Unlawful attack on a person by another is called **assault.** The assaulter may use a gun, knife, fists, feet, or other means of causing injury. You can help prevent an attack by following certain safety guidelines. Your best defense is common sense—if you feel a situation is unsafe, try to avoid it.

Some precautions to follow are to avoid walking in dark areas and deserted streets. When walking alone, act as if you know where you are going. Walk at a steady pace near the curb. Wear shoes you can run in, especially if you are out after dark. If you think you are being followed, turn and walk the other way. Do not go anywhere that you might be alone, such as in a public restroom or home to an empty house. Instead, stop at a store or a friend's home until you feel safe.

At home, keep your doors locked at all times. Do not open the door to strangers without a chain lock in place. If someone in trouble asks to use your telephone, have the person wait outside while you make the call. Never allow anyone who makes you feel uneasy to come into your home. If you should arrive home and find a door or window broken, do not go in. Go to the nearest neighbor or public phone and call the police.

Children alone or babysitters should know the safety rules for answering calls. Do not say you are alone. If someone phones asking for your parents, say ''Mom or Dad can't come to the phone right now.'' When strangers dial the wrong number, tell them only that they have dialed incorrectly. Don't give them your name or number. If you get a crank call, hang up immediately.

When driving, always lock your car doors and drive with plenty of gas in your tank. Try to leave your car in a well-lighted area or commercial parking lot. Always lock your car after parking. Before you open the car, look inside to make sure no one is hiding on the floor or in the back seat. If someone stops you under suspicious circumstances, drive away quickly sounding your horn.

Figure 25–11   Local organizations have helped to reduce crime in many neighborhoods.

If you think you are being followed, drive directly to a police, fire, or rescue station. If your car breaks down, raise the hood, wait in the locked car, and flash your lights until the police come.

Hitchhiking, or taking a ride with someone you do not know, is very risky. It is also against the law in many parts of the country. Instead of hitching a ride, try to find another form of transportation such as a bus, subway, or bicycle. You may also want to call a family member or friend for a ride.

If you are attacked, scream and run, if possible. Do not resist a robbery; your safety is more important than any money or jewelry. Try to get a good look at your attacker so that you can describe him or her to the police.

Preventing Rape

Forcing another person to have sexual relations is the crime of **rape.** Most victims of rape are young women, although young children and teenage boys, as well as older women, may also be raped. Most rapists hurt their victims out of a desire for power, not sex.

Rape is an extreme form of assault, and the guidelines to prevent an attack also apply. Sometimes other precautions are also needed. For example, more than half of all women who are raped are raped by men they know, if only slightly. In such cases, learn how to say *no* forcefully. Never let anyone do something or touch you in a way that makes you feel uncomfortable or scared. If you can, leave or tell the person to leave. Use common sense in avoiding situations that may send the wrong signals to people.

Reporting rape is not an easy thing to do, but it is necessary in preventing more rapes. Many communities have set up rape squads staffed by specially trained police officers to interview the victim and see that she or he receives medical care. Hospitals are taking notice of the special needs of rape victims. Most communities have established **rape crisis centers.** A rape crisis center is a community agency developed to help a victim get medical help or to provide emotional support during an investigation and trial. Sometimes a mental health specialist will be recommended for rape victims.

Health Bulletin

FBI statistics indicate that a rape is reported every 10 minutes. However, for every rape reported, nine others probably remain unreported.

Lesson Review

Crime and violence affect everyone. You can make your community safer by reporting any unusual or suspicious activity to the police. You can help keep yourself safe by following certain guidelines. If you are attacked, get medical help and report the attack immediately.

1 What are three precautions to take when walking alone?

2 If you get a crank call, what should you do?

3 What safety steps should you take if your car breaks down?

4 Which community agency helps rape victims?

Preparing for Disasters

Tornadoes, floods, hurricanes, and earthquakes can all cause disaster. A **disaster** is any sudden, unforeseen emergency that causes personal injury, death, or property damage. A natural disaster is one that has natural causes, such as a blizzard. In addition to natural disasters, there are other disasters that occur as a result of an action taken by people. These include fires, explosions, or nuclear accidents.

No one can control the weather or stop natural disasters. However, people can prepare for them to lessen the damage they cause to people and property.

Weather Preparation

With modern weather satellites and other equipment, it is now possible to forecast most severe weather conditions. Warnings are usually given before bad weather hits, so that you have time to prepare. Often, being prepared means stocking up on food, water, flashlights or candles, and any needed medicines. Always follow the instructions given by local or state authorities.

Lightning Lightning kills an average of 150 people in the United States each year and injures about 250. To keep yourself safe during a lightning storm, go indoors and stay there. Avoid metal objects, such as pipes and stoves. Always unplug electrical appliances and do not talk on the telephone unless it is absolutely necessary.

If you are outside when a lightning storm hits, seek shelter immediately. Because lightning often strikes the tallest or highest object in an area, do not take shelter under a tree or stand in the open. Automobiles offer good protection in a lightning storm because rubber tires, rather than any of the car's metal, are in contact with the ground. Avoid tractors and other farm machines that have metal attachments that touch the ground. If you are caught out in the open, lie down in the lowest place possible.

Figure 25–12 Lightning usually strikes the tallest object. Be careful that the tallest object isn't you!

Figure 25–13 Flooding can be caused by a hurricane or by rapid melting of heavy snows. If a flood warning is issued for your area, you may have to leave your home in a hurry.

Floods Flooding is a frequent result of severe rainstorms. Melting mountain snow in the spring may also cause floods along rivers and streams. If you are in an area that is likely to flood, have an emergency plan ready if any flood warning is issued. If you are in a car and it stalls because of high water, leave it immediately and get to higher ground.

Never disregard signs that warn about flooded bridges or low roads. Many people have drowned because they thought they could drive through a flooded street.

Hurricanes A tropical storm with heavy rains and winds of more than 75 miles per hour revolving around the center, or eye, is called a **hurricane.** In the United States hurricanes most often strike coastal areas between Texas and Florida and from Florida to the New England states. If a hurricane is forecast, keep informed by listening to local weather reports. Secure your living area by boarding up windows. Bring in items, such as lawn chairs, that could be tossed about in heavy winds.

Do not drive if the storm is close by. When driving after the storm be alert for tree branches, scattered bits of rocks, or holes in the road. Stay away from shore areas in case they are swept by high waters.

Tornadoes A whirling funnel-shaped windstorm that extends to the ground from a mass of dark clouds is a **tornado.** Tornadoes can cause great damage in seconds. Wind speeds inside the twisting cloud may reach as high as 400 miles per hour. Tornadoes have occurred in every state of the continental United States, but the central states have the most tornadoes. A **tornado watch** is issued when conditions are favorable for a tornado to devleop.

A **tornado warning** is issued when a tornado has been sighted by a person or on radar. If a tornado warning is issued for your area, seek shelter immediately. Open the windows on the side of the house away from the approaching storm. This will keep air pressure inside the house equal to the pressure outside. If you

Health **History**

Over 700 tornadoes hit the United States each year. The worst U.S. tornado occurred in 1925. Lasting three hours, it swept across the Midwest and killed 689 people.

have a basement, go to it. Otherwise, find the smallest room, usually a bathroom, with the strongest walls and no window on the lowest level of the house. If you live in a mobile home or are not near your house, you should go to the nearest shelter. In open country, move at right angles away from the tornado's path. Lie down in a ditch if there is no time to escape.

Blizzards Blizzards are the most dangerous snowstorms. **Blizzards** are snowstorms with winds at 35 miles per hour and temperatures of 20°F or lower. The snow whips around, making it difficult to see beyond a few yards. If a blizzard should strike your area, do not leave your school, business, or home. Because the winds of a blizzard often damage power lines, it is also a good idea to have another source of heat if you have electric heat.

If the heat at home goes off during a blizzard, there are several ways to keep yourself warm. Dress warmly and layer clothes. Wear a wool hat, especially when sleeping. Use several lightweight blankets rather than one very heavy one.

Carry blankets and snacks in your automobile during the winter. If you are trapped in a car during a blizzard, stay in the car. Run the motor for brief periods of time a few times an hour for heat. To avoid the build-up of carbon monoxide, open the windows slightly when the motor is running. Be sure the tailpipe is clear of snow, so that fumes will exhaust properly. Try to move around. Do not allow anyone to go to sleep. Turn on the light inside the car so that rescue groups will see you.

Earthquakes and Landslides

The earth's surface is made up of a crust of rock. A condition in which the rocks shift and move, and the ground shakes is an **earthquake.** In the United States, most of the earthquakes occur along the West Coast. Although they usually last only a few seconds, they can cause the collapse of buildings and bridges.

A **landslide** occurs when a mass of soil and rock slips or falls from a hillside. Landslides are often a result of earthquakes. Landslides may also be caused by a slow wearing away of soil due to freezing and thawing of water. Heavy rains can create landslides or mudslides where there are no trees or underbrush to hold the soil.

If you live in a known earthquake area, make sure that you have some emergency plans. For example, if you are indoors, hiding under a piece of heavy furniture might help protect you from any falling materials. If you are outside, stay in the open away from electrical wires and buildings. If you are in a car, stop the car but stay inside.

After the shaking of the earthquake stops, check your water, power, and gas lines. If they are leaking or broken, shut off the power source and report the problem. Have a battery-powered radio on hand so that you can listen to emergency bulletins. Stay out of damaged buildings until they have been inspected. The small shocks that often follow earthquakes may cause a damaged building to collapse.

Health **History**

In late 1985 in Mexico City, two major earthquakes struck within days of each other, killing and injuring thousands. Many died after being buried under collapsed buildings.

Figure 25-14 Many organizations provide assistance during a natural disaster. Which agencies are active in your community?

Disaster Plans

Most communities already have a disaster plan developed. The planners usually include police, fire, hospital, public health, Red Cross, and civil defense representatives. A civil defense agency is an organization concerned with protecting the community. When school buildings are used in the disaster plan, school officials are also represented.

Accident prevention is chiefly your individual responsibility. However, there are different agencies that can help you learn to prevent accidents and to know what to do if an accident should occur. The National Safety Council is a private agency that collects statistics on all types of accidental death or injury and works to prevent accidents. It has almost 100 state and local safety branches in the United States and Canada. The American National Red Cross works to increase safety throughout the United States. The Red Cross offers free courses in first aid, lifesaving, and small craft handling as well as aid in the event of a disaster.

Lesson Review

There are two kinds of disasters: natural disasters and those caused by human action. Although you cannot prevent natural disasters you can learn how to reduce their risks. Learn and obey the procedures to follow in the event of a disaster in your own community.

1 List three safety steps you should take during a lightning storm.

2 When is a tornado warning issued?

3 If you are in a car that stalls when a flood warning is in effect, what action should you take?

4 List two national safety organizations that provide information and programs to prevent accidents.

Chapter Review

Vocabulary

accident	electrocution	rape
assault	hurricane	rape crisis center
blizzard	landslide	tailgating
defensive driver	neighborhood crime watch	tornado
disaster	pedestrian	tornado warning
drownproofing	poison control center	tornado watch
earthquake		

Using Vocabulary

Questions 1–14. On a separate sheet of paper, write the term from the column on the right that identifies the phrase on the left.

1 group of people on the lookout for unusual activities or people in their area

2 condition in which the rocks in the earth's crust shift and move

3 death caused by an electric shock

4 funnel-shaped windstorm that extends to the ground from a mass of dark clouds

5 unlawful attack on a person by another person

6 unplanned event of a sudden nature

7 system of rhythmic breathing and vertical floating that helps save energy

8 person who travels on foot

9 place where information and help can be obtained when someone has taken poison

10 crime of forcing another person to have sexual relations

11 tropical storm with winds of more than 75 mph moving around an eye

12 person who is prepared for poor driving on the part of others and poor road conditions

13 mass of soil and rock falling down a hillside

14 sudden, unforeseen emergency that causes injury, death, or property damage

a assault
b pedestrian
c accident
d hurricane
e rape
f neighborhood crime watch
g poison control center
h landslide
i electrocution
j disaster
k defensive driver
l tornado
m drownproofing
n earthquake

Interpreting Ideas

1 Describe a neighborhood crime watch program: What is its goal; how is such a program set up; and how do its members function?

2 Identify five ways to prevent assault.

3 Describe four ways to avoid automobile accidents.

4 Why is it important to always wear a safety belt in an automobile? Why is it important to secure children in a child safety seat?

5 Describe two ways to prepare for severe weather conditions.

6 List four ways to prevent accidental poisonings in your home.

7 What can you do to protect yourself if you are outside when a lightning storm hits?

8 What are three causes of landslides?

9 List four ways that drowning can be prevented.

10 How can you protect yourself during an earth-quake? What measures should you take after the shaking of the earthquake stops?

11 List four safety guidelines to apply when handling a gun.

12 Identify three safety guidelines that should be followed by pedestrians.

13 What is the difference between a tornado watch and a tornado warning?

14 What safety guidelines should you follow when you are boating?

15 How can you make your home safe from falls?

16 What is the chief cause of burn deaths in homes? Describe five ways to guard against fires and burns in your home.

17 What pieces of equipment should be worn by a motorcyclist or a bicyclist to prevent fatal injuries from happening?

18 Identify three human factors that may play a role in causing accidents.

19 List two guidelines that apply specifically to the prevention of rape. What is the function of a rape crisis center?

20 How can you prevent electrocution?

Applying Concepts

1 Describe what you should do in each of the following situations: (a) you are stuck in your car during a blizzard; (b) you are walking home alone at night and believe that the person behind you is following you; (c) you are in your house when a tornado warning is issued for your area; (d) you get a crank call while baby-sitting or home alone.

2 In each of the following examples, explain what is wrong and why: (a) Edward decided to sample several kinds of wild mushrooms that he found on the field trip; (b) six-year-old Chris was delighted when the stranger offered him two chocolate chip cookies and a ride home; (c) Tanya used her blowdryer as she stood on the wet bathroom floor; (d) Marty generally smoked in bed whenever he had to study late into the night.

3 If someone has swallowed a poison, why should syrup of ipecac not automatically be given in order to rid the body of the poison?

4 At a recent party where your friend Bob became intoxicated, you called your parents to drive both of you home rather than have Bob drive. Now Bob feels humiliated and angry. What reasons can you give him for your action?

5 If you are jogging at night, which piece of clothing is the most important: regulation running shoes, a warm hat, or reflective clothing?

6 On a warm summer night Frank took his friend Alan water skiing in Frank's boat. Give two reasons why this was not safe.

7 Why is it better not to fight back if you are mugged? What action might you take instead?

Projects

1 Prepare a pamphlet for your classmates on electrical safety. You may wish to illustrate the following concepts: the use of electricity requires common sense and care at all times; electricity and water are a deadly combination; electricity is always trying to get to the ground, and you don't want to be part of that pathway.

2 Investigate the two kinds of smoke detectors—ionization and photo-electrical. Which responds to smoke by fast-burning fires? Which responds to smoke by slow, smoldering fires? Why is it advisable to install one type of detector in some rooms and the other type in other rooms?

3 On poster board, create a series of cartoons entitled "What Is Wrong Here?" In each frame, show the cartoon character violating an important personal safety rule.

4 With your family, set up an emergency escape plan in case of fire in your home. Figure out two escape routes for each bedroom, in case of a night fire.

5 With several classmates, investigate any local civil defense plans. Where are local emergency shelters located? In what situations you would use these shelters?

Critical Thinking

RESISTING PEER PRESSURE

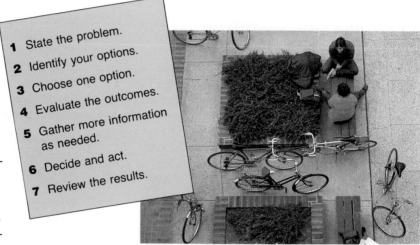

1 State the problem.

2 Identify your options.

3 Choose one option.

4 Evaluate the outcomes.

5 Gather more information as needed.

6 Decide and act.

7 Review the results.

"I didn't mean to. I didn't know it would turn out like this!" You are probably not surprised when people tell you that they regret their actions. At some time, everyone has made a decision without thinking of its effects. But considering the consequences of an action can lead to sensible decisions about health and safety so that apologies will not be necessary later on.

Probable Consequences

Probable means likely to happen or likely to be true. A consequence is an outcome that naturally follows from an action or a condition. Therefore, a probable consequence is something that is likely to happen if a certain action is taken.

Consider, for example, the following statement: Bicycling six miles a day will gradually increase the rider's leg muscles and lung capacity. The action in this example is bicycling. The probable consequence is increased leg muscles and lung capacity.

Before taking an action, it is wise to review the decision-making process presented in Chapter 1 and shown above.

Peer Pressure

Peer pressure plays a major role in decision-making. Your peers may try to persuade you to take many actions. Sometimes they may try to pressure you into a decision.

Peer pressure can have positive or negative outcomes. Playing softball to the best of your ability and studying hard to make the honor roll because you want your friends to admire you are positive outcomes of peer pressure. Driving too fast or abusing alcohol and drugs can be negative outcomes.

Learning to predict probable consequences is a good way of resisting peer pressure. Your decisions can affect the length of your life as well as the health and safety of other people.

Friends, classmates, and fellow workers are very important

to human well-being. However, in your need to belong and to be accepted, you cannot blindly follow what others do. You must carefully think through decisions affecting your health and safety. Predicting a consequence is better than paying for one.

In your health course, you have learned an abundance of health and safety information. Apply your knowledge from this course to each of the situations below. What is the probable consequence of each of the following actions? What answers would you give your friends if they made these suggestions?

1 A friend comes by to pick you up for school. "Hurry up! There's no time for breakfast. Why don't you leave now and eat a big lunch?"

2 Everyone in your neighborhood has started riding bicycles to school. Your friends encourage you to ride your bicycle instead of taking the bus.

3 You have been working out with weights to improve your muscle tone. Several friends have suggested that you take steroids as a way to increase the size of your muscles.

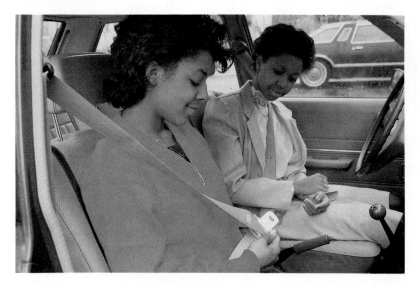

4 Your friends have started riding all-terrain vehicles. You don't own one, but a friend has offered to give you a ride on his.

5 You would like to go to a dance in another town. You don't have a ride, so several friends suggest that you hitchhike.

6 Your neighborhood has recently experienced several burglaries. In an attempt to cut down on crime, everyone has agreed to watch each other's houses more carefully. People agree that if there is a suspicious person in the neighborhood, they will call the police. Your best friend has encouraged you to join in, too.

7 A cookout with friends is threatening to become a disaster. Instead of bright sunny weather, it is pouring rain. Because it is so wet, you cannot get the fire started to cook the hamburgers. Your friends suggest that you use some kerosene to start the fire.

8 As a way of losing weight, your friends have decided to go

on a new low-carbohydrate diet. You would like to lose 10 pounds quickly and wonder if you should follow the diet.

9 Your friends are planning a canoe trip to an island in the middle of a lake. They ask you if you'd like to come and bring the beer.

10 In your state you can get your driver's license six months

earlier if you pass a driver's education course. All of your friends are taking the course. Should you, too?

11 You have had a strep throat, but have just recovered. Your best friend seems to be getting the same thing. Your friend asks if you will give him some of your medicine so he won't have to go to the doctor.

12 You have heard in the news about a teenager in a nearby town who committed suicide. You and your friends are upset about this and would like to do something to help. Two of your friends have volunteered to help coordinate a local suicide hot line. They are urging you to get involved.

First aid provides practical and immediate treatment for an injury or health emergency.

FIRST AID

What is First Aid?

First aid is practical and immediate care for an injury or sudden illness. First aid is administered until professional medical help is available. Such emergency care provides self-help in case of injury or illness. It is also critical in response to natural disasters.

First aid does not require elaborate training or special equipment. First aid training covers care for wounds and sudden illness, care for specific injuries, accident prevention, and emergency procedures. Knowing first aid is important for skill in handling emergencies and accidents effectively.

Any injury or illness can benefit from prompt first aid. Some conditions, such as minor wounds or bruises, require only simple first aid. Other conditions, such as choking or severe bleeding, are true medical emergencies. In a medical emergency, prompt first aid can make the difference between life or death, quick or slow recovery, and temporary or permanent disability.

Although first aid requires action, the first step in an emergency is to examine the situation carefully. In this way, you can spot any conditions that may threaten your safety or that of other bystanders.

The next step is to decide what action should be taken. A thorough knowledge of first aid makes it possible for you to provide the action that is needed. It helps you to know which emergencies should be handled first. It also gives you the confidence to remain calm and to help keep others calm.

How to Use This Manual

This manual is a guide to practical first aid steps to be taken until professional medical help is available. Following the introductory sections, there is an alphabetical listing of first aid situations. References to other relevant topics are also given.

Cardiopulmonary resuscitation (CPR) is included at the end of this manual, rather than with the alphabetical listings, because it requires special training. This manual does NOT teach CPR. Never attempt CPR unless you have completed a course.

The major sections of the manual are identified by general types of illness or injury. Each section is then divided into specific instructions regarding illnesses or injuries. The information in each part consists of a description of the first aid situation followed by first aid directions. The directions are numbered and should be followed in the order presented. Illustrations are included to help make the first aid directions clear.

To use this manual, find the section in the alphabetical reference list that describes the type of illness or injury. Open the manual to the correct page for the information you will need. Remember, it is best to read and study this manual before an emergency occurs. Prompt, effective first aid is more likely if you are familiar with the procedures.

In this manual, you will find the instruction "monitor ABCs". The A stands for *airway*, the B stands for *breathing*, and C stands for *circulation*. Monitoring ABCs involves three steps: (1) keeping the injured person's airway clear; (2) checking the person's breathing and using rescue breathing if the airway is blocked or breathing stops; and (3) checking circulation by feeling for a pulse and looking for signs of bleeding. If circulation has stopped, CPR should be given by someone trained in CPR.

In case of an accident or sudden illness, you should know where to call for help. Keep a list of emergency telephone numbers posted near your telephone. The emergency phone numbers should include your local emergency medical services (EMS), the police department, the fire department, a poison control center, and your family doctor. Some communities have a coordinated EMS system that can be contacted by telephoning 911.

FIRST AID REFERENCE

First aid procedures in this manual reflect the most recent guidelines recommended by the American Heart Association and the American Red Cross. These procedures did not appear in the original printing of this book. (January 1988)

What to Do in an Emergency

Any sudden illness or serious injury can create a first aid emergency. First aid care is always influenced by the type of injury or illness. However, in an emergency, it is important to have first aid priorities.

Observe these priorities when the facts of the situation are not known, when the extent of illness or injury is unclear, or when the injured person is unconscious or unable to explain:

1. DO NOT put yourself in danger. Examine the situation carefully and then determine the best and safest way to give help.
2. Remain calm.
3. Ask for help if you need it.
4. Send someone else to get professional help. The person telephoning for help should state the following information: the phone number of the telephone she or he is calling from, the location of the injured or ill person, the nature of the injury or illness, and the first aid being given. The person should not hang up until the other party has finished asking questions and has obtained all necessary information.
5. Examine the injured or ill person carefully in a systematic way, such as from head to toe.
6. Deal first with the most life-threatening condition, such as severe bleeding, absence of heartbeat, or breathing failure. If you are trained in CPR, be prepared to administer it.
7. Care for shock or act to prevent it.
8. Know your first aid limits. DO NOT attempt any procedure that you cannot do efficiently and confidently.
9. Protect the injured or ill person from further harm. DO NOT move an injured or ill person unless that person is in immediate danger.
10. Stay with the injured or ill person until professional medical help arrives.

Types of First Aid That Require Special Training

Prompt first aid can be very effective. Most first aid care is a set of practical procedures for nonprofessionals. Such emergency care helps the victim until professional medical help arrives or the person can be taken to a hospital. These emergency techniques usually do not require special training.

Occasionally special training is required to learn a first aid procedure. Cardiopulmonary resuscitation (CPR) is a lifesaving technique that cannot be learned from a book. CPR is a method of restoring breathing and heartbeat to a person who is no longer breathing and whose heart has stopped beating. The American Heart Association or your local Red Cross chapter can tell you where CPR instruction is offered in your area. Learn to recognize situations that require CPR, but do not attempt it without the necessary training. Individuals who attempt CPR without proper training may endanger the life of the victim.

Any additional training in correct first aid procedure is helpful to make a person confident and effective in an emergency. In addition, special programs are available in many communities to teach swimming, lifesaving, and water and boating safety. Such programs teach people to enjoy themselves, to prevent accidents, and to be prepared in case of an emergency.

First Aid and Good Samaritan Laws

Most states have some form of Good Samaritan law. These laws provide legal protection for people who aid victims of accidents or emergencies. The laws vary from state to state.

In one state, the law provides that any Good Samaritan who gives emergency aid shall not be held financially responsible for injury resulting from the emergency care. In another state, persons trained in CPR have legal protection for their rescue efforts unless their actions are deliberate misconducts of care. In a third state, it is unlawful for a knowledgeable person to ignore a victim of an accident or emergency.

Good Samaritan laws do not protect people from being sued. These laws do protect rescuers by specifying the limits of the rescuer's legal responsibility to the victim. All states require that once the Good Samaritan has begun to give care he or she must continue to give care until more adequate help arrives.

Bites and Stings

Animal Bites

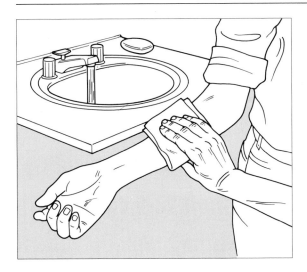

When a person is bitten by another person or by an animal, an infection can result. For example, rabies infection can be transmitted through animal bites. If a person is bitten by a land mammal that may have rabies, the incident and a description of the animal and where it was last seen should be reported to the EMS, the police, and animal control. Follow these first aid directions:

1. Before touching a wound, wash your hands.
2. Wash the wound with soap and water if there is not heavy bleeding.
3. Control any bleeding.
4. Tape a clean dressing over the wound.
5. Get medical help.

Insects, Spiders, Ticks

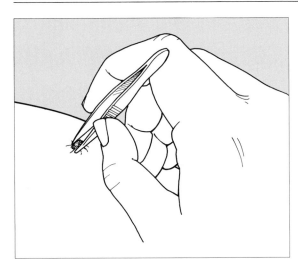

Insect or spider bites may cause allergic reactions such as hives, wheezing, difficulty breathing, and nausea. Also, ticks and certain insects may transmit disease. For allergic reactions, get immediate medical help. For bites by poisonous organisms, call a poison control center or go to the hospital.

Follow these first aid directions:

1. Gently scrape an insect's stinger out of the skin with the edge of a clean fingernail or blunt edge of a table knife. With tweezers, grasp a tick as close to the skin as possible. Pull steadily, trying not to crush the tick.
2. Apply cool, wet, clean cloths.
3. Get medical help for an allergic reaction.

Snakebites

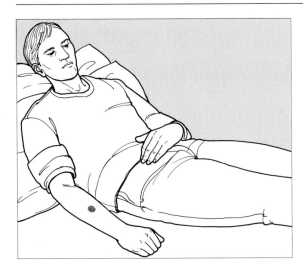

In the case of a snakebite, try to notice the appearance of the snake. There are four kinds of poisonous snakes in North America: rattlesnakes, copperheads, water moccasins (cottonmouths), and coral snakes. The first three have long fangs, which may leave puncture marks.

Follow these first aid directions:

1. Stay calm and keep the injured person calm.
2. Keep the person lying still with the bitten area immobile and below heart level.
3. Care for shock and monitor ABCs (page 512).
4. If you think the snake might have been poisonous, get medical help as soon as possible.
5. Do not try to remove venom or apply tourniquets.

Bleeding

Washing a Wound

In the absence of severe bleeding, washing a wound helps prevent infection.

Follow these first aid directions:

1. Wash your hands with soap and water.
2. Rinse the injured area with clean water.
3. Put soap on a moist cloth and gently wash the wound area. Rinse again with water.
4. DO NOT try to remove material that is embedded in the wound. DO NOT use antiseptics without consulting a physician.
5. Apply a clean dressing to the wound.
6. Seek medical help if matter is embedded in the wound, there is severe bleeding, the wound edges do not stay closed, or the wound involves a vital structure such as the eye.

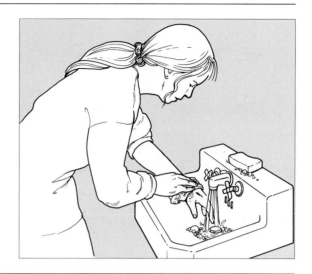

Direct Pressure

Rapid loss of blood should be stopped as quickly as possible. First, apply a clean dressing to the wound. Then press down firmly with the palm of the hand. Clean towels, gauze, or clothing can be used as a dressing. If no clean material is available, apply pressure directly with the hand.

Follow these first aid directions:

1. Cover the wound with a clean dressing.
2. Press firmly on the dressing.
3. DO NOT remove blood-soaked dressings, but keep adding dressing and applying pressure.
4. After bleeding stops, secure the dressing with a bandage.
5. If bleeding does not stop, get medical help.

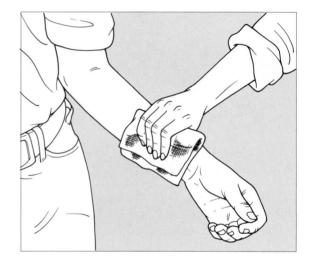

Elevation

Sometimes direct pressure alone cannot control the flow of blood from an open wound. Raising an injured limb higher than the heart will help stop bleeding.

A bleeding open wound on the head, neck, arm, or leg should be raised above heart level and direct pressure continued. If there is any possibility of a neck injury, DO NOT move the head. If there is any sign of fracture, DO NOT elevate an injured limb. DO NOT move an unconscious person.

Follow these first aid directions:

1. Apply direct pressure to the open wound.
2. If there is no sign of fracture, elevate an injured arm or leg higher than the heart.

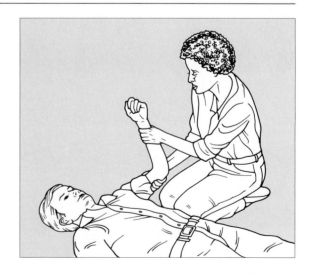

Pressure-Point Technique

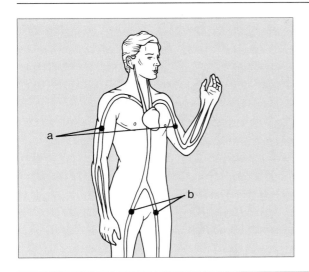

Pressure-point technique may be necessary if direct pressure and elevation are ineffective. This technique consists of applying pressure to a major artery at a point between the wound and the heart. This slows the flow of blood to the wound so that clotting can occur.

The use of pressure-point technique stops circulation within the entire limb. Stop using the technique as soon as bleeding is under control. For any case of bleeding that cannot be stopped, get medical help immediately.

The pressure points most often used to control bleeding are found on the arms and legs. These points are shown in the top illustration.

Internal Bleeding

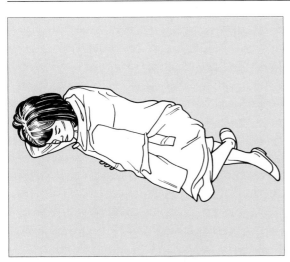

Closed wounds can result in internal bleeding instead of blood loss through the skin. A black eye is an example. Extensive internal bleeding and injuries to internal organs can be caused by the impact of a fall or a motor vehicle accident. Be alert for the following signs of internal bleeding: vomited or coughed-up blood and blood in the urine or stools.

Follow these first aid directions:
1. If the person is unconscious, vomiting, or bleeding from the mouth, place the person on her or his side to prevent choking.
2. Keep the person comfortably warm.
3. DO NOT let the person eat or drink.
4. Get medical help immediately.

Nosebleed

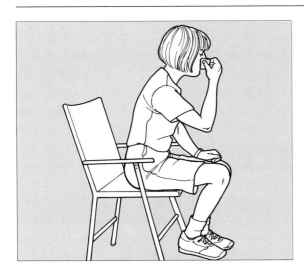

A nosebleed can be caused by an injury to the nose, a cold, a disease, or strenuous physical activity. A nosebleed is usually not serious. When the bleeding has been stopped, avoid activity that might start it again.

Follow these first aid directions:
1. Have the person sit down and lean forward, or if that is not possible, lie down with the head and shoulders raised.
2. Squeeze firmly the soft, flexible part of the nose for at least 10 minutes without releasing the pressure.
3. If necessary, apply cold compresses to the bridge of the nose.
4. If the bleeding continues, get medical help.

Breathing Problems

Causes of Breathing Problems

The body needs a continuous supply of oxygen to support life processes. Normal breathing supplies this oxygen. When air does not move freely in and out of the lungs, breathing problems result. Severe breathing difficulties can result in respiratory failure, a life-threatening emergency. For example, an object caught in the airway can obstruct breathing and cause respiratory failure.

Some breathing difficulties are associated with chronic medical problems. Some forms of heart disease can cause coughing and shortness of breath. Sitting upright may relieve these symptoms.

Asthma occurs when a person's airways are blocked or narrowed. Its symptoms include coughing, wheezing, and breathing difficulty. Asthma can be triggered by an allergy or a respiratory infection. Help the person remain calm. Give him or her an asthma medicine, if prescribed by a physician, and provide warm, moist air. If breathing difficulty continues or becomes worse, get medical help.

Croup is another type of breathing difficulty that is particularly common among young children. It causes narrowing of the larynx along with a barking cough and breathing difficulty.

Steam from a vaporizer or hot shower usually relieves the symptoms of croup. In rare cases, croup can become a life-threatening problem. If breathing becomes more difficult and exhausting, or if there is a sudden high fever or drooling, seek immediate medical help.

Hyperventilation

Hyperventilation (very fast breathing) is often caused by emotional stress. It may be confused with a heart attack or a mental disorder. Symptoms include a sense of not getting enough air; sharp, short pains in the chest or stomach; dizziness; and a "pins and needles" sensation in fingers, toes, and face. In an older adult, immediate medical help should be obtained for chest pain.

For a young, otherwise healthy person, follow these first aid directions:
1. Be calm and encourage slower breathing.
2. Have the person breathe into a paper bag or cupped hands to rebreathe the same air.
3. If symptoms continue, seek medical help.

Rescue Breathing

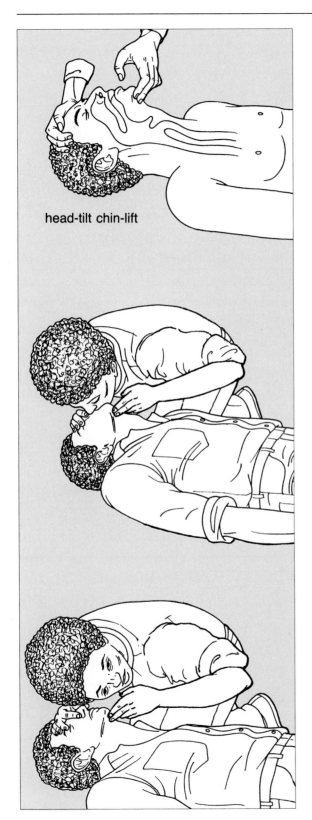

head-tilt chin-lift

In some cases of severe breathing problems, normal breathing stops or is ineffective. Respiratory failure is a life-threatening emergency that requires first aid.

Rescue breathing is a first aid procedure that forces air into the lungs. The mouth-to-mouth technique is considered the most practical and effective method. If rescue breathing is necessary, so is professional assistance. Send someone for immediate help. In cases of carbon monoxide poisoning, drug overdose, electric shock, rescue breathing may be needed for a long time. Remember the ABCs (page 512).

Follow these first aid directions:

1. Place the person on his or her back.
2. Open the airway. Tilt the injured person's head back with the chin pointed upward. Place one hand on the person's forehead. With the other hand, place your fingertips under the bony part of his or her jaw and lift the chin gently. This procedure is known as the head-tilt chin-lift. Be careful not to close the person's mouth completely. See top illustration.
3. Check for breathing. Watch the chest to see if it is rising and falling. Listen and feel for signs of breathing at the mouth and nose. Check for about five seconds. If there is no breathing, pinch the nostrils closed. See middle illustration. Take a deep breath and seal your mouth over the person's mouth as shown in the bottom illustration. Blow two full, slow breaths into his or her mouth, watching the chest rise with each breath. Between the two breaths, raise your mouth, take a breath, and watch the person's chest fall.
4. Check for circulation by feeling gently for the pulse in the groove on either side of the Adam's apple for five to ten seconds. Check also for bleeding.
5. Send someone to call EMS for an ambulance.
6. If there is a pulse and no sign of breathing, give one full, slow breath every five seconds. After each breath, when the person's chest is expanded, raise your mouth, turn your head toward the chest, take a breath, and watch the chest fall. Repeat blowing cycle. If there is no pulse and no breathing, CPR is necessary. If you have no CPR training, continue rescue breathing until qualified help takes over and administers CPR.

Burns

First- and Second- Degree Burns

Burns can result from exposure to the sun, hot liquids and objects, electricity, or chemicals. In a first-degree burn, the outside layer of skin becomes red. There may be mild swelling and pain.

In second-degree burns, the skin appears red and blotchy. Blisters and swelling often develop. Pain is more severe.

Follow these first aid directions:
1. Cool the burned area with cold (not ice) water until pain lessens.
2. DO NOT break blisters that may develop.
3. Cover the burn with a clean, moist dressing.
4. Seek medical care if burns are on the face, genitals, hands, feet, or more than one body part.

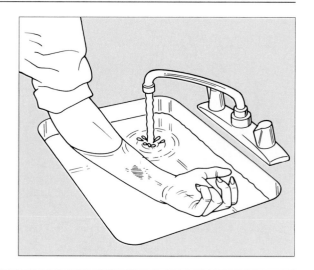

Third-Degree Burns

Third-degree burns, or burns that involve deep tissue and have open blisters, can be life-threatening. The skin may look leathery, white, or charred. There may be little or no pain. Burns of the face may be accompanied by respiratory burns and breathing problems.

Follow these first aid directions:
1. Care for ABCs.
2. Call EMS immediately.
3. Cool burned area with cold (not ice) water until pain lessens.
4. Cover burn with clean, moist dressing.
5. Keep burned arms and legs above heart level. DO NOT let the person walk.

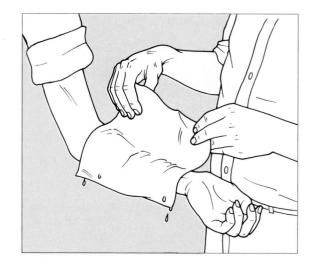

Chemical Burns

Skin injury caused by irritating chemicals is called a chemical burn. Household and garden products, such as fertilizer, bleach, ammonia, and many other cleaning agents, are frequent causes of chemical burns. It is important to read all product labels carefully. The aim of first aid is to remove the irritating substance as quickly as possible.

Follow these first aid directions:
1. Wash the area with large quantities of water for at least 20 minutes. Remove any contaminated clothing during the washing.
2. Cover the burned area with a sterile dressing to avoid infection.
3. Seek medical help.

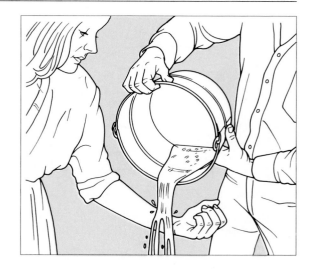

Choking

universal choking signal

Universal Choking Signal

A person who suddenly cannot breathe, cough, or speak may be choking. Choking occurs when an object lodges in any part of the airway. Choking can be a life-threatening emergency. The risk of choking is increased by chewing food inadequately, talking with a mouthful of food, wearing ill-fitting dentures, or drinking alcohol before eating. Be sure you know how to make and recognize the universal choking signal. Signs of choking include:

sudden collapse
ineffective coughing
wheezing or breathing
  with difficulty

bluish color of face,
  neck, or hands
inability to speak
unconsciousness
panic

First Aid for Choking

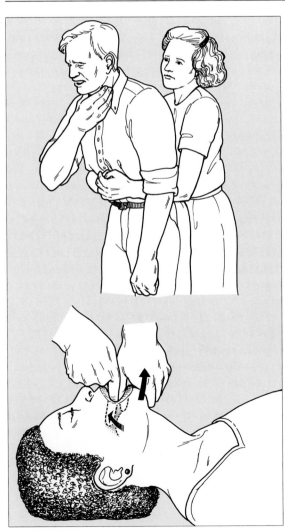

Encourage a choking person to cough. If the person coughs weakly or shows other signs of choking, give first aid immediately.

For a conscious adult or child, first aid consists of abdominal thrusts (Heimlich maneuver), as described below:

1. Stand or kneel behind the choking person with both arms around the waist.
2. Place the thumb side of your fist against the person's abdomen, halfway between the navel and the tip of the breastbone.
3. Grasp your fist with the other hand.
4. Press your fist into the choking person's abdomen with quick, hard, upward thrusts.
5. Each thrust should be a separate, distinct motion. Continue the thrusts until the person is able to cough forcefully or breathe, or becomes unconscious.
6. If the person loses consciousness, lay him or her down face up. Do a finger sweep: Grasp tongue and lower jaw with one hand; lift the jaw. With the other hand, slide a finger down the inside of the cheek to the base of the tongue. Sweep out the object.
7. Open the airway; give two breaths. If air does not go in, do six to ten abdominal thrusts.
8. Repeat the finger sweep, opening the airway. Give two breaths and repeat abdominal thrust steps until the airway is cleared, or an ambulance arrives.
9. A choking person can do self abdominal thrusts by leaning over the back of a chair and pushing up and in against the abdomen.

Common Injuries

Bruises and Minor Wounds

Bruises and wounds are injuries of the skin and underlying tissue. Ice wrapped in a clean cloth may reduce the pain and swelling. If the bruised area is on an arm or leg, keep the limb elevated above heart level. If pain and swelling continue or if the bruise is the result of a joint injury, seek medical help.

There are several types of wounds. A laceration, in which the skin is torn, is usually more severe than a smooth cut (incision). A puncture is a hole made by a sharp object, such as a nail. An abrasion is a scrape.

For minor wounds, first aid to stop the bleeding, clean the wound, and prevent infection may be the only treatment necessary. If there is a lot of bleeding, numbness, loss of motion, or additional injury, get medical help. Puncture wounds are especially susceptible to infection, including tetanus.

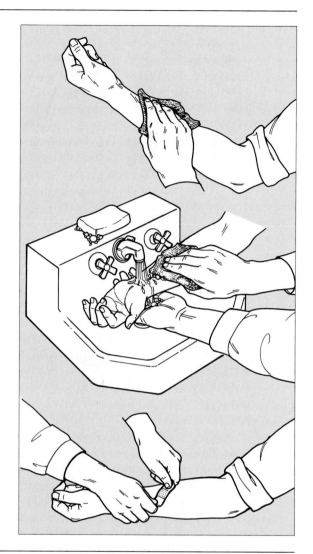

Follow these first aid directions:

1. Control bleeding with direct pressure and elevation.
2. Wash the wound thoroughly with soap and water to clean it. Vigorous washing may be necessary to remove embedded material from an abrasion.
3. Rinse the wound with clean water and pat it dry. If bleeding recurs, control it.
4. Cover the wound with a sterile dressing.
5. Watch for any signs of infection, such as pus, pain, redness around the wound, or a fever.
6. Check with the person's doctor to see whether a tetanus shot is needed.

Blisters

Protect unbroken blisters from pressure by applying a gauze wrap or bandage. Clean a broken blister with soap and water and cover it with a sterile dressing. Seek medical help if the blister is large, infected, or very painful.

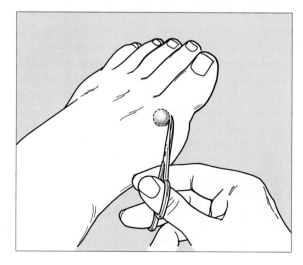

Follow these first aid directions to drain a blister that is likely to break:

1. Wash the area with soap and water.
2. Open the blister along the perimeter with clean, sharp scissors, such as cuticle scissors. Leave outer layer of skin in place.
3. Press out the fluid with a clean cloth.
4. Keep the open blister clean and covered.
5. Seek medical help if infection occurs.

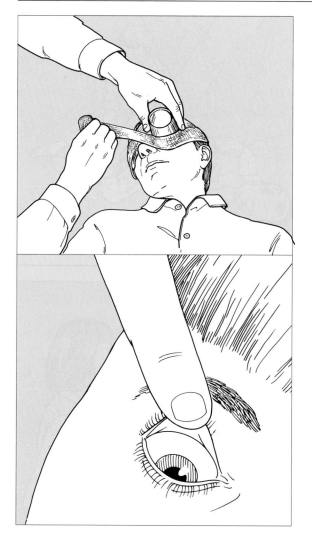

Eye Injuries

Causes of eye injury include a loose object in the eye, an embedded object in the eye, a chemical burn, and a direct blow to the eye.

With any suspected eye injury, DO NOT rub the eye and DO NOT try to remove contact lenses. Chemical burns should be flushed with water for 20 minutes. Then close and cover both eyes and get prompt medical help. An injury caused by a direct blow, such as a black eye, should be examined by a doctor. There could be damage inside the eye. An embedded object can be a serious emergency. Do not try to remove the object. The injured person should lie down. Place an inverted paper cup over the injured eye and secure with a bandage over both eyes. Get immediate medical help.

A loose object may be a particle or an eyelash. First try to flush it out with warm water. If it will not flush out, cover both eyes and seek medical help.

Follow these first aid directions to look for a loose object:

1. To examine the lower lid, have the person look up. With clean hands, gently pull the lower lid down.
2. If you see the particle, flush it out with water.
3. To examine the inner surface of the upper lid, have the person look downward and gently pull the upper lid up and out.
4. Flush out the eye with water, and let the lid down.
5. If irritation, tearing, or blurred vision continues after the particle is removed, get medical help.

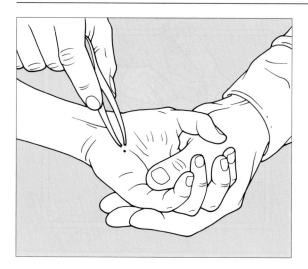

Splinters

To treat a splinter wound, follow the first aid directions for cleaning a wound. Quickly and gently, wash the area to remove any material that is not deeply embedded in the wound. If the splinter is large or deeply embedded, DO NOT try to remove it. Get professional medical help.

Follow these first aid directions to remove a splinter:

1. Using a clean pair of tweezers, pull out the splinter at the same angle it went in.
2. Wash the wound and cover it with a sterile dressing.
3. If there is an infection or difficulty removing the splinter, get medical help.

Head Injuries

Signs of Head Injury

Head injuries require immediate medical attention. There may be internal bleeding and brain damage. There also may be a neck injury, which could cause paralysis.

The signs of head injury may appear immediately or within 48 hours of an accident. A person who has received a serious blow to the head should be watched carefully for 24 to 48 hours.

Sings of possible head injury include:

drowsiness

loss of consciousness

paralysis

clear or bloody fluids
    from nose, ears, mouth

slurred speech

pupils of unequal size

vomiting

loss of memory

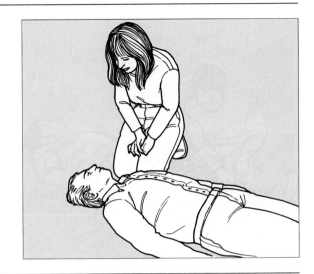

Scalp Wounds

A scalp wound is a type of head injury. Scalp wounds usually bleed a lot because of the scalp's rich blood supply. DO NOT try to remove foreign matter from a scalp wound, unless the matter is easily removed with soap and water. Get medical help as soon as possible. If there is a possible neck injury, DO NOT move the person.

Follow these first aid instructions:

1. Control bleeding.
2. Clean only very minor wounds.
3. Raise the person's head and shoulders. DO NOT bend the neck.
4. Cover the wound with a sterile dressing.
5. Get medical help.

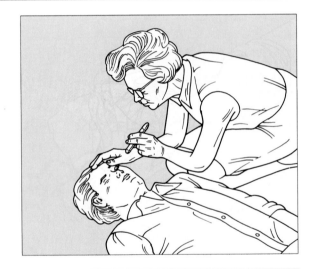

Concussions/Fractures

A blow to the head can cause the brain to shake against the skull. This may result in a loss of consciousness, or a concussion. A concussion may be accompanied by a crack, or fracture, in the skull.

Follow these first aid directions:

1. Keep the person lying down.
2. Call EMS for an ambulance.
3. Stabilize the injured person's head and neck as you found them by placing your hands along both sides of the head.
4. Keep an open airway.
5. DO NOT give food or drink.
6. Note the time of injury and the person's behavior just after sustaining the injury.

Muscle Injuries and Cramps

Muscle Strains

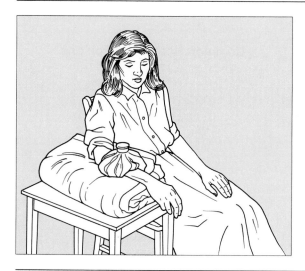

Muscle strains, or tears, are caused by over-exertion. The muscle feels tender and may become swollen and stiff. First aid care can provide relief for the pain and promote healing of the injured tissue. Get medical help if the area is badly swollen or very painful.

Follow these first aid directions:

1. Rest the muscles involved and avoid movement that causes pain.
2. Elevate the limb to minimize swelling of a strained arm or leg muscle.
3. Apply cold compresses or ice packs for 20 to 30 minutes at a time to relieve pain.
4. After 24 to 48 hours, apply warm compresses or heat to increase circulation.

Muscle Cramps

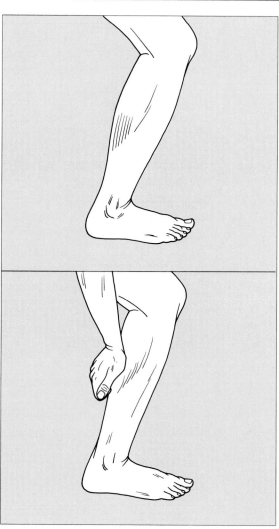

The sharp pain of a muscle cramp is caused by a sudden intense contraction of a muscle. A muscle cramp can occur during exertion or while the body is at rest. It may last from a few seconds to a few hours.

Muscle cramps are uncomfortable but rarely dangerous. They are common during pregnancy but are not significant. Leg cramps often disturb the sleep of older people.

Heat cramps are painful muscle spasms. They are most likely to affect abdominal or leg muscles. A person who experiences muscle cramps during exercise on a hot day may need to be treated for heat exhaustion as well as for heat cramps.

Any muscle cramp can be dangerous to a swimmer if he or she is incapacitated by pain or panic.

Most muscle cramps respond quickly to gentle massage and heat. If the cramps are not relieved by first aid or continue to occur, get medical help.

Follow these first aid directions to treat muscle cramps:

1. Gently but quickly stretch the cramped muscle. If the cramp is in an arm or leg, bend the limb gently back and forth.
2. Massage the knot in the stretched muscle with the heel of the hand.
3. For a cramp in the calf or the sole of the foot, straighten the leg while pointing the toes back up toward the body.
4. Apply a cold pack to the cramped muscle. Leave in place for 20 to 30 minutes.

Poisoning

Swallowed Poison

A poison is a substance that damages health and may cause death when it is swallowed or breathed. Many cleaning agents, house and garden plants, and garden products are very toxic when swallowed. Swallowed poison is also called poisoning by mouth. When poisoning has occurred or is suspected, first aid is needed quickly. Try to discover what product has been swallowed so that correct procedures can be followed.

Remove any poison from the person's mouth. A child may need to be prevented from eating or drinking more of the poison.

Call the local poison control center and follow their instructions. Keep this phone number posted near a telephone. If there is no local center, call the closest hospital emergency facility or a doctor. DO NOT rely on product labels for instructions. If there is no professional advice, be prepared to take steps to dilute the poison, maintain vital body functions, such as breathing and heartbeat, and get immediate medical treatment.

Care for shock until you have been advised by professionals. DO NOT induce vomiting if the person is unconscious or having convulsions; if the product swallowed was an acid, alkali, or petroleum product; or if it is not known what was swallowed. DO NOT give anything by mouth until you have checked with your local poison control center or EMS.

Otherwise, follow these first aid directions as appropriate:
1. Prevent shock (page 532). Rescue breathing or CPR may be necessary. Only a person trained in CPR should administer it.
2. DO NOT wait for symptoms to develop. Call the poison control center or EMS immediately. Follow their directions.
3. Save the label and/or container of the suspected poison.
4. Save any vomited material.

Poisoning is an emergency that can be prevented. Pills and medicines should be carefully labeled and stored out of the reach of children. Household and garden products that can be poisonous should be securely closed. These should then be safely stored out of the reach of small children.

Common Household Poisons

most drugs
some house plants
any spoiled food
alcohol
antifreeze
cosmetics
deodorant
ink
laundry detergent
matches
mothballs
nail polish or remover
perfume
peroxide
rat or mouse poison
suntan lotion
ammonia
bleach
corn and wart removers
dishwasher detergent
drain and toilet cleaners
lye
metal cleaner
oven cleaner
quicklime
rust remover
floor polish and wax
furniture polish and wax
gasoline
kerosene
lighter fluid
liquid naphtha
paint thinner
turpentine
wood preservative

Inhaled Poisons

Inhaled poisons are smoke, gases, and fumes. Warning symptoms of poisoning include dizziness, headache, and weakness. Before you enter a place where there might be poisonous smoke, gases, or fumes, make sure it is safe for you and other bystanders. Then move the injured person to fresh air. Send for immediate medical help and oxygen.

Follow these first aid directions:
1. Check the person's breathing. CPR training may be necessary to continue first aid.
2. Loosen tight clothing.
3. Prevent shock and care for other injuries.
4. If the person is conscious, elevate the head and chest to ease breathing.

Drug Overdose

A drug is a substance that affects the function of the mind or body. Drugs include alcohol, marijuana, hallucinogens, stimulants, and tranquilizers. Even drugs that are safe when used in small amounts may be poisonous when taken in large doses or over a period of time. Poisoning can be avoided by properly labeling and storing drugs. Keep ALL drugs away from small children.

A drug overdose can be a life-threatening emergency. Try to determine the type of drug taken, the amount, and the time it was taken. Call a poison control center or EMS and follow the instructions for specific care. If this center cannot be quickly identified, call a hospital emergency facility or a doctor. If there is no professional advice, be prepared to give general first aid.

Drug withdrawal after prolonged use can also produce severe symptoms. General first aid care is again important until professional medical help is received. In the case of drug overdose or withdrawal, get immediate medical help.

Follow these first aid directions:
1. Check the person's breathing. CPR training may be necessary to continue first aid.
2. Maintain an open airway and normal body temperature.
3. Care for a convulsion if necessary.
4. Be reassuring and keep the person calm. Try to keep her or him awake.
5. Follow directions for swallowed poison, if appropriate.
6. Get medical help.

Shock

Symptoms of Shock

Shock can result from any condition or injury that severely lowers blood pressure and vital body functions. Shock is not the same as electric shock, but a person can go into shock from a severe electric shock. Shock is a life-threatening emergency, even if the injury or condition that has caused it may not be fatal. Be alert for these possible symptoms of shock.

Early Symptoms of Shock:

pale, moist, clammy skin   rapid breathing

weakness and nausea   rapid, weak pulse

Advanced Symptoms of Shock:

unresponsiveness   unconsciousness

vacant look, dilated   mottled skin

   pupils

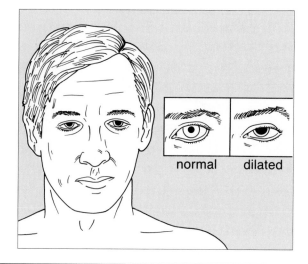

normal   dilated

Preventing and Caring for Shock

Prevention is an important part of treating shock. If signs of shock exist, act right away to alleviate them. Then take steps to prevent a more serious degree of shock. The injury or condition that causes shock is often severe, and may also require first aid.

Shock can be fatal, and even mild shock can become more severe without proper first aid. Improved circulation, adequate oxygen, and normal body temperature minimize the effect of shock. They are the objectives of preventing and caring for shock.

Follow these first aid directions:

1. To improve circulation, keep the injured person lying down in one of these positions:
   A. Flat on the back, if there is doubt about the correct position.
   B. On the side, if the injured person may choke on vomit, is unconscious, or has serious facial injuries.
   C. On the back with head and shoulders elevated, if this improves breathing or if there is no danger of choking and no sign of head, neck, or back injury.
   D. On the back with only the feet elevated, if this improves the condition.
2. To conserve body heat, place blankets or clothing over and under the injured person. DO NOT overheat the injured person.
3. DO NOT give anything to eat or drink.
4. DO NOT move the injured person if there is a possible neck or back injury.
5. Get immediate medical help.

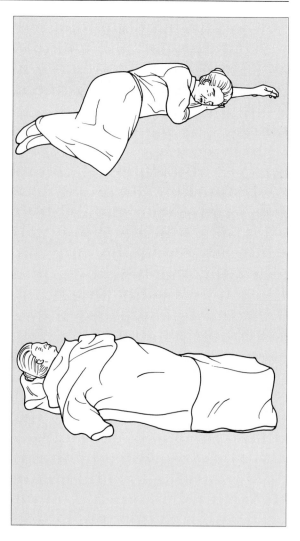

Poisonous Plants

poison ivy
reddish green stems; clusters of 3 shiny, teardrop-shaped leaflets

poison oak
clusters of three wavy-edged leaflets

poison sumac
leaflets pointed at both ends; one leaflet at the tip

Poison ivy, poison oak, and poison sumac cause allergic reactions in four out of five people. It is important to learn to recognize these plants, because they grow in suburban areas as well as in the woods.

Every part of the poison ivy plant contains oils that can cause a skin rash. A person may be exposed to the oils through contact with clothing, pet fur, or garden tools. The smoke from burning oils in poison ivy can be extremely dangerous to the lungs and eyes.

Carefully destroy poisonous plants with a chemical spray. Do not cut them down; they will grow back from the roots. After spraying, thoroughly wash all clothing.

Reactions to Poisonous Plants

The rash produced by the plants in the poison ivy group is characterized by redness, swelling, and itching. The rash may also produce oozing blisters and a burning sensation. The symptoms usually appear within 18 to 72 hours after contact.

Follow these first aid directions:
1. Remove contaminated clothing and set aside for later washing.
2. Wash all exposed skin very well with soap and water.
3. Get medical help for a severe reaction, a history of sensitivity, a rash on the face or genitals, or if plant parts were chewed or swallowed.

Other Skin-Contact Poisons

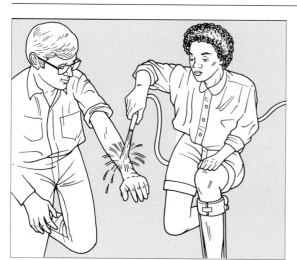

Other skin-contact poisons include harsh or corrosive chemicals often found in household and garden products. On contact with the skin, these poisons can produce a chemical burn. If the poisonous substance is a pesticide or a strong acid, emergency medical help is necessary. Otherwise, first aid for skin contact poisons is similar to that for chemical burns (page 520).

Follow these first aid directions:
1. Remove contaminated clothing.
2. Wash away the poisonous substance with large quantities of water for 20 minutes.
3. Get medical help in cases where the chemical burn is extensive.

Unconciousness

Possible Causes and First Aid Priorities

There are many possible causes of unconsciousness. Sometimes unconsciousness is brief—as in fainting—and not related to an injury. Other times, unconsciousness is related to an injury or medical problem. It can be caused by injury-related shock, respiratory failure, convulsions, drug use, head injury, or sudden illness. Unconsciousness can signal a medical emergency.

When a person is found unconscious, immediate first aid is important. Information about the events that resulted in unconsciousness may be limited or unavailable.

Remember the first aid priorities. Especially remember to avoid injury or danger to yourself or other bystanders and to protect the injured person from further danger or damage.

Medical treatment is always required unless the condition is very minor. Call the emergency medical services for help.

Follow these first aid directions before giving care for specific injuries:

1. Confirm unconsciousness. See whether the injured person responds to a shout or a firm tap on the shoulder.
2. Check for any sign of breathing. Rescue breathing or CPR may be necessary to continue first aid.
3. Call EMS for help.
4. Prevent and care for shock (page 532).
5. Check for injuries. If there are any, care for them appropriately.

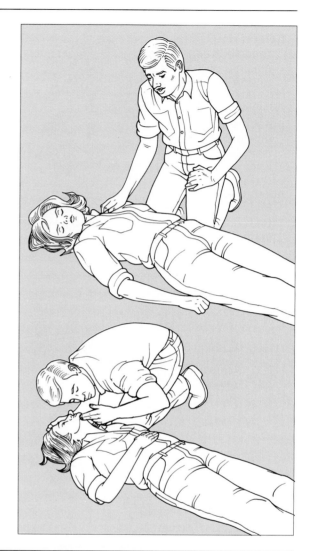

Fainting

When the blood supply to the brain is interrupted for a short time, the result can be a momentary loss of consciousness. Fainting can occur suddenly or be preceded by symptoms including dizziness, nausea, paleness, and sweating.

A person who feels faint should lie down or bend over with the head down.

Follow these first aid directions:

1. Act quickly to prevent injury from a fall.
2. Keep the person lying down with legs raised. Loosen any tight clothing.
3. Sponge the person's face and forehead with cool water.
4. Get medical help if recovery is not rapid.

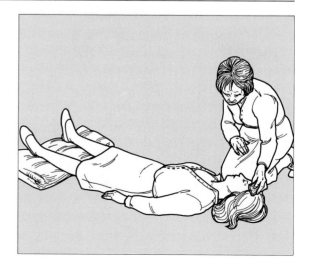

Heart Attack

Signs of a Possible Heart Attack

tight or crushing pain that lasts more than 2 minutes and may spread from the center of the chest to the upper abdomen, shoulder, left arm, neck, or jaw

shortness of breath

severe anxiety

weakness

sweating

pale or bluish skin or lips

nausea or vomiting

irregular pulse

If sudden constant chest pain occurs, suspect a heart problem. A heart attack is caused by the blockage of a coronary artery. An attack may be mild or result in sudden death. To reduce the risk of heart attack, maintain proper weight, keep blood pressure down, get regular exercise and medical checkups, and eat foods low in fats and cholesterol; avoid smoking.

Be alert for the signs of a possible heart attack. They include tight, crushing chest pain that can spread to arms, shoulders, or neck; severe shortness of breath; weakness; sweating; bluish color of skin or lips; and nausea. If a heart attack is suspected, the first step is to calm and reassure the person.

If there is any history of heart trouble or the chest pain is accompanied by other danger signs, treat the condition as a heart attack. Get immediate medical help and be prepared to give prompt first aid.

Follow these first aid directions:
1. Call EMS for an ambulance.
2. Have the person sit up or recline on pillows.
3. Loosen tight clothing and keep the person warm, NOT overheated.
4. Find out if the person has medicine for this condition. Help the person take this medicine, if he or she is conscious.
5. If the person loses consciousness, lay the person on his or her back and check for signs of breathing. CPR training may be necessary to continue first aid.
6. Stay with the victim until medical help arrives.

Stroke

A stroke occurs when a blood vessel in the brain ruptures or a clot restricts circulation. The type of damage that results depends on the area of the brain affected. Symptoms of a stroke include speech problems, weakness or paralysis on one side of the body, confusion, dizziness, or unconsciousness.

Follow these first aid directions:
1. Place the person on his or her side to prevent choking.
2. Keep the person lightly covered.
3. Check for breathing. Artificial respiration or CPR may be necessary.
4. DO NOT give fluids.
5. Get immediate medical help.

Cardiopulmonary Resuscitation

What is CPR?

CPR, or cardiopulmonary resuscitation, is a technique used to save a person who has stopped breathing and whose heart has stopped beating. CPR is a combination of rescue breathing and external chest compressions. Rescue breathing forces air into the lungs. External chest compressions circulate the blood. When the heart stops beating (cardiac arrest) and breathing stops, cardiopulmonary resuscitation is necessary. The purpose of CPR is to keep the victim alive until medical help arrives or until heartbeat or breathing return. Special training in CPR is required. CPR courses are also useful in learning to recognize the symptoms of cardiac arrest.

Who Needs CPR Training?

CPR training can mean the difference between life and death. It is a life-saving skill that anyone can learn. However, the information in this manual does not take the place of CPR training. The American Red Cross and the American Heart Association offer CPR instruction. Lectures and demonstrations by authorized CPR instructors, followed by practice sessions with manikins, are used to teach the procedure.

Cardiac arrest is a life-threatening emergency that can occur any time and any place. Medical professionals, police, firefighters, and paramedics get CPR training. Before they arrive, you may save a life if you are trained in CPR. Who needs CPR training? You do!

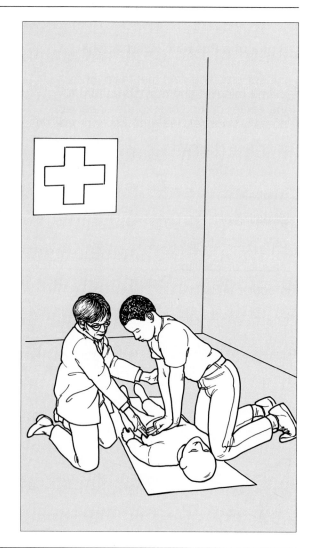

When CPR Is Needed

Follow these steps to see if CPR is needed:
1. To see whether the person can respond, tap the shoulder and shout. If there is no response, call EMS for an ambulance.
2. Check ABCs (see page 512). Open the airway and monitor breathing. If the person is not breathing, give two full, slow breaths (page 519). Check for circulation by feeling for a pulse and looking for signs of bleeding.

If the person has a pulse and is breathing, watch him or her until help arrives. If the person has a pulse and is not breathing, continue to give rescue breathing. If the person has no pulse and is not breathing, CPR is needed immediately.

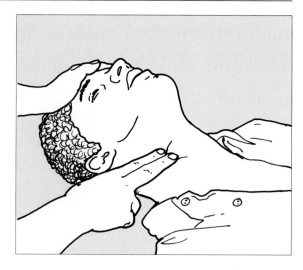

Cardiopulmonary Resuscitation

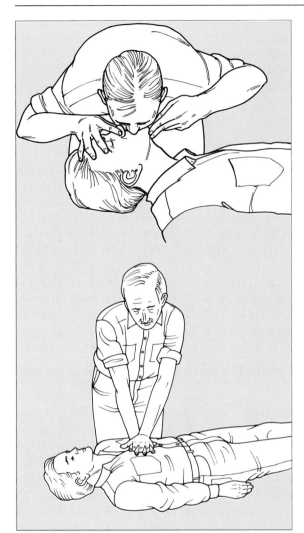

The Steps of CPR

CAUTION: If you have not had CPR training, DO NOT attempt to give CPR. If done improperly, CPR can cause further injury or death. If CPR is given to a person who has a pulse, it can cause cardiac arrest. CPR for children and infants is different than for adults.

A person trained in CPR checks for unresponsiveness, breathing, and pulse as described in "Where CPR Is Needed." Determine unresponsiveness and remember the ABCs (page 512). Call EMS for an ambulance.

If there is no pulse, a person with CPR training finds the correct hand position and gives 15 compressions in about ten seconds. This circulates blood to the brain and other vital organs. After every 15 compressions, the rescuer stops compressing and gives two full, slow breaths. The rescuer continues cycles of 15 compressions and two breaths.

The rescuer checks the victim's pulse after the first minute (or after four sets of compressions and breaths) and again every few minutes. If there is no pulse, the rescuer continues CPR. If there is a pulse but no breathing, the rescuer gives rescue breathing. If there is a pulse and breathing, the rescuer maintains an open airway and keeps checking pulse and breathing.

If two rescuers are available, one rescuer gives chest compressions while the other gives one breath after every five compressions. Two rescuers are more effective than one because two rescuers can give more frequent breaths and can change positions if one gets tired.

Respiratory Emergency Prevention

There are many causes of respiratory failure. Respiratory accidents often occur around water. By learning to swim and knowing about water safety, accidental drownings can be prevented.

Respiratory emergencies also can occur at home. Choking and suffocation are the leading causes of accidental death in infants less than a year old. Drowning is the second leading cause of accidental death in children between the ages of one and four. Some respiratory emergencies can be prevented by labeling medicines and poisons and storing them out of reach of children. Others can be prevented by discarding plastic wrappings. Never leave a child unattended in the bathtub.

First Aid Review

Vocabulary

abrasion	first aid	muscle strain
abdominal thrust	first-degree burn	open fracture
cardiopulmonary resuscitation	fracture	pressure-point technique
(CPR)	frostbite	puncture
choking	heart attack	rescue breathing
closed fracture	heat cramp	second-degree burn
concussion	heat exhaustion	shock
convulsion	heat stroke	splint
croup	Heimlich maneuver	sprain
dislocation	hyperventilation	stroke
electric shock	hypothermia	third-degree burn
emergency medical	incision	unconsciousness
services (EMS)	laceration	universal choking
fainting	muscle cramp	signal

Using Vocabulary

Questions 1–10. On a separate sheet of paper, write the term from the column on the right that matches the phrase on the left.

1 life-threatening condition in which blood pressure and vital body functions are severely lowered
2 practical and immediate care for an injury or sudden illness
3 first aid procedure that forces air into the lungs
4 a break or crack in a bone
5 upward thrusts on the abdomen, intended to dislodge an object that is causing choking
6 condition caused by the blockage of a coronary artery
7 a life-threatening condition involving very high body temperature, lack of perspiration, and rapid pulse
8 first aid technique for use when heart and lungs fail
9 lowered body temperature
10 type of wound in which a hole is made by a sharp object

a heat stroke
b CPR
c hypothermia
d abdominal thrusts
e heart attack
f fracture
g first aid
h shock
i puncture
j rescue breathing

Interpreting Ideas

1 What is the purpose of first aid? What are the advantages of a knowledge of first aid?
2 Why can animal or human bites be dangerous?
3 List three methods of controlling bleeding, in the order in which they should be tried.
4 What are the signs of choking? How can a choking person perform abdominal thrusts on himself or herself?

5 When should medical care be sought for a blister? When should a blister be drained? Describe the procedure for draining a blister.
6 What are the possible causes of an eye injury? What two actions should be avoided with any suspected eye injury? With chemical burns or invisible objects in the eye, what two steps should be taken before seeking medical care?

7 How should a splinter be removed?

8 How can you help to prevent injury and choking during a convulsion?

9 How can you protect yourself from the source of electricity when you are trying to care for an electric shock victim?

10 How can you avoid hypothermia?

11 Compare the symptoms of heat exhaustion and heat stroke. Which of these conditions is more serious?

12 What are the signs of a sprain? What parts of the body are most easily sprained?

13 List five signs of head injury.

14 What directions should be followed when a child has swallowed poison? How can poisoning be prevented?

15 What immediate procedure should you follow if you discover the victim of a drug overdose?

16 What are the early symptoms of shock? four advanced symptoms of shock? What are the objectives of preventing and caring for shock?

17 What are the signs of a possible heart attack? How can people reduce the risk of heart attack?

18 What are the symptoms of stroke? What steps should be taken to care for a stroke victim?

19 What is the purpose of CPR? What two procedures does CPR combine? What is the purpose of each procedure?

20 Why is it dangerous for a person without proper training to try to give CPR?

Applying Concepts

1 A two-year-old child awakened during the night with a barking cough and difficulty breathing, but no fever. What do you think is wrong with this child? How would you care for the condition?

2 How should burns be cared for?

3 Why is it dangerous to talk with a mouthful of food?

4 When frostbite occurs, why is it dangerous to rub the frozen area to help it thaw out?

5 Why do you think heat cramps are more likely to affect the muscles of the legs or abdomen first?

6 How can some people get a rash from poison ivy without ever having touched the plant?

7 How would you argue that everyone needs CPR training?

8 A high school basketball player who is about to make a speech at an awards banquet suddenly has chest pains and difficulty breathing. What is most likely to be the problem? How should it be cared for?

Decision Making

1 Tell how the following situation should have been handled: A child who was thought to have swallowed a household poison was promptly give syrup of ipecac in order to induce vomiting.

2 After football practice Tom noticed swelling around one of his ankles. As he walked home, the ankle became increasingly painful. To get the swelling down, Tom applied an ice pack to his ankle. What did Tom do wrong?

Projects

1 Make a poster showing poisonous plants, such as poison ivy, that grow in your area. What is the leaf color and arrangement? How does it change with the seasons? If the plant has berries, what color are they?

2 Prepare and distribute a safety booklet for young children. With words and cartoons, describe how to prevent accidents, including poisoning. Also show what to do if an accident does happen.

3 Create an eye-catching bulletin board that provides information on a group of related emergencies, such as sports emergencies. Include easy-to-follow illustrated steps for handling the emergencies and emergency phone numbers for getting the proper help.

4 Organize a series of skits in which you and several classmates act out medical emergencies such as choking, bleeding, or drowning. Demonstrate the proper first aid techniques.

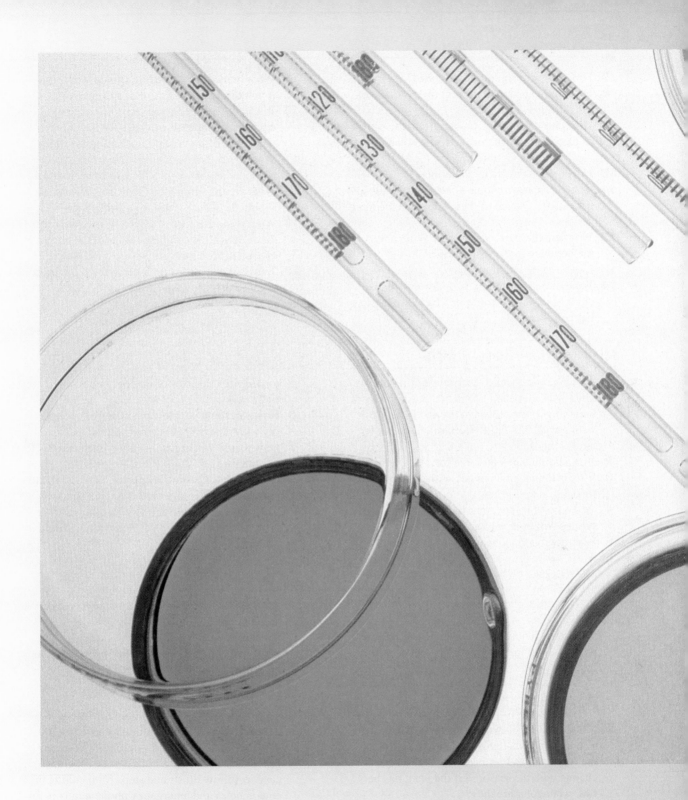

Health and Safety Almanac

Calories, Minerals, and Vitamins of Selected Foods

Food and amount	Energy (Calories)	Nutrients		Minerals		Vitamins				
		Protein (g)	Fat (g)	Calcium (mg)	Iron (mg)	Vitamin A (International Units)	Vitamin B₁ (thiamine) (mg)	Vitamin B₂ (riboflavin) (mg)	Niacin (mg)	Vitamin C (mg)
Apple, 1 medium	80	—	1	10	.4	120	.04	.03	.1	6
Applesauce, 1 cup, unsweetened	100	—	—	10	1.2	100	.05	.02	.1	2
Bacon, 2 slices, crisp	85	4	8	2	.5	—	.08	.05	.8	—
Banana, 1 medium	100	1	—	10	.8	230	.06	.07	.8	12
Beans, snap green, 1 cup, cooked	30	2	—	63	.8	680	.09	.11	.6	15
Beans, red kidney, 1 cup, canned	230	15	1	74	4.6	10	.13	.10	1.5	—
Beef cuts: Hamburger, 3 ounces	235	20	17	9	2.6	30	.07	.17	4.4	—
Rib roast, 3 ounces, boned	375	17	33	8	2.2	70	.05	.13	3.1	—
Sirloin, 3 ounces, boned	330	20	27	9	2.5	50	.05	.15	4.0	—
Beef stew with vegetables, 1 cup	220	16	11	29	2.9	2400	.15	.17	4.7	17
Beets, 1 cup, cooked	55	2	—	24	.9	30	.05	.07	.5	10
Breads: White, average slice, enriched	70	2	1	21	.6	—	.10	.06	.8	—
Whole wheat, average slice	65	3	1	24	.8	—	.09	.03	.8	—
Butter, 1 tbsp.	100	—	12	3	—	430	—	—	—	—
Cabbage, 1 cup, raw	15	1	—	34	.3	90	.04	.04	.2	33
Cake: Sponge, average slice	195	5	4	20	1.1	300	.09	.14	.6	—
Pound, average slice	160	2	10	6	.5	80	.05	.06	.4	—
Candies: Caramels, 1 ounce	115	1	3	42	.4	—	.01	.05	.1	—
Chocolate, milk, 1 ounce	145	2	9	65	.3	80	.02	.10	.1	—
Cantaloupe, ½ melon	80	2	—	38	1.1	9240	.11	.08	1.6	90
Carrot, raw, 1 average size	30	1	—	27	.5	7930	.04	.04	.4	6
Catsup, 1 tbsp.	15	—	—	3	.1	210	.01	.01	.2	2
Cheese: Cheddar, 1 ounce	115	7	9	204	.2	300	.01	.11	—	—
Cottage, 1 cup	235	28	10	135	.3	370	.05	.37	.3	—
Cream cheese, 1 ounce	100	2	10	23	.3	400	—	.06	—	—
Swiss, 1 ounce	95	7	7	219	.2	230	—	.08	—	—
Chicken, broiled, 3 ounces	115	20	3	8	1.4	80	.05	.16	7.4	—
Chicken, fried, ½ breast, 3.3 ounces	160	26	5	9	1.3	70	.04	.17	11.6	—
Cocoa, 1 cup, homemade	220	9	9	298	.8	320	.10	.44	.4	2
Coffee, black, 1 cup	—	—	—	—	—	—	—	—	—	—
Cola, carbonated, 12 ounces	145	—	—	—	—	—	—	—	—	—
Corn, average ear	70	2	1	2	.5	310	.09	.08	1.1	7
Corn flakes, 1 cup	95	2	—	3	.6	1180	.29	.35	2.9	9
Crackers: Graham, 4	110	2	3	11	1.0	—	.04	.16	1.0	—
Saltines, 4	50	1	1	2	.5	—	.05	.05	.4	—
Cream: Sour, 1 cup	495	7	48	268	.1	1820	.08	.34	.2	2
Whipped topping, 1 cup	155	2	13	61	—	550	.02	.04	—	—
Doughnut, 1 plain	100	1	5	10	.4	20	.05	.05	.4	—

Food										
Egg: Raw or cooked in shell, 1	80	6	6	28	1.0	260	.04	.14	—	—
Omelet, scrambled, 1	95	6	7	47	.9	310	.04	.16	—	—
Frankfurter, 1	170	7	15	3	.8	—	.08	.11	1.4	—
Fruit cocktail, 1 cup, canned	195	1	—	23	1.0	360	.05	.03	1.0	5
Grapefruit, ½	45	1	—	19	.5	10	.05	.02	.2	44
Haddock, breaded, fried, 3 ounces	140	17	5	34	1.0	—	.03	.06	2.7	2
Honey, strained, 1 tbsp.	65	—	—	1	.1	—	—	.01	.1	—
Ice cream, 1 cup	270	5	14	176	.1	540	.05	.33	.1	1
Jellies, 1 tbsp.	50	—	—	4	.3	—	—	.01	—	1
Lamb: Rib chop, boned, 4 ounces	400	25	33	10	1.5	—	.14	.25	5.6	—
Liver: Beef, fried, 2 ounces	130	15	6	6	5.0	30,280	.15	2.37	9.4	15
Luncheon meat, 2 ounces	165	8	14	5	1.2	—	.18	.12	1.6	—
Macaroni and cheese, 1 cup	430	17	22	362	1.8	860	.20	.40	1.8	—
Margarine, 1 tbsp.	100	—	12	3	—	470	—	—	—	—
Mayonnaise, 1 tbsp.	100	—	11	3	.1	40	—	.01	—	—
Milk: Whole, 1 cup	150	8	8	291	.1	310	.09	.40	.2	2
Skim (non-fat), 1 cup	85	8	—	302	.1	500	.09	.34	.2	2
Nuts: Almonds, 1 cup shelled	850	26	77	332	6.7	—	.34	1.31	5.0	—
Peanuts, roasted, 1 cup	840	37	72	107	3.0	—	.46	.19	24.8	—
Oatmeal, 1 cup, cooked	130	5	2	22	1.4	—	.19	.05	.2	—
Oils, salad, cooking, 1 tbsp.	120	—	14	—	—	—	—	—	—	—
Orange, 1 medium	65	1	—	54	.5	260	.13	.05	.5	66
Orange juice, frozen, 1 cup	120	2	—	25	.2	540	.23	.03	.9	120
Pancake, wheat, 1 average	60	2	2	27	.4	30	.06	.07	.5	—
Peach, 1 medium	40	1	—	9	.5	1330	.02	.05	1.0	7
Peanut butter, 1 tbsp.	95	4	8	9	.3	—	.02	.02	2.4	—
Peas, green, 1 cup	110	8	—	30	3.0	960	.43	.14	2.7	21
Pie: Apple, 4-inch wedge	345	3	15	11	.9	40	.15	.11	1.3	2
Lemon meringue, 4-inch wedge	305	4	12	17	1.0	200	.09	.12	.7	4
Pineapple, raw, 1 cup, diced	80	1	—	26	.8	110	.14	.05	.3	26
Pizza, cheese, 4¾-inch wedge	145	6	4	86	1.1	230	.16	.18	1.6	4
Pork: Roast, 3 ounces	310	21	24	9	2.7	—	.78	.22	4.8	—
Chop, with bone, 2.7 ounces	305	19	25	9	2.7	—	.75	.22	4.5	—
Potatoes: Baked, 1 medium	145	4	—	14	1.1	—	.15	.07	2.7	31
French-fried, deep fat, 10 pieces	135	2	7	8	.7	—	.07	.04	1.6	11
Potato chips, 10	115	1	8	8	.4	—	.04	.01	1.0	3
Rice: White, enriched, 1 cup cooked	225	4	—	21	1.8	—	.23	.02	2.1	—
Salad dressing, French, 1 tbsp.	65	—	6	2	.1	—	—	—	.1	—
Sardines, canned, 3 ounces	175	20	9	372	2.5	190	.02	.17	4.6	—
Spaghetti, 1 cup cooked	155	5	1	11	1.3	—	.20	.11	1.5	—
Spinach, 1 cup cooked	40	5	1	167	4.0	14,580	.13	.25	.9	50
Sugar, 1 teaspoon	15	—	—	—	—	—	—	—	—	—
Tomato juice, canned, 1 cup	45	2	—	17	2.2	1940	.12	.07	1.9	39
Tuna fish, 3 ounces	170	24	7	7	1.6	70	.04	.10	10.1	—
Yogurt, 8-oz., plain	145	12	4	415	.2	150	.10	.49	.3	2

Common Noninfectious Diseases and Disorders

Disease	Characteristics	Treatment
Acne	Overproduction of sebum causes blackheads, white-heads, and pimples over face, upper chest and back	Cleansing skin; medication for severe cases
Alzheimer's disease	Progressive dementia that may occur before age 60; brain cells gradually die; causes impaired language and motor functions and loss of memory and thinking ability	None; research under way to find effective treatments
Anemia	Disorder in which there are too few red blood cells or not enough hemoglobin; not enough oxygen reaches tissues; causes weakness	Depending on cause, iron supplements, vitamin injections, or transfusions
Anorexia nervosa	Psychological condition causing progressive weight loss; refusal to eat causes dry skin, brittle hair, dehydration, fainting, and irregular heartbeat	Counseling to change attitude toward eating and to resolve underlying conflicts
Appendicitis	Infection of appendix; causes severe pain in abdomen, vomiting, constipation, and fever	Surgical removal of appendix
Arteriosclerosis	Hardening of arteries; may cause legs to ache during physical activity, dizziness, and temporary loss of sight; may lead to stroke, heart disease, or senile dementia	Diet control; medication
Arthritis	A group of diseases in which joints in the body become inflamed, swollen, and sore	No cure; medications relieve symptoms; joint surgery; physical therapy
Asthma	Chronic respiratory disease; spasms of bronchi result in recurrent attacks of coughing, wheezing, and shortness of breath	Medication
Atherosclerosis	Build-up of fatty material such as cholesterol on artery walls; reduces blood flow; can lead to heart attack or stroke	Diet control; regular physical activity; quitting smoking
Bulimia	Eating disorder in which episodes of extreme overeating are followed by self-induced vomiting or use of diuretics and laxatives	Counseling to stop the binge-purge cycle and regain control over eating behavior
Cancer	Group of diseases characterized by uncontrolled growth of cells; caused by carcinogens; symptoms vary with type of cancer	Surgery; radiation therapy; chemotherapy; immunotherapy
Cerebral palsy	Disorder resulting from brain damage at or before birth; results in loss of muscle control, poor coordination, and speech and hearing problems	Exercise; supportive devices
Coronary heart disease (coronary artery disease)	Reduced flow of blood to wall of heart due to atherosclerosis; causes chest pains and possible heart attack	Diet control; regular physical activity, quitting smoking
Cystic fibrosis	Hereditary disease that affects mucus-secreting glands; causes coughing, poor digestion, diarrhea, increased susceptibility to respiratory infections	Respiratory therapy; antibiotics
Diabetes mellitus, insulin-dependent (Type I)	Hereditary condition in which the pancreas does not produce enough insulin, resulting in high blood sugar; causes frequent urination accompanied by thirst, fatigue, and rapid weight loss; if left untreated, can cause blindness, kidney failure, and death; onset usually occurs in childhood or adolescence	Insulin injections; special diet
Diabetes mellitus, noninsulin-dependent (Type II)	Condition in which the cells cannot take in glucose, resulting in high blood sugar; causes frequent urination, thirst, fatigue, blurred vision, and frequent infections; onset most common among overweight adults	Special diet; exercise; medication

Common Noninfectious Diseases and Disorders

Disease	Characteristics	Treatment
Emphysema	Condition of weakened lung tissue; lungs lose elasticity, resulting in difficulty in exhaling; usually related to smoking or air pollution	No cure; medicines, hormones, air pumps, and surgery help relieve symptoms
Epilepsy	Disorder of nerve cells in brain; seizures occur when cells release a sudden burst of electric energy	Medication
Glaucoma	Build-up of fluid pressure within the eye, causing the eye to become rigid; causes loss of peripheral vision and may lead to blindness if left untreated	Medication; surgery
Gout	Inflammation of joints due to build-up of uric acid; causes severe pain in elbow, knee, hand, or foot, fever, and inflamed skin; can lead to kidney disease and death if left untreated	Physical therapy; spinal brace
Hemophilia	Hereditary disease in which blood lacks factors necessary for clotting; bleeding cannot be stopped	Avoiding risk of injury; injections of a clotting factor
Hernia	Bulge of tissue pushing through muscle wall; a rupture; often of intestine through abdominal wall	Surgery
Hodgkin's disease	Cancer of the lymph nodes; occurs most often in young adults; produces enlarged lymph nodes, fever, weight loss, fatigue, and sweating	Radiation therapy; chemotherapy
Hypertension	High blood pressure caused by narrowing of blood vessels; no symptoms until blood pressure gets dangerously high; can lead to stroke or heart disease	Medication to control blood pressure; special diet
Leukemia	Cancer of the bone marrow, in which immature white blood cells multiply rapidly and crowd out mature white cells; immune system weakens; occurs most often in children	Chemotherapy
Migraine	Severe headache accompanied by nausea and sensitivity to light	No cure; medication; avoiding certain foods or stressful situations
Multiple sclerosis	Disease that slowly destroys nerve tissue; usually starts during childhood; causes paralysis and death	No cure; rest and physical therapy
Muscular dystrophy	Progressive weakening of muscles, usually starting during early childhood; causes deformed limbs	No cure; physical therapy
Osteoporosis	Loss of calcium from bone; results in weakened bones and rounded shoulders; common in older women	Diet rich in calcium; exericse
Parkinson's disease	Disorder of the nervous system; results in tremors, slower body movements, weakness, stooping posture, and weak voice	Medication
Schizophrenia	Mental disorder in which a person withdraws from reality, behaves in odd ways, and has hallucinations	Psychotherapy; medication
Scoliosis	Abnormal curvature of the spine that becomes noticeable during adolescence; can cause chest infections and shortness of breath	Physical therapy; spinal brace; electrical stimulation
Sickle-cell disease	Hereditary type of anemia in which red blood cells are deformed in shape, or "sickled"; causes severe pain, high fever, damage to body tissues, blindness, convulsions, paralysis, and loss of speech; occurs chiefly among Blacks	No effective treatment; experimental medicines
Stroke	Blockage or rupture of blood vessel in the brain; can cause loss of physical and mental abilities or death	Physical therapy

Common Infectious Diseases

Disease	Characteristics	Method of Transmission	Prevention/Treatment
Acquired immune-deficiency syndrome (AIDS)	Viral disease of the immune system; causes fever, fatigue, loss of appetite, loss of resistance to infection, and swollen glands; fatal	Sexual contact; transfusion of infected blood; use of unsterile syringes	Screening blood donors; changing sexual behavior; no treatment or cure
Athletes's foot	Fungal skin infection on the foot; skin becomes red and flaky, blisters develop between toes	Contact with contaminated objects such as showers and locker room floors	Cleaning and drying feet; antifungal medication
Botulism	Food poisoning caused by toxin released from bacteria; results in muscle weakness, dizziness, nausea, and paralysis of cardiac, respiratory, and central nervous systems	Eating vegetables and fruits that were canned improperly	Toxin destroyed by heating, so all foods canned or bottled should be boiled; antitoxin
Bronchitis	Viral or bacterial infection of membranes lining bronchi; causes deep cough that brings up gray or yellowish sputum, difficulty breathing, and fever	Close contact with infected person	Bed rest; antibiotics
Chancroid	Bacterial STD; painful chancre develops in genital area	Sexual contact	Antibiotics
Chicken pox	Viral skin infection; causes mild fever and itchy skin rash with blisters that form scabs	Close contact with infected person; airborne spread of virus	Skin lotions alleviate symptoms
Chlamydia	Bacterial STD; inflammation of urethra in males and vagina in females; symptoms similar to gonorrhea	Sexual contact	Antibiotics
Cholera	Bacterial infection of intestines; causes severe diarrhea, vomiting, and dehydration	Ingestion of food or water contaminated with sewage or vomit	Drinking treated water; replacement of body fluids; antibiotics
Common cold	Viral infection of upper respiratory tract; causes coughing, sneezing, and runny nose	Close contact with infected person; airborne spread of virus	Bed rest; hot liquids
Conjunctivitis	Viral or bacterial eye infection; results in tearing, inflammation, itching, burning, and pus in eye	Contact with discharge from eyes	Antibiotics
Diphtheria	Bacterial infection; results in sore throat, fever, and patches of grayish membrane on tonsils and throat; now most common in less developed countries	Direct contact with infected saliva or mucus	Vaccine; hospitalization; antitoxins; antibiotics
Gonorrhea	Bacterial STD; males experience painful urination, puslike discharge from penis; symptoms not as obvious in females	Sexual contact	Antibiotics
Hepatitis A (infectious hepatitis)	Viral liver infection; causes fever, fatigue, loss of appetite, abdominal pain, and jaundice; sudden onset	Person-to-person contact; eating contaminated food and water	Careful attention to hygiene; isolating patients during infectious period; bed rest
Hepatitis B (serum hepatitis)	Viral liver infection; symptoms similar to Hepatitis A, but more severe and with slower onset	Contact with contaminated syringes; contact with infected blood; sexual contact	Same as Hepatitis A
Hepatitis, Non-A, Non-B	Viral liver infection; symptoms similar to Hepatitis A and B, but milder	Contact with infected blood; sexual contact	Same as Hepatitis A

Common Infectious Diseases

Disease	Characteristics	Method of Transmission	Prevention/Treatment
Herpes Type I	Viral mouth infection; causes cold sores and fever blisters that appear most often on lips and mouth	Contact with infected saliva	Heals naturally; topical medications may ease symptoms
Herpes Type II	Viral infection of the genitals; sores on genitals	Sexual contact	No drug treatment or cure
Influenza	Viral respiratory infection; causes fever, chills, headache, muscle aches, runny nose, sore throat, and coughing	Person-to-person contact; contact with contaminated articles	Vaccine; bed rest; hot liquids
Legionnaire's disease	Bacterial lung infection; results in high fever, inflammation of lungs, coughing, and weakness	Contact with bacteria that grow in the water of air-conditioners	Antibiotics
Malaria	Caused by a parasite that lives in the blood; causes fever, chills, sweating, headache, and jaundice	Carried by mosquitoes; transfusion of infected blood	Preventive medications; drug therapy
Measles (rubeola)	Viral infection of skin and respiratory tract; results in fever, dry cough, runny nose, and rash; can lead to pneumonia and other serious complications	Contact with infected saliva or mucus; airborne spread of virus; highly contagious	Vaccine; bed rest
Meningitis	Viral or bacterial inflammation of the membranes around the spinal cord and brain; results in fever, headache, nausea, vomiting, and a stiff neck; may cause unconsciousness	Contact with infected saliva or mucus; airborne spread of virus	Vaccine or drug therapy for bacterial form; symptomatic treatment for viral form
Mono-nucleosis	Viral infection that spreads to many organs; causes high fever, fatigue, swollen glands, and sore throat; weakness and lack of energy noticeable for weeks	Kissing is suspected; other methods unknown	Bed rest; treatment of fever
Mumps	Viral infection of glands; causes headache, fever, vomiting, and swelling of glands in front of ears	Direct contact with saliva or contaminated articles; highly contagious	Vaccine; bed rest
Pneumonia	Viral or bacterial infection of lungs; causes inflammation of the lungs, chills, fever, chest pain, and coughing	Contact with infected saliva or mucus	Vaccine and antibiotics for bacterial pneumonia
Poliomyelitis	Viral infection of nerves; results in fever, headache, vomiting, muscular stiffness, soreness, and weakness; can cause paralysis that may lead to respiratory failure and death	Direct contact; eating contaminated foods	Vaccine; no specific treatment
Rabies (hydrophobia)	Viral infection of the brain; causes convulsions, paralysis, restlessness, fever, and excessive salivation; fatal unless treated in time	Contact with saliva from the bite of an infected animal (dog, cat, fox, skunk, racoon, bat, or rat)	Vaccine; see physician immediately for antirabies injections
Rheumatic fever	Caused by streptococcal bacteria; results in severe sore throat (strep throat), fever, inflamed joints, and body rash; can cause permanent heart damage	Direct contact	Antibiotics
Ringworm	Fungal skin infection; causes ring-shaped sores	Direct contact with fungus or contaminated articles	Careful laundering of clothing; good personal hygiene; antifungal compounds

Common Infectious Diseases

Disease	Characteristics	Method of Transmission	Prevention/Treatment
Rocky mountain spotted fever	Caused by tiny, bacterialike organisms; results in a high fever, severe headache, chills, body rash, and severe muscle weakness; if untreated, kidneys, liver, lungs, and blood can be damaged	Bite of an infected tick	Tick repellant; antibiotics
Rubella (German measles)	Mild viral disease; causes rash, fever, swollen glands around ears, neck, and throat; can cause birth defects if a pregnant woman contracts disease	Direct contact with saliva or mucus of infected person	Vaccine; bed rest
Salmonellosis	Bacterial food poisoning; causes acute diarrhea, abdominal pain, vomiting, and fever	Eating contaminated food, such as inadequately cooked meat, poultry, and egg products	Keeping raw meats refrigerated and cooking meat thoroughly; medication to relieve diarrhea and vomiting
Scarlet fever	Caused by streptococcal bacteria; results in severe sore throat (strep throat), fever, vomiting, headache, and body rash	Direct contact	Antibiotics
Shingles	Chicken pox virus attacks nerve roots; results in fever and scabby sores	Direct contact	Skin lotions
Staphylococcal food poisoning	Caused by bacterial toxin; results in vomiting and abdominal cramps; most common type of food poisoning	Eating contaminated food, such as tuna and chicken salads, cream-filled pastries	Keeping food cold; medication to relieve vomiting
Syphilis	Bacterial STD; causes open sore on genitals and body rash in early stage; more serious symptoms develop if left untreated	Sexual contact	Antibiotics
Tetanus (lockjaw)	Bacterial infection of nerve cells in spinal cord; causes painful tightening of the muscles; can be fatal	Bacteria enter the body through wounds	Vaccine; antitoxin
Trichinosis	Food poisoning caused by parasitic worms; causes diarrhea, fever, and profuse sweating	Ingestion of infected pork or game	Cooking pork thoroughly; bed rest; medication
Tuberculosis (TB)	Bacterial lung infection; causes coughing, weight loss, blood in phlegm, afternoon fevers, and heavy perspiration at night	Contact with saliva or mucus of infected person; ingestion of unpasteurized dairy products from an infected cow	Antibiotics
Typhoid fever	Severe form of salmonellosis; causes fever, headache, weakness, loss of appetite, skin rash, and constipation or diarrhea	Ingestion of contaminated food and water	Antibiotics
Vaginitis	Yeast or protist infection of vagina; causes vaginal inflammation, soreness, discharges, and itching	Yeast infection may develop with hormonal change or after use of antibiotics; protists can be spread by sexual contact	Antifungal cream; medication
Whooping cough (pertussis)	Bacterial respiratory infection; results in loss of appetite, mild fever, lethargy, hacking cough, followed later by violent coughing episodes and vomiting	Contact with saliva or mucus of infected person	Vaccine; antibiotics

Medicine Chest Know-How

A bleary-eyed man rummages through the bathroom cabinet, tossing various bottles and boxes aside until, with a sigh of relief, he finds the remedy for his indisposition.

This scene, enacted frequently in television commercials, may help sell the sponsor's product, but is not one to be recommended for the viewer's home. What's wrong with the picture is that the bathroom is not the proper place to store medicines. Bathroom cabinets are usually right over the sink and too accessible to young children. What's more, the warm moist air of the bathroom can cause some drugs to deteriorate. Not only that, but the clutter found in the man's cabinet, which obviously made it difficult for him to find what he wanted, suggests that he probably had more drug products than he really needed.

Of course, it's a good idea to have useful medical supplies on hand for emergencies and to treat minor ills, but the family medicine chest does not have to be a mini drug store. What should be kept in the average household will depend on the makeup of the family—for instance, when there are young children the medicine chest might include baby aspirin, antibacterial topical ointments, and medicine to treat symptoms of diarrhea. For that family, syrup of ipecac to induce vomiting and activated charcoal are important for emergency treatment for some accidental poisonings. Persons who are likely to use or administer them, however, should understand the types of poisoning for which they should not be used, as when a caustic agent has been swallowed, for instance.

Generally, medicine chests should include only those health care products likely to be used on a regular basis. Overstocking drugs in the household should be avoided. Some drug products lose their potency on the shelf in time, especially if they are opened. Milk of magnesia, for instance, dries out if it remains on the shelf for a while after opening.

Buying the large "family size" of a product not used frequently may seem like a bargain, but it's a poor economy if it has to be thrown out before the contents are used up. Ideally, supplies in the medicine chest should be bought to last over a period of no more than 6 to 12 months.

When it comes to storing these health care items, the cardinal rule is to keep all medicines out of the reach of children. In addition, be sure all medications have child-resistant caps. Elderly people who have difficulty opening such caps can ask the druggist for regular caps. However, they should be extra careful to see that young visitors can't get to these drugs.

Both prescription and non-prescription drugs should be kept in a cool, dry place away from foods and other household products. Some drugs may need to be kept in the refrigerator. This should be indicated on the label. If in doubt, ask the pharmacist.

Many people keep medicines on a high shelf in a hall or bedroom closet. Some experts suggest using a locking box. A word of warning: Be sure all responsible adults in the family know where the key is kept.

To avoid confusion, keep prescription and non-prescription drugs in separate boxes clearly labeled to distinguish one type of drug from the other. A list of what's in each box, attached to the outside if possible, will make it easier to find specific items, particularly in an emergency.

The medicine chest should be checked periodically to be sure supplies haven't run low and to get rid of drugs that may have gone bad or become outdated. Many drug labels have an expiration date beyond which the product should not be used. If there isn't a date, put a label on the container with the date of purchase and the date it was first opened. Then, if there are any questions in the future, a pharmacist can tell whether the product is safe to use.

Tablets that have become crumbly, medicines that have changed color, odor, or consistency, or are outdated should be destroyed. Empty the bottle of medicine into the toilet, flush it down, and rinse out the bottle. Don't leave leftover drugs in the trash basket where they can be dug out by inquisitive youngsters. Newly purchased drug products that don't look right should be returned to the pharmacy. Drug products that have lost their labels also should be destroyed.

Keep the telephone numbers of the local poison control center, physician, hospital, rescue squad, fire and police departments near every phone in the house. Tape the emergency phone list inside the medicine cabinet door and also keep it with the emergency supplies.

Each family's medicine chest is bound to contain some different items. For help in selecting appropriate health care supplies, check with a physician and a pharmacist.

Source: *FDA Consumer*

Glossary

Numbers in parentheses refer to the page on which the term is defined.

abrasion   a type of wound; a scrape (522).

accident   a sudden, unplanned event (490).

acid rain   precipitation that carries air pollution back to the ground (481).

acne   a skin condition in which an overproduction of sebum causes blackheads, whiteheads, and pimples (24).

acquired immune-deficiency syndrome (AIDS)   a fatal viral disease of the immune system (420).

addiction   a physical dependence upon a drug (348).

additive   a substance added to food to prevent spoilage or to improve appearance, texture, or taste (149).

adolescence   the period of human development during which children develop adult physical characteristics (66).

adoption   the legal process by which children become a part of a family (287).

adrenal glands   a pair of endocrine glands located at the top of each kidney that produce about 30 hormones (304).

adrenaline   a hormone released by the adrenal glands in response to danger, excitement, or stress; the hormone that prepares the body to fight danger or to flee from it (96, 304, 349).

afterbirth   the placenta that has been expelled from the mother's body after childbirth (323).

air pollution   contamination of air by harmful gases or particulates (231).

alarm stage   the immediate response to stress (96).

albinism   a hereditary condition in which the body does not produce the pigment melanin (331).

alcoholic   a person who is psychologically and physically dependent on alcohol (371).

alcoholism   a disease characterized by psychological and physical dependence on alcohol and the inability to control drinking (297, 374).

alimentary canal   the organs of the digestive system through which food passes (172).

allergy   a reaction of the body to an irritating substance (25).

alveoli   tiny air sacs in the lungs (229).

Alzheimer's disease   a type of dementia in which loss of brain cells results in memory loss, confusion, and a gradual weakening of the body (451).

amino acid   basic chemical unit of all proteins (136).

amnesia   the sudden inability to remember basic personal information (120).

amniocentesis   a procedure in which the amniotic fluid is tested for birth defects in the fetus (334).

amniotic sac   a protective membrane that surrounds the embryo (321).

amphetamines   a group of very strong stimulants (392).

amylase   an enzyme that begins the chemical digestion of complex carbohydrates (173).

amyl nitrite   a prescription drug used to lower blood pressure; often abused (399).

anemia   a blood condition caused by either too few red blood cells or too little hemoglobin to transport adequate oxygen to the cells (140, 226, 327).

anger   a strong feeling of displeasure (81).

angina pectoris   chest pains and a feeling of suffocation caused by a temporary lack of oxygen in the heart (438).

anorexia nervosa   an eating disorder characterized by constant dieting, rapid weight loss, and the feeling of being too fat in spite of the weight loss (162).

anterior lobe   the front part of the pituitary gland (303).

antibiotic   a medicine made from fungi or bacteria that fights disease-causing bacteria (420).

antibody   protein in the blood that produces resistance against pathogens or their toxins (418).

antisocial personality disorder   a condition in which a person has no respect for the rights of others (119).

anus   the muscular opening at the end of the rectum (176).

anvil   one of three small bones in the middle ear (48).

anxiety   fear of the future or the unknown (82).

anxiety disorder   a group of disorders in which anxiety is the main symptom (117).

aorta   the largest artery (217).

appendicitis   a condition in which an infected appendix becomes inflamed and swollen (180).

appendicular skeleton   the bones in the limbs (198).

appendix   a small pouch located near the junction of the small intestine and the large intestine (180).

appetite   a desire for food (156).

arch   the middle section of the foot that does not touch the ground (205).

arterioles   blood vessels that are smaller than arteries and branch into capillaries (218).

arteriosclerosis   hardening of the arteries (437).

artery   blood vessel with a thick muscular wall that carries blood away from the heart (217).

arthritis   a group of diseases in which the joints of the body become swollen and sore (206, 450).

artificial respiration   a first aid procedure that forces air into the lungs (519).

assault   an unlawful attack on one person by another (500).

asthma   a respiratory disorder characterized by spasms of the bronchi causing shortness of breath, wheezing, and coughing (230, 354).

astigmatism   an eye disorder in which an irregularly shaped cornea causes light rays to focus unevenly on the retina (43).

atherosclerosis   a condition in which fatty material builds up on the walls of arteries and blocks blood flow (222, 437).

athlete's foot   an irritating and sometimes painful fungal infection of the moist skin around the toes (26).

atrium   an upper chamber in the heart (217).

attitude   state of mind toward something in particular or life in general (74).

audiologist   a specialist in hearing problems and their treatment (50).

auditory nerve   a network of nerves in the ear that carry impulses to the brain (48).

autonomic nervous system   the part of the nervous system that controls involuntary responses (241).

aversion therapy   treatment that changes behavior by connecting it with unpleasant experiences (376).

axial skeleton   the portion of the skeleton consisting of the bones of the skull, the chest, and the spine (197).

axon   a long fiber that carries impulses away from the cell body to other neurons (236).

B cell   a white blood cell that forms antibodies (418).

bacteria   one-celled organisms made up of a very small amount of living matter surrounded by a thin cell wall (414).

ball-and-socket joint   a joint formed when the rounded end of one bone fits into a cup-shaped section of the bone joining it, such as the shoulder joint (201).

barbiturate   a strong depressant made from barbituric acid; often abused (393).

basal metabolism   the energy used by the body at rest and fasting to carry out basic functions (157).

behavior modification   a form of therapy that rewards good actions and punishes bad actions (122).

behavioral therapy   a form of psychotherapy that helps an individual change his or her behavior by using a system of rewards and punishments (122).

benign tumor   a tumor that does not spread (442).

benzopyrine   a deadly carcinogen found in cigarette smoke and coal tar (353).

bile   a thick yellow-green fluid released by the liver that helps the body digest and absorb fat (175).

biopsy   a medical test in which a tiny sample of tissue is surgically removed from the body (446).

birth defect   damage to the fetus (329).

birthmark   mark on the skin that is caused by either enlarged blood vessels or extra pigment (20).

blended family   a family made up of the father or mother, a stepmother or stepfather, and the children of one or both of the parents (287).

blindspot   the point on the retina at which the optic nerve joins the eye (40).

blizzard   a snowstorm with winds at 35 miles per hour and temperatures of 20° F or lower (504).

blood alcohol content (BAC)   a measure of alcoholic intoxication (368).

blood donor   a person who gives blood for another person to use (225).

blood platelet   small disklike structure in the blood that contributes to the process of clotting (223).

blood pressure   the force with which blood pushes against the vessel walls as it travels through the circulatory system (220, 436).

blood serum   blood plasma without the clotting agents (225).

blood transfusion   the process of taking blood from one person and putting it into the circulatory system of another person (225).

blood type   a classification of blood based upon the presence of several substances (225).

body composition   the amount of fat tissue relative to the other tissue in one's body (263).

body fat distribution   the pattern in which fat is stored in the body (264).

boil   a hard, painful inflammation or swelling caused by an infected hair follicle (25).

bolus   a ball of food that has been chewed and softened in the mouth (173).

botulism   food poisoning caused by the toxins given off by *Clostridium botulinum* bacteria (189).

brain dead   a condition in which the central nervous system has stopped functioning (248).

brain wave   change in electrical activity of the brain (245).

brainstem   the structure that connects the cerebrum with the spinal cord (239).

breech birth   a birth in which the baby's feet or buttocks enter the birth canal first (327).

bronchitis   an inflammation of the mucous membrane of the bronchi (230, 354).

bronchus   one of two tubes leading from the windpipe to a lung (228, 350).

bulimia   an eating disorder characterized by episodes of extreme overeating followed by self-induced vomiting or the use of laxatives (162).

bunion   a hard swelling where the big toe joins the foot (205).

bursitis   the painful inflammation of small sacs located near joints (204).

butyl nitrite   an illegal drug similar to amyl nitrite (399).

Caesarean section   a method of childbirth in which a doctor makes an incision in the mother's abdomen and uterus, and lifts the baby out (327).

caffeine   a legal stimulant that is found in coffee, soft drinks, and cocoa (392).

calculus   hardened plaque, often leading to periodontal disease (31).

calisthenics   gymnastic exercises designed to develop muscle tone (267).

Calorie   a measure of the energy content of food; the energy required to heat one kilogram of water one Celsius degree (134).

cancer   a group of diseases characterized by an uncontrolled growth of cells that invade and destroy healthy tissue (182, 353, 442).

canine   pointed tooth that tears food into smaller pieces (30).

capillary   a microscopic blood vessel with extremely thin walls (218).

carbohydrate   nutrients containing only carbon, hydrogen, and oxygen; sugars and starches (134).

carbon dioxide   a waste product that cells produce when breaking down glucose for energy (227).

carbon monoxide   a highly poisonous gas that has no odor or color (480).

carcinogen   any chemical, organism, or type of radiation that causes cancer (353, 442).

cardiac muscle   a kind of involuntary muscle found only in the heart (207).

cardiopulmonary respiration (CPR)   a first aid procedure that restores circulation and breathing to a person whose heart and lungs have stopped functioning (514, 536).

cardiorespiratory endurance   the ability of the heart, lungs, and blood vessels to send fuel and oxygen to the body's tissues during long periods of vigorous activity (257).

cardiovascular disease   disease of the heart and the blood vessels (436).

cartilage   a strong, flexible, supportive tissue that is mostly collagen (195).

cataract   a deterioration of the eye's lens (44).

cavity   a hole in the enamel of a tooth that results from decay (30).

cellular defense   a defense against pathogens involving certain cells of the body, especially white blood cells (417).

cementum   a sensitive, bonelike material that covers the root of the tooth (29).

central nervous system   the brain and spinal cord (237).

cerebellum   the part of the brain that coordinates muscular activity (239).

cerebral cortex   the outer layer of the cerebrum (238).

cerebral hemorrhage   a hemorrhage in the brain; may cause a stroke (439).

cerebral palsy   a birth defect caused by damage to the central nervous system that occurs before, during, or soon after birth (250, 329).

cerebrospinal fluid   a substance that fills spaces between the central nervous system's protective membranes (237).

cerebrum   the largest and uppermost part of the brain, which controls thought and conscious action (238).

cervical cancer   cancer of the opening of the uterus (444).

cervical vertebrae   spinal bones in the neck that support the head (197).

chancre   an open sore; a symptom of syphilis (429).

chancroid   a bacterial disease that causes painful genital sores; transmitted through sexual contact (430).

chemical digestion   the process of changing food into simpler substances, chiefly through the action of enzymes (172).

chemotherapy   the use of chemical medicines to treat disease (123, 447).

chewing tobacco   tobacco that is made of poor-quality leaves mixed with honey or molasses (344).

chicken pox   a viral disease characterized by an itchy rash and blisters that form scabs (424).

chief effect   the physical or mental change for which a drug is taken (389).

child abuse   physical violence or emotional pressure directed at children (296).

child neglect   not providing children with proper care (296).

child support   the money given to the parent who cares for the child to help pay for the child's expenses (295).

chlamydia   a sexually transmitted disease with symptoms similar to those of gonorrhea (430).

choking   the inability to breathe normally because of an obstruction in the air passages (521).

cholesterol   a waxy substance related to fats that may block the arteries, leading to atherosclerosis (135, 222, 437).

chorionic villus biopsy   a test in which a sample is taken from the wall of the amniotic sac (335).

choroid   the middle layer of eye tissue containing many blood vessels (39).

chromosomes   threadlike structures found within cells that carry the hereditary information from generation to generation (330).

cilia   microscopic hairlike structures that line the air passages and keep the lungs and other organs clean by trapping dust and foreign matter (228, 350, 417); microscopic hairlike structures in the Fallopian tube that sweep the eggs toward the uterus (309).

circulatory system   the body system composed of the heart, blood, and blood vessels (216).

circumcision   the surgical removal of the foreskin from the penis (314).

cirrhosis   a scarring of the liver that impairs its functioning (185, 374).

clinical depression   a mental disorder in which there are ongoing feelings of worthlessness and hopelessness (116).

cocaine   a stimulant that is extracted from the coca plant (392).

coccyx   tailbone, made of three to five fused vertebrae (198).

cochlea   a spiral tube in the ear that turns sound waves to nerve impulses and sends them to the brain (48).

codeine   a narcotic; a weak pain reliever (398).

collagen   a strong, flexible material produced by bone cells (19, 195).

colon   the lowest part of the large intestine (182).

colorblindness   a hereditary disorder in which a person cannot distinguish certain colors (43, 333).

coma   a deep unconsciousness from which a person cannot be awakened (248).

combination food   a food containing ingredients from two or more food groups (143).

common cold   an infectious disease caused by many different viruses, characterized by a runny nose, sore throat, and coughing (423).

compact bone   a layer of tissue in a bone, located under the periosteum (194).

compensation   a defense mechanism; making up for dissatisfaction in one area of life by excelling in another (87).

complementary combination   a mixture of two or more sources of incomplete protein that provides all the essential amino acids (137).

complex carbohydrate   a carbohydrate made of many sugars (134).

compound fracture   a bone fracture that breaks the skin, often with the bone protruding (202, 526).

compromise   the process by which opposing sides settle differences by both sides giving in a little bit (293).

compulsive personality disorder   a mental condition in which someone is constantly concerned with rules or standards (119).

concussion   an injury of the brain, resulting from a violent blow, that causes unconsciousness (247, 528).

conditioning   the shaping of behavior with punishment or reward (64); exercise that develops cardiorespiratory endurance or muscular strength (269).

cone   a photoreceptor that detects color, but is not very sensitive to light (39).

congenital heart disorder   an irregularity in the way the heart is formed (221).

conjunctiva   a clear membrane that lines the insides of the eyelid (39).

conjunctivitis   an inflammation of the inner lining of the eyelid (44).

conscience   the part of an individual that separates right from wrong (70).

constipation   a condition in which the bowel movements are difficult and do not occur often enough (177).

contraception   the prevention of pregnancy (294).

contusion   a bruise of the soft tissues of the body (247).

convulsion   an intense involuntary muscular contraction in which a person becomes unconscious and the body becomes stiff (524).

cool-down   a tapering-off period after exercise workout (269).

coordination   the ability to make many movements work together smoothly (243).

coping   dealing with a problem or difficult situation (96).

cornea   a nearly circular structure that serves as a window to let light into the eye (39).

corneal transplant   a surgical procedure in which a damaged cornea is removed and replaced with healthy cornea tissue from a donor (45).

corn   hard, thick area of keratin, usually on or near a toe, caused by rubbing or pressure (23).

coronary artery   the vessel that delivers blood to the heart muscle (219).

coronary artery bypass   a procedure in which doctors build a bypass around a blocked artery to the heart (440).

coronary heart disease   a disease that occurs when the coronary arteries become clogged from atherosclerosis; also called coronary artery disease (222).

cortex   the tissue in the adrenal glands that surrounds the medulla (306).

cortisol   a hormone produced by the adrenal cortex that controls the production of digestive enzymes and regulates the amount of sodium and potassium in body tissues (306).

crack   a rocklike form of cocaine that is smoked rather than sniffed (393).

cramp   a painful, involuntary muscle contraction (210).

cranium   part of the skull that protects the brain (197).

Crohn's disease   a chronic inflammation of the small intestine (181).

crosseye   a condition in which the muscles pull one or both eyes toward the nose (43).

croup   a type of breathing difficulty, particularly common among children (518).

crown   the part of the tooth above the gum line (29).

custody   the legal right of guardianship over a minor (287).

cuticle   the hard epidermis that surrounds the edge of a fingernail (23).

cystic fibrosis   a hereditary disease that affects the mucus-secreting glands (332).

dandruff   small flakes of dead skin from the scalp (26).

daydreaming   a defense mechanism; the creation of make-believe events that seem more pleasant or exciting than the real world (89).

deafness   total loss of hearing (49).

decibel   a unit that measures the loudness of a sound (50).

deductible   a flat fee that is subtracted from an insurance reimbursement for illness or injury (465).

defense mechanism   method of protecting oneself against emotional pain (87).

defensive driver   one who is always prepared for poor driving on the part of others and for poor road conditions (496).

deficiency   having too little of a necessary substance (138).

dehydration   a severe loss of water from the body tissues (142, 178).

delirium   a mental disorder that involves confusion and a loss of awareness of the environment (115).

delirium tremens (D.T.'s)   the uncontrollable trembling that alcoholics suffer during withdrawal (371).

dementia   a severe, irreversible loss of mental ability (116).

dendrite   fiber of a neuron that receives impulses and sends them to the cell body (236).

denial   a defense mechanism; refusal to recognize reality (90).

dental assistant   a person trained to examine teeth and gums, take x-rays, and clean teeth (461).

dental caries   tooth decay (30).

dental hygienist   a health care specialist who is qualified to treat tooth and gum disease (461).

dentin   the substance that makes up the body of the tooth (29).

depilatory   a hair-removing cream, lotion, or spray (22).

depressant   a drug that slows down the body's mental or physical abilities (143, 366, 393).

depression   a feeling of sadness, worthlessness, helplessness, or isolation (100).

dermatitis   a skin condition characterized by redness and swelling; may result from many causes (25).

dermatologist   a doctor who treats skin disorders (24).

dermis   the inner layer of skin (19).

despair   a feeling of complete hopelessness or loss of confidence (85).

detached retina   the separation of the retina from the choroid, the nourishing middle layer of the eye (44).

detoxification   the process by which a drug is withdrawn from a user's body (376).

diabetes mellitus   a condition characterized by high blood sugar and resulting from the body's inability to produce or properly use insulin (166, 449).

diabetic coma   a state of partial or complete unconsciousness brought on when the blood sugar level is very high and the insulin level is low (449).

diagnosis   the identification of a medical condition (456).

diaphragm   the chief muscle used in breathing; separates the chest cavity from the abdomen (228).

diarrhea   a condition in which the feces are watery and loose and the bowels move too often (178).

diastolic pressure   the force of the blood between beats, when the ventricles of the heart relax (220).

dietary fiber   a complex carbohydrate that cannot be digested by the human body (134).

disaster   a sudden, unforeseen emergency that causes personal injury, death, or property damage (502).

dislocation   injury in which the ends of bones are pulled out of a joint (203, 527).

displacement   a defense mechanism; shifting the expression of feelings about one person onto another person (90).

dissociative disorder   a condition in which the personality suffers sudden changes (120).

distillation   a process in which fermented liquids are evaporated and then cooled back to liquids, after allowing some of the water vapor to escape (364).

distress   stress that has a negative effect (103).

divorce   the legal ending of a marriage (295).

DNA (deoxyribonucleic acid)   a chemical substance that makes up chromosomes (330).

dominant gene   a gene that is expressed whenever it is present (330).

Down syndrome   a chromosomal disorder that usually causes mental retardation and slowed physical development (334).

driving while intoxicated (DWI)   the illegal act of driving a motor vehicle after drinking alcohol (379).

drownproofing   a system of rhythmic breathing and vertical floating that helps save energy in a water emergency (498).

drug   a chemical that causes changes in the body, mind, or both (386).

drug abuse   the use of any drug for other than medical purposes (386).

drug maintenance program   a method of treatment in which narcotics addicts receive a legal drug in place of the illegal drug (405).

duodenum   the first part of the small intestine (175).

eardrum a thin membrane stretched across the inside of the ear canal that vibrates when hit by sound waves (47).

earthquake a condition in which the rocks shift and move, and the ground shakes (505).

eczema a swelling and redness of the skin (25).

ejaculation the process by which muscle contractions push semen through the urethra and out of the penis (314).

electric shock the body's response to an electrical current; may include burns and the stoppage of breathing and heart activity (524).

electrocardiogram (ECG) a graph of the electrical impulses of the heart (440).

electrocution death caused by an electric shock (493).

electroencephalograph (EEG) an instrument that gives a visual record of brain impulses (245).

electrolysis a form of permanent hair removal (23).

embolism a process in which an artery in the brain is blocked by a blood clot or piece of cholesterol that moved through the circulatory system; a cause of stroke (439).

embryo a fertilized egg during the first two months (321).

emergency room a part of a hospital or medical center that receives victims of accidents and people suffering from sudden illness (462).

emotion the strong, immediate reaction that a person feels in response to an experience (80).

emphysema a respiratory disease caused by a weakening of lung tissue and characterized by a serious shortness of breath (231, 354).

emulsifier a food additive that makes food smoother (150).

enamel a white, compact material containing calcium that covers the crown of a tooth (29).

encephalitis an inflammation of the brain cells (250).

endocrine gland an organ that produces and releases hormones (302).

endocrine system the set of glands that produce and release chemical messengers in the body (302).

endometrium the lining of the uterus (310).

engram a special code a person's brain uses to remember the way to perform a task (244).

enriched food food in which additives are used to help replace nutrients that were lost during processing (149).

environment the sum of all physical and social conditions surrounding an individual or community (63, 479).

envy the discontentment caused by the desire for something that belongs to someone else (84).

enzyme a protein that speeds up the chemical activity of the body (172).

epidemic the rapid spread of an infectious disease (474).

epidermis the thin outer layer of the skin (19).

epiglottis a small flap of tissue that prevents food from entering the windpipe (173).

epilepsy a disorder marked by sudden surges of electrical impulses in the brain resulting in seizures (251).

episodic treatment center an independent clinic that provides primary care and treats minor medical emergencies (462).

erection a stiffening of the penis (314).

esophagus a muscular tube that connects the mouth to the stomach (173).

essential amino acid an amino acid necessary for a healthy body that must be supplied by the food one eats (136).

estrogen a hormone produced by the ovaries (307).

ethanol the kind of alcohol found in alcoholic drinks; the only alcohol that is safe to drink (364).

euphoria extreme happiness or sense of well-being (387).

Eustachian tube the passageway connecting the middle ear and the throat (48).

eustress stress that has a positive effect (103).

evaluate to weigh or judge information (7).

excretion the process that removes waste from the blood, tissues, and cells (183).

exercise duration the length of time spent doing a particular exercise (266).

exercise frequency the number of times one exercises over a given period (266).

exercise intensity how hard one exercises (265).

exhaustion stage stage of stress in which the body's defenses are used up (96).

expiration date the date after which a medicine may no longer be effective or safe (468).

extended family a household that contains relatives who are not part of the nuclear family (286).

extensor a muscle that extends or straightens a joint (208).

extrovert a person who is primarily interested in the world outside the self (62).

fainting a momentary loss of consciousness (534).

Fallopian tube the narrow tube through which eggs cells pass from an ovary to the uterus (309).

famine an extreme shortage of food (478).

farsightedness a condition in which the retina is too close to the front of the eye, causing an image to come into focus behind the retina rather than on it (42).

fat a nutrient that contains concentrated sources of energy (135).

fat-soluble vitamin a vitamin that dissolves in fat and can be stored in the body (138).

fear a scared feeling (82).

feces solid wastes (176).

fermentation the process by which yeast changes sugar into carbon dioxide and alcohol (364).

fertilization the joining of egg and sperm cells (320).

Fetal Alcohol Syndrome (FAS) a group of birth defects caused by drinking alcohol during pregnancy (329, 374).

fetus the name given to the developing baby from the third month until birth (322).

fibrinogen a blood protein that plays an important role in blood clotting (223).

fight or flight response the body's immediate response to stress (96).

first aid practical and immediate treatment of an injury or sudden illness (512).

first-degree burn a burn that injures only the epidermis and heals without leaving a scar (27, 520).

flexibility the ability to bend joints and stretch muscles through a full range of motion (261).

flexor a muscle that bends a joint (208).

fluoride a tasteless, odorless chemical that unites with tooth enamel to increase resistance to tooth decay (33).

focus the point at which light rays intersect (39).

food allergy a condition in which body cells, in response to certain foods, release certain substances that cause fluid to leak into the surrounding tissues (167).

food poisoning an illness caused by infected food (179).

foreskin   a flap of skin covering the end of the penis (314).

fortified food   food to which vitamins and minerals that are not naturally present have been added (150).

foster children   children who receive parental care from adults without being related to or legally adopted by them (287).

fovea   a small yellow spot at the center back of the retina (40).

fracture   a break or crack in a bone (202, 526).

fraternal twins   twins that develop at the same time but from different embryos (324).

frostbite   freezing of the skin (525).

frustration   a feeling of disappointment (81).

functional disorder   a mental disorder that is not connected to a physical cause (113).

fungi   small plantlike organisms (415).

gallstones   hard, stonelike particles that form from cholesterol and other substances in bile (181).

gender identification   having a sense of self that matches one's sex (68).

gene   the basic unit of heredity (330).

generic name   the common name of a substance (467).

genital wart   a sexually transmitted disease caused by a virus (431).

gingivitis   an early stage of gum disease that may cause inflamed and swollen gums (31).

glaucoma   a build-up of fluid pressure within the eyes, eventually causing loss of vision (45).

gliding joint   a joint that allows bones to slide over one another, such as the wrist joint (200).

glomerulus   a network of coiled blood vessels in the nephron (183).

glucose   blood sugar (134).

glycogen   a starch stored in the liver that maintains blood sugar levels between meals (176, 307).

goiter   a condition in which the thyroid becomes very large due to a lack of iodine (140, 304).

gonorrhea   a sexually transmitted disease that causes a discharge and painful urination in males (427).

gout   an inflammation of the joints due to a build-up of uric acid (185).

gray matter   the nerve cell bodies of the cerebral cortex (238).

greenstick fracture   a partial fracture that is common in children (202).

grief   a deep sorrow that is caused by the loss of someone or something (84).

group therapy   a form of therapy in which a psychotherapist meets with several people who have similar problems (123).

guilt   a feeling of regret caused by having done something wrong (86).

habit   an activity repeated so often that one does not think before doing it (74).

hair follicle   a bulb-shaped pocket in the dermis from which a hair grows (21).

hallucinate   to experience a hallucination (372).

hallucination   the sensation of seeing, hearing, or sensing something that does not exist (116).

hallucinogen   a drug that causes hallucination (396).

hammer   one of three small bones in the ear (48).

hangover   the unpleasant physical effects following the heavy use of alcohol (370).

hashish   a drug made from extracts of the marijuana plant (397).

Haversian system   a network of blood vessels that run through canals in the layer of compact bone (194).

health   the state of physical, mental, and social well-being (4).

health behavior   an action that affects health (5).

health food   a general term that means that the food is healthy (150).

health maintenance organization (HMO)   a medical group that provides a variety of medical services only for its members (465).

hearing impairment   partial hearing loss (49).

heart   the muscular pump that pushes blood through the circulatory system (216).

heart attack   a sudden, life-threatening malfunction of the heart muscle (222, 438, 535).

heart failure   a condition in which the heart is no longer able to pump a normal amount of blood (438).

heart rate reserve   the range between the rate of heartbeat at rest and at exhaustion (265).

heart transplant   a procedure in which a healthy heart is transferred from a person who has recently died into the body of the patient (440).

heat cramp   a cramp in the muscles of the legs or abdomen resulting from exposure to heat (525).

heat exhaustion   a condition resulting from exposure to heat in which there is excessive perspiration, headache, and nausea (525).

heat stroke   a life-threatening emergency resulting from exposure to heat in which there is a very high body temperature, hot and dry skin, lack of perspiration, and rapid pulse (525).

Heimlich maneuver   a method of abdominal thrusts and sharp blows used to stop choking (521).

helper T cell   a white blood cell that identifies the type of infection (418).

hemodialysis   a method of filtering blood directly through the bloodstream (184).

hemoglobin   an iron-containing substance in red blood cells that carries oxygen to all parts of the body (140, 223).

hemophilia   a hereditary disorder in which the blood lacks a substance that is necessary for proper clotting (333).

hemorrhoids   swollen veins in the anal area (181).

hepatitis   a serious disease caused by toxic agents of a virus that infects the liver, causing jaundice, nausea, fever, and pain in the abdomen (374, 426).

hepatitis A   a viral liver infection resulting from contact with infected food or water (426).

hepatitis B   a viral liver infection spread through the blood, usually by sexual contact with an infected person, or through the use of dirty hypodermic needles used to inject drugs (426).

herbal cigarette   a cigarette made from the leaves of herbs; may include tobacco (350).

heredity   the passing of biological characteristics from parents to child (5, 62).

hernia   a loop of intestines bulging through a weak spot in the muscle wall of the abdomen (211).

heroin   a powerful illegal narcotic (398).

herpes type II   a sexually transmitted disease caused by a virus, characterized by painful blisters and sores in the genital area (429).

heterosexual a person who is attracted to members of the opposite sex (290).

hinge joints joints that swing back and forth (200).

histamine a substance that increases the flow of gastric juices in the stomach and dilates the walls of small blood vessels (167).

hives bumps on the surface of the skin, usually caused by an allergic reaction to food or medicine (25).

Hodgkin's disease cancer of the lymph nodes (446).

homosexual a person who is attracted to members of his or her own sex (290).

hormone a chemical substance that is released into the blood stream and travels to other organs and tissues, where it stimulates growth and regulates activities (302).

hospice a system of medical care intended to make a dying patient more comfortable (463).

hospital clinic a part of a hospital that treats medical problems that are not emergencies (462).

hostility feeling and behaving in an unfriendly way (81).

hunger a strong desire for food (156).

hurricane a tropical storm with heavy rains and winds exceeding 75 miles per hour (503).

hydrocarbon a chemical compound that contains both hydrogen and carbon (480).

hygiene a set of healthful practices that help prevent disease (20).

hyperactivity a condition in which a child is in constant movement and is very easily distracted (116).

hypertension high blood pressure (166, 222, 436).

hyperventilation abnormally fast and deep respiration; may cause dizziness, pain in the chest or arms, sweating, and clammy skin (518).

hypochondria a strong belief that one is ill when illness is neither present nor likely (118).

hypoglycemia low blood sugar; a condition caused by too much insulin being produced by the body (167).

hypothalamus the part of the brain that regulates automatic functions, such as breathing, heartbeat, digestion, and the release of hormones (238, 302).

hypothermia lowered body temperature (525).

idealization a defense mechanism; an extreme form of identification (89).

identical twins twins that develop from the same embryo (324).

identification a defense mechanism; feeling connected and similar to someone else (88).

identity the particular parts of a person's personality by which he or she is recognized (69).

illegal drug a drug that is forbidden by law because its harmful effects outweigh any useful purpose (386).

illness stage the stage of disease in which the symptoms are fully developed (423).

immunity an inherited or acquired resistance to a specific pathogen (418).

immunotherapy a treatment that uses anticancer medicines to help the body's own immune system fight cancer cells (447).

impetigo a bacterial skin infection characterized by small blisters that form yellow crusts (25).

impulse message that is carried by neurons from one part of the body to another (236).

incisor a sharp front tooth used to cut food (29).

incomplete protein a food that lacks some of the essential amino acids (137).

incubation stage the stage of disease between the entry of the pathogen and the first appearance of symptoms (422).

incubator a special container that keeps the baby warm and protects it from disease (325).

indigestion the inability to digest food properly (178).

infantile autism a condition in which children do not react to people or their environment (116).

infatuation a short-lived burst of interest in a person (290).

infectious disease disease caused by a pathogen and passed from one person to another (414).

inflammation the redness, swelling, and tenderness in an infected area (417).

influenza an infectious disease caused by many different kinds of viruses, all of which bring on fever, aches, coughing, and a tired feeling (423).

inguinal hernia a condition in which tissue is pushed through an opening between the abdomen and the scrotum (314).

inhalant a drug that is drawn into the body through the nose (399).

inhibition check on the emotions (366).

initiator a small amount of a carcinogen, which activates a cell, but not enough to make it cancerous (443).

inpatient care medical care given to a patient staying overnight in a hospital (462).

insertion the point at which a muscle is attached to the movable bone (208).

insomnia the inability to sleep (246).

instinct an inherited pattern of behavior that does not need to be learned (62).

insulin a hormone produced by the pancreas that regulates the metabolism of sugar in the body (166, 307).

insulin-dependent diabetes a type of diabetes in which the pancreas does not make enough insulin (449).

insulin shock a condition in which there is a very low level of blood sugar and a high level of insulin; symptoms include dizziness, rapid pulse, excessive sweating, and paleness (449).

insurance a contract in which a company agrees to pay an individual for a loss or illness in return for a payment of a specified premium (464).

insurance policy a contract offering payment for certain health services in return for certain premiums (465).

intelligence the ability to learn and to deal with change (62).

interferon a protein that is produced by the body to protect cells from viruses (420).

interneuron a neuron that receives sensory messages and sends responses (237).

intoxication the set of bad effects that alcohol has on the body and mind (366).

introvert a person who is concerned mostly with his or her own thoughts (62).

iris the colored part of the eye that surrounds the pupil (39).

isometric exercise the contraction of muscle through resistance without moving the limbs (267).

isotonic exercises exercises that contract the muscles and move the limbs (267).

jealousy the fear of losing something you have (84).

joint the place at which two bones meet (199).

keratin   a fiberlike material filling the outer cells in the epidermis, making them strong and tough (19).

kidney   an organ in the urinary system that filters wastes from the blood (183).

kidney failure   a serious condition in which the kidneys cannot effectively remove wastes from the blood (184).

kidney stone   a urinary disorder in which solid particles build up in the kidney (184).

labor   the process of birth (322).

lactic acid   a waste product formed when glucose is broken down without using oxygen (210).

lactose intolerance   an inability to digest milk sugar, caused by the lack of the enzyme lactose (178).

landslide   a mass of soil or rock falling from a hillside (505).

large intestine   the part of the digestive system that extends from the small intestine to the anus; its main function is to absorb water (176).

larynx   the voice box, located in the upper trachea (228).

lead   a poisonous metal added to some gasolines (480).

learned behavior   the way in which a person behaves in response to his or her environment (63).

leavening agent   substance that makes breads rise (150).

legal drug   a drug that is considered useful enough to be sold (386).

legume   a plant that bears seeds in pods; a member of the pea family (137).

lens   a flexible structure that focuses light rays on the retina of the eye (39).

leukemia   cancer of the bone marrow (446).

leukoplakia   a disease of the mouth marked by leathery white patches on the cheek, gum, tongue, or lips (32, 352).

licensed practical nurse (L.P.N.)   a nurse who is responsible for patients' basic needs (460).

life change unit   a unit of measurement for the amount of stress (99).

life expectancy   the statistical average number of years that a member of a particular group may expect to live (5).

ligament   a thick strand of collagen fibers that binds bones together (200).

liver   a large organ that secretes bile, filters the blood, and stores carbohydrates (176).

long bone   a bone with large ends and a narrow middle (194).

love   an emotion of strong affection or deep concern for another person (80).

low tar, low nicotine cigarette   a cigarette with special filters that reduce the amount of tar and nicotine in the smoke (350).

lower respiratory tract   the organs of the respiratory system that extend from the windpipe to the lungs (227).

LSD   a very powerful hallucinogen (396).

lumbar vertebrae   spinal bones found in the lower back (197).

lungs   a pair of organs where oxygen is taken in from the air and carbon dioxide is released into the air (228).

lymph   the plasma that seeps out of capillaries; also fills the spaces between the cells (224).

lymph node   tissue that produces white blood cells; tissue that traps and filters out pathogens (225, 418).

lymphatic system   a system that returns fluids from body tissues to the blood stream and defends the body against infection (224).

lymphatic vessel   a small vessel that transports lymph (224).

mainstream smoke   smoke that has been inhaled and then exhaled by a smoker (356).

major medical insurance   an insurance plan that pays for large expenses not usually covered by other kinds of health insurance (465).

malignant tumor   a cancerous growth (442).

malocclusion   a condition in which the upper and lower teeth do not line up properly (31).

mania   an elated, impulsive mood (117).

manic-depression disorder   a condition in which mania and clinical depression alternate (117).

marijuana   a stimulant, depressant, and hallucinogen that comes from the leaves and seeds of the Indian hemp plant, *Cannabis sativa* (397).

mastectomy   an operation in which part or all of the breast is removed due to breast cancer (444).

maturity   the state of being fully grown (71).

maximal heart rate (HRmax)   the highest heart rate at which one can exercise safely (265).

mechanical digestion   the process of chewing, mashing, and breaking food into smaller pieces (172).

Medicaid   a public health insurance program that pays for the health care of low-income people (466).

medical center   a place containing groups of hospital services that can treat most medical problems (462).

medical doctor   a person who has earned either the degree of doctor of medicine (M.D.) or doctor of osteopathy (D.O.) (456).

medical history   a record of the medical problems and treatments of a person and his or her family (457).

Medicare   a federal health insurance plan for people 65 or older and others who receive Social Security benefits (466).

medicine   a substance used to treat medical problems or diseases (467).

medulla   the part of the brainstem that controls some of the most important functions of life, such as breathing, blood pressure, heart rate, and swallowing (239); a central core of cells in the adrenal glands (306).

melanin   a pigment in the epidermis (20).

melanoma   a type of skin cancer that usually begins as a dark mole and spreads throughout the body (28, 444).

memory cell   a cell that retains the ability to produce antibodies against a particular pathogen (418).

meningitis   an inflammation of the membranes around the brain and spinal cord (249).

menopause   the time of life when a woman stops menstruating (311).

menstruation   the monthly process in which an unfertilized egg cell and the inner lining of the uterus are discharged from a woman's body (309).

mental health   the state of well-being of the mind (62).

mental health counselor   a professional who helps people with mental or emotional problems (461).

mental illness   any disease of the mind that affects the emotions, thoughts, or personality of an individual (112).

mental retardation   a condition in which a person never develops the full mental abilities of an adult (374).

mental trauma   a violent shock that damages a person's mental health (114).

mescaline   a hallucinogen found in peyote (396).

metabolism the process by which the body uses food to release energy and uses the energy to build and repair body tissues (157).

metastasis the process by which cancer cells spread throughout the body (442).

methadone a synthetic narcotic taken by mouth and used to spare addicts from the pain of withdrawal (405).

methaqualone a tranquilizer with effects similar to those of barbiturates (393).

midbrain a part of the brainstem that controls certain involuntary actions such as pupil size and eye movements (239).

migraine a severe headache caused by a narrowing of blood vessels in the brain followed by an enlargement of these vessels (99, 247).

mineral a nutrient found in the environment that is essential to the body's functions (140).

miscarriage the process in which a nonliving embryo is expelled from the body (327).

modeling the process of learning by imitating another person, or role model (64).

molar a large tooth with several rounded points that grinds food into bits (30).

mole a raised growth of brown pigment (20).

mononucleosis a viral disease causing a sore throat and the swelling of the lymph glands and spleen (424).

mood disorder a condition in which a single, often painful, mood rules the whole personality (116).

morphine a powerful narcotic (398).

motor neuron a nerve cell that carries a response from the interneurons to the muscles, glands, and internal organs of the body (237).

motor skill skill of balance and control of movement (261).

mucous membrane a layer of tissue that lines the respiratory, digestive, and reproductive systems (228, 417).

mucus the thick liquid coating secreted by the glands in the mucous membranes (417).

multiple personality disorder a condition in which a single person frequently changes between two or more separate personalities (120).

multiple sclerosis a disease that slowly destroys the tissue that surrounds and protects nerve fibers (250).

muscle cramp a sudden, involuntary, and often painful muscle contraction (529).

muscle strain an injury in which the muscle fibers are stretched or torn (210, 529).

muscle tone the slight but constant contraction maintained by all muscles (210).

muscular dystrophy a hereditary disease that slowly destroys muscle fibers (211).

muscular endurance the ability to apply strength over a period of time (259).

mutagenic substance a substance that causes changes in genes leading to birth defects or miscarriages (483).

narcolepsy a disorder in which people fall asleep suddenly (246).

narcotic a powerful drug that depresses the senses; usually derived from the opium poppy (398).

nasal cavity the area that lies between the roof of the mouth and the floor of the brain cavity (227).

natural food food that contains no additives (150).

nearsightedness a condition in which the retina is too far from the front of the eye, causing an image to come into focus in front of the retina (42).

neck the part of the tooth just below the gum line where the crown and root come together (29)

negative attitude state of mind in which one expects the worst to happen (74).

negativism a defense mechanism; the act of always refusing to do what others suggest or ask (90).

neighborhood crime watch an organization of people who look out for unusual activities in their area (500).

nephron the main functioning unit of the kidney (183).

nervous system the complex group of organs and nerves that control all actions and thoughts (236).

neuritis an inflammation of the nerves (249).

neuron the basic unit of the nervous system (236).

neurotransmitter a chemical produced by nerve cells that passes across a synapse from an axon to a dendrite (237).

nicotine an addictive stimulant found in tobacco (347).

nicotine gum a prescription chewing gum containing nicotine (359).

night blindness a condition characterized by poor vision in dim light (43).

nitrous oxide an inhalant used as a mild painkiller (399).

nocturnal emission the process by which semen is released from the penis during sleep (314).

noninfectious disease a disease that is not caused by a pathogen (436).

noninsulin-dependent diabetes a form of diabetes in which the pancreas produces enough insulin but the cells cannot take in glucose (450).

nuclear family a family consisting of a mother and father and their children (286).

nuclear radiation invisible energy released from the nucleus of an atom (314).

nurse practitioner a registered nurse who has had further training in a specialty (460).

nursing home a health care center that provides long-term care for those who are chronically ill (463).

nutrient a substance found within food that the body needs to function properly (134).

nutrient density the amount of nutrients in a food compared to the number of Calories it contains (146).

nutrition the process by which the body takes in and uses food (134).

obesity a condition in which a person weighs 20 percent more than his or her highest comfortable weight (159).

obsessive-compulsive disorder a mental condition characterized by the presence of unwanted thoughts, emotions, or behaviors (117).

occupational therapy therapy that helps patients overcome problems by teaching them job skills (124).

olfactory nerve reactor receptor in the nasal cavity that is sensitive to smell (53).

oncogene a gene that can make cells grow without control (442).

opium a drug derived from the seed pods of a certain poppy; a narcotic (398).

optic nerve the cord of nerve fibers that carries messages from the eye to the brain (40).

oral cancer   a cancer of the mouth or throat (354, 444).

organ   a group of different kinds of tissues that perform a certain function (18).

organic disorder   a mental illness that is the result of a physical cause, often a chemical imbalance (112).

organic food   food grown on farms that do not use synthetic fertilizers and pesticides (150).

origin   the stationary attachment of one end of a muscle to a bone (208).

ossification   the process by which cartilage changes to bone cells and minerals (195).

osteoarthritis   a chronic condition in which the layers of cartilage in the joints become rough (450).

osteoporosis   the loss of calcium from bone (195).

outpatient care   medical attention for patients who are not staying in a hospital (462).

outpatient recovery program   a drug recovery program that allows drug abusers to live at home and visit the hospital for treatment (405).

oval window   a membrane that separates the inner ear from the middle ear (48).

ovarian cyst   a fluid-filled sac that may grow on the ovaries (312).

ovary   the reproductive organ that produces egg cells and releases sex hormones (307).

overdose   an excessive dose of a drug, often causing shock, coma, or death (386).

overgeneralization   the act of drawing a broad conclusion from one incident (101).

over-the-counter drug   a drug that may be purchased without a doctor's prescription (386, 468).

overweight   the state of being more than 10 percent over one's comfortable weight (159).

ovulation   the monthly release of an egg (309).

ovum   an egg cell (309).

pacemaker   a small mass of nerve and muscle cells that start each heartbeat (220); a small electric device placed under the skin to help the heart beat regularly (440).

pancreas   a long, soft gland lying behind the stomach that secretes digestive enzymes into the duodenum and releases hormones that regulate metabolism (175, 307).

panic disorder   a sudden unfounded attack of terror that is usually connected with a particular situation (117).

Pap test   an examination for cancer in which cell samples are taken from the cervix and vagina (312, 445).

paralysis   a loss of the ability to move a part of the body due to nerve or muscle damage (248).

paranoid personality disorder   an unfounded suspicion and mistrust of others (118).

paraplegia   the paralysis of the lower body and legs (248).

parasite   an organism that lives by feeding on or in another animal (415).

parasympathetic nervous system   the part of the autonomic nervous system that slows down the body's functions (241).

parathyroid gland   an endocrine gland that controls the level of calcium and phosphorus in the body (304).

Parkinson's disease   a malfunction of the nervous system that causes muscle stiffness and tremors in the body (451).

particulate   a type of air pollutant composed of tiny solid particles (480).

passive-aggressive personality disorder   a mental condition in which a person indirectly resists cooperating with others (120).

passive smoker   a nonsmoker sharing the same air with a smoker (355).

pasteurization   the process of heating liquids in order to kill germs (416).

pathogen   an organism that causes disease (414).

PCP (phencyclidine)   a depressant and a hallucinogen originally developed as a tranquilizer for animals (396).

pectoral girdle   the collarbone and shoulder blades (198).

pedestrian   a person who travels on foot (497).

pediculosis   a condition in which lice infest the hair (26).

peer group   group of people who are alike in age, status, or interests (69).

peer pressure   the urging from peers to follow the crowd (69).

pelvis   the sacrum and the hip bones (198).

penis   a male reproductive organ (314).

peptic ulcer   an open sore in the lining of the stomach or duodenum (181, 355).

periodontal disease   disease of the gums (31).

periodontitis   a serious gum disease characterized by inflammation of the gums and the destruction of bone tissue (31).

periosteum   a strong membrane covering the outside of the bone (194).

peripheral nervous system   the system that carries messages between the body and the central nervous system (240).

peripheral vision   the process of seeing objects at the sides of the eyes (41).

peristalis   the wavelike contraction of muscles that moves food through the digestive system (173).

personality   the behavior, attitudes, and feelings that make each person an individual (62).

personality disorder   a mental disorder that prevents a person from interacting with others in a healthy way (118).

personalization   the act of taking a remark or incident too seriously (101).

perspiration   a liquid made up of water, salt, and wastes that is excreted from sweat glands (19).

peyote   a hallucinogenic cactus that grows in the Southwest and Mexico (396).

phagocyte   a white blood cell that surrounds pathogens and destroys them (417).

pharmacist   a specialist who is qualified to prepare and sell medicines; a druggist (467).

phenylketonuria (PKU)   a genetic disease characterized by the inability to break down phenylalanine (332).

phobia   an unreasonable fear of a situation or object (117).

photoreceptor   a light-sensitive receptor in the retina (39).

physical dependence   addiction (348).

physical environment   physical surroundings (6).

physical fitness   the ability of one's heart, blood vessels, lungs, and muscles to work at their best (256).

physician's assistant   a person who works with a physician to provide certain types of health care (460).

pimple   a blocked pore that is infected and inflamed (24).

pituitary gland   the endocrine gland that produces hormones that regulate growth rate and coordinate the actions of other glands (302).

pivot joint   a joint in which one bone rotates around another, such as where the skull meets the backbone (200).

placenta a membranous organ that nourishes the developing embryo (321).

plaque a colorless layer of bacteria, saliva, and food particles that forms on teeth (30).

plasma the liquid part of the blood (223).

play therapy a form of therapy in which mental illness is studied and treated by observing children at play (123).

pneumonia a viral or bacterial infection that causes an inflammation of the lung tissue (229).

poison control center a place where information and help can be obtained when someone has taken poison (492).

pollutant an action or a thing that causes pollution (479).

pollution the dirtying of the air, water, or soil by chemicals, disease, or waste products (479).

pons a portion of the brainstem that links the cerebrum with the cerebellum and the right cerebral hemisphere with the left cerebral hemisphere (239).

pore tiny opening on the surface of the epidermis (19).

portal vein the vessel that carries blood from the small intestine to the liver (219).

positive attitude the ability to see the best in a situation and to expect that good things are to come (74).

posterior lobe the rear section of the pituitary gland (303).

preferred provider organization a form of health insurance that pays for medical costs if patients use certain specified doctors (465).

premature born before being fully developed (325).

premenstrual syndrome (PMS) a feeling of depression that occurs several days before a menstrual period begins (312).

premium a set amount of money paid each year in return for specified insurance coverage (465).

premolar a double-pointed tooth that tears and crushes food (30).

prenatal care medical care during pregnancy (326).

prescription drug a drug that may be legally purchased only with a doctor's written permission (386, 467).

preservative an additive that prevents food spoilage (149).

pressure-point technique a method of stopping severe bleeding by applying pressure on the artery supplying the affected limb (516).

preventive medicine practices that promote health and help avoid medical problems (465).

primary care medical care that includes preventive medicine, routine checkups, and the diagnosis and treatment of common problems (461).

private practice the patients of a doctor who is not on the staff of an organization such as a hospital (456).

problem drinker a person who drinks heavily and is psychologically dependent on alcohol (371).

prodromal stage the stage of disease during which the earliest symptoms appear but are not fully developed (423).

product date the manufacturer's estimate of how long the product will last before it spoils (150).

projection a defense mechanism; denying an unwanted trait by repressing it and assigning it to someone else (88).

promoter a substance that causes cells activated by an initiator to become cancerous (353, 443).

proof a measurement of the alcoholic content of beverages; twice the percentage of alcohol (364).

prostate gland a male gland that surrounds the urethra (314).

protein a chemical made up of amino acids that builds and repairs body cells (136).

protist a group of one-celled organisms with specialized internal structures (415).

psilocin a psychoactive drug found in certain mushrooms; a hallucinogen (397).

psilocybin a psychoactive drug found in certain mushrooms; a hallucinogen (397).

psychiatrist medical doctor who specializes in psychiatry (112).

psychiatry the medical study, treatment, and prevention of mental disorders (112).

psychoactive drug a mind-altering drug (386).

psychoanalysis a medical process that tries to reveal a person's unresolved conflicts (122).

psychological dependence the state of being dependent on something to the point of becoming emotionally upset without it; habituation (347).

psychologist a person who has earned an M.A. or a Ph.D. in psychology and is qualified to diagnose and work with people who have emotional problems (62, 461).

psychosomatic illness a physical disorder caused by stress rather than disease or damage to the body (97).

psychotherapy the treatment of mental, emotional, and nervous disorders (122, 376).

puberty the stage of human development in which the reproductive system matures (302).

pubic lice animal parasites found in the genital region; most often transmitted through sexual contact (431).

public health the effort to protect and improve the health of a group of people (474).

pulmonary circulation the pathway of blood from the heart through the lungs (218).

pulp soft tissue in a tooth containing small blood vessels and nerve fibers (29).

pulse point a place at which the pulse can be felt easily (265).

puncture a wound made by a sharp object (522).

pupil the round opening that allows light to enter the eye (39).

quackery the act of selling products as cures when they have little or no healing power (469).

quadriplegia paralysis of the body from the neck down (248).

quarantine a restriction that separates sick people from others to prevent an infectious disease from spreading (474).

radiation sickness illness resulting from exposure to nuclear radiation (484).

radiation therapy a cancer treatment in which a tumor is exposed to x-rays or other types of radiation (447).

radioactive waste waste material that gives off radiation (484).

rape the illegal act of forcing another person to have sexual relations (501).

rape crisis center a community agency that provides rape victims with medical help and emotional support (501).

rapid eye movement (REM) the dream stage during sleep, indicated by the back and forth movement of the eyes under the eyelids (246).

rationalization a defense mechanism; finding reasons to justify certain behavior (87).

reaction formation a defense mechanism; the expression of an emotion that is the opposite of what one feels inside (89).

receptor a nerve ending that sends or receives signals (39).

recessive gene   a gene that is expressed only if the dominant gene is not present (330).

recovery stage   the stage of disease in which the disease is overcome by the body's defenses (423).

recreational therapy   pleasurable activity that helps patients express themselves creatively (124).

rectum   the portion of the large intestine that stores solid wastes until the body is ready to expel them (176).

red blood cell   a cell that carries oxygen from the lungs to the body tissues and waste carbon dioxide from the body tissues to the lungs (223).

red bone marrow   bone tissue that makes red blood cells and some white blood cells (194).

reflex   a rapid, automatic response to the environment that occurs without action from the brain (242).

reflex action   involuntary response to a stimulus (242).

reflex arc   the route through the nervous system that an impulse travels during a reflex (242).

refugee   a person who flees to another country for protection or safety (478).

registered nurse (R.N.)   a graduate of a two-year or three-year hospital program, or college nursing program (460).

regression   a defense mechanism; retreating into childish or immature behavior (89).

relapse   becoming ill with a disease from which one has partially recovered (423).

releasing hormone   a hormone secreted by the hypothalamus that stimulates the pituitary gland to release specific hormones (302).

renal artery   the blood vessel that brings blood to a kidney from the aorta (219).

resin   a clear or yellow-brown plant material (349).

resistance stage   a stage of response to stress in which a person's body works against the stress (96).

respiratory system   the group of organs that enable oxygen and carbon dioxide to move between the blood and the air (227).

retina   the part of the eye that absorbs light rays and changes them into electrical messages (39).

Rh factor   a protein found in the red blood cells of some people (225).

Rh negative   blood that lacks the Rh factor (326).

Rh positive   blood that contains the Rh factor (326).

rheumatic fever   a disease caused by strep bacteria that can result in inflammation of the heart valves and muscle tissue (221).

rheumatoid arthritis   a disease in which the membranes in the joints become swollen (450).

ringworm   a fungal infection that causes round, red, scaly patches on the skin (26).

risk   the statistical possibility that something bad will take place (7).

rod   a photoreceptor that is sensitive to light but cannot distinguish colors (39).

role model   a person whom someone watches and copies (64).

root   the part of the tooth below the gum line that fits into the jawbone (29)

round window   an opening in the middle ear below the oval window that passes vibrations from the skull bones to the fluid of the cochlea (48).

rubella   German measles; a viral disease characterized by a skin rash, mild fever, sore throat, and a runny nose (424).

ruptured disc   a condition in which the cartilage between two vertebrae breaks and the inside pad slips out (204).

sacrum   the five fused vertebrae of the hip area (198).

saliva   a watery, tasteless liquid that moistens chewed food and begins chemical digestion (173).

salivary gland   an organ that produces saliva (173).

saturated fat   fat that is a solid at room temperature (135).

schizoid personality disorder   a condition of deep withdrawal from other people (119).

schizophrenia   a severe mental disorder in which a person withdraws from reality (121).

sclera   the white of the eye (39).

scoliosis   a condition in which there is a side-to-side curvature of the spine (206).

scrotum   a pouch of loose skin that houses the testes (313).

sebaceous gland   a gland in the dermis that produces oil and releases it to the surface of the skin (19).

sebum   an oil produced by the sebaceous glands (19).

secondary care   treatment of specific medical problems in hospitals (461).

second-degree burn   a burn that injures the epidermis and part of the dermis and may leave scars; blisters and swelling often develop (27, 520).

secondary sex characteristics   the physical traits that develop during puberty and distinguish men from women (308).

seizure   an attack of epilepsy (251).

self-concept   one's view of oneself and one's role in life (73).

self-control   control of one's actions by one's own will (68).

self-examination   a consideration of one's own thoughts or emotions (73).

semicircular canal   a fluid-filled tube in the ear lined with tiny hairs (48).

senile dementia   a group of disorders in which an older person becomes severely forgetful, confused, and out of touch with surroundings (451).

sensory neuron   a neuron that detects changes in the environment and sends signals to the spinal cord or brain (237).

separation   an act in which husband and wife agree to live apart while they try to work out their differences (295).

sex-linked disorder   a genetic disorder passed on by the X chromosome (333).

sexual abuse   illegal sexual activity between an adult and a child (296).

sexually transmitted disease (STD)   disease that is passed from one person to another during a sexual act (427).

shaft   the narrow portion of the bone between the ends (194).

shin splint   an aching pain on the front of the lower leg, caused by a muscle strain (275).

shingles   a disease in which the chicken pox virus attacks a nerve root (424).

shock   a serious slowing down of the circulatory and nervous system (532).

sickle-cell disease   a hereditary form of anemia in which abnormal hemoglobin causes red blood cells to have a long, curved shape; inhibits the transport of oxygen (226, 331).

side effect   an unexpected or undesirable reaction to a drug (389, 468)

sidestream smoke   smoke that comes directly from the burning end of a cigarette (356).

simple carbohydrate   a carbohydrate made of one kind of sugar (134).

simple fracture   a fracture in which the broken ends of the bone do not pierce the skin (202, 526).

single-parent family   a household in which only one parent lives with a child or children (287).

sinus   an air passage in the skull (197).

sinusitis   an inflammation and swelling of the sinuses (355).

skeletal muscle   a muscle connected to a bone and controlled consciously (207).

skinfold caliper   a tool used to measure the amount of fat on the body (263).

sleep apnea   a condition in which breathing stops periodically during sleep (246).

small intestine   a long, coiled digestive organ; part of the alimentary canal (175).

smog   a brown haze caused by the action of sunlight on air pollution (480).

smog alert   a warning that the level of air pollution may cause serious health problems (481).

smog index   a measure of the amount of pollution present in the air (480).

smooth muscle   involuntary muscle that surrounds many internal organs (207).

snuff   tobacco ground into a fine powder and inhaled through the nostrils or held against the gums (344).

social drinker   a person who drinks alcohol only at certain times and who can stop drinking without trouble (371).

social worker   a professional who helps people with mental or emotional problems (461).

socialization   the process of teaching behavior based on the belief and habits of the family and community (63).

somatoform disorder   a condition in which there are physical symptoms but no physical illness (118).

sperm   male reproductive cells that fertilize the egg (313).

spinal cord   the main nerve trunk of the body, extending from the medulla to just below the ribs (239).

splint   a long, stiff object used to support a fracture (527).

spongy bone   porous tissue found in the end of bones (194).

sprain   a joint injury in which the ligaments and tendons around a joint are stretched or torn (203, 527).

statistical risk   a mathematical calculation of the possibility that something will occur (7).

statistics   the branch of mathematics concerned with the probability that something will occur (7).

stereoscopic vision   the process by which the brain combines the images from two eyes to see in three dimensions (41).

stereotype   the belief that all members of a large group share the same characteristics in a fixed way (68).

sternum   flat bone in the middle and front of the chest (198).

steroid   a synthetic drug that is like the male hormone testosterone (399).

stillbirth   a delivery in which the fetus is born dead (327).

stimulant   a drug that speeds up the body's mental or physical activities (392).

stirrup   one of the three small bones in the ear (48).

stomach   a saclike organ of digestion (174).

strength   the ability of a muscle to exert force (258).

stress   the body's response to physical or mental demand or pressure (96).

stressor   an agent that causes stress (96).

striated muscle   skeletal muscle (207).

stroke   brain damage caused by a blockage or rupture of a blood vessel in the brain (439, 535).

structural defense   a form of protection against infectious disease resulting from the physical structures of the body (417).

sty   an infection surrounding an eyelash (44).

subcutaneous layer   the layer of tissue that binds the skin to the body (18).

sublimination   a defense mechanism; the replacement of an undesirable outlet for energy by a desirable one (91).

sulfur oxide   a type of pollutant; a foul-smelling gas released by the burning of coal and oil in factories and power plants (480).

sweat gland   a gland in the dermis that releases perspiration to the surface of the skin (19).

sympathetic nervous system   the part of the autonomic nervous system that works when one is active or under emotional stress (241).

symptom   a signal of the existence of illness (112).

synapse   a space between the end of the axon of one neuron and the dendrite of another (237).

synthetic drug   a drug created in a laboratory by combining other chemicals (386).

syphilis   a sexually transmitted disease caused by bacteria; early stages characterized by an open sore or rash (428).

systemic circulation   the circulatory vessels that move oxygen-rich blood to all parts of the body other than the lungs (219).

systolic pressure   the force of the blood pushing against the walls of the artery when the ventricles of the heart contract (220).

tactile corpuscle   a nerve ending that changes shape in response to outside forces, sending impulses to the brain or spinal cord (52).

tailgating   driving so closely behind another car that you cannot stop or swerve in an emergency (496).

tar   a dark oily mixture consisting mainly of carbon and hydrogen (349).

target heart rate   the rate at which one must exercise the heart to improve cardiorespiratory fitness (265).

taste bud   a tiny organ on the tongue that contains the taste receptors (52).

Tay-Sachs disease   a hereditary nervous disorder causing paralysis and ultimately fatal brain damage (332).

temperature inversion   a condition that occurs when a layer of cool air becomes trapped under a layer of warm air (480).

tendon   a band of collagen fibers that connects a muscle to a bone (200).

tendonitis   the condition in which a tendon becomes irritated and swollen (211).

tension   an uneasy feeling caused by mental or emotional stress (104).

testes   endocrine glands found in men, which hang in a small outer pouch just below the pelvis (307).

testicular cancer   a cancerous growth in the testes (445).

testosterone   a male sex hormone that is produced by the testes (307).

tetanus   a disease caused by bacteria that attack the nerve cells, causing painful tightening of the muscles (414).

thalamus   the part of the brain that relays sensory impulses to the cerebral cortex (238).

therapeutic commuity   a highly structured, drug-free residential program (404).

therapist   a person who has been trained to treat a physical or mental illness (122).

third-degree burn   a burn in which nerve endings and all layers of skin are destroyed (27, 520).

thoracic vertebrae   the spinal bones that help support the chest (197).

thrombosis   a process in which a blood clot blocks an artery; may cause a stroke (439).

thyroid gland   a large gland at the front of the neck that helps control the rate of chemical activity in the body (303).

tolerance   a resistance to the effects of a drug (347, 389).

tonsil   a reddish mass of lymphatic tissue at the back of the mouth (228).

torn cartilage   a serious condition in which cartilage has been pulled away from a bone or joint (203).

torn muscle   a rip in the muscle fiber (211).

tornado   a whirling funnel-shaped windstorm that extends to the ground from a mass of dark clouds (503).

tornado warning   a warning issued when a tornado has been sighted by a person or on radar (503).

tornado watch   a report issued when conditions are favorable for a tornado to develop (503).

tourniquet   an extremely tight bandage placed around a limb to stop the flow of blood (517).

toxemia   a life-threatening complication of pregnancy characterized by swelling, rapid weight gain, high blood pressure, protein in the urine, and stomach pain (327).

toxic   poisonous or deadly (138, 366, 483).

toxic shock syndrome   a serious illness characterized by a sudden, high fever and vomiting, a rash, faintness, and sometimes diarrhea (312).

toxin   a poison (414).

trachea   the section of the windpipe below the larynx (228).

tranquilizer   a drug that slows down nerve activity (393).

trichinosis   a disease caused by parasitic worms, usually transmitted by eating infected pork (415).

tuberculosis (TB)   an infectious disease caused by bacteria that attact the lungs (426).

ulcer   an open sore in the lining of the stomach or other parts of the digestive system (97, 181).

ulcerative colitis   an inflammation of the lining of the colon (182).

ultrasound   a technique that uses sound waves to make an image of a certain area of the body on a screen (334).

umbilical cord   a thick cord that connects the placenta to the embryo (321).

unconscious   the part of the personality that cannot be observed (122).

unconsciousness   the state of having temporarily lost full awareness (245, 534).

underweight   a condition of being 10 percent under one's comfortable weight (161).

undescended testes   a disorder in which one or both testicles fail to descend into the scrotum (314).

unit price   the cost per unit of measure (151).

universal choking signal   hand signal used to communicate the inability to breathe (521).

upper respiratory tract   the organs of the respiratory system that extend from the nose to the windpipe (227).

urea   a chemical end product of protein digestion (183).

ureter   a narrow muscular tube that connects the kidney to the bladder (183).

urethra   the tube from the bladder through which urine may pass out of the body (183).

uric acid   an end product of protein digestion (185).

urine   a form of bodily waste consisting of urea, water, salts, and other substances (183).

U.S. RDA   a guideline used to determine the amount of nutrients in foods (148).

uterus   the female reproductive organ that protects and nourishes a developing baby (308).

vaccination   a treatment in which the body is given a small dose of a disease, causing the body to build up an immunity against it (419).

vagina   a muscular tube that connects the uterus to the outside opening of the body (309).

vaginitis   an inflammation of the vagina caused by yeast or protists (430).

values   beliefs and standards that an individual feels are important to live by (70).

vas deferens   the tube that connects the testes to the urethra (314).

vegetarian   a person who chooses to eat no meat (147).

vein   a blood vessel that carries blood to the heart (217).

ventricle   a lower chamber in the heart (217).

venule   a small blood vessel that leads from capillaries to veins (218).

vertebrae   the bones that make up the spinal column (197).

villi   tiny fingerlike projections that line the walls of the small intestine (175).

virus   a single unit of genetic material in a protein shell (415).

visiting nurse   a health care specialist who cares for people who are ill or recuperating in their homes (463).

vitamin   a chemical substance that helps transform digested food into tissue and helps regulate body functions (138).

vitreous humor   a jellylike fluid in the center of the eye (38).

voluntary body movements   a series of muscular movements blended together to achieve a desired response (243).

wards of state   children who have been placed under the care of a guardian or the courts (288).

warm-up   slow, fluid motions used to increase circulation to the muscles (269).

water   a liquid that is essential for all life processes (142).

water-soluble vitamin   a vitamin that dissolves in water and cannot be stored in the body (138).

wellness   a condition of physical, mental, and social well-being (4).

white blood cell   a blood cell that guards the body against disease and infection (224).

white matter   the layer of the cerebrum below the cortex (238).

withdrawal   the discomfort that people suffer when they stop taking a drug to which they are addicted (348).

X chromosome   a female chromosome (330).

Y chromosome   a male chromosome (330).

Index

Illustrations are indicated by *italics*.

Acknowledgments, continued from page ix.

396 (right) Karlene Schwartz   397 © Leonard Lee Rue III/Photo Researchers Inc.   398 © Charles Marden Fitch/Taurus Photos   401 © J. Sloan/Gamma-Liaison   402 © Marcus Helevi/Wheeler Pictures   403 © Judy Porter/Photo Researchers Inc.   404 © Ralph Oberlander/Stock Boston   405 © Leonard Kamsler/Medichrome   408 © J. Berndt/The Picture Cube   409 (top) © Julie O'Neil/The Picture Cube   409 (bottom) © David Woo/Stock Boston   410-11 © David York/Medichrome   410 (left) © John McGrail   410 (top center) © Dr. A. Liepins/Photo Researchers Inc.   410 (bottom center) © Charles Gupton/Stock Boston   410 (right) © Don Smetzer/Click/Chicago   411 Cary Wolinsky/Stock Boston   412 © Jeff Reed/Medichrome   414 (left, center) © David M. Phillips/Visuals Unlimited   414 (right) Visuals Unlimited   415 (left, center) © L.V. Bergman & Associates   415 (right) Biophoto Associates/Photo Researchers Inc.   416 Dick Luria/The Stock Shop   419 Fisher Scientific Co.   420 © John McGrail   421 AP/Wide World Photos   423 © Billy E. Barnes/Click/Chicago   424 Beth Ullmann/Taurus Photos   426 Raul Hackel/Stock Boston   427 © Grace Moore/Medichrome   428 © Martin M. Rotker/Taurus Photos   430 © Don Smetzer/Click/Chicago   431 © Ed Reschke   436 © Susan Leavines/Photo Researchers Inc.   437 © Lou Lainey   438 © Eugene Richards/Magnum   439 © R.P. Kingston/The Picture Cube   440 © Martin M. Rotker/Taurus Photos   441 © Ellis Herwig/Stock Boston   444 Dr. A. Liepins/Photo Researchers Inc.   447 © Richard Wood/The Picture Cube   448 © David York/Medichrome   449 © John McGrail/Wheeler Pictures   450 PFIZER INC.   451 © Mark Sherman/Bruce Coleman Inc.   454 © Robin Hood   461 (top) © Peter LeGrand/Click/Chicago   461 (bottom) Alexandre/Leo deWys   462 © Charles

Gupton/Stock Boston   463 AP/Wide World Photos   466 © Richard Pasley/Stock Boston   467 © Hilary Wallace   469 The Granger Collection   472 © Eric Carle/Stock Boston   474 Rob Stepney/Photo Researchers Inc.   475 Ronald Thomas/Taurus Photos   477 (top) © Dan McCoy/Rainbow   477 (bottom) © Susan Meiselar/Magnum Photos   480 © Peter Menzel/Wheeler Pictures   481 Carlin/The Picture Cube   482 © Jean Gaumy/Magnum Photos   484 (top) David Falconer/Folio   484 (bottom left) © Don Smetzer/Click/Chicago   484 (bottom right) © Mike Malyszko/Stock Boston   488 © Dave Driscoll/Photo Researchers Inc.   493 (bottom) James Ballard   494 Cary Wolinsky/Stock Boston   495 Cezus/Click/Chicago   496 James Ballard   497 © Marcus Halevi   499 © Arthur Gray/Stock Boston   500 © George E. Jones III/Photo Researchers Inc.   502 © John Deeks/Photo Researchers Inc.   503 © Owen Franken/Stock Boston   505 © Tom McHugh/Photo Researchers Inc.   508 David Brody/Stock Boston   509 (top) © Bruce M. Wellman   509 (center) © Richard Pasley/Stock Boston   509 (bottom) James Ballard   510 © Wesley Bocxe/Photo Researchers Inc.   540–41 © Julie Houck/Stock Boston

Gregg Eisman (Ligature, Inc.) xi (bottom), 3, 17, 37, 56, 57, 59 (top), 79, 94, 95, 110, 111, 132, 133, 155, 171, 188, 193, 215, 235, 255, 257-263, 266, 285, 301, 319, 342, 343, 359 (left), 384, 385, 413, 455, 473, 489

Ken O'Donoghue: 160 (right)

Ralph G. Ragsdale: x (bottom), xvi (right), 23, 33, 81 (left), 97, 102, 107, 130 (right), 144 (bottom), 148, 151, 154, 157, 160, 210, 363, 434, 435, 458-59, 493 (top)